ECONOMICS
OF
LABOR RELATIONS

ECONOMICS

OF

LABOR RELATIONS,

GORDON F. BLOOM, Ph.D., LL.B.
Senior Lecturer, Sloan School of Management
Massachusetts Institute of Technology

HERBERT R. NORTHRUP, Ph.D.
Professor of Industry and
Chairman, Department of Industry
Wharton School of Finance and Commerce
University of Pennsylvania

Sixth Edition · 1969
RICHARD D. IRWIN, INC., Homewood, Illinois
IRWIN-DORSEY LIMITED, Georgetown, Ontario

SIXTH EDITION

First Printing, January, 1969

Second Printing, July, 1969

Third Printing, April, 1970

Fourth Printing, December, 1970

Fifth Printing, June, 1971

HD
4901
.B58

Library of Congress Catalog Card No. 68–30853

PRINTED IN THE UNITED STATES OF AMERICA

SUMNER H. SLICHTER (1892–1959)

Teacher and Inspiring Friend

PREFACE

Labor relations and labor economics in the 1960's have been dominated by the interrelated key issues of unemployment, poverty, race relations, and inflation. These issues are not only integrated into each chapter of our completely rewritten Sixth Edition, but in addition special chapters are devoted to unemployment and poverty, civil rights legislation, and the impact of union policies on inflation.

Because a complete revision was undertaken, current labor problems have been given great emphasis: the Reuther defection from the AFL–CIO, early retirement, union policies in regard to Negro workers, and the latest developments in wage theory are among the many issues discussed in detail. All materials dealing with labor relations, race relations in industry, labor force matters, and all figures, tables, and suggested readings have been brought up to date. In addition, at the suggestion of many kind adopters of the book and several reviewers, the writing has been tightened and the pages considerably reduced. In short, the authors have striven to make the Sixth Edition as new and fresh as the latest issue of the morning newspaper.

As in earlier editions, a major objective has been the integration of economic facts and economic analysis so that the student may acquire not only an awareness of labor problems, but also an understanding of conflicting views concerning their causes and possible solutions. Wherever possible the authors have incorporated in their discussion the latest views and approaches to various labor problems which have appeared in recent articles in professional journals. Considerable effort has been made to spell out clearly economic principles and the techniques of economic analysis.

The authors have not attempted to write a text with a general theme or a particular slant. Their main interest has been in making available to the teacher and student a text which discusses the field of labor problems in a clear, comprehensive, and interesting fashion. The material contained in the text has been organized in a manner which it was felt would make the study of labor problems both enjoyable and understandable to the beginning student. Part I, which contains a general introduction to the field of labor problems, is intended to orient the student to the subject matter. Parts II and III give a picture of labor history, union structure and government, and collective bargaining techniques and issues. Part IV uses the tools of economic analysis to illuminate a variety of labor problems. Part V discusses wage and hour regulation and the movement toward a shorter workweek. Part VI describes in detail various programs—governmental, union, and industry—for obtaining security for the aged, the unemployed, and the sick and injured.

Part VII deals with the increasingly important role of the government in labor relations. As in previous editions, it contains detailed, up-to-date analyses of all major labor laws, including the Taft-Hartley Act and the Landrum-Griffin Act. In addition, Part VII contains the chapter dealing with the federal equal opportunity law and similar state laws. Part VIII is devoted to concluding remarks of the authors; and as has already been indicated, important questions are raised as to the future role of unions in our economy.

As in early editions, many persons have been most helpful. Mr. W. Everett Allen, of the firm of Towers, Perrin Forster and Crosby, Inc., did the research and wrote the drafts of Chapters 17, 18, and 19. Mr. David Scott did some of the research work for Chapters 2–7. Mrs. Margaret E. Doyle and Mrs. Marie P. Spence typed parts of the manuscript, and Mrs. Doyle took care of numerous administrative problems as well. Mrs. Marjorie C. Denison and Miss Elsa Klemp did proofreading and the index, and Mrs. Denison also constructed some charts.

Over the years, many professors who have used the book have aided the authors by constructive suggestions. These include Professors Frank T. deVyver, Duke University; Charles Killingsworth, Michigan State University; Emanuel Stein, New York University; John P. Troxell, Stanford University; Russell S. Bauder, University of Missouri; Myles Hoffman, Temple University; Darrell S. Spriggs, University of Arkansas; Walter Galenson, Cornell University; and Edwin Young, formerly University of Wisconsin; and Dr. Jack Ellenbogen. Many helpful suggestions have been received from colleagues at the Wharton School, including Professors George W. Taylor, William Gomberg, Edward B. Shils, Charles R. Perry, Marten S. Estey, and Bernard Anderson, Dr. William N. Chernish, and especially Professor Richard L. Rowan. The staffs of the U.S. Bureau of Labor Statistics, the Wage and Hour and Public Contracts Division, and the Office of Labor Management and Pension Welfare Reports, all of the Department of Labor; the National Labor Relations Board; the Chamber of Commerce of the United States; and the National Industrial Conference Board were all most helpful in supplying materials and data.

The authors are grateful to the following organizations, publishers, and journals for permission to quote copyrighted material: National Industrial Conference Board, the Chamber of Commerce of the United States, McGraw-Hill Book Co., University of Chicago Press, Brookings Institution, American Economic Association, *Antioch Review, Southern Economic Journal,* Harper and Row, Houghton Mifflin Co., Twentieth Century Fund, W. W. Norton and Company, Inc., *Quarterly Journal of Economics,* The Macmillan Company, *Harvard Business Review,* the Bureau of National Affairs, Inc., *U.S. News and World Report, Industrial and Labor Relations Review, Industrial Relations, Fortune,* Yale University Press, and many others cited in the text.

This book represents a joint undertaking for which joint responsibility is shared. The authors hope that their combination of academic background and practical experience in the field of labor relations has enabled them to introduce into this text a viewpoint and ideas which will make the field of labor as vital and interesting to the student as it has been to them.

The opinions expressed herein are the responsibilities solely of the authors and are not to be attributed to any company or organization with which either author is now, or has been in the past, associated.

The first five editions of this book were dedicated to the late Sumner H. Slichter, who not only profoundly influenced both authors as well as the whole field of labor economics during our generation, but also gave to the undersigned his wise counsel and friendship. This edition is dedicated to his memory as a person, a teacher, and a friend.

December, 1968   GORDON F. BLOOM
                                   HERBERT R. NORTHRUP

TABLE OF CONTENTS

PART I. INTRODUCTION

Who Is Labor? Who Are Employers? Nonfarm Business: *Government. Agriculture*. The Labor Force: *Definitions. Statistics. Characteristics of the Labor Force. Projected Growth of the Labor Force. Quality of the Labor Force. The Changing Composition of the Labor Force. Youth. The Older Worker. Women at Work. Part-Time Workers. The Changing Status of the Negro*. Occupation and Socioeconomic Status: *The Decline in Agricultural Employment. The Shift from Goods-Producing to Service Industries. The Growth in White-Collar Employment. Government Employees*. What Is a Labor Problem? *Organized Labor and Labor Problems*.

PART II. UNION HISTORY AND GOVERNMENT

The Conditions of Organization. The American Environment: *Class Fluidity. Resources and Land. Wide Markets. Heterogeneous Population. Social and Legal Background*. The Beginnings, 1790–1825: *The Conspiracy Doctrine*. Citywide Movements, 1825–37: *Politics and Federation*. Reformism and Cooperation to National Organization, 1840–67. The Knights of Labor. The Rise of the American Federation of Labor: *Samuel Gompers. AFL Philosophy. The Injunction and the "Yellow-Dog" Contract. Industrial Relations, 1880–1914. The IWW*. World War I to the Great Depression: *Company Unions. The AFL Decays. William Green. Labor under the New Deal. The Founding of the CIO. The CIO Organizes Steel. Rubber, Automobiles, and Other CIO Drives*. World War II to the Korean War. Communist Unionism: *Party-Line Shifts*. Religious Leadership in Unions. Labor's New Disunity: *Merger Impact on Union Policies. American Unions Today. Concentration of Union Membership. Labor in Politics. Labor Unions and Politics in the Future. Labor Unions and the Negro*.

Organizational Structure and Its Determinants. Determinants of Union Government: *Administrative Determinants. Effects of Rival Unionism. Imitative Elements. Power Elements. Effect of Legislation and Court Decisions*. The National or International Union: *The Referendum. National Union Officers. Tenure of National Union Officials. Appointive Officials*. Intermediate Union Government. The Local Union: *Local Jurisdiction and Size. Local Union Officers. Duration of Local*

Distributed: *The Long-Term Trend in Real Wages. Labor's Relative Share in National Income. Effect of Union Organization upon Income Shares.* Wage Policy and Productivity Changes: *Wage Guideposts and Foreign Trade.* The Labor Dilemma. Unions and Wage Inflation: Do Unions Accelerate the Rise in Wage Levels? Negative View. *Factors Inflating Demand in the post–World War II Era. Wage Gains among Unorganized Workers.* Do Unions Accelerate Wage Increases? Affirmative View: *The Effect of Cost-of-Living Provisions in Union Contracts. Unions and Cost-Push Inflation.* Appraisal of the Dilemma.

The Extent of Unemployment: *Unskilled Workers. Youth. The Uneducated. Older Workers. Negro Workers.* Occupational Characteristics of the Unemployed. The Location of Unemployment: *Unemployment in the Cities.* Poverty and Unemployment. The Area Redevelopment Act. The Manpower Development and Training Act of 1962. The Economic Opportunity Act of 1964: *Industry Cooperative Programs.* Types of Unemployment: *Why the Unemployed Look for Work. Economic Classifications of Unemployment.* Cyclical Unemployment: *Characteristics of Cyclical Unemployment.* Technological Unemployment: *Possibility of Permanent Technological Unemployment. Technological Progress and Employment Opportunities. Automation and Unemployment.* Seasonal Unemployment. Frictional Unemployment. *Wage-Distortion Unemployment. Demand versus Structural Unemployment.* The Challenge of a High-Employment Economy.

PART V. GOVERNMENTAL WAGE REGULATION AND THE SHORTER WORKWEEK

The Federal Fair Labor Standards Act: *Superminimum and Prevailing Wages. State Minimum Wage Legislation. Procedure for Setting State Minimum Wages.* Minimum Wages and Employment: *Theoretical Effects of the Minimum Wage. Empirical Studies—The 25-Cent Minimum of 1938. The Effects of the 75-Cent Minimum. The Effects of the $1 Minimum. The 1961 Amendments. The 1965 Amendments. Minimum Wages and Poverty. Minimum Wages and the North-South Differential.* Emergency Wage Regulation. World War II Wage Stabilization: *Effects of World War II Stabilization.* Wage Stabilization during the Korean War: *The Wage Stabilization Board.* Analysis of Wage Controls of World War II and of the Korean War: *Different Economic and Psychological Conditions. The Changing Character of Labor and Management.* "Stabilization" by *Big Bargains.* Wage Restraint in Peacetime.

History of the Shorter-Hour Movement. *Shorter Workyear. Other Hours Legislation.* Basic Factors Affecting the Trend toward Shorter

Hours: *The Role of Unions.* The Arguments for Shorter Hours: *Health and Leisure. Purchasing Power Theory. Efficiency and Productivity. Akron Rubber Tire Industry. New York City Electricians. Moonlighting.* Hours Reduction and Employment: *Shorter Hours with Unchanged Basic Wage Rates. Reduction in Hours with Compensatory Wage Increases. Effect of Increasing the Number of Shifts. Interindustry Shifts. Shortages of Skilled Labor.* Nature of Unemployment. Costs of the Shorter-Hour Program. Automation and Hours. Long Vacations and Employment. Overtime and Employment: *Fringes, Overtime, and Turnover Costs.* Concluding Remarks.

PART VI. ECONOMICS OF THE SEARCH FOR SECURITY

The Economic Problems of Old Age and Premature Death: *Old Age. Loss of Breadwinner.* Public and Private Approaches to the Economic Problems of Old Age and Premature Death: *Public Approaches. Private Approaches.* The Old Age, Survivors, Disability, and Health Insurance Program (OASDHI): *Benefits. Eligibility. Financing. Administration.* Old-Age Assistance. Employer-Provided Retirement Benefits: *Types of Plans. Benefit Levels. Eligibility for Retirement Benefits. Termination of Employment Benefits. Funding Private Pension Plans. The Cost of Private Pension Plans.* Employer-Provided Death Benefits. Current OASDHI Issues: *Too Much OAA? Public Pension Protection for All. "Pay as You Go" versus Reserve Financing. "Earmarked" Taxes versus General Revenues. Compulsory Retirement.* Medicare. Current Private Pension Plan Issues: *Vesting. Minimum Funding. Reinsurance of Private Pensions. Portability of Pensions. Investment of Pension Funds.*

Unemployment Insurance: *Development of the Unemployment Insurance Program. Coverage of Unemployment Insurance Laws. Eligibility. Benefit Amounts. Duration of Benefits. Financing. Experience Rating. Some Future Prospects.* The Dismissal Wage: *Management's Attitude toward Dismissal Wages. Labor's View of Dismissal Wages. The Dismissal Wage and Wage-Employment Equilibrium. Appraisal of Dismissal Wage. Relation to Unemployment Compensation.* Supplemental Unemployment Benefits: *The Guaranteed Annual Wage. Supplemental Unemployment Benefit Plans. Comparison of Insurance Fund and Individual Account Plans. SUB and State Unemployment Compensation Laws. Appraisal of Supplementary Unemployment Benefit Plans.*

Workmen's Compensation: *The Development of Workmen's Compensation. The Nature of Workmen's Compensation Laws.* Nature of Benefits. Administration. *Second-Injury Funds and Special Provisions. Financing. Analysis of Workmen's Compensation. Accident Preven-*

tion and Rehabilitation. State Temporary Disability Legislation: *Development of Disability Insurance. Analysis of State Disability Legislation.* Health and Welfare Plans: *Unions and Welfare Funds. Analysis of Health and Welfare Plans.*

Were Affected: *Restrictions on Internal Union Affairs. Restrictions on Union Officials. Trusteeships. Restrictions on Union Organizing and Bargaining Tactics. Special Privileges for Unions in Construction Industry.* How the Individual Worker Was Affected: *The Bill of Rights. Fair Elections. Voting by Strikers.* How the Public Was Affected. Appraisal of the Act.

PART VIII. CONCLUDING OBSERVATIONS

INDEXES

PART I

Introduction

| Chapter | THE NATURE OF LABOR |
| 1 | PROBLEMS |

Unemployment, wage demands, strikes—these are issues of vital concern today. Hard-core unemployment of minority groups in our urban centers poses one of our most explosive current domestic problems. Continuing union wage pressure adds fuel to the mounting forces of inflation in our economy. And strikes—by teachers, municipal employees, and hospital workers, as well as industrial workers—raise perplexing problems of the extent to which a free society should attempt to curtail the individual's right to withdraw his labor from essential occupations. Through radio, television, and the daily newspaper, all of us have become increasingly aware of these and other labor problems which confront our economy. Labor problems have become everyone's problems. They affect every man, woman, and child—every consumer, employer, and employee.

WHO IS LABOR?

The term "labor" is used in many different ways. Sometimes, it is used as synonymous with "the civilian labor force." This group, as we shall see, includes all persons who work for a living. Such a definition, therefore, lumps together in the same category the banker and the ditch-digger, the independent storekeeper and the president of the United States Steel Corporation. This heterogeneous group has one common characteristic, namely, that its members work for a living. In this respect, they are distinct from other groups in the population, such as the housewives, students, pensioners, those too young or too old to work, the incapacitated, and those who, for one reason or another, find it impossible to seek work.

On the other hand, the term "labor" is sometimes used to refer to much more limited groups. For example, when we refer to "skilled labor," we normally mean skilled craftsmen who work for hire for others and who are neither white-collar workers nor professional personnel. This definition excludes both the typist in the office and the doctor in the hospital, although both may work for hire and have highly developed skills. Similarly, if one reads that "labor" opposes the use of the injunction

3

as a strikebreaking weapon, it is likely that the term is intended to apply to a limited group of men and women, skilled and unskilled, white-collar and nonwhite-collar, who either are members of unions or are in groups which lend themselves to union organization. The term "labor," therefore, may have various meanings and scope, depending upon the context in which it is used.

WHO ARE EMPLOYERS?

In order to understand the nature of the labor market in our economy and the factors which contributed to the development of trade-unions, one must understand who provides the jobs for our labor force. Today, most people work for someone else, whether it be a large farm operator, a giant industrial corporation, a governmental agency, or the corner drugstore. Self-employment has continually declined as a source of work. In 1900, about 36% of all workers with jobs were self-employed; today this percentage had dropped to less than 12%.[1]

NONFARM BUSINESS

There are about 5 million operating nonfarm businesses in the United States, and most of them are small in size, averaging only about 12.4 workers per firm.[2] If employment in the entire economy were evenly distributed among a great many such small firms, our labor market would be quite different from what it actually is, and it is conceivable that workers would never have felt a need for unions to protect their interests. Averages, however, are deceptive. While small business enterprises are abundant in wholesale and retail trade and in various service occupations, a relatively small number of giant companies employ a substantial portion of the entire nonfarm labor force. For example, if we take *Fortune* magazine's list of the 500 largest industrial companies, we find that this small group of companies accounts for almost one out of every five jobs in the nonfarm sector of the economy.[3] Manufacturing, in particular, is characterized by bigness, and generally bigness in corporate form. Approximately 3 out of every 4 workers in manufacturing are employed by corporations employing 100 or more persons.[4]

Most employees in nonagricultural establishments are employed by corporations. This means that they are employed by a legal entity, which

---

[1] F. A. Bogan and T. E. Swenstrom, "Multiple Jobholders in May 1965," *Monthly Labor Review*, Vol. LXXXIX (February, 1966), pp. 151–52.

[2] *Business in Brief*, Chase Manhattan Bank News Letter, October, 1966, p. 3.

[3] *Fortune*, June 15, 1967, p. 213.

[4] National Industrial Conference Board, *Economic Almanac*, 1967–1968 (New York, 1967), p. 233.

in turn is owned by stockholders, frequently numbering in the hundreds of thousands. Over 80% of all disbursements by private business for wages and salaries is accounted for by corporations; sole proprietorships, partnerships, mutual organizations, producer cooperatives, trade associations, and other forms of enterprise account for less than 20% of the total.[5] Large corporations control the bulk of our wealth and production; they set the tempo for wage adjustments; they establish the general framework of attitudes and policies which condition union-management relations in the economy as a whole.

Because of the wide holdings of stock in this country, it might be argued that the ultimate employer of labor in the United States is the stockholding public. They own the assets which provide employment and, moreover, as stockholders they normally have the right to elect directors and so influence corporate policies. As a practical matter, however, corporate decisions tend to be made by a class of persons known as management, who are employed by stockholders to manage the day-to-day business of corporations. Management includes executives such as the officers and directors of corporations, as well as personnel directors, department heads, and foremen. To the average workman in a large corporation, it is this group—and not the remote stockholder-owners—which constitutes the employer. We shall discuss at a later point how the separation of the management function from ownership in American industry and the growth in size of corporations has exercised a profound effect upon the nature of collective bargaining.

Government

We are accustomed to thinking of the automobile industry, the steel industry, and other durable goods producers as the major source of employment in our economy. Yet today in the United States there are as many persons employed by government—federal, state, and local—as by all durable goods manufacturing industries combined. Government employment has doubled since the end of World War II from 5,474,000 in 1947 to 11,479,000 in 1966. The major governmental employer is the municipality and other local governmental agencies, which in 1966 accounted for 6,407,000 jobs. Next in importance is the federal government, which employed 2,861,000 persons, and lastly state government, which provided 2,211,000 jobs.[6] If we add to the foregoing figures over 3 million members in the Armed Forces and about 6.3 million persons employed in private industry supplying goods and services purchased by various governmental agencies, we find that roughly 3 out of every 10 workers in the nonagricultural sector of the economy owe their jobs either directly

---

[5] National Industrial Conference Board, *op. cit.*, p. 110.

[6] U.S. Department of Labor, *Handbook of Labor Statistics, 1967* (Washington, D.C.: U.S. Government Printing Office, 1967), p. 69.

or indirectly to governmental action.[7] Since we tend to pride ourselves on the achievements of our private enterprise economy, it is sobering to consider the extent to which government expenditures and government decision making affect the level of employment.

Agriculture

Agriculture is the only major industry in which the majority of workers are self-employed or unpaid members of families. Hired workers, today, account for less than 1.5 million of total farm employment of 5.6 million. The number of farms has decreased from 5.3 million in 1947 to slightly over 3 million today, with the decrease concentrated among smaller farm units. However, most farms are still small; in fact, half of the nation's farmers do not hire any workers at all![8] Although the size of the average farm has risen substantially over the years, employment per unit is not following the same trend, primarily because the rapid application of new technology has resulted in spectacular accomplishments in saving of labor in farm work. Employment in large numbers per farm unit seldom occurs except during seasonal harvest periods. Farms having five or more year-round hired men—usually dairies, stock ranches, or poultry farms— are few and exceptional.

Large commercial farms have been growing in number and account for an ever increasing proportion of total agricultural output. In 1964, 89% of all expenditures for hired labor were on the 29% of farms that sold product valued at $10,000 or more.[9] Union organizers have been attempting to organize employees on some of the larger farms, particularly in California and in recent years have achieved some notable breakthroughs. However, organizing farm employees is extremely difficult because of the geographical dispersion of farms, the small number of workers per unit, and the fact that many of the workers are migratory or part time without a full-time attachment to a particular employer.

THE LABOR FORCE

Suppose we want to find out how many people are in the "labor force" of the United States? How would we go about obtaining this information? Obviously we need two things: first, a definition of what we are seeking, and, second, the statistics to fill our classifications.

Definitions

The classification of the labor force and its components most commonly used is that adopted by the Bureau of Census, which compiles

[7] U.S. Department of Labor, *Manpower Report of the President, 1967* (Washington, D.C.: U.S. Government Printing Office, 1967), p. 29.

[8] U.S. Department of Labor, *Manpower Report of the President, 1966* (Washington, D.C.: U.S. Government Printing Office, 1966), pp. 122, 126.

[9] *Ibid.*

statistics for the United States Bureau of Labor Statistics. These definitions have been changed from time to time,[10] but at this writing the following criteria are applied in classifying persons on the basis of activity during the survey week studied.

Labor Force: The sum of persons in the Armed Forces plus persons in the civilian labor force, whether employed or unemployed.

Civilian Labor Force (limited to noninstitutional population 16 years of age or more).

Employed persons include:

(1) all civilians who during the specified week did any work at all as paid employees or in their own business or profession, or on their own farm, or who worked 15 hours or more as unpaid workers on a farm or in a business operated by a member of the family;

(2) all those who were not working but who had jobs or businesses from which they were temporarily absent because of illness, bad weather, vacation, or labor-management dispute, or because they were taking time off for personal reasons.

Unemployed persons include those civilians who had no employment during the survey week, were available for work, and:

(1) had engaged in any specific job-seeking activity within the past four weeks, such as registering with employment offices, checking with friends and relatives, meeting with prospective employers, etc.;

(2) were waiting to be called back to a job from which they had been laid off; or

(3) were waiting to report to a new wage or salary job scheduled to start within the following 30 days.

Persons Not in Labor Force: This category includes all persons not classified as employed, unemployed, or in the Armed Forces who are 16 years of age or over and are not inmates of institutions. These persons are further classified as follows:

(1) engaged in own homework;

(2) in school;

(3) unable to work because of long-term physical or mental illness;

(4) other—this category includes persons who are retired, voluntarily idle, too old or temporarily unable to work, seasonal workers in

---

[10] For a discussion of current techniques and concepts, see *Concepts and Methods Used in Manpower Statistics for the Current Population Survey,* Bureau of Labor Statistics Report No. 313, June, 1967. In January, 1967, several important changes were made in labor force concepts and definitions:

1. The lower age limit for inclusion in official statistics was raised from 14 to 16 years of age.

2. To be counted as unemployed, an individual had to be available for work currently.

3. To be counted as unemployed, specific jobseeking activity was required during the prior four weeks.

4. Persons with a job were classified as employed, even though they were absent from their jobs during the survey week and looking for other jobs.

off season who are not looking for work, and persons who did not look for work because they believed that no jobs were available in the area, or that no jobs were available for which they could qualify.

The statistics based upon these definitions are widely used and enter into formulation of major governmental policy decisions affecting the economy in general and the labor market in particular. Unfortunately, many people who use these figures are unaware of the restrictive definitions upon which they are based. Much careful thought and research has gone into the establishment of the criteria listed above, yet for certain purposes the definitions may produce misleading results. For example, any study of Negro unemployment must take account of the fact that the Bureau of Census definitions tend to understate the true amount of such unemployment by categorizing persons as being "not in labor force" if they have given up looking for a job because of a belief that they do not have the necessary skills.

Statistics

Figures on employment and unemployment to be meaningful must be current. It is obviously impossible, therefore, to obtain such statistics through a massive survey such as that undertaken every 10 years for the federal census. The alternative adopted by the Bureau of Census in obtaining raw data for its labor force reports is monthly surveys of the population based upon a scientifically selected sample of households designed to represent the civilian noninstitutional population 16 years and over. Members of these households are questioned concerning activity or status during the calendar week Sunday through Saturday which includes the 12th of the month. This week is known as the "survey week."

Obviously, any sampling technique has certain shortcomings. Here again it is possible that the sampling technique may tend to understate the true dimension of Negro unemployment, since many Negroes have only a temporary attachment to households. This problem affects even the broader-based decennial census figures. One study has suggested that as many as 1.8 million men aged 15 to 64 were not counted in the 1960 census. Over 900,000 of these men were nonwhite.[11] It is apparent that statistics in the field of labor must be used with circumspection and caution.

Characteristics of the Labor Force

The civilian labor force is not a fixed group. It grows with the long-term growth of the population; it responds to the influence of economic forces; and it changes with the seasons. In July there are usually three or four million more job seekers than in January, as students look for summer jobs and housewives seek jobs in seasonal farm industries.

---

[11] *Manpower Report of the President, 1966, op. cit.,* p. 51.

December is another peak month, for it is the time when many persons take part-time jobs in department stores and other firms which do a heavy Christmas business. A surprisingly large proportion of adult men are in the labor force for only a part of the year. One recent study indicated that, of the men in the prime working ages of 25–64 years who were in the labor force during the year studied, about 10% were in it for less than a full 12 months.[12]

Because of the movement in and out of the labor force during a given year, many more persons are employed (and unemployed) during the course of a year than is indicated by the annual averages in Table 1–1. For example, in 1964 about 85 million persons are estimated to have worked at some time during the year,[13] yet Table 1–1 shows civilian employment averaged only a little more than 69 million.

As can be seen from Table 1–1, the rate of participation[14] in the civilian labor force at first glance appears to have been remarkably stable since 1947. However, this apparent overall stability masks some striking changes in the participation rates of various component groups within the labor force. For example, from 1948 to 1967 the participation rate for white males declined from about 86.5% to 80.7% while the rate for white females rose from 31.3% to 40.1%.[15] The decline in the male participation has been concentrated in the youngest and oldest members. Participation by young men has been reduced largely as a result of increase in school attendance. Participation by white males over 65 fell from 46.5% in 1948 to 27.1% in 1967,[16] reflecting the spread of public and private retirement programs, business policy aimed at compulsory retirement at age 65, and the diminishing importance of agriculture which historically had enabled older men to work, even if part time, to an older age than industry now permits. For women, the rise in participation rates has occurred almost entirely among married women. Changing social attitudes toward work by women and the increased utilization of laborsaving devices in the home have undoubtedly contributed to this change.

The relative stability in the ratio of the labor force to population is all the more remarkable when account is taken of the large number of men of working age who choose to remain outside the labor force at any given time. For example, in 1966, there were about 4.5 million men

---

[12] Samuel Saben, "Work Experience of the Population," *Monthly Labor Review*, Vol. LXXXIX (February, 1966), p. 155.

[13] *Ibid.*

[14] The rate of participation is the percentage of persons of working age in the population actually in the labor force.

[15] Albert Rees, "The American Labor Force," in William Haber, *Labor in a Changing America* (New York: Basic Books, Inc., 1966), p. 2; *Manpower Report of the President, 1968* (Washington, D.C.: U.S. Government Printing Office, 1968), Table A-4, p. 225.

[16] Rees, *op. cit.*, p. 2; *Manpower Report of the President, 1968, op. cit.*, Table A-4, p. 225.

TABLE 1-1. Employment Status of the Noninstitutional Population 16 Years and Over: Annual Averages, 1947-67
(Numbers in Thousands)

Year	Total Noninstitutional Population	Total Labor Force, including Armed Forces		Civilian Labor Force						Not in Labor Force
		Number	% of Noninstitutional Population	Total	Employed			Unemployed		
					Total	Agriculture	Nonagricultural Industries	Number	% of Labor Force	
1947	103,418	60,941	58.9	59,350	57,039	7,891	49,148	2,311	3.9	42,477
1948	104,527	62,080	59.4	60,621	58,344	7,629	50,711	2,276	3.8	42,447
1949	105,611	62,903	59.6	61,286	57,649	7,656	49,990	3,637	5.9	42,708
1950	106,645	63,858	59.9	62,208	58,920	7,160	51,752	3,288	5.3	42,787
1951	107,721	65,117	60.4	62,017	59,962	6,726	53,230	2,055	3.3	42,604
1952	108,823	65,730	60.4	62,138	60,254	6,501	53,748	1,883	3.0	43,093
1953*	110,601	66,560	60.2	63,015	61,181	6,261	54,915	1,834	2.9	44,041
1954	111,671	66,993	60.0	63,643	60,110	6,206	53,898	3,532	5.5	44,678
1955	112,732	68,072	60.4	65,023	62,171	6,449	55,718	2,852	4.4	44,660
1956	113,811	69,409	61.0	66,552	63,802	6,283	57,506	2,750	4.1	44,402
1957	115,065	69,729	60.6	66,929	64,071	5,947	58,123	2,859	4.3	45,336
1958	116,363	70,275	60.4	67,639	63,036	5,586	57,450	4,602	6.8	46,088
1959	117,881	70,921	60.2	68,369	64,630	5,565	59,065	3,740	5.5	46,960
1960*	119,759	72,142	60.2	69,628	65,778	5,458	60,318	3,852	5.5	47,617
1961	121,343	73,031	60.2	70,459	65,746	5,200	60,546	4,714	6.7	48,312
1962*	122,981	73,442	59.7	70,614	66,702	4,944	61,759	3,911	5.5	49,539
1963	125,154	74,571	59.6	71,833	67,762	4,687	63,076	4,070	5.7	50,583
1964	127,224	75,830	59.6	73,091	69,305	4,523	64,782	3,786	5.2	51,394
1965	129,236	77,178	59.7	74,455	71,088	4,361	66,726	3,366	4.5	52,058
1966	131,180	78,893	60.1	75,770	72,895	3,979	68,915	2,875	3.8	52,288
1967	133,319	80,793	60.6	77,347	74,372	3,844	70,527	2,975	3.8	52,527

* Not strictly comparable with prior years. The introduction of data from the decennial censuses into the estimation procedure in 1953 and 1962, and the inclusion of Alaska and Hawaii in 1960, have resulted in three periods of noncomparability: (a) Beginning 1953, as a result of the 1950 census, population levels were raised by about 600,000; labor force, total employment, and agricultural employment by about 350,000, primarily affecting the figures for totals and males; other categories were relatively unaffected; (b) beginning 1960, the inclusion of Alaska and Hawaii resulted in an increase of about 500,000 in the population and about 300,000 in the labor force, four fifths of this in nonagricultural employment; other labor force categories were not appreciably affected; (c) beginning 1962, the introduction of figures from the 1960 census reduced the population by about 50,000, labor force and employment by about 200,000; unemployment totals were virtually unchanged.

Source: U.S. Department of Labor, Manpower Report of the President, 1968 (Washington, D.C.: U.S. Government Printing Office, 1968), Table A-1, p. 221.

between the ages of 18 and 64 who were neither employed nor looking for work.[17] This group of men outside the labor force has increased both in absolute size and as a proportion of the population during the last decade. The proportion of men outside the labor force is greater among nonwhite than white men in all groups except those under age 24.[18]

Why do men and women stay out of the labor force? The reasons are varied: school attendance, physical or mental disability, family obligations, discouragement with job prospects, and other temporary circumstances. It is important to recognize that the group of men of working age outside the labor force is fluid and ever changing, and actually has a strong attachment to the labor force. For example, a survey of men age 25–64 who were outside the labor force at some time during the year studied revealed that less than one third were outside the labor force for the entire year.[19]

As has already been suggested in the discussion on page 8, prolonged inability to obtain jobs may cause men and women to drop out of the labor force. It is not surprising, then, that empirical research[20] suggests that the size of the civilian labor force may be inversely related to the level of unemployment. This implies that although some secondary workers enter the labor market when unemployment affects family earnings, more depart or delay their entrance until a more favorable labor market situation develops.

Projected Growth of the Labor Force

Population growth in the United States appears to be slackening. The birth rate has declined substantially over the past few years, and recently it has continued to decline despite a rising trend in marriages. Yet, despite this fact, we are facing a labor-force explosion of nearly unprecedented proportions as the high birth rates of the postwar years pour a tremendous increment of new workers into the labor market. In the 10 years from 1965 to 1975, the labor force is expected to increase by 15 million persons.[21] This will represent the largest increase for any 10-year period in our entire history. In the past decade, the labor force has been growing at the rate of 1.2% per annum. Between now and 1975, the labor force is expected to grow at a rate of about 1.8% per annum, with a labor force in 1975 projected at 93 million persons. This estimate assumes

[17] Susan S. Holland, "Adult Men Not in the Labor Force," *Monthly Labor Review*, Vol. XC (March, 1967), p. 5.

[18] *Manpower Report of the President, 1967, op. cit.*, pp. 131, 133.

[19] Holland, *op. cit.*, p. 7.

[20] See Glen G. Cain, "Unemployment and the Labor-Force Participation of Secondary Workers," *Industrial and Labor Relations Review*, Vol. XX (January, 1967), p. 292; Jacob Mincer, "Labor-Force Participation and Unemployment, A Review of Recent Evidence," in R. A. Gordon (ed.), *Prosperity and Unemployment* (New York: John Wiley & Sons, Inc., 1966), pp. 73–112.

[21] *Manpower Report of the President, 1967, op. cit.*, p. 271.

some increase in the labor participation rate, particularly among women. If current participation rates are applied to the estimated population for 1975, a labor force of about 91 million would result.[22]

During the 1960's, the most dramatic change in the composition of the labor force occurred in the number of workers under age 25. By the end of the decade, an estimated 6.6 million persons aged 14 to 24 years will have been added to the labor force for an increase in that bracket of 48%! During the same period, the number of workers in the age group 25 to 44 years will have increased by only 1.5 million or 4.9%. During the 1970's, the rates of growth will be reversed with the highest percentage increase occurring in the prime working age bracket and a more moderate rate of growth for younger workers. From 1970 to 1980, it is estimated that workers aged 14 to 24 years will increase by 3.7 million, or 18%, while workers aged 25 to 44 will rise by 10 million or 30%.[23]

Quality of the Labor Force

A nation's labor force is the source of its strength and wealth. But these attributes cannot be measured in terms of numbers alone. More important are the educational attainments and skills of the people who compose the labor force. Are they adequate and responsive to the fast-changing needs of our dynamic economy?

Examination of only a few basic statistics in this regard indicates that we face a massive job of retraining and educating our workers so that they can become an *effective* labor force. It is true that during the past decade the average educational attainment of the labor force has continued to rise. The proportion of workers aged 18 to 64 with high school diplomas rose from 45% to 56% in the 12 years from 1952 to 1964. Yet, in 1964, over 17 million workers—one out of every four—had no more than eight years of schooling, and about 2.6 million had not even finished fifth grade. Lack of education is a particularly serious problem for Negro workers. About two out of every five nonwhite workers have no more than an eighth grade education—almost twice the proportion for whites.[24]

Despite the obvious advantages that accrue to the educated worker, almost one out of every three school enrollees drops out of school before graduating from high school. The impact on employment and earnings of such action is painful indeed. The unemployment rate for young workers who fail to finish high school is about two-thirds higher than for those with high school diplomas, and those dropouts who do find employment are likely to be employed in occupations with the lowest wage rates.[25]

Continued improvement in the duration and scope of our educa-

---

[22] *Economic Potentials of the United States in the Next Decade* (New York: National Industrial Conference Board, 1965), p. 6.

[23] *Manpower Report of the President, 1967, op. cit.,* p. 269.

[24] *Manpower Report of the President, 1966, op. cit.,* pp. 91, 92.

[25] *Ibid.*

tional programs will be reflected in a better educated labor force in the future. Yet, despite such progress, it is expected that as late as 1975 the number of so-called functional illiterates (i.e., persons with less than five years of formal schooling) in the labor force will still approximate 2 million.[26] The federal government is cognizant of the seriousness of this problem and is engaged in financing a wide variety of educational and training programs with related supporting activities broadly identifiable as "manpower development." Excluding general aid to education and Armed Forces programs, there are 35 federal laws containing provision for direct financial assistance to persons while enrolled in educational or occupational training programs. In 1965, over 6.7 million persons were enrolled in some type of federally assisted education or training manpower development program at a total cost of approximately $1.8 billion. In the same year, over $500 million was appropriated for manpower development under the Economic Opportunity Act alone, which is designed to meet the needs of persons within the poverty population.[27]

The Changing Composition of the Labor Force

The foregoing brief statistical review suggests the need for a more careful analysis of the changing composition of the labor force as it grows over time. Differences in the rate of growth of various groups within the labor force will tend to produce or to aggravate special problems affecting such segments of our working population. But even if a particular group is growing at a relatively lesser percentage rate than at other times in its development, the absolute increase in its numbers may still present acute problems in terms of available employment opportunities. In the following discussion we shall take a look at certain of the major components of the labor force and consider the special problems facing each of them in the years ahead.

Youth

The number of young people in the labor force has been increasing at an amazing rate. In 1970 there will be 48% more workers under the age of 25 than at the beginning of the decade.[28] These are the wartime babies coming to maturity. The increase in the number of young workers has been occurring despite increased school enrollment, which normally would postpone entrance into the labor market. However, a remarkable phenomenon of the past decade has been the increase in the number of young people who work while attending school. Some 5.3 million stu-

[26] Harold Goldstein, "Projections of the Labor Force in the United States," in G. L. Mangum (ed.), *The Manpower Revolution: Its Policy Consequences* (Garden City, N.Y.: Doubleday & Co., Inc., 1965), p. 17.

[27] U.S. Department of Labor, Manpower Administration, "Federally Assisted Manpower Development Programs," undated, pp. 2, 3.

[28] *Manpower Report of the President, 1967, op. cit.,* Table E–3, p. 269.

dents age 14 to 24 were in the labor force in October, 1966, nearly 2 million more than in 1960.[29]

Of special significance is the fact that the Negro segment of the young adult group in the labor force has been growing at a much faster rate than the white segment. Between 1965 and 1970, nonwhite members of the labor force aged 14 to 24 years are expected to increase by 28%, while the comparable white group will increase by only 19.6%.[30] The number of Negro teen-agers in cities rose by over 50% in the five-year period, 1960–65, about twice as fast as the teen-age population nationally.[31] These teen-agers will now be seeking jobs in the labor market. These unprecedented increases in numbers of young people—many of them now jobless, out of school, and living under substandard conditions —are a potential source of social dynamite in the slums.

While the percentage increase in young workers in the labor force will not be as great during the decade of the 1970's as during the 1960's, nevertheless there will be no letup in the number of young job seekers in the foreseeable future. The 18-year-old population will remain at about its present level of 3.5 million for a few years and then begin to rise slowly to about 4 million by 1973.[32] Not only must jobs be provided for the millions of young new entrants to the labor force, but employment must also be found for the young people who have been working part time but will now require full-time work.

The problem is a staggering one. Thus far, we have not succeeded in providing adequate job opportunities for our teen-agers. In 1967, about 13% of our young people aged 16 to 19 were unemployed—more than three times the average unemployment rate for the entire civilian labor force. The unemployment rate for Negro teen-agers is even higher— 26.5%.[33] While unemployment rates have always been higher for young people because of lack of experience, lack of protection by seniority provisions, and the frequency of transitional part-time employment, nevertheless the existence of such a high rate of unemployment at a time when this age group is growing so rapidly in the labor market poses a social problem of serious proportions.

The Older Worker

Another significant trend in composition of the labor force involves the increase in the number of older workers. The "older worker" is

---

[29] Vera C. Perrella, "Employment of School Age Youth," *Monthly Labor Review*, Vol. XC (August, 1967), p. 20.

[30] *Manpower Report of the President, 1967, op. cit.*, Table E–5, p. 271.

[31] *Manpower Report of the President, 1967, op. cit.*, p. 91.

[32] *Manpower Report of the President, 1967, op. cit.*, p. 43.

[33] U.S. Department of Labor, Bureau of Labor Statistics, *Employment and Earnings, January, 1968* (Washington, D.C.: U.S. Government Printing Office, February, 1968), pp. 10–11.

defined in our youth-oriented economy as a person 45 years of age or over, an identification related to the special unemployment problems which workers in this age classification experience. It is rather ironic that a society which has achieved such marked success in prolonging the average life-span should relegate workers in their productive middle years to the category of "older workers."

Between 1960 and 1970, it is expected that the number of persons in the labor force aged 45 to 64 will have grown by almost 5 million—an increase of about 17% since the beginning of the decade. During the 1970's, there will be a significant slackening in the rate of growth in this component of the labor force with the number of persons in this age group increasing by only 1.7 million during the entire decade.[34]

Our concern with this group of workers rises out of the difficulty they experience in obtaining employment once they lose their current jobs. The rate of joblessness among workers over 45 is actually less than the average rate for the labor force as a whole. However, once unemployed, the older worker tends to remain unemployed longer, because many employers impose arbitrary restrictions which impede the hiring of older workers. Furthermore, older workers dislike changes in occupation, industry, or place of employment and are frequently unwilling to undergo the training necessary to fit them for new jobs. In a period of rapid economic and technological change, it is obvious that older workers may be faced with many problems to which they may be unwilling or unable to adapt.

Women at Work

Today about 36% of all workers are female. By contrast, in 1950 only 27% of all workers were female.[35] It is evident that more and more women have been entering the labor force. As a matter of fact, in the decade of the 1960's, slightly more women were added to the labor force than men—6.6 million women and 6.3 million men. The number of women in the labor force is continuing to grow, though at a somewhat diminished rate. From 1960 to 1970, the number of women in the labor force will have increased by about 28%; the anticipated growth from 1970 to 1980 is 21%.

The movement of women into gainful employment represents a long-run trend of great significance for our economy. This trend has been closely associated with a number of changes, such as the reduction in the size of families, the transfer to the factory of much productive work formerly done in the home, the increased utilization of laborsaving equipment and conveniences in the home, and the increasing desire of women

---

[34] *Manpower Report of the President, 1967, op. cit.,* Table E–3, p. 269.

[35] *American Women, Report of the President's Commission on the Status of Women* (Washington, D.C.: U.S. Government Printing Office, 1963), p. 28.

for economic independence. Furthermore, the shift of population from rural areas to towns and cities has placed more women in geographic locations where job opportunities are expanding in manufacturing and in clerical, sales, and service jobs. The opportunities for women to secure work outside the home have also been greatly augmented by the increasing acceptance of women in the professions and in clerical, sales, and similar fields of employment.

The composition of the female labor force has also been undergoing a surprising change. The typical female worker is not the young girl who pounds a typewriter until she can "catch a man." The average woman worker is 39 years old, and more than 60% are married. There is a marked correlation between women's interest in employment—and success in obtaining it—and the extent of their education and training. In 1965, the proportion of women in the labor force was only 31% among those with eight years of schooling, 45% among high school graduates, 54% among four-year college graduates, and 72% in the group with five years or more of college.

Despite the progress which women have made in recent years in gainful employment, they are still faced by major handicaps in the labor market. The range of jobs open to women is still limited; three out of every five women workers end up with jobs classified as clerical, operative, or service. About one third of all women workers are found in just seven occupations: secretary, saleswoman, private household worker, elementary schoolteacher, bookkeeper, waitress, and professional nurse.

Women generally have lower earnings than men, even when employed in comparable occupations. In saleswork they earn about two fifths as much as men; in clerical and professional occupations, where the income gap is smallest, they earn about two thirds as much as men. Likewise, their unemployment rate is consistently higher than the rate for men.[36] As will be further discussed in Chapter 24, the federal government, 33 states, and the District of Columbia have enacted laws requiring equal pay for equal work, but the problems noted above persist nonetheless. The disadvantages women experience in the labor market reflect a variety of circumstances which are not likely to change markedly in the near future: interrupted work experience,[37] emphasis on traditional occupational choices, limitations on education and training, limited physical strength, and socially accepted stereotypes about "women's jobs" and "men's jobs."

[36] For the statistics noted in the text and other data on women in the labor force, see *Manpower Report of the President, 1967, op. cit.*, pp. 134–39.

[37] The fact that men generally have more seniority in jobs than women accounts for some of the differential in pay between men and women in similar jobs. A Bureau of Labor Statistics study of eight office and three plant locations found that the average job tenure of male clerical workers was nearly twice that of women. *Monthly Labor Review*, Vol. XC (December, 1967), p. 43.

Part-Time Workers

Part-time employment is generally defined as employment for fewer than 35 hours a week. Part-time workers are making up an increasing proportion of the nation's labor force. Between 1950 and 1965, the number of persons working primarily full time during the year increased by one fifth, while over the same 15-year period, part-time workers increased by two thirds.[38] In 1967, over 10 million men and women were employed voluntarily on a part-time basis.[39] Both supply and demand factors have combined to produce this increase in part-time employment. On the one hand, there has been a sharp increase in the number of workers seeking part-time employment, particularly middle-aged women and youth. For example, the number of teen-age boys working part time more than doubled between 1950 and 1965.[40] On the other hand, the extension of legislation requiring overtime pay, continuing consumer demand for more shopping hours in the evening, and climbing fringe benefits for full-time workers have made it more desirable and less costly for employers to hire part-time workers than to utilize full-time workers for the same hours of employment.

Two classes of part-time employment can be distinguished—that which is voluntary on the part of the worker who just does not want to work full time and that which represents an involuntary reduction from full-time schedules for economic reasons. Over 80% of all part-time workers fall in the former category. They are primarily housewives and students who because of other obligations are not willing or available to work full time.

Part-time unemployment of the economic type represents a failure by our economy to utilize its human resources fully. In December, 1967, an estimated 2.4 million workers were employed part time but would have preferred full-time employment.[41] Part-time employment of this kind fluctuates with the business cycle, rising in periods of recession when companies are cutting work schedules to save costs and diminishing as business conditions improve. Such part-time employment is most common among semiskilled and unskilled workers.

Part-time employment—both voluntary and involuntary—is particularly common among the very young (under age 18) and those over the age of 65. Likewise, in almost every age class, women are more likely to be employed part time than men. Part-time employment is most preva-

---

[38] U.S. Department of Labor, Bureau of Labor Statistics, *Work Experience of the Population in 1965* (Special Labor Force Report No. 76 [Washington, D.C., December, 1966]), p. 1375.

[39] *Employment and Earnings, op. cit.*, Table A–7, p. 41.

[40] *Work Experience of the Population in 1965, op. cit.*, p. 1375.

[41] *Employment and Earnings, op. cit.*, Table A–22, p. 50.

lent among nonwhite workers, and as might be expected, involuntary part-time employment also bears heavily upon this group. Although nonwhite workers constitute only about 11% of the total labor force, they account for 26% of involuntary part-time employment.[42]

The Changing Status of the Negro

Approximately 11% of the civilian labor force is classified as nonwhite—i.e., Negro, Oriental, or American Indian. Over 90% of this group is Negro. We shall therefore use the terms Negro and nonwhite interchangeably in the discussion in this text.

In recent years, there has been a gradual breaking down of some of the age-old barriers between white and nonwhite in terms of education, occupation, and social status. Nevertheless, important differences remain in the characteristics of the white and nonwhite components of the labor force. Thus, nonwhite persons go to work at an earlier age and remain in the labor force to a greater extent after 65 years of age; nonwhite women have a greater tendency to remain in the labor force after marriage; and because of high mortality and heavy toll of disability on the job, nonwhite workers have a considerably shorter average working life.

A majority of Negro families still live in the South, but there has been a heavy migration of Negroes to the metropolitan areas of the North. Negroes in metropolitan areas (both in the North and the South) are concentrated in the central cities, where 56% of all Negroes now live, whereas whites live predominantly outside the core city—in the suburbs or smaller towns. Negroes are increasing as a percent of the total population in almost all large cities and today represent 26% of the population in cities of metropolitan areas with a million or more people, compared to 13% in 1950.[43] The exodus of Negroes from the South to the North is in part a reflection of the movement of colored workers from a sharecropping existence on the farm to the industrial life of the big cities. It also represents a movement of people seeking better economic opportunities in an environment where they hoped the barriers of discrimination would be less rigid than in the society they left. The move from agriculture, where underemployment is chronic but total unemployment is comparatively rare, has brought new problems to Negroes, for every recession falls with special force upon them. Moreover, the occupational stratification which has developed as a result of their lack of skills, on the one hand, and discriminatory practices by both employers and unions, on the other, has made them particularly vulnerable to unemployment.

Over the past decade, nonwhite workers have made important strides in entering occupational fields formerly unavailable to them. For

[42] *Manpower Report of the President, 1967, op. cit.,* p. 128.

[43] U.S. Department of Labor, Bureau of Labor Statistics, *Social and Economic Conditions of Negroes in the United States* (Report No. 332 [Washington, D.C., October, 1967]), pp. 9, 10.

example, employment of nonwhites in professional, technical, and kindred occupations has increased more rapidly over the past decade than in any other major occupational group and much faster than employment of white workers in these fields.[44] Despite these gains, nonwhite workers tend to be disproportionately concentrated in the less skilled blue-collar and service industries. As can be seen from Table 1–2, almost one out of every

TABLE 1–2

Occupation Group of Employed Persons, by Color, November, 1967
(Percent Distribution)

Occupation	White	Nonwhite
White-collar workers	49.6	23.9
Professional and technical	14.4	7.6
Managers, officials, and proprietors	11.0	2.7
Clerical workers	17.5	11.8
Sales workers	6.6	1.9
Blue-collar workers	35.4	42.3
Craftsmen, foremen	13.8	7.8
Operatives	17.9	23.7
Nonfarm laborers	3.7	10.8
Service workers	10.5	28.8
Private household workers	1.5	9.4
Service, except private household	9.0	19.4
Farm workers	4.6	4.9

Source: U.S. Department of Labor, Bureau of Labor Statistics, *Employment and Earnings* (Washington, D.C.: U.S. Government Printing Office, December, 1967), p. 28, Table A–17.

two white workers has found employment in the rapidly growing white-collar occupations, but for nonwhites the ratio is less than one out of every four. Relatively few Negroes have been able to find employment as managerial or sales workers; in 1966, Negro workers constituted only about 3% of the 12 million employees in these occupations.[45]

Because of the changing structure of the job market, employment in the occupations in which Negroes are now concentrated will be growing more slowly than in other fields. As a consequence, if nonwhites are to continue to improve their employment situation in the future, they will have to gain a larger proportion of the jobs in the white-collar and skilled occupations even faster than heretofore. Projections made by the U.S. Department of Labor indicate that if nonwhites merely continue to hold

[44] Joseph L. Russell, "Changing Patterns in Employment of Nonwhite Workers," *Monthly Labor Review*, Vol. LXXIX (May, 1966), p. 89.

[45] U.S. Department of Labor, *The Employment Situation for Negroes* (Washington, D.C., September, 1967), p. 14.

the same proportion of jobs in each occupation that they held in 1965, nonwhite employment will grow to 9.1 million in 1975, but the nonwhite proportion of total employment would decline because of the slower growth rate of occupations in which nonwhites are concentrated. The result of maintaining the status quo in occupational distribution would be an estimated nonwhite unemployment rate of about 15%—which would, of course, be intolerable. Even if the proportion of nonwhite workers in each occupation should continue to change between 1965 and 1975 at the same rate as during the 1958–65 period, employment of nonwhites would rise only to 10.2 million in 1975, and the 1975 unemployment rate for nonwhites would still be twice that for the labor force as a whole.[46]

It is obvious that there must be an acceleration in the rate of transfer of Negroes from blue-collar jobs to growth-oriented white-collar occupations if any substantial improvement is to be effected in reducing the already high Negro unemployment rate. The need for opening up additional job opportunities for Negroes is made even more pressing by the fact that the Negro work force will be growing at a faster rate in the future than the white. It is anticipated that by 1980, the total nonwhite labor force will have risen by 41% (compared with 1965), while the white labor force will show only a 28% increase in the same period. This projected difference in growth is primarily attributable to the expected greater rate of population growth among nonwhite youth.[47]

Throughout the postwar period, unemployment has consistently fallen most heavily on the Negro worker. Nonwhites are only 11% of the civilian labor force but usually account for over 20% of the jobless total, and their unemployment rate has typically been at least double the rate for white workers.[48] Furthermore, when employed, nonwhite workers generally receive lower earnings than white workers in similar occupations. This comes about from two circumstances. In the first place, in any particular occupational grouping, Negro workers tend to have the jobs at the bottom of the ladder—the most menial and least skilled. In the second place, even on the same jobs, Negroes will frequently earn less because of lesser seniority or because of discriminatory practices. It is significant that in occupations such as mail carriers, protective service workers, and bus drivers—in which workers are largely municipal or federal employees and under fair employment practice regulations—the earnings of nonwhite men are equal to or close to those of white men of similar education.[49]

[46] Russell, *op. cit.,* p. 89.

[47] Sophia Cooper and Denis F. Johnston, "Labor Force Projections by Color, 1970–80," *Monthly Labor Review*, Vol. LXXIX (September, 1966), p. 965.

[48] *The Employment Situation for Negroes, op. cit.,* pp. 14–15.

[49] *Nation's Manpower Revolution* (Hearings before the Subcommittee on Employment and Manpower of the Committee on Labor and Public Welfare, U.S. Senate, 88th Cong., 1st sess., May 20, 1963 [Washington, D.C.: U.S. Government Printing Office, 1963]), Part II, p. 404.

The foregoing statistics highlight the problem faced by the Negro worker in the American economy. Negro leaders believe that at the root of such problems is the persistence of discriminatory employment practices in American industry. Beginning with New York and New Jersey in 1945, 34 states have passed laws prohibiting discrimination based on race, religion, or national origin, and a federal law became effective in July, 1965. A detailed discussion of these state and federal laws is found in Chapter 24.

The future of the Negro worker is tied inextricably with the fate of our central cities. We have already mentioned that the Negro population is tending to concentrate in the core city areas. These are also areas where poverty, substandard housing, and unemployment rates two or three times the national rate are commonplace. One recent survey of 10 slum areas in major cities found that three out of every four unemployed workers were nonwhite.[50] An understanding of Negro unemployment can be obtained only after an examination of the problems of poverty, unemployment, and substandard employment which confront the residents of the nation's slum and depressed areas. We shall consider this problem in detail in Chapter 14.

OCCUPATION AND SOCIOECONOMIC STATUS

We live in an evolutionary economy in which basic trends are constantly at work changing the composition of the labor force, the manner in which it is employed, and even the locus of its employment. The labor market itself is in a constant state of flux. New industries are born, old ones decline, rendering old skills obsolete and creating demands for new ones. Today, while the level of overall employment in our economy is at an all-time high, stubborn pockets of unemployment remain in many areas of our country. While it is facile to equate such unemployment to a lack of job opportunities, it is more perceptive to recognize that a substantial amount of unemployment is attributable to the fact that the industry mix in our economy has changed rapidly in recent years and has not been matched by a comparable adaptation in the skills of our labor force. In the following discussion, we shall examine in detail some of the major trends which are affecting the nature of employment in our economy and altering the occupational and socioeconomic status of our labor force.

The Decline in Agricultural Employment

As laborsaving machinery has taken over the backbreaking work which used to be required on the farm, the surplus population from our large farm families has gravitated to the cities to work in industry. Thus, as industrial employment has risen, agricultural employment has fallen

---

[50] *The Employment Situation for Negroes, op. cit.,* p. 18.

drastically. In 1900, about one out of every three persons gainfully employed was engaged in farming or other agricultural pursuit. In 1967, agriculture accounted for only 3,844,000 employees out of a total of 74,372,000 employed in both agriculture and nonagricultural industries, or about 5% of employment.[51] Agricultural employment has been declining at the rate of about 200,000 workers per year over most of the past decade, but in 1966, farm employment dropped by a surprising 400,000 as the lure of high-paid city jobs quickened the movement from farm to the urban centers.[52]

The sharpest drop over the years has been in the number of farm operators and unpaid family workers, which declined from 7.9 million in 1945 to 4.1 million in 1965—a reduction of 48%. Employment of hired workers has decreased more slowly—from 2.1 million in 1945 to less than 1.5 million in 1965, a decline of about 30%. The dynamic factor which has revolutionized agriculture has been the application of modern technology to farming. Through the use of giant machines, it has been possible to curtail employment and at the same time increase output. Man-hours of labor used on the farm fell by more than half between 1947 and 1965, while farm output increased by over 40%. Most of the labor now required in agriculture is now seasonal, part time, or migratory. Only about 300,000 hired workers are employed year-round on our farms.[53]

The agricultural work force is expected to continue to decline at a rate of about 4% per year.[54] Most of the decline in employment is projected to occur among the self-employed and family workers. The number of hired workers will remain relatively stable. As the work force declines further and even more sophisticated machines are used on the farm, workers with training and skills will be much in demand. It is significant to observe, therefore, that in agriculture, as in industry, future developments will place a premium on skill and training.

The Shift from Goods-Producing to Service Industries

A surprising aspect of our machine-oriented industrial economy is the decline in importance of the goods-producing sector as a source of employment opportunities. Table 1–3 shows how employment was divided between the goods-producing and service sectors of the economy in 1947, 1957, and 1966, and how the division of employment is projected to look in 1975. Whereas in 1947 about 42% of all workers in nonagricultural establishments were employed in the production of goods, by 1966 the proportion had fallen to 36%, and projections for 1975 suggest that

[51] *Manpower Report of the President, 1968, op. cit.,* p. 221.

[52] *Manpower Report of the President, 1967, op. cit.,* p. 37.

[53] For the statistics referred to in the text and other data on agriculture, see *Manpower Report of the President, 1966, op. cit.,* pp. 120–21.

[54] Phyllis Groom, "Today's Farm Jobs and Farmworkers," *Monthly Labor Review,* Vol. XC (April, 1967), p. 3.

TABLE 1-3

PERCENT DISTRIBUTION OF ACTUAL AND PROJECTED EMPLOYMENT IN NONAGRICULTURAL
ESTABLISHMENTS BY INDUSTRY DIVISION, 1947, 1957, 1966, AND 1975

Industry Division	1947	1957	1966*	1975†
Total	100.0	100.0	100.0	100.0
Goods-producing industries	42.1	39.6	36.0	32.3
Manufacturing	35.4	32.5	29.9	26.0
Durable goods	19.1	18.6	17.5	15.1
Nondurable goods	16.3	13.8	12.4	10.9
Mining	2.2	1.6	1.0	.8
Construction	4.5	5.5	5.1	5.5
Service-producing industries	57.9	60.5	64.0	67.7
Transportation and other utilities	9.5	8.0	6.5	6.0
Trade	20.4	20.6	20.7	21.2
Finance, insurance, and real estate	4.0	4.7	4.8	4.9
Services and miscellaneous	11.5	12.8	15.0	17.1
Government	12.5	14.4	17.0	18.5
Federal	4.3	4.2	4.0	3.5
State and local	8.2	10.2	13.0	15.0

NOTE: Individual items may not add to totals because of rounding. Data include Alaska and Hawaii beginning 1959 and are therefore not strictly comparable with previous years.
* Preliminary.
† Projected.
SOURCE: U.S. Department of Labor, *Manpower Report of the President, 1967* (Washington, D.C.: U.S. Government Printing Office, 1967), pp. 248, 274.

the continuing decline will bring the percentage down to about 32% in that year. Even if we include agriculture in goods producing (not so indicated in Table 1-3), it is still true that approximately two out of every three American workers are employed today in the service sector of the economy.[55]

Manufacturing is still the single most important source of employment opportunities, but until the last few years, employment in manufacturing had shown little growth. In 1963, for example, there were fewer persons employed in manufacturing than in 1957. However, with the pickup in rate of economic growth in the past few years, manufacturing has provided a significant increase in new job opportunities. Thus, in 1966, manufacturing added one million net new jobs for the largest annual gain since the early 1950's.[56]

The increase in overall employment which we have witnessed in recent years has come about primarily in the mushrooming service, government, finance, and trade sectors of the economy. Since 1947, the service-producing sector of the economy has accounted for more than three fourths of all new jobs created in the nonfarm economy.[57] Most

[55] Harry I. Greenfield, *Manpower and the Growth of Producer Services* (New York: Columbia University Press, 1966), p. vii.
[56] *Manpower Report of the President, 1967, op. cit.*, p. 20.
[57] *Manpower Report of the President, 1967, op. cit.*, p. 23.

people are aware of the increasing importance of consumer service industries, such as retail trade, recreation, and finance. There is also another part of the service sector which has been growing rapidly—producer services, or what one writer[58] defines as "those services which business firms, nonprofit institutions, and governments provide and usually sell to the producer rather than to the consumer." In this category fall such services as data processing, rental of equipment, and cleaning and maintenance of buildings, all of which reflect the tendency to increased specialization in every aspect of industry. It is significant to note that while consumer services typically have a high concentration of female employment with relatively low pay scales, producer services have a greater percentage of male employment and higher average earnings than are shown for the labor force as a whole.[59]

If we look ahead to 1975, it is anticipated that the service-producing industries will provide three fourths of the increase in jobs which will occur between the present and that date. The service sector will be employing larger and larger proportions of the labor force, and its requirements will be mainly for skilled, well-educated workers.

The Growth in White-Collar Employment

A third significant trend has involved a shift in employment toward white-collar occupations, such as professional, managerial, clerical, and sales work, and away from the blue-collar occupations of craftsmen, operatives, and laborers. This change in the nature of the occupational content of jobs has been associated with the shift from goods-producing to service-producing industries and with the rapid growth of employment in the governmental sector of the economy, which creates jobs primarily for white-collar workers.

This trend toward more white-collar employment has been evident in our economy since the turn of the century and is part of the normal evolution of economic development which shifts labor resources from agriculture to manufacturing and then to services. The increasing importance of white-collar jobs is not, however, just another manifestation of the shift from goods-producing to service industries; for even within manufacturing industry itself, nonproduction white-collar employment has grown faster than production employment.

White-collar jobs have made rapid gains in recent years. By the middle of the 1950's, white-collar workers began to outnumber blue-collar workers; by 1975, white-collar jobs are expected to be almost 50% more numerous than blue-collar jobs.[60] Within the white-collar and blue-collar categories there will be a further restructuring of the labor market toward higher skill requirements. As can be seen from Table 1–4, between

[58] Greenfield, *op. cit.,* p. 1.

[59] *Ibid.*

[60] *Economic Potentials of the United States in the Next Decade, op. cit.,* p. 7.

TABLE 1-4. ACTUAL AND PROJECTED EMPLOYMENT BY MAJOR OCCUPATION GROUP, 1960 TO 1975

Major Occupation Group	Actual				Projected*				Change, 1960–65		Change, 1965–75	
	1960		1965		1970		1975					
	No. (000)	%	No. (000)	%	No. (000,000)	%	No. (000,000)	%	No. (000,000)	%	No. (000,000)	%†
Total employment‡	66,681	100.0	72,179	100.0	81.2	100.0	88.7	100.0	5.5	8.2	16.5	22.8
Professional, technical, and kindred workers	7,475	11.2	8,883	12.3	11.0	13.5	12.9	14.5	1.4	18.8	4.0	45.2
Managers, officials, and proprietors, except farm	7,067	10.6	7,340	10.2	8.4	10.3	9.2	10.4	.3	3.9	1.9	25.3
Clerical and kindred workers	9,783	14.7	11,166	15.5	13.1	16.1	14.6	16.5	1.4	14.1	3.4	30.8
Salesworkers	4,401	6.6	4,715	6.5	5.3	6.5	5.8	6.5	.3	7.1	1.1	23.0
Craftsmen, foremen, and kindred workers	8,560	12.8	9,221	12.8	10.4	12.8	11.4	12.9	.7	7.7	2.2	23.6
Operatives and kindred workers	11,986	18.0	13,390	18.6	14.3	17.6	15.0	16.9	1.4	11.7	1.6	12.0
Service workers, including private household	8,349	12.5	9,342	12.9	11.1	13.7	12.6	14.2	1.0	11.9	3.2	34.5
Laborers, except farm and mine	3,665	5.5	3,855	5.3	3.7	4.6	3.7	4.2	.2	5.2	–.1	–3.0§
Farmers and farm managers, laborers, and foremen	5,395	8.1	4,265	5.9	3.9	4.8	3.5	3.9	–1.1	–20.9	–.8	–18.9

* Based on an assumption of 3-percent unemployment.
† Based on data in thousands where available.
‡ Represents total employment as covered by the monthly household survey of the labor force.
§ Employment is projected at about the level of the past decade; however, because 1965 employment was unusually high, reflecting a sharp increase in manufacturing, the projected percent change from 1965 indicates an apparent decline.
SOURCE: *Manpower Report of the President, 1967*, Table E–8, p. 274.

1965 and 1975 it is anticipated that professional, technical, and kindred workers—white-collar occupations requiring a high degree of skill—will increase by 45.2%, while salesworkers—a lower-skill occupation—will increase by only 23%. Similarly, within the blue-collar classification, craftsmen, foremen, and kindred workers (high skill) will increase by 23.6%, while laborers, except farm and mine (low skill) are expected to decrease by 3%. It is clear that the industrial and occupational trends foreseeable in the next decade will underline for all young people entering the labor market the need for increased education and training so that they can qualify for the challenging jobs ahead.

Although technological progress has been changing our economy into a nation of employees, it has not been building a proletariat. Scientists, supervisors, artists, teachers, professional workers, and other white-collar workers have been increasing at a much faster rate than the working population as a whole. The increasing importance of middle-class occupations has tended to strengthen the forces of conservatism and to some extent has made more difficult the task of union organization. White-collar workers often ally themselves with management groups in their thinking on economic matters; by and large, they have looked upon union organization as a blue-collar movement. Unions have found white-collar workers difficult to organize. Union members are a minority of the 16 million clerical and sales workers.[61] Recent successful organizing drives among teachers and other government employees have made some inroads in the white-collar group,[62] but most white-collar workers still remain outside the union fold. Union leaders, faced by the changing composition of the labor force, must find some way of attracting white-collar workers as members. Failing this, organized labor will decline in importance in the years to come.

Government Employees

Another trend of great significance has been the vast growth in government employment, which has been increasing at a much faster rate than nongovernmental employment. Total government employment increased from 6,556,000 in 1945, to 11,479,000 in 1966. The largest growth has occurred in state and local government, which jumped from 3,181,000 in 1945 to 8,618,000 in 1966. Projections for the 10-year period 1965–75 indicate that state and local government employment will jump by almost 50% over this period, while federal employment is expected to rise by only 11%.[63]

Government employment is one area in which the changing compo-

[61] However, unions in government employment are among the fastest growing in the nation. See Chapter 23.

[62] About 1 out of every 12 union members is now on a government payroll, and the percentage is increasing. *Business Week*, October 21, 1967, p. 76.

[63] For the statistics in the text and other data on government employment, see *Manpower Report of the President, 1968, op. cit.*, pp. 180–81, and *Handbook of Labor Statistics, op. cit.*, p. 69.

sition of the labor market tends to favor union organization. The militancy demonstrated by unions which have become entrenched among key groups of government employees portends major problems of public policy in the years ahead. We shall explore some of these problems in depth in Chapter 23.

WHAT IS A LABOR PROBLEM?

We have reviewed briefly the composition, characteristics, and projected growth of the labor force. That term, as most commonly used, refers to the civilian labor force and therefore includes all of the gainfully employed persons in the country, whether they be bank presidents or common laborers. "Labor problems" typically involve only a certain segment of the civilian labor force. A simple illustration will serve to indicate the criterion which separates the group with which we are concerned from other members of the labor force. Consider the case of John Jones, the independent grocer, who owns his own store and is self-employed. His income depends upon the margin between his sales receipts and the cost of his wares, after covering expenses of operation. Suppose competition from other grocers compels him to reduce prices so that, as a consequence, his income is cut in half. John Jones may now complain that his labor is not being adequately compensated; yet ordinarily, this circumstance would not be considered a labor problem.

Now, change the facts slightly. John Jones employs 10 clerks in his store. Competition forces him to cut their wages in half. Here, we have a labor problem. What is the essential difference between the two cases? The difference lies in the fact that John Jones is self-employed, while his clerks work for wages and are therefore dependent upon their employer for their livelihood. Labor problems grow out of the economic activity of that part of the working population which offers its services for hire to *others* and receives its compensation in the form of wages or salaries. Because they are dependent upon others to offer them employment, wage and salary earners are subject to the risk of unemployment. Because they are dependent upon employers for their daily income, their interests frequently clash with those of the latter group. The result is strikes, lockouts, slowdowns, and other manifestations of labor strife. Finally, because they have this common bond of dependence upon others for their employment and income, a certain feeling of solidarity tends to exist among members of this group, despite the diversity of their occupations. This sense of a common status has led many of them to join together in unions to present a common front to their employers and to the owners of the means of production.

Organized Labor and Labor Problems

While much of the theoretical discussion in later chapters of this book concerning the labor market, supply and demand, and related considerations is applicable to all persons who work for hire, our major emphasis will be upon organized labor and the problems which arise between unions and management in the collective bargaining process. The reason for this emphasis is clear. While only one out of every four workers is a union member, nevertheless union actions and union policies affect the working of the entire labor market. We have already noted that large corporations control the bulk of our industrial assets and employ the majority of our workers in manufacturing. For the most part, these giants of industry are unionized. As a consequence, agreements reached by management and union representatives in these companies profoundly affect production, income, prices, and employment throughout the economy.

In the manufacturing field, practically all our key industries are strongly unionized. Today virtually no one works at production jobs in the steel, automobile, rubber, can, flat glass, men's clothing, and women's garment industries except on terms agreed to by some union. The same is true for the railroads, air transport, and in many parts of the trucking, construction, electric light and power, and paper industries. While, as has been pointed out earlier in this chapter, the growing importance of white-collar employment and the diminishing importance of production workers in our economy may in the long run weaken the position of organized labor, at the present time and for the foreseeable future organized labor exercises—and will continue to exercise—a major influence on trends in the labor market.

There would undoubtedly be labor problems without unions. For example, we experienced strikes, large wage increases, and a wage-price inflation in 1919 when unions were weak and industry was largely unorganized. But the fact remains that in our economy today the labor problems that make the headlines and require our study are primarily problems in which unions play a key role. We shall, therefore, begin our study of labor problems by reviewing the history and development of organized labor in this country so as to understand better the motivation, objectives, and policies of organized labor.

In the following discussion, it is important to keep in mind a fundamental consideration which has shaped the nature of the labor problems which we shall be studying. Labor problems, as a phenomenon of American industrial development, have arisen from voluntary employer-employee relations in a free labor market. Labor problems are a manifestation of freedom of choice in economic activity. Strikes and lockouts, for example, are concrete demonstrations of the freedom of the employee not to work, and of the corresponding privilege of the employer not to hire. Strikes, unemployment, wage demands, and other aspects of labor problems in America are phenomena which can exist only in a democratic society. Communists boast that in Russia there is no unemployment, no strikes, no conflict over wages. The reason is there is little freedom of choice. Both management and labor are shackled by the arbitrary whim of a dictatorial bureaucracy.

QUESTIONS FOR DISCUSSION

1. Discuss the various meanings which can be attached to the phrase "labor force." Consider how the following factors might affect the size of the labor force: war mobilization; massive unemployment; increased social security benefits; elimination of discrimination in employment.
2. How does the changing occupational structure of employment affect the problem of providing jobs for Negroes in our economy?
3. Karl Marx predicted that the growth of capitalism would produce an industrial proletariat, squeeze out the small businessman and shopkeeper, and therefore set the stage for Communist revolution. To what extent has the development of capitalism in the United States differed from this prediction?

SUGGESTIONS FOR FURTHER READING

Economic Report of the President, January, 1968. Washington, D.C.: U.S. Government Printing Office, 1968.

An invaluable source of current information on labor, population, business, and other economic trends and statistics.

REES, ALBERT. "The American Labor Force," in William Haber (ed.), *Labor in a Changing America*, pp. 1–11. New York: Basic Books, Inc. 1966.

An excellent analysis of the changing participation rates of various groups within the overall labor force.

RUSSELL, J. L. "Changing Patterns in Employment of Nonwhite Workers," *Monthly Labor Review*, Vol. LXXXIX (May, 1966), pp. 503–509.

An informative discussion of how the changing occupational structure in the American economy complicates the problem of reducing Negro unemployment.

U.S. DEPARTMENT OF LABOR. *Manpower Report of the President, 1968.* Washington, D.C.: U.S. Government Printing Office, March, 1968.

A concise explanation, supported by up-to-date statistics, of the changes which have occurred and are continuing in population, labor force, and employment.

PART II

Union History and Government

Chapter	HISTORY OF THE AMERICAN
2	LABOR MOVEMENT

Unions today have a profound effect on the American economic system. The allocation of economic resource, the sharing of the product of industry, political attitudes and alignments, employment and unemployment, legal rights and duties, business stability, technical prog-

FIGURE 2–1

CHANGES IN UNION MEMBERSHIP, 1950–68

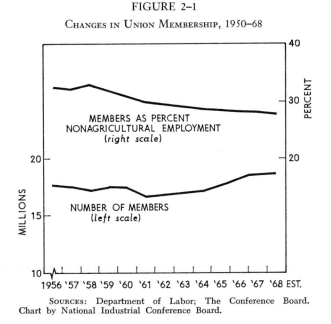

SOURCES: Department of Labor; The Conference Board.
Chart by National Industrial Conference Board.

ress and the rate of innovation in industry, and the policies and attitudes of government of all levels—all are influenced by union policies and programs. Despite the failure of union membership growth to keep pace with the growth in the labor force, union membership today is at an all-time peak (see Figure 2–1), and union power remains strong. Obviously, economic analysis must concern itself with union policy and practice if such analysis is to present a realistic contemporary picture.

THE CONDITIONS OF ORGANIZATION

Despite differences, all labor movements have certain characteristics in common. Labor movements arise initially out of the separation of the worker from his tools. When a man becomes an employee instead of a self-employed person, he loses control over the terms and conditions of his employment. With the development of a factory system of labor and a concentration of ownership employing large numbers of workers, the individual finds his influence over working conditions steadily lessened. Workers tend to show interest in organizing unions when they feel that their immediate opportunities for advancement in the organizational hierarchy to the employer class are limited. The acceptance of unionism by a worker in a society like ours, with its relatively fluid class lines, does not mean that the worker will reject future opportunities to rise above the working group. It merely means that the worker believes that his present economic situation will be best served by union activity.

Workers also join unions to obtain a voice in their wages, hours, and working conditions. Even those satisfied with what they are paid form unions, often in order to participate in the determination of the conditions under which they work.

A fundamental condition for the existence of trade-unionism everywhere is the existence of freedom of speech, press, and assembly. The so-called "unions" which operate in dictatorial or totalitarian countries are, in fact, organs of the state, controlled and operated by the state, and lacking in power to act except to transmit state orders. We shall be concerned with unions in the traditional sense: organizations of workers which function primarily as the agent of employees in collective bargaining with employers or management over the terms and conditions of employment. Such unions may engage in a variety of supplementary activities, but their primary interest is in collective bargaining, and they are free, subject to some legal limitations, to act unrestricted by state control or domination.

Once the initial conditions are met, labor organizations emerge among employees who have bargaining power which the employer must respect. They are workers possessing a hard-to-replace skill, e.g., toolmakers; or those located at critical spots, e.g., teamsters or longshoremen. They may form a union solely of their own, or they may find it necessary or wise to bring in their less strategically located fellow employees. The skilled are the essentials of unionization.

The speed with which a labor movement organizes is a product of economic and political conditions. American labor unions have made their greatest gains in periods of rising prices and labor shortages (1863–72,

1896–1904, 1917–20, 1941–45, and 1965–67), and in periods of political unrest (1827–36, 1881–86, and 1933–37). When prices are rising and labor is in short demand, union growth occurs as employer resistance to large wage increases is tempered by high profits and difficulties of obtaining sufficient employees. In recent years, expansion of industries with compulsory union agreements has also spurred union growth.

Union expansion during periods of political unrest represents worker dissatisfaction with the manner in which the economic system is working. For example, in the 1930's, the widespread feeling that depression layoffs were not fairly handled greatly spurred interest in unions.

THE AMERICAN ENVIRONMENT

If, however, the conditions of union organization and growth are similar in various lands, the environment is not; and it is the uniqueness of the American scene which has made American labor unions unique. America was settled by a wide variety of races and nationalities who inhabit a wide area rich in natural resources. The results have been an unparalleled high standard of living for the masses, great opportunities for individual advancement, a huge market for industry's products, an abundance of living space, racial and national rivalries, and relative freedom from legal restraint on business and labor. The effect on the American labor movement has been profound.

Class Fluidity

A fundamental characteristic of the American scene has been the comparative fluidity of classes. Penniless immigrants arriving in the United States have seen their sons become business executives, labor leaders, statesmen. In America, one is not born in a status. Since class lines are not hard and fast, workers have been able to advance as individuals. American workers have, therefore, been less interested in trade-union organization. Indeed, it was not until the Great Depression of the 1930's that large numbers of workers decided that they needed unions at all.

America's loose class lines have not only hindered union development but have shaped unionism as well. In being interested primarily in improving labor's conditions within the capitalistic system, American unions reflect their members' basic belief that this is still the land of opportunity.

Resources and Land

The rich resources of America have, of course, aided in preventing the rise of hard class barriers by providing the opportunities for advancement. Moreover, the traditional "rugged individualism" of American employers stems from the same sources. In labor relations, employer "individualism" has featured opposition to government or union "interference" in the operation of business and the refusal to recognize unions of employees or collective bargaining until compelled by law.

One of America's great resources has been abundance of land. The westward migrations drained off potential city proletariat. Many workers went West to seek individual fortunes instead of remaining in the East and joining unions to seek group advancement. The movement of industry from urban areas to suburban and rural environments in recent years has further hindered unionization by decentralizing plants and work forces.

Wide Markets

The size of the American market has been an important factor contributing to the growth of American unions. To protect the workers under its jurisdiction, a union cannot raise the price of labor too far beyond that which competitors of the company are paying. A union must organize the length and breadth of the market. Otherwise, nonunion plants, by paying lower wages, may take business away from the union plants and thus imperil the jobs of the union workers. In the 1830's, a union did not have to organize much more than a citywide market. Poor transportation made the city relatively immune from competition of other areas. Today, however, the market is more likely to cover a far greater area, or even be national in scope. A union, therefore, must often become a national union of tremendous size in order to be a successful union in a national market.

The development of the national market not only stimulated national labor organization but paradoxically made that organization more difficult. With a continental market, nonunion competitors can be a thousand miles apart. The resources which American unions require in order to organize an industry are thus very great.

Moreover, the large American market permitted the breaking down of jobs into small specialized units of the mass-production process. Thousands of workers are employed in unskilled or semiskilled jobs, their efforts combining to perform a task done in smaller countries by a single skilled worker. Since the semiskilled and unskilled are easier to replace than the skilled, the bargaining power of labor was correspondingly reduced, and the ability of unions to compel a reluctant management to recognize their existence was considerably lessened.

Heterogeneous Population

Another factor hindering the development of labor organization is the existence of many races and nationalities without common heritage, with rivalries, suspicions, and often without obvious mutuality of interests. Such heterogeneity presents a labor force which is much more difficult to weld into a labor movement than one in which the labor force is homogeneous in ethnic background and composition. To the natural suspicions has been added the tendency of American employers to play up these differences in order to prevent unionization. The policy of many factories in employing a "judicious mixture" of ethnic groups, or the practice of substituting a new wave of immigrants when an older wave showed signs of becoming restive with the status quo, kept these rivalries alive and made the task of the union organizer all the more difficult. Current animosities among white and black workers attest to the continued existence of the racial problem in union organization.

Social and Legal Background

The legal and social system in the United States, itself a result of the environmental factors of the American scene, has strongly conditioned American labor. The strong support of private property among the masses, the high esteem of businessmen in the population as a whole, and the consequent unpopularity among the dominant middle class of trade-unionism, which is often pictured as "antibusiness," have all helped to make the American labor movement difficult to build and to shape its policies as well.

THE BEGINNINGS, 1790–1825[1]

Records of local labor unions and of strikes antedate the Revolutionary War, but labor organizations in colonial times were very short-lived. Commencing in the 1790's, however, came the first known unions which survived for a number of years—shoemakers, carpenters, printers, bakers, tailors, longshoremen, and teamsters formed organizations of their crafts and groups. Sometimes organization was defensive against the merchant-capitalist, a new functionary who bought and sold in large quantities over wide areas and therefore broadened the scope of competition. This often either compelled master craftsmen to discontinue independent work and hire out as journeymen or else forced the master to reduce the wages of his journeymen. On other occasions, organization was spurred by the shortage of skilled labor and the desires of craftsmen to take advantage of the demand for their services.

These early unions were composed entirely of skilled or strategically located (teamsters, longshoremen) workers. In fact, throughout history, this group has always been the first to organize. Those who, by reason of skill or strategic location, can exert pressure or inflict a loss by withdrawing their services possess the ability to secure employer recognition long before their less favorably placed fellow workers.

[1] Although the authors accept full responsibility for interpretations, they have frankly based the historical section on secondary sources, including the pioneer works of John R. Commons and his associates, R. F. Hoxie, and Norman J. Ware, but especially on the admirable synthesis of Professor Royal E. Montgomery— H. A. Millis and R. E. Montgomery, *Organized Labor* (New York: McGraw-Hill Book Co., 1945), pp. 1–242. The lack of detailed documentation is for reader convenience and is not intended to understress our great debt to these authors.

Early unions did not engage in collective bargaining as we know it today. Customarily, the union "posted its prices," i.e., announced the wages and working conditions for which its members would work. If the employer refused to agree, a strike would ensue, and perhaps a compromise would be worked out. Only slowly did the custom develop of joint employer-employee conferences at which bargaining occurred prior to direct union action. Even in the later part of the 19th century, when collective bargaining as we know it today was well under way, unilateral union posting of wage schedules was not uncommon.

The Conspiracy Doctrine

Early unions were not received with complacency by employers. The latter found a firm ally in the judiciary, which throughout the 19th century stood firmly with the well-to-do class from which its members were recruited. The ancient doctrine of conspiracy was brought out and applied to "labor combinations in restraint of trade." Although "there was nothing unlawful in combination itself, nothing unlawful in an individual's refusal to work, and nothing unlawful in a workman's desire to obtain better standards of employment,"[2] the early judges found it all added up to a conspiracy. Thus, in the famous Philadelphia Cordwainers' case,[3] the learned judge declared: "A combination of workmen to raise their wages may be considered in a two-fold point of view: one is to benefit themselves . . . the other is to injure those who do not join the [combination]. . . . The rule of law condemns both. . . ." Hence the workers were jailed and fined.

The judges were reasoning from their socioeconomic point of view. As time wore on, however, more reasoned justice asserted itself. In 1842, the Massachusetts Supreme Court dealt the criminal conspiracy doctrine a mortal blow by ruling in effect that the legality of a strike depended upon the end sought, and that the mere purpose of requiring all workers to join a union (closed shop) was not per se illegal.[4]

CITYWIDE MOVEMENTS, 1825–37

Andrew Jackson rode into the Presidency on a wave of agrarian and urban revolt against that era's prevailing economic and political inequalities between different classes. Most rankling to the urban wage earner was the length of the workday (sunup to sundown), imprisonment for debt, compulsory militia service from which the rich could buy excuse, absence of mechanics' lien laws to protect workers in case of employer bank-

[2] Charles O. Gregory, *Labor and the Law* (2d rev. ed.; New York: W. W. Norton & Co., Inc., 1961), p. 19.

[3] An 1806 case. Cordwainers were shoemakers, originally those who worked on cordovan leather.

[4] *Commonwealth v. Hunt*, 4 Metcalf 111 (1842).

ruptcy, property qualifications for voting, and lack of a free educational system.

Workers in New York, Philadelphia, and other seaboard centers attempted to cope with these problems through their unions. The battle was fought both by direct economic action and by political action. The former technique was utilized to improve wages and working conditions, especially by reducing hours to a straight 10 per day.

Politics and Federation

It was in the political field, however, that the unions of this period made their most spectacular efforts. Workingmen's parties were formed in New York, Philadelphia, and other centers; and, particularly in the two largest cities, they held the balance of power between the Federalists and the Democrats for several years, and elected several officials. More important, however, was their effect on the Democrats. Anxious to secure the workers' votes, New York's Tammany Hall adopted the basic workers' program—free public education, universal suffrage, and mechanics' lien laws were adopted or strengthened, and compulsory militia service for the poor only commenced to disappear. By 1834, the workingmen's parties had folded, but their imprint remained.

The local unions in the cities formed central trades organizations to coordinate their activities, and some attempts were made to consolidate them into a national organization. A National Trades Union was formed in 1834, but it lasted less than five years. It did successfully agitate for the establishment of the 10-hour day in government employment. The workers' problems were primarily local, however, and they were unwilling to cede authority to a national body. The same factor hindered the establishment of national craft unions, although at least five crafts attempted to form national unions in the 1830's.

A feature of the labor movement in these early years was the prominent role played by intellectuals. Robert Dale Owen, son of the English industrialist-philanthropist; Frances Wright, our first women's suffragist; and the brilliant pamphleteer, Thomas Skidmore—all left their imprint on the labor movement, and all saw their programs promoted at one time or another by the unions. As the unions grew, however, a gulf between the practical needs of workers and the Utopian dreams of reformers developed.

REFORMISM AND COOPERATION TO NATIONAL ORGANIZATION, 1840–67

The depression which began in 1837 was one of the severest in American history. The ranks of unions thinned out and disappeared in the face of mass unemployment. The experience and records of 20 years were lost, and the labor movement had to start anew. The decade of the 1840's saw the formation of many new unions; but too frequently their interests were diverted toward reformist programs which were often more well-meaning than practical. The spokesmen of various brands of socialism, land reform, consumer and producer cooperation, farmer-labor parties or political action, the eight-hour day, and free land all attempted to win labor's support.

Adherents of cooperation were especially prominent in this era. The thesis that labor's problems can be solved by placing the ownership of the means of production into the hands of the worker and then having the worker take his share in profits has always had a great appeal to reformers of every era. But in the 1840's, as before and later, attempts at cooperation ran into difficulties. Workers found that it takes more than work to run a business. There are problems of organization, problems of sales, and problems of finance, among others. Budding cooperatives too often lacked these technical necessities.

More important, however, the cooperative often could not supply better conditions of employment than the capitalist, and all too often the cooperative could not even produce the goods as cheaply. Consequently, it was the practical trade-unionist who won out. He alone could deliver something more substantial than the promised millennium to cope with the problems of wage earners—problems made more severe by the commencement of the "American Industrial Revolution." For it was about 1840 that the use of anthracite coal stimulated the rise of the steel industry, that railroad development began, and that increased industrialization and urbanization went forward rapidly. This decade also saw rapid increases in population, wealth, and prices, and a consequent increased demarcation between the property holders and the propertyless.

Unionism of this time was confined to the skilled, but it was vigorous and firmly rooted. Beginning in 1852 with the founding of the International Typographical Union,[5] during the following two decades at least a dozen organizations were formed which survive to this day. The Civil War, separating North from South, and dislocating industry and the economy, at first seriously set back the new unions; later, however, by creating a shortage of labor and stimulating industry, it fed union growth. By 1867, the union movement was ready for a serious attempt at national federation. The result was the National Labor Union, founded in that year.

Knowing nothing of the early struggles of labor for freedom from political domination, and beset by the problems of rapid post–Civil War industrialization, the union founders of the National Labor Union permitted political as well as labor organizations to affiliate. When, moreover, the organization's propaganda led to the adoption of the eight-hour day in

[5] Unions are called "international" in the United States because they have locals in Canada.

federal employment within one year, a naïve faith in political action, often since reiterated, developed. Other panaceas or reform objectives, however, failed of attainment. States did not, as hoped, pass eight-hour laws; producer cooperation or worker ownership of industry failed to materialize; and "cheap money" or the Greenback movement brought no success to worker aspirations. Slowly, the unions dropped out, and the National Labor Union grew purely political, until in 1872 it became defunct.

THE KNIGHTS OF LABOR

Even before the National Labor Union was engulfed by politics, seven tailors met in Philadelphia determined to found an organization which would transcend the narrow limits of craft unionism and unite all workers under one banner, regardless of race, sex, nationality, or creed. Thus was created the Noble Order of the Knights of Labor, which as a secret society spread slowly through industrialized Pennsylvania.

Gradually, the secrecy became a liability. Secret organizations were in ill-repute in Pennsylvania as a result of the activities of the Molly Maguires, a terroristic group which attempted to achieve social justice by murdering company officials. The Mollies were uncovered by a Pinkerton detective, who managed to become a Molly official and thus achieve fame as the first in a long line of labor spies. Several Molly officials were hanged for murder, but a question remains as to whether the real culprits were punished.

The Knights' secrecy was formally abolished in 1879, when Terence V. Powderly became the "Grand Master Workman." He insisted that this be done so that the official approval of the Catholic Church could be secured for the new organization. Thereafter the Knights grew rapidly.

The Knights of Labor was an interesting cross between a union and an uplift society. It attempted to weld together all elements of the working classes; and to do so, it permitted craft unions to affiliate directly with its "general assembly" (national organization) and also organized "mixed assemblies," i.e., local organizations composed of a variety of workers organized on either an industrial or a heterogeneous basis.[6] Its program stressed political reform and was closely allied with the agrarian revolt of this period which is known as the "Great Upheaval." T. V. Powderly, for many years leader of the Knights, was a kindly, friendly Irishman who had a keen sense of social justice, a yearning for a better life, and a firm belief in the common virtues and the American system of private property. Some of his allies, however, were more radical, and they

---

[6] An industrial union includes all workers in a plant, an industry, or industries, regardless of craft or trade, whereas a craft union includes workers of one craft or trade, regardless of the plant or industry in which they are employed. Heterogeneous unions are those which take membership on any basis.

gave the Knights its tone, for local autonomy ruled under the Knights' bylaws.

The Knights of Labor reached its apex in 1886 after a strike on the Wabash, Missouri-Kansas-Texas, and Missouri Pacific railroads had forced Jay Gould, the financier who controlled these railroads, to grant recognition. From 100,000 the previous year, the Knights' membership rose to 700,000. Members came in so fast that it was necessary for the central office to suspend organizing to assure that no lawyers, bankers, gamblers, liquor dealers, or Pinkerton detectives—the only barred groups—would join the Knights.

The decline of the Knights was as rapid as its ascent. Losses in a number of strikes, including defeat in a second Missouri Pacific walkout, and the separation of the skilled men into a rival organization, later known as the American Federation of Labor, turned the tide. In 1888, the Knights claimed only 222,000 members; in 1890, 100,000; and in 1893, but 75,000. From then till the official dissolution 20 years later, their central office was engaged primarily in reform propaganda, often allied with the agrarian Greenback and Populist parties.

The structure and program of the Knights was ill-suited to the job of running a labor organization. Local organizations, known as "assemblies," often took in all comers, regardless of job or place of employment. The assumption was that all workers had the same interests and needs. The leadership of the Knights spent much of its energy, enthusiasm, and financial resources promoting producer cooperation and various monetary proposals such as Greenbackism and Bryan's "free silver" program. Meanwhile, day-to-day needs of wages and working conditions, and especially organization building, were neglected.

The membership of the Knights was very unstable. It was composed mainly of unskilled workers who flocked in and out so fast that it was once described as a "procession instead of an organization." These workers, being totally inexperienced in unionism, were great strikers but poor union members. Eager to join in a strike, the inexperienced masses disappeared from the organization as soon as a conflict was finished. Some flocked in when the Knights won a strike; more were scared away when a strike was lost. At first, the skilled craftsmen and their unions were attracted to the Knights; but the ineffectiveness of the Knights in the day-to-day bread-and-butter unionism led the craftsmen to bow out and seek an organization suited to their special needs and ambitions.

THE RISE OF THE AMERICAN FEDERATION OF LABOR

While the Knights of Labor was achieving its great boom, a group of trade-union leaders met in 1881 and formed what was first called the Federation of Organized Trades and Labor Unions and then, after 1886, the American Federation of Labor (AFL). Led by Samuel Gompers and

Adolph Strasser of the Cigarmakers' International Union, this group was composed primarily of representatives of the skilled trades who not only did not desire to be submerged in the mass movement of the Knights of Labor but feared that the net result of the Knights' activities would be the destruction of trade-unionism as they conceived it. They believed that trade-unionism could best succeed if confined to those who were able to organize themselves—in other words, to skilled or strategically located groups; and that trade-unionism should limit itself to the immediate issues of improving workers' wages and working conditions rather than work for a socialist Utopia or become entangled with other political movements or "uplift" campaigns.

The program of the AFL leaders was thus a pragmatic one, grounded firmly in the principles of American capitalism. They were out to improve the conditions of those whom they represented, and they represented the skilled workers or workers who, because of their strategic location, had bargaining power sufficient to command employer recognition. To the great mass of workers, they said, in effect: "Organizing will help you, but until you are ready for organization, we can best aid you by pulling up our wages and thus indirectly influencing yours to rise also."

Samuel Gompers

Samuel Gompers and his fellow founders of the AFL did not come to their conclusions concerning the type of labor movement that could prosper in America without patient study and experience. Gompers was a self-educated man. The son of Dutch-Jewish immigrants, he was brought to this country as a child; and as a youngster, he went to work in the slum tenement cigar factories in New York. Early in his working career, he became acquainted with the German Socialists, mainly refugees from the unsuccessful European revolution of 1848. Through them, he became familiar with the writings of Marx and the other literature of socialism. Often the cigarmakers worked in groups of 10 or 15, with one of the workers spending the entire day reading to the rest and the other workers making up his wages out of their own. At the same time, Gompers took an active role in the developing Cigarmakers' Union, and thus he acquired the practical experience of a trade-unionist.

Although sympathetic with the aims of socialism, Gompers and his fellow trade-unionists were thoroughly convinced that a labor movement founded as an arm of the Socialist party, or even espousing socialist principles, could not survive in America. Gompers saw clearly that any organization which made a frontal attack on private property would alienate the dominant American middle classes and would find little support even among employees, who were less class-conscious and more interested in getting ahead as individuals than any of the European Socialists had been able to comprehend.

During the first years of the AFL, growth was slow but steady. As the Knights of Labor declined, the Federation forged ahead. Socialists made attempts to convert the AFL into an appendage of their organization. In one year, 1894, they did succeed in defeating Gompers for the presidency. They were unable, however, to place their man at the helm for more than one year, and Gompers was returned to the office, which he held every year thereafter until he died in 1924. Later the Socialists changed their program and attempted to form a rival organization known as the Socialist Trade and Labor Alliance. This organization failed, however, to gain a mass following, consisting mainly of hardworking pamphleteers and rigid doctrinarians in New York City.

In order to insure control of the AFL by national unions, Gompers was careful to reject affiliation offers by political groups. The constitution of the AFL maintained the national unions as autonomous organizations, each with exclusive jurisdictional rights in its territory. An executive committee, composed at various times of 5 to 15 persons, elected from affiliated national unions, plus a full-time president and secretary, governed the Federation between annual conventions. Representation in the AFL conventions was based on dues-paying membership. A combination of a few larger unions could thus control the AFL. The president's office had little authority. By leadership, force of personality, and an astute sense of politics, Gompers gave the AFL presidency vitality and power until his later and less vigorous years.

AFL Philosophy

The American Federation of Labor, as the true counterpart of American capitalism, has traditionally opposed government intervention in industrial relations matters. Samuel Gompers and business exponents of laissez-faire were one in their belief that the government should confine its role in labor relations to policing and the maintenance of order and should not interfere in industrial relations matters or in the internal affairs of labor or business. Thus, Gompers opposed government intervention in labor disputes even to the extent of opposing government facilities for mediation and voluntary arbitration,[7] foreseeing that such intervention might lead to compulsory arbitration. Moreover, he wanted no part of government assistance in union organization. He did not think the government should outlaw discrimination against workers because of union membership, believing that such government aid would lead to government control.[8]

In social welfare matters, Gompers likewise stood for "voluntarism."

[7] Mediation or conciliation is the process whereby a third party attempts to secure settlement of persuasion and compromise. Arbitration involves the use of a third party to decide a dispute.

[8] This was no idle fear. Twelve years after the prounion Wagner Act was passed, Congress enacted the Taft-Hartley law, which has definite union control features, and then 12 years later came a true union control law—the Landrum-Griffin Act.

No less than businessmen, he was against a government minimum wage
for men, and against government unemployment insurance and other
forms of governmental social security. He believed that such welfare
programs would weaken democracy by making citizens too dependent
upon the state; that a minimum wage would tend to become a maximum
and thus limit union action; and that minimum wages, unemployment
insurance, and other social security measures could best be provided by
the workers themselves through trade-unions. The only exception to this
rule, he felt, was maximum hours and minimum wage legislation for
women and children, and for government employees. These groups had
little bargaining power and were therefore, he felt, in need of special
government protection.

The Injunction and the "Yellow-Dog" Contract

Of all the forms of government intervention, few have been resented
by labor as bitterly as the "injunction." It became prominent in labor
disputes in the latter half of the 1800's and was a carry-over from the
common law, where it was devised to grant continuing relief where
damages would not suffice to remedy a continuing harm. For example, if a
farmer who depended upon a brook for water observed his neighbor
upstream damming up that brook, he might, under certain conditions, go
to court, present a bill to a judge, and, without prior notice to the
neighbor, secure a temporary injunction requiring him to cease work on
the dam, to maintain the status quo, and to appear in court in a given
period, usually a week or 10 days, to show cause why the injunction
should not be made permanent. At the hearing, both parties had the right
to plead before the judge as to what his course of action should be. The
judge would then render an opinion, either dissolving the injunction or
making it permanent. In any case, any party who fails to comply with an
injunction, whether temporary or permanent, is in contempt of court and
subject to penalties which the judge may impose without trial by jury.

Employers soon saw in the injunction an ideal weapon to curb the
activities of labor unions. An employer who felt that a strike was impending could scurry to a judge with a complaint and rather easily secure an
injunction requiring the union to stay any action on the ground that grave
damages would befall the employer. Then the employer could discharge
union members and otherwise undermine the organization so that by the
time the hearing was held, the question whether the injunction was to be
made permanent or to be dissolved was irrelevant. Judges sometimes
showed a ready disposition to grant injunctions on the flimsiest requests.

To supplement the injunction, a legal technique was developed
which was soon termed by organized labor, and is now known generally,
as the "yellow-dog" contract. This is an agreement between an employer
and a worker whereby, as a condition of employment, the worker agrees
not to join the union. Unionists maintained that this was not a legal

contract, since the worker was coerced into signing it. The courts of New York State upheld this contention by refusing to enforce it, but the federal courts and those in most other states maintained that the mere fact of inequality of bargaining power did not necessarily render a contract unenforceable. Thus, if an employer had signed up his workers to yellow-dog contracts, he might get an injunction requiring the union organizer to cease attempting to induce employees to break their legal contracts! This was truly an effective antiunion device.

The climax of government by judiciary came when the Supreme Court ruled that the Sherman Antitrust law, enacted in 1890 to curb cases of business combination, was applicable also to labor combinations and that employees who had instituted a nationwide boycott against a hat manufacturer could be successfully sued for the treble damages provided in the law.

This was the background which led to the 40-year AFL campaign to end "government by judiciary" and to "neutralize" the courts. Gompers appealed to Congress to take action in this regard. He argued that he was not abandoning the principle of neutral government or "voluntarism" but rather that he was asking Congress to implement it; for the courts, in his opinion, were firmly on the side of the employer. In 1914, when Congress passed the Clayton Act, which Gompers thought removed unions from the jurisdiction of antitrust laws, he believed that he had won his aim; but the courts whittled away this law by interpretation. Not until 1932, with the passage of the Norris–La Guardia Act, did the AFL's great legislative drive achieve fruition—only to be partially annulled later with the passage of the Taft-Hartley Act of 1947 and the Landrum-Griffin Act of 1959.

Industrial Relations, 1880–1914

The years of the great upheaval were also years which saw the first attempts at modern collective bargaining. National agreements negotiated in the stove, glass, and pottery industries, the beginning of regional collective bargaining in the bituminous coal industry, a large number of agreements in the building and printing trades, all showed promise of a conciliatory tone in industrial relations between labor and management. Under the leadership of John Mitchell, president of the United Mine Workers and one-time Gompers "heir apparent," the anthracite coal industry was organized and a working agreement achieved after two long strikes and federal intervention in the form of a fact-finding commission had forced the "hard-boiled" operators to negotiate.[9]

---

[9] Among them was George M. Baer, president of the Philadelphia and Reading Company, who immortalized himself with this statement: "The rights and interests of the laboring man will be protected and cared for not by labor agitators but by Christian men to whom God in his infinite wisdom has given control of the property interests of the country."

In the 1890's also, industrialists and bankers under the leadership of Mark Hanna, President William McKinley's campaign manager and later a senator from Ohio, joined with Gompers and other AFL leaders in founding the National Civic Federation. This body sought agreement between labor and industry on broad principles, promoted collective bargaining contracts, and maintained voluntary machinery for mediation and arbitration of labor disputes. By promoting collective bargaining, the Civic Federation aided the immediate interests of the AFL. It frowned, however, on aggressive unionism. Since the latter was needed to organize the unorganized, unskilled masses, the Civic Federation's influence was more friendly to established unions than to union growth.

If, however, the AFL had established a beachhead in industry through agreements and "class collaboration" in the Civic Federation, it found no warm welcome on industry's shores. This was especially true in the new mass-production industries. Andrew Carnegie, rising genius of the steel industry, had at one time been anxious to deal with the Amalgamated Association of Iron, Steel and Tin Workers. He reasoned that by encouraging the union, he would encourage stability of prices; and since he figured he could outsell his competitors if he held them to equal costs, he promoted unionism to promote sales.

As Carnegie grew in the industry, however, his love for unionism declined. In 1892, he dealt the Amalgamated Association a terrific blow when he ousted it from his Homestead plant (near Pittsburgh, Pennsylvania) in a bloody strike. The course of unionism in steel from then on was downward; and as steel went, so went unionism in mass production. The United States Steel Corporation, which was formed in 1901, principally by Carnegie and Morgan interests under the latter's domination, refused to recognize the steel union, defeated it in its attempt to force recognition by a strike, and then gradually eliminated it from the plants where it had already been recognized. Mass-production industries which grew up between 1900 and 1933 followed the lead of the steel corporation. Detroit, the automobile capital; Akron, the center of rubber products; the Pittsburgh–Ohio Valley steel center; Chicago, the heart of the meat-packing combines—all kept unionism from their gates except for the briefest of periods during World War I, and other industries followed their lead.

As their spokesman, the antiunion interests found the National Association of Manufacturers an excellent crusader, with its campaign for the "open shop," which, to the NAM, meant the elimination of trade-unionism. Between 1900 and 1914, the American Federation of Labor was on the defensive. It held its own in industries in which workers had strong bargaining power, such as building, printing, glass, stove foundries, and to some extent bituminous coal mining; and its membership increased to 2 million by 1914. Nevertheless, it failed to keep pace with our growing industrial economy. Even in those industries such as glass, where it had a firm foothold, the AFL unions were confined largely to the skilled employees. Coal mining was one of the few union strongholds among semiskilled and unskilled employees.

The effect of the NAM drive was both swift and long-lasting. In 1901, the National Metal Trades Association, which one year before had entered into a national agreement with the International Association of Machinists, broke off relations and continued its nonunion policy for nearly 40 years thereafter; in 1904, the National Founders' Association broke off its relations with the International Molders Union; and in 1905, the National Erectors Association and the Bridge and Structural Iron Workers Union broke off relations. The employer who maintained union relations was termed a "traitor to his class"; and the "moral duty" of the employer to defend the worker's "right to work" was emphasized as the basic cause of the employer opposition to unions.

The antiunion drive of the NAM and its allies served to give most of the new large corporations formed at the turn of the century the opportunity to utilize labor without restraint from unions. The worker who did not like his treatment, or who rebelled, could look elsewhere for a job; that was his only recourse against the power of the giant corporation. Of course, many employers had good cause to reject unionism around 1900. The history of industrial relations provides many examples of unions during 1880–1900 refusing to sign written agreements, adhering to "quickie" strikes, and placing restrictive rules on expanding industries. Industry, however, had the opportunity to work out an understanding with the AFL, but the "fight unionism" program of the National Association of Manufacturers prevailed over the cooperative program of the National Civic Federation.

The IWW

To American radicals at the turn of the century, the success of the antiunion crusade and the support which it elicited from the general public were evidence that "narrow" dollars-and-cents unionism of the AFL type could not succeed in working out a compromise with the capitalistic system. At the same time, the failure of the AFL to interest itself in the needs of the unskilled workers and the workers in such frontier industries as metal mining and logging and lumber drove these groups to seek a solution of their problems outside the AFL's orbit. The metal miners, who for a time had affiliated with the AFL, took their union, the Western Federation of Miners, out of the AFL in 1897. Lack of success in their own fierce labor struggles and an increased radical bent within the organization and among its leaders led the Western Federation of Miners and its allies from the West to make common cause with the Socialist Trade and Labor Alliance and with various dissident AFL locals. In June, 1905, these groups launched the Industrial Workers of the World.

The direct-action, nontheoretical Westerners, who represented the only group with a sizable membership, soon split with the theoretical Socialists from the East, and by 1908 the latter were eliminated from the organization. From then on, the IWW was truly the representative of the unskilled masses, intervening in strike situations or leading strikes of harvest workers, logging and lumber mill employees, and longshoremen, or wherever a labor upheaval occurred. The IWW befriended the newly arrived immigrant worker, carried on "free speech" campaigns where the right of speech and association was denied, and generally acted as the champion of the underdog whom no one else would champion.

The IWW was the champion of the unskilled, but it never built an organization for them. It would not sign agreements, which it regarded as a form of capitalistic enslavement. The IWW depended on mass action used directly and without restraint. It hid nothing and apologized to no one for its anticapitalistic views.

The IWW organizers were agitators who either stirred up trouble or took charge of trouble when it broke out. They often performed yeoman service in securing better wages, hours, and working conditions in particular situations. Once, however, their initial objectives were secured or lost, the IWW leaders were off to another trouble spot, leaving the local organization to wither away. The press built up the "wobblies" as a tremendous organization. Their strength was more carefully appraised by a scholarly observer of the labor movement after he had witnessed their 1913 convention:

The first significant fact revealed by this convention, and by the whole history of the IWW as well, is that this body, which claims as its mission the organization of the whole working class for the overthrow of capitalism, is pathetically weak in effective membership and has failed utterly in its efforts to attach to itself permanently a considerable body of men representative of any section of American workers.[10]

IWW leaders energetically opposed the American entrance into World War I and preached sabotage to prevent it. As a result, many of the leaders were indicted and the organization was proscribed. What was left of the membership was pretty thoroughly broken up by the post–World War I red witch hunts of the then United States Attorney General, A. Mitchell Palmer.

WORLD WAR I TO THE GREAT DEPRESSION

The "New Freedom" of the Wilson administration promised organized labor many gains. One of these was the Clayton Act to restrain labor injunctions, which Gompers hailed as the Magna Charta of labor, only to

---

[10] R. F. Hoxie, *Trade Unionism in the United States* (New York: D. Appleton-Century Co., 1924), p. 139.

be disappointed by the Supreme Court's interpretation of this law. As the war approached, the Wilson administration became more and more solicitous of labor support. Gompers, who at first had demonstrated a vigorous antiwar philosophy, soon was preaching for Wilson preparedness. A threatened strike by the four railroad brotherhoods for an eight-hour day was averted when President Wilson secured the passage of the Adamson Act, guaranteeing the eight-hour day without loss of pay from the previous 10 hours to all operating employees of railroads (hence, not extending the benefits to the still unorganized nonoperating group). As war neared, tripartite, public-labor-industry labor relations boards were established in critical industries, and the AFL was given official recognition as a representative of labor. In return, the Federation put aside voluntarism and cooperated thoroughly with the government.

When war finally broke out, President Wilson called together representatives of labor and industry; and they hammered out an agreement providing, among other things, for the establishment of a tripartite National War Labor Board, an agreement guaranteeing the right of organization, and a freeze on the closed-shop issue which stated that open shops were to remain open and closed shops closed for the duration. Aided by the shortage of labor, the official recognition by government, and a truce with industry, organized labor's ranks shot up to 5.5 million, which proved to be the highest membership figure prior to 1935.

World War I was followed by serious industrial strife. The nation had a coal strike in 1919 and an industrywide steel strike (which was mainly a demand for the end of the 12-hour day in blast furnaces and for recognition of the union). The strike failed after being portrayed as a "red menace." Serious stoppages also occurred in other industries such as meat packing, with the result that, similar to another postwar year, 1946, the year 1919 was one of the costliest in terms of per capita days lost from work because of strikes.

The year 1919 was also an inflationary year with prices soaring, which, of course, was one of the serious reasons for labor discontent. High prices continued into 1920 and then fell sharply as the country experienced a short but serious depression. Labor's gains of the war evaporated as war industries closed and unemployment set in. Industry took the offensive with the "American plan," a version of the open shop dressed up by the first ingredients of personnel administration.

Company Unions

During the war, American industry had realized the high cost of hit-or-miss personnel policies. Industry became concerned for the first time over high labor turnover, foreman training, scientific salary administration, and other personnel policies which Frederick Taylor had been preaching for 20 years. Moreover, the public was demanding more democracy in industry, and the more forward-looking industrialists saw that they must have something to meet the trade-union challenge besides the famous remark attributed to the chairman of the United States Steel Corporation: "We do not deal with unions as such."

Out of this developed many elaborate schemes of employer representation and company unions. They were deficient in many ways. Certainly, the company union cannot give the worker the bargaining power to stand up and fight for an enlargement of his share, since it ultimately owes its strength to company toleration. Nevertheless, during the 1920's, it was the forward-looking, liberal employer who sponsored the company unions and the employee representation plans. The rest of the employers did not permit even such organization of their workers. Company unions also played a role in training future union leaders, in teaching employees to discuss their rights, to learn about business, and eventually to realize the impotence of company unions as bargaining agents.

The AFL Decays

American trade-unionism was in a state of decadence during the 1920's, despite the fact that 30 years later the AFL was still led by some of the leaders who were prominent during the 1920's. Some of them were old in spirit and unreceptive to new ideas by 1920. The Federation was unwilling and unprepared to organize the great mass of employees. As technological and mass-production methods reduced skills and converted jobs into semiskilled operations, the AFL continued to hold on merely to the craft unions and made no serious attempt to organize the great body of workers. Membership slowly fell from the wartime peak to less than 3 million in 1932. The coal miners' union, which had been the largest in the AFL, not only failed to organize southern West Virginia and Kentucky, but it was eliminated from most of the northern mines as well. Even the building-trades unions, which were the bulwark of the AFL, lost their grip on San Francisco and failed to penetrate such new industrial areas as Detroit. Charges of corruption within its leadership, attacks by liberals and left-wing groups, and the effective antiunionism of employers all took their toll.

William Green

Samuel Gompers held on to his post as AFL president long after his prime, till he died soon after the 1924 convention, at the age of 74. The choice of William Green, then secretary-treasurer of the United Mine Workers, and third vice president of the AFL, was engineered by John L. Lewis, president of the United Mine Workers. Lewis had too many enemies to win the job for himself. He therefore made a deal with the other "Indianapolis boys"—President William Hutcheson of the Carpenters' Union and President Daniel Tobin of the Teamsters' Union, which, like the miners' and typographical unions, then had their headquarters in Indianapolis. The deal placed William Green, a compromise candidate, in the AFL president's chair, and he was successfully reelected every year until his death in 1952.

Although William Green owed his AFL presidency to John L. Lewis more than to any other one person, the decline in membership in the miners' union in the 1920's forced Green to rely more and more for political support on the building trades. As a result, when the big controversy over union structure and power broke after the New Deal, Green was an ally of the craft unionists of many years' standing rather than of the miners.

In 1932, on the eve of the New Deal, the AFL was losing members rapidly and had neither the finances, the structure, nor the will to recoup its losses. Nevertheless, in that very year, Congress passed the Norris–La Guardia Act, ending "government by injunctions" by making it extremely difficult for an employer to secure an injunction from a federal court in a labor dispute and by denying federal court enforcement of yellow-dog contracts. Thus, at the bottom of its fortunes the AFL won a great legislative triumph.

Labor under the New Deal

The Roosevelt administration, which came to power in 1933, brought gains to labor which were unprecedented in American history. In the wake of such legislation as the National Recovery Act, the National Labor Relations (Wagner) Act, and the amendments to the Railway Labor Act, trade-union organization increased to an all-time high, which, with the final impetus of war, continued prosperity, and shortage of labor, drove union membership to a figure of 18 million.[11]

The first great New Deal law, the National Industrial Recovery Act, may be regarded as a sort of general handout to the different pressure groups in the country. Business and agriculture were encouraged to plan scarcity in order to raise prices, and labor was given the right to organize without management interference. Labor's right was not enforceable to a very important extent, but energetic unionism took immediate advantage of it. Gambling the last $75,000 in the miners' union treasury, John L. Lewis sent expert organizers throughout the country's coal fields, and within three months he had enrolled 400,000 coal miners, including those in the previously impregnable antiunion strongholds of Kentucky and southern West Virginia. The International Ladies' Garment Workers' Union resurrected and expanded itself, as did the Amalgamated Clothing Workers in the men's clothing industry. Unionism sprang up in the mass-production industries, unaided, unguided, and confused; but if some organizations sprang into action under the magic of NRA, most of the AFL lay quiet and asleep. Not until after considerable prodding did AFL organizers appear on the scene to help unionization in previously unor-

---

[11] Discussion of legislation on collective bargaining is reserved for Part VII.

ganized industries. Then, in industries such as rubber and automobiles, where no AFL affiliate had general jurisdiction, the Federation chartered directly AFL-affiliated or "federal" locals.

Without a central organization, however, these new locals were often inept in bargaining. Moreover, craft unions of carpenters, electrical workers, machinists, etc., claimed the right to, and often did, demand that craftsmen in newly organized federal locals be turned over to them. The effect was usually to destroy the federal local and to estrange the transferred craftsmen from the labor movement until organizations suited to their purposes were founded.[12]

In the steel and meat-packing industries, AFL unions did exist. The Amalgamated Association of Iron, Steel and Tin Workers, however, had had an unbroken record of failures since the Homestead strike in 1892, and its leadership had neither the resources nor the capacity to undertake a large-scale organizing drive. Except for a short World War I interval, the Amalgamated Meat Cutters and Butcher Workmen never had penetrated the major meat-packing centers. Until revitalized in the late 1930's, it appeared content to confine its organization to the small packing establishments and to retail butchers.

The Founding of the CIO

The AFL's failure to organize mass-production industries gave impetus to a movement led by John L. Lewis to issue industrial union charters to organizations in the mass-production industries. Both Lewis and the craft union adherents realized, of course, that if thousands of new recruits came into the AFL, the power balance within labor's rank would change, and Lewis, with a revitalized miners' union and the recognized champion of the industrial unionists, would be in a strong position. In 1935, for the third time, the craft unionists refused to permit the issuance of industrial union charters. The issue was fought in terms of union structure, but the basic issue was power in the AFL.

Thwarted within the AFL, Lewis went ahead anyway. The industrial union group, under his leadership and that of David Dubinsky of the Ladies' Garment Workers' Union, Sidney Hillman of Amalgamated Clothing Workers, and Charles P. Howard of the Typographical Union (acting as an individual), and including unions in the oil, textile, and metal mines industries, met and formed the Committee for Industrial Organization for the avowed purpose of organizing unorganized workers within the AFL. The original unions were soon joined by others, such as the rubber, flat glass, automobile, shipbuilding, and electrical appliance workers' unions, who had pleaded in vain with the AFL for industrial union charters. The CIO immediately offered the AFL $500,000 to organize the

[12] The story of the AFL efforts in the automobile industry during this period is recounted in scholarly detail in Sidney Fine, *The Automobile under the Blue Eagle* (Ann Arbor, Mich.: University of Michigan Press, 1963).

steel industry. When the latter's Executive Council turned it down, Lewis succeeded in inducing the leadership of the virtually dormant Amalgamated Association of Iron, Steel and Tin Workers to put itself in a receivership to a newly organized Steel Workers Organizing Committee headed by Philip Murray, then vice president of the United Mine Workers.

The AFL viewed these developments with alarm. Its Executive Council ordered the CIO to disband. When the latter refused and Lewis resigned as a vice president of the AFL, the AFL Executive Council suspended the CIO affiliates for "promoting dual unionism." The haste with which the Executive Council acted and the probable lack of constitutionality in its suspension were not seriously challenged by the CIO unions, except the Ladies' Garment Workers' Union.[13] The CIO group had given up the possibility that mass-production industries could be organized within the framework of the AFL. Hence, when the AFL convention met in 1936, the CIO unions were not represented, and the action of the Executive Council was sustained. Two years later the CIO unions were formally expelled.

The CIO Organizes Steel

The CIO challenge to the antiunion policies of the steel industry was met vigorously by the steel companies. Once more, men were spied on and fired for union activity; the rights of assembly and free speech in company-dominated towns were curtailed; and violence, bloodshed, and death erupted on the industrial scene.

The steel companies also used more refined tactics in trying to overcome the new union threat to their traditional methods of controlling labor relations. Large sums were spent on a nationwide advertising campaign condemning unionism as a threat to the country. And considerable effort and money were expended to form and to maintain company unions.

This time, however, the steel companies met more than their match. The CIO drive had behind it money, effort, and above all, the organizing know-how of union organizers who had already penetrated antiunion citadels as tough as those established by the steel companies. The tactics and flair for showmanship demonstrated by Philip Murray and his aides were superior to those put on in any previous organizing campaign.

[13] In 1935, the AFL constitution said nothing about Executive Council jurisdiction to suspend an affiliate. Unions could be expelled only by a two-thirds convention vote. If the CIO unions had been represented at the 1936 convention, no two-thirds vote would have been possible. The 1936 convention was reminded by several delegates that the Executive Council was "in such a hurry" to suspend the CIO that the procedure was questionable. Matthew Woll, leading exponent of the Executive Council viewpoint, later defended the suspension as follows: "The fact is that if the Council had not acted there would have been possible disintegration within the American Federation of Labor which would have been disastrous. The Council acted not so much to punish those who had formed the CIO, but rather to prevent disintegration from within." (*The Hat Worker*, June 15, 1939, p. 11.)

SAMUEL GOMPERS
President, AFL, 1886–94 and
1895–1924

Photograph by Rogers Studio, Seattle

WILLIAM GREEN
President, AFL, 1924–52

Photograph by Maurice Seymour, Chicago

JOHN L. LEWIS
President, UMW, 1920–60
Chairman and President, CIO,
1935–40

Photograph by Chase-Statler

PHILIP MURRAY
President, CIO, 1940–52

Photograph by Chase, Washington, D.C.

WALTER P. REUTHER
President, UAW, 1946—,
and CIO, 1952–55

Photograph by Chase, Washington, D.C.

GEORGE MEANY
President, AFL, 1952–55
and AFL-CIO, 1955—

Photograph by Fabian Bachrc

For example, the CIO realized that the nationwide advertisements sponsored by the companies gave the organizing campaign widespread publicity which it could not otherwise have obtained. Hence, in its rejoinder to the company publicity, which was often so extreme as to alienate the public, the union replied softly.

The year 1936 was an election year for the Roosevelt administration. The Republican candidate for President, Alfred M. Landon, was a relative of a prominent United States Steel Corporation official. The CIO allied itself fully with President Roosevelt's reelection campaign and made much out of Landon's family connection with Big Steel and the support given Landon by many officials of steel concerns. The overwhelming reelection of President Franklin D. Roosevelt was followed by a large influx of steelworkers into the CIO.

Because the CIO drive in steel was well financed by the miners and needle-trades unions, it could afford to, and did, waive all union fees and dues until company recognition was secured. This promoted confidence among steelworkers who, in the past, had paid out union dues but never received anything to show for their support.

Toward company unions, Philip Murray, leader of the CIO drive, also adopted a new tactic. Instead of regarding them as archenemies, he saw company unions as a training ground. The CIO people attacked them by trying to get control and succeeded in a large measure. The United States Steel Corporation's money spent for company union agitation frequently served to promote the CIO. By January, 1937, it was apparent that the new steel union could close down Carnegie-Illinois, U.S. Steel's biggest subsidiary, if it so chose.

At this point, probably through the friendly offices of President Roosevelt and Senator Joseph Guffey of Pennsylvania, Myron Taylor, chairman of the board of U.S. Steel, and John L. Lewis were brought together. The result was an agreement recognizing the CIO as bargaining agent for its members in all U.S. Steel subsidiaries in the iron and steel industry. The archopponent of unionism thus came to an agreement with a new CIO union, a triumph for the latter that insured its existence.

The CIO drive in steel was temporarily slowed down by the defeat of its recognition strikes against several of the major "Little Steel" companies.[14] Four years later, in 1941, however, the steel union came back to win bargaining rights in all these concerns. Today, under the name of the United Steelworkers of America, this union has a membership of over one million and contracts covering nearly all major steel concerns, as well as numerous companies in related industries.

Rubber, Automobiles, and Other CIO Drives

While the steel drive was getting under way, labor erupted in the rubber and automobile industries. These unions were not started from the

---

[14] Bethlehem, Republic, Youngstown, and Inland, all giant corporations.

top down, as in steel, but grew straight from the rank and file. Using a new technique, the "sit-down" strike, workers in the rubber and automobile industries took possession of plants of such giant corporations as Goodyear, Chrysler, and General Motors. This unorthodox and undoubtedly illegal procedure won recognition from these corporations because of general public sympathy with the objective of union recognition. (There never was any attempt by the unionists to seize permanent control of the plants.) The lawlessness involved in the sit-down, however, soon became sufficiently apparent to react against unionism. It was shortly abandoned as an approved tactic, so that by early 1938, sit-downs virtually disappeared from the American scene—until revived as a tactic by college students in the mid-1960's!

In the rubber industry the CIO won bargaining rights at United States Rubber, Firestone, and Goodrich in the 1930's, but the status of the union at Goodyear was not officially recognized until 1941. Today the CIO Rubber Workers' Union is not only dominant in this industry but has spread out in the cork, linoleum, floor tile, and plastic industries as well.

Although sit-down strikes won the CIO recognition at Chrysler and General Motors, Ford did not yield until 1941, when a strike closed down the great plant at River Rouge. Today the Automobile Workers, after expanding into the aerospace and agricultural implement industries, boast a membership well in excess of one million.

CIO unions also organized the packing houses and stockyards in the large centers, as well as the bulk of the electrical manufacturing industry. The old Western Federation of Miners, now known as the International Union of Mine, Mill and Smelter Workers, near extinction in 1935, became a CIO charter member and gained over 20,000 workers 10 years later, principally in the western silver and copper mines and smelters. A new union, the National Maritime Union, started from remnants of the then decadent International Seamen's Union, AFL, brought unionism to the East Coast seamen for the first time since World War I.

The revolt of the East Coast seamen also did something else. It forced the AFL to reorganize its seamen's union, in effect dissolving the International Seamen's Union and forming in its stead the Seafarers' International Union. To a lesser degree, the CIO had the same general effect on the AFL as the formation of the National Maritime Union had on the AFL seamen's organization. Forced to meet an energetic rival for the first time since it outdistanced the Knights of Labor (the IWW of pre–World War I was no great threat organizationally), the AFL and its constituent unions got out of their easy chairs and really went to work. Although the CIO surpassed the AFL in membership in 1937 and 1938, it never did after that. For the first time, AFL unions such as the Machinists and the Teamsters really made an effort to take in the thousands of workers within their jurisdictions. By 1953, membership in the AFL included almost half of the 16.9 million unionized. By then the CIO, having lost the Ladies' Garment Workers and the United Mine Workers, and having expelled the Communist-led unions, as will be narrated below, could claim but 4.5 million, with the remaining unionized found in non-affiliated unions.

Once the CIO was firmly established in the mass-production industries, the AFL leaders made no more pretense of opposition to industrial organization. Indeed, if only as a defensive measure, the AFL accepted industrial organization wherever the alternative might be loss of jurisdiction to the CIO. For example, the Machinists were granted exclusive AFL jurisdiction in aircraft manufacturing to counteract the CIO Automobile Workers' drive in the same industry. But although acceptance of industrial unionism was admittedly eliminated as a basic thorn in the side of labor unity, it was replaced by concurrent jurisdictional claims as both the AFL and the CIO lost little time in chartering rival unions in jurisdictions dominated by affiliates of the other, and opening their doors to dissident groups of the other. The CIO chartered groups in such AFL-dominated areas as building construction, railway shop crafts, and pulp and paper. The AFL, in turn, welcomed rump groups from the CIO-dominated automobile and rubber industries, and tried mightily to gain a foothold in the CIO industrial union stronghold of steel.

Throughout the 1930's and early 1940's, numerous discussions between AFL and CIO leaders occurred seeking labor unity, but the will was lacking for success. Meanwhile, each side was building up vested interests in the form of jobholders dependent upon disunity, and each side was further encroaching upon the jurisdictional claims of the other.

In 1938, the CIO set up a permanent organization, the Congress of Industrial Organizations. The International Ladies' Garment Workers' Union, one of the CIO's founders, however, declined to enter the permanent body and after two years of independence returned to the AFL. David Dubinsky, then president of the ILGWU, charged (with considerable evidence) that the main stumbling blocks to labor unity were John L. Lewis and the Communists in the CIO; but certainly, other factors—the establishment of rival unions by each group, the interest of labor officeholders in maintaining their vested interests and jobs, and the "standpatism" of old-line AFL leaders—were also important.

WORLD WAR II TO THE KOREAN WAR

World War II was a period of expanding union membership. Soon after our entrance into the war, a National War Labor Board was established with union and management as well as public representation, the union groups being divided equally between the AFL and the CIO. Despite the stresses and strains, the NWLB maintained a high record for peaceful settlement; and apart from numerous "quickie" strikes, labor observed its no-strike pledge. The tight labor market and expanding industry aided union membership to grow steadily. But the large number of small stoppages, combined with the few large ones, particularly the miners' strikes under John L. Lewis, saw public opinion turn against unions.

The end of war and the lifting of economic controls resulted in a psychological outburst on many fronts. Labor's response was strikes— 1946 was the greatest strike year in American history in terms of man-days lost. Wherever the responsibility may have belonged, the public blamed labor; the result contributed to the congressional election sweep of the Republicans in 1946 and to the passage of the Taft-Hartley Act in the following spring.

Nevertheless, unions won great gains in money wages during the first post–World War II decade. Wages rose dramatically—7–20-cent-per-hour increases spread annually through the economy. In spite of wide variations, the pattern of increases granted by such industrial giants as United States Steel or General Motors to equally large CIO unions was followed by hundreds of small concerns and unions in collective bargaining. Yet postwar rising prices reduced the wage gains in terms of purchasing power. Labor fought postwar inflation by matching it with wage gains—which aggravated it.

The severity of the postwar strike wave came as a surprise to both union and management leaders. During the war a strike was a signal for a flurry of government and management activity to get the men back to work. As a result, wartime strikes were of short duration.

When the postwar strike wave started, management did not think that unions could hold out for a long period, and the unions did not think that the strikes would last long. Neither could have been more wrong. The General Motors employees were out on strike for nearly three months in the coldest part of the year, from December, 1945, to March, 1946; Westinghouse employees stayed out almost four months; strikes in steel, coal, and other industries were also of long duration. Yet the workers did not seem to give serious consideration to returning to work without their union approval. Managements, fortified by the knowledge that economic losses resulting from strikes could be partially made up by offsets on previous years' excess profits taxes, were in no hurry to settle until certain that the government would not continue its short-lived attempt to hold the price line after the war as it had done during the war.

Unlike the strikes after World War I, those after World War II were conspicuous for the lack of violence and bloodshed. The spectacle of the employer having doughnuts and coffee served to pickets in front of his plant was a sharp contrast to those who remembered the armed conflicts between pickets and strikebreakers during earlier years.

Despite the fact that most large postwar strikes resulted in substantial wage increases for the strikers, unions did not gain in favor or significantly in membership during the period between the end of World War II and the beginning of the Korean War. Much-publicized CIO and AFL drives to organize the South were almost completely unsuccessful. Gains in membership which the CIO and AFL recorded during this period resulted mainly from the expansion of employment in plants already unionized. Price increases which generally followed large wage increases were blamed often by press and public upon the unions.

Labor's poor public relations were especially bad in the rural areas and small communities. The antiunion drive at the turn of the century was not overcome 50 years later. State legislatures, dominated by rural interests, appeared eager to pass legislation designed to curb unions. And the most popular of these laws echoed the NAM's 50-year-old campaign to maintain the "worker's right to work" by outlawing the union shop or any variation thereof which requires union membership as a condition of employment. Such laws now exist in 19 states, all in the South and Midwest.

COMMUNIST UNIONISM

The Russian Revolution has had profound effects on the American trade-union movement, although these effects have undoubtedly been mild as compared with the effects in many other democratic and once democratic lands. The American Communist party was organized in 1919 and secured the adherence of William Z. Foster, a brilliant organizer who had led the great, unsuccessful steel strike in 1919.

In the 1920's, Foster led the Communists in a move to capture the unions in the needle trades. Communist sympathizers did take over the fur workers; then, after almost succeeding, they lost out completely to the anti-Communist leadership of David Dubinsky in the Ladies' Garment Workers' Union.

In the 1930's, however, John L. Lewis, an old enemy, gave the Communists a new opportunity in the labor movement. The new CIO was in need of organizers, and Lewis, against the advice of David Dubinsky, hired Communists to fill hundreds of CIO jobs. They organized well, but they also used their positions to seize power and to convert some of the new unions into propaganda transmission agencies for their communist views.

When the Nazi–Soviet Russia pact of 1939 opened the way for the Nazi attack on Poland, the Communists opposed the defense program, fomented strikes to interfere with it. This led to considerable tension within the CIO. Here again, they found common cause with John L. Lewis. He was a confirmed isolationist, with a gradually growing hatred of President Roosevelt, which began in 1937 when the President declined to support the Little Steel strike as strongly as Lewis wished him to. Lewis thus opposed Roosevelt in 1940 for reasons very different from those of the Communists. Nonetheless, when Lewis announced that he would support the Republican candidate, Wendell Willkie, and would resign from the presidency of the CIO if Roosevelt were reelected, his support came mainly from the Communists in the CIO. True to his promise, Lewis resigned at the CIO convention following the 1940 national elections, and Philip Murray succeeded him.

Party-Line Shifts

At first, the Communists obstructed Murray at every turn because he supported the war effort, and agitated for Lewis' return to power. Then, after the German invasion of Russia in 1941, the Communists deserted Lewis. Murray, who in his own words, "was in the estimation of some people in 1940 down in the bottomless pits of hell" because he had supported the defense program, suddenly found that "there came a day, the 23rd of June [when Germany invaded Russia] and I was still supporting my country. I was dragged by these same citizens from the bottomless pits of hell and lifted to a veritable sainthood."[15]

Henceforth, Murray effectively assumed the helm of the CIO and remained also president of its strongest affiliate, the United Steelworkers. Lewis gradually dropped into the background of CIO affairs; and then, in 1943, he took the United Mine Workers out of the organization which it had done so much to create. With Lewis went "District 50," a nationwide branch of the Mine Workers which was set up originally for coke and by-product workers but was later expanded to take in any industrial group it could organize.

Reasonable cooperation between the AFL and the CIO in an all-out war effort featured the war years 1942 to 1946, with the Communists preaching full cooperation with industry and government. Then the left and the right in the CIO grew steadily worse as the right wing backed the Marshall plan for European reconstruction and opposed the third, "Progressive," party of Henry Wallace, while the left opposed the former and promoted the latter. Aided no little by the anti-Communist requirements of the Taft-Hartley Act and the leadership by Walter P. Reuther of the United Automobile Workers, the right wing of the CIO administered a series of drubbings to the Communists.

Reuther ousted the Communists from the automobile union and then opened his union's doors to many locals seceding from the Communist-dominated Mine, Mill and Smelter Workers', Electrical Workers', and Farm Equipment Workers' unions. Joseph Curran, president of the National Maritime Union (CIO), and Michael Quill, president of the Transport Workers' Union (CIO), both at one time fellow travelers of the Communists, broke with the party and wrested control of their unions from it.

[15] *Steel Labor,* March, 1948.

During 1948 and 1949, the split between CIO leaders and the leaders of the Communist-led unions widened. At the CIO's 1949 convention, the Farm Equipment Workers were expelled for not merging with the UAW. Instead, this union merged with another Communist-led union, the United Electrical, Radio and Machine Workers, which also left and merged. The CIO promptly set up a rival union for the electrical product jurisdiction, the International Union of Electrical, Radio and Machine Workers, which soon established itself as the major union in this jurisdiction. Later the UAW took over the farm equipment group.

At the 1950 convention, action was begun which led to the expulsion of nine other Communist-controlled unions.[16] Since then, only two of these unions have not disbanded or been absorbed by other unions: the United Electrical, Radio and Machine Workers and the International Longshoremen's and Warehousemen's Union. The former has shrunk from 600,000 to 125,000 members; the latter, still under the leadership of Harry Bridges, has a membership of 50,000 as compared with a high of 65,000, but it retains its grip on waterfronts of the West Coast and Hawaii, and on the plantations of Hawaii as well.

Today, the Communists are not a significant factor in the American labor movement. They never had a mass following, but their strength was concentrated in a few unions. They lost out when they chose to subvert trade-union objectives to Communist party policy.

RELIGIOUS LEADERSHIP IN UNIONS

An important factor in many unions has been the Association of Catholic Trade Unionists, which, since its founding in 1937, has grown in numbers and influence. The ACTU has not aimed at building a Catholic trade-union movement, such as exists in many European countries. Rather, it has devoted its energies to the direction and support of workers seeking aid to unseat unsatisfactory leadership or needing help in organization. In the first capacity the ACTU played a notable role in helping the New York City subway workers, a predominantly Catholic group, rid themselves of Communistic leaders. And in the fight against the mass of racketeers who have preyed upon longshoremen, the ACTU was for many years the only effective opposition to the mobsters.

The Protestant and Jewish churches maintain no group similar to the ACTU, but they have been active in the labor field. A special section of the National Council of Churches of the Protestant churches is devoted to the task of bringing the church and labor together. Labor institutes,

---

[16] Mine, Mill and Smelter Workers; United Office and Professional Workers; United Public Workers; International Fur and Leather Workers; Food, Tobacco and Allied Workers; Marine Cooks' and Stewards' Association; Fishermen's Union; International Longshoremen's and Warehousemen's Union; and American Communications Association.

interpretation of labor's aims to the churches, and the church's to labor, and various acts of assistance to labor union problems have been among the functions performed by the Protestant group.[17]

Jewish groups were once active in the labor field to an even greater extent than the ACTU, but the Jewish organization, the United Hebrew Trades, was not developed under the leadership of Jewish synagogues. Rather, the UHT served as an organization and communications vehicle between the Jewish immigrants working primarily in the New York City needle trades and the AFL. UHT leadership was an important factor in saving the Ladies' Garment Workers' Union from Communist domination in the 1920's.

When Samuel Gompers assisted in organization of the United Hebrew Trades in 1888, he had serious qualms about the propriety of organizing a separate Jewish group because he did not believe in organizing workers along religious lines. Gompers, however, supported the United Hebrew Trades on the ground that "to organize Hebrew Trade Unions was the first step in getting these immigrants into the American Labor movement." Gompers was proved right in believing that the UHT would draw Jewish immigrants into AFL unions rather than separate them from such unions.

Questions have been raised whether the Association of Catholic Trade Unionists will split American unionism along religious lines. Those who believe that it will point to the separate Catholic unions in European countries and among French-Canadians. Thus far, however, the ACTU has exhibited no tendency toward promoting a separate Catholic union movement. The social fabric of the United States would seem to preclude such an event.

LABOR'S NEW DISUNITY

In November, 1952, within two weeks of each other, Philip Murray, president of the CIO, and William Green, president of the AFL, passed away. Walter Reuther, president of the United Automobile Workers, succeeded to Murray's office. George Meany, onetime Plumbers' Union official, and later secretary-treasurer of the AFL, succeeded Green. Reuther and Meany immediately initiated action toward achieving a no-raiding pact, which was ratified by the AFL and CIO conventions. In February, 1955, Reuther and Meany negotiated an agreement which brought the CIO back into the AFL fold. By the end of 1955, both AFL

---

[17] See Phillip Taft, "The Association of Catholic Trade Unionists," *Industrial and Labor Relations Review*, Vol. II (January, 1949), pp. 210–18; Will Herberg, "Jewish Labor Movement in America," *Industrial and Labor Relations Review*, Vol. V (July, 1952), pp. 501–23, and October, 1952, pp. 44–66; and James Meyers, *Do You Know Labor?* (New York: John Day Co., Inc., 1940), chap. xviii, for backgrounds of religious organizations.

and CIO conventions had ratified the pact. A new organization—known as the American Federation of Labor and Congress of Industrial Organizations—was born, with George Meany as its head.

In order to achieve labor unity, Meany and Reuther had to overcome two pillars of the AFL foundation which heretofore had been too great a stumbling block—the principle of exclusive jurisdiction and the principle of the autonomous national union.

The doctrine of exclusive jurisdiction provided that each affiliated national union should have a clear and specified job territory and boundary ordinarily defined in terms of work operations, crafts, trades, occupations, or industrial grouping of jobs, and occasionally defined in terms of geography.[18] Under this doctrine, no two unions were supposed to have jurisdiction over the same work operations or area. As a corollary, the AFL, by determining union jurisdictions, also determined the union which the individual employee should join. Of course, since the passage of the National Labor Relations Act (now known as the Taft-Hartley Act) in 1935, workers have designated by election the union that they desire to represent them. Since workers may not follow the dictates of the federation as to union jurisdiction, the principle of exclusive jurisdiction was never fully operative after 1935.

Meany and Reuther did not attempt to merge competing unions when the AFL and CIO merged. Instead, the merger agreement simply provided that jurisdiction actually exercised by each affiliate at the time of merger was to be preserved intact and that established collective bargaining relationships supplanted historical jurisdiction as a basis for unions' territorial or organizing rights. For unorganized groups, or for groups outside of the merged federation, a union was supposed to organize on the basis of its historical jurisdiction, with the federation determining priorities and rights in case of a dispute.

After the merger, a few competing unions in the paper, chemical, insurance, and government fields did merge, but most unions did not, so that there are usually at least two competing AFL–CIO unions in one jurisdiction.

The second significant alteration in the fundamental concept of American unionism as developed originally by the American Federation of Labor has been the modification of the principle of autonomy by the requirement that national unions shall be free of corrupt and totalitarian influences if they are to maintain AFL–CIO affiliation. The AFL–CIO set up codes of ethics and an Ethical Practices Committee, but it could only enforce its codes by expelling an affiliate. This it did, in 1957, with three unions, including the country's largest, the Teamsters. Under James R. Hoffa, however, the Teamsters declined to purge its ranks of persons of ill

---

[18] John T. Dunlop, "Structural Changes in the American Labor Movement and Industrial Relations System," in Industrial Relations Research Association, *Annual Proceedings* (New York, 1956), p. 13.

repute and proceeded to compete with some success for the right to represent workers in virtually any jurisdiction. The AFL–CIO has not again shown a disposition to expel recalcitrant affiliates, despite ample evidence of its existence in such unions as the Brotherhood of Painters, Paperhangers and Decorators.[19] With Hoffa in prison, new leadership may return the Teamsters to the AFL–CIO, although racketeering influences continue to be present in this union.[20] Meanwhile, in many areas, locals of the Teamsters and of AFL–CIO affiliates continue to work closely together in matters of joint interest.

Other unions which have remained outside of the AFL–CIO fold include the surviving organizations which were expelled from the CIO for Communist domination, and the United Mine Workers, whose membership in the coal mines declined with employment from 500,000 to about 125,000. (District 50, formerly UMW, still organizes wherever it can and now boasts a membership in excess of 200,000.) In March, 1968, the UMW disaffiliated District 50 over the latter's support of atomic energy fuel expansion which the UMW opposes. Additional nonaffiliated unions are found in the petroleum, chemical, and railway industries. Two of the four original Big Four railroad brotherhoods—the Brotherhood of Locomotive Firemen and Enginemen and the Brotherhood of Railroad Trainmen—affiliated with the AFL–CIO soon after its merger for the first time in their history. So have two small railroad unions, the American Train Dispatchers and the Railroad Yardmasters, which were also heretofore independent.

Although the AFL and CIO merged, no real unity was achieved. Not only have most competing unions continued to go their separate ways, but basic rivalries have only sporadically been abated. For example, the building-trades unions and the former CIO affiliates have regularly been at odds over whose members should perform plant maintenance and construction work.

More significant have been basic philosophical differences between George Meany and Walter Reuther. Mr. Meany, who has continued to head the merged federation although he is now in his seventies, has pursued a traditional business union course, coupled with strong support for Johnson administration foreign policy. His course has had overwhelming support from the leadership of AFL–CIO affiliates. Mr. Reuther, who at 60 years of age, obviously saw his opportunity to head the merged federation fading, has campaigned for more vigorous organizing activities and involvement in social welfare and civil rights causes, and has been

---

[19] Numerous defalcations in various locals and a series of murders in San Francisco have featured activities in this union in the 1960's. A summary of such activities is found in the syndicated column of Victor Reisel, December 8, 1966.

[20] For some recent developments, see *The Wall Street Journal*, January 15, 1968, detailing racketeering control of New York City area locals of the Teamsters. The causes of labor racketeering are discussed in Chapter 3.

more critical of Johnson administration foreign policy. Without support even from all former CIO affiliates, Reuther in 1968 led the UAW, the country's second largest union, out of the AFL–CIO, much as John L. Lewis led the Mine Workers to independent status two decades earlier. Like Lewis, Reuther may try to organize workers in industries outside the jurisdiction of his union and thus attempt to create a new federation, in alliance with the Teamsters.

Merger Impact on Union Policies

The merger of the AFL–CIO had direct effects on union policies despite the lack of real unity. For example, it furthered cooperation between unions, including coalition bargaining—an arrangement whereby all unions which deal with one company attempt to coordinate their efforts in order to obtain better bargains. Such bargaining resulted in a number of serious strikes in 1967 and 1968, as unions sought both to enforce coalition bargaining on companywide bases, and to obtain very large wage and benefit increases, and companies resisted both. With Reuther's departure from the AFL–CIO, the coalition program suffered a severe setback, for the UAW and the UAW-led Industrial Union Department financed and led most coalition efforts.

The merger had other effects. Competition is good for everybody, and the union movement is no exception. The competition of the CIO brought the AFL out of the doldrums, and each pressed the other to do a better job for its members. When the workers are dissatisfied with their union leadership, they can change the leadership within the union or change it by throwing out the union for a new one. Organic unity all but eliminated that second possibility, which is so important in keeping union leadership the servants rather than the masters of the rank and file. Reuther's departure may return the competitive drive to organizing.

American Unions Today

Table 2–1 shows the growth of union membership from 1930 to 1968 and the percentage of the labor force unionized. The great periods of growth were during World War I (which gains were substantially lost during the 1920's) and the periods 1935–39 and 1940–44. Union membership rose slowly for the first 12 years after World War II, but these gains did little more than to keep pace with the increase in the labor force. Judging from the fact that the nonunion groups of 1944 were still largely nonunion in 1956, it would appear that union growth in the 1944–56 period stemmed principally from expansion in employment by unionized firms.

Union membership reached a peak of 17.5 million in 1956—one year after the AFL–CIO merger—and then began to decline, not only as a percentage of the labor force but in absolute numbers as well, until 1962. The years between 1956 and 1962 saw the membership roles of former

TABLE 2–1

UNION MEMBERSHIP IN THE UNITED STATES
SELECTED YEARS, 1930–1968

		Membership as a Percentage of:			
Year	Union Membership (000's)	Total Labor Force		Employees in Non-Agricultural Establishments	
		(000's)	%	(000's)	%
1930	3,401	50,080	6.8	29,424	11.6
1940	8,717	56,180	15.5	32,376	26.9
1950	14,267	64,749	22.0	45,222	31.5
1953	16,948	67,362	25.2	50,232	33.7
1956	17,490	70,387	24.8	52,408	33.4
1958	17,029	71,284	23.9	51,368	33.2
1960	17,049	73,126	23.3	54,203	31.5
1963	16,586	74,681	22.2	55,515	29.9
1966	17,892	78,893	22.7	63,864	28.0
1968	17,900	79,000	22.6	65,000	27.5

SOURCE: U.S. Department of Labor, and authors' estimates.

CIO affiliates especially hard hit, as, first, recession unemployment occurred, and then automation and increased productivity permitted increased production without increased employment.

After 1962, union membership increased until in 1966 it passed the previous 1956 peak. Industry expanded, and union membership followed suit in the high prosperity of the era. Unions also made great gains among government employees and among some professional groups, notably public school teachers. Nevertheless, union growth failed to keep pace with the expansion of the labor force. The shift in the labor force from hourly to salaried, the shift in employment to service from goods producing, and the failure of unions to organize the salaried masses and the service industries have been the principal causes of the decline in the percentage of employees unionized.

Since the mid-1950's, union membership has been closely tied to the business cycle, as it has in history most always, except during the depression of the 1930's, when government intervened massively on the union side. Both the decline in the 1950's and the expansion in the 1960's resulted principally from fluctuations in industrial blue-collar employment. The rise in the 1960's was also aided by growing unionization among government employees, a result both of favorable federal and state government policies and rising discontent among government employees with their wages and working conditions. A fast-growing union in this era has also been the Retail Clerks' International Association, which now boasts more than half a million members in supermarkets, drug and department stores, and other such establishments. Yet heavy, sustained layoffs in the automobile, rubber tire, electrical products and steel industries would again result in reductions in union membership roles.

Future union membership growth will depend, therefore, on the state of the business cycle and the ability of unions to continue to expand in the government sector, where great potential for unionization still exists. This assumes that the salaried workers will remain largely unorganized; for there seems to be little evidence that salaried employees, who have been a majority of the labor force since the mid-1950's, are anxious to align themselves with the blue-collar unions, except for special groups such as retail store clerks and some government employees. It also assumes that unions will continue to make only slight progress in organizing the few remaining bastions of nonunion industry, such as the southern textile industry. Should these assumptions prove erroneous, union membership could increase even if industrial employment declined.

Meanwhile, unions remain a tremendous and powerful force. Despite the decline in the proportion of the labor force which they represent, they are the dominant influence in wage determination and in determining the rules and regulations under which people work. For the nonunion sector is heavily influenced by union policies and follows closely (or jumps ahead) of that which unions obtain for their members.

Concentration of Union Membership

In 1968, the six largest unions had approximately one third of the total union membership. These unions—the Teamsters, the Automobile Workers, the Steelworkers, the Machinists, the Carpenters, and the International Brotherhood of Electrical Workers—all claimed more than 700,000 members, with the first three claiming more than one million each.

It is interesting to note, as set forth in Table 2–2, that over the years the six largest unions have generally accounted for about one third of the total union membership. Although the makeup of the six largest has changed from time to time, the Carpenters have always been represented in the group, and the Miners were represented until very recently.

The elimination of the United Mine Workers from the Big Six is a direct result of the decline in employment in the coal mining industry. On the other hand, the Brotherhood of Carpenters and Joiners has been able to maintain its place in the Big Six not only because of the postwar boom in building construction and the continued importance of this trade but also because this union has branched out and organized, on an industrial basis, woodworking and furniture plants and lumber workers.

The International Association of Machinists with 840,000 members and the International Brotherhood of Electrical Workers with a membership of 875,000, like the Carpenters, are former craft unions which have branched out and organized factory workers on an industrial basis. For

TABLE 2-2

THE SIX LARGEST UNIONS, 1900–1968

Year	Six Largest Unions (In Order of Membership)	Membership of Six Largest	Total Union Membership	Percentage of Total Union Membership in Six Largest
1900	Miners Carpenters Railroad Trainmen Cigarmakers Locomotive Firemen Locomotive Engineers	335,800	868,500	38.7
1920	Miners Carpenters Machinists Railway Clerks Railroad Trainmen Railway Carmen	1,649,000	5,047,800	32.6
1929	Carpenters Miners Railroad Trainmen Electrical Workers* Clothing Workers Painters	1,028,200	3,442,000	29.8
1953	Automobile Workers Teamsters Steelworkers Machinists Carpenters Miners	5,750,000	16,948,000	34.4
1964	Teamsters Automobile Workers Steelworkers Machinists Electrical Workers* Carpenters	5,850,000	16,800,000	34.2
1968	Teamsters Automobile Workers Steelworkers Electrical Workers* Machinists Carpenters	6,000,000	17,900,000	33.6

* International Brotherhood of Electrical Workers.

SOURCE: Leo Wolman, *Ebb and Flow in Trade Unionism* (New York: National Bureau of Economic Research, 1936), for data for 1900–1929; U.S. Department of Labor, for 1953 and 1964; authors' estimates for 1968. Canadian membership excluded from total membership.

example, the Machinists now include skilled and unskilled employees of aircraft factories and a great variety of metalworking shops. The Electrical Workers include not only electricians but also employees of all classes in public utilities and electrical and communication products manufacturing. In 1967, it passed the Machinists in membership for the first time in 30 years.

The Automobile Workers and the Steelworkers are the only former CIO unions in the Big Six. Their size is largely the result of the size of the basic industries whose employees they represent, but they have augmented their growth by spreading into related jurisdictions. The automobile union now includes aerospace employees and the bulk of the workers engaged in agricultural implement manufacture. The Steelworkers have enrolled thousands in metal fabricating, metal mining, etc. Both unions have expanded substantially since 1962 as a result of expansion in their basic jurisdictions.

The Teamsters' Union is likely to be the first in America to boast 2 million members. Not only is there a substantial number of unorganized employees in the distribution and service industries over which the Teamsters' Union has jurisdiction, but the Teamsters' Union has been giving every indication of willingness to invade the jurisdictions of other unions when occasion arises.

Besides being the country's largest union, the Teamsters' Union is probably the most powerful. If the truck drivers stop work, nothing can move to its destination. Produce and manufactured goods remain at the farm, the plant, the railroad station, the airport, or the seaport. The last step in distribution is the truck drivers. Their strategic location insures the power of their union. If the Teamsters can clean their ranks of questionable personnel and rid themselves of a corrupt and lawless image, their appeal to employees and their potential for expansion could be even greater.

There is a possibility that unions in the textile, white-collar, or government employee fields can overtake the present Big Six. For a textile union to accomplish this, it would be required to organize the southern textile industry rather completely. The immediate prospects for this to occur do not appear bright. The textile unions continue to fail to overcome southern employer resistance and worker disinterest. A white-collar union—the Retail Clerks—could possibly grow substantially if it branched out into other white-collar areas and scored more successes than have occurred heretofore. Retail trade remains a very fertile area of white-collar unionization, so that there is a real possibility that by 1970 the Retail Clerks International Association will become one of the six largest.

In view of the strides made by the American Federation of State, County and Municipal Workers in recent years—its membership has doubled in 10 years and now exceeds 300,000—and in view of the fact that

10 million employees work in its jurisdiction—it could be the country's largest organization. At the present rate of growth, this could well happen in a decade.

Labor in Politics

American unions were never completely unified on political matters, but the political split was never as deep as was the organizational one in the days of AFL–CIO competition. Except for the Communists, basic union political philosophies do not now differ materially from those of Samuel Gompers; but the tactics have, of course, been modernized.

Gompers' "voluntaristic" philosophy advocated separation of unions and political parties—but not union aloofness from politics. Thus, under Gompers' leadership the AFL avoided involvement with any political party but attempted to throw its weight to any candidate with a prolabor record or platform, and against those considered antilabor, regardless of the party to which the candidate belonged.

The political program of most American unions has not varied significantly from the Gompers tradition. True, the CIO was always more active in support of political candidates and policies than the AFL, and now the AFL–CIO appears heavily committed to the Democratic party. On state and local levels, however, unions sometimes support Republican candidates, and "liberal" Republican senators and congressmen also on occasion gain AFL–CIO backing.

Although tied closely to the Democratic party, the unions cannot always claim to control the votes of the party on crucial issues concerning which the general public is aroused. The American two-party political system would seem to leave the unions no place to go. They are dissatisfied with their present lack of dominant influence; their ability to deliver votes is often questionable; and their failure to organize the expanding salaried groups could reduce this influence. Unions appear anxious to increase their political role, and their strong support of the Democratic party in national elections will undoubtedly continue as a means of accomplishing this aim. Yet, the Democratic party is, and will undoubtedly continue to be, made up of many diverse interests which preclude it from becoming a party operated and controlled by organized labor.

Labor Unions and Politics in the Future

Despite their increased interest and activities in politics, American unions still rely primarily on economic action—that is, collective bargaining—rather than upon political action as a means of achieving gains for the membership. This is likely to continue to be the case, if only because bargaining has been so successful. Having won so much through bargaining, there is no reason why unions would want to shift their tactics. At the same time, conscious that bargaining is aided by a favorable political climate, union officials are not likely to neglect political activities.

In this respect, unions are not different from corporations. Corporation officials utilize primarily economic weapons, both in their dealings with labor and in the other facets of their business relations. Like union officials, corporation officials are conscious of the political world about them and of the desirability of a favorable political climate. Lest it be assumed that labor unions are the only special-interest group active in politics, it is well to remember not only the activities of businessmen, but also those of farm organizations, the American Medical Association, and other professional societies, as well as a host of others, all of whom are laboring hard for a favorable political climate in which to carry on their basic economic activities.

Because America remains a land of plenty, replete with opportunity, its labor unions remain conservative. Today, unions are as uninterested in socialization of business as they were in 1900. Likewise, the aims of American unions have not changed over the years. The words of Samuel Gompers could describe the basic aims today as they could 50 years ago—"the best possible conditions obtainable for the workers . . . more —always more."

In refusing to accept the highest standard of living ever achieved by workers anywhere as being beyond improvement, American labor is following in the footsteps of its forefathers. America has been built by those who refused to be satisfied with the best that existed, and then did better. This applies to worker, businessman, farmer, and professional man. The worker who wants more wages, the businessman who goes after record profits, the farmer who seeks higher corn prices—all are acting like perfectly normal Americans.

Labor Unions and the Negro

Unions have supported broad social programs since the early New Deal days of the 1930's, including those designed to upgrade the economic and social status of Negroes. Yet, at the local level, unions and union members, and particularly those very visible ones in the building trades, have more often than not opposed practical equal opportunity for Negroes. As a result of this, relations between Negro groups and unions have become very strained in recent years.

The Negro-union relationship could well become further embittered in future years because, in our affluent economy, union members, by reason of their high wages, are becoming more and more a middle-class group, out of sympathy with those at the bottom of the income scale where Negroes predominate. The result could seriously weaken unions, despite the existence of the thousands of Negro union members, because it would mean that a strong voting bloc and pressure group would turn against unions, and support curbs on the union movement.

QUESTIONS FOR DISCUSSION

1. Do you think union growth will be faster or slower in 1975–1980 than it was in 1960–65? Support your answer.
2. Could an organization built upon the structure and principles of the Knights of Labor survive today?
3. If you were the president of the Brotherhood of Locomotive Engineers, an independent union, would you support affiliation with the AFL–CIO? Why, or why not?
4. Has the Teamsters' Union been damaged by its expulsion from the AFL–CIO? If so, in what manner? If not, why not?

SUGGESTIONS FOR FURTHER READING

EGGERT, GERALD G. *Railroad Labor Disputes: The Beginnings of Federal Strike Policy*. Ann Arbor, Mich.: University of Michigan Press, 1967.
    A history of 19th-century unionism and federal labor policy on the railroads.

FINE, SIDNEY. *The Automobile under the Blue Eagle*. Ann Arbor, Mich.: University of Michigan Press, 1963.
    A detailed account of the attempts of automobile workers to organize in the early days of the New Deal.

GALENSON, WALTER F. *The CIO Challenge to the AFL*. Cambridge, Mass.: Harvard University Press, 1960.
    An examination of the effect of the rise of the CIO upon the policies and activities of the AFL.

ROWAN, RICHARD L., and NORTHRUP, HERBERT R. (eds.). *Readings in Labor Economics and Labor Relations*, Part II, "Some Aspects of the History of the American Labor Movement," pp. 41–125. Homewood, Ill.: Richard D. Irwin, Inc., 1968.
    Various articles by leading authorities on the development and history of the labor movement.

ULMAN, LLOYD. *The Rise of the National Trade Union*. Cambridge, Mass.: Harvard University Press, 1955.
    A cogent account of the emergence and development of national unions.

CASE STUDY READING

Under the guidance of your instructor, read a book or a series of articles about unionism and industrial relations in a particular industry. How does the growth of unionism in the industry you studied compare with the growth of unionism in the country as a whole?

Chapter 3

UNION STRUCTURE AND GOVERNMENT

The governments of American unions, like those of nations, run the gamut from democracy to dictatorship. The type and structure of a union organization have traditionally depended upon a wide variety of industrial and personal factors, but with the passage of the Labor-Management Reporting and Disclosure Act of 1959 (also known as the Landrum-Griffin Labor Reform Act), federal law became a most important factor shaping union government. Since union government and structure have important repercussions both on union policies and on the economy as a whole, a knowledge of union structure and government is an essential background to the economics of labor.

ORGANIZATIONAL STRUCTURE AND ITS DETERMINANTS

Union organization usually commences on either a "craft" or an "industrial" basis, but it soon expands beyond these limitations. Today there are very few craft unions which confine their membership to a particular craft, and very few industrial unions which have not expanded beyond their original industry. Thus the International Brotherhood of Electrical Workers takes into membership building-trades electricians, railroad shop electricians, shipyard electricians, and electricians wherever else they are employed; but it has also organized all employees of telephone, electrical machinery, and electronic concerns. Likewise, the original jurisdiction of the United Automobile Workers included all employees in and around automobile plants, whether janitor, electrician, tool and die worker, assembly worker, or anything else; now, as the United Automobile, Aerospace and Agricultural Implement Workers, its activities embrace these additional industries also.

Some unions have expanded even further. The Teamsters, or District 50, formerly of the United Mine Workers, will literally accept employees in any occupation or plant. Being outside the AFL–CIO, these unions have no compulsion to respect the jurisdictions of other organizations.

Sometimes, as in the case of the Teamsters or District 50, organiza-

73

tion structure is determined by leadership power conflicts. More often, technical, market, or government factors are determinative. Early craft unions found that if they did not accept the helpers into their unions, the helpers would take their places in case of strikes. The AFL failed to organize the mass-production industries, partially because it would not accommodate organization structure to organizational needs. The CIO forced the AFL to adopt a more realistic approach.

Technological factors compel changes in union structure. Several craft unions—the Brotherhood of Blacksmiths, Drop Forgers and Helpers, for example—have disappeared from the scene because jurisdiction has been shrunk or obliterated by technical change.

Government policy alters union structure. The National Labor Relations (Taft-Hartley) Act removes some jurisdiction rules from the hands of union leaders and places them in the hands of the workers themselves and the National Labor Relations Board. For example, if a group of textile workers wish to be represented by the Rubber Workers' Union, and if the leaders of that organization are agreeable, they can petition the National Labor Relations Board for an election. The NLRB then decides who is eligible to participate in the election and holds it. If the workers vote for the Rubber Workers' Union, it is that union, which is the legal representative of the workers for collective bargaining, with which the employer must deal, regardless of what union jurisdictional rules provide.

As noted in Chapter 2, the constitution of the AFL–CIO recognized the realities of jurisdictional control under the NLRB by, in effect, giving organized labor's sanction not only to whatever jurisdiction a member union had successfully organized but also to contests among member unions for newly organized groups where two or more unions could demonstrate historical interest. The principle of exclusive jurisdiction as determined by the AFL died, in fact, in 1935 when the Wagner Act became law; the AFL–CIO recognized its burial in the merger agreement 20 years later.

The AFL–CIO constitution did not end either jurisdictional difficulties among unions or jurisdictional conflicts between the rules of the merged federation and the Taft-Hartley Act as interpreted by the National Labor Relations Board. To settle quarrels within the federation itself, a board, headed by an outside impartial umpire, was established as part of the no-raiding agreement which preceded the merger. This board has had considerable success in reducing union raiding and jurisdictional disputes. The NLRB now gives the board an opportunity to settle raiding disputes before it takes action in such a dispute between two or more AFL–CIO affiliates.

The decisions of the National Labor Relations Board affect union structure in other ways. For example, if the NLRB declines a union request to separate skilled from unskilled workers, the petitioning union has the choice of opening its doors to the unskilled as well as the skilled or facing the possibility of losing the right, as a result of the adverse votes of the unskilled, of representing either the skilled or the unskilled. This does not mean that craft unions have to take on an industrial character because of rulings of the National Labor Relations Board. The NLRB, as we shall point out in Chapter 21, has been careful to maintain the rights and jurisdiction of craft unions where that is desired by workers and where the craft is clearly a distinct work group.

In many situations, union jurisdictional lines are not clear. In an industry organized along craft union lines, as is the building industry, technological change and the substitutability of one material for another lead to conflicting jurisdictional claims and to jurisdictional strikes—that is, strikes of one craft against another craft doing the work. On the outcome of such strikes depends which group of workers will do the work and perhaps which union will grow in strength and size. Often in history, conflicts over jurisdiction have led to eventual merger of the contesting organizations. In any case, the outcome of jurisdictional disputes has a significant effect on the structure of the organizations involved, for the structure conforms to the needs of the various groups in the union.

A dispute over which union will represent workers is different from a jurisdictional dispute, since no matter which union wins out, the same workers will continue to work. In representation matters, the accidents of location often determine the result and therefore the union structure.

If, for example, a metal-fabricating company is located in Detroit, where the United Automobile Workers is strong, it will probably be represented by the UAW; if it were in Pittsburgh, the United Steelworkers would probably win bargaining rights; in Minneapolis, the Machinists, etc. In each case, the friends and relatives of the plant workers are likely to be in the dominant union of the area, and so that union is likely to be chosen by the workers in the metal-fabricating plant to represent them. Union structure then develops according to the needs of members and the organization.

DETERMINANTS OF UNION GOVERNMENT

As a union grows and takes into membership workers with different interests, not only its structure but also its government is shaped to meet the needs of the members and to take advantage of the experience which develops. For example, the division of the membership along craft, industry, racial, or geographical lines often results in semiautonomous division within unions and in special provisions for representation for specific groups. Thus, all executive board members in the United Automobile

Workers' Union are elected from various geographic areas except two, who are elected "at large" but who, by tacit consent, are a Negro and a Canadian.

Administrative Determinants

Practical administrative problems also determine union regulations. For example, unions discovered at an early date that strike control would have to be centralized to some extent if the unions were to be preserved. This proved necessary to prevent "quick on the trigger" locals from striking on the slightest provocation and thus costing the union and members thousands of dollars for strike benefits, legal and publicity charges, etc. Strike control by national unions takes two forms. In many cases, no strike can be called without approval of the national executive board. In others, any strike which is called without national union approval deprives the strikers of strike benefits or other such national union help.

Effect of Rival Unionism

The development of rival unionism on a mass scale in the 1930's materially affected union government. In many cases, the advent of rival unions forced existing unions to open their doors to members previously barred. For example, a number of unions which admitted only skilled workers (Flint Glass Workers and the International Molders and Foundry Workers' Union of North America) admitted unskilled workers in order to prevent their organization by the CIO. A number of other unions, such as the Hotel and Restaurant Workers and the Commercial Telegraphers' Union, removed bars to Negro membership because of the threat of rival unions. On the other hand, the existence of a union with discriminatory racial policies has often caused a rival union which ordinarily does not discriminate to "soft-pedal" its equalitarian program in order not to alienate the dominant white membership. The merger of the AFL and the CIO has, of course, reduced the effects of rival unionism on union policy and government.

Imitative Elements

Many union constitutional provisions result merely from the fact that the writers of the constitutions copy similar provisions from the constitutions of older organizations. The constitution of the first permanent union, the Typographical Union, was copied from that of the Right Worthy Grand Lodge of the Independent Order of Odd Fellows, and then it was gradually amended to suit the needs of the union. Likewise, nearly all the railroad union constitutions bear a strong resemblance to the constitution of the oldest—the Brotherhood of Locomotive Engineers.

Power Elements

A number of union constitutional provisions can be explained only by the desire to increase the power of given individuals or groups. Thus, James Hoffa was able to have the constitution of the Teamsters substantially rewritten to transfer power from subordinate officials to the union presidency. John L. Lewis had great power given the presidency of the United Mine Workers and reduced the union districts to impotency. Provisions in such union constitutions as the Carpenters' which give a greater vote to craftsmen than to members of industrial locals are aimed at retaining power for the former even though they might not make up a majority of the union's membership.

Effect of Legislation and Court Decisions

Union government, like union structure, is often shaped by laws or the decision of administrative bodies or courts. For example, the adoption of civil rights legislation has forced unions to delete racial bars from their constitutions. Decisions of the National Labor Relations Board, placing certain groups of workers in bargaining units, have compelled unions to alter their admission policies, as we have already noted. Likewise, the courts have ruled that union leadership did not have authority under certain union constitutions to take specific acts—for example, to expel a member. In a number of instances the union has thereupon amended its constitution, granting the officers additional authority.

But no act of government has so affected union government as has the Labor-Management Reporting and Disclosure Act of 1959 (Landrum-Griffin). Under this law, members of labor unions are guaranteed basic rights of free speech, free assembly, and access to financial information, and their officers are required to maintain records and to account for union funds. In addition, unions are required to amend their constitutions, if necessary, to conform to this legislation. The law spells out procedures for the election of officers of unions, their terms of office, and frequency of election, and provides rules for the conduct of elections. Why this was necessary and how it might work out in practice can best be understood by looking at the operations of union government at the national, intermediate, and local levels.

THE NATIONAL OR INTERNATIONAL UNION

The "top" organization of American unions is the national or international union. The officers of the national unions are selected either by a convention or by referendum, or by a combination of the two, whereby the convention nominates, with the actual contest being determined by a referendum of the entire membership. It is common today for unions to have conventions every two to four years, although the Landrum-Griffin Act requires that they "need" be held only once every five years.

Although union conventions generally provide for representation of every local, many locals do not send delegates because of the cost. Some internationals have paid the local union convention expenses, but the expense of so doing is usually considered too great. As a result, large segments of the membership can be unrepresented at union conventions.

Because the convention is the supreme governing body of most unions, a fair procedure for electing convention delegates is a requisite of democratic union government. Yet most national union constitutions had very little, if anything, to say about how delegates to conventions were to be selected prior to the passage of the Landrum-Griffin Act, which contains regulations for fair election procedures. Even now, however, top union officials can assure a friendly convention by paying expenses of delegates from locals friendly to them and refusing to pay similar expenses for others—as was done at the 1964 United Mine Workers conclave.

Some conventions are truly deliberative bodies; others are just captive audiences assembled to hear union officers and special guests talk, and to affirm action already decided upon. Even if the convention is truly deliberative with wide participation by the delegates in formulating, discussing, and adopting or rejecting policies and rules, the real work is done in caucus or committee. In some unions, there is an air of the perfunctory at the convention when actually there has been heated debate and wide participation by delegates in caucuses or committees. The fact that the conventions often have so many delegates increases the need to do work by committees.

To control the convention committees may be to control the convention. A credentials committee will have a powerful voice in determining which of two contesting groups of delegates can be seated with a vote in the convention and who is to be denied access to that vote. The resolutions committee may be able to bottle up some proposals, and report out others, thus controlling the priorities and nature of the floor discussion. The appeals committee hears those who have been disciplined by union locals or officers or who otherwise have a grievance against union judicial machinery. Other committees may perform equally strategic functions. Since either the international president or executive board almost always appoints the convention committees, the delegates must overturn the convention machinery to change the convention committees.

If, however, the convention delegates elected their committees after arrival, they would probably have either to accept their officers' recommendations because candidates for committee assignments would not be generally known to the delegates, or, as in one convention of the International Association of Machinists, to spend nearly a week bickering over committee assignments and transact almost no other union business. The

IAM abandoned direct delegate election of committees after this experience.

The Referendum

About one fourth of the country's unions elect their officers by direct referendum. The referendum can be a useful tool in promoting union democracy, where the membership has a tradition of participation and a high sense of responsibility, such as in the case of the International Typographical Union, or where procedures for getting nominated and insuring fair and honest elections are carefully adhered to. It is, however, no real substitute for a convention. Union members frequently do not take an interest in referendums, so that the decisions made as a result of them have largely been the decisions of active minorities who took the trouble to vote. And furthermore, the referendum denies the membership sufficient opportunity for the type of discussion of the pros and cons of issues which features many union conventions. Finally, substituting referendums for conventions permitted a few unions, such as the Tobacco Workers' International Union and the Laborers' International Union, to go for periods of over 30 years without holding a convention.

National Union Officers

Most national unions are officered by a president, a secretary-treasurer, occasionally a director of organization, and one or more vice presidents. The number of vice presidents will be determined by many factors, e.g., whether regional directors bear that title. In addition, most unions have a national executive board which is theoretically the top governing body between conventions. Members of the executive board are often the regional directors or vice presidents.

Although the president, or whoever the chief executive officer of the union may be, is almost always technically subordinate to the executive board, more often than not he is likely to control it. There are, of course, exceptions. In most cases, however, the constitutional power of the union's chief officer is very great; and if he is a forceful personality, he may reduce the executive board to complete subordination, as James R. Hoffa or John L. Lewis did, or simply dominate it, as does Walter Reuther, by stature and force of personality.

Tenure of National Union Officials

The tenure of national union officials has traditionally been long. Indeed, opposition to national union officials in election contests has traditionally been rare. John L. Lewis was president of the United Mine Workers from 1920 to 1960; William Hutcheson, of the Carpenters from 1915 to 1952; Daniel Tobin, of the Teamsters from 1907 to 1952; William D. Mahon, of the Amalgamated Association of Street, Electric Railway and Motor Coach Employees of America from 1893 to 1946; and Walter Reuther, of the United Automobile Workers since 1946. Most unions have been dominated by one man for many years.

In any election the incumbent has a tremendous advantage. He is already well known to the membership, and his every action is news. The challenger must make himself known outside of his locality and must have an issue which differentiates him from the incumbent. Patronage, the union journal, and other avenues of communication are controlled by the incumbent. In the fairest of elections the challenger faces heavy odds.

In one union, however, contests for the presidency have been the rule rather than the exception. The International Typographical Union stands out for the number and vigor of officer contests. Only three times since 1898 has the ITU presidency been uncontested, and most elections have been determined by narrow margins. Although this is decidedly an exceptional case, there have been an unusually large number of contests for top union offices in recent years. James B. Carey of the International Union of Electrical, Radio and Machine Workers; David McDonald of the United Steelworkers; and leaders of the State, County, and Municipal Workers; the Oil, Chemical and Atomic Workers; and the Retail Clerks International Association have all been defeated for office or have decided to step aside as opposition mounted.

Does this presage a new infusion of political opposition and democracy within unions? Certainly, provisions of the Landrum-Griffin Act relating to fair elections make opposition to the incumbent less likely to result in economic or physical harm to the challenger and reduce the potential for stealing elections. James B. Carey's henchmen announced in 1964 that he had been reelected president of the International Union of Electrical, Radio and Machine Workers by a margin of 2,193 votes. After court action, and a recount by the U.S. Department of Labor, pursuant to the Landrum-Griffin Act, the Department of Labor announced: "The ballots were miscounted by the [union] Trustees . . . instead of winning the election by 2,193 votes, as reported by the Trustees, Carey lost the election by 23,316 votes. . . ."[1]

One can, however, doubt that the trend toward long tenure of, and little opposition to, union chief executives will be radically altered by the Landrum-Griffin procedures, or by any changes in union institutional mores. For the most part, union incumbents do not depend on stolen elections to keep them in power. Landrum-Griffin Act regulations which provide for honest elections and make provisions for recall and impeachment are not, therefore, likely materially to reduce the length of incumbency of union chiefs. The comparatively large number of union chief executives who were replaced in recent years is the result of several

---

[1] U.S. Department of Labor, Office of Labor-Management and Welfare Pension Reports, *Interim Report of Election of National President, International Union of Electrical, Radio and Machine Workers,* April, 1965.

unique combinations of factors. Opposition to Carey and McDonald grew within their respective union hierarchies as much over their personalities as their policies. The rapid growth and membership change of the State, County and Municipal Workers led to the overthrow of that union's founder-president; and in other unions, the age of the incumbent in contrast to a young and more vigorous local leadership and rank and file has sparked the changes. New leadership is likely to settle down to long periods of unchallenged incumbency.

In several unions, nepotism has marked leadership change. The Carpenters, the Plasterers, the Painters, the Structural Iron Workers, and key locals of the Longshoremen are among the unions where sons succeeded fathers as president. The nepotism and long-term incumbency of top union officials are, of course, not unique in American life. Corporation and university officials frequently are in power for long terms, and there are advantages therefrom. In industrial relations, it may promote stability and understanding between labor and management. A union official who does not fear for reelection may be in a position to act more realistically with management than one who must constantly bear in mind the effect of collective bargaining on his tenure. That experience is a valuable asset, few would deny.

Nevertheless, the advantages of active opposition appear to outweigh the disadvantages. It is difficult to believe that an organization is strengthened when an individual who leads it refuses to subject himself to a membership election or otherwise declines to test his responsiveness to the wishes of the membership. Only in an election can members register complaints or otherwise make their wishes effectively known.

Appointive Officials

In addition to elected officials, most national unions have a sizable staff of paid, appointed personnel. They include two groups: the specialists or professionals, and the international representatives. The former are the lawyers, economists, statisticians, research and educational directors, etc., whom modern trade-union organizations must employ in order to engage in what has become the highly technical business of running a union and engaging in collective bargaining with management. The latter nearly always come from the ranks of union members.

Professional employees of unions sometimes become key figures in union administration or collective bargaining. This is especially true of lawyers. Ralph Helstein assumed such prestige for giving free legal advice to workers during the depression and later as legal adviser of the former CIO United Packinghouse Workers of America that in 1946 he was elected president. Usually, however, the lawyer remains in the background as a chief adviser of top officials. And if these officials fail to secure reelection, their lawyers and other professional advisers are usually swept out of office by the new administration. However important the advice of professionals is to labor leadership, that advice can always be purchased as well from those whose loyalty is above question as from those who served the outgoing administration. With extremely few exceptions, professional personnel have discovered that working for a union permits less deviation from the official administration line than does working for government or business.

International representatives have three main functions: First, they are assigned to organize unorganized shops in the union's jurisdiction; second, they assist local unions in negotiations and collective bargaining; and third, they act as political representatives of those responsible for their appointment.

The first of the international representatives' functions is self-explanatory, but the other two require further explanation. Much has been said and written about "interference" by national union officials who prevented local unions from settling controversies except on terms dictated by the national union. For example, the 1967–68 copper strike, which lasted about eight months, involved basically a demand by national leaders of the Steelworkers that the companies agree to companywide or industrywide bargaining, an issue of much less interest to the local membership.[2]

Frequently, however, the national union is a force for peace. Its officers know the costs of strikes, and its staff builds up prestige by successful, peaceful settlements. Local union officers often are too fearful of the consequences of their actions and too inexperienced. The local officers "get out on a limb" from which they cannot rescue themselves. At this point the international representative can step in and use the prestige of the national union to sell the membership on the fact that the local leaders have secured a very good deal, despite the fact that it is less than was promised.

International representatives have little job security, although they may win it for the rank and file through collective bargaining. Theirs is a political appointment (which does not cast aspersions on their abilities), and they must aid the political fortunes of those who appoint them if they are to retain their jobs.

The power of patronage in government is always an important weapon in the hands of the incumbent. So also is it in a union. A union official who gave no heed to politics would not last long in office. He must make friends in order to assure his reelection. One of the best ways to do that is to appoint to jobs people who have contributed to his success and who will continue to work for his interest. The international representative is a political appointee and thus the political emissary of the person responsible for his appointment. For, basically, the union is internally a political organization. It could not be otherwise if it is to be in any way

---

[2] The strike was finally settled after much government intervention, and the unions did not obtain this demand.

democratic. And no democracy or dictatorship has ever been managed without "political machines" built upon a patronage foundation.

Union international representatives, like employees of business, revolt against insecure working conditions. The decline in union membership between 1956 and 1962, the AFL–CIO merger, and resultant layoffs of organizers have led to the formation of unions by union representatives, and demands that such bodies as the AFL–CIO, the Ladies' Garment Workers' union, and others negotiate with unions of *their* employees. The reaction of labor's top officialdom has been remarkably like that of management 30 years ago—rejecting recognition. The unions of union organizers have been forced to go to the National Labor Relations Board, which has ordered labor unions to recognize unions of their own employees.

INTERMEDIATE UNION GOVERNMENT

To coordinate the activities of local unions, and to act as an intermediary form of government between the local and the national, most unions have established what are termed regional offices, district councils, joint boards, etc. In industrial unions the regional office is the most common. Its jurisdiction varies with the concentration of the industry. For example, the state of Michigan is divided into numerous regions by the United Automobile Workers, and the rest of the country has proportionately many fewer regions because the industry is concentrated in and around Detroit. Similarly, the districts of the United Mine Workers are contiguous with the various coal fields; those of the United Steelworkers are heavily concentrated in the Pittsburgh–Ohio Valley area; and those of the United Rubber Workers follow the concentration of the rubber industry in Akron, Ohio.

Building-trades unions, which are organized on a craft basis, frequently have all local unions in an area represented in a coordinating district council. The garment unions call a similar organization a joint board; railroad unions generally coordinate their locals on a single railroad in what they call a system federation.

Whatever the name, the general purpose of these intermediate forms is the same: coordination of local union activities and joint action of locals in dealing with management. Generally, the regional office is headed by an official elected either by the entire union membership or by the membership of the district or region only. In some unions, regional chiefs have the title of vice president; in others, such as the building trades, the head of the district council may be merely the secretary-treasurer of that council. In any case, the regional office is an important union position which many local union officials covet. The turnover in regional officers is less frequent than in the local officers, and the former jobs carry considerably more prestige in most instances than do local offices.

THE LOCAL UNION

The local union is the part of union structure which the member contacts directly. The conduct of affairs on the local level is thus frequently the means by which the member judges his union. Like the government of municipalities, there is much in local union government which is heartening to those interested in democratic ways and much that is unsavory; and the latter, as in municipal affairs, is most often attributable to the failure of the citizenry, or members, to concern themselves with the conduct of their organization. In short, local union government, like municipal government, too often depends on the character of the small minority who are willing to bear the burden of operating the organization.

Local Jurisdiction and Size

The jurisdiction and size of local unions do not follow a fixed pattern. Most commonly, the local has jurisdiction over a single plant, and thus the size of its membership depends upon the size of the plant. One of the largest locals is No. 600, United Automobile Workers, which has jurisdiction over the 40,000 workers employed in the River Rouge (near Detroit, Michigan) works of the Ford Motor Company. Other one-plant locals have only 10 to 100 members.

There are, however, many variations from the one-plant local. Craft union locals commonly have jurisdiction over an area. Thus, the Bricklayers' Local No. 1 of Louisiana is composed of all union bricklayers in New Orleans. In larger cities, like New York or Chicago, two or three such locals may divide the jurisdiction.

Local union membership may also be divided on racial or national lines. Thus, in many southern cities, building-trades mechanics are found in separate racial locals. In New York, certain locals of the International Ladies' Garment Workers' Union have been confined to Italian-Americans. Locals of Spanish or of Mexican-Americans are sometimes found in the Southwest and in the Pacific states. As a result of the Civil Rights Act of 1964, separate locals based on race or nationality are disappearing, for they have often involved an additional barrier to jobs for racial minorities.

Industries in which average plant employment is small are frequently characterized by multiplant or "amalgamated" locals. Thus, in the Detroit tool and die jobbing shops, which employ an average of less than 25 employees per shop, two United Automobile Workers locals have jurisdiction—No. 155 on the East Side and No. 157 on the West Side. In such cases, one shop is considered too small to function as a unit.

Amalgamated locals may also develop for other reasons. A separate local of the United Automobile Workers has jurisdiction over all automobile plant office workers in the Detroit area, apparently because it is thought that the peculiar problems of white-collar personnel are better handled through a centralized local than through the plant locals, which contain mainly production employees. A number of unions have amalgamated locals which are quite large, apparently to centralize control. Under the amalgamated system, each plant in the large locals is represented on an executive board. Control of the executive board secures control over all plants. By concentrating all their strength on a few small plants, one faction can win a majority on the amalgamated executive board and hence have complete control over the local.

Local Union Officers

If a local union is small, it usually cannot afford full-time officials. In such cases, its officers work at their jobs but, by agreement with management, take time off for union business. The union compensates them only for actual expenses, which include time off from their jobs at the job rate. In many instances the international union assigns a full-time representative to aid local unions in the conduct of their affairs. The international representative is of special importance where the local cannot afford full-time officers of its own.

The larger local unions usually have one or more full-time officials, who are compensated completely from the local treasury. The top-ranking official may be the president, or the latter may be only a figurehead, with the chief power in the hands of a business agent or manager, or a secretary-treasurer. Custom, accident, and the strength of individuals who have occupied or are occupying these positions are the determining factors.

Only the largest local unions can afford appointed officials to assist elected ones. A few of these do, however, have organizers and other "local representatives" on their payroll. Such appointees help organize new shops, assist in negotiating and administering collective bargaining contracts, and aid the union political fortunes of those elected officials who are responsible for their appointment. They function on a local basis similarly to international representatives on a national basis.

Duration of Local Union Office

Most commonly, local officials are elected for a term of one or two years. In contrast to the situation in the national union, the turnover of local officials is high. This is especially true in the smaller locals, where the leaders and the membership are close and challenges to local leadership do not involve expensive campaigning. On the average, it is not likely that the tenure of local office exceeds two to four years. Some of the turnover is accounted for by advancement to higher union positions; some, by the fact that local union officials often accept managerial positions—for example, become foremen; but most of the turnover is accounted for by the desire of the electorate for a change in administration.

Local union officials often have few compensations for their jobs. Their salaries as a rule are not particularly high, and often not very much in excess of what they can earn as workers. There are of course exceptions, with some local officials inordinately overpaid. In the main, however, status is likely to be more important for the full-time official, for full-time union work is more appealing to many than a factory job of equal pay. Against that, however, are the long hours, the necessity to work nights when factory employees are free, and the constant reminder that tenure in office is likely to be short.

The Shop Steward

Besides compensated officials, nearly all local unions have shop stewards or committeemen, who are the union representatives in the plant. They are usually elected by the group they serve. These officials work full time at their jobs; but in addition, they collect dues, handle grievances with management foremen, and generally look after union affairs in the shop. They carry the union's message and represent the union in its daily contacts with members. Their relations with foremen often determine the type of industrial relations which exist in a plant; for whatever may be the union-management relationship at the top level, stewards and foremen are the persons who must carry it out on the shop level where it counts.

Membership Apathy

Despite the evidence that the great majority of local union officials are both undercompensated and honest, a significant number have obviously been neither. Therefore the obligations for fair procedure set forth in the Landrum-Griffin Act specifically apply to local unions as well as to national unions. Local unions must now elect officials by secret ballot at least once every three years. Various guarantees are set forth to insure free elections by secret ballot, reasonable opportunity to nominate candidates, a fair notice of election prior to elections, no discrimination in use of membership lists or campaign literature distribution, and safeguards for a fair count of ballots.

If, however, the Landrum-Griffin Act is to achieve its full effect, the average union member will have to attend union meetings much more consistently than he ever has before. The outlook for such a turnabout in behavior is not promising.

The business of the local is generally conducted at meetings which are either called by local officials or held at stipulated intervals. Unfortunately, these meetings are not, as a rule, either interesting or well attended. The average union member takes his responsibilities as a member lightly. After a hard day's work, he is much more likely to stay home with his family or to engage in recreational pursuits than to attend a union meeting which may be quite unexciting. In short, his attitude toward his union duty is like that of the average citizen toward his responsibilities as a stockholder, organization member, or citizen.

TRUSTEESHIPS

Constitutions of many international unions authorize the international officers to suspend the normal processes of government of local unions and other subordinate bodies, to supervise their internal activity and assume control of their property and funds. These "trusteeships" (or "receiverships" or "supervisorships," as they are sometimes called) are among the most effective devices which responsible international officers have to insure order within their organization. In general, they have been widely used to prevent corruption, mismanagement of union funds, violation of collective bargaining agreements, infiltration of Communists—in short, to preserve the integrity and stability of the organization itself.

In some instances, however, trusteeships have been used as a means of consolidating the power of corrupt union officers, of plundering and dissipating the resources of local unions, and of obstructing the development of free speech, free assembly, and free elections within local unions. The fact that most union constitutions are vague on the explicit terms and powers of trusteeships has permitted and abetted misuse of the trustee function.

The reasons why trusteeships may be initiated are typically vague and indefinite, and provide the international president or executive board more often than not with almost blanket authority to take over a local union or even to subvert the will of the local membership. For example, the constitution of the United Mine Workers provides as follows: "Charters of districts, sub-districts and local unions may be revoked by the international president, who shall have authority to create a provisional government for the subordinate branch whose charter has been revoked." Under this provision, John L. Lewis and his successors instituted trusteeships and maintained them for over 40 years without permitting a resumption of district union governments.

Title III of the Landrum-Griffin Act sets forth detailed regulations for the conduct of trusteeships. Undoubtedly, the existence of this law has curtailed abuses in trusteeship administration by limiting the right of unions to impose trusteeships and by requiring the reporting of facts concerning trusteeships and providing for appeal and possible court reversal of arbitrary actions. Nevertheless, the trusteeships imposed by John L. Lewis in the 1920's were still in effect in 1968. Although the U.S. Department of Labor finally announced in 1964 that it would sue in court to force an end to this undemocratic practice, no significant change has as yet resulted in the government of the mine workers.

UNION FINANCE

Operating a union in modern American society is an expensive undertaking. Officer and employee salaries, office rent, traveling expenses, postage and other communications costs, publicity, and legal and research activities are some of the daily routine expenses which must be met. In addition, a reserve must be built up; for a long strike, with its increased demands on ordinary services, plus the cost of strike benefits, extra legal and publicity help, etc., can drain the union treasury of several million dollars. The United Automobile Workers spent $33 million on strike benefits in the 1967 strike against the Ford Motor Company.

Dues and Fees

The funds necessary to operate a union and to service its memberships come primarily from the monthly dues paid by the members themselves. In addition, unions derive income from initiation fees and assessments, also paid by members, and from government bonds, property, or other securities in which excess or reserve funds are invested.

In general, the older unions have the highest dues and initiation fees. There are two reasons for this. First, these unions are primarily craft organizations composed of skilled workers. They combine high earning potential with work-scarcity consciousness. To a large extent, high dues and fees are justified by these unions on the ground that newcomers should compensate the union which has raised wages and standards in the craft, especially since the present high wages permit "Johnny-come-lately" to pay his share so easily. A high initiation fee also serves to discourage applicants and thus give union men a greater part of the available work. The use of the initiation fee as an exclusionist policy is only feasible if entrance to the trade can be controlled by the union. With a few exceptions, only craft unions can exert such control. An industrial union which depends for its bargaining strength on organizing all employees of the industry or firm would defeat its purpose by raising its fees high enough to limit membership.

The second reason why dues and fees tend to be higher in the older unions than in the newer ones is the greater stress by older organizations on union-sponsored benefit systems. Many of the older unions have always paid death benefits; and some also pay disability, old-age, and sickness benefits as well. A few, the Big Four railroad brotherhoods in particular, have elaborate life insurance schemes. Dues and initiation fees in such unions are higher because they include the contributions of members to benefit plans.

Welfare programs developed by the newer unions do not directly affect union dues and initiation fees. Usually, these programs are the result of collective bargaining and are paid for either by direct payroll deduc-

tions on employees plus an employer contribution or by the latter alone.
On the basis of the data filed with the U.S. Department of Labor
pursuant to the Landrum-Griffin Act, the authors estimate that national
unions had receipts of approximately $1 billion in 1968. In addition,
several billions more are now channeled annually into union-controlled or
union-management welfare and pension funds. Table 3–1 summarizes
financial information for certain unions, including the six largest, several
very wealthy ones, and some whose assets are dwindling as their membership declines—e.g., the Railway Conductors. It does not, however, include

TABLE 3–1

UNION FINANCIAL INFORMATION, SELECTED UNIONS, 1967

Union	1967 Membership	Monthly Per Capita Dues	Total Receipts	Net Worth
Teamsters	1,651,240	$1,821,185	$26,345,980	$53,210,998
Automobile Workers	1,402,700	4,201,099	57,784,975	83,977,550
Steelworkers	1,068,000	2,668,956	67,041,220	25,472,079
Electrical Workers IBEW	875,000	2,837,366	66,610,746	24,403,086
Machinists	836,163	1,862,601	30,124,379	36,104,206
Carpenters	800,000	1,224,073	20,847,953	31,336,058
Hod Carriers	474,529	471,703	10,255,299	23,489,304
Electrical Workers IUE	320,000	654,105	8,135,114	4,150,899
Operating Engineers	330,000	545,941	11,140,697	24,299,890
Plumbers	284,707	628,895	11,991,251	10,643,254
Rubber Workers	170,437	458,387	5,801,758	9,409,319
Mine Workers	125,000*	459,519	12,174,482	84,982,160
Oil, Chemical, Atomic	165,329	392,612	5,638,899	2,181,160
Railway Clerks	270,000	369,355	7,148,512	18,246,520
Railroad Firemen	45,000	237,138	3,303,473	649,767
National Maritime Union	45,000	313,960	6,571,961	10,773,233
Railroad Conductors	18,780	64,897	968,818	988,376

* Excludes District 50, disaffiliated in 1968.
SOURCE: U.S. Department of Labor, Bureau of Labor Statistics and Office of Labor-
Management and Welfare Pension Reports.

information on union welfare and pension funds, the assets of which have
been estimated at 50 times those of unions.[3]
    Initiation fees tend to vary from double the monthly dues to much
more. Many of the older craft unions charge $100 or more for an entrance
fee, usually payable in installments. Where initiation fees of $500 or a
$1,000 have been asked, e.g., in some of the skilled crafts of the motion-
picture industry, such fees are as much bars to admission as they are actual
charges.
    The extent of union assessments varies considerably. Generally, they
occur as a result of an emergency expenditure, for an organizing cam-

[3] By Frank M. Kleiler, Director, Office of Labor-Management and Welfare
Pension Reports, U.S. Department of Labor, *Daily Labor Report*, February 8, 1968.

paign, or for strike benefits. For example, the United Automobile Workers, despite possession of the largest net worth of any American union, enacted a $25 per month assessment in 1967 to help defray expenses related to the strikes, particularly the one involving the Ford Motor Company.

The Problem of High Fees

Generally, complaints of high union fees refer to initiation fees rather than to dues. Moreover, as has been pointed out, the basic problem is admission policy and not initiation fees. Any legal attack on what is considered antisocial union fees must be directed to the root of the problem—the extent to which unions should be permitted to exclude persons from employment by excluding them from the union.

There is no one criterion for a "too high" initiation fee. One hundred dollars appears a quite reasonable fee for the Air Line Pilots Association, whose members may earn more than $35,000 per annum; the same fee is outrageous when charged by the Hod Carriers', Building and Common Laborers' Union. A fee is large or small relative to the benefits expected, which include primarily prospective earnings.

Most union fees are not excessive by this standard. The main exceptions are found in the building and amusement industry unions. In these industries, union power is great, and union control over jobs extraordinarily complete. Those who are in the unions are thus afforded an unusual opportunity to inflict heavy charges on such applicants as they permit to join.

Section 8(b) of the Taft-Hartley Act makes it an unfair labor practice for a union to charge "excessive or discriminatory" fees. The act further requires the National Labor Relations Board to consider "among other relevant factors, the practices and customs of labor organizations in the particular industry, and the wages currently paid to the employees affected" in determining whether a fee is excessive or discriminatory. The NLRB has had comparatively few complaints under this section, and has ordered fees reduced or discontinued in only a few instances.

The Landrum-Griffin Act attacks the problem of union dues and fees from another direction. It prohibits unions from raising dues or initiation fees, or from levying assessments, unless a majority of the members of a local union so vote either in a referendum, or by secret ballot at a special meeting for which due notice has been given or unless a national union votes by referendum or at convention, for which appropriate due notice has been given. Failure to follow these provisions has forced a few unions to rescind dues increases or assessments.

Salaries

Unions are, in general, not distinguished as high-salaried organizations. The average union staff member received less than his counterpart in industry, in terms of salary, benefits, and expense allowances. Actually, union officials are paid on the more modest scale which typifies employees of other nonprofit institutions. Of course, the income of the union representative is usually greater, often substantially, than he would earn in his trade. More often, however, the prestige and interest of the office, rather than the money, are the lures which impel a man to seek union office.

As the data in Table 3-2 show, there are, however, a few union officials who receive fairly high salaries and allowances. A salary of from

TABLE 3-2

UNION PRESIDENTS AND THEIR SALARIES, SELECTED UNIONS, 1967

Union	Membership	President	Salary	Other Compensation
Teamsters	1,651,240	James R. Hoffa	$87,163.68	$11,054.66
Automobile Workers	1,402,700	Walter P. Reuther	28,149.92	4,202.11
Steelworkers	1,068,000	I. W. Abel	50,000	11,489.76
Electrical Workers IBEW	875,000	Gordon M. Freeman	36,333	6,041
Machinists	836,163	P. L. Siemiller	28,750	8,011
Carpenters	800,000	M. A. Hutcheson	37,700	11,374.71
Hod Carriers	474,529	Joseph V. Moreschi	50,000	6,841
Electrical Workers IUE	320,000	Paul Jennings	25,499.91	7,180
Operating Engineers	330,000	Hunter P. Wharton	55,000	18,026.64
Plumbers	284,707	Peter T. Schoeman	36,000	21,650
Rubber Workers	170,437	Peter Bommarito	17,712.70	5,616.05
Mine Workers	125,000*	W. A. Boyle	50,000	7,796
Oil, Chemical, Atomic	165,329	A. F. Grospiron	17,500	8,322.29
Railway Clerks	270,000	C. L. Dennis	50,000	1,657
Railroad Firemen	45,000	H. E. Gilbert	24,416	5,742
National Maritime Union	45,000	Joseph Curran	79,350.07	3,332
Railroad Conductors	18,780	C. F. Lane	57,123.55	3,631.38

* Excludes 230,000 in District 50, disaffiliated in 1968.
NOTE: George Meany, president of the AFL–CIO, was paid a salary of $50,000 and had extra compensation of $20,000 in 1967.
SOURCE: U.S. Department of Labor, Bureau of Labor Statistics and Office of Labor-Management and Welfare Pension Reports.

$25,000 to $50,000 does not seem large when compared to one varying from $100,000 to $500,000 paid to an industrialist. But unions are, after all, nonprofit organizations whose expenses are paid for by workers' monthly dues; and sometimes, those dues come from workers whose income is very small. Thus, the $50,000 salary of Joseph V. Moreschi, long-time president of the Hod Carriers and Building Laborers, is paid for mainly by laborers. And as the number of seamen and railway clerks has declined, the salaries of Joseph Curran, president of the National Maritime Union, and C. L. Dennis, president of the Railway Clerks, have gone up.

The largest unions do not necessarily pay the highest salaries, although the Teamsters is first in both respects. National Maritime Union's 45,000 members paid Joseph Curran $82,682.07 in salaries and expenses, but Peter Bommarito's 170,437 Rubber Workers paid him only $23,328.75. With more than one million members, the United Automobile Workers paid their president only $32,352.03; with less than 25% of the UAW's membership, the Operating Engineers paid $73,026.64, or more than twice as much, to Hunter Wharton, their president.

We may conclude that union salaries vary with the interest of the chief executives in the subject. Some union officials want more money than others. And because the salaries of the rest of the union bureaucracy depend upon what the top man receives, there is always interest in more money for the top man if he is willing to countenance his subordinates pushing up the scale.

Union Financial Methods

A union with a membership of 100,000 and dues of $10 per month would have a monthly dues income of $1 million and expenditures for numerous items, most of which are purchased in bulk. Obviously, it is imperative that unions operate with careful bookkeeping and accounting methods which account for every penny to the membership. Many unions have always done this, but others have not. In addition, local union accounting practice was often inadequate. Careful practices such as were adopted by the Steelworkers, the Ladies' Garment Workers, or the Machinists were not sufficiently common, especially at the local level. The passage of the Landrum-Griffin Act in 1959, and pension and welfare control laws in 1958 and 1962, were designed to safeguard union and welfare funds, now amounting to several billions of dollars.

As a result of these laws, union financial practices have been substantially improved. Nevertheless, congressional investigators have found that millions of dollars of union and welfare fund assets have been siphoned into the hands of questionable characters,[4] or used, as James R. Hoffa did, for questionable investments in questionable projects run by equally questionable characters.[5]

In many cases, employer representatives have closed their eyes to union dishonesty; too often, they have handed over to corrupt union leaders large amounts which the employers knew or should have known would never be used for the welfare of the employees represented. It is difficult to believe that such employers do not share the guilt of any resulting malfeasance. In a recent case, both Hoffa and employer representatives on a Teamster welfare fund were convicted of conspiring to misuse funds.

---

[4] See, for example, "Diversion of Union Welfare-Pension Funds of Allied Trades Council and Teamsters Local 815," in *Hearings before the Permanent Subcommittee on Investigations of the Committee on Government Operations*, (U.S. Senate, 89th Cong., 1st sess., 1965).

[5] Ralph and Estelle James, *Hoffa and the Teamsters. A Study of Union Power* (Princeton, N.J.: D. Van Nostrand & Co., 1965), pp. 213–320.

Union Assets

Based on reports to the United States Department of Labor, the authors estimate that international unions had approximately $2 billion in assets in 1968. This does not include the tremendous assets of local or intermediate union bodies; nor does it include the assets of welfare and pension plans, many of which are wholly or partially union controlled, and have assets estimated, as already noted, at "fifty times greater than the assets of all the labor organizations in the United States."[6]

Union assets are enormous, but they do not approximate the wealth of corporations. The assets of major corporations are in billions; those of unions, in millions. A few companies have more assets than all unions combined.

Unions are generally conservative financial managers. Most union funds are invested in low-return government bonds. Union financial managers want their assets liquid for emergencies, and they want to avoid criticism that could come if they invested in stocks of companies with which they might deal. Attempts to persuade unions to invest in socially desirable projects, such as low-cost housing, or to diversify their investments have not been successful.[7]

Two conspicuous exceptions to this rule are the Mine Workers and the Teamsters. The former union has invested in a variety of enterprises, including several coal companies, and has working control of the third largest bank in Washington, D.C. The Teamsters have invested in a variety of deals, including real estate, gambling casinos, and hotels. Many of these Teamster deals have shown little return and are the basis for a continuing investigation of relations between Teamster officials and the promoters of these ventures.

Union assets vary with the fortunes of an industry. The booming automobile industry of the early 1960's made the United Automobile Workers the wealthiest union; the declining fortunes of the railroad industry have reduced the assets of several railroad unions substantially. The assets of the United Mine Workers remain high despite the decline in coal mining employment from 500,000 to about 150,000 because the union has converted itself into a virtual investment holding company. Its investments in coal companies raise interesting conflict of interest problems.

ADMISSION POLICIES AND THE RACE ISSUE

The great majority of American unions admit any applicant to membership. "If he is good enough to work in the plant, he is good enough to join the union" sums up the prevailing union practice and attitude.

[6] See note 3, *supra*.
[7] *Business Week*, January 13, 1968, pp. 104–106.

But unions also tend to accept prevailing practice. The union is the servant of its members, not an innovator. If discrimination exists, it is likely to be satisfactory to white union members. That is why Negro organizations and unions often are at loggerheads. That is why much antagonism exists today between many union and Negro groups.

Although the AFL preached against discrimination in its early period, many of its constituent unions did practice discrimination. Negroes were antagonistic to organized labor in the pre-1932 period because of this fact. But when the CIO was organized, it made a practice of encouraging Negro membership. This, in turn, forced the AFL and its unions to adopt a more tolerant attitude. Unions, and especially the CIO, received heavy Negro support during the next 15 years.

But as Negro unemployment rose in the late 1950's and the drive of the Negro for more equal status on all fronts continued, the gulf between the aspirations of Negroes and unions widened. Racial equality programs ran counter to the vested interests of white union members—and they control most unions. The attempts of Negroes to end this discrimination, and the "white backlash," have further antagonized Negro and white workers.

The reasons for racial discrimination by unions lie in the basic economic and technological conditions of a particular industry. The unions which readily admit all applicants—the United Automobile Workers, the United Steelworkers, the International Ladies' Garment Workers' Union—are organized on an industrial basis, the only type of union structure feasible in a mass-production industry. Such unions derive their bargaining power by admitting all the workers in their industries to membership and by bargaining for them without discrimination. If they excluded any racial or ethnic group, they would weaken their bargaining power. Exclusion would invite the excluded group to join another union and to break strikes. Racial exclusion by unions in mass-production industries is not only impractical, but it endangers the union's very existence.

On the other hand, equal admission practices do not necessarily mean equality of treatment. Union seniority rules often institutionalize existing discrimination in promotion practices, or even add new discriminatory practices. In the steel industry, the United Steelworkers has done little or nothing to open up rolling mill jobs, traditionally a white man's preserve, to Negroes. Nor has the United Auto Workers, at least until very recently, substantially aided efforts of Negroes to expand their opportunities among the skilled craftsmen of the industry.

There are craft unions that do not discriminate, and industrial unions that do. Many other factors are involved; and in each case, they are mixed in different ways. In the case of the railway unions, for example, much can be explained by their character as fraternal societies. The first two railway unions (the Brotherhood of Locomotive Engineers and the Order of Railway Conductors of America) were fraternal and benevolent societies, and discriminatory rules are traditional in many areas of the fraternal field. As other railway unions came into existence, they copied the bylaws of the older organizations, including the discriminatory rules, as a matter of course, even though they may have become by then more important as bargaining than as fraternal organizations.

More recently, however, economic factors have been most important in maintaining the discriminatory practices of the railway unions. Employment on the railways has been declining, and the railway unions have been trying to shift to Negro workers, whom they bar from membership, the burden of unemployment. The Brotherhood of Locomotive Firemen and Enginemen and the Brotherhood of Railroad Trainmen have succeeded in getting nearly every railroad in the South either to limit the number of Negroes hired as brakemen and firemen or, more often, to eliminate Negroes from these jobs altogether within a few years. Negroes are thus being deprived of jobs which have been open to members of their race since the southern railroads were built and which were once among the highest-paying jobs to which they could aspire in the South.

The AFL–CIO takes a strong position against discrimination in its constitution and in all of its official actions. Nevertheless, it admitted to membership both the Locomotive Firemen and the Railroad Trainmen, after exacting promises that these organizations would delete the offending clauses from the constitutions—which they did, but significantly without altering their practices. Moreover, the AFL–CIO has no effective authority to force a constituent union to alter its practices.

There are many unions which expressly protect the right of workers to join, regardless of race. Such provisions vary from explicit provisions that "no worker otherwise eligible to membership shall be discriminated against or denied membership because of race" (Woodworkers), or that any discrimination because of race will be punishable by a fine of $100 (Bricklayers), to simple provisions that all eligible members, "regardless of race," shall be admitted (United Mine Workers).

Except in the building trades, racial admission policies are determined and controlled by the national union. There have been important exceptions. Locals of the United Automobile Workers have discriminated against Negroes, despite contrary national union policies; and locals of the Machinists and Boilermakers have admitted Negroes on an equal basis, in spite of national union discriminatory rules. These local variations have been the exception rather than the rule.

In the building trades, locals have on many occasions refused to admit Negroes despite some national officer pressure. This industry is still featured by strong local autonomy—and internal racial discrimination. As a result, building-trades local unions have been the targets of numerous civil rights demonstrations and court cases brought by state human relations commissions and by the federal government pursuant to the 1964 Civil Rights Act. Few matters have caused so much bitterness between unions and civil rights groups as the obvious and overt discriminatory practices of the building-trades unions.

The failure of the building-trades unions to admit Negroes, and the resultant agitation, has led to a reappraisal of the situation by the AFL–CIO, and the development of a program by the AFL–CIO and the government to further Negro training in the building-trades industry. A number of unions, such as the plumbers, which hitherto had declined to take any affirmative steps in this regard, have now gone on record as determined to change the situation. Instrumental in bringing this about has been the threat of the federal government and a number of state governments as well, that construction contracts would be denied contractors and unions which discriminated against Negroes. By mid-1968, it was too early to determine the success of this program, but at least the machinery had been adopted to end what has been one of the most serious obstacles to Negro employment—the opposition of the AFL–CIO building-trades unions.

Despite the progress in eliminating it, racial discrimination by some unions remains a blot on the labor movement. The fact that the record of the labor movement is about equal to that of most other facets of American life in race relations does not reduce the need to eliminate race discrimination in unions.

CLOSED UNIONS

Sometimes, unions refuse admission to any newcomers or accept only a favored few, e.g., relatives of members. Such unions are found almost exclusively among the highly skilled or strategically located groups who alone are in a position to control entrance to the trade. In addition, closed unions may be found in industries where employment is casual or seasonal (maritime, garments). In a case in Philadelphia, one man has been trying in vain to gain entrance to the motion-picture projectionists' local for about 50 years—an extreme case involving skilled work in a casual trade.[8]

The closed union is usually a local organization. Generally, national unions are opposed to a policy which limits union membership and may create a sizable group of potential strikebreakers. The local leadership, however, is under pressure to give preference to local members—even at the expense of members from other locals—and closing the union books is one way to achieve this result.

Sometimes, closed unions give limited work permits to nonmembers. This has developed into a racket in many instances, with permit holders charged high fees to work; and sometimes, permit holders are allowed to work for a fee while regular members are out of work.

[8] *Philadelphia Inquirer*, December 2, 1962, p. 32. Investigation in 1968 indicated that he had never been admitted.

The extent to which the closed union exists is not known. It is most common in the building, amusement, and printing trades, the local delivery business, diamond cutting, and mirror manufacturing. In periods of depression, it has extended to the seasonal and casual trades, and even to such industries as mining.

Reasons for Union Exclusionary Policies

The fact that some trade-unions limit their membership should not be regarded as too extraordinary. A great many barriers against economic opportunity are sought by a wide variety of organizational groups—farm, business, and professional as well as labor organizations. Moreover, the policies used by unions to bar admission are like those of other groups. Consider, for example, the successful attempts of the American Medical Association to limit the number of doctors (or to use the AMA's terminology, "prevent overcrowding of the profession"). Constituent groups of the AMA have used licensing laws, race discrimination, discrimination against aliens, denial of licenses to out-of-state doctors, and other equally antisocial means of preserving the medical profession for those who are already in it.

Whether a labor organization, a professional society, or a business organization, the reasons for restricting entry are usually the same: work-scarcity consciousness, dictated by fear of unemployment. For example, unions are more likely to close their books in depressions than in prosperity. Also, it is true that race prejudice is only one factor in the discrimination against Negroes. Undoubtedly, a most important reason for such discrimination is the fact that the color line provides a convenient method of limiting the market.

Public policy generally condemns closed unions. Nevertheless, the case is often not a clear-cut one. For example, in depressed times, when unemployment among union members in the maritime industry is significant, unions typically "close their books." Because of the hiring hall system, whereby men are employed in rotation for available jobs, the effect of admitting new members would result in a further sharing of unemployment in a particular industry where unemployment among those already attached to the industry is severe and where employment even in ordinary times is casual and intermittent. Nevertheless, if the union books are closed to some, but not to others, on the basis of race, creed, or color, or by some other invidious method, then the action is clearly indefensible—and today also illegal.

JUDICIAL PROCEDURE IN UNIONS

In the conduct of their affairs, unions have found it necessary to establish a list of offenses for which penalties may be assessed against the members. Union constitutions give officers considerable authority to impose a wide variety of sentences upon their own initiative, or after a trial has found the member guilty. Many of the offenses are general in character (action unbecoming a union member is such an offense); others are more specific (strikebreaking, for example).

The penalties vary from a modest reprimand to the serious ones of heavy fines or expulsion from the union, which can mean a virtual blacklist for employment. Union judicial processes are thus a serious matter from the point of view of public policy—namely, to what extent should private governments, such as unions, be permitted to levy fines and to deny persons work?

Anyone familiar with the realities of union organization realizes that unions must have some protection against those who would convert the union into instruments of outside organizations, e.g., the Communist party, or those who are agents of the employer, labor spies, or provocateurs. Moreover, if unions were unable to enforce any penalties whatsoever against members, workers who violate collective bargaining agreements could not be disciplined by the union.

On the other hand, the vagueness and general character of offenses found in union constitutions are a grave peril to the civil rights of its members. One of the worst abused is the prohibition against slander. No constitution defines "slander." Yet, it has often been invoked to insulate union officialdom against criticism. The same is true of "creating dissension" or discussing "union business" in public. Such events contributed to the passage of the Landrum-Griffin Act's "bill-of-rights" sections, guaranteeing members' rights to free speech.

Procedure

Charges against a union member are typically filed by another member. Invariably, they must be in writing and be served on the accused. A trial committee is then usually appointed by the local president or elected by the local. The committee hears testimony and renders a decision, which usually is reported to the local membership for action. A guilty verdict often requires more than a majority vote—two thirds or three fourths—usually by secret ballot. Penalties vary from reprimands and light fines ($5) to expulsions and heavy fines ($100–$500).

Virtually all unions provide for appeals through the union hierarchy. A frequent course is for appeal to the regional office, thence to the international president and/or executive board, and finally to the international convention.

In addition to this procedure, a number of unions grant their international president specific authority to initiate and/or hear charges against local members or local unions. Other unions permit the president to order a local to try a member and to take action if the local refuses to comply.

Unfortunately, most union constitutions do not provide for a stay of execution of the penalty pending appeal. Thus, even if a member eventually won a case on appeal, he could be denied union membership (and work) in the interim, which could be as long as four years. The ability of unions thus to discipline members has been reduced somewhat by the provisions of the Taft-Hartley Act, which do not interfere with the right of a union to expel a member but prevent that expulsion from causing the member's discharge, except for nonpayment of dues; and by the bill-of-rights sections of the Landrum-Griffin Act, which have provided much more ready access to the courts for redress if a member is wronged. Studies of the impact of these laws in terms of actual redress to the individual indicate, however, that restoration of job rights is often not effectively accomplished; or else that the costs of litigation are too formidable for the individual to undertake.[9]

Analysis of Union Judicial Procedure

Justice requires trial before an impartial jury, a full and fair hearing, and speedy determination of cases, including the appeal. Union judicial procedure has not stood up well under these criteria. There have been some significant exceptions to this judgment. The International Typographical Union constitution shows great concern for due process and independent judicial determination for those charged with offenses against the union.

The United Automobile Workers goes even further. It has set up a public review board composed of seven well-known citizens who have no other relationship with the union. The review board receives copies of all complaints lodged with the UAW international executive board. If a union member is dissatisfied with the decision of the executive board, he may then appeal to the public review board, which has not hesitated to overturn the executive board on a number of occasions. Moreover, the public review board has authority to act directly on a matter "if it concludes that there is substance to the original complaint and that the action of the International Executive Board does not satisfactorily meet the problem."

The UAW's public review board system thus attempts to provide a means of maintaining a constant surveillance over the judicial decisions of local and national union officials by a body whose independence is unquestioned. The Upholsterers' International Union is the only other union with a similar public review system.

As a matter of fact, those who bring charges under union constitutional processes more often than not may control the staffing of the trial

[9] See, for example, the articles by Bernard L. Samoff, Regional Director of the NLRB Philadelphia office, "The Impact of Taft-Hartley Job Discrimination Victories," *Industrial Relations*, Vol. IV (May, 1965), pp. 77–94; "Taft-Hartley Job Discrimination Victories," *Labor Law Journal*, Vol. XVII (November, 1966), pp. 643–63; and Cyrus F. Smythe, Donald P. Schwab, and Robert Madigan, "Individuals' Procedural Rights in Union Disciplinary Actions," *Labor Law Journal*, Vol. XVII (April, 1966), pp. 226–40.

committee appeal bodies. Thus, local officers who may bring charges in most unions either are most usually on the trial committee or appoint that body, this being the case in 77 of the 136 unions studied by the Bureau of Labor Statistics. However, 56 of these unions denied a place on the trial committee and appeal body for anyone who was an accuser or defendant. In addition, the defense is often prevented access to information, and witnesses are sometimes intimidated from testifying for the defense, or prompted to testify for the prosecution. The infliction of the penalty prior to the completion of an appeal has also been a severe hardship in many cases. An appeal to a convention which may not meet for five years is often an empty right, especially if the penalty is enforced meanwhile.[10] Moreover, conventions are large legislative bodies, basically unable to give the time and study to appeals from disciplinary actions or other judicial functions. Since convention committees are usually appointed by union officers, such committees usually recommend denial of appeal from rulings made by these same officers.

Traditionally, the courts have regarded unions as private bodies without a vested public interest. Hence they would not intervene on behalf of a worker disciplined by a union unless the worker was denied the forms of a fair trial, i.e., fair according to the union rules, or else fair in general terms if the union rules contravene public law or policy. Moreover, the courts frequently required union members to exhaust internal remedies before accepting a case—which meant appealing first up the union hierarchy to a convention before bringing the case to the courts. Court litigation is, moreover, costly and uncertain in outcome because of the numerous technicalities involved.

Congress, therefore, intervened by passing the Landrum-Griffin Act, which requires guarantees of freedom of speech and assembly, freedom to resort to the courts or administrative agencies without reprisal, and safeguards against disciplinary action (except for nonpayment of dues) unless served with written charges, given time to prepare a defense, and afforded a fair hearing, regardless of any contrary provision in a union constitution. Moreover, if the union procedure takes longer than four months, the judicial requirement to exhaust internal remedies is waived so that court appeal is facilitated. Nevertheless, appeals to the courts continue to be costly and lengthy, although an increasing number of union members are using this avenue of redress.

DEMOCRACY AND BUREAUCRACY

Democratic government is frequently confused with "good" or efficient government. Some of the best-run unions in the country from the

---

[10] For examples of high-handed and unfair procedure in locals of the plumbers' union in St. Louis and Philadelphia, see, respectively, "Big Man in Town," *Wall Street Journal*, February 2, 1968, p. 1; and Gaeton Fonzi and Greg Walter, "Plumber's Friend." *Philadelphia Magazine*, Vol. LVIII (October, 1967), pp. 46–49, 134–44.

point of view of economic returns to membership, responsibility, financial integrity, etc., cannot be considered democratic. The Amalgamated Clothing Workers and the United Steelworkers are cases in point.

Centralization should also not be confused with dictatorship. Although James R. Hoffa's efforts to centralize the Teamsters' government and bargaining were based on undemocratic premises, most centralization is dictated by economic, not bureaucratic, requirements. Moreover, national union control can have democratic effects; for example, national officers are usually more liberal on the race issue than their local counterparts.

The excessive delegation of authority, both executive and legislative, to union officials, who in turn employ a large appointive bureaucracy, is not necessarily a structural defect of large political units. It endangers democratic principles but is not proof of lack of democracy.

Moreover, union constitutions meet fairly well the key structural requirements of democratic government—general suffrage, free election of legislators, and control by the legislators of expenditure of funds and other executive actions. To be sure, the governments of unions frequently vary widely from the constitutional forms; and in actual fact, most unions are operated by political machines, the members of which have a vested interest in perpetuating themselves in office.

The existence of political machines, however, is not an antidemocratic element per se. Political machines are an important element in all democratic governments. "If the advent of democracy depended on the dissolution of all informal political groupings (machines) and on the appearance of pure-hearted leaders, we should wait a long time. Actually, democracy requires only that there be reasonably free competition among rival machines, and that the self-interest of union leaders be canalized in directions beneficial to the membership."[11]

Where general suffrage and free elections exist, the existence or lack of democracy cannot be tested by the extent to which leadership acts in the "interest of the membership." The plain fact is that neither the members, the leaders, economists, nor newspaper editors can be certain where the "interest" of the membership lies. The demands of the rank and file can lead to costly strikes which a union dictator might have avoided to the economic benefit of all.

The really basic test of a democracy is found in the principles set forth in the Bill of Rights—the first 10 amendments to the Constitution of the United States. To test whether a union—or any other organization— is democratically operated, we can use the Bill of Rights to lay down these standards:

1. Do the members have freedom of speech, assembly, and press to the extent that they are free to criticize their leaders and to work openly

[11] Lloyd G. Reynolds, *American Economic Review, Proceedings,* Vol. XXXVI (1946), p. 381.

for the defeat of their leaders at the next election, without fear of reprisal?

2. Is there a judicial system within the organization which effectively insures the dissenter against reprisal and which effectively insures a free trial for those accused of crimes against the organization?

These are the standards by which Congress, based on evidence similar to that presented in this chapter, found unions sufficiently wanting so as to require a bill of rights for union members imposed by law.

Gradual Bureaucratization

How do unions become undemocratic?

We have already noted the tendency for power to concentrate at the top as unions grow. This seems to be a natural evolutionary process which is only aggravated or hurried by the thirst for power of strong individuals. The rank and file seem to lose touch as the union grows large, its functions and responsibilities multiply, and the art of collective bargaining becomes more technical and embraces a wider area.

Centralization at the top seems to grow as the union gets older and the administration of union affairs becomes bureaucratized. The union's affairs are administered by a select group, partly professional or quasi-professional employees, partly "the administration," elective officials who have been in office so long as to have practically nothing in common except their antecedents with the rank and file. The net effect is likely to be more efficient administration, the creation of a special privileged caste of administrators within the unions, the limitation and virtual extinction of self-government, and the restriction of the civil rights of the members.

It should be emphasized again that the strangulation of democracy by bureaucracy is an impersonal process. The root cause is the indifference of the rank and file. With the union efficiently run, the average worker has little to get him excited. Like the average citizen or the average stockholder, he is content to let the machine run things as long as conditions are good. "Why waste time going to meetings? We pay officials to run the union," sums up the attitude.

LABOR RACKETEERING

Deficiencies in trade-union government which have been discussed in this chapter do not necessarily involve "racketeering," as the term is commonly used. What racketeering involves is the conversion of the union to the private benefit of the union official. A union official may engage in all sorts of undemocratic practices and still not convert the union into an instrument utilized primarily for his own benefit. John L. Lewis is a conspicuous example of a union leader who did not hesitate to use extremely undemocratic methods. Even Lewis' enemies, however, did not accuse him of robbing the union treasury or of using bargaining sessions to obtain bribes for himself instead of wage increases for the miners.

In contrast, consider the case of Dave Beck. Born in poverty, he worked himself up from laundry driver to the presidency of the country's largest union, the Teamsters. Not satisfied with the power, prestige and affluence of office, he used the union as a vehicle for personal moneymaking, greedily turning almost every opportunity to his profit. Finally, he was forced out by Senate committee revelations and an indictment for income tax evasion, for which he was later convicted.

Or take the case of Anthony (Tony Pro) Provenzano, a Teamster vice president and ardent Hoffa supporter from Hoboken, New Jersey. A one-time truck driver, he rose through the ranks to his vice presidency, allegedly with the aid of violence, underworld connections, and Hoffa support. A young ex-Marine who opposed him was summarily murdered. Other Tony Pro opponents have been beaten up or have disappeared and are presumed dead. Finally, Tony Pro was convicted of extortion, and the U.S. Department of Labor sued to have his reelection as a local president voided because of numerous irregularities in violation of the Landrum-Griffin Act. Interestingly—and typically—Tony Pro, the convicted extortionist, never won his men as good a contract as those of honestly run neighboring locals.[12] Shortsighted employers sometimes find it cheaper to pay off a racketeer than to deal with an honest unionist.

Not all labor racketeers grow up in the labor movement. Some are full-fledged lawbreakers before they become union functionaries. An example is Johnny (Dio) Dioguardi, alleged Mafia member, who was brought into the Teamsters by Hoffa. Dioguardi created a number of "paper" local unions which sold protection to employers, and which also gave Hoffa the votes to control the New York City District Teamsters' Council. More recently, Dioguardi has been accused of a "stranglehold" on airfreight utilizing New York's Kennedy airport.[13]

Causes of Racketeering

Labor racketeering is likely to flourish in those industries in which employment is unstable and strikes are extremely costly. In such instances, notably trucking, the building trades, the longshore, and the amusement industries, the labor force changes so fast that opposition to leadership is difficult. More often than not, there are more men than jobs, so that the power of dispensing jobs is great, and the fear of unemployment inhibits opposition. When opposition within the union arises, a beating or a murder can squelch it. Employers, meanwhile, acquiesce in order to avoid strikes, property damage, or physical beatings.

[12] See *New York Times*, June 16, 1963, for an account of the Provenzano career.

[13] See, for example, the syndicated news column of Victor Riesel of January 8, 1968; and *Wall Street Journal*, January 5, 1968.

Racketeering and Public Policy

Racketeering is thus a cancerous growth on the labor movement. It affects only a small portion of unions, but a significant enough group to be of public concern. Moreover, union racketeering is often a part of a larger setup featuring crooked business and political deals.

Obviously, such racketeering is more of a police than a labor relations matter. Too often, local authorities are unable or unwilling to cope with the situation; and sometimes, state officials are in no better position. A bistate authority established by New York and New Jersey is now trying to control crime on the New York City waterfront. Among the laws it must enforce is one barring those recently convicted of felonies from serving as union officials. A similar provision has been incorporated in the Landrum-Griffin Act. It has made it more difficult for racketeers to utilize unions as fronts for rackets but has certainly not ended the problem.

THE GOVERNMENT OF THE AFL–CIO

The government of the American Federation of Labor reflected the deliberate desire on the part of the founders of that organization to lodge the principal power in the hands of the national unions. The AFL constitution gave its president no authority to intervene in the affairs of its constituent unions. Consequently, a mild-mannered leader like William Green took refuge in his lack of authority when pressured to act against an affiliate. Stronger personalities, like AFL founder Samuel Gompers or George Meany, used the prestige of office to assert leadership when an affiliated union misbehaved, without violating the technicality that national unions are autonomous bodies.

Since the CIO was organized by former AFL unions, it is not surprising to find that its constitution was similar to that of the AFL. Thus the CIO constitution gave the president no statutory authority over affiliated unions. Until the death of Philip Murray in November, 1952, however, the CIO executives, Murray and John L. Lewis before him, had great influence over affiliated unions. This was true because Lewis and Murray had, each in his own way, strong leadership personalities, and because both were the heads of powerful affiliated unions besides heading the CIO itself: Lewis of the Mine Workers, which he later took out of the CIO which he did so much to found; and Murray of the Steelworkers. It was also true because Lewis and Murray helped to organize many of the unions affiliated with the CIO, and other leaders in the CIO looked up to them and greatly respected their judgment. After Walter Reuther succeeded Murray as CIO president, he had the backing of the auto workers of which he remained president, but much less complete support among other CIO unions. This perhaps contributed to his willingness to merge the CIO with the much larger AFL.

Figure 3–1 describes the formal governmental structure of the AFL–CIO. It is much like that of the AFL (and the CIO, which was modeled on the AFL). The Executive Committee is a new development, which stems partially from the fact that the Executive Council was almost doubled in size after the merger.

FIGURE 3–1

STRUCTURE OF THE AFL–CIO

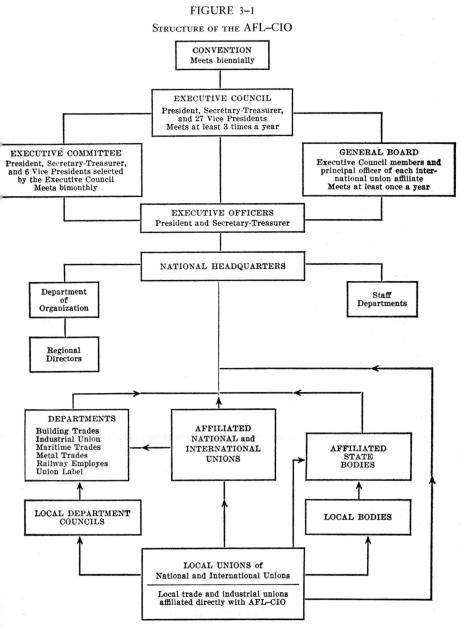

SOURCE: U.S. Department of Labor, Bureau of Labor Statistics.

The supreme governmental body is the convention, which meets biennially. Between conventions, the federation is ruled by its Executive Council, composed of the heads of 27 union officials who are vice presidents of the federation, plus the AFL–CIO's only two full-time salaried officers, the president and the secretary-treasurer. The Executive Committee, which meets bimonthly, is a committee of six members of the Council, elected by the Council, plus the president and the secretary-treasurer. AFL–CIO vice presidents receive no salaries from the federation.

National union control of the AFL–CIO conventions is insured by the method of representation. Each national union is entitled to send delegates to the convention in accordance with a formula based upon the membership for which monthly per capita tax has been paid to the AFL–CIO.

In contrast, directly affiliated locals—that is, local unions which are affiliated with no national union but are attached directly to the federation —are accorded just one delegate, as are city and state federations and departments.

Most delegates to AFL, CIO, and now AFL–CIO conventions are officials of affiliated unions. The rank and file are more apt to be represented directly at conventions of affiliates. This does not, of course, imply that the AFL–CIO conventions do not represent rank-and-file opinion.

The AFL and CIO organized local unions for direct affiliation only when no affiliated national union had jurisdiction over the persons involved. After the merger, most of these unions were turned over to a national union. City and state councils are coordinating bodies which were chartered by the AFL and the CIO in cities and states for the purpose of giving direction and leadership to affiliated unions and to represent the AFL or CIO point of view before city and state officials. Often the leaders of these central bodies have considerable influence in their areas. They assist unions with bargaining, represent them before public bodies, and generally aid and coordinate their activities. The merger agreement provided the state and city AFL and CIO organizations had until December, 1957, to merge voluntarily. After that, the AFL–CIO was supposed to force merger. By the deadline, less than half had merged. It was 1963 before Meany finally forced some recalcitrant state and local bodies to merge, and as late as 1968, some which did merge either split apart, or former AFL or CIO unions disaffiliated from state or local bodies.

The Industrial Union Department was created to give the CIO unions a coordinating body within the merged federation. Other unions with industrially organized segments have since joined this department, but it remained principally a focal point for the old CIO group, and a platform for Walter P. Reuther, head of the department, to expound his views as he formerly did when president of the CIO, and to coordinate organizing, negotiating, and research efforts. In the 1960's, the Industrial Union Department attempted to coordinate bargaining among unions which deal with the same company or industry. Such "coalition" bargaining tended to transfer the locus of union power from the various local and national unions to the Industrial Union Department and greatly to enlarge the scope of bargaining, and therefore the impact of strikes. The decision of Reuther to lead the UAW out of the AFL–CIO may mark the demise of the Industrial Union Department and aid opposition to coalition bargaining by employers who have been emphatically against expanding negotiations on companywide or industrywide bases.[14]

With the exception of the Union Label Trades Department, which is a propaganda organization to promote the use of union-made goods, the other federation departments act as coordinating bodies for craft unions which operate in the same industry. Their independence and importance varies considerably. Thus, the Railway Employees Department is composed of the six (seven until 1952, when the Boilermakers and the Blacksmiths amalgamated) unions which have organized the railway shop employees. It is the most independent of the departments, having its headquarters in Chicago instead of in Washington, where the AFL–CIO headquarters are located. The Railway Employees Department, through local divisions on each railroad on which it has unionized the shops, acts as the collective bargaining agent for the shop employees.

The Metal Trades Department and the Building Trades Department are less closely knit organizations. The former operates principally in shipyards; the latter, of course, in the building trades. Both establish local councils which act as the bargaining coordinator or agent for the unions involved. Both these departments play an important role in ironing out jurisdictional disputes among their members and often act as bargaining agents for unions which have locals in their geographic areas.

It is possible for one international union to be a member of several AFL–CIO major departments. In fact, the International Brotherhood of Electrical Workers has memberships in four departments, and other unions are members of at least two or three.

The AFL–CIO services its affiliates with a wide variety of functions. It attempts to decide disputes among them; it coordinates and supplements their organizing work; it supplies them with a series of news publications, maintains a legal department, and acts as official representative in political matters, although it has been careful not to back a particular political party because of the differences of views among its members. In actual fact, its political activities are largely concentrated in promoting prolabor legislation in the states and in Congress, and in opposing legislation considered generally detrimental to labor.

The AFL–CIO receives its funds from the per capita tax of 4 cents per month which each international union pays, supposedly, on each of its

---

[14] This issue will be further discussed in Chapter 4.

members. We say "supposedly" because sometimes the larger unions tend to report to the AFL–CIO a membership considerably less than they have in order to keep down their cost of belonging to the federation. As a result, AFL–CIO membership figures which are based upon the per capita taxes received may not be accurate.

The power of the AFL–CIO over its affiliates is greater than that which was held by the old AFL, but it remains limited despite the vigorous leadership of George Meany, president of the AFL since 1952, and of the combined federation since the merger. Article VIII (7) of the AFL–CIO constitution establishes procedures to implement the doctrine, adopted in the new merger constitution, that affiliated unions shall be free of corrupt influences and totalitarian agencies. The Executive Council is empowered to conduct an investigation, to direct an affiliated union to take action on these matters, and on a two-thirds vote to suspend an affiliate pending action by the convention. This was the procedure followed in the suspension of the Teamsters' Union and other unions which the convention then expelled.

The AFL–CIO, for a short period, regulated the conduct of its affiliates to a degree not even considered by the AFL of William Green's recent, yet bygone, days. The passage of the Landrum-Griffin Act, however, lessened federation interference in the affairs of its affiliates. For with the enactment of legislation, the government took over the policing of union government and finances, and did so after the AFL–CIO expulsion of the Teamsters had demonstrated the basic lack of ability of the AFL–CIO to curb large affiliates which could "go it alone" after expulsion—the federation's most drastic penalty. Evidences of racketeering in such affiliates as the Painters have since elicited no action from the AFL–CIO headquarters.

QUESTIONS FOR DISCUSSION

1. Explain why the tendency toward increasing centralization of unions has occcurred.
2. What do you think is the greatest weakness in union government? What remedies would you propose?
3. Why do you think discrimination and racial prejudice exist among unions?
4. Go to a local union meeting. Observe the conduct of affairs. Compare it with the local's constitution, and report to your class who runs the local—and how.

SUGGESTIONS FOR FURTHER READING

Cook, Alice H. *Union Democracy: Practice and Ideal.* Ithaca, N.Y.: Cornell University Press, 1963.

    An analysis of four large local unions in New York City, in terms of democracy, participation of members, and the democratic ideal.

Rowan, Richard L., and Northrup, Herbert R. (eds.). *Readings in Labor Economics and Labor Relations*, Part III, "The Structure and Government of Unions," pp. 129–56. Homewood, Ill.: Richard D. Irwin, Inc., 1968.

A series of articles by noted authorities on various aspects of union government.

Sultan, Paul. *The Disenchanted Unionist.* New York: Harper & Row, Publishers, 1963.

The story of why one-time union members leave unions, and their experiences with union government.

"Union Policies and Programs for Equal Opportunity," in *The Negro and Employment Opportunity* (eds. Herbert R. Northrup and Richard L. Rowan), pp. 167–206. Ann Arbor, Mich.: Bureau of Industrial Relations, University of Michigan, 1965.

Four articles dealing with various aspects of Negro union relations and problems.

PART III

Collective Bargaining

Chapter	ORGANIZING AND
4	NEGOTIATING

How do workers become organized in a union? What happens when collective bargaining begins? What are the wage and nonwage issues which concern labor and management in the collective bargaining process? What about strikes, "industrywide bargaining," "coalition bargaining," and "labor monopoly"? These vital questions will be the subject of our discussion in this and the following three chapters.

ORGANIZING

When a union representative sets out to unionize a group of workers, what does he do? There are probably as many organizing techniques as there are organizers, but some general patterns have emerged.

The unorganized plant may be called to the union's attention in a variety of ways. Often employees contact the union to interest it in establishing a local union for them. Other times the employers with whom the union deals stress the competition of nonunion firms and give the union representatives names and places as well as facts and figures. And frequently, the union will itself map out a drive to bring the nonunion plants within the fold.

The nature of the organizing campaign will depend upon the skill of the union leadership and the nature of the objectives. For a small group, the union drive may consist exclusively of personal contact of workers by the union representative. Organizing campaigns involving large companies include radio and newspaper publicity, leaflet handouts, large public meetings, and other methods of arousing enthusiasm in addition to the essential personal contacts.

As soon as possible, the organizers attempt to establish contact with sympathetic workers in the plant. Such workers act as volunteer organizers within the plant and form the nucleus of the budding union organization. As the union following increases, membership meetings are held, and a program for building a local union is developed.

Most union organizers recognize today that their job is growing progressively more difficult. In most industries, the large firms have been organized. Future increase in membership can come only from the laborious task of organizing hundreds of smaller firms with relatively small labor forces. Where large companies still remain unorganized, they are "tough nuts to crack." If they have held out this long against the onslaught of union organization drives, they apparently know all the tricks of defeating attempts to organize. Today the employees of government, federal, state and municipal, and of nonprofit institutions, such as hospitals, are the most inviting organization targets. These groups include large numbers of unorganized employees who have recently demonstrated a strong interest in unionization.

Unions are often careful to select organizers who fit in with local requirements. Sending a New Yorker to the South is not likely to achieve as good results as employing a native Southerner for the job. Organizers of the same ethnic or racial groups as the plant workers often find it easier to gain recruits than do those of other stock. The smart organizer tries to gain the allegiance of the natural leaders within the plant—those who are respected and who will be listened to by their fellow workers.

Winning Union Recognition

Before the passage of the Wagner Act in 1935, if unions wished to win the right to represent workers, and if management did not voluntarily agree to recognition, the only way to settle the question was a strike. If the union won the strike, it was recognized as the bargaining agent for the workers, at least until such time as management could oust it. If the union lost the strike in the first place, as was typical, there would be no union recognition as bargaining agent. Under such conditions, union organizing strategy was directed mainly toward organizing key workers whose skill or strategic position enabled them to cripple production by a strike.

Today procedures are provided under both federal and some state laws[1] for peaceful determination of collective bargaining representatives. The Wagner Act, and later the Taft-Hartley Act, provided that "representatives . . . selected for the purposes of collective bargaining by the majority of the employees in a unit appropriate for such purposes shall be the exclusive representatives of all the employees in such units for the purposes of collective bargaining. . . ." Congress gave to the National Labor Relations Board the power to conduct elections or otherwise to determine what union, if any, shall represent a given group of workers for collective bargaining. Once a union is certified by the NLRB as the bargaining agent, an employer must deal with it.

WHEN THE UNION ENTERS

A union organizing campaign, by its very nature, upsets existing relationships and unbalances emotions within a plant. The job of the union

[1] See Chapters 21 and 23.

organizer is in many respects that of initiating the transfer of the employee's loyalty from the employer to the union. To accomplish this, he is likely to point up existing or imagined grievances, to promise extraordinary and often unattainable benefits, to appeal to the worker to join with his fellows at the peril of being a social outcast, and to give impetus to the impulse of aggression and hostility which exists dormantly within most individuals.[2]

The purpose of the union, of course, is to win the representation election conducted by the National Labor Relations Board, or otherwise to gain recognition from the employer as the bargaining agent. To accomplish this purpose, the union must sell itself to the workers; and as in political campaigns, almost no holds are barred. Under such circumstances, the employer finds himself under extraordinary temptation to develop a keen emotional animus toward the union and its personnel. Many employers believe that they should keep the record straight for their employees, that they should advise their employees to vote in representation elections so that decisions will not be made by default, and that they should correct grievances which are called to their attention by the union organizing campaign. Employer communication to employees in such situations is becoming more and more common.

Employers who attempt to convince their employees that they are better off without a union may be charged with violating the Taft-Hartley Act by intimidating workers in the free exercise of their rights to choose their bargaining agent. Union organizers, on the other hand, complain that they are often denied equal opportunity and facilities to get their viewpoint across to employees; and when they stage mass rallies or picket at the factory gate so as to influence employees leaving or entering the plant, they may find that the employer has obtained an injunction prohibiting such activity. Some of these problems involved in the exercise of free speech by employers and picketing for organization purposes will be discussed in Chapter 21 in connection with analysis of the Taft-Hartley Act.

In recent years, the National Labor Relations Board has increasingly permitted unions to obtain bargaining rights if they can induce a bare majority of the affected employees to sign cards favoring the union. Since cards often contain misleading language as to their purpose, or are signed just "to get the union organizer off the worker's back," or even as a result of coercive tactics on the part of union adherents or organizers, this procedure has been widely criticized by neutral observers and by the courts. Many employers feel that this NLRB policy greatly increases the need for them to communicate to employees about employee rights as well as about the employer view of unionization. National Labor Relations Board policies are discussed in detail in Chapter 21.

<hr>

[2] B. M. Selekman, *Labor Relations and Human Relations* (New York: McGraw-Hill Book Co., 1947).

Problems of Early Adjustment

When the election is over, and if the union wins bargaining rights, the parties sit down at the conference table to negotiate an agreement which will govern their relationship for the next few years. Then there is a real need for clear heads and mutual understanding, not name calling and emotionally generated heat. But such a change in attitude, although undeniably beneficial to stable labor relations, cannot be achieved overnight. Charges, recriminations, and abusive remarks made in the heat of the preceding battle are not quickly forgotten. The union has the job of making good on as many promises to the employees as it can, and of establishing itself firmly not only with those employees who voted against it but also with those who have been lukewarm. The union representative, therefore, is likely to make extravagant demands and to be unwilling to compromise.

The employer, on the other hand, often retains the view that the employees were better off without the union, and he is disinclined to yield any concessions which would strengthen the union position and thus indicate to employees who were either lukewarm in their adherence to the union or who voted against union representation that there are substantial benefits to be gained through retention of the union as bargaining agent.

As a matter of fact, stable bargaining relations are not likely to be achieved until two developments occur: (1) management accepts the idea that the union is in the plant to stay, and (2) union members and leaders understand that their union is not all-powerful but instead that the basic job of running the business is still largely a management function. Until the new union and management learn to understand their new relationship and achieve a *modus operandi* within this relationship, there is likely to be some strain and strife in union-management dealings.

Management has the opportunity to start bargaining relations off on the right foot by dealing with the union honestly and fairly as a permanent institution and by forgetting any unpleasantness that developed during the organizing campaign. Management can also be helped by employing competent advisers who are experienced negotiators and who understand the significance of the first contract in the long-time union-management relationship. Otherwise management may concede issues that seriously interfere with the profitable operation of the business while fighting the union on other issues which, in the long run, may be less significant. For example, it may be far less costly to grant demands for extra vacation benefits rather than to concede to the union a veto over how many persons are required to man certain machines or whether new and more productive equipment may be introduced, even though a concession on these latter points does not involve any immediate cash outlay.

Union leaders can also ease the tensions by sending in new personnel to conduct negotiation of the contract—persons who cannot be charged with responsibility for any false accusations or violence which may have occurred in the course of organizing the plant—and by having the courage to explain to extremists among its members that some demands are out of the realm of the possible.

Negotiating the Contract

Negotiation of a contract, whether by a new union or an established union, is both a battle of effective preparation before negotiations commence and a battle of wits between the representatives of management and the representatives of the union. In many cases the general pattern of the contract will have been set before the negotiators even sit down at the conference table. This is true not only of the amount of any wage adjustment sought by the union but also with respect to the general content of the contract. Quite often the union will present the employer with a form of contract used by other organized employers in the same industry or by the same union in another industry. Or it may be that the employer will submit a form of contract which contains various clauses taken from other contracts in the industry or area.

Even if neither party presents a proposed contract, the "big bargains"—like those between the United Automobile Workers and General Motors, the United Steelworkers and United States Steel—or the big bargain in the particular industry or area may well have decided the general tenor of the agreement. But even where the general pattern has been set, the course of bargaining between the employer and union representatives will determine the extent to which the general pattern will be modified to suit the needs and peculiarities of the particular firm involved.

Collective bargaining has been facetiously referred to as "collective arguing." Since both parties sit down together with the intention of bargaining, they may try to conceal the ultimate position they are prepared to take and commence bargaining from extreme positions. If the union is prepared to settle for a 10-cent-an-hour increase, it may submit a demand for 30 cents an hour. Although the union's intention, when it makes such extravagant demands, is usually apparent to a skillful management representative, submission of such demands at the outset of negotiations accomplishes two useful purposes from the point of view of the union. In the first place, there are always certain extreme elements in the union who vociferously urge that large wage adjustments, such as 30 cents an hour, be obtained. The union negotiators must, therefore, present such a demand and retreat from this extreme position only after they appear to have made a last-ditch stand in the face of overwhelming employer opposition. In the second place, human nature is so constituted that management may be readier to settle at 10 cents an hour, and management representatives will feel that they have done a better job of bargaining, if the union demand starts at 30 cents an hour than if it starts at 10 cents. The employer cannot, of course, know precisely what the union minimum demand really is. By starting from a high figure, therefore, the union hopes to improve its chances of picking up a few cents an hour which it might not otherwise have obtained had it started at a figure closer to the true minimum.

This method of bargaining is not always either smart or successful. Experienced management negotiators often refuse to make a genuine offer until the union "gets realistic." Often the only result of fantastic union demands is a delay in negotiations or an increase in bad feeling. In both the rubber and automobile negotiations of 1967, the union negotiators did not recede from such demands until after a long strike. Apparently these union officials believed that this approach was necessary to convince the rank and file of their militancy.

Collective bargaining frequently looks like a show. Sometimes the purpose of the oratory and gesticulations is to impress the parties on the other side of the table. Sometimes, there may be an actual audience, as is the case when the union business agents bring with them a large negotiating committee representing the membership. Then the business agents are anxious to impress the negotiating committee with their skill as negotiators and the fact that the employer is a tough party to deal with. So they play to the galleries. Occasional walkouts by the union or management representatives from the bargaining table have come to be accepted as part of the byplay of collective negotiations.

The union, of course, does not have a monopoly on "acting ability." Employers also have become efficient in the art of predicting dire consequences if compelled to grant the union demands. When a representative of an employer association, or an outside consultant or lawyer, handles the company negotiations, he may also engage in theatrics to impress management personnel on the negotiating committee. Sooner or later, however, both sides get down to business, and usually a contract is hammered out. (See Figure 4–1 for the index of subjects covered in a typical agreement.)

Dissatisfaction with the "haggling" approach to collective bargaining has induced some employers to come to the bargaining table with a carefully researched and thought-out proposal, offer it to the union, and at the same time announce it publicly to the employees. The bargaining offensive in this instance reverts to the employer, and the bargaining which does occur usually is concerned with possible or minor modifications in the company offer. The effect of this tactic is to force the union to justify to its constituents any attack on the employer's position, for management has communicated its position directly to employees. This approach has been utilized with great success by a few large companies, where it has resulted in agreements very close to proposals by the compa-

FIGURE 4–1

Index to a Typical Collective Labor Agreement, Showing the Range of Subjects Covered

INDEX

FIGURE 4–1—*Continued*

nies, with few serious work stoppages over the years. This approach is known as "Boulwarism," after L. R. Boulware, a former vice president of General Electric Company where this approach has been utilized.

Satisfying the Constituents

No matter how smart the union may be or how fair the employer (an employer's being fair does not mean inept bargaining on his part), there will always be some employees in the plant who will be dissatisfied with the results. Usually, they are groups to whom the union promised something that was not obtained. They are the union's problem as well as the employer's. Moreover, difficulties in the home may cause some employees to discover "grievances" which are merely figments of their imagination, for their private lives may have upset them emotionally.

These problems require sincere, sympathetic, and honest treatment by both management and union officials. Grievances must be settled, not won. It does no good to prove that a grievance did not really exist. Pent-up grievances, however imaginary, are the sparks that flame into "quickie" strikes. A real attempt must be made to find the sources of the difficulties and to correct them, even if they are totally unrelated to the grievances presented; otherwise, dissatisfaction continues. Even under the best conditions, a new relationship between management and labor may be hindered by an occasional "wildcat" stoppage led by irresponsible elements who cannot be controlled by union officials. As elected officers who desire to retain their positions, union leaders cannot be too tough on contract breakers.

If, however, wildcat strikes or slowdowns continue despite company patience and good faith, it may be because understanding has degenerated into appeasement. Then a firm management hand, discipline of those who violate the contract, and a "no more nonsense" discussion with the union are usually the best methods of ending the trouble.

THE ECONOMIC SETTING OF COLLECTIVE BARGAINING

The labor relations policies of the textile and pulp and paper industries in the South are completely opposite in most instances despite the fact that both are located in the same region and often in the same or neighboring communities. The textile industry fights unionization tooth and nail, whereas the pulp and paper industry has stressed accommodation, peaceful union recognition, and high wages.

The answers to this seeming paradox lie in the different economics of the two industries. The textile industry has a high labor content, with its ability to operate profitably heavily dependent upon the availability of a large supply of semiskilled labor. Unionization presents a threat to the profitable operation of the enterprise and to the ability of the industry to meet foreign competition, with its much lower labor costs.

In contrast, the economics of the pulp and paper industry is featured by huge investments in buildings, equipment, and timber reserves, a relatively low turnover of capital, and a low percentage of labor costs relative to total costs. With fixed costs so high, there is tremendous pressure on the pulp and paper industry to operate its facilities 24 hours per day, seven days per week. To accomplish this with a minimum of interruptions, the industry has extended voluntary recognition to unions and paid high wages. The unions in turn have given the companies relatively a free hand in plant operations and have generally cooperated in peaceful settlements. In addition, the unions have aided in recruiting personnel to the often inaccessible locations where mills must be located.

The nature of collective bargaining is always heavily dependent upon its economic setting. The employment relationship is an economic relationship. The character and extent of competition, the relation of wage costs to total costs, the demand for the product, the capacity of the industry to pass on higher costs to the consumer (that is, the elasticity of demand for the product), and the size of the market all directly affect the nature and results of collective bargaining. Misjudging any of these factors can directly and adversely affect the demand for the product and thus for labor. Hence not only the results of bargaining but also the organization of bargaining arrangements (or lack thereof as in the case of the textile industry) reflect the economics of the industry. Whether, for example, employers bargain for themselves or through an association, as will be discussed in Chapter 7, depends largely upon these economic variables. The ability of a company to set up subsidiary plants where unions are weaker instead of concentrating them in one area where a strike can close down the entire company can depend on the capacity of the company to afford more than one operation and the investment required to make a plant profitable. A company whose plants manufacture unrelated products has much more bargaining power than one with assembly operations and parts plants all of which are interdependent. A company which supplies parts, such as glass or rubber tires, to another industry which, like the automobile industry, cannot operate without these parts, is usually reluctant to take a strike which could shut down its big customer. In such industries wages are usually very high.

Other examples could be given to show the dominance of the economic setting in collective bargaining. Within the economic constraints, other factors are significant. The social setting of collective bargaining illustrates this fact.

THE SOCIAL SETTING OF COLLECTIVE BARGAINING

The attitudes and issues which develop in the process of collective bargaining are profoundly affected by the social environment in which workers and employers live and work. Although collective bargaining technically concerns only the conditions and terms of work in a particular plant or company, the demands made by workers and the reactions of employers to such demands may reflect broad sociological patterns affecting the community, or even the country as a whole. The struggle between management and unions is to some extent a struggle for status—for recognition and respect and security. This contest is not confined to the factory. It can be seen in the attempts of labor and management to gain the favorable attention of public opinion. It is likewise to be seen in attempts of labor and management groups to influence the election of public officials. Union officials who live in a small-town atmosphere of hostility to unions are not likely to sit down with management with anything other than an attitude of suspicion and distrust.

Ethnical and cultural patterns in the community leave a characteristic imprint on collective bargaining relations. Steelworkers have frequently been Italian-born or Polish-born; garment workers, Jewish and Italian in background; automobile workers, often Southerners, white and Negro. These diverse cultural and ethnic backgrounds undoubtedly influence union policies and the course of collective bargaining in particular industries and localities.

Likewise, some of the frictions which develop in a plant may be attributable to deep-rooted tensions in the community growing out of racial conflicts. Antagonism between Negro workers and white foremen may merely mirror the broader struggle for status of underprivileged Negro citizens who are discriminated against in the community and of white citizens taught early in life to "keep the Negro in his place."

The social patterns which affect collective bargaining are not limited to the local community. The changing composition of the population in terms of age, for example, affects the type of issue which will arise in collective bargaining. By 1970, it is estimated that from 19 to 20 million persons will be over 65, whereas in 1950, those over 65 numbered only 11.5 million. The growing number of older persons in the population adds new impetus to the drive of unions for pensions. The substantial increases negotiated in pensions in recent labor negotiations reflect this emphasis on retirement benefits.

Similarly, the scope and content of federal and state legislation have a far-reaching effect upon the nature of union objectives in collective bargaining. It is probable that if employers had joined with labor in urging that the old-age and survivors insurance program be liberalized and made more inclusive, the movement for employer-financed pension plans would never have gained momentum. However, with a retired worker entitled to only $26 a month from the government prior to the 1950 liberalization of the Social Security law, it was inevitable that unions would seek to bring pensions into the scope of collective bargaining. If the Social Security Act had been liberalized earlier, industry might not have been forced into the present haphazard patchwork of varying pension benefits.[3]

The young men who are now entering the labor force are quite different from the men who entered the labor force at the beginning of the century. They are, for the most part, American-born, for the great influx of immigrants has ended. They are better educated than ever before. They have grown up in an era of full employment, rising standards of living, and prosperity. They have seen unions stall great industries and union leaders command the respect of management and public officials. But they are questioning many policies of unions and companies. Excessive stress on pensions and security, for example, seems unnecessary to them in the light of their experiences and value scales. They want high

[3] Pensions are discussed in Chapter 17.

wages and they want them now. When unions have not delivered to their satisfaction, they have not hesitated to reject settlements and to stay on strike. Sometimes, such rejection is more a revolt against union leadership than unhappiness with the proposed agreement. But an active, restive, well-educated and uninhibited rank and file adds a new dimension to collective bargaining.[4]

Such a change in rank-and-file sentiment from the relatively docile to the uninhibited is obviously disturbing to the status quo. It has added to labor strife and probably will add to it for a time. In the long run, however, it seems certain to presage a change for the better in which union leadership demands reflect accurately the needs of the rank and file, and management is conscious of that fact.

THE COLLECTIVE AGREEMENT

A collective bargaining agreement today is customarily a lengthy document, often drawn in final form by an attorney, which sets forth the basic rules and standards which will govern the relationship of the employer and employees for the duration of the contract. The contract terms are binding not only on union members but also on all employees, whether members of the union or not, who are included within the bargaining unit. Union contracts customarily include clauses governing wages and hours, vacations, grievance procedure, union security, rights and responsibilities of management and union, promotion, layoff and discharge, and various working conditions peculiar to the plant or industry, as indicated by the table of contents of the contract reproduced in Figure 4–1.

Bargaining during the Life of the Agreement— Grievance Disputes

The typical union-management agreement, contains provisions— grievance machinery—for the settlement of disputes arising out of contract interpretation and application. The grievance machinery usually includes a series of steps, with a higher level of union and management authority participating at each step. To induce settlement without a work stoppage, more and more contracts provide for a terminal step of arbitration, to which are referred disputes which the parties cannot settle in any of the earlier stages. This type of arbitration is found in more than 90% of the contracts negotiated in recent years.

---

[4] For an illuminating study of why the rank and file reject agreements negotiated by union and management officials, see the talk at the University of Chicago by the Director of the Federal Mediation and Conciliation Service, William Simkin, "Refusals to Ratify Contracts," November 17, 1967. A total of 14.2% of the 7,193 cases studied by FMCS involved rank-and-file rejections of settlement in 1967.

The grievance procedure is in fact more than a process which provides for the peaceful settlement of disputes arising out of contract interpretations. It is also a mechanism through which misunderstandings can be straightened out and problems solved. It permits representatives of management and labor to meet regularly and to obtain greater understanding of each other's problems. Finally, it is a vehicle for continued collective bargaining.

Collective bargaining does not end when the agreement is signed. It simply takes a different form. Union officials are just as alert to the possibility of obtaining additional benefits for their membership after a contract is signed as before. If, for example, the union can induce management to make an exception on vacation policy for one worker, that exception can be made the basis of a demand for liberalization of vacations in the next contract negotiations, either with this company or with other companies with which the union deals. Various groups in the shop may try to gain by direct action or pressure what they failed to achieve in bargaining over the new contract. If a rival for the union leadership can make gains in this manner, he might insure his election to the top union job next time.

Management may also do more than rest upon the contractual status quo. Plant managers and supervisors, anxious to maintain their control and profit positions, sometimes attempt to water down the agreement in practice. The contract is, in a real sense, only a temporary resting place.[5]

In most instances, bargaining during the life of the contract is different from bargaining over a new contract. That is true because the bargaining after the contract has been signed is basically over the interpretation and administration of the agreement, whereas before the agreement is signed, it is the language of the agreement which is in dispute. Thus some observers liken the negotiation of the agreement to the legislative function of writing laws, and the interpretation and administration bargaining which goes on after the agreement is signed to the judicial function of interpreting laws which the legislature has enacted. Like judges, the parties can substantially alter meaning and intent by interpretation.

Nevertheless, the attitudes of unions and managements toward interpretation and toward bargaining over new contracts are in many ways quite different. For example, whereas, as already noted, most agreements provide for the arbitration of grievance disputes—that is, disputes over contract interpretation—only about 2% provide for the arbitration of disputes over new or reopened agreements. In other words, unions and managements are willing to allow a third party to settle a dispute over an interpretation of an agreement when they cannot agree on the interpreta-

---

[5] For an excellent analysis of bargaining and group pressures through the grievance procedure, see James W. Kuhn, *Bargaining in Grievance Settlement: The Power in Industrial Work Groups* (New York: Columbia University Press, 1962).

tion; but when it comes to the actual negotiation of the agreement, they want no outsider to do it for them.

Now, this is sensible, because no one is as qualified to write a contract as the parties who have to live with it. On the other hand, if the company is going to get out production, and if the workers are to receive steady pay, then the parties have to agree on a practical method which insures that production will not be interrupted by disputes over contract interpretation and administration. Then, if either party is too dissatisfied

FIGURE 4–2

GENERAL PATTERN OF GRIEVANCE MACHINERY IN LARGE PLANTS

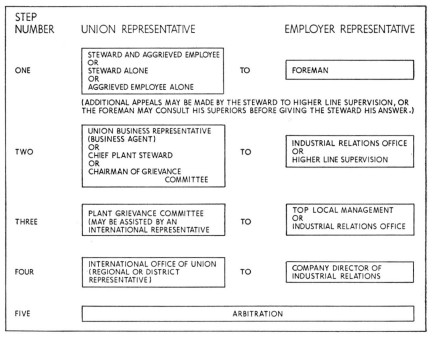

STEP NUMBER	UNION REPRESENTATIVE		EMPLOYER REPRESENTATIVE
ONE	STEWARD AND AGGRIEVED EMPLOYEE OR STEWARD ALONE OR AGGRIEVED EMPLOYEE ALONE	TO	FOREMAN
	(ADDITIONAL APPEALS MAY BE MADE BY THE STEWARD TO HIGHER LINE SUPERVISION, OR THE FOREMAN MAY CONSULT HIS SUPERIORS BEFORE GIVING THE STEWARD HIS ANSWER.)		
TWO	UNION BUSINESS REPRESENTATIVE (BUSINESS AGENT) OR CHIEF PLANT STEWARD OR CHAIRMAN OF GRIEVANCE COMMITTEE	TO	INDUSTRIAL RELATIONS OFFICE OR HIGHER LINE SUPERVISION
THREE	PLANT GRIEVANCE COMMITTEE (MAY BE ASSISTED BY AN INTERNATIONAL REPRESENTATIVE	TO	TOP LOCAL MANAGEMENT OR INDUSTRIAL RELATIONS OFFICE
FOUR	INTERNATIONAL OFFICE OF UNION (REGIONAL OR DISTRICT REPRESENTATIVE)	TO	COMPANY DIRECTOR OF INDUSTRIAL RELATIONS
FIVE	ARBITRATION		

with the results of the decision of the outside arbitrator who interprets the disputed clause in the agreement, that party can attempt to have the contract altered at the next negotiation.

Figure 4–2 shows typical grievance machinery from the time a grievance is raised until it is settled by arbitration. Lest the reader misunderstand, it should be stressed that the typical grievance is settled at the first step. This is particularly the case after the union-management relationship has matured. Once the shop foreman and the union stewards or committeemen get used to each other and to living under a contract, they are likely to work out a *modus operandi*. For every grievance which goes to arbitration, thousands are settled by the parties themselves in the shops.

The disputes which do go to arbitration, however, are likely to be important ones, or ones in which both parties feel they have too important a stake to compromise. That is why the provisions of the contract which concern the arbitration machinery are so important.

Before an arbitration can occur, the arbitrator, or in some cases, board of arbitrators, must be selected. Some agreements provide either for a permanent arbitrator selected by the parties, or a permanent number of arbitrators who rotate by case. More often the arbitrator is selected for each case, or group of cases. Most contracts provide that if the parties cannot agree on a selection, either the Federal Mediation and Conciliation Service, or a private, nonprofit organization, the American Arbitration Association, will be asked to submit a panel from which the arbitrator can be chosen, or even to name the arbitrator.

The Arbitrator's Jurisdiction and the Courts[6]

Historically, agreements to arbitrate grievance disputes carefully restrict the arbitrator's jurisdiction. Some contracts state that the arbitrator cannot rule on certain subjects or cannot add to or subtract from the agreement. Until recently, it was also assumed by most practitioners in the collective bargaining field that rights not specifically dealt with by the contract were, in effect, reserved to management. This view was buttressed in many contracts by a general "management rights" clause, which reserved to management all rights that were not limited by the agreement with the union.

Then, in 1960, the United States Supreme Court ruled that unless there is a specific exclusion in a written agreement or "the most forceful evidence" indicating that the parties intended the arbitration clause not to be applicable, all issues arising between parties to a contract were arbitrable.[7] Such matters as plant moves or the contracting-out of work, over which the union failed to gain a voice in contract negotiation, were thus nevertheless made arbitrable by these Supreme Court rulings.

This ruling was greeted with great dismay by employers, who saw it as another successful attack on their "prerogatives" (which are discussed later in this chapter) and on the ability to compete profitably. Coming at a time when employers have been faced with difficult decisions arising out of automation and intensified competition, including foreign competition, the result has been additional effective union pressure in a broad range of issues relating to managerial decisions affecting plant, equipment, products, and other factors, which, of course, have an effect on employees.

---

[6] For a more complete discussion of this subject, see Herbert R. Northrup and Gordon F. Bloom, *Government and Labor* (Homewood: Richard D. Irwin, Inc., 1963), pp. 124–29.

[7] *United Steelworkers of America* v. *American Manufacturing Co.*, 361 U.S. 564 (1960); *United Steelworkers* v. *Warrior and Gulf Navigation Co.*, 363 U.S. 574 (1960); and *United Steelworkers* v. *Enterprise Wheel and Car Corp.*, 363 U.S. 593 (1960).

Another effect of these Supreme Court decisions has been management's insistence on restricting the arbitrator's discretion by inserting very specific exclusions in contracts.

Typical Grievance Cases

So far, all this may be a bit abstract to a person not familiar with collective bargaining issues. Let us therefore look at a few typical cases.

In a certain year, two important holidays—July 4 and May 30 (Memorial Day)—came on Saturdays. What happened if the contract called for provisions for special pay or for leave with pay on these days and Saturday was not a workday? The answer is that it all depends upon what the contract says. For if a dispute over contract interpretation goes to an arbitrator, his job is to decide the dispute in the light of what the contract actually says and means.

This dispute arose at the Hanson & Whitney Company of Connecticut, which deals with the Electrical, Radio and Machine Workers. Here the decision went with the company's contention that it was not obligated to pay for these holidays not worked because the contract stated (1) that the regular workweek was Monday to Friday, inclusive, and (2) that the company would pay for time lost in observance of holidays which were observed during the regular workweek. Obviously, in the light of this language, the union's claim for pay for a Saturday holiday not worked could not stand up.

The same issue arose before the same arbitration board in the case of the New Britain (Connecticut) Gas Company and District 50, formerly United Mine Workers, but here the language of the contract was quite different. This contract provided that holidays were to be paid whether falling within the workweek or not; and furthermore, that holiday hours were to accumulate and be counted in determining hours worked for the purpose of computing overtime pay. Since the holiday came on Saturday after the employees had worked 40 hours during the week, the arbitrator decided that the language of the contract required not only pay for the Saturday holiday but pay at the overtime rate of time and one half.

Seniority is another area in which disputes are frequently hotly contested. This is especially the case when the issue involves the promotion of a junior man over a senior one under a contract clause which says that both seniority and ability will be factors in promotion.[8] For example, in a case involving the Hercules Powder Company and the Chemical Workers' Union, the action of the company in promoting an employee with less than top seniority was sustained because the contract read that seniority would prevail "*only if* factors of ability, aptitude and training are relatively equal." The words "only if" made it clear that seniority was a secondary, not a primary, criterion for promotion. On the other hand,

---

[8] Seniority is discussed in Chapter 6. The terms "senior" and "junior" are used to denote length of service with a company, not age or experience.

the action of the Southern Bell Telephone Company in promoting a junior employee was overturned by the arbitrator in a dispute with the Communication Workers because the pertinent contract clause read that "seniority shall govern if other necessary qualifications of the individuals are substantially equal"; but the company wrongly interpreted the clause to permit it to promote the best qualified who was not "substantially" superior to the most senior employee in line for promotion.

Among the most difficult cases are those involving discipline. Often the issues are not sufficiently clear, and the evidence is blurred. For example, an employee may have deserved to be discharged for his conduct; but if the employer does not follow the procedure outlined in the contract, the arbitrator may have to reinstate the employee because contract procedure must be followed if an action is to be sustained in arbitration. In other cases, union officials will carry discharge cases to arbitration because the rank and file demands that officials fight for the membership, right or wrong. Even if the arbitrator sustains the discharges, the union official can take credit for putting up a good fight.

These cases illustrate not only how grievance disputes are settled but also why contract interpretation is so important to both labor and management during the life of the agreement. By settling disputes over interpretation and administration, and by working out disagreements, labor and management use the grievance machinery to turn a dry-reading contract into a way of working together.

Grievances are important to the union leadership in other ways. They afford an opportunity to gain the workers' loyalty and support by effectively arguing workers' causes with management in the many disputes which are processed through the grievance machinery. Furthermore, operation of the grievance machinery provides opportunities for thousands of workers to serve as union stewards and committeemen, and thus to gain familiarity with the process of collective bargaining. Several hundred thousand union members now serve in these minor positions. By participating in the grievance machinery, these men are training themselves for future union leadership and at the same time doing something which raises them above the monotony of tending a machine.

Management's representatives in the shop, the foremen, usually find that dealing with a union makes their job much more difficult. Once the union is in, the foremen's commands are subject to union challenge. But the foreman who learns to deal effectively with the union is training himself for a bigger job—for this foreman has learned to deal with people in a situation where not command but persuasion is the means of getting things done.

Bargaining during the Life of the Agreement—New Issues

The traditional and commonsense view of labor contracts has been that once the contract is signed, no new issues may be brought up and discussed until the contract is up for renegotiation. We have, however, already noted that where a union fails to win a demand for the inclusion of a provision limiting a management action—for example, the subcontracting of work—it may still force management to arbitrate a dispute arising over the exercise of this management action.

Now the National Labor Relations Board has carried this a step further. It has ruled that a company commits an unfair labor practice if it takes action based upon economic grounds, again using the subcontracting of work as an example, without first bargaining with the union, even though subcontracting is not mentioned in the union agreement and no attempt is being made to discriminate against the union or the union members.[9]

In other NLRB cases the Board has ruled that where a matter was not discussed in bargaining, it can be brought up during the life of an agreement; and again, the employer must bargain. Thus, if a pension plan was not discussed in negotiations, presumably the union could demand that such a plan be inaugurated during the life of the contract.

Such NLRB rulings have, of course, disturbed employers, many of whom now often demand that unions waive the right to bargain over or to arbitrate issues which management feels it must control to protect the profitability of the business. Employers now frequently also insist that unions waive the right to bring up new matters when the agreement is signed in order to protect their costs and economic stability against pressures for new and higher charges unforeseen at the time the labor agreement was signed; but under the Supreme Court's new ruling for arbitration, even such waivers do not protect an employer from having the issues involving new matters submitted to bargaining and arbitration.

LONG-TERM CONTRACTS

In 1948, a new bargaining style was established when General Motors Corporation and the United Automobile Workers negotiated a two-year contract, and then followed in 1950 with a five-year agreement. In 1951, 70% of the union contracts examined by the Bureau of Labor Statistics were of one year's duration. Five years later, the Bureau reported that only 35% of the contracts in its file were for a one-year or less period, whereas 65% covered periods of two years or more. By 1964, the Bureau's records indicated that contracts for periods of two years or more were the overwhelming favorite of unions and companies, and this practice has continued.[10]

The reasons for the popularity of the longer contracts lie in the desire of both labor and management to avoid possible interruptions in their relationships every year. Longer contracts insure workers job oppor-

[9] National Labor Relations Board policies are discussed in Chapter 21. The subcontracting issue is discussed in Chapter 6.

[10] Data from U.S. Bureau of Labor Statistics.

tunities without strikes for two or three years and permit management to schedule production and deliveries without fear of upset by labor trouble for the life of the contract.

Since 1958, however, the trend has definitely been away from the "formula bargaining" devised by General Motors and the United Automobile Workers in 1950. This formula provided for quarterly cost-of-living adjustments based upon movements of the consumer price index plus annual wage increases regardless of the movement of prices.

The recession of 1958 caused a good deal of soul searching in management circles as to the advisability of long-term agreements. The steel industry, for example, had committed itself in 1956 to substantial wage increases payable in 1958. When these increases came due, sales and employment were down as much as 40% from the 1956 pinnacle. Certainly, no such large increases would have been negotiated for a recession year if the negotiations had occurred during that year.

Despite the 1958 experience, the steel industry did not return to a one-year agreement after its long 1959–60 strike. As the country emerged from the recession, opposition to long-term contracts in management circles also declined. The prospects of avoiding the uncertainty and disturbances of annual negotiations continued to offset other unfavorable factors. But the new long-term agreements have usually omitted or strictly limited any cost-of-living adjustments, except in the automobile and farm equipment industries, where the United Automobile Workers is the bargaining agent.

The rise in the cost of living in the mid-1960's induced unions again to demand cost-of-living adjustment provisions. This has resulted in some increase in the number of such agreements. Even in the automobile industry, however, the cost-of-living feature was no longer open-ended after 1967. The maximum amount that employees may now receive was limited by the 1967 automobile agreements, and adjustments are henceforth to be made annually instead of quarterly, thus limiting the amount, frequency, and probable impact of cost-of-living wage increases.

Human Relations Committees

Following the 1959 steel strike, the United Steelworkers and the Kaiser Steel Corporation set up a committee composed of three well-known arbitrators plus representatives of each side to try to work out some of the problems which had led to the strike. Later the larger companies in the basic steel industry and the Steelworkers established a joint Human Relations Committee to meet regularly on joint problems. Before the 1963 negotiations, General Electric and the various unions with which it deals established joint study committees. Similar committees were discussed in the automobile and other industries.

These committees achieved much publicity and had seemingly good results of disposing of troublesome issues without resort to strike. Most of them have worked quietly on particular problems which required considerable analysis and discussion before a settlement could be reached and which therefore could have caused problems in negotiations if not handled carefully. Others, particularly the Kaiser program, were aimed also at special problems—and because of the participation of well-known personages received considerable publicity.

Although interest in such activity waned after the human relations program in the steel industry was scuttled by a new union administration, there is still interest among industrial relations scholars and practitioners as to whether (1) year-round negotiating sessions on joint problems would contribute to improved labor relations; and (2), as in the Kaiser experiment, so called "neutrals" should be utilized to assist labor and management to solve their problems.

An examination of the experience of the joint study committees, whether neutrals are involved or not, demonstrates that they were established to solve particular or pressing problems. Their success in this regard does not necessarily commend them to general application. In these cases, the parties, to their credit, recognized the need to seek solutions—and did. But the same problems or issues are not generally present or, if they are, are not susceptible to the same solutions. Most joint study committees soon disappeared when the problems which caused their birth were mitigated. A collective bargaining system, as the next few chapters will emphasize, grows out of the experience of the parties, which, in turn, is based upon the structure and problems of the industry involved, the general economic situation, the personalities at work, and a host of other things. What is applicable in one place may not be in others. There is no panacea for the solution of problems. They must be met, examined, and handled, and no two groups do that exactly alike.

As to the use of neutrals, there can be no doubt that there are situations where an objective study, a different point of view, or a new look can be most helpful and appropriate if a particular problem or problem area is to be handled to successful conclusion. There is, however, no substitute for experience, and no crutch for responsibility. Management and union officials cannot, in the final analysis, share their responsibility and accountability. If the business is not profitable, it is the management's responsibility; if the union members are dissatisfied with their contract or its administration, they hold the union leadership accountable. Third parties or neutrals may help to bring agreement, but those responsible must achieve the agreement and live with it.

THE SCOPE OF BARGAINING AND MANAGERIAL PREROGATIVES

Union policy with respect to wages has always been phrased in terms of "more—always more." Management fears that unions intend to apply this same policy to the scope of collective bargaining. Recent actions by the courts in expanding the jurisdiction of arbitrators, and of the National Labor Relations Board in requiring bargaining over actions, such as the contracting-out of work, which are initiated on purely economic grounds, have, as noted, added to management's fears and sharpened the debate over "management's right to manage" and the unions' right to encroach thereon.

Managerial prerogatives may mean different things to different people. For the most part, however, the term is used by the group in society who may be termed the "professional managerial class." These are the managers of large corporations, as distinguished from the stockholders, who are the owners. These people, who include in their ranks the whole array of business executives and administrators from president down to foreman, are a group set apart from both labor and owners. In a very real sense the conflict over managerial prerogatives and functions is part of the struggle of this group for status and recognition—a struggle which is as important to this group as is the struggle by union leaders for recognition and public respect. Some take the view that the function of the union is primarily one of limiting the power of the managerial class to determine the distribution of the total product of industry and the share of individuals and groups in it.

But the conflict over managerial prerogatives is also a part of the conflict between management's desire and need to innovate and employees' attempts to achieve "security" by institutionalizing the status quo. The history of labor relations is replete with examples of employees, acting through unions, "winning security" by restricting management's freedom to innovate or to change, only to find that their "victory" created a high-cost situation which lost the very jobs they sought to protect. For if innovation and change are blocked in one plant or industry, other companies will innovate and change, with resulting cost differentials and consequent effects on sales, profits, and employment.

Nevertheless, there is no clear pattern of practice from one industry to another as to what is solely a management function. In Chapters 5 and 6, we shall find that unions have been able to influence—or, on occasion, to control—a wide variety of actual managerial problems which relate to both the wage and the nonwage aspects of collective agreement. Thus unions assist in advertising and distribution; influence and affect price policies, directly or indirectly; control or limit entrance to the trade; act as employment agencies or otherwise control hiring; affect the rate of technological advancement and, therefore, management organization of the factors of production; and in other ways participate in what management traditionally has considered its proper functions. Obviously, a definition of managerial functions which would have any real meaning would be very difficult.

Actually, collective bargaining affects all phases of business activity.

Paradoxically, the companies which recognize this fact are the ones which have been best able to retain "management's freedom to manage." Before making decisions on plant location, contracting-out, work scheduling, or even new-product development and manufacturing, companies such as General Motors or Armstrong Cork consider the employee relations aspects and work to eliminate complications and problems which might otherwise arise. They thus avoid challenges in sensitive areas and are prepared to meet opposition if it arises, not on an emotional but on a factual basis.

Looking at the problem another way, it is important to recognize that unions are, in a real sense, a management-regulating device. The extent to which this management regulating or restraining becomes participation is sometimes only a matter of degree. This is true despite the fact that most unions disclaim any desire to participate in management as vehemently as management denies the right of labor to participate in management. Yet in the light of the vast participation of unions through collective bargaining machinery in activities which directly or indirectly affect all phases of company management, there is already labor participation in management.

The extent to which labor participation should exist in management decisions, or whether it is socially desirable, remains a matter of debate. Certainly, solution of the problem of the extent of union participation and influence in management is one of the great problems of our time. In fact, the issue of union impingement on managerial prerogatives is merely another aspect of a greater issue—namely, the role of unions in our society. One may therefore agree with the view (often expressed in anger or sorrow by businessmen) that there are in fact no limits to union interests in management. Union penetration of former managerial prerogatives is likely to be greatest in the areas most closely associated with industrial relations. Personnel management is thus today much less a sole management function than is business finance. Since, however, industrial relations affect all aspects of a business, union interest in corporate financial methods should not be surprising. Nor is such interest new. The railroad unions, for example, have criticized the financial methods of the railroads, charging that they carry an oversized bonded indebtedness which tends to siphon off earnings and thus to permit the railroads to plead inability to pay wage increases. Many other examples could be cited involving production, sales, engineering, and other management functions in which unions have taken an effective interest.

But although unions have taken an *interest* in management functions beyond the personnel field, that interest has not altered management decisions, at least in the mass-production industries. Thus the decisive considerations in the automobile or steel industries, both before and after the spread of unionism, have been economic and center in the advantages which accrue to the largest producers by virtue of their ability to spread their costs. The unions have effected changes and altered ways of thinking, but the basic decisions outside of the personnel field are made by management and controlled by the economics of these industries. When management has lost this control, or when the economics of the situation have been disregarded, the inevitable result has been economic loss—sales, profits, and employment have declined, or the companies have gone out of business.

SETTING UNION POLICY FOR COLLECTIVE BARGAINING

Who sets union policy in collective bargaining—and how? There is, of course, wide variation among unions, but several clear trends have developed over the years. One is the shift of control from local unions to national unions. This is in line with the trend toward centralization of national union power, which we noted in Chapter 3.

The Shift to National Control

The trend toward national union control of collective bargaining is not new; it was noticeable at the turn of the century. In recent years, however, it has gained momentum, for several reasons.

In the first place, national unions have been forced to take over authority from locals in order to insure that uniform wage and working conditions and policies pertaining thereto will be followed where the national union believes such uniformity is essential. This is especially important when union members travel, as in the case of musicians, actors, or building workers. Although these unions negotiate on a local basis, their negotiations are often either guided by the national union or controlled by the national union to insure uniformity within limits and to prevent jockeying to secure superior settlements.

Even where the tradition of local control is strong, national unions sometimes regulate the limits of local union bargaining. Local agreements in the Typographical Union must be submitted to national headquarters for approval. The United Automobile Workers has created national union-dominated departments which do the primary bargaining with such multiplant concerns as General Motors, Ford, and Chrysler.

When collective bargaining goes from the local to the national stage, the power of the local union wanes. Centralization of authority within the United Mine Workers has obviously been furthered by the development of national collective bargaining. On the other hand, regional systems of collective bargaining, such as exist in the parts of the pulp and paper industry, have the effect of creating semiautonomous departments within national unions. Especially if the region is large, it becomes self-sufficient and needs little national assistance in bargaining. Its officers and members are then not likely to submit meekly to close national union supervision. Moreover, even when bargaining is nationwide, purely local conditions are left for local bargaining. The coal mines are a case in point.

Too tight national union control of local bargaining has often brought strong local reactions. Agreements made by national union leaders have on a number of occasions been repudiated by local union members who felt either that their interests were insufficiently considered or that they were not sufficiently consulted beforehand.

Within a single organization, there may be conflict between "high-wage" and "low-wage" locals over the extent of national control. The former, fearful that they will lose business to the latter, are likely to desire strong national control in the interests of uniformity. Because of the marginal character of many employers with whom the low-wage locals deal, they are likely to oppose these policies. The fight between these two groups is a feature of many Typographical Union conventions.

Federation Control

As noted in Chapter 2, certain departments of the AFL–CIO have taken over a significant role in the collective bargaining process. For many years, the Railway Employees Department has coordinated bargaining for the railroad shopcraft unions; the Building Trades Department and the Metal Trades Department have local or regional affiliates which perform the same task in local or regional bases. By such departmental confederations, craft unions have been able to deal on an industrial basis with employers. But historically, the coordinating department official has had little authority or power except to carry out the desires of the national or local unions.

An attempt at more far-reaching coordination, or coalition, was undertaken by the Industrial Union Department, which attempted to bring into one bargaining group industrial and craft unions which deal with one company or one industry. Under this coalition program, the representative of the Industrial Union Department assumed a key role in the bargaining, became the key strategist, and often the key spokesman as well. The aim of the program was to bring maximum union pressure on the company and to promote union mergers and amalgamations by demonstrating the effectiveness of coalition efforts.[11] If successful, this program would result in taking the bargaining process and its control one step further from the local union and would, of course, dilute national union control of bargaining as well.

The Formulation of Demands

Although negotiations may be controlled to a considerable extent by the national officers, it is typically the local members who formulate demands. Actually, of course, most demands other than those for higher

[11] For a frank statement of the aims of coalition bargaining by the then officials of the Industrial Union Department, AFL–CIO, see Jack Conway and Woodrow L. Ginsburg, "The Extension of Collective Bargaining to New Fields," *Proceedings of the Nineteenth Annual Winter Meeting, Industrial Relations Research Association* (San Francisco, 1966), pp. 303–11.

wages or specific working conditions are usually articulated by union officials, or in the case of many unions, developed by the leadership. Sometimes union officials even push demands that are not popular with the rank and file. In times of unemployment, it is not uncommon, for example, for the leadership to be demanding shorter hours and work division while the rank and file that is working want more overtime. In general, however, the leadership must keep its ear to the ground and attempt to articulate what is of interest to the rank and file. Otherwise both the political support of the officials and the opportunities for contract settlement are endangered.

Customarily, demands are formulated at local meetings, in some cases on the basis of leadership proposals, in others after presentation by a special committee, and in still others after direct suggestions from the floor. When more than one local is involved, union rules often call for joint committees of the locals to unify demands. Regional bargaining requires machinery similar to that of the Pacific Coast paper unions, where organizers of the two collaborating unions draw up proposals which form the basis for discussion in the local unions. The locals submit their amendments to a general meeting held just prior to bargaining conferences. Demands of unions engaged in national bargaining are usually formulated at national conventions (miners, steelworkers) or at special national conferences (railway employees).

One of the effects of rank-and-file formulation of demands is likely to be that the demands are excessive, both in number and in amount. Everyone has his favorite recipe. This, in turn, leads on occasion either to disgruntlement with results or to strikes because extraordinary demands either are not met or are insisted upon in the face of employer resistance.

Negotiating Personnel and Its Powers

The negotiating committee in most unions is appointed with an eye to representation of the various groups within the organization. The various crafts, geographical areas, races, or nationalities are likely to be represented on any negotiating committee. It is quite common for union constitutions to require that negotiating committees provide for adequate geographical or trade representation. Craft groups in industrial unions especially insist on representation. Only a few unions, such as the International Hod Carriers', Building and Common Laborers' Union, grant almost blanket power to union officials to act automatically as the negotiating committee.

In actual practice, negotiations are frequently carried on by a subcommittee of the negotiating committee. This is often a practical necessity, since negotiating committees are frequently too large and negotiations become unwieldly when all members participate. Some union constitutions provide for the election of a subcommittee. Others do so in practice. In still others, the union president becomes the subcommittee, particularly where he has a considerable standing and prestige with both employers and the membership.

The power of negotiating committees or subcommittees varies considerably. At the local level the committee is rarely given full authority to settle without rank-and-file approval of the terms. However, it is quite usual for the rank and file to give a negotiating committee power of settlement after negotiations have proceeded for some time or have reached an impasse where a prompt decision is essential.

In general, it is probable that most local leaders would not want complete power of settlement. The reason is that if they make an agreement without specific rank-and-file approval, they will be held strictly accountable for the results, and the net effect of the accounting may well be defeat for reelection.

On the other hand, most national leaders would prefer the power to settle. They feel that they are capable of securing the best settlement possible, and that the rank and file, which is often without knowledge of the peculiar problems involved in negotiations, will demand more than can possibly be obtained and thus force the union into costly strikes which it has no hope of winning.

The case for granting union officials the power of settlement is formidable. Nevertheless, the requirement that all terms be referred to the rank and file is a power check on union leadership which is probably best retained. Moreover, even in cases where union leadership possesses the right to settle, rank-and-file revolt may effectively curtail that right. In 1966, the membership of the International Association of Machinists repudiated an agreement negotiated under the auspices of President Johnson at the White House, and kept six airlines shut down for several weeks as a result. In previous years, other national union leaders have been surprised by rank-and-file rejections, and as already noted, such rejections have no longer become exceptional. It is not unlikely that these rejections indicate a lack of communication and understanding between older union officials and the largely youthful rank and file.

Another reason why granting full power of settlement to the leadership is undesirable sociologically, even if economically the leadership would reach the soundest bargain, is that there is a great deal of educational value in worker participation in collective bargaining. With the exception of times when there are political contests within the union, negotiations for new contracts cause the greatest turnout to meetings and the greatest general worker interest. Service on negotiating committees, participation in discussion over terms of settlement, and the interest which these activities arouse build union leadership for the future and assure an element of democracy in unions.

National collective bargaining, however, does not appear to afford the opportunity for full discussion for settlement on the local level unless it is possible to have the contract discussed and voted upon at local meetings all over the country. With hundreds of locals involved, as in the case of the United Steelworkers, this is impractical. Moreover, the refer-- endum is no substitute, since it does not permit argument and discussion, which are the essence of the educational process. A truly representative national bargaining committee with an effective voice in negotiations appears to be the most practical body to approve or reject contracts where national or regional collective bargaining exists. The difficulty of obtaining effective rank-and-file participation in national collective bargaining is one reason why local strikes have become so common in such industries as automobiles after the national bargaining has been concluded. Local issues and local participation require consideration that cannot be given at the national level, and a strike may be the only method of effective participation for the local rank and file. Under such circumstances, the settlement of the national contract may be only the beginning of labor problems for the company, not the end.

SETTING MANAGEMENT POLICY FOR COLLECTIVE BARGAINING

"When employees want to deal with management through a union, the most fundamental question is how far management should be guided by definite policies."[12] The absence of policies means that all decisions are made on a spur-of-the-moment or opportunistic basis. The usual result in such cases is that management sacrifices the long-run needs of the business to maintain its competitive position for assurances of uninterrupted production at the moment. For example, in the 1940's and early 1950's, the Studebaker Corporation of South Bend, Indiana,[13] and the Alexander Smith Carpet Company of Yonkers, New York, were cited as outstanding, liberal companies which handled union relations well. By 1966, both were out of business. Opportunistically attempting to buy good labor relations, these and many other companies allowed their costs to grow until they could not compete. Not only were the stockholders and business managers losers—their employees lost their jobs, and the local unions representing these employees lost their members.

A management guided by well-thought-out policies does not mean a rigid management. New situations and problems constantly arise, and

[12] Sumner H. Slichter, J. J. Healy, and E. R. Livernash, *The Impact of Collective Bargaining on Management* (Washington, D.C.: Brookings Institution, 1960), p. 10.

[13] When the UAW's Walter P. Reuther in 1945 reported to General Motors' chief negotiator that Studebaker had granted a substantial wage increase, the General Motors spokesman retorted: "I wouldn't want our plants run like Studebaker's are run" (Robert M. MacDonald, *Collective Bargaining in the Automobile Industry* [New Haven: Yale University Press, 1963], pp. 364–65). Professor MacDonald's study, in contrast to earlier, less incisive ones, found Studebaker featured by costly and poorly administered labor practices, brought on chiefly by inept handling of labor relations by top management and by inadequate training of supervision.

experimentation is necessary. But such experimentation is far different than action by opportunism, or than complete concern with the immediate and disregard of the future. As the authors of an outstanding work noted:

> A few firms are in a position to dictate the nature of their relationship with the union; many small firms must take what conditions the union offers and get along as best they can; most firms, however, are more or less an equal match for the union, and the quality of their relationship with the union depends on the skill shown in negotiating and administering the agreement. The best goal for most firms is a stable relationship with the union on terms that permit the firm to be competitive and to adapt itself to changing conditions.[14]

This "stable and competitive" relationship can be achieved only if the top management of a company understands its importance and is willing to invest the time, talent, and funds to obtain this objective. Only top management can make some of the necessary decisions. For example, will the company be willing to take a strike in order to prevent it from being saddled with a work rule which one day might weaken its competitive position? "Unless top management takes a firm position in advance against accepting uneconomic practices, subordinate officials will tolerate them rather than assume the responsibility of failing to meet production standards."[15]

MANAGEMENT ORGANIZATION

To implement its policies, management must set up an organization capable of handling both union relations and other aspects of the personnel function. Because union relations involve a time-consuming process, and a talent not necessarily held by production or sales executives, a special management representative or department is usually assigned to handle personnel. If union relations are conducted on a part-time or offhand basis, the net effect is likely to be expensive concessions made to the union "so we can get back to our main business of cutting metal or shuffling paper." Small companies which cannot afford full-time personnel departments often hire skilled lawyers or consultants for this purpose.

The companies noted for the most successful administration of their labor relations assign this responsibility to executives of stature and resourcefulness, compensate them and afford them status accordingly (for example, name a vice president to the top personnel post), and see that they are a part of the top councils of the concern. Such persons can recommend policies or changes in policies, argue with other top executives about the merits of various issues, and see that the labor relations point of view is considered in basic production and sales policies. Problems can then be met and handled before controversies arise.

---

[14] Slichter, Healy, and Livernash, *op. cit.*, p. 11.
[15] *Ibid.*

Keeping Line Supervisors Informed

Equally as important as setting policy and putting effective leadership in charge of union and personnel relations is the need for top management to make clear to its subordinate officials, supervisors, and foremen what it expects of them in handling the union relationship. Unless this is done clearly and effectively, policies at the shop level will bear little relation to the pronouncements from company headquarters, for the foremen will work to "get along," at whatever cost it requires. Such "getting along" can mean quiet but costly concessions which, in practice, whittle away managerial control of the shop, reduce productivity and efficiency, and injure the competitive position of the company.

The best managed companies, therefore, spend considerable time, effort, and money on foremen selection and training, in an effort to insure effective management, including employee relations management, at the shop level. Foremen, are instructed in such companies on techniques of handling people, grievance settlement, and union contract interpretation.

It is most important, also, that top management back up its supervisors and practice what it preaches. If executives of a company advise foremen to take a strong stand against a union demand or action and then yield to the union under the threat of a strike, the word will go through the shop grapevine that management does not mean what it says. The union will take the action to mean that it can induce a change in company policy by a show of force, and foremen will see such executive inconsistency as advice to them to concede readily and quietly to union demands.

The Management Bargaining Committee

From the point of view of the employer, bargaining with the union may be on an individual plant basis or on a companywide basis, or the employer may be one of a number of employers who bargain together in an employers' association. If bargaining is between a local union and a single plant of a large corporation, negotiations may be conducted by the local personnel director and/or the plant manager, subject to instructions from company headquarters. On the other hand, if all of a number of plants of a company are involved, the industrial relations director of the company is likely to conduct negotiations. In regional or industrywide bargaining, employers are usually represented by committees or officers designated by the employers' association. On all levels of collective bargaining negotiations, employer representatives may include the company attorney or consultant, whose function may be to participate actively in negotiations, to give advice behind the scenes, or in some cases merely to reduce to contract form the bargain reached by the parties.

As in the case of unions, there is considerable diversity in the amount of authority given the management representatives at the bargaining table. In some cases, they may be able to make final decisions on all aspects of the contract; in other situations, they may be able to agree only to minor changes and concessions, and they must obtain the approval of the president before committing the company to anything substantial. Large outlays, such as those involved in the establishment of a pension system, sometimes require approval of the board of directors as well as of the president.

Within the management organization, some of the same type of pulling and hauling for the power of decision making occurs as goes on within the union. In some cases, the financial officer exercises powerful influence whenever a money matter is involved. In other companies the dominant voice is that of the top production man; in still others the top sales executive exercises the most influence. The extent to which the advice of the chief personnel official is accepted in such situations is a measure of the standing and influence of both himself and his function.

Whenever a company must determine whether to take a strike or to accede to a union demand, a decision must be made on the basis of the current position of the company and the prospects and choices involved. Obviously, the final determination in such matters must be made by the top executive of the company. In such instances the current sales and the financial and production situations must be evaluated. The decision cannot be made on the basis of industrial relations alone but must be made on the total needs of the company. A company which can stockpile inventory is obviously in a stronger position to resist union pressure than one which sells a nonstorable service. Automobiles or steel can be warehoused or built ahead; daily newspapers, air transport companies, or restaurants cannot accomplish this. The demand for some products can be postponed; for others it cannot. Management decisions must reflect the realities of the company's industrial situation.

Because a strike involves losses now and concessions *may* be serious in the future from the point of view of a company's competitive position, there is a great temptation for businessmen to decide questions involving labor relations on a short-run basis. Yet the failure of management to evaluate correctly the long-run implications of costly concessions made to avoid labor strife has been fatal to many companies. Undue concessions made at the point of a strike threat, or actual strike, are too often an invitation to further strife. For by yielding to such coercion, management is in effect telling union officials and members that a strike threat or a strike pays off. If this feeling becomes general, it can easily result in a long, bitter strike at some future date—if not a series of shorter walkouts —but in any case, it can be quite costly to the business.

Moreover, if a company yields to an uneconomic demand, or a series of demands, it may be digging its grave by incurring a cost which does not permit it to compete in the product market. This can mean not only loss of profits but also loss of jobs and hence union members. A short-run decision which ignores long-run considerations can be disastrous to both employer and union.

Of course, not all business decisions, any more than all union decisions, are based upon economic calculation. Instances of businessmen forcing a strike to win leadership over rivals in their own firm are not unknown. Likewise, industrial relations decisions based upon emotions rather than economic facts occur every day in managerial ranks. Businessmen, like union leaders, are people, and anything but infallible.

QUESTIONS FOR DISCUSSION

1. If you were the personnel manager of a plant and a union began an organizing campaign, what actions would you take? If you were a business agent of a union, how would you attempt to recruit workers?
2. Why do you think long-term contracts have become so important? What are the economic implications of this development?
3. What are managerial prerogatives? Is it a good idea to define them by law? If you were a manager, how would you protect your prerogatives?

SUGGESTIONS FOR FURTHER READING

GARBARINO, JOSEPH W. *Wage Policy and Long-Term Contracts.* Washington, D.C.: Brookings Institution, 1962.

An economic analysis of the effects of long-term contracts on wage policy.

ROWAN, RICHARD L., and NORTHRUP, HERBERT R. (eds.). *Readings in Labor Economics and Labor Relations,* "Organizing and Negotiating," pp. 259–84; "Strategy in Collective Bargaining," pp. 321–67. Homewood, Ill.: Richard D. Irwin, Inc., 1968.

A series of six articles by various scholars and practitioners on aspects of collective bargaining.

SLICHTER, SUMNER H.; HEALY, J. J.; and LIVERNASH, E. R. *The Impact of Collective Bargaining on Management,* chaps. i–ii, xxi–xxx. Washington, D.C.: Brookings Institution, 1960.

These chapters of this outstanding work deal with management issues in collective bargaining, grievance handling and arbitration, and managerial handling of industrial relations.

Chapter 5	THE CONTENT OF COLLECTIVE BARGAINING: WAGES

Collective bargaining is basically a method of determining wages and working conditions for employees. In this chapter, we shall examine the wage content of collective bargaining; in the following chapter the working conditions which form the "industrial jurisprudence" of bargaining will be our subject. Then, in Chapter 7, we shall discuss some key questions resulting from the bargaining process.

WAGE—A COMPLEX TERM

A better insight into the nature of the collective bargaining process is provided by considering just what is encompassed by the term "wage." There is a natural inclination to use this term as if it were a rather simple component and as if the only variable which had to be determined in setting the wage was its amount. Actually, however, the wage is a highly flexible form of compensation and may vary considerably both as to form and as to content. For example, it may be based on payment by the piece, payment by the hour, or participation in a complex profit-sharing plan. It may or may not include group insurance, pensions, and similar fringe benefits. For example, a labor-management negotiation may result in a 15-cent-per-hour "package," composed of 5 cents in wages, 5 cents in pension improvements, 3 cents in insurance and miscellaneous benefit improvements, and 2 cents in holiday and vacation allowances.

Only the first item—the change in the wage rate itself—relates directly to what has traditionally been termed wages, whereas the other items of the wage package fall in the category of supplementary or fringe benefits. Moreover, to the company wages are a cost whereas to the worker they are income. Those who think in terms of social needs regard wages as a right to income, not payment for work. Demands for guaranteed annual wages reflect the merging together of wages paid by the hour and salaries paid by the week, month, or year, with guaranteed income for present hourly as well as for salaried workers. The importance of wages is further emphasized by the fact that wages and salaries comprise about 65% of national income, a potent factor in national income determination and in the impact on the business cycle and the state of the economy. What some of the major forms of wage payment are, and management and labor attitudes toward them, will be considered in this chapter. As a background, it will be useful first to consider the various types of wage data which are published, so that the reader may be familiar with the content as well as the limitations of such statistics.

ANALYSIS OF WAGE DATA

The union leader, bargaining with an employer, may be primarily interested in setting a high rate for a particular job in the collective bargaining agreement. The employees, on the other hand, may be more interested in their actual take-home pay. And the employer is likely to be concerned with the overall cost of labor, including all fringe benefits paid by him. Because of these varied interests in employee compensation, a number of statistical series are published which analyze wage changes from different points of view. Seven major types of data can be distinguished.[1]

1. *Wage rates* represent the actual price for particular jobs. Because of the great diversity of such rates, not only from industry to industry but also from company to company within the same industry, there are no overall compilations of such rates published regularly by any agency of the government or by private research organizations. However, the Bureau of Labor Statistics of the U.S. Department of Labor publishes studies from time to time of wage rates in particular industries and for various occupations in selected metropolitan areas.[2] Such studies report the average rates in plants, often by occupation, occupational groups, and area. These are often the wage rates agreed upon in bargaining by companies and unions. Extra compensation resulting from tips or overtime work are usually excluded from such data.

2. *Straight-time average hourly earnings* are the average wages earned, exclusive of overtime pay. They include incentive pay, but generally exclude payment for work on weekends, holidays, and late shifts. From time to time, the Bureau of Labor Statistics publishes studies of straight-time earnings for particular jobs in various industries.

3. *Gross hourly earnings* include all wage payments to employees, including overtime, premium pay for holidays and weekend pay, etc., and therefore normally exceed straight-time earnings. Some statistical series report earnings *per hours worked*, and some report earnings *per hours*

---

[1] An excellent and still current discussion of this subject is contained in Jules Backman, *Wage Determination* (Princeton, N.J.: D. Van Nostrand Co., Inc., 1959), pp. 18–29.

[2] The U.S. Bureau of Labor Statistics studies are reported or summarized in the *Monthly Labor Review*, published by the U.S. Department of Labor, and often issued in more complete form as separate bulletins.

paid for. If a man is paid for a holiday on which he does not work, should the hours in the holiday be added to hours worked during the rest of the week to obtain the hours figure to divide into total earnings so as to arrive at average hourly earnings? The Bureau of Labor Statistics says yes; the Bureau of the Census says no. As a result, hours of work as used by the Bureau of the Census in its series have averaged about 5% less than hours paid for as reported by the Bureau of Labor Statistics.[3] The most complete gross hourly earnings data are published in the form of a monthly series by the Bureau of Labor Statistics covering 21 broad manufacturing industry groups, about 300 manufacturing industries, and 30 nonmanufacturing industries, including trade, construction, and mining.[4]

4. *Weekly earnings* reflect the average number of hours worked per week in relation to gross earnings per hour. Weekly earnings data are published from time to time by the Bureau of Labor Statistics and are also compiled by various state departments of labor, and trade associations.

5. *Weekly take-home pay* refers to the amount left in the weekly pay check after deductions for federal, and in some areas state and/or local income taxes, social security taxes, union dues, health and welfare programs, group insurance, and other benefits. The Bureau of Labor Statistics publishes a monthly calculation of "spendable average weekly earnings," which is defined as gross average weekly earnings less an amount estimated for federal income and social security taxes.[5] By excluding other deductions from paychecks, this average overestimates take-home pay.

6. *Annual earnings* of employees are not published in any regular series. Studies of various industries are made from time to time by the U.S. Bureau of Labor Statistics. In addition, the U.S. Department of Commerce publishes data for 84 industries and industry groups for "full-time equivalent" employees.[6] These are not actual earnings figures but rather computed figures derived by dividing wages and salaries in an industry by the number of full-time workers. For industries having a substantial number of part-time employees, the U.S. Department of Commerce reduces these to an equivalent number of full-time employees.

7. *Fringe benefits* run the whole gamut of pay from "coffee-break time" to employer payments for unemployment insurance. There are no reliable statistical series showing the cost of fringe benefits for industry as a whole, or even for all manufacturing industries. Since 1947, the Chamber of Commerce of the United States has made a biennial sample study of the extent and nature of fringe benefits.

[3] The significance of this difference in methodology in relation to fringe benefit payments is explored later in this chapter.

[4] See Table C–1, in *Monthly Labor Review*, each month.

[5] See Table C–2, *ibid.*

[6] Published as a supplement to the U.S. Department of Commerce monthly publication, *Survey of Current Business.*

BASIC WAGES

Since many different types of payment are included in labor's total compensation, it is convenient to distinguish two major categories which together make up total compensation: basic wages and supplementary (or fringe) benefits. Basic wages may be defined as the payment for hours actually worked, based on time or output. This includes payment at a higher rate for overtime and premium pay for working night shift, Saturday, or Sunday, and so forth. Supplementary benefits cover all other types of compensation, including vacation pay, Christmas bonuses, pension benefits, dismissal pay, and so on.

Basic Wages: Time Payment

The great majority of American workers are paid by the hour, day, week, or month—i.e., by time. For manual workers, rates are typically set by the hour or the day; for white-collar and supervisory workers in private industry, by the week, half month, or month, or, less frequently, by the year. White-collar and supervisory workers in government employment are often paid at an annual rate of pay. Workers paid on an hourly or daily basis (as well as those who are on an incentive basis where the incentive is computed on the basis of hourly or daily output) are usually referred to as "wage earners." Workers paid by the week or longer time interval are usually referred to as salaried workers.

Time pay customarily varies to provide extra compensation to employees who have to work at undesirable hours. The payment of premium rates for work performed on Saturday and Sunday, or on the sixth or seventh day of the work week, has become a common feature of collective bargaining agreements. Nearly all contracts now provide time and one half or double time for work on the sixth and seventh day of the workweek, and also for extra compensation for the evening and night shifts.

The major criticism advanced by employers against time payment is that output and earnings are not directly related—there is no "incentive" on the part of the worker to produce. Unions frequently prefer time pay because it compensates workers on a uniform basis and prevents the speedier workers from making it hard for the slower members of the union. On the other hand, the idea of paying by results—for example, the number of pieces produced—is deeply ingrained in managerial philosophy.

Nevertheless, union and managerial attitudes toward the form of wage payment are more the reflection of economic, technological, and historical conditions than of a basic ideological preference for one type of payment rather than another. For example, the United Automobile Workers is widely credited with eliminating incentives in the automobile industry. Yet, incentive plans at Studebaker and Kaiser-Willys were abandoned at managerial insistence after they became unworkably high-cost —a move reluctantly acquiesced to by local unions after much strife.[7]

Payment on the basis of time work prevails in more than 70% of manufacturing industry, and throughout the building and service trades, public utilities, and transportation, although the last industry also incorporates such factors as mileage and trips in its pay scale. It seems likely that most workers are paid on a time basis simply because this is the most practicable method of payment for most jobs in the business world.

Basic Wages: Incentive Payment

Piecework and other forms of incentive payment relate compensation and output, so that earnings fluctuate more or less in accordance with actual output, thus providing a direct financial stimulus to workers to increase their efforts and output. About 30% of workers in manufacturing receive their basic wages through some form of incentive payment. Such payment is common in apparel, textiles, footwear, and some of the metalworking industries. There is frequent variation, however, even among companies in the same industry. Bonuses and commissions are also frequently paid in retail and wholesale trade as a stimulus to the efforts of individual salesmen.

In general, incentive systems work out best in industries where labor cost is a large percentage of total cost, where competition is keen, and where the output of the individual worker is easily discernible. Clothing and textiles are good examples of industries which meet these requirements. In general, incentive compensation is not practical where emphasis is on quality rather than quantity, where individual output or performance cannot be measured with precision, and where mechanical contrivances control the speed of employees' work. Automobile assembly, chemical manufacture, and machine tool design are examples of industries in which these conditions apply. Automation and improvement in methods or machine design cause earnings of employees paid on an incentive basis to increase rapidly and get out of line with others in the plant. This is a frequent cause of labor strife. Those receiving the high wages resist change, others resent the out-of-line wages, and management must often take a strike in order to get the incentive rates (and labor costs) back into line. Otherwise a company risks loss of business because of noncompetitive prices resulting from the runaway incentive payments.

Incentive plans vary from simple payment by the piece, or unit of work, to complicated formulas which provide a bonus for production in excess of an established norm. The most common of the latter are standard hour plans. In such a plan, a piecework rate of 20 cents per piece

[7] Robert M. MacDonald, *Collective Bargaining in the Automobile Industry* (New Haven, Conn.: Yale University Press, 1963), pp. 112–31.

multiplied by a 10-piece-per-hour standard equals $2. Workers would be expected to produce this under normal conditions at a normal workpace. For higher production, a bonus or incentive would be paid. Incentive payments of 15% to 30% are common. Such plans as the Bedaux, Emerson, Wennerlund, Halsey, and Gantt fall in this category, although they differ in details. Standard hour plans have the advantage of providing incentives with guaranteed base earnings. Their identification in workers' minds with "speedup" tactics and their complex figuring systems, which confuse employees and increase bookkeeping costs, are their main disadvantages.

Incentive plans may be figured on the basis of an individual's output, which is most common, but also on the output of a related group, or even on the output of an entire plant. Group incentives are applicable only to closely related operations where individual performances are linked. Plantwide incentives have the advantage of keeping all employees interested in high production, but since it is difficult, if not impossible, to relate the work of many employees, for example, maintenance personnel, to output, it is possible for some employees to loaf and still reap the bonus.

Union Attitudes toward Incentive Wage Methods

Popular writers have frequently pictured all unions as bitterly opposed to piecework and incentive plans. Despite considerable union opposition to incentives, this is far from correct. Union policy toward incentives has always varied considerably from industry to industry, and is far less important in determining the extent of incentives than are the basic economic and technological forces in the industry; or, as in the case of steel, the historical fact that the industry grew up with this form of payment is in contrast, for example, to the aerospace industry, which started and adhered to a time method of payment.[8] There is no evidence that the United Steelworkers has made any attempts to alter the basic method of payment.

The United Mine Workers does not oppose piecework partially because of strong nonunion competition in bituminous coal. Nonunion competition has historically been an important circumstance conducive to union acceptance of incentives. Before the needle trades were so thoroughly organized, the threat of nonunion competition was one of the most important reasons why the needle trades not only did not oppose incentives in piecework but actually promoted them. In addition, the Amalgamated Clothing Workers, which has been as favorably disposed toward piecework as any union, has promoted its installation because only through piecework could the workers in the clothing industry increase earnings without increasing labor costs. If wages in clothing had been pushed up without an increase in production, the net effect would proba-

---

[8] See R. B. McKersie, G. F. Miller, Jr., and W. E. Quarterman, "Some Indicators of Incentive Plan Prevalence," *Monthly Labor Review*, Vol. LXXXVII (March, 1964), pp. 271–76.

bly have been a decline in employment, which would have taken away from the workers what they would have gained in wages.

In general, unions accept the method of payment in an industry. They may favor incentives where manual skill and labor costs are extremely important, where nonunion competition exists, where the unit of production can be defined with precision, where standards of work are fairly stable, and where piecework incentives have worked reasonably satisfactorily over a long period of time. The great majority of unions do not take a strong stand either for or against incentives as such, but instead they attempt to exert influence over how incentives work in practice—which, if successful, can have profound effects on the results of incentives.

Union Control of Incentive Systems

The United Mine Workers requires payment for "dead work" and compensation for other unfavorable conditions; the Textile Workers' Union fights management on the work load or stretch-out issue without opposing incentives per se; and the United Steelworkers is vitally concerned with methods of computing tonnage rates without attacking the basic system itself. A strong union, by placing numerous restrictions on the incentive system, may succeed in "demoralizing" it—creating substantial inequities in earnings and effort; raising substantially average hour yields or bonuses; and effectively divorcing productivity and earnings by instituting various guarantees which insure high "incentive" bonuses, whether or not production quotas are met. Usually, union pressure to accomplish this is accompanied by relaxed managerial control and managerial impatience to "get production out of the door no matter what the costs"—which can be substantial.[9]

A union drive to control an incentive system usually takes a number of years. As a rule, the battle for control is waged on two fronts—through negotiation for changes in the contract and the day-to-day shop operations revolving around rate setting on new jobs and the grievance procedure. By gradually winning guarantees for machine downtime, by negotiating out-of-line rates and then bringing other rates up to those already out of line, by harassing supervision and time-study departments with grievances, and by slowdowns or walkouts at critical delivery periods, the standards can be effectively reduced, and the incentive system can be turned into a featherbedding device for higher pay with less work. Unless management is eternally vigilant, an experience can develop such as that at a ball-bearing plant in Philadelphia where each day the employees stopped work after five or six hours and just loafed because they had made a "day's pay" under the demoralized incentive. Only the purchase of property in Tennessee and plans to relocate there ended this practice—which grew up as a result of union pressure and ineffective managerial response. Although sound collective bargaining relationships exist in numerous plants where incentive systems are utilized, there is considerable evidence that incentive plans do complicate industrial relations and can contribute to industrial strife. So many factors, frequently intangible and unmeasurable, affect a worker's earnings that unless mutual goodwill exists, continued bickering is often the result. For example, if a machine breaks down or materials stop flowing, should the worker receive base pay or average hourly earnings of a previous period?

Another problem arises from the fact that in the average plant an incentive system can be applied to only a part of the employees; maintenance personnel and employees whose speed of work is entirely machine controlled—e.g., assembly-line operators—must usually remain on time work. As the pay of incentive workers rises, it creates inequalities with that of other workers in the same plant who feel they also contribute to production. A further source of grievances arises from the fact that employers frequently substitute incentive systems for good management and rely on incentive workers to keep machines going, even though they are improperly maintained by management.

Incentives can be an effective management tool to increase production. They are not, however, a substitute for good management. Indeed, experience demonstrates that installation and effective administration of an incentive system requires increased management ability and frequently substantial additions to management payroll in order to provide the staff people—the accountants, time-study experts, and personnel men—who are needed to make the plan work.

Measured Daywork

The realization that incentive systems have disadvantages as well as advantages for management has encouraged the search for a method of wage payment which combines the simplicity of time payment with the control of worker efficiency which is a feature of effective incentive systems. This interest has been furthered by technological advances which reduce worker control over speed or effort. In most plants, however, many employees with remarkably little effort can raise their efficiency considerably.

As a result, more plants are turning to measured daywork—that is, pay by the hour in association with some type of control of worker efficiency by means of production standards.[10] To make such a system work, management must establish meaningful standards, be able to justify their fairness and objectivity, and adhere to the standards under pressure. If the standards are to be meaningful, they must be met, and those who refuse to meet them must be disciplined. Otherwise, no one will make an

---

[10] *Ibid.*, pp. 530 ff.

effort to meet them. This, in turn, requires managerial objectivity and fairness in setting standards, for if the employees as a whole do not think the standards are fair, then a concerted effort to break them can often succeed.

If, however, management is convinced that the standards are fair, and remains so convinced after carefully evaluating grievances concerning them, it must be willing to back up this opinion. To many companies, this means defending their position before arbitrators. Other companies feel even stronger about the need to maintain control over production standards, which can indeed mean control over productivity and hence profits and competitive position. The General Motors Corporation, for example, regards such control as so significant that it prefers to permit unions to strike over production standards in order to exempt such disputes from arbitration. General Motors management believes that this results in better production standards from the company point of view, not only because it leaves production standard determination in the hands of management but, equally important, because the importance of standards setting is emphasized by this procedure. If the standards are set too loose, the cost and competitive position of the plant or operation are jeopardized; if they are set unfairly, a costly strike can occur. Plant management is thus under exacting pressure to set proper standards at all times.

Production Standards and Effective Employee Relations

"Details of working agreements do not make headlines. . . . They are undramatic, and hence they receive little public attention. . . . Yet we all know companies where a few changes in such areas as bumping rights, tryout periods or the enforcement of work standards would contribute more to the health, success and profitability of the enterprise than a reduction of several cents in hourly wage rates."[11]

Actually, loose work standards and inefficient methods not only contribute to a lack of profitability of the enterprise but also do not usually result in sound employee relations or to the absence of strikes. As the authors of the most authoritative book on collective bargaining's impact on management point out:

> Logically it might be expected that a fairly high task level, creating a strong competitive position for a plant, would lead to serious union-management conflict. While the possibility of conflict cannot be ruled out, observation tends to support the view, when reasonably qualified, that the reverse is true. It is the demoralized incentive plans and the poor daywork plans that are associated with union-management conflict. Efficient plans tend to have satisfactory to good union-management relations.[12]

[11] Quoted by MacDonald, *op. cit.,* p. 365. From a speech by a Ford Motor Company executive.

[12] Slichter, Healy, and Livernash, *op. cit.,* p. 551.

The reasons for this apparent paradox become clear, if they are not already, as the reader's study progresses through the many facets of industrial relations and labor economics. Among them are the following:

1. Loose standards, whether incentive or daywork, lead inevitably to high costs and poor competitive position, and result in layoffs and unemployment. The effect is to generate insecurity, poor morale, unrest, and strife.
2. Loose standards usually are proceeded by managerial yielding to short strikes, threats of strikes, or slowdowns in order to keep production going. But by yielding to this pressure, management incites more of it. Eventually, the employees go too far, and a long and bitter strike does occur.
3. Loose standards create inequities. People doing similar work are paid different rates or earnings. This creates unhappiness, unrest, and constant demands for changes.
4. Well-run plants, in contrast to poorly run ones, feature uniform treatment of people similarly situated. Threats of force to change what is considered proper are firmly resisted. By experience, employees learn that such action will not yield results; hence, they do not resort to it. Where this is combined with cost-consciousness and sound and humane management, the result is steadier work and well-understood conditions. Feeling secure and knowing where they stand, employees and their union representatives are more likely to work things out with management on a peaceful, logical basis because they have learned that it pays to do it that way.

PROFIT-SHARING PLANS

Incentive systems, whether they be piece-rate or group plans, are generally related to physical production. Profit-sharing plans attempt to go a step further and distribute to workers a share in the profits of the business after all ordinary costs, such as wages, materials, and overhead, have been met. Profits have no necessary or close relation to physical production or employee effort—and this is one of the inherent weaknesses in profit-sharing plans. Employees may exert extra effort, yet profits may decline because competitive conditions compel a reduction in prices; on the other hand, physical production may decline, yet profits may rise because the employer has made a favorable purchase of raw materials, or for many other reasons.

Despite the lack of close connection between employee effort and profits, many employers believe that profit sharing is the best means to obtain maximum cooperation between labor and management and to eliminate friction in labor relations. Profit-sharing plans of one kind or another have been in existence for about 150 years. A 1967 study by the U.S. Bureau of Labor Statistics found that, in terms of worker coverage, profit sharing had doubled in the last decade. Over 2 million persons—

12% of plant and 22% of office workers—in medium-sized and large establishments within all metropolitan areas are now covered by profit-sharing plans.[13]

About 81% of all profit-sharing plans studied by the Bureau of Labor Statistics provide for deferred sharing. Under federal tax regulations, employers are allowed to count as a wage cost, and therefore a deduction from income, profit-sharing payments up to 15% of total employee compensation. If such payments are put into a trust, and paid to employees upon retirement (or after they leave the company, so long as the payments have remained in the trust a required number of years), the employee pays no income taxes on his profit-sharing payments, even if paid to him in a lump sum. Rather such payments are taxed as long-term capital gains in which the maximum rate is 25%. Profit-sharing plans are thus spurred by federal tax law and can be a factor not only in attracting, but also in holding, employees.

Where Profit Sharing Is Likely to Occur

An analysis of the distribution of profit-sharing plans found that the extent of profit sharing could be expected to vary with the following factors:[14]

1. Profit sharing is likely to be widespread only in industries where profits are consistently large or "excessive." The photographic apparatus industry, dominated by Eastman Kodak, which has long had a successful profit-sharing plan, is the leading example.[15]

2. Where there is seasonal instability of the labor force, profit sharing is not likely to occur. Such industries usually employ large numbers of unskilled or semiskilled employees who may not be attached to a particular firm and therefore are not likely to be motivated by profit sharing.

3. Industries with high turnover costs often use profit sharing to retain key personnel or those who must be especially trained for the job. If such personnel leave, they lose; under some plans, shares of profits are set aside for them and are collectible only after specific waiting periods.

4. Profit-sharing plans are not likely to occur where "the conditions in the factor and product markets are such that demand is relatively inelastic (bilateral monopoly or oligopoly in the labor market). . . ." Such conditions are typified in the automobile, steel, and agricultural and heavy electrical equipment industries.

5. Profit sharing is not likely to occur in industries where unions are strong.

[13] Gunnar Engen, "A New Direction and Growth in Profit Sharing," *Monthly Labor Review*, Vol. XC (July, 1967), pp. 1–8.

[14] Charles Schotta, Jr., "The Distribution of Profit Sharing Plans: An Analysis," *Southern Economic Journal*, Vol. XXX (July, 1963), pp. 45–49.

[15] Eastman Kodak also has not been unionized. Sears Roebuck, another company with an outstanding profit-sharing plan, is also largely nonunion. See point 5.

Unions and Profit Sharing

Unions have traditionally opposed profit sharing. Samuel Gompers, William Green, and John L. Lewis were all on record against it.[16] Partially, this is because profit sharing is often advocated as a means of obtaining an employee-employer "partnership" through a joint interest in profits, thereby lessening the influence of unions.

More important, however, is the knowledge of sophisticated union leadership that profits can be and are affected by managerial actions which are beyond the pale of collective bargaining. Thus, one union official recently stated that under a profit-sharing plan, a union either

. . . must demand a voice in areas where it has never demanded a voice before and where in general it does not want such a voice; or it must be willing to have its return for its employees under that plan regulated unilaterally by company decisions. For example, . . . the company could double the number of foremen . . . raise executive compensation, executive bonuses, stock options. . . . Decisions whether to borrow money, whether to expand . . . on depreciation, tax changes . . . and all affect the results of a profit-sharing plan. Therefore either the union has to have a voice [in these matters] or have to be agreeable to having its compensation set unilaterally. And the Steelworkers Union is not interested in doing either.[17]

Such union opposition to profit sharing is remarkably similar to that expressed by management of large enterprise. Noting that it abolished profit sharing for wage earners because "an individual employee seemed to realize that his performance on the job had little or no effect on what he got from the general profit-sharing plan," the General Electric Company added this statement: "Wage earners do not have direct control over pricing policies, design, manufacturing technology, credit and collections, managerial efficiency and a host of other factors and forces that contribute to profit or loss. So wage earners should not be penalized when a company loses money nor rewarded by a share of the profits when a company makes money."[18]

A widely publicized exception to union opposition to profit sharing was the experiment of the United Automobile Workers and American Motors which began in 1961. American Motors hoped to exchange profit sharing for union surrender of restrictions on efficient production. The UAW saw profit sharing at American Motors as a wedge to lucrative arrangements at the more profitable Big Three automotive companies, General Motors, Ford, and Chrysler. The decline in the sales of American Motors products and losses by the company, plus union unwillingness to provide concessions demanded by the company in work rules, resulted in

[16] Schotta, *loc. cit.*

[17] Statement of Marvin Miller, then assistant to the president, United Steelworkers of America, before the National Industrial Conference Board meeting of January 16, 1964.

[18] General Electric Company, *Union Relations Bulletin*, January 16, 1958.

mutual disenchantment. No other automobile company has indicated any interest in pursuing a similar plan, nor has the UAW promoted it seriously.

GAIN SHARING

The American Motors profit-sharing plan has one significant thing in common with different types of plans which have been developed in recent years to modify pay practices—it was developed to overcome or to "buy back" uneconomic work practices which were adversely affecting the competitiveness and profitability of the company. Some of these programs date back to the 1920's and were known as "union-management cooperative" plans. Basically, they were designed to improve productivity through joint union-management attack on wasteful practices and a joint drive for improved methods. Most often, such programs arose when the competitive position of the firm and hence the jobs of the employees were in serious jeopardy, and waned as the threat to employment waned, or died if the business lost out anyway.[19]

In recent years, and especially during the period 1958–62 when unemployment affected several union strongholds rather heavily, a number of similar programs were developed to deal with problems generated by unemployment and/or new technology. Among those have been the plans associated with the West Coast longshoremen and with the Kaiser Steel Corporation. Similar, but developed earlier, are the so-called Scanlon plans.[20]

Buy-Out Formulas

"Buy-out" formulas are essentially antifeatherbedding deals—designed to alter bad past practices and provide for the unobstructed introduction of new technology. They usually also involve work guarantees and payments of various sorts to cushion technological employment. Hence such deals affect wage payment and administration. Essentially, they call for an employer payment to a fund over a period of time to be used for welfare payments and work guarantees in return for union agreement to end uneconomic practices and/or opposition to technological advancement.

One of the most widely known of such formulas is that involving the West Coast longshoremen. The International Longshoremen's and Warehousemen's Union gave up various restraints on productivity and its opposition to technological change in return for various benefits, includ-

---

[19] See William Gomberg, "Special Study Committees," in John T. Dunlop and Neil W. Chamberlain (eds.), *Frontiers of Collective Bargaining* (New York: Harper & Row Publishers, 1967), pp. 235–51.

[20] Plans associated with the management consultant Allen W. Rucker are also similar to this group.

ing the establishment of a fund, supported by employer contributions, for various welfare, disability, and retirement benefits.[21]

Scanlon Plans

The Scanlon plans are basically plantwide cost-saving programs which are designed to give employees an incentive to improve production methods and to suggest cost savings. The Scanlon plans were developed by the late Joseph Scanlon, onetime Steelworkers' union official, from his experience in trying to save the jobs of union members by improving the competitive position of high-cost steel-fabricating firms.

Many Scanlon plans are put into effect as a substitute for demoralized incentive plans. A plantwide incentive—or bonus—potential replaces the existing incentive with the aim of producing teamwork efforts to achieve higher efficiency and productivity. "The incentive toward teamwork is provided most commonly by giving the employees a large share (usually three-fourths) of the savings in labor costs. The savings are measured by ascertaining the extent to which the ratio of payroll to sales value of production is reduced below the previous normal ratio."[22]

Scanlon plans require a great deal of mutual trust and cooperation among employees, unions, and management if they are to work. They have been most successful among small firms which have been in trouble competitively, and in which employer-employee relations have been on a high plane of mutual confidence. On the other hand, such plans are not without problems, since bonuses are paid to all, regardless of the contribution of each to the savings. Moreover, under such plans there is a tendency for the parties to become overimpressed with initial successes and to believe that necessary overhead, such as industrial and methods engineers, maintenance outlays, and adequate supervision, can be dispensed with because "the worker knows best how to cut costs." Under such conditions a Scanlon plan can become as demoralized as an incentive plan and can result in the payment of bonuses which would not have been paid if proper consideration had been given to expenses required to maintain future profitability. This seems to have occurred in the case of the widely publicized Scanlon plan at the LaPointe Machine Tool Company.[23]

[21] For an account of the West Coast longshore agreement, see Thomas Kennedy, *Automation Funds and Displaced Workers* (Boston: Harvard University Graduate School of Business Administration, 1962), pp. 70–101. The basic agreement has been twice renewed since this account was written, each time with more liberal benefits.

[22] Slichter, Healy, and Livernash, *op. cit.*, p. 865. This explanation is given: "Suppose the normal ratio is found to be 35 per cent, which means that if a plant were selling $1 million of goods a year, payroll would normally be $350,000. If the workers by improving their efficiency were able to produce $1 million of goods for a payroll cost of $310,000, three-fourths of the saving or $30,000 would be paid to them as a bonus."

[23] For an analysis of the LaPointe situation, see Herbert R. Northrup and Harvey A. Young, "The Causes of Industrial Peace—Revisited," *Industrial and Labor Relations Review*, Vol. XXII (October, 1968).

Kaiser Plan

The Kaiser plan was developed by a tripartite committee headed by three well-known arbitrators: Professors George W. Taylor and John T. Dunlop, and Mr. David L. Cole. It is based on a "gain-sharing" formula. The key feature of the plan is a complex formula that matches each month's material, labor, and supply costs against a base. Kaiser pays the same wages as do other basic steel companies. The Kaiser plan has, therefore, resulted in a bonus above regular earnings which is paid monthly. The original agreement, negotiated in 1961, has since been liberalized and renewed.[24]

One of the original objectives of the Kaiser plan was to replace a demoralized incentive plan. Employees on incentives were, however, allowed to forego the plan for the existing incentive if they so desired—and many who were receiving high individual incentive payments declined to change over. As in Scanlon plans, the cost reduction effectiveness of the Kaiser plan seemed to wane with time. The bonuses, however, continue to be paid, thus assuring worker support. The fact that the plan guarantees the company against strikes even if other companies in the industry are struck, and the wide and favorable publicity resulting from the working of the plan, are strong factors behind the company's desire to continue it. Significantly, the Kaiser Plan has had only one emulator, and that company has expressed serious reservations about its own experience, indicating that the returns to the company have been less than the costs.[25]

FORMALIZATION OF WAGE STRUCTURE

In most of American industry, wages are tailored to the job rather than to the man. Management could, of course, attempt to pay each worker an amount equal to management's estimate of the worth of the individual, taking into account his age, health, skill, length of service, and similar factors. This practice is followed to some extent with respect to supervisory and executive employees and in the hiring of employees such as musicians and radio performers, whose individual talents vary greatly. In a large industrial establishment, however, such piecemeal establishment of a wage structure would be expensive, time-consuming, and impracticable. As a consequence, most industrial establishments have adopted formalized wage structures.

Formal wage structures are generally of two kinds. A "single-rate

[24] See Harold Stieglitz, *The Kaiser Steel Union Sharing Plan* (Studies in Personnel Policy, No. 187 [New York: National Industrial Conference Board, 1963]); *New York Times*, October 1, 1967; *Business Week*, March, 1967, pp. 149–50; and *Daily Labor Report*, December 18, 1967, No. 244, p. A–11.

[25] See Robert F. Groves, *Alan Wood Joint Economic Expansion Plan*, speech prepared for presentation at Philadelphia Technical Meeting of American Iron and Steel Institute, October 26, 1966. Mr. Groves is vice president—personnel, Alan Wood Steel Company.

establishment" pays the same rate to all experienced workers in a job classification. This means that a lower rate may be set for apprentices, but once a man has acquired what is considered the minimum experience necessary to qualify him for journeyman or experienced worker rates, he is paid the same rate as all other experienced workers performing the same work, regardless of variation in length of service and other factors. A "rate range establishment," on the other hand, sets up a range of rates for a particular job and provides that specific rates for individual workers within the range are to be determined by merit, length of service, and similar considerations.

The adoption of formal wage structures has greatly eliminated controversy over intraplant wage relationships. Whereas, prior to World War II, grievances over the relation of one person's job rate to another's were common, the spread of "job evaluation" and the improvement of wage administration have greatly diminished such disputes.[26]

Job evaluation involves the establishment of a rational internal wage structure. Although such an evaluation may be accomplished in many ways, it usually is done in three steps: Jobs are described in terms of duties, responsibilities, and characteristics; the jobs are then point-rated by a formula giving due account to skill, responsibility, working conditions, effort, etc.; and finally, jobs are grouped into a hierarchy of grades and wage rates or ranges established for the grades. A similar procedure is utilized for salaries.

Job evaluation developed as a management device aimed at simplifying the wage structure and its administration, and preventing "whipsawing" of rates—that is, using one out-of-line job to gain a wage increase and then using that wage increase to press for others. Job evaluation received a great impetus during World War II as a means of relieving pressure on the National War Labor Board to grant "intraplant inequity" wage increases.

Except in a few industries, such as steel, job evaluation has not enjoyed formal union support. It does, however, usually gain union acceptance. This occurs because whereas the introduction of a job evaluation plan upsets internal wage relationships and thus is often not politically supportable by union leadership, once the plan is introduced, it stresses payment on a job rather than on a personal basis, and hence reduces friction and dissension among union ranks. For employers, job evaluation simplifies wage administration and helps to prevent individual supervisors from letting individual wage rates rise out of line.

Within job evaluation plans, most unions prefer single rates to rate ranges. In the automobile industry, union pressure has virtually eliminated rate ranges.[27] Many employers prefer ranges, with the right to reward merit within the range. Other employers have found that ranges of this

---

[26] Slichter, Healy, and Livernash, *op. cit.*, pp. 538 ff.
[27] MacDonald, *op. cit.*, pp. 83–133.

type can be maintained only by strict control because otherwise pressure on the foremen to recommend increases within the range soon puts most employees at the top of the range. Some ranges are, in effect, just nominal, for the contract may provide that employees receive a wage increase every few months until they reach the top of the grade. The most effective rate range plans place strict limits on the manner and/or number in the grade who can achieve the top rate, and permit automatic increases only to the midpoint of the range—if at all. Since the midpoint of the rate range is, theoretically, the same as a single job rate would be, an average of the workers' rates in any grade which exceeds the midpoint means that the plant is paying more for a range rate than it would for a single-rate structure.

SUPPLEMENTARY OR FRINGE BENEFITS

Wage supplements, commonly called fringe benefits, commenced their growth during World War II, when wages were controlled but benefits were permitted generally free rein. In the immediate postwar period, John L. Lewis set the style for the union drive for fringe benefits by winning a health and welfare plan for the coal miners paid for solely by employer contributions. Fringe benefits, which began modestly, mushroomed and now constitute a substantial portion of total labor costs in American industry. In recent years, employers have granted to their employees, health and accident insurance, life insurance, holidays and vacations with pay, pensions, paid sick leave, annual wage guarantees, and many other fringe benefits.

Because supplementary benefits have become costly to employers and attractive to employees, they are a potent source of friction between labor and management. Moreover, the general adoption by industry of various types of welfare plans affects business costs and so may have important repercussions on the level of employment and income in the economy.

Nature and Extent of Supplementary Benefits

There is no reliable statistical series published showing the cost of all supplementary benefits for industry as a whole, or even for manufacturing industries. This is understandable when we consider that supplementary benefits include such things as pay for "coffee-break" time, suggestion awards, free meals, and a whole gamut of similar benefits. Few employers have the time to calculate the cost of all these miscellaneous benefits. Despite the increasing emphasis placed upon fringe benefits in union negotiations, many employers have only the haziest idea of the costs their companies have assumed with respect to such benefits.

If we include in supplementary benefits only employer contributions legally required for various types of social insurance, such as old-age and survivors insurance, unemployment insurance, railroad retirement insurance, and the like, and in addition, employer contributions to private pension and welfare funds, we can turn to the U.S. Department of Commerce, which publishes such fringe benefit data in its National Income Statistics. Figure 5–1, which is based on U.S. Department of Commerce statistics, indicates that in 1966, employers spent in the neighborhood of $35 billion on such payments.

FIGURE 5–1

Employer Payments for Employee Security
(Private Industry)

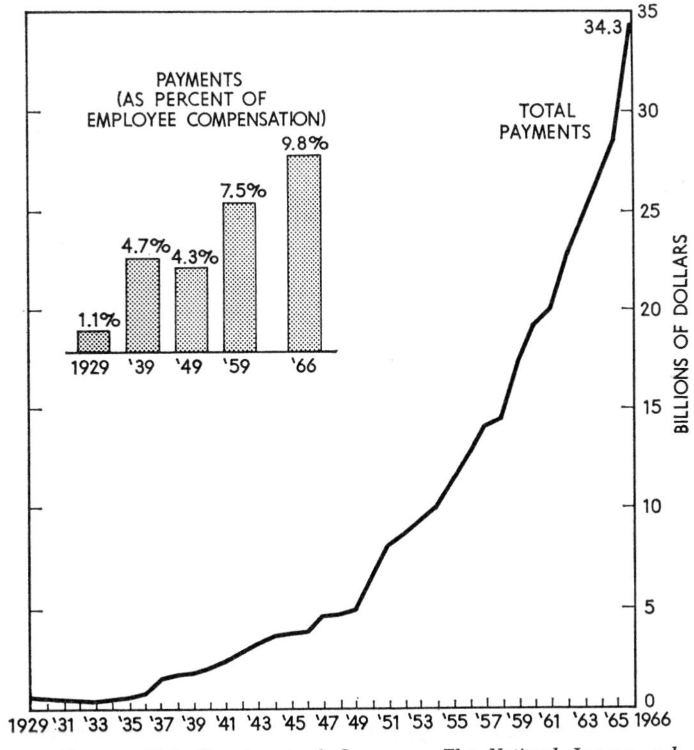

Source: U.S. Department of Commerce, *The National Income and Product Accounts of the United States, 1929–1965* and *Survey of Current Business*, April 1968.

The data in Figure 5–1 reveal a big jump in fringe benefit costs in the late 1930's, following enactment of the Social Security law, and again in the 1940's, when private pension, insurance, and welfare plans became increasingly important. The trend since then has continued almost steadily upward, and promises to do so as long as union negotiators stress "security" in their bargaining.

But the data in Figure 5–1 tell only part of the story. Biennial studies by the Chamber of Commerce of the United States indicate that payments for vacations, holidays, rest periods, and other time not worked constitutes almost one half of total fringe benefit costs. Such payments for time not worked are not included in the data in Figure 5–1.

The growth of fringe benefit costs, as well as the importance of the various types, is shown in Table 5–1, which is based upon data supplied by 79 identical companies in each of the Chamber of Commerce's biennial surveys since 1947. As can be seen from the figures in Table 5–1, fringe payments rose from 16.1% of payroll in 1947 to 29.9% in 1967, an increase of 86%. Because wage rates were also rising during this same period, fringe benefits calculated on a cents-per-hour basis and on an annual-dollars-per-employee basis increased more rapidly than on a percent-of-payroll basis. Fringe benefits for these companies increased from 22.1 cents per payroll hour in 1947 to 103.1 cents in 1967, an increase of 368%! On a dollars-per-year-per-employee basis, such benefits rose from $450 in 1947 to $2,132 in 1967—an increase of over 374%.

As can be seen from Table 5–1, the two major classes of fringe benefits are "pension and other agreed-upon payments" and "payments for time not worked." The former rose from 4.8% of payroll in 1947 to 10.4% in 1967; the latter rose from 5.5% to 9.9% during the same period.

Payments for pensions and other agreed-upon payments, as used in the Chamber of Commerce survey, include pension plans; life insurance; sickness, accident, surgical, medical care, or hospitalization plans; contributions to supplementary unemployment benefit plans; and dismissal or termination pay allowances. All of these have been very much in the forefront of union demands during this entire period. The phenomenal growth of such benefits during these years was due to a number of factors—the freezing of wages during World War II, NLRB decisions holding that such benefits were subject to collective bargaining, and favorable tax treatment under federal income tax legislation accorded to employer-sponsored programs. These factors, together with a growing acceptance by employers of responsibility for worker security, accounted for the tremendous growth of these plans during this period.

Today fringe benefits are so pervasive in American industry that paid holidays and vacation are almost universally provided, and over 90% of employers make payments for welfare programs of various kinds. Moreover, each year the liberality of these programs increases. Whereas health plans once covered only basic hospital care, now some include dental and psychiatric care and free eyeglasses; 6 holidays with pay have advanced to 10 and 12 and one week's vacation to four with even a three months sabbatical at intervals; time off with pay and benefits seem not only to expand but find new ways of expression.

The Future of Fringe Benefits

Union interest in fringe benefits and employer willingness to accede to some of the union demands is attributable in part to the peculiar tax

TABLE 3-4

COMPARISON OF 1947–67 EMPLOYEE BENEFITS FOR 79 COMPANIES

Item	1947	1949	1951	1953	1955	1957	1959	1961	1963	1965	1967
All industries (79 companies)											
1. As percent of payroll, total	16.1	17.5	19.4	21.0	22.3	24.2	25.1	27.1	28.6	28.1	29.9
a) Legally required payments (employer's share only)	2.7	2.6	2.8	2.6	2.8	3.1	3.7	4.2	4.8	4.1	5.0
b) Pension and other agreed-upon payments (employer's share only)	4.8	5.7	6.0	7.0	7.6	8.2	8.6	9.2	9.8	10.1	10.4
c) Paid rest periods, lunch periods, etc.	1.6	1.6	1.8	2.1	2.5	2.5	2.2	2.5	2.5	2.4	2.5
d) Payments for time not worked	5.5	6.1	7.1	7.5	7.6	8.6	8.8	9.3	9.3	9.5	9.9
e) Profit-sharing payments, bonuses, etc.	1.5	1.5	1.7	1.8	1.8	1.8	1.8	1.9	2.2	2.0	2.1
2. As cents per payroll hour	22.1	27.1	35.0	43.2	48.3	54.9	63.5	73.9	86.2	88.3	103.1
3. As dollars per year per employee	450	551	718	893	999	1157	1287	1530	1794	1874	2132
All manufacturing (45 companies)											
1. As percent of payroll, total	14.3	16.0	17.3	19.3	20.9	23.4	24.0	26.3	27.8	27.7	28.7
a) Legally required payments (employer's share only)	2.9	2.7	2.8	2.6	3.1	3.2	3.9	4.3	4.9	4.2	5.2
b) Pension and other agreed-upon payments (employer's share only)	3.5	4.6	5.3	6.2	6.9	7.7	7.8	8.7	9.2	9.7	9.8
c) Paid rest periods, lunch periods, etc.	1.6	1.6	1.7	2.2	2.4	2.5	2.2	2.5	2.6	2.6	2.5
d) Payments for time not worked	4.8	5.5	6.1	6.7	6.9	8.1	8.4	9.2	9.1	9.5	9.8
e) Profit-sharing payments, bonuses, etc.	1.5	1.6	1.4	1.6	1.6	1.9	1.7	1.6	2.0	1.7	1.4
2. As cents per payroll hour	20.2	24.9	33.1	40.2	46.4	54.2	63.4	73.6	82.1	88.9	99.3
3. As dollars per year per employee	416	508	690	842	966	1165	1269	1533	1861	1896	2064
All nonmanufacturing (34 companies)											
1. As percent of payroll, total	18.8	20.3	22.4	23.5	24.5	25.0	26.8	28.2	29.8	28.4	30.8
a) Legally required payments (employer's share only)	2.5	2.5	2.8	2.7	2.6	3.0	3.5	4.0	4.6	4.0	4.8
b) Pension and other agreed-upon payments (employer's share only)	6.8	7.8	7.0	8.1	8.6	8.8	9.8	10.1	10.8	10.4	10.8
c) Paid rest periods, lunch periods, etc.	1.6	1.7	1.9	1.9	2.5	2.4	2.3	2.4	2.3	2.2	2.5
d) Payments for time not worked	6.5	7.0	8.7	8.8	8.7	9.0	9.2	9.5	9.5	9.5	10.1
e) Profit-sharing payments, bonuses, etc.	1.4	1.3	2.0	2.0	2.1	1.8	2.0	2.2	2.6	2.3	2.6
2. As cents per payroll hour	25.1	30.5	37.9	47.9	51.4	55.3	63.6	74.3	88.3	87.5	105.3
3. As dollars per year per employee	506	617	763	972	1056	1135	1316	1524	1751	1798	2165

SOURCE: Chamber of Commerce of the United States, Biennial Survey of Employee, or Fringe, Benefits.

status presently accorded to fringe benefits under federal law. If an employer were to pay an employee an additional salary with the understanding that the employee would use the money to buy himself a retirement annuity or purchase life insurance, the amount paid to the employee would be deductible by the employer as an expense in calculating taxable income, but it would be taxable as income to the employee for federal tax purposes. If, however, the employer does not give the money directly to the employee but instead sets up a group pension plan or purchases group life insurance, the employee can get substantially the same protection as long as he remains an employee of the company; but the provision for such benefits made by the employer, although deductible by the latter as a business expense, is not taxable to the employee at the time such provision is made. If tax preference of this type continues with employee interest in security, the trend to ever larger fringe costs will proceed. The 1964 tax revisions limited to $50,000 the amount of tax-free group life insurance which any employer may provide for an employee for 1964 and later years. This law might be the beginning of legal limitations on fringe benefit tax preferences—but so far it has not been extended.

Fringe benefits have now become such an accepted part of the wage structure that we are apt to overlook the revolutionary change which has occurred in the entire concept of compensation. For example, wages used to be paid for time worked. Today, there are few employers who do not pay wages of some kind for time *not worked:* paid vacation, sick leave, holidays, etc. As already noted, some statistical series report earnings *per hours worked*, and some report earnings *per hours paid for*. If earnings are measured per hours worked, increases in paid holidays, paid vacations, paid sick leave, and similar fringe benefits increase average hourly earnings. On the other hand, the Bureau of Labor Statistics figures usually are based on earnings per hour paid for. Therefore, in the BLS series, increases in paid vacations, holidays, and sick leave do not raise hourly earnings. In one year, for example, hours at work as measured by the Bureau of the Census were 5.4% lower than hours paid for as reported by the Bureau of Labor Statistics. This difference by itself would cause earnings per hour of work to be 5.4% higher than earnings per hour paid for.[28] The growing importance of fringe benefits in labor's compensation makes it vital for the student of labor economics to examine carefully the basic theory upon which statistical series of earnings have been constructed.

It is apparent that, bit by bit, American industry is obligating itself to underwrite the economic needs and the economic risks of the worker. Industry today is close to being saddled with a cradle-to-grave security

---

[28] Albert Rees, "Patterns of Wages, Prices, and Productivity," in American Assembly, *Wages, Prices, Profits, and Productivity* (New York: Columbia University Press, 1959), p. 12.

program for employees similar to the government program in England. As more and more costs go into fringe benefits, payment by the hour for time actually worked will become less important. Does this mean that our traditional modes of payment will eventually be outdated? These are questions which cannot be answered today but which are a matter of concern to business and labor leaders alike.

The Growing Gap between Wage Costs and Employee Take-Home Pay

At the same time as the employer's cost of employing a worker has been increasing because of fringe benefits, employee take-home pay has been subjected to major deductions in the form of withholding for federal income taxes, state income taxes, union dues, charitable contributions, etc.

TABLE 5–2

Item	Weekly Cost to Employer
Federal Old-Age, Survivors, and Disability Insurance tax	$ 4.40
Unemployment insurance taxes	2.95
Workmen's compensation premium	1.00
Private pension contribution	8.00
Group insurance contribution	3.00
Supplemental unemployment benefit plan contribution	2.00
Pay for holidays, vacations, rest periods, and the like	15.00
Employee facilities, services, and other miscellaneous benefits	2.50
Total	$38.85

The result has been a growing gap between spendable earnings and labor costs.

For example, assume that a company employs a worker at $125 weekly pay. The company could have, in addition to this direct wage cost, indirect costs associated with the employment of this worker as shown in Table 5–2.

On the other side of the coin, the employee's paycheck might well reflect deductions such as those in Table 5–3.

In this company, therefore, the employer looks upon his labor costs as $163.85 for this particular employee, while the employee only receives $98 in his pay envelope. The employee is, of course, aware of these various indirect benefits and of the manner in which his pay has been diverted. The problem facing industry, however, arises from the fact that to some extent, some of these amounts are discounted in the employee's thinking. Although "package" settlements, which provide that the bulk of a bargain wage adjustment shall be taken in the form of fringes, are especially popular with employees who are security-conscious, even such employees also tend to think in terms of "take-home" pay—that is, the

TABLE 5-3

Item	Weekly Cost to Employee
Statutory deductions (income tax withheld; contributions to federal Old-Age, Survivors, and Disability Insurance; contribution to state disability insurance)*	$14.50
Union dues	1.00
Contributions to group insurance and company pension plan	3.50
Group insurance premiums for dependents' coverage and contributions to company thrift plan and charitable drives	8.00
Total	$27.00

* Four states—California, New Jersey, New York, and Rhode Island—have disability insurance programs in effect.

amount actually received in the pay envelope. Continued emphasis on fringes, therefore, can tend to increase the cost to the employer without increasing the satisfaction of the employee.

Fringe Benefits and Employment

A characteristic of many fringe benefits is that they are attached to the individual employee rather than to the overall wage bill of the employer. Thus the worker receives vacations, holidays, pensions, group insurance, etc., whether he works 35 hours, 40 hours, or 50 hours per week. Of course, his earnings may change the amount he receives as benefits; but within broad limits, such fringes are often like the government social security program (old age): After a basic amount of payroll cost, there is no additional charge.

This means that fringe benefits can make it cheaper to work employees overtime than to hire new employees. For example, assume that fringe benefits cost an employer 25 cents per hour and government-imposed benefit programs (social security, and unemployment and workmen's compensation) add another 10 cents. Add to these the costs of recruiting, indoctrinating, and employing new personnel, which can be substantial, and frequently employers find that it is cheaper to employ existing employees at overtime rates (time and one-half basic rates) than it would be to hire new employees. This fact accounts for proposals to increase the overtime rate to double time as a means of discouraging overtime. Such proposals were strongly advanced in the early 1960's when unemployment was quite heavy in many industrial centers.

Fringe benefits, by adding to the employers' marginal costs, may adversely affect both the amount of employment and its character—that is, whether existing employees are worked more hours or new employees are added to the payroll. The cost of security for some may be less employment—and less security—for others. Whether, however, adding to the cost of overtime, and hence to the employers' overall cost, would lessen or increase the propensity to employ is, of course, very doubtful.

We shall return to this issue in our discussion of the hours of work question in Chapter 16.

SUMMARY

We have seen that the wage issue is not a simple question of how many cents per hour a worker should be paid. Wages—in the sense used in this text—can encompass a wide range of benefits, from maternity care for a worker's wife to extra pay for working after 6 P.M. Wages are naturally important to a worker because they mean purchasing power for him and his family. But wages also have another dimension in our society which should not be overlooked. The worker, in common with other members of the community, views his wage as a symbol of his standing in the community. It is an aspect of his status in our economic society. That is why benefits such as a third week of paid vacation, for example, are so important. If John Jones is at home cutting the lawn while Bill Smith is working at the plant because his company did not give the third week of vacation, you can bet that Mrs. Jones and Mrs. Smith are discussing the injustice of it all and that Bill Smith—and eventually his employer—will hear about it!

In the next chapter, we shall consider other problems arising out of the employer-employee relationship which do not directly involve wages but are important issues in the collective bargaining process.

QUESTIONS FOR DISCUSSION

1. Discuss the various forms of incentive payment. Is it true that unions oppose piecework and favor time payment? Support your answer.
2. Discuss the pros and cons of profit sharing versus gain sharing.
3. Discuss the relationship of fringe benefits as a cost to the employer and a return to the employee. Do you think the trend of fringe benefit costs will continue to rise; and if so, what are some of the implications of this trend?

SUGGESTIONS FOR FURTHER READING

ALLEN, DONNA, *Fringe Benefits: Wages or Social Obligation.* Ithaca, N.Y.: Cornell University Press, 1964.
> An analysis of the role of fringe benefits in compensation theory and practice.

DOUTY, HARRY M. *Trends in Labor Compensation in the United States, 1946–1966.* Washington, D.C.: U.S. Government Printing Office, 1967.
> A succinct summary of wage and compensation trends and changes in the 20 years following World War II.

ENGEN, GUNNAR. "A New Direction and Growth in Profit Sharing," *Monthly Labor Review*, Vol. XC (July, 1967), pp. 1–8.
> An analysis of profit sharing by types of plans, reason for growth and outlook for the future.

LEVINSON, HAROLD M. *Determining Forces in Collective Wage Bargaining.* (New York: John Wiley & Sons, Inc., 1966.)

A scholarly analytical study of wage changes in four industries, emphasizing the power factors in collective bargaining which have contributed to the wage trends.

SLICHTER, SUMNER H.; HEALY, J. J.; and LIVERNASH, E. R. *The Impact of Collective Bargaining on Management,* chaps. xvii–xx. Washington, D.C.: Brookings Institution, 1960.

These chapters of this outstanding work contain comprehensive and realistic analyses of wage incentives, measured daywork, evaluated wage structures, and other wage structure considerations based upon extensive field work and careful evaluations of the problems encountered.

THE CONTENT OF
COLLECTIVE BARGAINING:
INDUSTRIAL JURISPRUDENCE

The process of collective bargaining, as we have seen from the previous chapter, is a method of determining the price of labor, that is, of fixing wages. An additional important function of collective bargaining is to formulate the rules and regulations governing the employment relationship.

Where there is no union, management's labor policies may be liberal or restrictive; but in either case, they are *management's* policies. Management is free to discharge, to promote, to hire, or to lay off in any legal manner in which it desires. But when a union represents the employees, these functions and many others which were once the prerogative of management become subject to a variety of rules. Some of the rules are written into an agreement between union and management; others are simply accepted by both parties and remain unwritten; and still others are embodied in federal, state, or municipal laws, often as a result of pressure by unions or employers.

Whatever the form of the rules, they embody the system of "industrial jurisprudence" by which the relation of union and management is regulated.[1]

No Uniformity of Rules

The rise of a system of industrial jurisprudence is traceable to a number of factors. Basically, however, it is the result of American workers' demands that industrial relations be conducted according to rules which labor has had a voice in formulating. Only if such rules are in effect do unions and employees feel that persons equally situated will be guaranteed equal treatment in promotions, layoffs, discipline actions, and in meeting technological change; and only if such rules exist can the union in most situations influence substantially the handling of people and maintain

---

[1] As the term was used by the late Professor Sumner H. Slichter in his pathbreaking book, *Union Policies and Industrial Management* (Washington, D.C.: Brookings Institution, 1941), p. 1. A new edition, completed by Professor Slichter just prior to his death in 1959 and coauthored by Professors J. J. Healy and E. R. Livernash, was published in 1960 under the title, *The Impact of Collective Bargaining on Management* (Washington, D.C., Brookings Institution).

its own status as a significant organization capable of exerting effective pressure on managerial decision making.

The type of rules developed in a particular industry or shop reflects the problems encountered there. The industrial pattern—including the extent of product competition, the character of the labor market, the degree of union and nonunion competition, the rate of technological change, and a host of other socioeconomic factors—determines particular union policies. What one union finds suitable in a particular situation, another in a different locale will reject as unworkable. Union policies are a function of their environment. Hence we find a wide variety of policies pursued by various unions. Popular statements to the effect that "all unions desire the closed shop" or "all unions favor seniority" or "all unions oppose incentive systems" have no basis in fact.

Union Security[2]

A primary aim of most unions is "union security," and this usually involves some form of compulsory union membership and automatic dues checkoff. Whether a union will demand a "closed shop" (under which employees must join the union as a prerequisite to employment) or a "union shop" (under which the employer may hire anyone he chooses, but after a probationary period of 30–90 days all employees must join the union as a condition of employment) will vary with the type of employment and labor market. In general, the closed shop is found among skilled and strategically located trades and in industries in which employment is casual and intermittent. The closed shop differs from the union shop primarily in that it is not only a means of "union security" but also a method of controlling entrance to the job or trade. Other forms of union security, including methods of "checking off" dues and thus assuring unions of a flow of funds, are described in Table 6–1. Approximately 80% of the nearly 18 million persons covered by collective bargaining agreements work under some form of union security provisions.

Except in underdeveloped countries, union security provisions are not common outside of the United States and Canada.[3] In America, the closed or union shop became a necessary weapon for union survival. Only with such protection could the union count on effective protection from employer discrimination against union members. In many cases the closed- and union-shop provisions were necessary to induce workers to join the

[2] For a more complete analysis of this subject, with emphasis on the legal and public policy aspects, see Herbert R. Northrup and Gordon F. Bloom, *Government and Labor* (Homewood, Ill.: Richard D. Irwin, Inc., 1963), chap. viii.

[3] In many underdeveloped countries, unions have found that it is impossible to collect dues and to maintain an organization without at least a checkoff. In New Zealand and in some of the Australian provinces, workers are required by law to maintain membership and to pay dues to the union which represents them before state arbitration courts.

TABLE 6-1

TYPES OF UNION SECURITY AND CHECKOFF

UNION SECURITY TERMS	CHECKOFF TERMS

UNION SECURITY TERMS

Closed Shop—Employer agrees that all workers must belong to the union to keep their jobs. He further agrees that when hiring new workers he will hire only members of the union.

Union Shop—Employer agrees that all workers must belong to the union to keep their jobs. He can hire whom he wants; but the workers he hires must join the union within a specified time (usually 30 days) or lose their jobs.

Modified Union Shop—Employer agrees that all present and future members of the union must remain in the union for the duration of the contract in order to keep their jobs. (Present workers who are not in the union and who do not join the union in the future can keep their jobs without union membership.) The employer further agrees that all new employees must join the union within a specified time (usually 30 days) or lose their jobs.

Agency Shop—The employer and the union agree that a worker shall not be forced to join or stay in the union to keep his job. The worker has the choice of joining or not joining. But if he elects not to join he must pay to the union a sum equal to union dues. This sum represents a fee charged him by the union for acting as his agent in collective bargaining and in policing the union contract.

Maintenance of Membership—Employer agrees that all present and future members of the union must remain in the union for the duration of the contract in order to keep their jobs. (Workers who are not in the union and who do not join the union in the future can keep their jobs without union membership.)

Revocable Maintenance of Membership—Employer agrees that all present and future members of the union must remain in the union to keep their jobs. But he specifies that workers can leave the union during specified periods (usually 10 days at the end of each year) without losing their jobs.

Preferential Hiring—Employer agrees that in hiring new workers he shall give preference to union members.

CHECKOFF TERMS

Voluntary Irrevocable—Employer agrees to deduct union dues and other monies from the worker's wages only if the worker signs a form authorizing him to do so. This generally requires that the worker's authorization shall not be irrevocable for more than 1 year or beyond the termination date of the contract, whichever is sooner.

Year-to-Year Renewal—Employer agrees to deduct dues and other monies from the worker's wages if the worker signs a checkoff authorization. If the worker does not revoke his authorization at the end of a year or at the contract termination date, it goes into effect for another year.

Voluntary Revocable—Employer agrees to deduct union dues and other monies from the worker's wages if the worker signs a form authorizing him to do so. The worker can revoke this authorization any time he sees fit.

Automatic—Employer agrees automatically to deduct dues and other monies from the worker's wages and turn the money over to the union.

Involuntary Irrevocable—Employer agrees that to secure and keep his job a worker must sign a form authorizing the employer to deduct union dues and other monies from his wages.

SOURCE: J. J. Bambrick, *Union Security and Checkoff Provisions* (Studies in Personnel Policy, No. 127 [New York: National Industrial Conference Board, 1952]). Mr. Bambrick's definitions have stood the test of time and remain current.

union, not so much because of their reluctance to join but because of their fear of consequences in the form of employer retaliation if they joined voluntarily.

In other democratic countries, unions found little need of union security, for they often grew at a more rapid rate than those in the United States and encountered much less employer opposition. Complete union membership was achieved not by union security provisions in contracts but by direct action among employees. Men unwilling to join unions in European democracies are usually compelled to do so either because union men will not work with them or because they find that failure to join unions means social ostracism or other types of effective pressure. Such methods proved ineffective in America because of employer opposition to unions and the lack of class-consciousness on the part of employees.

Theoretically, the passage of the National Labor Relations (Wagner) Act in 1935 eliminated much of the need for union security. This act outlawed employer discrimination against workers because of union membership and required employers to bargain with duly certified unions. Nevertheless, union security demands lost none of their intensity. This was true partly because union leaders and members believed, often with considerable justification, that employers were opposed to unions and could circumvent the law; partly because, emotionally, they could not imagine successful unionism without the closed or union shop; and partly because of a new development—the rise of rival unionism on a scale theretofore unknown. The existence of a union security provision deters raiding by rival unions and thus gives unions "security" from another angle. The merger of the AFL and the CIO in 1955 further outmoded this union argument in favor of security needs.

Like union arguments in favor of union security, which attempt to couch the issue in terms of the survival of collective bargaining, employer arguments against compulsory unionism are usually set forth in highly emotional language—that is, in terms of individual liberty, "right to work," or "freedom from domination by union bosses." In actual fact, there is a very real power issue involved which the emotional arguments all but obscure. The power issue has two related aspects: power of a union in relation to its members and power of a union in bargaining with management. These are vital concerns of both labor and management.

Power over Members

That the union security issue is concerned with union coercive power over its members seems undeniable. Power over the membership involves, of course, the right of a union to fine, to discipline, or to effectuate the discharge of a member for violation of union rules or conduct, or for the completely indefensible reasons of opposing, antagonizing, or otherwise offending union leadership. Students of labor relations have always recognized that a union must have some authority over its members, particularly when a majority has taken a legitimate position in favor of a legitimate objective. Otherwise, anarchy in industrial relations could result. For example, few disagree with the right of a majority to accept a settlement offered by an employer, or to reject the settlement and to choose a strike. But should a union have the power to fine or to discipline a member who crosses a picket line and returns to work during a strike, and thus makes the achievement of the strike goal more difficult for the majority? Questions like this involve complex moral and economic issues which each citizen may answer differently and which the legislatures and the courts likewise find difficult to determine. The U.S. Supreme Court, by the narrow margin of five Justices to four, ruled that a union could fine members for refusing to stay on strike.[4] The complexities of such questions and their difficulty of resolution have induced the Congress and state legislatures to move into this field of regulation—either by a "bill-of-rights" guarantee, such as is contained in the Landrum-Griffin Act, or by limiting or controlling union security provisions. The latter approach stems from the obvious reason that union security provisions give the union leadership greatly added power over its members.

The Taft-Hartley Act of 1947—which is discussed in detail in Chapter 21—outlawed the closed shop, placed restrictions on other forms of union security, and expressly permitted the states to legislate in this field, regardless of federal law. Once a union security provision was legally negotiated, the union was not restricted in its admission or disciplinary actions, but the teeth were withdrawn from the latter by the requirement that a union could require the discharge of an employee pursuant to a legal union security provision only on the ground that the employee had failed to tender the regularly required initiation fee or dues.

Discharges and Checkoff

Expelling a man from a union for nonfiscal reasons, or for declining to pay a special fine or assessment, cannot thus expel him from his job unless an employer conspires with a union to violate the act. Undoubtedly, this happens when the parties mutually agree to rid themselves of a "troublemaker" to both. Nevertheless, the existence of this provision has restrained arbitrary union discipline of members, and especially arbitrary union-inspired discharge of members.[5]

The Taft-Hartley Act in this respect did not attempt to protect a person's right to belong to a union. It protected the person's right to remain on the job under a union-shop provision as long as he tendered his

---

[4] *National Labor Relations Board* v. *Allis-Chalmers Mfg. Co.*, 65 LRRM 2449, U.S. Supreme Court (1967).

[5] That there is still considerable use of union security provision to deny job opportunities, but much less than before Taft-Hartley became law, is indicated by a recent study. See Mack A. Moore, "The Conflict between Union Discipline and Union Security," *Labor Law Journal*, Vol. XVIII (February, 1967), pp. 116–23.

regular union dues. The sections of the Landrum-Griffin Act dealing with individual union rights, which are discussed in Chapter 22 added protection to the individual against arbitrary expulsion from the union.

Closely allied to this union security restriction in the Taft-Hartley Act was the act's ban on the compulsory checkoff. The checkoff of membership dues was made lawful only where individual employees execute a written assignment of wages for not longer than one year, or for the duration of the applicable union contract, whichever is shorter. In general practice, such assignments are in effect until revoked. But it is now unlawful for an employer and union to agree to turn over a portion of an employee's wages to a union without that employee's express written permission—certainly a highly defensible public policy.

Ban on Closed Shop

The Taft-Hartley Act outlawed the closed shop (see Table 6–1, page 171, for definitions) and other forms of preemployment preferential treatment of union members. The writers of the act were impressed with the fact that unreasonable denial of work had occurred as a result of union control of hiring, and this they were determined to eliminate.

There is general agreement, however, that this provision tended largely to drive the closed shop underground instead of out of existence. We shall examine in following sections of this chapter why control of hiring through the closed shop is so vital to unions in the building, maritime, and other trades where employment is intermittent. In Chapter 3, we also noted how the closed shop is used to bar persons deemed unacceptable to the members—for example, to discriminate against Negroes. There is no question that unions in the building trades, for example, have used the power inherent in closed-shop arrangements to deny Negroes job opportunities.

Despite the obviously discriminatory activities of the building trades unions, Congress in 1959, while enacting the Landrum-Griffin Act to promote union democracy, actually loosened Taft-Hartley restrictions applied to the construction industry. It legalized "prehire" agreements (that is, arrangements to employ union personnel before a job starts). Such agreements may now make union membership compulsory 7 days after employment (rather than 30 days, as is the Taft-Hartley requirement in other industries), provided that the state law permits union security provisions. Construction union contracts also can require an employer to notify the union of job opportunities and to give the union an opportunity to refer qualified applicants for employment, and can specify minimum training or experience qualifications for employment. The net effect of these provisions was to restore a considerable amount of legality to the actual practice in the construction industry. Then, five years later in 1964, Congress enacted a Civil Rights Act, Title VII of which forbids discrimination by unions or employers on grounds of race, color, creed, or sex. The net effect has been a flood of street demonstrations and of lawsuits aimed at unions and contractors in the building industry, and massive federal programs aimed at forcing unions and companies in this industry to open up jobs for Negroes and to cease using the closed shop as a device for racial discrimination.

The Taft-Hartley Act also provided that a union could negotiate legal forms of union security only after a special vote of the membership. This was based on a belief that employees would reject compulsory unionism. The opposite proved to be the case. Between 1947 and 1951, when these elections were conducted, over 75% of the 6,545,001 eligible employees voted for the union shop and authorized negotiations for it in 97% of the cases.[6] The net effect was twofold—a bipartisan movement to repeal this voting requirement, which was accomplished by the Taft-Humphrey amendments of 1951; and a general spread of union-shop agreements throughout industry. Companies such as General Motors and United States Steel, which had accepted maintenance-of-membership provisions only under National War Labor Board compulsion, now agreed to the union shop after their employees had voted in favor of it.

"Right-to-Work" Laws and the Union-Management Power Relationship

In the long run, the most significant provision of Taft-Hartley relating to union security is probably Section 14(*b*), which provides that "Nothing in this Act shall be construed as authorizing the execution or application of agreements requiring membership in a labor organization as a condition of employment in any State or Territory in which such execution or application is prohibited by State or Territorial Law." This provision ran counter to the usual principle that state laws are superseded by federal legislation on the same subject matter. The Taft-Hartley Act not only applied the state law but declared further that the state law should apply to employers engaged in interstate commerce, as well as those whose business was purely local.

Thus the clear purpose of Section 14(*b*) was to give states the right to legislate in this field; and many did, outlawing union security provisions altogether. Nineteen states now prohibit such agreements;[7] and a twentieth, Louisiana, which once had such legislation, repealed it, except insofar as it applies to agriculture. Indiana also repealed its law. The issue of whether a state should outlaw union security provisions is very much alive in several states and highly emotional. The use of the term "right-to-work laws" is indicative of the emotional content. These laws give no

---

[6] Data from *Monthly Labor Review*, August, 1953, p. 837. An analysis of these votes is presented in Northrup and Bloom, *op. cit.*, pp. 236–41.

[7] Alabama, Arizona, Arkansas, Florida, Georgia, Iowa, Kansas, Mississippi, Nebraska, Nevada, North Carolina, North Dakota, South Carolina, South Dakota, Tennessee, Texas, Utah, Virginia, and Wyoming.

one a right to work—except insofar as union security provisions interfere with that right.

Because of the emotional content of the arguments pro or con, the union security issue, and hence right-to-work laws, some observers have expressed the belief that the issue itself is largely symbolic and political rather than economic and significant in the union-management relationship.[8] Yet, even the Taft-Hartley union-shop polls found a significant minority of workers who declined to support the union shop. This minority—about 23%—is a substantial number of members (and dues)— enough to affect a power balance, to pay the costs of a lot of strike benefits, or to employ a squad of union organizers.[9]

Other investigations support the view that in the absence of compulsory union provisions, a significant minority of employees in bargaining unions remain nonunion.[10] By restricting union income, state right-to-work laws must certainly affect the union-management relationship more basically than in a symbolic manner.

CONTROL OF ENTRANCE TO THE TRADE

Attempts to control entrance to the trade are limited largely to craft unions. Except for a few, such as the United Mine Workers, who have been able to utilize license laws in a few areas, industrial unions do not find it feasible to control entrance. Their members learn their tasks by experience. They permit the employer to recruit the work force and exert their control in other ways.

Craft unions, however, have found that control of entrance is an effective method of increasing their bargaining power. Their efforts take two principal forms: regulation of apprenticeship and support of licensing legislation.

Regulation of Apprenticeship

Apprenticeship is a way by which young men who meet certain standards of age, education, and aptitude learn a trade by working at it under close supervision and usually combine such practical learning with appropriately related part-time schooling. Nearly all unions whose membership includes journeymen, for which apprenticeship is customary, attempt to regulate the terms and conditions under which apprentices are employed.

Apprenticeship is, however, only one of the many ways in which a

[8] This seems to be the conclusion of Professor Frederic Meyers, "*Right to Work*" *in Practice* (New York: Fund for the Republic, Inc., 1959). For a critique of Meyers' conclusions, see John M. Glasgow, "The Right-to-Work Law Controversy Again," *Labor Law Journal*, Vol. XVIII (February, 1967), pp. 112–15.

[9] See Northrup and Bloom, *op. cit.*, pp. 235–38; and Glasgow, *loc. cit.*

[10] *Ibid.*

vocational aptitude may be gained. Indeed, in most occupations, training is acquired by other means: in other countries (immigration), in trade or vocational schools, in the armed services, in federal or state training courses, by working informally as an understudy (for example, as a hod carrier to a bricklayer and thereby learning bricklaying), or just picking up the trade piece by piece in various shops or locations. Consequently, only about one fourth of American unions actually participate in apprenticeship regulation. From a pre–World War II figure of 17,300, the number of apprentices grew to a high of 230,823 in 1950 and then has declined steadily to 158,616, where it appears to have stabilized.[11] This recent decline in the number of apprentices reflects the drop of new apprentices in the building trades, and particularly in carpentry and bricklaying. The building trades account for 65% of all registered apprentices, with another 15% in metal trades, 8% in printing trades, and the balance scattered thinly throughout industry. Despite a substantial increase in building-trades journeymen between 1950 and 1960, apprentices in this industry fell in all trades except electrical work.[12]

The most common method of regulating apprenticeship is to control the proportion of apprentices to journeymen. This protects journeymen against any tendency on the part of employers to displace journeymen with apprentices. Agreements in the building or printing trades normally contain provisions for the employment of one apprentice to every four to eight journeymen. In addition, many unions negotiate agreements which place an absolute limit on the number of apprentices who can be hired.

In addition to controlling the number of apprentices by a direct limitation, unions can also control apprentice training by controlling the wages of apprentices. The higher the wages of apprentices are set, the more costly it is for the employer to use apprentices. Thus a liberal ratio of apprentices to journeymen may be nullified by an unreasonable rate for the use of apprentices.

Few unions require the serving of an apprenticeship as a condition of membership. Perhaps more would do so if they completely controlled entrance to their trade. The fact of the matter is, however, that so many Americans either pick up a trade without formal training or have secured their training by other means that unions could not sustain a requirement that apprentice training be an absolute prerequisite to membership.

[11] See F. F. Foltman, "Public Policy in Apprenticeship Training and Skill Development," in *Nation's Manpower Revolution* (Hearings before the Subcommittee on Employment and Manpower of the Committee on Labor and Public Welfare, U.S. Senate, 88th Cong., 1st sess., May 20, 1963, *et seq.* [Washington, D.C.: U.S. Government Printing Office, 1963]), Part 6, p. 2163; and U.S. Department of Labor, *Manpower Report of the President, 1964* (Washington, D.C.: U.S. Government Printing Office, March, 1964), Table F–7. See also, Richard L. Rowan, "Discrimination and Apprentice Regulation in the Building Trades," *Journal of Business*, Vol. XL (October, 1967), pp. 435–47.

[12] Phyllis Groom, "Statistics on Apprenticeship and Their Limitations," *Monthly Labor Review*, Vol. LXXXVII (April, 1964), pp. 392–93.

The reasonableness of union apprentice regulation varies from industry to industry. There has been considerable evidence in certain trades, including building and printing, that union apprentice regulations have been utilized to prevent newcomers from winning a place in the industry; and in other cases, such limitations have actually created artificial shortages of labor. Moreover, in many of these trades, apprentice regulations have been utilized to confine apprentice training to friends or relatives of journeymen and to exclude Negroes and other minority groups from participation.

Discrimination against Negroes in apprenticeship participation has been a serious matter because there are few other ways in which Negroes can learn these trades. Not having friends and relatives in jobs, except in the southern trowel trades (bricklaying, plastering, and cement finishing) where there has been a tradition of Negro craftsmen since slavery days, Negroes have been compelled to depend upon formal training if they desired such skilled work. Informal training based on working with family or friends, or otherwise picking up the trade, a common method of instruction, depends on contacts largely unavailable to Negroes. Yet the formal plans in such fields as building construction have been in practice reserved for whites only, with very few exceptions until recently.

Now that the bars are beginning to be lifted and the federal and several state governments are making a strong drive to open up apprenticeship jobs to Negroes, qualified Negro applicants are very scarce. Those with the requisite backgrounds, particularly in high school mathematics, are as their white counterparts, more likely to be interested in a college education than in apprenticeship training. Many Negroes whose schools are either in the city slums or in largely segregated southern areas, find that their training has been inferior. Special training and assistance is now recognized as required if Negroes are to gain a fair share of skilled craft work, and several plans are now in operation to provide this. Moreover, it appears that the national building-trades unions now realize that they must admit Negro apprentices, although many locals are still reluctant to move forward.

Unions perform some definite services in regard to apprentice training. For one thing, the existence of a strong union prevents an employer from keeping an apprentice on a particular task he has mastered instead of giving him a well-rounded mechanical education. The temptation for employers to confine apprentices to a small section of the mechanic's job is very great, for in such cases they are receiving work of mechanic's quality for apprenticeship wages. In addition, apprentices who jump their training usually find the existence of a union a bar to attempts to pass themselves off as journeymen. This protects the public and the employer against poorly trained mechanics.

On the other hand, unions have tended to maintain or even to extend the terms of apprenticeship when they have become obsolete. Thus, it is highly doubtful whether today four or five years is a necessary term for learning many of the building crafts which require apprenticeships of that duration. It would appear probable that these terms could be shortened, but unions fear to do this because their rules and restrictions are based on the number who can be expected to become journeymen after four- and five-year apprenticeships. Any reduction in the terms would probably be accompanied by a reduction in the percentage of apprentices permitted in union agreements.

Apprentice training as a whole is not likely to be a very efficient method of providing qualified labor when it is needed. Typically, during periods of depression, no apprentices are trained, so that in following periods of prosperity, there is a great shortage of skilled labor. Then in the prosperity period the number of apprentices being trained increases tremendously. By the time some of these apprentices become qualified journeymen, business conditions and their opportunities for employment have worsened. If apprenticeship training is to be continued, it may have to be done at public expense in order to insure a continuous supply of skilled craftsmen. If that is done, however, care should be taken not to institutionalize some of the deficiencies of the apprenticeship system.

Licensing Legislation

A number of unions have sought to limit entrance to the trade by means of licensing legislation. Most prominent among them have been the plumbers, electricians, barbers, miners, stationary engineers and firemen, and motion-picture operators. These unions have sponsored state laws and municipal ordinances which require workers in the trade to pass tests as a condition of employment therein. Generally, these laws give unions and employer associations prominent places in their administration. Ostensibly, they are enacted in the interest of the safety of the consumer. Actually, their real purpose from a union point of view is to limit entrance into the trade and to increase union bargaining power by making it more difficult for employers to employ strikebreakers.

Few careful studies of licensing legislation have ever been made.[13] Such evidence as is available, however, indicates quite clearly that licensing laws are frequently abused and that their value to the consumer varies considerably. For example, such laws may be used as a vehicle for race discrimination, or to restrict artificially the number of qualified mechanics.

The problem of licensing legislation extends beyond the limitations of unions. The medical, legal, dental, and the other professions which

---

[13] Two excellent studies are, Elton Rayark, *Professional Power and American Medicine: The Economics of the American Medical Association* (Cleveland: World Publishing Co., 1967); and F. Marion Fletcher, *Market Restraints in the Retail Drug Industry* (Industrial Research Unit Study No. 43 [Philadelphia: University of Pennsylvania Press, 1967]).

advocate licensing legislation have encountered the same problems. Studies of the practices of physicians and pharmacists indicate that there is considerable use of licensing laws to limit competition and to monopolize services and markets.[14] Licensing laws which are sold to the public as a means of protecting the consumer are easily perverted into tools for enhancing restrictive practices.

CONTROL OF HIRING

In an unorganized labor market the employer controls both hiring and layoffs. When a union enters the picture, it must secure some voice in at least one of these vital matters. Otherwise, the union can be of little service to members who fear discrimination because of union membership or who want hirings and/or layoffs conducted by rules rather than by employer fiat.

Methods of Controlling Hiring

The most common method of controlling hiring is by means of the closed shop, requiring employers to hire only members of the union or, if no union members are available, persons willing to join the union. Some agreements go further by requiring the employer to hire only through the union office or through a hiring hall which may be controlled by the union, by the union and the employer in cooperation, or by a third body, for example, a government bureau.

Control over layoffs often involves indirect control over hiring, especially if, as on the railroads, employment is declining on a secular basis. In the railroad industry the seniority agreements provide for preference for furloughed men in rehiring in the order of the furloughed men's seniority, i.e., length of service with the company. If there is a large pool of furloughed men, the employer's freedom to hire is restricted almost as severely under this type of seniority agreement as under the closed shop.

As in the case of control over entrance to the trade, control over hiring is practiced mainly by the craft unions. The main exceptions involve, first, such control over hiring as result from control over layoffs (for example, seniority provisions); and, second, control over hiring by industrial unions in industries where employment is casual and intermittent or seasonal, as in the maritime or needle trades. Most other unions do not operate in labor markets which permit them to exert control over hiring. Hence, except indirectly through seniority provisions, most industrial unions concentrate on control of layoffs and do not attempt to restrict employer control of hiring.

Hiring Halls

It is quite common in many industries where the average employer is small and the unions are organized on a craft basis for the employer to

[14] *Ibid.*

hire through the union office. Sometimes, this custom arose more as a convenience to employers who wanted a central hiring office than as a means of union control. Generally, however, it is a result of union demands, provoked by special market conditions. In trades or industries where employment is intermittent or casual—for example, building or maritime—hiring through the union is the only method by which the union can secure equal division of work for its membership and end systems whereby a small portion of the membership secures the bulk of the available work.

Although unions may demand that employers hire through them in order to avoid abuses, the net effect may be the substitution of new abuses for old. For example, in the building trades the business agent has frequently substituted his favoritism for that of the contracting foreman. The opportunities to use job dispensations as a means of building up one's personal political machine within the union are immense, and the temptation is frequently succumbed to. In order to protect themselves against such methods, the rank and file of many unions may require officials to rotate jobs on a first-come, first-served basis. This, however, can place a heavy burden both on employers and on the most efficient men. It severely restricts the right of employers to choose men whom they deem competent. And since, especially in the building trades, where the unions do not control layoffs, the least efficient are the first fired and thus the first in line for new jobs, the efficient men are at a disadvantage once they are laid off.

In the garment trades, where employment is highly seasonal, unions control hiring but permit employers latitude in rejecting employees. Thus a typical agreement provides that employees of a given craft may be sent in rotation, but the employer has the right to discharge without union complaint during a two-week probationary period. Contracts in other industries vary, some giving the employer the right to reject at least two persons sent by the union office for a job; but upon rejection of a third, the union may challenge the employer to prove incompetency through the grievance machinery.

Formal hiring halls are most common in the maritime industry. Because employment in this industry is casual, there is usually a larger labor force attached to it than there are jobs at a given time. This has encouraged a host of antisocial hiring practices and racketeering at the expense of the workers, such as selling jobs, forcing employees to borrow money at exorbitant rates or to patronize retail establishments in which employers have an interest, etc. Repeated exposures of these practices led the states of New York and New Jersey, in 1953, to establish a bistate waterfront commission to run hiring halls in the port of New York. On the West Coast, such halls were established in 1934. They are formally under joint union-management control, but since the dispatcher is a union man, the union is the dominant factor in their control. Most seamen's unions also operate hiring halls.

Closed Unions and Hiring Halls

The union which is "closed"—that is, which will not admit new applicants to membership—is generally painted as antisocial. Like all generalizations in labor relations, this is not always so. In the maritime industry, some restriction of entry is actually desirable. One of the causes of favoritism and racketeering in hiring on the waterfront is the fact that, especially in depressed times, unemployed workers drift there, often attracted by the high hourly rates. If the "drifters" are granted free entry into the organization, the hiring hall becomes a vehicle for sharing poverty rather than sharing work. The unions must therefore either refuse admission to newcomers or enforce some sort of seniority regulations which modify rotation schemes and give preference to the workers who have been longest attached to the industry. The former policy is more often pursued because the admission to membership of workers for whom there are no jobs provides a hard core of opposition to incumbent union officers. Moreover, the "unemployed brothers" are likely to congregate in the union hall and to be able to attend all meetings. They thus are in an excellent position to control union policy out of proportion to their numbers.

CONTROL OF LAYOFFS

The interest of a union in layoff policy stems from two sources: the worker's desire to know where he stands—to know what chance he has of retaining his job in case of a reduction in the labor force—and the union's desire to maintain some control in the employment process, which it can do only by a voice either in hiring or layoffs. Since, for reasons already noted, few unions can control hiring, most attempt to have a strong voice in the procedure which governs layoffs. The most common method of handling layoffs is by seniority.

Seniority

Seniority agreements generally provide that employees in a plant or subdivision thereof shall receive preference in layoffs and rehiring in the order in which they were hired. In some cases, as on the railroads, seniority agreements are quite rigid, the only requirement being ability to perform the job. In other cases, seniority provisions are much weaker, giving the employer the opportunity to select a more competent person over one with greater seniority. A few agreements provide for retention by the employer of a small percentage of personnel in slack times, regardless of seniority, so that the plant will be manned by a key basic work force. Many agreements place the union shop steward or committeeman at the head of the seniority roster.

Seniority is most common in the railroad, automobile, iron, steel, rubber, electrical products, and other mass-production industries. In the mass-production industries the extent of the seniority district or unit varies considerably. Sometimes the seniority district is the plant, sometimes a plant division, or a department, or an occupation, or some combination thereof. In general, management prefers the smallest possible seniority districts, with no provisions for workers to hold seniority in more than one district. Under such regulations, layoffs and rehiring do not involve much dislocation in the plant and hence do not interfere materially with the efficient organization of personnel.

Union and employee preference as to the size of seniority districts varies considerably. In general, in times of unemployment, skilled workers prefer wide seniority districts and unskilled workers narrow ones. This is because skilled workers can replace unskilled ones but not vice versa. Hence the wider the seniority district in times of layoffs, the greater the chance for the skilled worker to find a spot by exercising his seniority, and the greater the chance that the unskilled worker will be pushed out of a job. In times of prosperity the opposite is likely to be true because expanding employment gives unskilled workers the opportunity to advance in the occupational hierarchy, and this they like to do without sacrificing their seniority in their former jobs. On the other hand, skilled workers see in expanding employment more competition for jobs when times become depressed. Hence they favor narrow seniority districts during prosperous periods.

Seniority and Race

A combination of narrow seniority districts and discriminatory employment practices has been used for many years in the southern pulp and paper and tobacco industries, as well as in iron and steel plants in many parts of the country, to confine Negroes to less desirable jobs in these industries. The seniority practices in these industries were not discriminatory per se. Rather they were developed out of the needs of the industry. For example, in pulp and paper, a person worked his way up the paper machine hierarchy of jobs to the top job of machine tender. No one else in the plant could bid on any paper machine jobs except the lowest one, no matter how much plantwide seniority he had, unless he was in the paper machine line of progression. The nature of the job requires long service on the machine to be able to hold the top job. But Negroes were historically denied the right even to bid on the lowest paper machine job. Then when the Civil Rights Act was passed, they had to start at the bottom. This has led to the suggestion that Negroes who were denied previous job rights be given a "seniority credit" in order to help them to achieve their "rightful place" in the job hierarchy—that is, the place where they would perhaps have been if they had not suffered discrimination. The problem, of course, is that many of the jobs, such as those on the paper machine line, require long years of experience, and the job has to be mastered before any seniority credits can be of practical aid. At least, however, the problems caused by the use of seniority to enforce and to perpetuate discrimination are being recognized by government, and remedial action is being taken to prevent the continuance of an inherently discriminatory system.

In the automobile industry, seniority districts are very broad, since more than one half of the jobs are semiskilled. It is easy for persons to move from job to job and for relatively unskilled personnel to master many of the operations. This is a significant reason why the automobile industry is one of the largest, if not the largest, employer of Negroes, who, as we have noted, are relatively less educated and less well represented in jobs requiring a high skill.[15]

Other Effects of Seniority

The widespread use of seniority provisions in industrial relations has other salutary and unfortunate effects. The most important argument in favor of seniority is that it affords the worker knowledge of his position vis-à-vis his fellow workers. Although seniority is frequently confused with security, it should not be, since, if the plant in which the worker holds seniority ceases to operate, seniority is of little value. Moreover, for every worker whom seniority retains on the payroll, another must be discharged. Seniority, however, is an impersonal criterion and rules out the personal favoritism workers fear so much. And it does have a sort of rough justice, since it gives preference to those who have worked the longest and who presumably have the greatest equity in their jobs. These are the sources of its popularity.

On the other hand, it cannot be denied that seniority puts a premium on mediocrity. The person who is least willing and able to take advantage of opportunities in other plants, or who has least ability and therefore does not receive such opportunities, is the one who stands the greatest chance of reaching the top of a seniority roster. For those who like to get ahead by standing still, seniority is a godsend. For those who yearn for the opportunity to advance quickly on merit, seniority is a bane.

In some instances, seniority may improve managerial efficiency. The fact the employers can no longer discharge workers at will forces them to improve selection and training facilities. Moreover, union controls prevent the degrading practice of buying favors from foremen and other such favoritism on the job.

From the community point of view, seniority gives the not-quite-so-efficient worker an opportunity to improve instead of being cast out, often prematurely, as unemployable. And it protects the older worker

---

[15] Herbert R. Northrup, *The Negro in the Automobile Industry* (Racial Policies of American Industry, Report No. 1 [Philadelphia: Industrial Research Unit, Wharton School of Finance and Commerce, University of Pennsylvania, 1968]).

with many years of efficient service from being laid off in times of slack employment.

Seniority causes many internal union problems. For example, there is frequently dispute over what constitutes length of service. Occasionally, service is interrupted for one reason or another, and a wide divergence of opinion is likely to arise both between employer and union and among employees as to whether breaks in seniority for one or another reason should be overlooked. On numerous occasions, internal union disputes over seniority provisions and their interpretation have resulted in lengthy and costly litigation.

Seniority provisions have an effect on strikes. Generally, senior men are less willing to strike because they have more to lose. Once on strike, senior men are likely to be apprehensive at the slightest hint that their jobs are being filled. At the same time, junior men are likely to be strongly tempted to return to work in order to leap from the bottom to the top of the seniority roster. Once men return to work, strikes may drag on over the issue of whether the strikebreakers can maintain their positions or place on the seniority roster.

Juniority

Pay to employees who are not working has now reached a stage in some industries where it literally almost pays not to work. In the rubber tire and automobile industries, for example, the differential which a worker receives for working (that is, wages less paycheck deductions) as compared with what a laid off employee gets from state unemployment compensation plus supplemental unemployment pay, can amount to as little as $10 to $25 per week.[16] In view of this fact, agreements between the United Rubber Workers and the major tire manufacturers permit a senior employee to take layoff instead of working where the layoff is involuntary. The senior employee cannot choose just not to work, but he can substitute for a junior employee who would otherwise be laid off. Thus the junior man can get the job, the senior man, the enforced leisure with pay. This is the first recognition in union contracts that layoffs may be preferable to working and that the penalty for juniority may be a requirement to stay on the job.

Division of Work

In a number of industries, division of work is either substituted entirely for the seniority principle or combined with it. The garment trades provide the outstanding example of the complete use of division of work as union layoff policy and the almost complete absence of the seniority principle. The reason is that the average worker in the garment trades is employed not by one company but by several during a given

---

[16] Unemployment compensation and supplemental unemployment pay are discussed in Chapter 18.

year. The industry is highly seasonal, so that a worker who has 25 years' experience in the labor market may be the last one employed by a shop which is no longer able to operate at full capacity. The seniority principle would work a hardship on the more experienced worker because he happened to be the last hired during a particular season. Hence most contracts in the garment trades provide for complete division of work among all but probationary employees in the shop, regardless of length of service.

Division of work was once much more widely utilized as a layoff control than it is today. The reason is the combination effect of higher layoff benefits and higher paycheck withholding. Division of work can reduce take-home pay very close to the level of benefits paid under state unemployment compensation systems. When supplemental unemployment benefits are added to state benefits, as in the automobile and steel industries, take-home pay under a division-of-work system can even be less than benefits for not working. Since division of work is also usually less efficient than laying off unnecessary men, it now has little popularity except in special situations.

There is, however, one situation in the automobile industry where a form of division of work is used and combined with a special form of unemployment pay. Instead of laying off assembly-line workers, companies now often put their labor force on two- or three-day weeks. Employees then receive "short-week pay" to make up some of the lost pay. Manufacturers prefer this because they do not have to slow up the line and reassign each and every job that is left. If, however, business does not improve in time, then layoffs are made and jobs restructured accordingly.

Dismissal Wages

In addition to seniority and division of work, recent years have seen a considerable increase in interest in dismissal wages. Dismissal compensation is fundamentally a device to mitigate losses resulting from permanent dismissal rather than temporary layoffs. It is utilized in instances in which employees are severed from the payroll as a result of plant abandonment or movement to another area, or as a result of a permanent decrease in the working force. In cases of permanent severance of employees who are near, but have not achieved, the retirement age, a dismissal wage may be used to make up earnings until the employee reaches the age when he is eligible for a pension. Dismissal pay usually provides a schedule of payments based upon length of service. It is very common in the newspaper industry, which has seen many concerns go out of business in recent years. In many other industries, companies and unions have negotiated a dismissal pay schedules after the decision has been made to go out of business or to close a plant. Dismissal wages are discussed further in Chapter 18 with other measures designed to give security against unemployment.

PROTECTING AGAINST LAYOFFS

Seniority, division of work, and dismissal wages are all means to *mitigate* the effects of layoffs. But unions also strive to protect their members against layoffs. Among the methods utilized to do this are provisions for retraining, limiting of contracting-out, and "make-work" or "featherbedding" restrictions.

Retraining

Widespread displacement of blue-collar employees in the mass-production industries during the late 1950's generated considerable interest in retraining by industry, unions, and government. The federal government began a program in 1961. Vocational education by government is not new, but the Manpower Development and Training Act of 1962 and the Area Redevelopment Act of the previous year marked a broader entry into the training and retraining field which was especially aimed at the unemployed and which more recently has been designed to help "disadvantaged" persons, particularly Negroes and members of other minority groups, obtain jobs in industry. The steel industry and the United Steelworkers, in cooperation with the government, have launched a widespread program to help those on the payrolls, and potential but disadvantaged recruits. Those selected for training do not have sufficient education or training to go beyond laborer jobs. They are aided in acquiring the necessary skills by a combination of classroom work and on-the-job training. A similar program has been started in the building construction industry by the Carpenters' Union and various contractors. Most of those being trained in such programs are Negroes or members of other minority groups.

From the union point of view, interest in training already displaced workers or those never employed is secondary to attempting to gain retraining for those still on the job but threatened by displacement. In the last decade, the authors have observed an increasing union interest in provisions designed to give training (often at employer expense) to employees to qualify them for new opportunities.[17] In addition, many of the larger companies make available opportunities for employees to take appropriate training on their own time and at their own expense. If the pace of technological change continues, one may expect a rising interest in such retraining, and perhaps it may become a major focus of union demands in some industries.

Another union proposal—the training of blue-collar personnel for

---

[17] For a study of a broad retraining and resettlement program in the meat-packing industry in which there has been considerable technological displacement and plant closings, see George P. Shultz and Arnold R. Weber, *Strategies for the Displaced Worker* (New York: Harper & Row Publishers, 1966).

white-collar jobs—is likely to meet with more employer resistance. Many blue-collar workers do advance to white-collar jobs. But industry is likely to go slowly to advance union-oriented factory workers to its as yet largely unorganized office work force.

Contracting-Out and Part-Time Work

Few issues in recent years have generated more heat both between companies and unions, and among unions themselves, than has the contracting-out of work. Most manufacturing enterprises do not make everything they assemble. They "contract out" or buy parts from various suppliers. In turn, such companies may make parts for other companies if they have capacity in some departments. The reasons for this are manifold but basically fall into two categories: (1) The ability to make parts or items better and cheaper varies among companies; therefore, it is often not good business for a concern to make all of its parts. (2) Some parts or components are not required in sufficient volume to make it profitable for a company to tool up, purchase equipment, or employ or train labor in order to make them itself. And of course, much contracting-out takes place because firms often find parts companies who have lower labor costs and can do the job for less.

From time to time, also, the ability to make parts varies. Capacity might be reached so as to force a company to contract out work in order to meet delivery dates. When orders decline, work previously contracted out may be done within the company. Loading and manning factors also may force contracting-out. For example, one department may be overloaded while another is short of work. Yet the short-of-work department may not have the skills or equipment to aid the overloaded one.

In recent years, there has been an increase in another type of contracting-out—that of such services as typing and secretarial work, janitorial service, plant guarding, even engineering work, and in some chemical and petroleum concerns, all maintenance work. Companies have found that it is cheaper to pay an agency to supply temporary office help in order to meet peak loads than it is to have employees on the payroll who cannot be kept busy. High wages and fringe benefits have raised the costs of employing guards and janitors to a point where it is economic to contract out such work.

Companies supplying contract labor have had no difficulty in finding workers who desire this type of employment. Temporary employees are the fastest growing segment of the labor force, with almost 10 million persons so occupied. The married woman who wants to work only a few days per week, or a few hours each day while her children are in school, the teacher or fireman who "moonlights" during off hours for more income, the student putting himself through college, all swell the part-time labor force. Unions in industrial plants are opposed both to contracting-out and to using part-time labor. Being responsive to fears of the people in the plant that contracting-out costs them jobs, and finding that part-timers have little interest in becoming union members or dues payers, unions have naturally put pressure on management to restrict such practices. Some of these restrictions are very tight and deny essential managerial flexibility required to maintain delivery schedules or profitable operations. Other clauses simply require management to notify unions why contracting-out is necessary. Many managements do this anyway, in order to allay fears and otherwise avoid controversy or support for restrictive union demands. As has already been noted, the National Labor Relations Board now requires that management bargain on the decision to contract out as well as on the impact of such contracting-out on employees; presumably also, such decisions are subject to arbitration under the contract unless the agreement contains a specific disclaimer to the contrary.

The building-trades unions, in contrast to those in industrial plants, not only are unopposed to contracting-out or to the use of temporary help, but enthusiastically support such measures as a means of furthering the employment of their members. The building-trades unions have worked with a number of contractors to promote the idea of having all maintenance work done by contract labor, and this policy has been adopted by a large number of petroleum and chemical firms. The companies using contract maintenance have been well satisfied with it and believe that it provides a sound solution to their needs for a varying number of maintenance employees at different times.[18] The industrial unions, of course, regard contract maintenance as an invasion of their jurisdiction and a method of denying work to their members. Because of such opposition, contract maintenance is most likely to be found in new or unorganized plants in the future.

"MAKE WORK" OR "FEATHERBEDDING"

Insecurity of the worker in modern industry has led employees to "make work" by adopting a variety of policies. These make-work or "featherbedding" arrangements often exist among unorganized as well as organized employees, but the entrance of a union can have the effect of formalizing and strengthening them.

Restrictions on Output

Restrictions on output, direct or indirect, are the most common make-work practice. Formal restrictions are not very common in industry, although reference to them sometimes occurs in union literature or even in collective bargaining contracts. Usually, however, the restrictions are disguised as health protective devices or, more likely, simply based on tacit understanding among employees. Restrictions, both formal and in-

[18] See James H. Jordan, "How to Evaluate the Advantages of Contract Maintenance," *Chemical Engineering*, Vol. LXXV (March 25, 1968), pp. 124–30.

formal, are more often found under incentive than daywork systems because workers often fear that a "world beater" among them will earn so much that he will force the more average employees either to quit or to work at an exhausting pace.

Restrictions on output and other forms of make-work policies are also the result of fear on the part of employees that they will work themselves out of a job. Most employees believe that there is a given amount of work and that by stretching it out, each employee will receive more. This notion is, of course, fallacious. If employees restrict production, the result is higher costs and higher prices; consumers buy less of the product; and in the end, employment opportunities are diminished. In industries such as building construction, however, the individual worker may stretch out his immediate employment by slowing up on the job, even though the long-run effect of the slow down may well be less work because of resultant high costs.

Limits set on output are usually enforced by social pressure rather than by union rule. True, sometimes men have been fined for getting out too much work. More often, whether the plant is unionized or not, the speed of work deemed appropriate by the majority is enforced by their refusing to engage in social relationships with other workers who "speed up." The latter, finding themselves outcasts from the groups to which they belong, are likely to conform to the "social output" very quickly.

Limits on output frequently become more obsolete as machinery improves and worker efficiency rises. As time passes, such restrictions are often self-defeating. The result may be either loss of membership in the union or inability to organize nonunion shops because the lack of restrictions in the latter establishments can permit nonunion employee earnings to rise above union earnings. Since the national union leadership is likely to be more interested in organizing nonunion shops than is local union leadership, severe restrictions on output favored by locals are often vigorously opposed by national unions.

Restrictions on output may be effected by indirect methods. Thus, instead of setting a quota, the same results may be achieved by retarding speed of performance—for example, by limiting the number of machines a man may attend or, as in the case of the Painters' Union, limiting the width of the brush or size of the roller.

Restrictions on output may also be achieved by excessive safety or quality controls. When the New York bus drivers want to slow down, they observe all safety regulations. The result is to put buses an average of 30 minutes behind schedule on moderately long runs. The various building-trades unions have adopted a variety of rules on quality and safety performance which often go beyond the requirements of appropriate authorities or of fire insurance underwriters. The object is quite apparently "make work"; but in addition, these regulations serve as a fertile source of graft for unscrupulous business agents of building-trades unions.

Many instances have occurred in which the business agent will demand that the employer pay a fine or bribe so that construction work will not be interrupted by a strike called because of a "rule" infraction.

Unnecessary Work and Unnecessary Men

Some of the most obvious featherbedding results from union requirements that unnecessary work be done, that work be done by time-consuming methods, or that unnecessary men be hired. The building, amusement, and railroad industries are characterized by a good deal of such union policies. For example, it is standard practice for the Plumbers' Union to require that pipes be threaded on the job, even though it is far more economical to do the threading in the shop. The International Typographical Union requires that when plates or papier-mâché matrices are exchanged, as they frequently are, the matter be reset, read, and corrected within a stipulated period, and that proof be submitted to the union chairman in the office. The Meat Cutters often require that pre-wrapped meat be rewrapped on the job. In 1968, the Brotherhood of Railroad Trainmen demanded that railroads eliminate the use of radio telephones by crewmen and go back to the hand signals and lanterns of the age of the coal-burning locomotives. According to the union, this would mean more jobs and would increase safety!

The employment of unnecessary men is typified by the manner in which the Brotherhood of Locomotive Firemen and Enginemen was able for years to maintain a "fireman" on diesel engines, even though his firing function did not exist; or by the excessive complements carried by American ships—about one third more than by foreign ships. By refusing to permit workers to do jobs outside of their narrowly defined craft jurisdictions, unions in the building, amusement, and railway industries likewise prevent the most effective utilization of manpower and thus require the employment of unnecessary men.

Seniority, Job Ownership, and Featherbedding

Featherbedding was once considered primarily a problem involving craft unions and craft-organized industries. But it appears also in manufacturing enterprises organized by industrial unions. The avenue by which featherbedding most often enters such an industrial situation is through an expansion of the concept of seniority.

The argument goes like this: If a man has seniority in a particular occupation, then he alone can perform the work, even though other persons are qualified to do it. By seniority, he acquires exclusive ownership in his job. Then only a person in that craft can be assigned to the job if the person who "owns" the job is not available.

Similarly, according to this reasoning, if an employee "owns" a job, the employer is no longer permitted to contract it out; and if, in the exercise of what he thinks is his management function, he does so, the employee is entitled to be paid for not working. In a similar view, the National Labor Relations Board has ruled that no contracting-out can be undertaken without consultation with the union—presumably to protect the employees' rights to their seniority.

Few managements could have believed that signing a seniority agreement would mean turning over job ownership as well. Although in the past, industrial unions generally have not sought such an interpretation of seniority, they are increasingly doing so. The pressure is strongest in times of layoffs, when the principle of job ownership can save a man's job. Of course, the added cost involved may eventually result in additional unemployment, including the worker whose job was supposedly saved. But this possibility usually does not seem imminent to those advocating restrictions.

A related idea is that of job confinement—if a job is owned by a particular craft, its limits must be confined or circumscribed. Recently, a strike over this issue occurred at a large machine shop, when some small groups of chippers and flame gaugers were instructed to squirt oil on castings so they could see where they were working. Through their local unions the groups charged that squirting oil from a can was outside the jurisdiction of their jobs, and demanded that somebody else do the work.

In no industry are job ownership and make-work practices more prevalent than in newspaper publishing. Yet such practices have certainly not brought with them worker security. Rather, by adding on to costs and decreasing productivity, they have no doubt materially contributed to the decline of firms in the industry and to the demise within three years of four newspapers in New York City alone.

Make-Work Legislation

A number of laws have been passed at the prodding of special-interest groups which are ostensibly in the interest of the consumer but actually go considerably beyond that. In this category are a number of building codes and railway "safety" legislation. The former frequently discriminates against prefabricated materials, even where prefabrication products are equal to, or in many cases superior to, on-the-job construction. In addition, particularly in plumbing and electrical work, building codes stipulate that certain jobs be done by licensed mechanics and include therein work which is obviously unskilled and can be performed with no danger by the average homeowner. These codes carry on the policy of many building unions of attempting to secure as much work as possible for their crafts, even though much of it is easily performed by unskilled or semiskilled labor.

The railroad unions have expended much effort to secure "full-crew" and train-length-limit legislation. The former requires a minimum crew on all trains, ostensibly in the interests of safety but quite clearly often resulting in the employment of unneeded personnel. The latter limits the number of cars which can be attached to a single train. In a series of court tests a number of train-length laws have been declared unconstitutional. The full-crew laws keep unnecessary firemen and trainmen on trains.

Comments on "Make Work"

Make-work rules are a wasteful method of dealing with the problems of unemployment and insecurity, since they add to the cost of production and, as a result, probably often curtail total employment. In many cases, make-work provisions so raise costs that wages are lower than they might otherwise be. An excessive use of make-work rules may seriously limit a union's effectiveness, for it may cause internal dissension between those favoring limits and those favoring higher earnings. Also, as already noted, limits on work may permit nonunion earnings to exceed union ones and thus prevent a union from organizing nonunion workers who are not interested in decreased earnings.

Make-work rules do not eliminate the intermittent employment which is found in the building and amusement industries, where their use is common; nor have make-work rules halted the secular decline in railway employment. Actually, by attracting more labor to an industry than is needed, make-work rules aggravate these evils.

Make-work policies present a difficult problem in terms of public policy. One method of attempted regulation is illustrated by the Taft-Hartley Act and a few similar state laws. Section 8(*b*) (6) of the Taft-Hartley Act makes it an unfair labor practice for a union "to cause or attempt to cause an employer to pay or deliver or agree to pay or deliver any money or other thing of value in the nature of an exaction, for services which are not performed or not to be performed." This clause was sometimes referred to as the "antifeatherbedding" provision; but actually, its scope has been construed by the courts and the National Labor Relations Board to be much more limited than the practice of make-work rules which is ordinarily encompassed within the term "featherbedding." Although make-work rules are wasteful and costly to the public, it is doubtful whether they can be dealt with effectively by legislation. What agency, for example, is to pass judgment on how fast a man should work, or how many men should be required to operate a given machine, or at exactly what point a job requires a skilled craftsman and at what point little skill is necessary?

To be sure, extreme cases are easy to detect. Legislation, however, would have to leave extraordinary discretion to a government bureau. To do its job, that bureau would be compelled to pass judgment on a variety of labor relations matters and would thus end up regulating industrial relations to a degree which neither labor, business, nor the public would find desirable.

There is another aspect to make-work rules and public policy which cannot be ignored. Restriction of output on the part of labor organizations is only one type of such restriction in the economy. Many businessmen restrict output in order to keep prices high. Numerous professional societies have urged enactment of legislation which would permit only licensed personnel to pursue a profession, but the definition of the profession often goes beyond the need for professional competence. In New Jersey the State Bar Association attempted unsuccessfully to have the negotiation of labor-management contracts declared the practice of law. If the attempt had succeeded, nonmembers of the state bar would have been unable to compete with lawyers for the right to aid labor and management unless no compensation was accepted. Farmers continually restrict production, plow under crops, and let fruit rot on the trees in order to bolster prices. Indeed, farmers are often encouraged to do this by law! Should only labor restrictions be regulated? Equality of treatment under the law would seem to require that all groups be equally affected or unaffected by legislation.

Before advocating legislation, it is well to realize that many featherbedding practices are the result of managerial mistakes or inadequacies. For example, the fireman issue on the diesel engine arose because railway management believed in 1936 that diesels were only a special-purpose engine that would never replace steam. "Bogus" work in printing derived from managerial desire to charge advertisers a full rate and was once actually encouraged by newspaper publishers. Wasteful ship crew and longshore complements grew out of cost-plus practices during World War II and employer profits on such overmanning. Numerous other featherbedding rules have resulted from managerial failure to make decisions on a long-run instead of an immediate-profit basis. Why should government be called upon to bail out managerial incompetence?

Moreover, despite the restrictions in American industry, effective utilization of labor is far greater here than elsewhere in the world. Some commentators believe that the shortage of labor abroad is artificial, being the result of wasteful practices. This does not condone the practices described here, but it does help keep them in perspective.[19]

TECHNOLOGICAL CHANGE AND AUTOMATION

The introduction of new machinery or methods may be beneficial to union members by easing the physical strains or improving the safety of

[19] For example, "There is no shortage of labor [in Britain]. Virtually every employer in British industry is underemployed. . . . In the British culture at this moment, a rather high proportion of the work force takes a substantial part of his wages not in money but in leisure, most particularly in the leisure that is taken at the place of employment. . . ." From a report by the American consultant W. W. Allen, first published in the *London Sunday Times* and reproduced in part in *Fortune*, May, 1964, pp. 62 and 67.

the job, or by bringing in more work and hence increasing employment. In some cases, unions have agitated for technological improvements. Thus the Brotherhood of Locomotive Firemen and Enginemen went to the Interstate Commerce Commission in order to force railroads to adopt the automatic stoker for coal-burning engines. Light, faster trucks have created more jobs for truck drivers; and larger, faster airplanes have made more jobs for pilots. There are many other such examples.

On the other hand, many technological developments affect workers adversely, at least immediately. They make the job more hazardous or more difficult, or they may reduce employment in particular plants. For example, paint spraying can cause lead poisoning; the substitution of the one-man streetcar for two-man operation certainly makes the job of the operator more difficult; the introduction of the continuous strip mill resulted in the abandonment of many hand-rolled steel mills; and the diesel engine eliminated the need for firemen.

Obstruction

The adverse effects of technological change have led a number of unions at various times actively to oppose shifts in methods of production. Opposition to technological change may take several forms. The most common is refusal to work with new machines. Workers can also reduce output, demand prohibitive pay, or even ask for legislation in their fight against change.

Few industrial unions adopt obstruction policies, although occasionally some of their locals may do so. The reason is that the average technological development does not affect all members of an industrial union; and therefore, it cannot go "all out" for the interests of a minority of its members. On the other hand, all members of a craft union are likely to be directly affected by an alteration in the methods of production.

In some cases, obstruction has been successful. Thus, plumbers have prevented the use of pipe-threading machines, and the bricklayers of automatic bricklaying equipment. But this "success" has been limited in the case of the plumbers by the use of tubing instead of piping, and connections by soldering and other means which avoid threading; and in the case of bricklaying by other means of facing, such as glass, poured concrete, or aluminum.

Opposition to technological change can rarely be successful for long, for if the new methods are superior, some enterprising manager will find a way to use the new technique or to surmount the old one by a substitutable process or technology. Then the union will have to decide whether to give up its opposition or to see its members unemployed. At this point, national union leaders, anxious to preserve the union, may find themselves at odds with members or local leaders whose prime objective is to work out their lives—or as long as possible—on the old techniques and methods which they know.

Worker opposition to technological change dates back at least to the Industrial Revolution, when the textile workers of Lancashire smashed newly installed machines.

The appearance of something new, whether in the form of a new labor-saving device, a new incentive system, a new kind of supervision, or a new process, seems to sound an alert among men at work; they mount guard, as it were, suspicious in advance that the change bodes them no good. The problem that emerges becomes particularly baffling when time and time again it appears immaterial whether an innovation affects the workers adversely or not. Indeed, even when it promises them substantial benefit, they still may pull and haul and balk.[20]

Union policies of obstruction are basically reflections of workers' fears that changes will affect them adversely. The union acts to solidify the obstruction or to fight it, but not to create it. Moreover, in many instances, union obstruction has served a good purpose. Opposition of the streetcar motormen to the one-man car led to the invention of the safety-door brake; the fight against the paint spray has helped to develop effective "waterfall" and blower systems to control fumes; and numerous other examples exist of safety measures taken to offset union claims of "health hazards" which, in fact, stem largely from rank-and-file opposition to change.

Perhaps even more important than forcing improvements in machines, union obstruction policies have compelled industry to consider human costs in introducing new methods. Abandoning a plant or eliminating a skill causes tremendous hardship to those affected. By slowing the process or forcing management to make concessions, union obstruction to technological change has reduced the number of employees rendered temporarily useless by progress.

On the other hand, there are many cases, particularly in the building, printing, and other trades, where union obstruction policies have increased consumer costs without apparent benefit to the community.

Competition

If a union finds that a policy of obstruction is failing (usually because nonunion shops are utilizing the new technique and causing unemployment in the union shops), it may attempt to compete with the new method. This takes the form of wage or working rule concessions to employers who retain the old techniques or, in rare instances, of the formation of cooperatives by displaced employees who seek to maintain old methods of operation.

Essentially, the policy of competition is a short-run device adopted for the purpose of slowing the advancement of new techniques and

[20] B. M. Selekman, *Labor Relations and Human Relations* (New York: McGraw-Hill Book Co., 1947), p. 111.

preserving the working lives of employees who would otherwise be displaced. If the new technique is sufficiently superior, wage and working rule concessions are not likely to halt its introduction. Nor can cooperative plants producing by less efficient methods hope to compete permanently with more modern plants.

A policy of competition, nevertheless, is not without social benefit By providing temporary employment for workers who might otherwise be unemployed, it mitigates the hardships of change. Moreover, as in the case of obstruction policies, competition forces improvement in new machines, which are often crude when first introduced, and therefore a policy of competition can result in the reduction of costs and of prices.

Control

In most cases, opposition to technological advancement and union attempts to compete with new techniques are temporary measures. Sooner or later, the union members must decide whether they want the union to survive. If they do, they must work out an agreement with management which permits use of the new invention. In short, the union must adopt a policy which gives it some control over the working conditions which develop under the new technique.

The policy of control may take many forms. In the supermarket industry, for example, the Amalgamated Meat Cutters and Butcher Workmen has generally obstructed the concept of central meat cutting instead of having butchers in each store. Some locals, however, have provided in their contracts that if central meat cutting is introduced, butchers in the stores will receive first opportunity for the jobs and their union will be recognized as bargaining agent in the central plants.[21] In the steel industry, the United Steelworkers has insisted that some of the benefits of machinery go directly to the workers. This has been used as a talking point in wage negotiations and also to implement union arguments that men laid off as a result of new techniques should be given the first opportunity for new job openings. In other cases, unions have negotiated dismissal compensation for men laid off. This tends to lessen rank-and-file opposition to a policy of control. A final method of control is for the union to negotiate high wage rates for work on new machines, which slow down the introduction of the new technique by making it relatively more expensive. As a result, the effect on the working force may be temporarily lessened—unless the net effect is to make the whole operation so high cost that everyone concerned loses his job.

The willingness of a union to adopt a policy of control depends on a variety of factors. Industrial unions are more likely to favor control policies than are craft unions because a new technique often helps one

[21] Herbert R. Northrup and Gordon R. Storholm, *Restrictive Labor Practices in the Supermarket Industry* (Industrial Research Unit Study No. 44 [Philadelphia: University of Pennsylvania Press, 1967]).

part of the industrial union membership even though it hurts another part. Moreover, craft unions may be unwilling or unable to organize employees operating the new machines, or their members may be unwilling or unable to learn new techniques or to work on new machines. Even if workers are willing and able to be retrained, the new technique may be started in a new plant or industry, and the opportunity to work the new technique may simply be unavailable to those utilizing the old methods or equipment.

Unions are much more willing to accept new techniques and methods if jobs are visibly at stake. Competition of nonunion or foreign plants, or of substitute methods or products, and consequent loss of sales and jobs, make clear to employees that costs must be lowered if jobs are to be saved. As such competition strikes closer to home, opposition to technological change tends to decline.

The vast number of technological improvements which have been introduced and their initial ill effect on workers raise the question of why more unions have not adopted policies of obstruction rather than control. The main reason appears to be that most inventions are introduced in times of prosperity and full employment, and indeed contribute to the prosperity. In such times, reemployment of displaced men is more easily effected, and opposition to new techniques is consequently lessened.

AUTOMATION FUNDS AND DISPLACEMENT

Automation

Technological developments since World War II have moved along three basic lines. These developments, termed "automation," can be divided into three fundamental groups.[22]

1. The integration by means of mechanical engineering techniques of conventionally separate manufacturing operations into lines of continuous production untouched by human hands.
2. The use of "feedback" control devices or servomechanisms which permit individual operations to be performed, tested, and/or inspected, and controlled without human control by means of electrical engineering or electronic techniques.
3. The development of computing machines which can record and store information and perform complex mathematical operations on such information largely by means of electrical engineering developments.

The effect of automation on labor utilization has been and is potentially spectacular. Labor displacement in some industries has been severe and in other industries promises to have effects that are even more drastic. In the longshore industry, for example, where ships have been loaded and unloaded by substantially the same methods for many years, an innovation

[22] These definitions were first set forth by G. B. Baldwin and G. P. Shultz in "Automation: A New Dimension to Old Problems," in Industrial Relations Research Association, *Annual Proceedings* (Detroit, 1954), pp. 114–28.

known as "containerization" has been developed. This is the principle whereby products to be transported in ships are loaded in large, fully enclosed containers at the factory or warehouse and the containers are moved directly by cranes from the dock into the vessel (and unloaded by the same method), thus eliminating all manual loading and unloading of ships at the dockside. Adoption of this method affords major reductions in costs and improvement in efficiency of stevedoring operations.

Meat packing is another industry in which automation has already had profound effects on employment. Manual handling of carcasses has been replaced by conveyors; dressing knives are driven by electric motors; hand curing of bacon and ham has given way to "pickling" by needle injections; automatic machines slice, weigh, and package bacon, and stuff and pack sausage. As a result, employment in the meat-packing industry has declined by about 50,000 in an era in which the consumption of meat has steadily risen.

Such problems have led to special collective bargaining action. The West Coast longshore agreement in effect provided that the employers "buy out" the restrictive practices and opposition to technological change by establishing a fund for improved pension and welfare benefits, provisions for early retirement, and other additions to the welfare package of the longshoremen. Since this contract was first negotiated in the early 1950's, employment on West Coast docks has actually risen because of general prosperity and its impact on shipping, because of the requirements of the Vietnam war, and also because of the new efficiency on the docks resulting from improved methods.[23]

Armour and Company and two unions of meat-packing employees also set up a fund. Its purpose has been to study the effects of automation and to attempt to transfer and to retrain employees, or to otherwise improve the opportunities of the displaced. As a result of such efforts, some success has occurred in retraining and relocation of displaced packinghouse employees.[24]

Automation funds of lesser magnitude, or arrangements of a similar nature, have been developed by the American Federation of Musicians, the United Mine Workers, the International Ladies' Garment Workers' Union, and the East Coast longshoremen's union.[25] In addition, the Kaiser and Scanlon plans, discussed in the preceding chapter, have similar aspects insofar as they are attempts to deal logically and consistently with the problem of technological displacement. Likewise, the efforts of unions in the steel and brewing industries to negotiate long vacations or "sabbati-

[23] For a brief discussion of the situation on the West Coast docks, see "Two Views of the Longshore Situation," *Monthly Labor Review*, Vol. XIC (January, 1968), pp. 1–13.

[24] See Shultz and Weber, *loc. cit.*, for a discussion of the Armour program.

[25] A discussion of the various automation funds is found in Thomas Kennedy, *Automation Funds and Displaced Workers* (Boston: Graduate School of Business Administration, Harvard University, 1962).

cals" are motivated principally by the desire to mitigate the impact of technology on employment by sharing the work.

But basically, neither automation funds nor the other arrangements discussed emphasize benefits for displaced workers. Rather, the benefits are designed either entirely or primarily for the purpose of sharing the savings of automation with those employees who are retained on the payroll. Thus such funds are like an extension of the basic policies of unions such as the United Mine Workers which concentrate on high wages for those left on the payroll. Since both managements and unions are interested in present and future employees, not former ones, this should not be surprising—but it should also emphasize that automation funds are designed primarily for those who remain to share in the fruits of technology, and not to care for the displaced. In effect, automation funds are a method of union control of technological change; contributions to the fund add to industry's costs of innovating and can therefore slow it down without completely obstructing the innovation.

Actually, the effects of automation on labor force and skills may well be much greater than their effects on employment. Earlier in this chapter, we noted how automation is tending to change the training needs in industry, rendering obsolete some skills and creating new ones. In Chapter 2, we noted further that automation has helped to reduce the importance of the hourly worker in the labor force and to increase the relative importance of the salaried worker, so that today the hourly worker is in the minority. We also noted that unions have been unable thus far to organize any significant percentage of the salaried employees. This means that even if unions succeeded in controlling the rate of technological progress and automation, such control would affect a sector of the economy continually declining in importance.

EFFECT OF UNION ORGANIZATION ON EFFICIENCY

In many firms, prior to the advent of union organization, management depended upon payment of low wages to keep costs down to a competitive level. Union organization, by removing wage rates from the competitive sphere, can produce a desirable change in emphasis from wage levels to production costs and thereby diminish the divergence in technical standards between the least efficient and most efficient firms in the industry. If the effect of union wage pressure is to make inefficient managers better innovators, the general level of efficiency in industry will benefit. And of course, to the extent that the least efficient firms are eliminated, an automatic increase occurs in the statistical average efficiency of firms left in industry.

Union organization may increase "social efficiency" by slowing down managerial action designed to displace persons or by forcing managers to consider such things as retraining existing employees instead of replacing them. The net effect can be to prolong the working life of people and thus to add to the overall ability of the population to support itself.

Union organization, by raising wages in union plants, increases the cost advantage of nonunion competitors and compels union firms to increase efficiency in order to remain in competition. Moreover, the presence of a strong union with alert shop stewards compels management to justify many production methods and rates, and therefore encourages a more careful examination of costs and production policy. Although union wage pressure probably produces a small net gain in labor efficiency, the difficulties encountered by union plants in holding their markets indicate that the gain is insufficient to offset the increased price of labor.

Union influence upon technical efficiency has a time dimension. Probably the greatest increase in efficiency is forthcoming when an industry is newly organized. Then the wastes may be more obvious and abundant; but after a while, when the backlog of waste is largely exhausted, a point of diminishing returns must be reached. Furthermore, as unionism itself matures and its power in industry grows, it is more likely to bring its own wastes to industry. As a general rule, the more strongly entrenched the position of a union in an industry, the less it is concerned with the efficiency of the individual firms under its jurisdiction. Consequently, even though the possibilities of raising the level of industrial efficiency are considerable, there is room for skepticism regarding the contribution which unionism will make in this respect in the future. Managements in the railroad, printing, and clothing industries have been subjected to union wage pressure over a long period, but it is doubtful whether they are conspicuously more able, thorough, and alert to technological developments than managements in other industries.

UNFAVORABLE EFFECT OF UNION RULES

On the whole, union organization will probably tend to diminish industrial efficiency rather than improve it. The rise of unionism has led to a multiplication of union rules and restrictions which limit the freedom of the employer to revise costly operations and to introduce improved techniques of production. There is no immediate prospect of eliminating the many needless make-work rules which are found at present in organized plants in various industries. Although union wage pressure affords some stimulus to invention and technological progress, it is doubtful whether general union wage adjustments occurring more or less simultaneously over a broad area of industry provide much stimulus to the rate of mechanization. Moreover, whatever stimulus is forthcoming from this source tends to be offset by the restrictive influence of union policies which retard the rate of introduction of laborsaving methods and machinery.

Despite the fact that the leaders of organized labor condemn opposition to laborsaving machinery, the policy still is practiced by individual unions. It is easy for leaders to generalize in sweeping terms about the futility of attempting to stem the advance of progress; but if the individual worker sees in his union a possible barrier to introduction of a new improvement which threatens his job, he is likely to use it. Union organization has not altered the feelings or attitudes of the average worker toward laborsaving machinery, but it has given him the strength to resist or retard technological change, whereas previously he could only voice weak protest.

Management, by and large, is compelled by the profit motive to be interested in reducing costs and improving the quality of the product. These twin objectives of employers ordinarily place management on the side of efficiency in the collective bargaining process. Unions—at least where nonunion competition is not a major problem—are interested primarily in improving earnings and working conditions, and in introducing order, tenure, and stability into the employment relationship. These objectives have important value from the point of view of the community and society; but we should recognize that in many cases, they will conflict with productive efficiency.

QUESTIONS FOR DISCUSSION

1. Do you feel that a union is ever justified in opposing technological change? Can you support your answer from experience?

2. Why is contracting-out so emotional an issue? How is it concerned with union policy and management rights? Why is it so much more in controversy today than formerly?

3. Why is apprenticeship so important to Negroes? What would you do to attempt to increase the number and proportion of Negro craftsmen?

4. Seniority has many ramifications. Discuss its relation to job security and union security, and how it can affect these two objectives of most unions.

SUGGESTIONS FOR FURTHER READING

CHANDLER, MARGARET K. *Management Rights and Union Interests*. New York: McGraw-Hill Book Co., 1964.

 A detailed account of the contracting-out issue, with emphasis on the sociological aspects.

MARSHALL, F. RAY, and BRIGGS, VERNON M., JR. *The Negro and Apprenticeship*. Baltimore: Johns Hopkins Press, 1967.

 A study of the problems involved in the attempts to open up apprenticeship to Negroes.

NORTHRUP, HERBERT R., and STORHOLM, GORDON R. *Restrictive Labor Practices in the Supermarket Industry.* Industrial Research Unit Study, No. 44. Philadelphia: University of Pennsylvania Press, 1967.
An analysis of featherbedding and restrictive union practices in an industry which directly affects the consumer.

ROWAN, RICHARD L., and NORTHRUP, HERBERT R. *Readings in Labor Economics and Labor Relations,* Part IV (c), "Issues in Jurisprudence." Homewood, Ill.: Richard D. Irwin, Inc., 1968.
Three articles on the union shop, featherbedding, and property in work.

SLICHTER, SUMNER H.; HEALY, J. J.; and LIVERNASH, E. R. *The Impact of Collective Bargaining on Management,* chaps. ii–xii. Washington, D.C.: Brookings Institution, 1960.
The basic work on industrial jurisprudence.

Chapter 7	# MULTIUNIT BARGAINING, STRIKES, AND THE LABOR MONOPOLY ISSUE

In this chapter, we continue our discussion of collective bargaining practices, taking up three of the most controversial issues—multiunit bargaining (often called industrywide bargaining), strikes, and the question of whether unions are monopolies.

MULTIUNIT BARGAINING

Multiunit bargaining is simply a term used to denote a collective bargaining arrangement which covers more than one plant. Multiunit bargaining takes many forms. One such form occurs when a single management controls two or more plants which are organized by a single national union. Negotiations between the United Automobile Workers and the General Motors Corporation or between the United Steelworkers and the United States Steel Corporation are two of the best-known examples of this type of bargaining. Both negotiations are between one management and one union, but they each establish basic wages and employment conditions for many separate plants throughout the country. Moreover, the settlements reached in these bargaining conferences provide the key wage bargains for much of the economy.

A second type of multiunit collective bargaining involves bargaining between one or more national unions and a representative of two or more managements in a single industry. For discussion purposes, such bargaining is usually subdivided on a geographical basis into local, regional, and national types. Local multiunit bargaining is by far the most common. It occurs in service industries of many kinds, building construction, amusements, retail stores, clothing, and many other industries in which the competitive market is predominately local. Frequently, it is difficult to distinguish the practical difference between the second type of bargaining on a national basis where the employers are represented by an association or other bargaining representative and the situation where a national union bargains at one and the same time with a number of multiunit employers. This is the situation in the steel industry. Each of the steel companies theoretically bargains independently with the United Steelworkers; but as a practical matter, they all look to the United States Steel Corporation to set the pattern.

Among the industries in which regional multiunit bargaining is common are pulp and paper, lumber, nonferrous metal mining, and maritime and longshore work.

The third geographic subdivision of multiunit bargaining between one or more trade-unions and two or more employers is national collective bargaining. Such bargaining is frequently termed "industrywide" bargaining, but the latter term is inaccurate in most cases. Even the widely known bargaining in the railroad industry, which is national in scope and very inclusive, is not actually completely industrywide.

National collective bargaining is itself divisible into two groups. In the first type a sizable segment of an industry throughout the country bargains with a national union or unions. The gradual extension prior to World War I of bituminous coal bargaining from local areas to districts and hence regionwide agreements, climaxed by the "central competitive field" agreements covering mainly Pennsylvania, Ohio, Indiana, and Illinois; the disintegration of this system in the 1920's because the unionized mines could not compete with the nonunion southern mines; and finally, the rise of national bargaining after 1934, afford the most vivid and well-known example of this development. Then, in the late 1940's, this bargaining split into northern and southern groups.

Railroad history provides another example. Single railway system bargaining developed, under the impetus of union "concerted movements," into regional conferences; then, during World War I, when the federal government took over the railroads, national bargaining was adopted. It relapsed into regional bargaining in the early 1920's, but national bargaining was again revived by the railroads in 1931 for the purpose of securing nationwide decreases. Since then, national bargaining has continued.

The railroad and bituminous coal situations have one significant difference which derives from the structure of their respective unions. Bituminous coal deals with one industrial union. Its negotiations settle matters for all employees at one time. Railroads deal with 20-odd craft unions. On most occasions the railroad unions have split into two, three, or four groups. National conferences are held with each group by the carriers. A settlement with one group must be made with the demands of the others in mind, thus greatly complicating bargaining.

Quite different either from the bituminous coal or the railroad situations, where most workers in an industry are involved in the national bargaining, is the second type of industry-wide bargaining. This is the situation where only one craft of workers bargains, as in wire weaving, tile laying, sprinkler installation, elevator installation and repair, and wallpaper crafts. Despite the fact that only a small segment of a particular employer's work force is involved, the bargaining is national in scope. A small, well-organized craft, desirous of maintaining its standards throughout the country, and an important industry segment providing nationally used products and/or services, participate in these multiunit bargaining arrangements.

Still another type of multiunit collective bargaining cuts across industry lines. In such cases, bargaining occurs between an employer association, or division thereof, representing numerous industries and the union or unions holding bargaining rights for the workers in these industries. Bargaining of this type has developed most fully in the San Francisco metropolitan area and has spread to several other western cities and to Hawaii. In San Francisco the aggressiveness and scarcity of labor led employers to organize and bargain on an area-wide basis as early as the "Gold Rush" days, but modern master agreements date from the union drives of 1934. Then the use of "whipsaw" tactics by unions—striking employers one at a time in order to raise wages—led to the formation of the San Francisco Employers Council in 1938. Today the Council supervises all negotiations for its members.

The newest type of multiplant bargaining is coordinated, or coalition, bargaining. As noted in previous chapters, this form has been developed by the AFL–CIO Industrial Union Department as a means of increasing union leverage on companies which deal with a number of unions at various plants throughout the United States and Canada. The IUD has attempted to coordinate efforts of unions to obtain common termination dates of contracts with a particular company, or with several companies in an industry, and then threaten to shut down all the plants if the managements refused to deal on a coalition basis. Despite widespread claims of success, the IUD drive had been successfully resisted for the most part by industry as of mid–1968. An eight-month strike against the nonferrous mining industry, and shorter strikes involving Union Carbide, Minnesota Mining and Manufacturing, General Electric, and Westinghouse had not achieved these goals for the IUD coalition approach.[1]

The Extent of Multiunit Collective Bargaining

Table 7–1 summarizes the findings of a survey as to the extent of multiunit collective bargaining. Because of the variations within industries, it has been necessary to include some industries under more than one heading.

In the left-hand column, titled "Single Company," are listed industries in which exist significant numbers of companies having several plants which deal on a companywide basis with unions. These industries are mostly the so-called "heavy" or "basic" industries, characterized by large investments, mass production, and a small number of large multiplant companies.

[1] A forthcoming book by William N. Chernish, to be published by the University of Pennsylvania Press, contains a detailed discussion of the coalition movement.

TABLE 7–1
Extent of Multiunit Collective Bargaining*

Single Company	Multicompany National	Multicompany Regional	Multicompany Local Area	Multi-industry
Automobile	Anthracite coal	Bituminous coal	Building construc-	San Francisco
Electrical supplies	Iron and steel	Fishing	tion	Tacoma
and equip-	(basic)	Canning and	Building materials	Reno
ment	Railroads	preserving	Longshoremen	Sacramento
Farm equipment	Pottery	foods	Trucking (local de-	Los Angeles
Office equipment	Flat glass	Lumber	livery)	Phoenix
Rubber	Pressed and	Pulp and paper	Warehousing	Denver
Meat packing	blown	Agricultural	Amusements and	Hawaii
Rayon textiles	glass	growing	theaters	Albuquerque
Shipbuilding	Glass con-	and har-	Hotels and restau-	
Woolen textiles	tainers	vesting	rants	
Nonferrous metal	Trucking	Clay sewer pipe	Laundries	
manufactur-	(over the	Cement	Cleaning and dyeing	
ing	road)†	Maritime (all	service	
Nonferrous metal	Wire weaving	classes)	Building service	
mining	Wallpaper	Seamen	Retail stores	
Pulp and paper	Tile laying	Longshore-	Department stores	
Tobacco	Sprinkler fitter	men	Charitable organ-	
(cigarettes)	installa-	Furniture	izations	
	tion	Motion-picture	Radio parts as-	
	Elevator in-	production	sembly	
	stallation	Hosiery	Metal job shops	
	and repair	Cotton textiles	Machine	
	Men's and	Woolen textiles	Tool and die	
	boys'	Dyeing and	Pattern	
	clothes	finishing	Foundry	
	Work clothes	textiles	Steel products	
	Stoves	Cotton gar-	(nonbasic)	
		ments	Jewelry and	
		Leather	silverware	
		(tanned,	Newspaper printing	
		curried,	Book and job print-	
		and fin-	ing	
		ished)	Women's clothes	
		Shoes	Millinery	
		Trucking	Fur	
			Leather products	
			and gloves	
			Shoes	
			Confectionery	
			products	
			Meat packing	
			Dairy products	
			Baked goods	
			Malt liquors	
			Beverages	
			(nonalcoholic)	
			Tobacco (cigars)	
			Furniture	
			Knit goods	
			Silk and rayon	
			textiles	
			Paper products	
			(boxes, etc.)	
			Garage main-	
			tenance men	

* Coordinated or coalition bargaining has been attempted in many industries, notably electrical manufacturing, nonferrous mining and manufacturing, chemicals, and drugs.
† One national agreement which may not be respected.

The three center columns are devoted to multicompany, multiunit bargaining. It will be noted that in only a few industries does national collective bargaining exist.

Local multiunit bargaining embraces by far the greatest number of industries. Multi-industry bargaining, as in San Francisco, is confined to western areas and Hawaii.

From this table, it is clear that multiunit bargaining in the United States embraces an enormous portion of American industry. Multiunit bargaining also varies according to issues. Pensions, for example, are bargained nationally in electrical construction, but most other issues are bargained locally. A wide range of such varied practices exists in industry.

Reasons for Development of Multiunit Collective Bargaining

The reasons for the development of the various types of multiunit collective bargaining vary from industry to industry. Sometimes the union is responsible for initiating such bargaining. In other cases the employers take the initiative.

Equalizing wage costs has been an important reason why unions have supported multiunit collective bargaining. In the railroads, for example, the brotherhoods found that the individual railroads were using the competition of other lines as a reason for objecting to wage increases. This led them to support first regional and then national bargaining. In the needle trades, wages are the most important cost factor. Both the unions and the employers discovered at an early time that unionism could not exist unless it equalized wage costs. This resulted in marketwide bargaining in the various branches of the industry; since most markets are local in scope, bargaining is local in scope. The exceptions are the men's clothing industry, which has expanded into a national bargaining situation, and the work clothes industries, where the union label has induced various manufacturers throughout the country to enter negotiations with the United Garment Workers.

The equalization of competition has played an important role in the development of multiunit collective bargaining in lumber, pulp and paper, pottery, and the various branches of the glass industry. In some of these industries, initiation came from the employers' side. In such industries as electronic manufacturing, the metal jobbing shops of various types, and book and job printing, as well as others, the pattern is similar to that in the garment trades. Wages are a significant, if not the most significant, cost item, the plant labor force is small, and the degree of competition high. All these factors tend toward the development of multiunit collective bargaining once the workers become unionized.

In industries in which an employee typically works for more than one employer, multiunit collective bargaining is virtually essential for both employer and union. These industries include the maritime trades, the building trades, and the needle trades. In such industries, failure to equalize wages and working conditions would have the effect of permitting some employers to pay less wages to workers who also work for other employers paying higher wages. From the union point of view, this is an intolerable situation, and it is equally so from the employer's viewpoint. For example, in the building industry the low-wage employer would be able to outbid high-wage competitors—and solely because the union allowed him a favorable rate. This would injure the union's relations with other employers. Hence the only solution from the point of view of both employer and union is multiunit bargaining over the extent of the market.

Another reason why both unions and employers prefer multiunit bargaining is that it eases contract enforcement. From the union point of view, this is very important in such industries as building or trucking, or in any others where the size of the firm is small and the employees bear a very close personal relation to their employers. There is a tendency in such industries, particularly when work is slack, for the employer to ask, and often to receive, wage concessions from his workers and to keep the concessions secret from the union. This enables the employer to get more work at the expense of his competitors. It also, however, takes business from the more contract-conscious competitors and threatens the entire union wage structure. Under a multiunit arrangement, such local deals are more difficult, especially since most arrangements contain explicit provisions enumerating severe penalties for any deals or kickbacks.

Multiunit bargaining simplifies negotiations in industries where there are scores of small employers. It also enables small companies represented by an association to employ skilled attorneys and industrial relations specialists whom they could not afford on an individual plant bargaining basis.

Unions like multiunit bargaining because it makes it more difficult for a rival union to gain a foothold in the industry. A history of bargaining with an employers' association will tend to induce the National Labor Relations Board to designate the multiplant group as the appropriate unit for bargaining purposes and thus block the efforts of a rival union to pick off individual plants. Employers also favorably regard the protection against rival unions afforded by multiunit bargaining, since the resultant stability of labor relations in the industry may produce moderation on the part of union leaders who feel sufficiently secure against rivals to display economic statesmanship. Of course, if a rival union can win a majority of votes for the entire multiplant unit, it can take over bargaining rights for all of the plants even though it might lack a majority in some of them. This is what a newly formed union, the Association of Western Pulp and Paper Workers, was able to accomplish in the western pulp and paper industry in 1964 after these employees had been represented by AFL–CIO unions for 30 years.

Multiunit bargaining alters the power structure within a union. Thus, James R. Hoffa pushed for national bargaining in the over-the-road trucking industry as a means of cementing his power in the union. By concentrating power for negotiations at the national level, the national leaders reduce the importance—and the independence—of the local and regional leadership. National and regional negotiations greatly enhanced centralization of authority in the United Mine Workers. It could have been expected to encourage a similar trend in the Teamsters' Union, which is one reason, now that Hoffa is in jail, that the union vice presidents and regional directors are encouraging a return to regional bargaining.

One of the most important reasons why employers have initiated or defended multiunit bargaining is the protection it gives them against loss from strikes. In industries such as transportation, building construction, amusements, services, or retail trade, a strike can result in a loss of business which is never regained because the company deals in a perishable good or service. If the union can pick off employers of such industries one at a time, employers are, more often than not, helpless to prevent the union from achieving even the most outrageous demands. But when employers form a common front, the union power is blunted because a strike means a strike of the entire industry. This, in turn, results in a serious loss of employment to all union members; and, perhaps even more important, no employer benefits from the loss of business of an employer who is struck. The logical development of such a situation has occurred in the West Coast maritime industry, where strikes have been answered either by industrywide lockouts or by the payment of benefits to struck concerns.

On the other hand, many employers who have their employee relations well controlled oppose multiunit bargaining because it might permit the union to spread throughout the industry gains won from weaker bargaining companies. The automobile companies oppose joint bargaining because the larger the group involved, the greater the propensity for government intervention, which often takes the form of pressure on the companies to give more to avoid a work stoppage.

The accident of location is also important. Multiunit bargaining is more common on the Pacific Coast than in any other area in the United States. The importance of the maritime and lumber industries and the historical shortage of labor in that area have probably been important factors. But the development of a citywide multiunit system in San Francisco has encouraged a similar development in other western cities and in Hawaii.

Multiunit Bargaining as a Problem

The basic public interest in multiunit bargaining arises out of the effects of work stoppages and of wage increases. A strike which shuts down either a whole industry or a major portion thereof causes serious public inconvenience. A wage increase which is achieved by a large number of workers under conditions which insure widespread publicity, such as when the Steelworkers' Union bargains with United States Steel, can result in public dissatisfaction with the large multiunit strike and with the wage bargain. Such settlements, particularly when effectuated by use of the strike weapon on a large scale, may be highly inflationary, give rise to charges of union monopoly, as discussed later in this chapter, and encourage government intervention in negotiations and strikes. Although government intervention is designed to protect the public interest, it has, in fact, often encouraged higher and more inflationary wage settlements because government officials are usually interested primarily in avoiding strikes and pressure employers to offer additional benefits in order to keep the peace.

Multiunit bargaining, by its very nature, tends to remove the bargaining from local pressures. Although this may have some advantages in creating an atmosphere conducive to reasonable settlement, it also frequently results in ignoring key local issues, or in referring them back to the plant level for further negotiations. As a result, there has grown up in such industries as automobiles and rubber products a situation which poses a double threat to industrial peace. Negotiations are held on the national level at which basic economic issues (wages, holidays, vacations, and benefits) are settled, together with other items of national significance. Other issues are handled locally after national negotiations. Management is then faced with bargaining over a host of problems, such as work standards, seniority, and other work rules, which the literature of collective bargaining calls "noneconomic," but which may be very costly indeed. Such items have a direct effect on productivity, number of labor hours needed, and equipment utilization, all of which help to determine the profitability of the enterprise. Yet, because wages and benefits have already been determined, local managers often have no funds for counter offers, nor can they do much but oppose further increases in costs. Long local strikes, disgruntled local employees, and a high turnover of local union officials who cannot "produce" for the rank and file are frequent results of multiplant bargaining even though agreement at the national level may have been achieved.

Multiunit bargaining can also involve the entire bargaining group in disputes which are of interest to only one small part. For example, an issue over discipline in one can factory in 1965 almost shut down most of the industry because local union officials in that plant had extracted a promise of action there from national leaders as a condition of settlement. Frequently in such national negotiations, days will be spent discussing such an issue, and then it will be referred back for local determination anyway. If issues of this sort get out of hand, or if either party is spoiling for a fight, the entire multiunit bargaining group can have a strike. The stakes are higher and the damage greater in multiunit bargaining when labor peace fails.

STRIKES

To many Americans, the strike epitomizes the union. Headlines are made in industrial disputes. They are the sensational aspects of union policies and managerial counterpolicies. Yet, strikes are surprisingly few in comparison to either man-days worked or the number of collective agreements negotiated. (See Table 7–2.) For example, the average annual

TABLE 7–2

STRIKES AND LOCKOUTS IN THE UNITED STATES,
SELECTED YEARS, 1917–67

Year	Number of Stoppages	Number of Workers Involved (Thousands)	Man Days Idle (Million Days)	Percentage of Working Time Lost[1]
1917	4,450	1,227	n.a.	n.a.
1919	3,630	4,160	n.a.	n.a.
1921	2,385	1,099	n.a.	n.a.
1925	1,301	428	n.a.	n.a.
1929	921	289	5.4	0.07
1933	1,695	1,168	16.9	0.36
1937	4,740	1,860	28.4	0.43
1941	4,288	2,363	23.0	0.32
1944	4,956	2,116	8.7	0.09
1946	4,985	4,600	116.0	1.43
1947	3,693	2,170	34.6	0.41
1950	4,843	2,410	38.8	0.40
1952	5,117	3,540	59.1	0.57
1956	3,825	1,900	33.1	0.29
1959	3,900	1,850	68.0	0.61
1961	3,367	1,450	16.3	0.12
1963	3,614	941	16.1	0.13
1965	4,405	1,960	25.4	0.19
1967	4,595	2,870	42.1	0.30

SOURCE: U.S. Department of Labor, Bureau of Labor Statistics.
[1] Private, non-farm.

number of man-days lost in the United States because of strikes during 1935–36—a period of great labor unrest—was 16.9 million, or 0.27% of the total annual estimated working time. In 1946, the worst strike year in our history, total man-days lost were 116 million, or 1.43% of the annual estimated working time. In 1959, despite the impact of a steel strike that shut down that industry for several months, total man-days lost were 68 million, or only 0.61% of the annual estimated working time.[2] Almost every hour while strikes occur, a collective bargaining agreement is being peacefully negotiated by a union and a company.

During the last two decades—with a few exceptions—there has been a reduction in both the number of strikes and the amount of time lost by strikes. In the period prior to 1958, this reflected in part the rise of the long-term contract, and both management's willingness to concede gener-

[2] See strike data in Table 7–2. But it should be noted that these strike data do not take account of those laid off because of strikes in other plants. Thus a railroad strike affecting 100 people could close down an industrial plant employing 5,000 workers—but only the 100 would be counted in the strike data.

ous terms and its ability to pass along costs to the consumer. In the 1958–64 period, it probably reflected the ability of management to reduce costs by improved technology and methods, and labor's willingness to accept smaller gains as a result of unemployment and companies' determination to control costs. Later in the 1960's, companies were often willing to concede large wage increases without a strike as a means of keeping the peace and of maintaining production. In 1967, however, there were an unusually large number of long, major strikes which made that year the worst strike year since 1959. Whether this indicates a general upward trend in strikes, only time will tell. Strikes have always been more frequent in periods of rising prices. The upward push of prices and the continuation of a tight labor market since 1965, high corporate profits since that time, and the restlessness among labor's young rank and file could all combine to produce a heavy strike year.

Strikes not only vary from year to year, but also seasonally. They most commonly occur in the months from March to September, when the majority of contracts come up for renegotiation. Workers are understandably more willing to take an enforced layoff and to picket in the summer sunshine than in the winter cold.

Despite their relative numerical unimportance, strikes have a vital effect on the economy. A strike in a key motor parts plant can and has shut down a large segment of an automobile company which depends upon that plant to supply certain parts. Strikes in missile bases can affect our national defense. These are matters of vital public concern and are discussed as such in Part VII. These problems also raise the question of why strikes arise out of labor-management disputes.

Classification of Work Stoppages

Strikes may be classified in three general categories: (1) economic strikes, concerning wages, hours, and working conditions; (2) strikes to achieve recognition or to eliminate unfair labor practices by employers; and (3) strikes involving conflicts between unions.

The first category—the "bread-and-butter" type of strike—has consistently been the major type of strike in this country, except during the period from 1934 to 1941, when the great upsurge of union organizing effort pushed to the forefront the second category of strikes. Wages are the most usual but by no means the only reason for economic strikes. For example, the longest major strike in the last several years—that affecting the nonferrous metal industry—was, as already noted, over an unsuccessful demand of the unions for industrywide and companywide bargaining.

Strikes of the second category are intended to eliminate an unfair labor practice by an employer, such as refusal to bargain or discrimination against union activity. Organization strikes, which also fall in this category, have become relatively unimportant in recent years as a result of the high percentage of organization already achieved in industry, the consequent retardation in the rate of growth of unions, and the existence of peaceful methods of determination of a collective bargaining representative under state and federal law. An exception is in the area of public employment, where an increasing number of strikes have occurred over the recognition issue in states which provide no machinery for this purpose.

The third class of strikes is a result of union rivalries over jobs and membership. It includes the jurisdictional strike, which involves a contest between unions as to which group of workers will perform a specified piece of work. It also includes the rival union organization strike, in which rival unions seek to compel the employer to recognize the one rather than the other as the exclusive bargaining agent for certain or all of his employees. Despite the fact that both voluntary machinery through the AFL–CIO and public methods provided by the National Labor Relations Board and state agencies are available to settle such disputes, they continue to exist. Disputes over construction and maintenance work in industrial plants between industrial and building-trades unions, involving the already discussed contracting-out issue, show no signs of abating.

The Taft-Hartley law makes it an unfair labor practice for a union to engage in a strike or refuse to work on goods or perform services where an object is "forcing or requiring any employer to assign particular work to employees in a particular labor organization or in a particular trade, craft, or class rather than to employees in another labor organization or in another trade, craft, or class, unless such employer is failing to conform to an order or certification of the Board determining the bargaining representative for employees performing such work." The same law also forbids strikes aimed at compelling an employer to bargain with one union where another union has been certified by the National Labor Relations Board as the proper representative of the employees. Despite these provisions in the law and the efforts of the AFL–CIO, jurisdictional and rival-union strikes will undoubtedly continue to inconvenience the public from time to time. The question of whether the Carpenters or the Metal Workers should install metal frame windows may seem to be a small reason to tie up millions of dollars of building construction; yet, to the workers involved, it is an emotionally charged issue upon which their very daily bread may depend in years to come. However, strikes over such issues are relatively unimportant in the overall strike picture. Since 1942, jurisdictional and rival-union strikes have aggregated less than 6% of all strikes from labor-management disputes each year.[3]

Strikes are usually classed in terms of union demands or objectives, but this does not mean that all strikes are the "fault" of the unions. Some strikes probably can be more properly classed as management lockouts. Suppose, for example, that the steelworkers, through negotiations with the

[3] Data from monthly reports of the U.S. Department of Labor, Bureau of Labor Statistics.

steel companies, have won agreements for wage increases of 10 cents an hour; then suppose that one of the companies refuses to go along with the arrangement. Even if this employer has good reason to balk, he knows that the union cannot agree to give his company such a special deal. He would, in effect, be inviting the union to strike, for it could probably do nothing else and still retain the loyalty of its members. Yet the actual decision to strike would be made by the union. Consequently, the strike would be classed as an economic walkout, even though it might be a truer description of the facts to call it a management lockout.

Noneconomic Factors in Strikes

There have been a number of attempts to state a theory of industrial disputes in terms of purely economic calculation. The assumption is that such calculation is utilized by the parties to determine whether a strike would be advisable. If the parties correctly determine each other's propensity to resist and to concede at given wage rates and strike-length periods, then, according to such analyses, they will come to an agreement without a strike at the precise point beyond which neither would concede further without a strike.

The main fault with this analysis is that it does not go far enough. The decision whether to strike for higher wages or to accept a peaceful settlement at a lower rate does, in fact, depend to a considerable extent on the parties' estimates of the relative resistance or recessions which they can expect of the other. But in addition, such a decision is also influenced by many noneconomic considerations which in some circumstances may make a strike for an additional cent an hour necessary, even though it is unsound on a purely economic basis.

The union is not a purely economic unit; it is a body politic. Its first consideration is ever the strength of the organization and/or its leadership. The long rubber products strike of 1967 was designed to win a virtual annual wage for the membership and renown for the United Rubber Workers' recently elected president. The nonferrous metal strike of 1967–68 had as its main objective the strengthening of the bargaining position and reputation of the Steelworkers, which had recently merged the Mine, Mill and Smelter Workers into its ranks. In each case, it will take the members many months, even years, to recover their economic losses from such strikes. Yet union leaders talk about "gains" resulting from such strikes—gains which are only such if the union or its leaders are considered separately from the rank and file.

Even where a dispute revolves solely around the size of the wage increase, unions will frequently go out on strike for a few cents more per hour, despite the fact that it is apparent that the wage loss incurred during the strike will far exceed the benefit which may be won in the final settlement. The union—particularly one in the formative stage—may derive more benefit from a wage increase of 50 cents a day after a strike than it would from a wage increase of $1 without a strike. The union leaders may need the rallying power of a strike to solidify the sentiment of the membership and to consolidate their own control.

Work stoppages may also result from noneconomic preferences of employers. The willingness of employers to take a strike over a principle cannot be measured on an economic calculation chart. What, for example, is it worth to a company to refuse to grant the union shop even if that involves a strike?

Whatever the cause of strikes, the computation of their costs in terms of lost wages or production is not simple. In some industries which produce a perishable or nonreproducible product or service—such as the amusement trades, passenger transportation, and newspaper publishing— business lost can rarely be regained, and therefore the cost of the strike will bear a close relationship to the revenues and wages lost during the duration of the walkout. On the other hand, in other industries, time lost by strikes may be made up during the year. Most coal strikes, for example, have not caused miners to lose more working time during an average year than they would otherwise lose from overcapacity in the industry. The average number of days worked per miner per year remains approximately the same in heavy strike years as in years of labor peace. Although this is an extreme case, the situation is somewhat comparable in all industries which produce a storable or postponable product, i.e., a product which, if not produced and sold today, can nonetheless be produced and sold tomorrow.

This illustrates the point that the "real" cost of strikes is higher in times of full employment than in periods of less than full employment. For in the latter periods a strike may only determine when idleness, which would occur anyway, will take place.

Strike Tactics

Unions attempt to time a strike so that it will put the greatest pressure on the employer to settle. For this reason, union negotiators attempt to have the term of a collective bargaining agreement end in the employer's busiest season. Employers, of course, prefer to have contract negotiations and any strike action fall in their slack season.

Generally, a strike is preceded by a formal strike vote adopted by the union membership at a meeting at which the last offer of the employer is presented. Occasionally, the membership does not go along with the union leadership and votes to return to work; but usually, most union members support their leadership on a strike vote because they view the vote as a tactical move which psychologically strengthens the hand of their representatives in dealing with the employer.

Strikes sometimes develop without any preliminary formal action. Such unpremeditated walkouts, usually called "wildcat" or "quickie" strikes, are generally of short duration and are a way in which workers let off steam as a result of tensions and grievances which build up in modern industry. In some situations, however, frequent "spontaneous" walkouts of a few hours' duration may be part of a plan by the union leadership to gain concessions from management during the term of the contract without technically violating a no-strike pledge contained in the contract. Although picket lines are informational in theory, they also carry with them a threat of force. In most strikes, workers tend to support the walkout and do not attempt to work. Moreover, employers often do not attempt to operate during a strike unless they do so with salaried employees and supervisors. Where workers attempt to work, however, they are often met with force or threats for which police protection is more likely to be inadequate than protective.[4] Recently, the United States Supreme Court has strengthened the hands of unions in dealing with members who oppose strikes by ruling that a union could fine employees who crossed picket lines and then institute legal proceedings to collect those fines.[5]

Automation and Strikes

Automation has had a profound effect on union strike tactics in several industries. Several strikes in oils and chemicals have resulted in severe union defeats, since supervisory employees can keep the plant running at near capacity because of the ease of operating automatic equipment. Long-distance dialing has made telephone strikes virtually entirely ineffective for the same reason. Electric light and power strikes now occur with no interruption of service. To the extent that automation operates equipment with minimum manual requirements, unions are finding that the strike is becoming an outmoded weapon.

Strike Benefits

Union leaders recognize that the ability of a union to withstand a long strike depends in major part on its members' economic staying power. Since the average union member's savings are quickly exhausted by a strike, most unions pay strike benefits. Some, like the United Automobile Workers pay benefits to all workers on a strike authorized by the international union executive board. Other unions, such as the United Steelworkers, pay benefits only to those in need. Strike benefits rarely exceed $25 per week and are often less, but even so, quickly use up large strike funds. Both the Auto Workers and the Steelworkers adopted extra assessments to cover strikes in 1967–68, with the Ford strike costing the former nearly $35 million in benefits, and the latter about as much for payments for nonferrous metals strikers.

During a strike, unions frequently receive gifts or borrow from other unions to help to defray the costs of strike benefits, publicity, legal

---

[4] On this point see Frank H. Stewart and Robert J. Townsend, "Strike Violence: the Need for Injunctions," *University of Pennsylvania Law Review*, Vol. CXIV (February, 1966), pp. 459–86.

[5] *National Labor Relations Board* v. *Allis-Chalmers Manufacturing Co.*, U.S. Supreme Court, 65 LRRM 2449 (1967).

fees, and other expenses which accompany a strike. In large strikes, such fund raising is sometimes coordinated by the AFL–CIO, whose direct resources to assist striking unionists are meager.

The meager amount of most strike benefits requires that the average unionist depend heavily on his own resources. The government has frequently aided those on strike with welfare payments, food stamps, and other handouts, thus preventing privation but on occasion prolonging the strike by reducing the pressure of the rank and file on the union leadership to settle. Merchants, anxious to hold on to the strikers' patronage, also usually extend credit. Little assistance to strikers from the outside is, however, necessary for members of the Air Line Pilots Association or the International Typographical Union. These organizations pay such substantial benefits that their members have no great incentive to return to work. It is likely that the rash of recent newspaper strikes by members of the Typographical Union as well as their length are not unrelated to the fact that striking members of this union receive benefits approximating their take-home pay. Such strikes also idle members of other unions in the newspaper industry who receive no such benefits from their unions.

State unemployment compensation can also support a strike. In a few states and in the railroad industry, employees may receive unemployment compensation even while on strike. This is true in New York after the strike has lasted six weeks. Again, it worked to support the striking Typographers. That payments designed to protect workers against involuntary unemployment should support them when they voluntarily withdraw their services is one of the anomalies of our unemployment compensation system, which is discussed in detail in Chapter 18.

Employer Strike Funds

Employers, too, have been searching for and finding ways to strengthen each other in a common stand against strong unions. One new technique which has elicited considerable employer interest was developed in the airline industry. The Civil Aeronautics Board has approved as being in the public interest a mutual assistance pact among several major airlines. Under the terms of this pact, airlines which have been shut down by a strike will route prospective passengers to other lines. Participating companies pay over to the struck lines their increased receipts less expenses. Members of the Hawaiian Sugar Planters Association, who bargain on an industrywide basis, also have a mutual support program intended to distribute long-term strike losses evenly among the 26 island plantations. Other groups who have developed strike insurance plans include the railroads and the five largest manufacturers of rubber tires.[6] There also

---

[6] For studies of the airline and railroad strike insurance plans, see two articles by Vernon M. Briggs, Jr., "The Mutual Aid Pact of the Airline Industry," *Industrial and Labor Relations Review*, Vol. XIX (October, 1965), pp. 3–20; and "The Strike Insurance Plan of the Railroad Industry," *Industrial Relations*, Vol. VI (February, 1967), pp. 205–12.

appears to be increased interest by employers in industrywide bargaining and bargaining through employer associations. Courts have sanctioned the right of all employers in a joint bargaining group to shut down when the union strikes one of the group in an attempt to divide and conquer.

The right of labor to strike and the right of management to resist such strikes by lockout and other measures are rights which are entitled to protection so long as they do not create a war of attrition inimical to the public interest. The continued existence of the right to strike as we know it may well depend upon the moderation with which this weapon is used in the next few years. Unfortunately, the decision to strike and to tie up an entire industry now frequently devolves upon one or two men, because of the growing scope of industrywide bargaining. The pressures on such leaders of management and labor are often such that considerations other than the general public interest are dominant. This brings us to the important question of whether or not unions are monopolies.

UNIONS AND MONOPOLY POWER

The growing strength of organized labor and the power of unions to shut down large segments of our economy through strikes have led many writers and statesmen to ponder whether restrictive measures are not necessary in order to prevent unions from destroying or seriously impairing the free enterprise system in this country. Persons dealing with this problem frequently justify their recommendation for action by labeling unions as monopolies. In some cases, their concern is with the supposed harmful *results* of union bargaining power; in other cases, with the *power* of unions, whether or not in fact exercised, to harm the general public. Some critics of unions assail the strike as the aspect of unionism most inimical to the public welfare; others attack industrywide bargaining or the power of exclusive representation granted unions which are certified as bargaining agents under the National Labor Relations Act. One thing emerges clearly from the epithet hurling and name calling—there is a need for a reexamination of the whole question of whether or not unions are monopolies and, if so, whether or not unions wield monopoly power which is detrimental to the public welfare.

Aspects of Union Monopoly Power

There are certain ways in which it might be said that unions act like a monopoly:

1. In economic theory, one test of a monopolist, as contrasted with a pure competitor, is the ability to fix prices. Unions and monopolists are alike, since they both fix prices and both hope to sell as much of their respective "product" at the fixed price as they can. It is true that the union does not attempt to fix the price of labor with the same objectives in mind as those which motivate a monopolist in setting the price of his

product. Presumably, a monopolist fixes a price which will maximize his profit, and in determining this price, he takes account of the fact that the quantity of his product demanded will be less at a high price than at a lower price. Unions, however, are not profit-making organizations. They are not motivated in all cases by purely economic objectives. Unions do not consistently seek to obtain the highest wage possible or the highest maximum income for their membership or the wage consistent with the largest number of jobs for the membership. Often, unions will strike for another cent or two above what employers have been willing to concede, even though it is apparent that the strike is bound to cost the membership money when the gains achieved are balanced by the losses sustained during the strike. Moreover, recent studies suggest that in fixing wage rates, except in situations of sharp nonunion competition, unions do not take account of the fact that the higher the wage rate, the smaller may be the employment of union members. In other words, unions do not behave like the calculating monopolist of economic theory.

However, strong unions do, within limits, have the power to fix the price of labor. It is in this "monopoly power" that some writers find the great threat to the continuance of the free enterprise system. Charles E. Lindblom, for example, in his book entitled *Unions and Capitalism*, wrote: "The union is a monopoly because it can and does raise the price of labor to levels which will in a competitive price system inevitably cause waste, unemployment, inflation, or all combined."[7] Lindblom stated that the foundation of union monopoly power is the strike. He found that unions were able to maintain a monopoly price for union labor even though there was competing labor available at a lower price by coercing the employer into submitting to the union. "Union monopoly regulates the wage rate therefore not by sustained control of supply but by control of the buyer who is the employer. The technique is the strike."[8]

Lindblom viewed the strike not as a refusal to work but as a punitive measure designed to force the employer to submit to the union. To him, the strike with its concomitant picket line was a means of shutting out the competition of union workers. Lindblom's conclusion was, that by use of the strike weapon, unions can force up the price of labor so high as seriously to misallocate resources, restrict output in expanding industries, and threaten the economy with continuing inflation and unemployment.[9]

2. A union is like a monopoly because, once certified by the National Labor Relations Board (and unless decertified), a union has, by law, an area of operation in representing workers in the bargaining unit in which competition from other unions is prohibited. Under the Taft-Hartley Act, employees bargain through unions of their own choosing which the

[7] Charles E. Lindblom, *Unions and Capitalism* (New Haven, Conn.: Yale University Press, 1949), p. 22.

[8] *Ibid.*, p. 58.

[9] Whether union wage policies cause inflation will be discussed in Chapter 13.

employer must recognize as the exclusive bargaining agent. A majority of persons voting in the election determine the bargaining agent for all of the workers in the bargaining unit. As long as a union remains the certified bargaining agent, it has the exclusive right to represent workers in their relations with the employer. When this power is combined with a union shop, which requires new workers to join the union as a prerequisite to holding their jobs, the union has, in effect, obtained a monopoly over job opportunities with the particular employer. Nonunion workers or members of other unions cannot work for the employer. We noted in Chapter 6 how compulsory unionism increased the power of union leadership both over the rank and file and in its relation to the employer.

3. A monopoly which controls the source of supply of a product essential to the public can cause the public serious inconvenience and harm by shutting off the supply of that product. Unions frequently are accused of exercising this type of monopoly power, particularly when a strike shuts down an entire industry. In recent years, there seems to have been a growing feeling in some circles that the basis for this type of union power lies in the practice of multiunit collective bargaining. To many people, major strikes involving multiunit arrangements in steel, automobiles, and other industries seem like a battle between Goliaths from which the public is certain to emerge as the major loser.[10]

4. Monopoly in the public mind is frequently associated with great aggrandizement of financial and economic power. The power of large unions to affect economic activity through the use of strikes is well known. Unions have also become great financial institutions. National union assets, including those under their control in welfare funds, now exceed several billion dollars, as we noted in Chapter 3. When unions with such assets as the Teamsters or the United Automobile Workers bargain with the individual employer who is not one of the major corporations, the scales may be so tipped in favor of the union that the individual employer can do little else but acquiesce to any demands made by the union, however illogical or uneconomic.

5. Under the antitrust laws of the United States, the test of monopoly is the power to restrain interstate commerce. The actions of unions frequently have this effect. As a matter of fact, any large-scale strike is likely to halt the free flow of products in interstate commerce. Furthermore, unions have frequently taken action deliberately aimed at restricting the flow of goods in interstate commerce. Thus, for example, the United States Supreme Court ruled that it was unlawful for Local No. 3 of the International Brotherhood of Electrical Workers to agree with New York City electrical contractors to purchase equipment only from local manufacturers with whom it had closed-shop agreements and to

---

[10] The issues of public policy raised by so-called "emergency" strikes are discussed in Herbert R. Northrup and Gordon F. Bloom, *Government and Labor* (Homewood, Ill.: Richard D. Irwin, Inc., 1963), chaps. xii–xv.

agree with such manufacturers to sell only to contractors who dealt with Local No. 3. *But the Court, in effect, held that if Local No. 3 accomplished this without conspiring with employers, then it was permissible!*[11] The extended immunity granted to labor from the antitrust laws was carried to its logical conclusion in other decisions. The American Federation of Musicians was permitted to maintain a nationwide boycott of recordings by refusing to have its members make such recordings;[12] a hod carriers' union was permitted to prevent usage within its jurisdiction of a low-cost cement-mixing machine except under conditions which made the use of such machines financially impossible;[13] building-trades unions were permitted to boycott materials because they were produced by companies where rival unions were bargaining agents or because they were prefabricated instead of being put together on the job;[14] and unions were allowed to picket or boycott a company solely on the ground that it dealt with a rival union and despite the fact that if the employer recognized the picketing or boycotting union, he would violate the National Labor Relations (Wagner) Act.[15]

6. Unions have been able to destroy individual businesses and deprive persons of their livelihood with impunity. In the famous case of *Hunt v. Crumbach*,[16] a union refused to permit members to work for one particular employer and refused to permit his employees to join the union. As a result, they completely destroyed his business in revenge for his previous hostility. The majority of the U.S. Supreme Court held that this was a legitimate exercise of the unrestricted right of concerted action with which labor organizations have been endowed by federal law. In a vigorous dissent, the late Justice Jackson pointed out that with this decision "the labor movement has come full circle. . . . This Court now sustains the claim of a union to the right to deny participation in the economic world to an employer simply because the union dislikes him. This Court permits to employees the same arbitrary dominance over the economic sphere which they control that labor so long, so bitterly, and so rightly asserted should belong to no man."

Both the Taft-Hartley and the Landrum-Griffin Acts restricted aspects of untrammeled union monopoly power.[17] Recent lawsuits undertaken pursuant to these laws against such unions as the Teamsters and the Mine Workers for breach of contract, closing down nonunion operations

---

[11] *Allen-Bradley Co. v. Local 3, International Brotherhood of Electrical Workers*, 325 U.S. 797 (1945).

[12] *United States v. American Federation of Musicians*, 318 U.S. 741 (1943).

[13] *United States v. International Hod Carriers' Union*, 313 U.S. 539 (1941).

[14] *United States v. Building & Construction Trades Council*, 313 U.S. 539 (1941).

[15] *National Labor Relations Board v. Star Publishing Co.*, 97 F. (2d) 465 (1938).

[16] 325 U.S. 821 (1945).

[17] See Chapters 21 and 22 for a discussion of these laws.

by force, or other now illegal acts have cost union treasuries hundreds of thousands of dollars. In addition, the U.S. Supreme Court has ruled in a case involving the United Mine Workers that a union forfeits its exemption from the antitrust laws when it is clearly shown that the union has agreed with one set of employers to impose a wage scale on other bargaining units. One group of employers may not conspire to eliminate competitors from an industry, and the union is liable, along with the employers, if it becomes a party to the conspiracy.[18] On the other hand, the same Court ruled that there was nothing illegal in a union forcing all stores to refrain from selling meat after 6 P.M. even though the stores remained open![19] Litigation in this area continues to fix the boundaries of legality for union conduct, but in view of some of the excesses of union power illustrated by these cases, it would not be surprising if Congress further limited union power.

In summary, then, the charges against unions are that they fix the price of labor through the use of coercion and force, that they have a monopoly of job opportunities, that they can shut down whole industries, that they have become financial giants by reason of their tax-exempt status and the use of the checkoff of dues, and that they hold the power of life or death over thousands of individual businesses. Labor's answer is that despite the alleged power of unions, the average worker with a family still does not have sufficient take-home pay to maintain an adequate standard of living, that the union shop is simply another application of the democratic principle of majority rule, that industrywide bargaining is necessary to stabilize wage rates between competing employers, that the assets of unions are minute compared to the assets of the giant corporations with which they must bargain, and that while some employers may get hurt by union actions, unions use their power to serve millions of workers, not a privileged few.[20]

Unions, however, can hardly expect that their monopoly power can continue to be exercised without restriction in an economy which is generally committed to the principle of fostering competition. Certainly, it is realistic to assume that new regulations of trade-unions will come. The direction which such regulation should take, however, is a subject on which there is little unanimity among labor critics. The great danger is that general legislation will be passed which will cause great harm rather than improvement.

For example, some want a blanket application of the antitrust laws to labor. Yet, these laws are most complex. Tomes have been written as to their application to business, but their meaning in specific cases is often

[18] *United Mine Workers* v. *Pennington*, U.S. Supreme Court, 59 LRRM 2369 (1967).

[19] *Local 189, Meat Cutters* v. *Jewel Tea Co.*, U.S. Supreme Court, 59 LRRM 2376 (1967).

[20] "The Labor Monopoly Myth," *Labor's Economic Review* (AFL–CIO publication), February, 1956.

not clear. Meanwhile, proponents of laissez-faire complain that the anti-trust laws have not ended business combinations.

We have already noted in Chapter 6 that attempts to legislate against make-work practices are likely to be both ineffective and dangerous to the free enterprise system because of difficulties of distinguishing feather-bedding from legitimate practice. Likewise, blanket condemnation of multiunit bargaining—also a favorite of those desiring remedial legislation—could well put small businesses at the mercy of unionism, instead of having the opposite effect. For if small business cannot present a united front against union demands, it often cannot obtain an equitable bargain.

Breaking up unions into local bodies is also a much talked-about remedy. This is a variation of the prohibition of multiunit bargaining which ties up entire industries and has led to proposals that industrywide bargaining be banned. Labor contracts would be required by law to be negotiated only between individual employers and local unions. Obviously, this proposal, if adopted, would disrupt long-standing relationships in many industries and would also prohibit bargaining through employer associations, which many management spokesmen feel has done much to stabilize labor-management relations. It can be argued that thus breaking up unions might actually cause them to be even more monopolistic in determining the selling price of labor. For example, if there were four or five separate unions in the automobile industry, each dealing with a separate employer, each company would still find that it was dealing with a monopoly which could cut off its labor supply. On the other hand, the individual unions would vie with one another to get the highest wage possible from their particular employer. The union in General Motors would be able to push its demands without regard to the ability of Ford, Chrysler, or American Motors to meet those demands. While industry-wide strikes might be lessened, the restraint now present in union negotiations, which leads to more or less uniform settlements with the most prosperous as well as the least prosperous companies in the industry, would be removed. The result would probably be a strengthening of the tendency of unions to raise wages and to generate increases in money incomes.

Outlawing compulsory unionism is another proposed solution to union monopoly power. This would probably weaken unions because of its effect on union income, but it would not remove union power over product markets, necessarily reduce the potential for industrywide strikes, or otherwise solve many of the abuses discussed in this chapter.

The problem of union monopoly power thus has many complicated facets. It requires most careful analysis, as well as a general review of existing labor relations law, rather than wholesale attack by oversimplified remedies. In Part VII of this book, we shall discuss our basic labor laws and how they have evolved. The approach of utilizing specific laws, or sections thereof, to attack specific abuses will be seen to be more satisfactory than would a generalized approach through the antitrust laws.

QUESTIONS FOR DISCUSSION

1. If Congress outlawed multiunit bargaining, what would be the effects on industries which now bargain on such a basis?

2. Are unions monopolies? Explain your answer, and compare unions with such aggregations of capital as American Telephone and Telegraph, United States Steel, and General Motors.

3. Do you feel that the future will see more and greater strikes, or less? Why? Would you expect such strikes, however many or few, to be accompanied by more or less violence than in the past?

SUGGESTIONS FOR FURTHER READING

BOARMAN, PATRICK M. *Union Monopolies and Antitrust Restraints* (Washington, D.C.: Labor Policy Association, Inc., 1963).
The case for putting unions under the antitrust laws.

"The Labor Monopoly Myth," *Labor's Economic Review* (AFL–CIO publication), February, 1956.
Labor's official answer to the union monopoly charge.

ROWAN, RICHARD L., and NORTHRUP, HERBERT R. (eds.). *Readings in Labor Economics and Labor Relations*, Part V (B), "Labor Monopoly and Wage Inflation," pp. 431–72. Homewood, Ill.: Richard D. Irwin, Inc., 1968.
Three articles by economists dealing with the monopoly aspects of union power and its impact.

PART IV

Economics of the Labor Market

Chapter 8

THE LABOR MARKET

In the market for labor, as in the market for wheat, buyers and sellers meet and bargain over the price at which a sale is to be made. In the wheat market, one price is ultimately arrived at, determined by supply and demand, which "clears the market." Sellers who want a higher price must accept the market price or they cannot sell their product; buyers who want to pay less than the market price cannot find sellers. Does the market for labor function like the market for wheat? If not, why not? What is the explanation for the great diversity which exists in rates of wages and salaries? These are the questions which we shall seek to answer in the following discussion.

DEFINITION OF LABOR MARKET

The concept of a "labor market" has been given many definitions by various writers, depending upon their points of view and the problems with which they were attempting to deal. On the one hand, the labor market can be viewed as a process by which supplies of a particular type of labor and demands for that type of labor are balanced or seek to obtain a balance. On the other hand, the labor market can be considered in the sense of a manufacturing or trading center, or some other geographical area. During World War II, the War Labor Board defined a labor market area as one in which the wage structure and levels in an industry were fairly uniform. The War Manpower Commission defined a labor market as the widest area in which employees with fixed addresses would accept employment.

The foregoing definitions have the common characteristic of viewing a labor market as a definite geographic area. Some economists, however, feel that the element of locality as a characteristic of the labor market is of limited significance insofar as the determination of wages is concerned. It is argued that unions often make wage decisions without reference to supply and demand influences in a particular geographic area. Thus the wage demands of the Rubber Workers' Union in a small town in the Midwest will be determined not by supply and demand factors within

229

the local area or even in the same industry but may be related to a pattern of wage increases granted by the steel and automobile industries in other parts of the country.

Even though it may be necessary to go beyond a particular geographic area to find the forces or criteria which determine wage levels within that area, the concept of the labor market as a geographic area is still a useful one. In this discussion, the term "labor market" will be used in the sense of the geographic area within which a particular group of employers and wage earners buy and sell services. For some forms of labor, the geographic area may be a town, whereas for other forms of labor, such as a talented violinist, the geographic limits of the labor market may be the entire Western world.

DIFFERENCES BETWEEN LABOR MARKETS AND COMMODITY MARKETS

Labor markets differ from commodity markets. Each buyer is distinguished from every other buyer. Even if the United States Steel Corporation and the John Brown Tool Company were to offer the same basic rate to machinists, the offers would differ in attractiveness to different workers. Some men like to work for a large company; some like to work for a small company. There are literally hundreds of other respects in which different employers may be distinguished in an employee's mind. Because the sale of labor involves a continuing, and not merely a temporary, relationship with the "buyer," these intangibles are frequently more important in the employee's mind than the employer's offering price.

Diversity of Rates

Diversity of rates for the same type of labor is the norm, not the exception, in the labor market. In this respect, the labor market resembles certain retail product markets. Recent theories of the functioning of the latter type of market explain that each seller of a particular type of product is in a sense a monopolist, having his own clientele and being able to vary prices within a certain range; yet, he is also in competition with all other monopolists selling similar products. Hence the term "monopolistic competition."[1] Because each seller has some degree of control over his own market, he is frequently able to charge a higher price for the same product sold by a different firm at a lower price. The supermarket may sell a can of beans for 10 cents while next door the delicatessen sells the same product for 15 cents. The exclusive hat shop may sell a hat for $50, while a copy can be obtained for $5 in a poorer section of town. That these differences in prices for the same product can persist is attributable

[1] E. H. Chamberlin, *The Theory of Monopolistic Competition* (5th ed.; Cambridge, Mass.: Harvard University Press, 1946).

in part to buyer ignorance and in part to the fact that even if buyers had full knowledge of the price difference, they might not want to alter their customary buying habits.

Similarly, as we shall see in the following discussion, differences in wages for the same job may exist in the same area because workers do not have full knowledge of other job opportunities; and even if they did have accurate knowledge, the differences might still persist because of the reluctance of workers to leave their places of work to start anew in a different firm. Thus, inertia, ignorance, and immobility are of major importance in the labor market. Furthermore, because of differences in the race, sex, or length of service of employees performing the same job, diversity in wage rates for the same job may exist even within a single plant.

A labor market may also have monopsonistic as well as monopolistic aspects. This is particularly true in a small town where one employer may dominate the labor market. The buyer of labor may then set the price—at least within a certain range—provided that the supply of labor is ample and no union exists or threatens to upset the status quo.

Wage Fixing in the Labor Market

Wage fixing, analogous to a quoted price in the product market, is characteristic of the labor market. Whereas, in the commodity market, it is normally the seller who sets the asking price, in the labor market (in the absence of unions) the buyer of labor normally sets the price. The price that is set tends to be "fixed" for some length of time. Employers do not want wage rates to fluctuate with every change in supply and demand conditions. Stability in wage rates is essential for satisfactory business operations. Constant change in the wage schedule of the average company would cost more than it is worth. Moreover, stability is also desirable from the point of view of employees. Frequent changes in wage rates would cause friction and suspicion and would make employees feel insecure. Therefore, in changing wage rates, employers customarily grant general wage adjustments to all employees instead of adjusting rates to individual demand and supply conditions, or at least grant individual wage increases according to some plan or custom.

The majority of multiplant companies do relate their wage scales either to those paid by other firms in the area or to rates for the same industry in the area; some, however, pay the same wage scales regardless of the size of the city or the region of the country in which their plants are located, and others have uniform scales for each region or zone. Still others pay community wage rates, but grant the same adjustments, regardless of area. Some companies raise wages with increases in the cost of living and increases in length of service, while other companies do not. Such differences in company wage policies, in employer evaluation of particular jobs, and in stress on various wage factors all contribute to the existence of a diversity of wage rates rather than a single rate for any grade of labor in a particular locality.

Lack of Mobility

Until recently, many economists assumed that there was enough mobility from job to job among workers within a geographic area so that if one firm paid a higher wage for a given job than other firms in the area, workers qualified for that job would attempt to get employment at the high-wage plant. The influx of applicants to this plant would tend to pull down the wage offered there and at the same time force other employers to raise their wages until equilibrium between the high-wage and low-wage firms was achieved, perhaps at some rate between the wages formerly paid by each. Recent studies indicate, however, that in the absence of collective bargaining, employers will continue indefinitely to pay diverse rates for the same grade of labor in the same locality under strictly comparable job conditions.

The labor market, therefore, is not characterized by a norm of pure competition. There is no wage which will clear the market, toward which a labor market under actual conditions even in the absence of collective bargaining is tending. The labor market is characterized by stability and lack of fluidity and a diversity of rates for similar jobs. A rise in the price of labor offered by a particular employer does not cause employees in other firms who are receiving less than that amount to leave their jobs and flock to the high-wage employer. Sufficiently large differentials will, of course, induce a movement of labor; but within a substantial range, changes in rates by a particular employer may have little effect in causing workers to leave other firms to seek work in the high-wage firm. In order to understand why this is so and why diverse wage rates for the same jobs can continue to coexist in the same area, some understanding of labor mobility is required.

THE NATURE OF LABOR MOBILITY

Labor is not an easily transportable factor of production. It does not flow readily or easily in response to small changes in its remuneration. One reason is that work—having and keeping a job—is a central status symbol in our profit-oriented society. Losing one's job brings with it more than a loss of income; in the eyes of the average wage earner—and his family—such a calamity means a definite loss of status. Workers' psychology, therefore, has an important impact upon labor mobility. In the following discussion we shall consider how mobility of labor in practice differs from the theoretical norm and therefore makes possible continuation of diversity of wage rates among firms, industries, and regions.

Problems of the Job Search

For most workers the choice of the first job is a matter of accident or coincidence. John Jones graduates from high school and needs a job. Usually, he hears of an opening through a friend or relative and goes to work there without making a systematic canvas of available opportunities in the labor market. Typically, information about job vacancies is obtained through informal channels.[2] A surprising reluctance exists among many workers to use state employment agencies. Only if they are laid off and are forced to register for unemployment insurance are they likely to utilize state employment offices. With both employers and employees, state employment offices apparently have, to an unfortunate degree, the reputation of supplying less satisfactory labor and less satisfactory jobs. Therefore, workers are likely to depend upon informal and chance methods of finding jobs or, occasionally, to utilize private employment agencies.

In a perfect labor market, job opportunities would be generally known and available workers would gravitate toward the better paying jobs for which their skills qualified them. In the actual labor market, this process is only dimly visible because information about the various job vacancies and the merits and disadvantages of particular jobs are not generally known. To a large extent, job attachments result from chance, rather than careful economic appraisal.

The lack of knowledge about job opportunities is particularly acute among slum residents. Newspapers, radio, TV advertisements, and placement offices all fail to reach out sufficiently in slum areas, and most employers do not actively seek help from such areas. Since people living in poverty areas generally have contact only with their friends and neighbors in low-level occupations, this kind of communication does little to widen their knowledge of job opportunities. Moreover, because of lack of confidence in their own ability and disillusionment with employment prospects, residents of slum areas rarely take the direct route of "knocking on doors" to find a job. For example, a study of 450 disadvantaged youth in Philadelphia revealed that two fifths of these youth had never made a single contact with an employer.[3]

The high unemployment rate of slum residents is visible evidence that impediments in the labor market are preventing it from effectively matching available jobs with available workers. The federal government is

---

[2] For a study of the many informal methods by which employers spread word of job vacancies, see Albert Rees, "Information Networks in Labor Markets," *American Economic Review, Proceedings of 78th Annual Meeting, Supplement,* May, 1966, pp. 559–66.

[3] *Manpower Report of the President, 1967* (Washington, D.C.: U.S. Government Printing Office, 1967), p. 86.

now seeking through a number of programs to help workers in slum areas to get more accurate information about job opportunities. A network of Youth Opportunity Centers have been established in War on Poverty target areas by the federal-state employment service system. These YOC's provide services for all young people seeking work and also reach out to disadvantaged youth in order to increase their employability. In addition, so-called Human Resource Development Programs have been begun in a number of cities by the Federal Employment Service in cooperation with business and minority groups and community agencies to ascertain by a door-to-door check what employment needs and employment opportunities exists in slum neighborhoods. Since a number of other federal, state, and local agencies are also working in the same direction, it is apparent that there is a great deal of overlap and wasted effort in such programs. However, the concept of improving the flow of information about job opportunities in slum areas is basically sound and much needed. It is bound to yield results in the long run in terms of reduced unemployment and higher incomes for slum residents.

Changing Jobs

Even after a worker has found a job, his new status as an employee does not broaden his horizon of knowledge about other job opportunities markedly. Generally, wages, hours, and working conditions in other plants are either vague or unknown to him. The lack of knowledge on the part of employees attaches them more firmly to their present jobs. They do not think in terms of changing jobs because they do not know what the alternatives are. They know the conditions under which they work, and they fear to take a chance on the basis of their inadequate knowledge of conditions elsewhere.

Once workers have had experience on the job, their ideas as to what they want in a position tend to crystallize. Of prime importance, of course, is an adequate wage rate. Employees are likely to judge wages by two criteria: first, what standard of living the wage permits them to enjoy; and second, how it compares to what they regard as a fair rate for the job. In addition to wages, workers tend to place a good deal of importance on such intangibles as the independence permitted them in their job, relationship with fellow workers, fairness of treatment by employer, the extent to which the work is interesting, and the physical characteristics of the job. All of these considerations, other than wages, it should be noted, are difficult to ascertain except by those who are already working in the particular plant. Lack of knowledge by employees of the merits of other jobs, therefore, is attributable not only to the failure of workers to inquire more thoroughly into alternative job opportunities but also to the fact that such knowledge is inherently difficult to obtain prior to actual employment in such other jobs.

Most workers are reluctant to change jobs even if they know that a higher wage can be obtained at a different plant or in a different occupation. One reason is that there is a transfer cost in making such a change. There may be a period of layoff between jobs, or additional training may be required, or perhaps the worker will have to physically move himself and his family to a new city or to a new residence in a different part of a city. All of these costs impose barriers to movement. The fear of a layoff, in particular, pervades the thinking of working people who rarely have any substantial amount of savings to fall back upon. For most of them, a basic objective is to work their way into a secure position where they will be protected in the event of slack work. Since a job change may mean loss of seniority and accrued rights under pension plans, employees are generally reluctant to leave a job as long as they regard their conditions of employment generally "fair," even though they may not be the best.

How long does, in fact, the average employee stay with a given job or employer? A survey of job attachment of workers made by the U.S. Department of Labor in January, 1966, indicated that employees stayed with the same job or employer an average of 4.2 years. Job tenure varied directly with age; workers under age 35 averaged only about 1.5 years on the current job while those over 35 years averaged 8 years. The longest job tenure was among skilled craftsmen outside the construction industry who were on the same job an average of 11 to 13 years. This long job duration reflects the influence of two major factors in job tenure—skill and age. Nearly half of these skilled workers were over 45. The shortest job tenure for men is found among farm and nonfarm laborers, carpenters, service workers, and sales employees.[4]

Determinants of Occupational Mobility

Why do workers change jobs? The motivation of occupational mobility is not clearly understood, and much field research is required on this subject if we are to have a satisfactory understanding of movements in the labor market. However, we do have available considerable statistical data suggesting definite interrelationships between worker mobility (both voluntary and involuntary) and age, sex, color, education, type of job, and character of employment. As has already been suggested in the previous section, occupational mobility declines as the age of the worker increases. Much of the occupational change among younger workers is probably voluntary and associated with "shopping around" for jobs, casual occupational attachment while in school, and tenuous home town ties. As workers grow older, mobility is impaired by stronger occupational ties, job seniority rights, age discrimination in hiring, higher in-

[4] Harvey R. Hamel, "Job Tenure of Workers" (Special Labor Force Report No. 77 [Washington, D.C.: U.S. Department of Labor, Bureau of Labor Statistics, 1967]), p. 34.

comes that reduce incentives to move, and the fear of change itself. Among the older worker group, job shifts are more likely to be involuntary than voluntary.[5]

Statistics suggest that men, both white and nonwhite, are more apt to change occupations than women. This is true both with respect to full-time and part-time employment. Furthermore, as can be seen from Table 8–1, part-time workers are more mobile occupationally. This is to

TABLE 8–1

OCCUPATIONAL MOBILITY RATES[1] BY FULL-TIME[2] OR PART-TIME[3]
WORK STATUS: OCCUPATION AND SEX, JANUARY 1966

	Men Usually work		Women Usually work	
Occupation in January, 1966	Full Time	Part Time	Full Time	Part Time
Total, 18 years and over.........	9.7	12.9	7.0	6.5
Professional, technical and kindred workers......................	6.4	8.4	3.2	5.5
Farmers and farm laborers...........	3.4	6.5	5.6	1.1
Farmers.......................	1.9	2.2	([5])	([5])
Farm laborers....................	7.5	([5])	6.5	1.6
Managers, officials, proprietors, except farm....................	7.5	3.0	5.9	([5])
Clerical and kindred workers.........	13.6	20.8	8.3	9.3
Sales workers.....................	8.3	11.8	7.1	10.1
Craftsmen and kindred workers.......	8.6	11.8	12.3	([5])
Operatives and kindred workers.......	12.7	21.4	7.4[4]	3.9[4]
Service workers, including private household....................	11.3	14.7	7.4	5.3
Private household................	([5])	([5])	4.9	3.0
Other service workers.............	11.1	14.4	8.2	7.5
Laborers, except farm..............	17.3	16.6	([5])	([5])

[1] Proportion of persons employed in both January, 1965, and January, 1966, who had a different occupaton in January, 1965.
[2] Includes persons who during the survey week worked 35 hours or more, those who worked less than 35 hours but usually work 35 hours or more, and persons with a job but not at work.
[3] Includes persons who during the survey week worked 1 to 34 hours and usually worked less than 35 hours a week.
[4] Includes a small number of laborers.
[5] Rate not shown where base is less than 100,000.
SOURCE: Samuel Saben, "Occupational Mobility of Employed Workers" (Special Labor Force Report No. 84 [Washington, D.C.: U.S. Department of Labor, Bureau of Labor Statistics, 1967]), Table H, p. A–11.

be expected since this group includes a large percentage of younger workers, Negroes, and the less skilled. Surprisingly, however, statistics indicate that women have about the same occupational mobility whether on part-time or full-time jobs.

[5] This section of the discussion draws heavily on Samuel Saben, "Occupational Mobility of Employed Workers" (Special Labor Force Report No. 84 [Washington, D.C.: U.S. Department of Labor, 1967]), pp. 31–38.

Negro men show a higher mobility rate than white men. The difference in rate between Negro women and white women is inconclusive. The difference for men reflects the fact that mobility is characteristically higher in the job categories where Negro employment is most pronounced. However, the statistics also suggest a more troublesome finding—that is, that many Negro occupational changes are aimless and involuntary. Studies reveal that (*a*) in intraplant occupational changes, few Negroes move upward in the skill-grouping of occupations; (*b*) when Negroes move to higher paid occupations, they tend to enter in the least skilled categories at the lowest earnings levels; (*c*) that there is a tendency for mobile Negro workers to move to lower earnings levels, particularly Negro men aged 25 to 34 years old, when the propensity to change occupations is high.

Nearly half of the men and women who changed jobs in 1965 came from occupations requiring little or no skill—operatives, service workers, and farm and nonfarm laborers. These are also occupations in which unemployment rates are relatively high. It seems odd that occupations with high unemployment rates should have the most entrants from other occupations—but they do simply because they do not require lengthy periods of education or training. Occupational change occurs least among persons who have completed four years or more of college. Simply stated, the person who has spent seven years in universities preparing for a career as a lawyer is likely to stay in that occupation, while the untrained high school graduate who gets a job as a gasoline station attendant is likely to shift frequently from one occupation to another.

One other important factor must be considered in any analysis of job changes—that is, that many of them are not wholly economically motivated. Reasons of health, residence, family, friendship, and many other factors all can contribute in motivating an employee to make a job change. These noneconomic factors further lessen the correlation between wage changes and employment in the labor market.

Types of Mobility

Job mobility may take different forms. An employee may change jobs within a particular company. He may change his occupation, his industry, and his employer, or there may be various combinations of these factors. Finally, he may or may not change the geographic location of his employment to the extent of moving across county lines.

Recent studies by the U.S. Department of Labor indicate that four out of five workers who change occupations also change employers.[6] Furthermore, the same survey found that 7 out of 10 of the men and three quarters of the women who changed occupations between January, 1965, and January, 1966, also changed the industry in which they were work-

---

[6] Saben, *op. cit.*, p. 36.

ing.[7] Although job changes which involve change of employers are probably more common than those that do not, as suggested by the above statistics, it is likely that job changes within the confines of a given employer are less likely to be reported, and therefore Department of Labor and other governmental statistics may tend to underestimate the actual mobility which occurs within the firm.[8]

Although we are known as a "nation on wheels," geographic mobility of workers—defined in terms of moves across county lines—is remarkably small. The U.S. Department of Labor Bureau of Labor Statistics found from a sample study of a group of men aged 18 to 64 that only 7% had moved across a county line during the year. One interesting fact revealed by this study is that professional and technical workers accounted for 19% of the migrants, but for only 12% of all employed men.[9] One has only to read the want ads in *The New York Times* to understand that engineers, physicists, and other technical and professional workers are responding to a labor market which for this group at least is national in scope. Persons with considerable educational attainments are likely to have high geographic mobility rates, although their occupational changes are relatively few.

The Trend in Quit Rates

We have seen that in the labor market both employer and employee are frequently more interested in job stability than mobility. The employee prefers stability in job tenure so that he is not exposed to income loss while changing jobs and can build up rights in valuable job fringes based upon seniority. The employer prefers stability because it means that costs of hiring and training new employees are minimized and he can plan production and operation schedules with the knowledge that adequate personnel are available. Yet, from the point of view of the needs of a dynamic economy with a constantly changing mix of job opportunities, a higher rate of mobility may be required in order to achieve a better utilization of the labor force and to minimize shortages of labor and bottlenecks in production as the economy achieves high employment levels.

Is labor mobility increasing or decreasing in our economy? One way of measuring this trend is to examine so-called "quit rates." Voluntary quits are defined as persons who leave the employ of a company upon their own volition for any reason except to retire, enter military service, or to transfer to another establishment of the same company. Series of such data per 100 employees are available for manufacturing industries

[7] *Ibid.*, p. 37.
[8] For an excellent study of mobility within a firm, see H. M. Gitelman, "Occupational Mobility within the Firm," *Industrial and Labor Relations Review*, Vol. XX (October, 1966), pp. 50-65.
[9] *Business Week*, October 3, 1964, p. 61.

over a long period of years. Unfortunately, they are collected only for manufacturing industries, although labor turnover is undoubtedly higher in some nonmanufacturing industries. As the figures in Table 8–2 reveal,

TABLE 8–2

QUIT RATES AND LAYOFF RATES IN MANUFACTURING,
AND UNEMPLOYMENT AS PERCENT OF LABOR FORCE:
ANNUAL AVERAGES, SELECTED YEARS, 1947–67

| | Per 100 Employees | | Unemploy- |
Year	Quit Rate	Layoff Rate	ment Percent
1947	4.1	1.1	3.9%
1949	1.9	2.9	5.9
1950	2.3	1.3	5.3
1951	2.9	1.4	3.3
1954	1.4	2.3	5.5
1955	1.9	1.5	4.4
1958	1.1	2.6	6.8
1960	1.3	2.4	5.5
1965	1.9	1.4	4.5
1966	2.6	1.2	3.8
1967	2.3	1.4	3.8

SOURCE: Unemployment rates from *Employment and Earnings*, January, 1968 (Washington, D.C.: U.S. Government Printing Office, 1968), p. 34; quit and lay-off rates from *Handbook of Labor Statistics, 1967* (U.S. Department of Labor Bulletin No. 1555 [Washington, D.C.: U.S. Government Printing Office, 1968]), p. 76, and *Manpower Report of the President, 1968, op. cit.*, p. 278.

quits are relatively small and tend to vary inversely with layoffs and the rate of unemployment. The statistics in Table 8–2 also suggest that the quit rate in manufacturing has gradually been declining. For example, in 1947 with an overall rate of unemployment of 3.9%, the quit rate was 4.1, whereas in 1966 with almost the same unemployment rate, the quit rate had fallen to 2.6%. The diminution in the quit rate is even more noticeable if recent figures are compared with those in the decade of the 1920's.[10]

The factors we have already mentioned—namely, seniority and pensions—have undoubtedly had some influence on this trend. On the other hand, it should be recognized that most workers who quit jobs are young and therefore are the least affected by seniority rules and pension rights. Other factors include:

1. *The Spread of Unionism.* In preunion days the most common

[10] For a statistical and mathematical analysis of voluntary quit data purporting to substantiate the proposition that there has been a decline in voluntary mobility in manufacturing over the past several decades, see John E. Parker and John F. Burton, Jr., "Voluntary Labor Mobility in the Manufacturing Section," *Monthly Labor Review*, Vol. XCI (April, 1968), pp. 33–56.

method of expressing dissatisfaction with a job was to quit. With the growth of unions, workers could air their discontent through grievance procedures and still retain their jobs.

2. *The Aging of the Labor Force.* The number of older persons in the labor force has increased during this entire period; and there is, of course, a strong correlation between age and the quit rate.

3. *Stability of Manufacturing Employment.* To a large extent, new entrants to the labor force have been going into the trade and service industries, while manufacturing employment has been relatively stable. As a consequence, manufacturing labor may be aging faster than the total labor force.

4. *Sociological Factors Making It Important to Keep a Job.* Today, many young men fall into the sociological pattern of marrying young, having children early, and taking on a heavy burden of installment debt to pay for the home, automobile, television set, and other essentials of modern-day living. The bill collector may be as important as the union business agent as an explanation of the reduction in quit rates in manufacturing.

It should be reiterated that the foregoing discussion applies only to manufacturing. Data are not available for other sectors of the economy, and it is quite possible that a different trend may exist there. In any case the great influx of young workers under 25 who are now appearing on the labor market may alter this trend of quit rates, although the anticipated stability of employment in manufacturing may hold quit rates in this sector of the economy down, while those in the service industries, which are expanding, may rise.

LABOR MARKET STRUCTURE

In analyzing various labor markets in this country, we may distinguish them by their geographic location—for example, the West Coast labor market differs materially from that in other parts of the country—or we may distinguish labor markets according to their "structure." A labor market structure has been defined as

a set of "established practices" which are applied consistently in carrying out the various employment functions of recruitment, selection, assignment to jobs, wage payment, transfer, separation, and the like. Established practices are created by law, contract, custom, and managerial policy. Their function is to establish the rights and privileges of employees and to introduce certainty and regularity into the handling of personnel—in short, to create a "rule of law" in employment matters. Their main effect is to limit managerial discretion.[11]

---

[11] Orme W. Phelps, "A Structural Model of the U.S. Labor Market," *Industrial and Labor Relations Review*, Vol. X (April, 1957), p. 403. The writers have drawn heavily on this excellent article for the analysis contained in this section.

In terms of the foregoing definition, labor markets range all the way from the highly structured to the unstructured, depending upon the presence or absence of rules or practices governing the employment relationship. Thus, public employment characterized by detailed civil service regulations would be an example of a highly structured labor market where managerial prerogatives have been severely restricted. By contrast, the market for domestic servants would be unstructured to a high degree, with great flexibility in the type of relationship which can be worked out between employer and employee.

Structured Labor Markets

Structured labor markets fall into three general categories: (1) the market for public employees, which is structured from entry to exit by legislation and administrative rules; (2) the nonunion labor market in the large firm, in which the structuring aspect emanates from the employer's personnel policies, formulated and administered by a personnel department; (3) the labor market, in which "established practices" derive from collective bargaining agreements and union work rules.

The market for public employees is impersonal, technical, and highly classified. Emphasis is on security of tenure rather than on pay. Entrance requirements are frequently based upon competitive examination. A high proportion of regular, permanent public employees are eligible for civil service status, which carries with it advantages of tenure and opportunities for promotion. However, despite the fact that government, in theory, has unrestricted authority to vary the terms and conditions of employment, as a practical matter the hands of the government administrator in charge of a particular agency are securely tied with the red tape of governmental regulation, so that the public labor market has many of the characteristics of a highly unionized labor market in the private business sector of the economy. The increasing importance of collective bargaining among public employees may further accentuate the formalized structuring of wage and employment practices in this field.[12]

The nonunion structured labor market dominated by employer personnel policies is to be found in three major areas: the large unorganized industrial firm, which, although somewhat exceptional, still exists; the large unorganized firm in the white-collar industries—banks, department stores, insurance companies, etc.; and nonunion employees outside the bargaining unit in large companies which are organized. Large industrial firms which are unorganized retain unilateral control over employment policies but, in practice, are likely to follow rates and policies of their organized competitors so as not to make themselves a target for union organization. In addition, restraints on wages and conditions are imposed

---

[12] See Chapter 23 for a discussion of collective bargaining by government employees.

by state and federal laws. Large white-collar companies are still the stronghold for structured employment policies dictated by management. This group has become more important in the present decade in terms of share of the total labor market because of the shift of employment toward trade, finance, and related fields, in which this type of structure predominates. White-collar workers in organized companies who are outside the bargaining unit do not have the full protection of the union, but nevertheless benefit in many ways from gains secured by the union for organized employees. Obviously, management cannot afford to have major inequities develop between the two groups of employees, which would either have a bad effect on morale or constitute an invitation to union organization.

Most unionized employment is manual, hourly rated, blue-collar work. The employee either may work on a permanent basis for a large industrial concern or may be employed in one of the casual trades, such as construction, where his association with any one employer may be brief. The structure of such a labor market is, in theory, bilateral, resulting from the bargain made by the employer and the union. Where the employer is small and the union strong, as in the building-trades or trucking industry, the union may often dictate the rates of pay, the hours of work, job assignments, promotions, and other aspects of the employment relationship. In larger firms the personnel department may still make policy decisions, but these are generally subject to review and consultation with the union through collective bargaining.

Unstructured Labor Markets

The unstructured labor market is, in general, the market of individual bargains, in which there are few if any rules or regulations affecting employment practices, except governmental enactments setting minimum wages, prohibiting discrimination, etc. This market includes farm labor, domestic help, professional office employees, and employees of small business firms. It has been estimated that this market covers about one third of the civilian employed labor force (excluding proprietors, self-employed, and unpaid family labor). Employment in these markets is apt to be on a personal basis, with little emphasis on formal policies and procedures. Union organization is largely absent, fringe benefits are few, and in many cases the employer is not even subject to the minimal structuring provided by various federal statutes, since most such statutes—the Taft-Hartley Act, the Fair Labor Standards Act, and similar laws—provide exemptions for small local businesses.

DIVERSITY IN WAGE RATES

We have already observed that even in a local labor market, divergent wage rates may prevail for similar jobs. It is not surprising, then, that diversity is also found when cities are compared with towns or the South with the North, or one industry with another industry. Indeed, diversity of rates is characteristic of the labor market however that term is defined. In the following discussion we shall consider such diversity from four principal points of view: geographical, interindustry, interfirm, and personal.

Geographical Diversity: The North–South Differential

Regional location is an important factor in determining pay levels. It is frequently stated that "wages are lower in the South." This statement is open to several interpretations. The North–South differential may mean that wages in particular industries are lower in the South than in other parts of the country. This is true in some industries, but not in others. Among 26 manufacturing industries studied recently by the U.S. Bureau of Labor Statistics, the southern wage level ranged from 38.6% below the rest of the country in meat packing to more than 9% above in synthetic fibers.[13] Likewise, in nonmanufacturing industries the differential ranged from about 30% below in service industries, such as laundries, restaurants and hotels, to only 5% below in bituminous coal. In the basic steel and automobile assembly industries, regional rate differentials have been largely eliminated by collective bargaining agreements.[14]

The North–South differential may mean that the average wage of all workers in the one region is lower than the average wage of all workers in the other. This is obviously a crude measurement because it compares wages regardless of intraregional industrial mix and variations in skills, city size, and so forth which can affect wage levels. One recent study concluded that average hourly earnings in the non-South are about 25% higher than in the South. About one third of this differential is attributable to regional differences in the labor force as measured by color, age, sex, and education; about one third is related to regional differences in city size; and about one third of the differential remains, after adjusting for labor force composition and city size.[15]

Many explanations have been advanced as to why this residual differential exists. Some claim that southern labor is less efficient, but after adjusting for educational differences, there is little evidence to support this claim. Union leaders argue that the weakness of union organization in the South accounts for the differential, but North-South wage differentials are much too complex and diverse for such a simple explanation. Differentials vary widely in amounts from industry to industry, whether the industries are unionized or not.

[13] H. M. Douty, "Wage Differentials: Forces and Counterforces," *Monthly Labor Review*, Vol. XCI (March, 1968), p. 74.

[14] *Ibid.*, p. 75.

[15] Victor R. Fuchs, "Hourly Earnings Differentials by Region and Size of City," *Monthly Labor Review*, Vol. XC (January, 1967), p. 25.

Actually, the most logical explanation of the southern wage differential is the fact that there is an oversupply of labor relative to capital in the South—or to put the matter another way, a relative shortage of capital. The oversupply of labor seems to be particularly acute with respect to unskilled labor. Statistics indicate that the differential between wage rates in the South and in the rest of the nation is much greater for unskilled labor than for skilled.[16] It is not surprising, therefore, that the regional differential in wages for nonwhite workers is greater than for all workers, since nonwhites tend to be concentrated in the unskilled category of occupations. It is possible, too, that there is more market discrimination against Negroes in the South, and this factor tends to add still another dimension to the regional wage differential.

The historical basis for the economic maldistribution begins with the use of land and unskilled labor as the main focus of development in the South, rather than the combination of capital goods and skilled labor. A relative shortage of capital, therefore, exists in the South even today. While, over the past few decades, there has been a net migration of labor out of the South and a net capital flow in, the southern labor force has been growing at a more rapid rate than that of the rest of the country. Furthermore, Bureau of Labor Statistics projections to 1980 indicate that the southern labor force will continue to grow at a faster rate than will be true for the labor force in the rest of the country.[17] As a consequence, the relative surplus of labor is likely to persist and the southern wage differential will decline very slowly.[18]

Union Policy and Regional Differentials

In general, union policy has opposed regional wage differentials. The United Mine Workers, for example, has succeeded in equalizing basic wage rates between the northern and southern Appalachian coal regions; the Steelworkers, with the cooperation of United States Steel and Republic Steel, began to eliminate area differentials in the late 1940's, and the job was pretty much completed in the 1950's. The UAW has ended all area differentials at Chrysler and Ford, but General Motors has continued to pay community-oriented rates despite UAW pressure. The Rubber Workers have been unsuccessful in their attempts to eliminate the regional wage spread. In the early 1960's, however, James R. Hoffa was successful in achieving a uniform national rate for over-the-road truck

---

[16] Victor R. Fuchs, *Differentials in Hourly Earnings by Region and City Size, 1959* (Occasional Paper No. 101 [New York: National Bureau of Economic Research, 1967]), Preface.

[17] Douty, *op. cit.*, p. 80.

[18] *Ibid.*, p. 78, finds that "over the past 60 years there has been little change in the general differential in wages between the South and the remainder of the country." Other investigators, however, have found some evidence that the differential is narrowing. See *Monthly Labor Review*, Vol. XCI (April, 1968), p. 44.

drivers, eliminating thereby several differentials, including one in the South.

On the other hand, many unions have not opposed southern wage differentials where they regard them as justified by certain circumstances. Because of a poor grade of coal and higher transportation costs, the United Mine Workers continues to sanction wage differentials between the Alabama and the Appalachian bituminous areas. The Textile Workers' Union of America has sanctioned differentials between Virginia and the New York metropolitan area. Very often, local unions in a strategic bargaining situation have been called upon by the national union to forego the maximum wage increase which they might have been able to obtain from local employers simply because the national policy was to establish uniform rates which would be borne by employers generally over a wider geographic area. Uniform wages, these unions feel, increase union solidarity and lessen cleavages within the union ranks.

The difficulty of organizing workers in the South, combined with the low wages of this area, has served as a brake on North-South wage differentials in certain industries. Unable to organize the South, the hosiery and the textile workers have seen lower southern rates keep down their wage gains in the North; other unionized mills in the North have either migrated South, where they operate nonunion, or gone out of business. The failure of the United Mine Workers to organize southern coal mines in the 1920's almost destroyed the union. The northern mines were forced to break with the United Mine Workers in order to compete with the low-wage South. The rising number of southern Appalachian mines which now operate nonunion at lower wage and fringe benefit rates is again a severe problem for the UMW.

In these cases the problem of the regional differential to the union is the problem of union and nonunion competition. The problem of the North–South differential is less acute when the unionized high-wage employers are located in and sell to a market such as the Far West, which, because of distance and geographic factors, is primarily local and is not sensitive to southern competition.

Geographical Diversity: City Size

While average hourly earnings are generally highest in the West and lowest in the South, within each region of this country it has been found that city size has a major impact upon wages no matter what kind of labor is being hired: men or women, white or nonwhite, skilled or unskilled, well schooled or uneducated.

As Figure 8–1 shows, the bigger the city the higher the wage. The city-size wage differential is largest in the South and among Negroes and workers with limited education. A man in the South, regardless of race, living in or near a city with a population of more than a million, makes 35% more than the average wage earned outside metropolitan areas. A

FIGURE 8-1

THE BIGGER THE CITY, THE HIGHER THE WAGE . . .

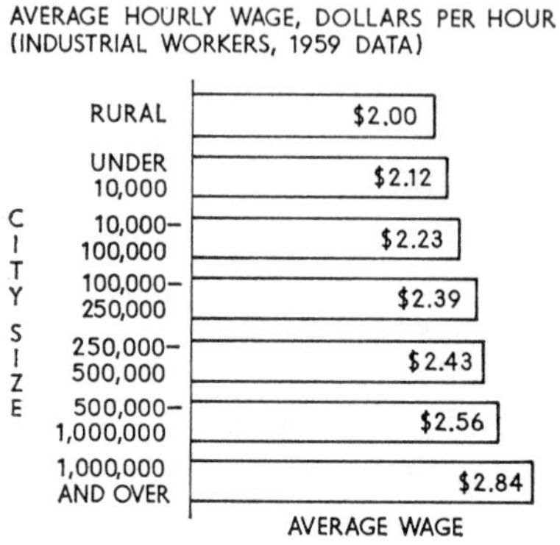

. . . BUT RACE AND LOCATION COUNT TOO

AVERAGE HOURLY WAGE, DOLLARS PER HOUR
(INDUSTRIAL WORKERS, 1959 DATA)

CITY SIZE	AVERAGE WAGE
RURAL	$2.00
UNDER 10,000	$2.12
10,000–100,000	$2.23
100,000–250,000	$2.39
250,000–500,000	$2.43
500,000–1,000,000	$2.56
1,000,000 AND OVER	$2.84

AVERAGE WAGE

Dollars per Hour [1959]

City Size	South		Outside of South	
	White	*Non-white*	*White*	*Non-white*
Rural.........	1.80	1.06	2.22	1.80
Under 10,000...	1.98	.99	2.31	1.62
10,000–100,000	2.14	.99	2.40	1.84
100,000–250,-000.........	2.34	1.13	2.56	1.90
250,000–500,-000.........	2.46	1.28	2.52	2.13
500,000–1,000,-000.........	2.54	1.37	2.71	2.18
1,000,000 and over.........	2.86	1.54	2.96	1.96

Data: National Bureau of Economic Research.

SOURCE: *Business Week*, March 11, 1967, p. 175. By permission of McGraw-Hill, Inc.

big-city Negro in the South will make 37% more, and a person with fewer than four years of schooling, 63% more.[19]

The reasons for differentials of this magnitude are not fully understood. While differences in cost of living have some relevance to this problem, statistical studies show that intercity differences in cost of living are relatively small compared to differentials in hourly earnings. Another possibility is that productivity is the explanation. Are big-city workers more productive, better educated, better motivated? One writer speculates that there is a "labor market disequilibrium" between the small towns and the large cities: Capital is scarce relative to labor in small towns, keeping wages low; capital is abundant relative to labor in big cities, pushing wages up.[20]

Whatever the explanation, the fact remains that these differentials do exist and attest to a lack of fluidity of labor and capital between geographical areas, which is somewhat surprising in our dynamic economy. In recent years, there has been some tendency for industry to move out of the central cities, motivated by the desire to avoid the traffic congestion and high tax rates of those areas as much as anything. This move, if it

[19] *Business Week*, March 11, 1967, p. 175.

[20] Victor R. Fuchs, *Differentials in Hourly Earnings by Region and City Size, 1959, op. cit.*, p. 34.

continues, coupled with the tendency of labor to move to the big cities, could in time narrow the differentials which now exist.

Between 1954 and 1965, almost two thirds of all new industrial building (measured by valuation) and a little over half of all new stores were constructed outside the nation's central cities.[21] Between 1947 and 1967, total employment in seven large central cities rose by only 50,000, while employment in the metropolitan rings surrounding these same cities increased by 900,000. This movement by industry has further complicated the difficult task of finding employment for slum residents who find it costly to travel from the heart of the central cities to the suburbs to work. By the same token, however, the development of pools of unemployed labor in the central cities coupled with the movement of new plants to suburbs and smaller towns will tend to reduce the differential in wages pictured in Figure 8–1.

Interindustry Differentials

Marked differences in rates and earnings prevail among various industries for similar jobs in the same geographical area. Table 8–3 shows

TABLE 8–3

AVERAGE HOURLY EARNINGS OF TRUCK DRIVERS IN METROPOLITAN
AREAS OF THE NORTHEAST BY INDUSTRY DIVISION, 1966

Retail trade	$2.77
Manufacturing	3.14
Nonmanufacturing	3.10
Transportation, communication, and public utilities	3.20
Wholesale trade	3.01
Selected services	2.41

SOURCE: U.S. Department of Labor, Bureau of Labor Statistics, *Handbook of Labor Statistics, 1967* (Washington, D.C., 1967), pp. 170–73.

that even in a highly unionized occupation like trucking, average hourly earnings will vary all the way from $2.41 to $3.20. These differences reflect in part competitive pressures from the product market which affect the ability of employers in various industries to compensate their employees. One might think that if truck drivers consistently earned more in manufacturing firms than in service-oriented companies, there would be a tendency for employees to move from the latter to the former with the ultimate result that rates and earnings would tend to be equalized between the two industries. Undoubtedly there is some tendency in this direction. But the fact that differentials continue to persist over long periods of time between industries is further evidence of the lack of mobility in the labor market and the divergence of the actual labor market from the theoretical norm.

[21] *Manpower Report of the President, 1967, op. cit.,* p. 87.

Industrial differentials can be compared in terms of hourly or weekly earnings, on the one hand, and annual earnings, on the other hand. The latter statistic gives greater weight to continuity of employment. Actually, one can understand industrial differentials only by considering both classes of figures. For example, in 1965 average hourly earnings in mining were $2.92. This was one of the highest rates among the various industry groups (see Table 8–4). But this high hourly rate was intended in part to compensate for the erratic employment which prevails in this industry. Average annual earnings of full-time employees in mining were actually less than those of employees in wholesale trade, although, as can be seen from Table 8–4, the latter received $0.31 less per hour.

The existence of industrial differentials does not necessarily mean that workers performing comparable jobs are paid at different rates in different industries, though this is sometimes the case. One industry may pay lower rates on the average than another because less skill is required in the industry; because of the larger percentage of women, Negroes, or part-time workers employed; because of the location of plants in small towns or rural areas rather than in metropolitan areas; or because of the lack of union organization.

There appears to have been no significant trend toward the broadening or narrowing of industrial differentials in hourly earnings since 1939.

The data in Table 8–4 support the thesis of the persistence of inter-industry wage differentials, especially insofar as hourly rates are concerned. There are, of course, changes as some industries decline in employment or profitability and others advance, or new ones arise. But the overall picture seems to be one of maintenance of differentials. A recent study by the U.S. Bureau of Labor Statistics found that industry differentials in pay in 1967 were somewhat smaller than in previous years, but the array of industries from highest to lowest had not changed since 1961.[22]

The interindustry wage differential does not seem to have been narrowed substantially by unionism. Yet pattern bargaining, followed by major unions and major industries, may tend to equalize wage adjustments among major industries. This is not contradictory—first, because the adjustments made in bargains tend to be equal but not to equalize the wage structures upon which they were added; and second, because the persistent low-paying industries are often not pattern bargainers even if unionized, which they frequently are not. Thus the lower wage structure of the latter group of industries tends to be maintained by the interrelated economic and power structure upon which it rests.

Interfirm Differentials

Even within the same industry and geographic locality, different firms will pay different rates for similar jobs. The reason is that an

[22] *Monthly Labor Review,* Vol XLI (April, 1968), p. 44.

employer offers more than a wage to compensate his employees. There may be more "prestige" in working for one employer than another. Or the plant may be newer, or more accessible. Management representatives, such as foremen, may be more skilled in dealing with employees. It takes a mixture of many qualities to build up the reputation of a company as a good place to work. The wage, therefore, is only one part of the total package of benefits which the employer holds out to his employees.

TABLE 8–4

AVERAGE HOURLY EARNINGS AND AVERAGE ANNUAL EARNINGS IN SELECTED
INDUSTRIES, 1947 AND 1965

Industries	Hourly Earnings		Annual Earnings	
	1947	1965	1947	1965
Mining	$1.47	$2.92	$3,113	$6,783
Electrical equipment	1.44	3.21	2,876	6,643
Machinery	1.34	2.96	3,112	7,280
Rubber manufactures	1.30	2.61	3,085	6,246
Wholesale trade	1.22	2.61	3,322	7,236
Chemicals	1.22	2.89	3,119	7,553
Stone, clay, and glass	1.19	2.62	2,672	6,275
Apparel	1.16	1.83	2,327	3,907
Paper and allied products	1.15	2.65	2,903	6,645
Food and kindred products	1.06	2.43	2,669	5,806
Textile products	1.03	1.87	2,338	4,558
Leather and leather products	1.03	1.88	2,313	4,229
Tobacco manufacture	0.90	2.09	1,950	4,807
Retail trade	0.90	1.82	2,368	4,719

SOURCES: National Industrial Conference Board, *Economic Almanac, 1967–1968* (New York: Macmillan Co., 1967), p. 80; and U.S. Department of Labor, *Handbook of Labor Statistics, 1967* (Washington, D.C.: U.S. Government Printing Office, 1967), pp. 147–49. The figures for average annual earnings represent annual wage and salary payments per man-year of full-time work. The figure is derived by dividing wages and salaries paid by the sum of (1) the number of full-time employees and (2) the number of part-time employees reduced to an equivalent number of full-time employees. The average hourly earnings represent average hourly earnings of so-called "production workers" in the respective industries.

Some companies have a deliberate policy of paying more than the market, or more than their competitors, for labor, believing that in the long run this will bring them a better type of worker and greater productivity. One investigation based upon a study of metalworking and soft-goods industries found that despite some industry variation, wage differentials based on size of establishment in the order of 20%–25% on a national basis were fairly typical for most of these industries, except textiles and clothing. In large establishments, compensation in the form of fringe benefits averaged about double in cents per hour what was paid by small establishments.[23]

[23] Richard Lester, "Pay Differentials by Size of Establishment," *Industrial Relations*, Vol. VII (October, 1967), p. 66.

Unions are under considerable pressure from their membership to reduce interfirm wage differentials where they exist in the same industry. Because of interfirm product competition, the low wages paid by some firms constitute a threat to the jobs of the higher paid men, and therefore there is pressure for equalization.

Personal Differentials: Sex and Race

While jobs may be alike, no two workers are the same. They bring to their respective jobs different skills, education, motivation, physical strength, and other attributes. We can understand why two workers with different educational backgrounds will be compensated at different rates. We may sympathize with the less educated worker and attempt to provide additional training for him, but there is no national policy which frowns on wage differentials based upon such factors. However, as a matter of national policy we do not approve of wage differentials based solely upon sex or race. Nevertheless, such differentials continue to persist in the labor market.

The earnings of women in recent years have been about half of those of men. However, the differential varies considerably from one industry or occupation to another. Women's earnings compare favorably with men's in contract construction, mining, transportation, communications, public utilities, and the service industries. Women's earnings are particularly low relative to men in manufacturing and retail trade—and the latter two industries employ about two thirds of all women workers.[24] The differential in earnings, however, results not so much from the payment of different rates for the same jobs as from the restriction of job opportunities. Since many women work only part time or prior to marriage, they do not gain seniority, acquire skills, or obtain promotion to higher paying jobs. Moreover, as a matter of custom, women have generally been afforded employment in jobs which pay less than jobs available to men.

The earnings of Negro workers are substantially less than those of their white counterparts. Here, too, there is considerable variation among industries and occupations. Generally, where Negroes and whites do the same work in a given plant, the racial differential, once prevalent, has been eliminated. But, as was indicated in Chapter 1, Negroes are concentrated in the lower paying jobs, receive less pay for the same education, and have a higher unemployment rate. As a result of an intensification of some of these factors, a growing income gap has developed between the income of Negroes and that of whites—an income gap which is the direct result of the racial-occupational differential and the differential in opportunities for employment. Recent studies document the fact that even at the lowest

---

[24] See *American Women, Report of the President's Commission on the Status of Women* (Washington, D.C.: U.S. Government Printing Office, 1963), pp. 38–39.

end of the occupational ladder, the impact of racial discrimination affects Negro earnings.[25]

Sex and race differentials are largely the result of mores and customs. By insisting on equal pay for equal work, unions have undoubtedly eliminated such differentials in particular plants. They persist, however, for unions do not alter basic institutional and hiring arrangements of this type, except in rare instances. Rather, they tend to institutionalize them, for the union becomes the organ of the majority. It remains to be seen how such differentials will be affected by recently enacted equal pay and equal opportunity laws (which we shall discuss in Chapter 24).

Differences in Occupational Remuneration

In 1965, the average annual salary of attorneys rated as "Class VII" by the U.S. Department of Labor was approximately $25,000.[26] In the same year, the average full-time worker in manufacturing earned approximately $6,386 on an annual basis.[27] What is the reason for this great disparity of earnings? Does the variation in earnings in a capitalistic society reflect differences in ability, or are other factors responsible?

If conditions of work (other than wages) were equally attractive in all occupations, if all workers had the same mental and physical abilities, and if all occupations were equally easy to enter, then, in a perfectly competitive labor market, wages in every occupation for every worker would be equal. In the actual labor market, of course, none of these conditions is present. If we remove restrictive assumptions one by one, we shall be able to gain an understanding of the causes contributing to the differences in wages which exist in the business world.

EQUALIZING DIFFERENCES

Not all occupations are equally attractive to workers. Therefore, even if every worker had freedom of choice as to the type of work he would perform, we would expect that certain jobs which were less attractive would have to offer higher pay in order to attract workers, while positions in which working conditions were particularly satisfactory would be able to obtain workers at lower wages. In other words, a part of the differences in wage rates which we observe in the labor market represents a factor which equalizes the attractiveness of various occupations. For example, the low salaries of college professors are partially

[25] See David P. Taylor, "Discrimination and Occupational Wage Differences in the Market for Unskilled Labor," *Industrial and Labor Relations Review*, Vol. XXI (April, 1968), pp. 375–90.

[26] U.S. Department of Labor, *Handbook of Labor Statistics, 1967* (Washington, D.C.: U.S. Government Printing Office, 1967), p. 155.

[27] National Industrial Conference Board, *Economic Almanac 1967–1968* (New York: Macmillan Co., 1967), p. 80.

offset by the short hours of work, the long vacations, and the opportunity for research and study. Women who work as domestics in homes frequently receive more than women who perform clerical tasks in business because, according to our social mores, working as a servant is looked upon as somewhat degrading, and therefore additional compensation must be offered in these jobs to equalize their attractiveness with other positions these women might obtain.

There are many other equalizing factors which balance differences in wages. For example, the clerk in the head office of a large company will be willing to start at a lower wage than a day laborer in the same plant because the opportunities for advancement open to the clerk make up for the deficiency in his entrance salary. Similarly, an occupation in which there is a chance, however small, of making very great earnings—as in the practice of law—is able to attract applicants who are willing to start as clerks at little or no wage. Hazard to life is another factor producing wage differences—the pilot who tests new planes for an aircraft company receives a very high wage in order to compensate him for the risk to life involved in his work.

Another important equalizing difference is the expense of training. The doctor expects a higher remuneration for his work than a carpenter because the expense of his training is so much greater. Thus a part of the higher remuneration of the professional class generally is reimbursement for the long years of study. However, as we shall see, differences in remuneration may exist which are not merely equalizing but are out of proportion to the expenses of training.

In actuality, most differences in wages in the labor market do not seem to be of an equalizing character. Indeed, they are more often the reverse. Instead of the most unattractive work being the best remunerated, it is usually the poorest paid. It is the ditchdigger and the garbage collector—not the movie actor—who receive the least remuneration for their labor.

NONEQUALIZING DIFFERENCES

Broad differences in wages prevail which bear no relation to the relative attractiveness of the work involved. The first great source of such differences is the lack of uniformity in physical and mental capabilities among the working population. Even if every worker had freedom of choice to enter any occupation, it is obvious that few would have the talents—physical or mental—to be great scientists, writers, or boxers. The extent to which such abilities are a result of training and environmental factors is still a subject of debate among psychologists, but it is evident that all workers are not equally gifted by inheritance. Those talents which are prized most highly by the community and which are least common among workers tend to be remunerated with the highest earnings.

Even in more humdrum occupations, such as machine operation or assembly production, differences in ability and dexterity among workers will be reflected in large variations in earnings if the workers are paid by the piece or on an incentive basis. Industrial psychologists have found that individual differences in dexterity, for example, are very great. It is not at all uncommon for some pieceworkers on a job to earn twice that of others doing the same work.

Another important cause of differences is the fact that all occupations are not equally easy to enter. Even in our free enterprise society, in which class lines are not firmly drawn, social strata emerge which render it difficult for the poor son of a laborer to rise to be the head of a great corporation. Examples of such spectacular successes are often cited, but they represent the exception, not the norm.

Differences in ability and in training account for only a part of the wide variations which exist in compensation of members of the labor force. Sometimes the amount of money a person receives for his work will depend more on who his father is or what business his relatives control than upon his own ability or training. Nepotism—favoritism shown to relatives in employment—is a factor not only in politics but also in the labor market. It extends not only to business, but to unions as well, with father succeeding son in both. The union may even make jobs available only to sons of craftsmen.[28]

Noncompeting Groups

The labor market is characterized by a vast number of noncompeting groups, as will be more fully explained at a later point in this discussion. However, in terms of occupational differentiation, five broad strata can be distinguished in the ranks of employees. At the lowest level, in terms of pay and social position, is the common laborer, working either on the farm or in industry and performing work which requires a minimum of skill and a maximum of brawn. His wages are low because there are very many persons in the labor market who can do such simple work and can do no other. Many workers find an entry into such occupations who would be excluded from other types of positions. Thus the Negro, the immigrant, and various other minority or foreign-born groups make up a large proportion of this lower stratum.

At a somewhat higher wage come the semiskilled. These are workers who have ordinarily had some education and have acquired some knowledge of a technical art but who, for one reason or another, have not served the necessary years of apprenticeship to become skilled artisans.

[28] See the enlightening article in *The Wall Street Journal*, April 1, 1964, "The Son Also Rises," as to business favoritism of family ties. See above (Chapter 3) for union leadership nepotism. Being a relative or son is almost necessary to gain an apprenticeship in many craft unions.

Above them come the skilled workers—carpenters, boilermakers, bakers, and so on. Most of these men have union cards and the benefit of a considerable period of apprenticeship behind them. That they consider themselves in some respects superior to less skilled fellow workers is demonstrated by the clannishness of the skilled craftsmen in the American Federation of Labor, which, for many years, refused to accept unskilled workmen into membership.

The next group on the ladder of social status—the clerical workers —are frequently below the skilled and sometimes below the semiskilled, in terms of remuneration. Yet, in outlook and social allegiance, they are allied with the professional and capitalist class. This is a major reason why union organization has made slight inroads in the clerical group.

The top group in the labor market, in terms of pay and social prestige, are the professional workers—the doctors, dentists, lawyers, architects, engineers, professors, and others who have generally trained for their occupations in college and through advanced study—and the managerial groups and self-employed businessmen.

Although there is considerable movement between these groups, nevertheless, to some extent the strata become self-perpetuating. In other words, the son of a doctor is likely to become a member of a profession, while the son of a common laborer is more likely to be a laborer or, at best, a skilled worker. A recent study by the Bureau of Labor Statistics of mobility in the labor market found that there was comparatively little shifting from blue-collar (craftsmen, operatives, and nonfarm laborers) to white-collar (professional, managerial, clerical, and sales) occupations. Only about 12% of the men who changed occupations and held white-collar jobs in 1966 had been blue-collar workers a year earlier; for women the comparable proportion was only 5%.[29]

The greatest barrier to movement up the social ladder is the cost and time required for education and training. The poor laborer would like his son to go to college, and it may be that the son is bright enough to win a scholarship. But all too frequently, a career is blighted because the son must leave school in order to go to work and earn money toward the support of the family. Family income is related to occupational status. It is obvious that the farm operator, unskilled worker, or service worker will have great difficulty in sending a child to college. The GI Bill of Rights had a major effect on the degree of mobility between these various groups. It afforded higher education to thousands of men who would otherwise have been denied the opportunity because of lack of funds. These men will want their children to have the same opportunity, and they will be better able to give them this opportunity because they themselves have left schools and colleges equipped for higher paying jobs in industry.

[29] Saben, *op. cit.*, pp. 34–35.

There has been a tendency in this country toward a narrowing of differentials in earnings between occupational groups. Thus, for example, the relative spread between wage rates of skilled and unskilled workers was cut by nearly one half during the first 50 years of this century.[30] Although the emphasis of industrial unions, such as the United Automobile Workers, on cents-per-hour increases, which raise rates of lower paid workers relative to higher paid workers, undoubtedly contributed to the narrowing of the differential between skilled and unskilled, other more basic forces were also at work to bring about this change. Even in the building trades, which are organized and bargain on a craft basis, there was a marked narrowing of differentials between skilled and unskilled workers.

One basic reason for the relative improvement in wages of unskilled workers has been the metamorphosis in the type of work performed by "unskilled" workers. The ditchdigger now uses a machine; unskilled labor is now being combined with more capital than in the past, with the result that its productivity and wages have been substantially increased. In this connection, it is perhaps significant that after World War II, the U.S. Bureau of Labor Statistics discontinued its annual survey of the entrance rates of male common labor because of the increasing difficulty of obtaining reasonably comparable reporting among firms and industries for a "common labor" classification of workers.

Another important reason for the relative rise in wages of lower paid workers has been the substantial reduction in immigration in the past decade. In years past, many of the foreign-born could be attracted at low rates to jobs doing manual unskilled work.

In addition to these two influences, the following factors have also contributed to the decline in occupational differentials between 1900 and 1950: (1) a comparatively long inflationary period, characterized by large increases in money wages, primarily on a cost-of-living basis, which was preceded by a period of new unionism, with emphasis on higher pay for the lowest income workers; (2) a definite tendency throughout this period to apply adjustments, including "cost-of-living" increases, on a cents-per-hour basis.

At the same time as the gap between unskilled and skilled workers has been narrowed, the differential between unskilled and white-collar workers has also been reduced and in some cases eliminated. Some professional groups now find their average hourly earnings below those of skilled workers, or even below those of essentially unskilled groups such as over-the-road truck drivers. On the other hand, industrial unions, which once concentrated on raising the rates of the unskilled, are now emphasizing percentage wage adjustments to increase the skill differentials

---

[30] W. S. Woytinsky and Associates, *Employment and Wages in the United States* (New York: Twentieth Century Fund, 1953), p. 342.

as a result of pressure from the craftsmen within their ranks.[31] In some recent settlements, this pressure has resulted in separate and larger adjustments for skilled workers who otherwise threatened not to abide by the union agreement. The changing character of industrial union pressure during the last decade is probably one reason why percentage differences in pay between skilled and unskilled jobs in manufacturing industries have remained the same since 1953.[32]

These shifts in the labor market reflect the dynamic aspect of our economy, which continually changes the values accorded by our society to individual skills and capabilities. It also reflects the changing bargaining position of various groups as a result of union organization, or of the pressures within unions.[33]

The concept of noncompeting groups is helpful in explaining the broad economic strata into which the labor force is divided. In actual practice, however, there are not five but literally hundreds of noncompeting groups in a given labor market. These groups generally have as their basis a particular skill, sometimes attachment to a particular industry, sometimes a common ethnic or racial background. For example, pools of labor are often grouped around the operation of foundries or machine shops and in the lumber products or other industries. Employees in such groups may be practically noncompeting, and shutdowns in one industry affecting one pool of labor may have no direct influence on rates of other groups, unless the shutdown lasts for a considerable period. Then unemployment affects wage levels in the area generally. Furthermore, investigators have found that although on first analysis the rates paid in a given labor market may seem to be highly diverse, when the workers are grouped according to these submarkets or noncompeting groups, a more uniform pattern becomes discernible.

Unions and Wage Differentials

Traditionally, it was thought that the competitive norm in the labor market was uniformity of rates for comparable jobs and that only imperfections in the market permitted differentials to persist. Based on this premise, it would seem to follow that the introduction of a union into a labor market—since it represents a departure from free competition in the market—would produce even greater variation in wage rates for similar jobs. What has been the effect of unions in practice?

[31] See, for example, Robert M. MacDonald, *Collective Bargaining in the Automobile Industry* (New Haven, Conn.: Yale University Press, 1963), pp. 134–205.

[32] "Occupational Wage Relationships in Metropolitan Areas," *Monthly Labor Review*, Vol. LXXXVI (December, 1963), p. 1431.

[33] A recent study has found that in several countries, including the United States, "the long-term decline in [occupational] differentials . . . may soon be reversed." The data on the United States used in this study are heavily weighted by the building trades and may not be conclusive. See H. Günter, "Changes in Occupational Wage Differentials," *International Labor Review*, February, 1964, pp. 136–55.

In the first place, in the individual firm the advent of the union compels the employer to reexamine and justify his internal wage structure. As a result, management in organized plants has been compelled to set up job evaluation plans and in general to eliminate unjustified differentials between similar jobs. "Personal differentials have largely been eliminated or brought under formal control in unionized sectors."[34]

In the second place, when unions bargain with a number of companies in an industry, they have—as we have already observed earlier in this discussion—exerted strong pressure to achieve uniformity in rates for similar jobs in the various companies with which they bargain. This has affected area differentials as well as differentials within the same labor market and has tended to eliminate or to reduce both.

Occupational differentials have also tended to diminish over time. Here, the effect of union policies is probably a factor, but other forces in the labor market are likely to have had the most substantial effect.

Interindustry differentials have continued to persist over long periods of time. They do not seem to be substantially narrowed by unionism. Likewise, differentials on the basis of race or sex continue to endure.

The interesting question that remains is: Have unions tended to introduce a new type of differential in the labor market—a differential between union and nonunion companies? On this subject, there is considerable controversy among economists. One of the difficulties in ascertaining an answer to this question is that it is extremely difficult to isolate the effect of union organization alone. For example, larger companies usually pay higher rates than smaller companies for similar jobs. Since unions have, by and large, organized the larger companies in various industries first, a comparison of rates in organized and unorganized plants in such industries will generally show that the unionized plants pay higher rates. Obviously, such a comparison is no real indication of a union-caused wage differential. One study sought to eliminate the effect of such factors as size of company by comparing wage rates in 1950 of time workers in nonunion and union establishments in comparable plants in the same metropolitan area in seven industries: paints and varnishes, furniture, footwear, cotton textiles, hosiery, automotive parts, and women's dresses. This study found that for the industries and occupations considered, there were no significant differentials between the rates of workers in union and nonunion plants.[35] However, this study suffers from the defect that the unionized firms may have set a pattern in the local labor market which is followed by nonunion companies to forestall possible union organization.

If, in order to eliminate this interrelationship of rates which occurs

[34] Clark Kerr, "Wage Relationships—The Comparative Impact of Market and Power Forces," in John T. Dunlop (ed.), *The Theory of Wage Determination* (London: Macmillan & Co., Ltd., 1957), p. 181.

[35] John E. Maher, "Union, Nonunion Wage Differentials," *American Economic Review*, Vol. XLVI (June, 1956), pp. 336–52.

within a given labor market, we compare union rates in a particular industry in one city with nonunion rates with the same industry in a different city, we run into the problem of regional wage differentials, which obscures the effect of union organization. Since it is difficult to compare union and nonunion rates at the same point in time and eliminate various factors which may affect the relationship of the two, one writer has sought to throw light upon this problem by comparing changes in wages and income in a "nonunion period," 1923–29, with a so-called "union period," 1947–57. He found that real average hourly earnings of production workers in manufacturing in the union period rose over twice as rapidly as in the nonunion period, although the increase in productivity in manufacturing, as measured by change in physical output per man-hour, was actually greater in the nonunion period.[36] Here again, however, we run into problems of interpretation. This result may simply mean that production workers in manufacturing fare better in a period of labor scarcity and inflation, such as characterized the years after the end of World War II, than they do in normal times under stable prices, such as existed from 1923 to 1929. The same writer points out that the rate of increase in average annual incomes of white-collar workers in manufac-turing far outdistanced that of production workers in the same industries in the nonunion period, while, by contrast, in the union period the rate of increase in average annual incomes of production workers exceeded that of white-collar workers.[37] Is this an index of the influence of union pressure or of the different demand and supply conditions which pre-vailed for white-collar versus blue-collar workers in the two periods?

Another economist studied two industries in detail—cigars and men's and boys' shirts—using Bureau of Labor Statistics data for the years 1955–57. He found that even after the influence of establishment size and city size was eliminated, there was still a significant differential between organized and nonorganized plants.[38] Since the industries examined are highly competitive, one is led to ask: How could such a wage differential persist? Was the union labor more productive? Did the higher wages in the unionized firms tend to make management more efficient so that they could continue to compete? Did the unions simply eliminate monopsony profits of the unionized employers?

It should be apparent from this brief discussion that the effect of union organization on the level of wage rates is a subject of controversy in the economic literature. We shall consider this problem in more detail in subsequent chapters. At this point, it can be stated, however, that even those economists who do not believe that unions can alter basic wage

---

[36] Robert Ozanne, "Impact of Unions on Wage Levels and Income Distribu-tion," *Quarterly Journal of Economics*, Vol. LXXIII (May, 1959), p. 195.

[37] *Ibid.*

[38] David E. Kaun, *Union-Nonunion Wage Differentials Revisited* (Reprint No. 87 [Washington, D.C.: Brookings Institution, 1964]), p. 404.

relationships so as to be a source of comparative advantage to their members will concede that unions can alter wage relationships to the benefit of their members in three special circumstances: (1) where unions are new and aggressive, and may be offsetting prior monopsony power of employers; (2) where there have been periods of substantial unemployment and in the absence of union contractual arrangements wage rates would tend to fall; and (3) where craft unions control the supply of labor and thereby push up the wage.[39]

Whatever the facts, "we are here working with a very tangled web of forces."[40] The union influence and the market influence are difficult, and often impossible, to separate. If we recall the persistence of inter-industry differentials, and the small impact of unionism on occupational differentials as contrasted with the major impact of unionism on personal and area differentials, the possibility of either overstating or understating union influence is apparent.

Supply and Demand in the Labor Market

We have seen that the labor market differs materially from the market for wheat, which we considered at the beginning of this chapter. Diverse rates, rather than a single rate, typically prevail for a given type of labor in the labor market. There is no one market price—even for a particular grade of labor. Buyers and sellers are able to make bargains at a variety of rates.

How, then, do supply and demand fit into this picture? It will be recalled that we have defined the labor market in terms of a geographical area. Because labor is highly immobile, unemployed workers in a labor market tend to remain in the area rather than to seek jobs in a different market. The existence of this excess labor supply has a downward effect on wages—felt more strongly by nonunion than by union workers, but by both nonetheless.

Despite the existence of noncompeting groups, therefore, if there is a decline in business, and therefore in demand for labor in a particular area, which produces some unemployment, this change in demand will ultimately make its influence felt on the whole structure of wage rates in the community. Likewise, if the supply of labor in a local market is reduced, say, by drafting men for the army who would otherwise become additions to the labor force, this influence, too, will have its ultimate effect on wage levels.

Supply and demand—two traditional conceptual tools of economists—have not, therefore, been rendered useless by our changed conception of the labor market. Supply and demand do not interact to produce a single rate in the market, but they do influence the level of the whole

[39] Kerr, *op. cit.*, pp. 180–81.
[40] *Ibid.*, p. 192.

structure of diverse rates that characterizes the actual labor market. In the next two chapters, we shall consider in detail what demand and supply mean in terms of labor and the labor market.

QUESTIONS FOR DISCUSSION

1. What factors are responsible for the existence of diverse rates for similar jobs in the same labor market? What effect would you expect union organization to have upon such diversity of rates? Why?
2. Discuss the theory of noncompeting groups. Of what value is this theory in explaining actual differences in remuneration in the labor market?
3. If you were an employer, would you pay national rates or community rates if you had plants in both North and South?

SUGGESTIONS FOR FURTHER READING

BLAU, PETER M., and DUNCAN, OTIS D. *The American Occupational Structure.* New York: John Wiley & Sons, Inc., 1967.

   An empirical analysis of the determinants of occupational position and mobility of American workers, with special attention given to the effects of race, religion, migration, and farm background on occupational status.

GALLAWAY, LOWELL E. "The Significance of the Labor Market," in ROWAN, RICHARD L., and NORTHRUP, HERBERT R. (eds.), *Readings in Labor Economics and Labor Relations*, pp. 421–30. Homewood, Ill.: Richard D. Irwin, Inc., 1968.

   A discussion of the relationship of the labor market, unemployment, and economic growth.

Monthly Labor Review, Vol. XCI (March, 1968).

   A special issue on "Labor in the South," discussing manpower, employment, wage differentials, and other important factors in the southern labor markets.

REDER, M. W. "The Theory of Occupational Wage Differentials," *American Economic Review*, Vol. XLV (December, 1955), pp. 833–52.

   A theoretical and empirical analysis of factors creating occupational wage differentials in the United States.

TAYLOR, DAVID P. "Discrimination and Occupational Wage Differences in the Market for Unskilled Labor," *Industrial and Labor Relations Review*, Vol. XXI (April, 1968), pp. 375–90.

   An analysis of the effect of discrimination on wage levels at the lowest end of the occupational ladder.

ULMAN, LLOYD, "Labor Mobility and the Industrial Wage Structure in the Postwar United States," *Quarterly Journal of Economics*, Vol. XXIX (February, 1965), pp. 73–97.

   A discussion of various institutional barriers in the labor market.

Chapter	THE SUPPLY OF LABOR
9	

We have seen that the labor market is the area in which the supply and demand for particular types of labor seek to obtain a balance. But what do we mean by the phrase "supply of labor"? For conceptual purposes—as, for example, in drawing the diagram Figure 9–1 on page 265 showing the relationship between the "supply of labor" and wages—it is sometimes convenient to think of labor as being composed of homogeneous units. Nothing, however, could be farther from the truth. Not only is there a multitude of types of labor, running the gamut of professions, skills, and trades, but also no two workers are precisely alike even though they may both work in the same trade side by side at similar machines in the same plant. Yet despite such differences in skills and abilities, there is a degree of substitutability of one kind of labor for another. As one writer puts it, "Labor is a heterogeneous factor of production such that one type may be substituted for another and that one type may be converted into another by training and/or through experience."[1]

Significance of the Heterogeneity of Labor

Recognition of the heterogeneity of labor is important in assessing the adequacy of labor supply. For example, if all labor were homogeneous, employers could not complain about a shortage of labor as long as one man remained unemployed. Yet in the labor market today we observe, on the one hand, continuing unemployment of large numbers of workers—particularly among disadvantaged groups—while at the same time shortages exist of qualified workers in many occupations. At this writing a shortage exists of engineers, nurses, physicians, teachers, social workers, draftsmen, tool and die workers, machinists, and other skilled craftsmen, particularly in metalworking industries. In many occupations, the shortages which exist are not absolute but relative—relative in the sense that men are available but employers do not consider that they are qualified.

[1] H. M. Gitelman, "Occupational Mobility within the Firm," *Industrial and Labor Relations Review*, Vol. XX (October, 1966), pp. 64–65.

In a profession such as medicine it is conceivable that at a given time in a given locality there may be no unemployed persons available who have graduated from a medical school. But in a trade such as that of a machinist there is likely to be at all times men available with some knowledge of the craft; yet employers may not consider them suitably qualified for employment. Obviously, at any time in any occupation, the men left unemployed are likely to be less qualified than those who are working. However, in an economy operating at a high level of production and employment, employers can produce an artificial labor shortage by maintaining hiring standards at too high a level or by being unwilling to invest sufficient funds in training or additional supervision to utilize less qualified applicants.

The point is that the heterogeneity of labor makes the concept of "labor supply" a difficult one to perceive, even when we deal with a single "type of labor." In a manufacturing plant, for example, the supply of machinists available to the employer really consists not only of the qualified craftsmen who are available in the labor market, together with those who are already in his employ, but also those less qualified men who with training and supervision could learn to do the job. Employers are beginning to realize now that by imposing arbitrary hiring requirements—such as, for example, a high school diploma—they have effectively excluded from labor supply many persons from disadvantaged groups who with additional training may be quite capable of performing the jobs in question satisfactorily.

Labor supply, therefore, is not something simple or constant—nor can you go out into the labor market and neatly count the number of persons available in a given occupation. There are all gradations of skills and abilities, and the supply of labor as seen by an individual employer is, in fact, materially affected by his own hiring standards. Whenever in the following discussion we refer to "labor supply" in terms of so many units of a given type of labor, it must be understood that this is an oversimplification utilized only to illustrate a principle which exerts its influence in the labor market.

CLASSIFICATIONS OF LABOR SUPPLY

The supply of labor can be considered from four points of view:

The Supply of Labor Available to an Individual Firm. This may be large or small, complex or relatively homogeneous, depending upon the size of firm, the ramifications of its operations, and the diversity of its products and plant locations. The labor supply of the United States Steel Corporation, for example, would represent a cross section of the working population. It would include miners, merchant seamen, scientists, bookkeepers, and salesmen, in addition to the great variety of skilled and unskilled workers who are required to operate modern steel rolling mills and blast furnaces. By contrast, the supply of labor to the corner drugstore would probably include only a pharmacist and some clerks.

The Supply of Labor Available to an Industry. An industry may be defined, for our purposes, as a group of firms producing approximately the same product. The supply of labor to an industry will ordinarily represent a broader class of skills than the supply of labor to an individual firm because of the variation in methods of production used by firms making the same product in different parts of the country. The supply of labor to an industry may, however, be quite limited if the industry draws upon a relatively scarce type of skilled labor. For example, there are comparatively few qualified violin makers in this country. Consequently, the supply of labor available to this *entire industry* in the United States is less than the supply of labor available to an individual firm in other industries (such as, for example, the United States Steel Corporation).

The Supply of Labor Available to a Particular Locality. This will represent workers of all types employed in a variety of industries within the particular locality. Unless employment in the locality is highly specialized, the supply of labor will normally include a greater variety of skills and classes of workers than either the supply of labor to an industry or the supply to the average firm. Availability of new workers will depend upon the mobility of workers from other areas and upon the extent to which persons in the area, not normally members of the labor force, can be induced to enter employment.

The Supply of Labor Available in the Economy as a Whole. This is *the* labor force, including workers of all types in all industries in all sections of the country. Since immigration is relatively unimportant, the availability of additional workers in the short run will depend upon the extent to which persons not ordinarily part of the labor force can be attracted into employment.

VARIATIONS IN LABOR SUPPLY

Labor supply is subject to a diversity of influences. Moreover, some influences will affect one element in labor supply (such as hours of work) without affecting another element (such as number of workers available). It is therefore useful to distinguish, on the one hand, the various *causes* of variations in labor supply and, on the other hand, the *components* of labor supply which are subject to variation. We may then select the particular relation between cause of variation and components of labor supply which we wish to study.

The components of labor supply are number of workers, hours of work (i.e., length of workday and workweek), and efficiency. Causes of variation in labor supply include variations in the wage rate, family income, willingness to work, physical strength of the worker, conditions of work, and similar factors. A rise in family income, for example, may influence all three components of labor supply. A rise in family income may make it possible for Johnny to go to college, thus reducing the number of men available for work; it may enable the family breadwinner to buy a cottage at the beach and therefore interest him in securing a reduction in the workweek so that he can spend his weekends at the beach; and it may enable him to eat better, and to see the doctor and dentist more regularly, so that his physical efficiency will be improved.

In the following discussion, we shall be primarily concerned with all three components of labor supply but with only one of the causes of variation: the wage rate. Holding the other causes constant (with the exception of family income), and changing only the wage rate, we shall attempt to ascertain how the amount of labor supplied will vary. This is the conventional way of studying changes in labor supply in the labor market.

Role of Nonwage Factors

It seems probable that the most important single cause of *variation* in the short-run supply of labor is change in the rate of compensation for jobs. The level of wages is, of course, not the only factor employees consider in seeking employment. We know that proximity of the place of employment, congenial atmosphere, employment with friends or relatives, regularity of work, security, and prospect of advancement are all important elements affecting the attractiveness of a job to the individual worker. However, it is the level of wages which normally fluctuates frequently, and it is therefore easier to correlate changes in labor supply with this cause of variation than with others. Any relationship, of course, is going to be rough and approximate; for as we have seen in Chapter 8 in our discussion of the labor market, employees do not normally have accurate information either about existing wage levels in various firms or of changes in such rate levels. Nevertheless, over a period of time, higher wage rates will attract more employees.

Therefore, in the following discussion, supply curves have been drawn in terms of changes in wage rates. We might also have drawn supply curves in terms of changes in regularity of employment, changes in prospects for promotion, or similar conditions. These and other circumstances make their influence felt on the supply of labor. Although, in the following discussion, we have, for the sake of simplicity, dealt with changes in supply of labor in terms of its relationship to changes in wage rates, it might be helpful to consider wage rates as standing for the "net attractiveness" of the job. Or looked at another way, if we assume that other things are held constant (i.e., all aspects of the job relationship other than wages), then a change in wage rates must itself change the net attactiveness of the job.

Short-Run Supply of Labor

Variations in labor supply may be considered from either the short-run or the long-run point of view. The short-run supply of labor may be defined as the schedule of the varying amounts of labor that would be supplied at varying wage rates. Geometrically represented, the schedule is a curve on a diagram on which the wage rate is measured along the ordinate (*Y* axis), and the number of workers, or units of labor, is measured along the abscissa (*X* axis).

As has already been mentioned, the supply curve may be drawn from the point of view of an individual firm, an industry, a locality, or the economy as a whole. For the purpose of explaining geometric representation of supply conditions, we may assume that Figure 9–1 represents

FIGURE 9–1

SHORT-RUN SUPPLY CURVE OF LABOR

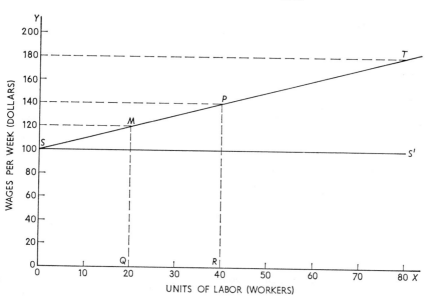

supply curves of labor to a firm. The same type of representation, however, can be used to show supply conditions from the point of view of an industry, a locality, or the economy. Figure 9–1 shows two hypothetical supply curves of labor. The line *SS′* has been drawn parallel to the *X* axis and intersects the *Y* axis at a wage of $100 per week. Since *SS′* is parallel to *OX*, it indicates that at a wage of $100 per week the employer anticipates that he can get 20 workers or 40 workers or 70 workers. In other words, as much labor as the employer requires can, within limits, be obtained at the same wage rate. Economists describe this situation by saying that the supply curve of labor is perfectly "elastic." Increasing amounts of labor can be obtained without raising wage rates. As we shall see in the following discussion, this is frequently the case when unemployment exists in the labor market.

Suppose, now, that a war crisis arises suddenly and large numbers of workers are drafted into the army. Our employer's supply curve for labor may now be changed abruptly to one which looks like the line *ST* in Figure 9-1. Because of the shortage of labor in the market, the employer now finds that to get more labor, he must offer a progressively higher wage rate to attract workers away from other firms and to draw persons out of retirement into his factory. Thus, while 20 workers (*OQ*) can be hired for a wage of about $120 per week, if the employer wants to double his labor force to 40 workers, he may find that he will have to raise wages to $140 per week (*RP*). Such a supply curve, which correlates higher wage rates with increased labor supply, is known as a supply curve of less than perfect elasticity.[2] This usually means that the supply of labor is limited relative to buyers' demands and that additional workers or additional hours or units of labor can only be obtained by raising rates of pay.

The more "elastic" a supply curve is, the greater will be the increase in labor associated with a given increase in wage rates. Looked at another way, the steeper the slope of the supply curve, the less elastic it will be. In Figure 9-1, curve *SS'* is more elastic than curve *ST*, and curve *ST* has a steeper slope than curve *SS'*. If the supply curve is vertical, meaning that no matter how wage rates rise or fall, there will be no change in the amount of labor available, the supply curve is said to be "perfectly inelastic" or of "zero elasticity." On the other hand, if the supply curve is horizontal, as in the case of curve *SS'* in Figure 9-1, any amount of labor (within limits) can be obtained at a constant wage rate. Such a curve is called "perfectly elastic."

The short-run supply schedule is drawn up on the assumption that population remains constant. Population growth enters into the long-run supply curve, which will be discussed later in this chapter.

Classification of Variations

Much confusion arises in discussions of labor supply because of a failure to distinguish properly between a shift in the entire supply curve and a movement along the curve. The former should be referred to as a "change in labor supply," since "supply" means the whole schedule. The latter should be designated as a "change in the amount of labor supplied," that is, a movement from one *point* on the supply curve to another. This

---

[2] The concept of elasticity will be utilized from time to time in the following chapters in connection with both supply curves and demand curves. The elasticity coefficient is equal to the percentage change in quantity divided by the percentage change in price (or wage). Algebraically, this relation can be expressed as $(\Delta Y / \Delta X)$ X/Y, where Y equals quantity and X equals price.

distinction will be clarified if variations in the availability of workers, labor time, and labor efficiency are considered from the viewpoint of whether they do or do not involve an actual shift in the supply curve:

1. A change occurs in the number of workers available in the market.

a) Such a change may be attributable to factors other than a variation in wage rates. For example, the end of the war in Vietnam would add thousands of GI's to the ranks of the civilian labor force. Where the change in numbers of workers is attributable to nonwage causes, the whole supply schedule of labor shifts its position, either to the right or to the left, depending on whether there has been an increase or a decrease in the number of workers available at given rates.

b) Additional workers may be induced to enter the labor market by the attraction of high wages. To the extent that this is true, there has been a movement along a given supply curve.

2. A change occurs in hours of work.

a) During World War II, hours of work of nonagricultural employees increased from 41 hours in 1940 to a peak of more than 46 hours per week in 1943. In part, the willingness to work these longer hours was motivated by a desire to bring the war to a speedy and successful conclusion. That is, the motive of patriotism would have actuated workers to accept some lengthening of the workweek with no increase in hourly wage rates. To the extent that this was true, there was a shift to the right in the labor supply curve.

b) Workers increase hours of work because of availability of work beyond 40 hours at a premium rate of time and a half. This represents a movement along a given supply curve.

3. A change occurs in efficiency.

a) Music is played in a factory during working hours; and as a result, output increases. There has been a movement of the entire supply curve.

b) On the other hand, if additional efficiency is forthcoming simply as a result of a piece-rate system which rewards additional effort with additional compensation, there has merely been a movement along a given supply curve.

The same distinction in terminology, of course, applies to shifts of the demand curve for labor and to movements along that curve.

THE SUPPLY CURVE OF LABOR TO THE FIRM

As has already been mentioned, the supply of labor may be considered in relation to a particular firm, an industry, a locality, or the economy as a whole. The last three types of supply curves are "objective." That is, they represent the "actual" changes in supply of labor which would accompany given changes in the rate of wages, if such variations in supply could be isolated from the general flux in the labor market and measured. The supply curve of labor to the individual firm, however, is of quite a different nature. The supply curve of labor to the individual firm, as this concept is normally used by labor economists, is a subjective concept, not an objective fact. It represents the *expectation* of the individual employer as to what the relationship of wage rates and labor supply *will be*. Analysis of employer actions in the field of labor—as in economics in general—depends on understanding the subjective estimates of the employer as to the interrelation of costs, prices, and other variables. The supply curve of labor to the individual firm represents the employer's estimates as to what wage rates he will have to pay to obtain varying amounts of labor.

Of course, we could draw up an objective supply curve of labor for the individual firm. The slope of such a curve would reflect, among other things, differences in worker preference for specified combinations of money income and working conditions, attachment of workers to a familiar workplace or residence, and the size of the firm in question. It is more useful, however, for most economic problems to draw up a hypothetical curve analogous to the demand curves which represent employer expectations. These expectations will be derived in part from past experience; and therefore, many of the elements which would determine the shape of the objective supply curve will enter into the employer's estimation of the shape of the supply curve of labor as he imagines it to be.

Labor Supply to a Large Firm

Because the supply curve of labor to the individual firm reflects the estimates of the individual employer, its slope will depend upon the size of the particular firm involved. A very large firm may have to recognize that any attempt by it to obtain more labor is likely to affect the prevailing wage rate in the locality. In order to obtain 1,000 more workers in a local labor market where there may be only 10,000 qualified workers available in all, a large firm will have to raise wage rates sufficiently to induce workers to leave other jobs. Workers will be reluctant to leave jobs in other firms without such an inducement, since by leaving their current employment, they are likely to lose seniority rights and preferential status with regard to future promotion, health benefits, pensions, and so forth. But when the large firm offers higher wages to attract additional workers, this is likely to produce an increase in wage rates in the community generally, since other employers will also find it necessary to raise wages in order to induce employees to remain. The large firm is thus placed in such a position that any increase in rates it may offer to attract additional workers will likewise have to be offered to all employees already on its own payroll; for if other employers raise rates in retaliation, the large firm would not be able to hold its own employees at lower rates. Moreover, if the workers in the large firms are organized, the union will undoubtedly require uniformity of pay among employees of the same skill. Even if the plant were unorganized, management would probably consider it impracticable from the point of view of employee morale to raise rates for new employees without making a corresponding adjustment in the rates of old employees.

The result in such circumstances is that the addition to the total labor cost of the firm incidental to the employment of an additional worker will exceed the direct labor cost or wage paid to that man. In technical language, this means that the marginal cost of labor (i.e., the addition to the total cost of labor attributable to the addition of one more unit of labor) will exceed the supply price of labor (i.e., the wage offered to the additional worker). Assume that the going rate for labor in the firm is $3 an hour and that 100 men are employed at that wage. In order to attract additional workers, the wage paid to new workers has to be raised to $3.20. The supply price of additional labor, as indicated by the labor supply curve, therefore will be $3.20. But if, as a result of this rise in the wage, all workers already on the payroll have to be given an increase from $3.00 to $3.20 an hour, the additional cost of $23.20 ($0.20 × 100 + $3.20) attributable to hiring an additional worker will be substantially in excess of his wage ($3.20).

Labor Supply to a Small Firm

The small firm will tend to view its supply curve of labor as being perfectly "elastic" over the relevant range—that is, the employer considers that he can obtain all the additional workers he may need without raising wages. His demand is so small relative to the total supply of workers available that his need for additional workers will not affect wage rates generally. This condition of perfect elasticity may also typify the supply curve for labor in a large firm in times of substantial unemployment. However, the supply curve of the small firm is likely to be perfectly elastic even if there is full employment. For even under condition of full employment, there are some workers leaving other employment for one reason or another, and the small firm may figure it can satisfy its needs from this pool of workers without the necessity of paying higher wages to draw men away from other firms. Consequently, if the small firm had been paying $3 an hour to its employees, it estimates that it can get additional workers for $3, and therefore the marginal cost of the additional labor and its supply price or wage will be the same. The fact that the supply curve for labor to the small firm will tend to be perfectly elastic, while the supply curve to the large firm is more likely to be less than perfectly elastic, influences their respective employment policies. This problem will receive attention in Chapter 10, dealing with the demand for labor.

Why the Labor Supply Curve Slopes Upward

Perhaps the most common cause of an upward slope for the labor supply curve is the need for paying higher wages in order to attract workers away from other firms. As we have seen, insofar as this is the reason for the lack of perfect elasticity in the supply curve, it is more likely to be characteristic of a large than a small firm. But there are other conditions which can produce an upward slope in the labor supply curve, and these are to be found in large and small firms alike. For example, an employer may have to pay penalty rates for overtime if he wishes to get more hours out of his existing labor force. Additional units of labor time have to be remunerated at a higher price, which means that the supply curve for labor to the firm is rising. Another condition which will produce an upward sloping labor supply curve is a scarcity of qualified workers. If additional workers can be obtained at the prevailing wage, but these workers are less efficient, the firm is, in effect, paying an increased price per "efficiency unit." A further possible reason for an upward sloping labor supply curve is increasing "fringe" expenses made necessary by the employment of additional workers. For example, if the only additional workers available are women, the employer may be compelled to expend funds upon separate lavatory facilities, rest rooms, and so forth. The result will be that the marginal cost of employing these additional workers will exceed the wage paid to them.

Effect of Union Organization on Supply Curve

Union contracts customarily fix the wage rates for particular types of labor for a given period of time, usually a year. Once the rate is fixed in the contract, the employer is obligated to pay it, regardless of the amount of labor he employs. Thus, theoretically, a union contract creates a perfectly elastic supply curve for labor.

In practice, however, the results are sometimes different. In a tight labor market the employer may find that even with a union contract, the only way to get more labor is to hire substandard workers and pay them the union rate or to work more overtime. In both cases, his supply curve of labor would be upward sloping: in the former case, because he has to pay more for less efficient labor; in the latter case, because the additional hours worked would have to be compensated at premium rates. On the other hand, in times of business depression the employer may find that the union will insist on maintaining rates in the contract but will acquiesce in actual cuts below the contract rate. If the employer reduces employment, he thereby increases competition for the remaining jobs and is likely to find that the fewer workers he needs, the lower the wage he will pay—indicating an upward sloping supply curve of labor. Unions have, however, reduced the tendency for competitive wage cutting among workers which characterizes an unorganized labor market; and to that extent, they have contributed to a greater elasticity in the labor supply curve.

THE SUPPLY CURVE OF LABOR TO AN INDUSTRY

The elasticity of supply of labor to an industry will depend primarily upon the mobility of workers who can be drawn into this industry from other industries. Because most skills in modern industry can be fairly quickly acquired, an industry can ordinarily draw workers away from other industries if it offers sufficient inducement in the form of higher wages.[3] The supply curve of labor for an industry will ordinarily be more elastic than the supply curve for labor in a given locality, because there will be less resistance to the movement of workers away from industry to industry within a given locality than there will be to movement away from or into the locality. The supply curve of labor for an industry will ordinarily be more elastic than the supply curve of labor for the whole economy, because it will be easier to induce employees to leave other industries to work in this particular industry than it will be to induce additional men, women, and children who are not normally members of the labor force to enter the labor market.

The supply curve of labor for an industry will be of zero elasticity —i.e., more workers would not be attracted to the industry no matter how high a wage was offered—only in the rare case when the industry uses a type of highly skilled labor which is not employed by other industries and when the skill is not one which can be easily acquired in a short period. It should be observed that even if the elasticity of labor supply to a particular industry was zero, an individual employer in such an industry might still imagine that the supply curve of labor to his firm was perfectly elastic. He might calculate that even though the industry as a whole could not obtain more workers, his own needs were so small relative to the amount of labor available to the industry that he would be able to attract a few additional workers without being compelled to offer a higher wage.

THE SUPPLY CURVE OF LABOR TO A LOCALITY

The slope of the supply curve of labor to a locality will depend in large measure upon the nature and location of the locality in question. If a shortage of labor were to develop in New York City, additional workers would be attracted from all over the country because of the advantages (other than the job opportunity) which New York has to offer. On the

[3] According to a study made by the U.S. Department of Labor, about 5½ million Americans were employed in January, 1966, in an occupation different from the one in which they were employed in January, 1965. Three out of four of those workers changing occupations changed their industry as well. See Samuel Saben, *Occupational Mobility of Employed Workers* (Special Labor Report No. 84 [Washington, D.C.: U.S. Department of Labor, 1967]), pp. 31, 38.

other hand, if a labor shortage were to develop in a little mill town in a backwoods region, even a very high wage rate would not induce many workers to migrate there, leaving their present homes and occupations.

Although many workers, particularly older ones, are reluctant to sever local ties, nevertheless there is a considerable amount of geographical mobility in this country. On the average, during each year over 6% of the civilian population moves its residence across county lines and 3% across state lines.[4] During prosperous periods, the rate of mobility out of labor-surplus areas is higher than in periods of depression. But it is also true from our observation, that lower income groups are often the least willing to relocate.

Many of the characteristics of the supply curve of labor to a locality are also true of the supply curve to the economy as a whole; therefore, these aspects can be conveniently considered together in the discussion below.

THE SUPPLY CURVE OF LABOR FOR THE ECONOMY

The short-run supply of labor for the economy as a whole is likely to be somewhat inelastic above the prevailing wage. That is, a rise in the rate of wage offered will not substantially increase the number of workers available. As soon as all average workmen are employed, the amount of labor supplied can be increased only by bringing in submarginal workers or people who are not ordinarily part of the labor force—such as women, youths, and older men. The additions which can be expected from these sources in peacetime, within normal wage ranges, are not very large. During World War II, patriotism and the lure of very high wages did attract many of these groups into the labor market. Indeed, the degree of expansion in the labor force for the economy as a whole was surprising. Yet, because of the relative immobility of labor, bottlenecks continued to develop in particular areas which were unable to attract sufficient labor despite the attraction of high wages. In other words, the elasticity of labor supply was greater for the economy as a whole than it was for particular localities. Under ordinary circumstances, however, the contrary would be expected. The elasticity of labor supply in a particular locality depends on the mobility of labor both in and out of that locality and in and out of the labor force, while the elasticity of labor supply for the economy as a whole depends only upon the latter—the movement of particular groups of labor in and out of the civilian labor force.

In Figure 9–2, the prevailing wage rate is indicated along the Y axis, while units of labor supplied are measured along the X axis. The curve lettered SS' represents an approximation to the short-run supply curve of labor for the economy in normal times.

---

[4] *Economic Report of the President, January 1964* (Washington, D.C.: U.S. Government Printing Office, 1964), p. 100.

If we assume that wage rate OP is a bare subsistence wage, then below that rate, workers will not be strong enough to work as many hours or in as great a number as at wage OP, and the supply curve will therefore reflect this diminution in the number of units of labor supplied by sloping sharply to the left. At and slightly above wage OP, we may assume that earnings are very low relative to the standard of living; and as a consequence, workers with families will be compelled to send their children to work at an early age. Also, many women will have to work at this low wage in order to help their husbands support their families. As the wage rate is raised to a more satisfactory level, men are better able to maintain their families on their own wages. Thus, at a wage of OQ, earnings of the family breadwinner will be sufficient so that children can remain in school for more extended education and women can remain in

FIGURE 9-2

SHORT-RUN SUPPLY CURVE OF LABOR
FOR THE ECONOMY

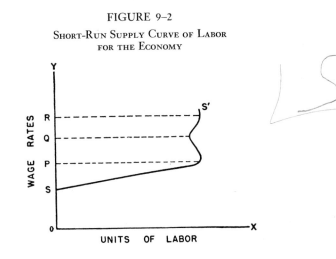

the home. Consequently, the amount of labor offered on the market will tend to diminish, and the supply curve will slope to the left. As the wage becomes very high—as was the case during the war years—women and children will again be induced to enter the labor market. Youths will put off entering college for a few years in order to "cash in" on the high wages. Older men who were ready to retire will postpone the event in order to enlarge their nest eggs. Therefore the supply curve may again slope to the right, as indicated at wage OR. But again, when the wage becomes extremely high, the man of the family will prefer to send his children to school and college, and he himself will be less inclined to work long hours. As a result, there may be a diminution in the amount of labor supplied, and the supply curve may slope backward to the left.

The above analysis of the behavior of the supply of labor at high wages is purely speculative. There is some evidence that within a given range of wage rates where the rise in wages is associated with an increased availability of jobs, additional workers are attracted into the labor force. These additional workers are primarily females and male workers under 25 or more than 54 years of age.[5] The problem, however, is that a rise in wages invokes conflicting responses from various groups in the population. Actually, we know very little about what motivates people to work. Why is it, for example, that a millionaire may drive himself so that he works seven days a week and hardly has time for his family, while a day laborer may refuse to work on Sunday even at triple time?

Economists describe (but do not really explain) the decision-making process between work and leisure by saying that there is both an income effect and a substitution effect to be considered. At any given level of income, a worker is assumed to have achieved a balance between his desire for leisure and his willingness to work at the prevailing wage. If wages are increased, the substitution effect will tend to induce him to substitute work for leisure, since higher wages will now make work more attractive. On the other hand, the income effect of higher wages may lead him to reduce his hours of work because with higher income he now can afford to buy a boat, have a summer cottage, etc., and he therefore needs additional time to use these acquisitions. The actual changes in labor supply which we observe over time in the economy reflect the complex decisions made by millions of persons both in and outside of the labor force in which the balancing of the desire for income versus the desire for leisure is undoubtedly a major consideration.

Statistical Investigations into the Supply Curve for Labor

Various attempts have been made to determine what would happen to labor supply if earnings were lower or higher than the prevailing rate. These studies have generally been based on one of two approaches: Labor force size is measured at different moments of time as earnings vary, or simultaneous measurement is made of labor force and earnings in different labor markets to determine what, if any, is the normal interrelationship. One of the earliest investigations in this field was made by Paul H. Douglas, who used the latter approach and, after examining earnings and labor force size in 38 large cities, found evidence of an inverse relationship.[6] Clarence D. Long, who published a comprehensive study of this problem, confirms that variations in the proportion of a city's population in the labor force, i.e., its participation rate, appear to be inversely associated with variations in its average income per equivalent adult male

---

[5] See the discussion by Otto Eckstein in R. A. Gordon (ed.), *Prosperity and Unemployment* (New York: John Wiley & Sons, Inc., 1966), p. 48.

[6] Paul H. Douglas, *The Theory of Wages* (New York: Macmillan Co., 1934), chap. xi. See also Paul H. Douglas and Erika Schoenberg, "Studies in the Supply Curve of Labor," *Journal of Political Economy*, Vol. XLV (February, 1937), pp. 45–79.

worker.[7] When the Douglas and Long results are averaged for the years 1900 to 1940, there is some evidence that whenever real earnings per adult male equivalent worker increase by 1%, the labor force, standardized for age and sex, decreases by about one sixth of 1%.[8] However, there are so many years in which there is no association, and so many other inadequacies and inaccuracies in the earnings and labor force data, that the shape of the instantaneous labor supply curve still remains conjectural.

A somewhat allied question is the problem of what happens to the labor force in times of depression. If there is an inverse relationship between earnings and labor supply, then, as earnings diminish in times of depression, additional workers should be expected to enter the labor force in an attempt to supplement family income. This "additional workers" theory, as it is called, is held by many economists, but has also been rejected by others. Recent empirical research suggests that labor supply is inversely related to the level of unemployment. This implies that as wages drop and unemployment rises, although some secondary workers enter the labor market in order to supplement family income, more depart or delay their entrance until a more favorable labor market situation develops.[9] Thus, the converse of the "additional workers" theory is the "discouraged workers" theory, which in effect postulates that labor force participation will fall as unemployment rises because lack of jobs in the labor market will cause persons to delay entry into, or to withdraw from, the labor force.

Hours of Work

The slope of the short-run labor supply curve will depend in part upon the relationship between the rate of wages and the number of hours employees are willing to work. Here again we are faced with the conflicting influences of the substitution effect and the income effect. A longer workday or longer workweek not only spells greater fatigue for the worker but also means that he will have less time to devote to his family, recreation, education, and other pursuits. It is understandable, therefore, why premium pay is offered for longer hours of work. On the other hand, we also know that as take-home pay rises, some workers become more interested in a reduction of hours worked so they can have more time for leisure. It is apparent that this is an area of complex motivation. The subject of hours of work will be discussed in greater detail in Chapter 16.

[7] Clarence D. Long, *The Labor Force under Changing Income and Employment* (National Bureau of Economic Research General Series No. 65 [Princeton, N.J.: Princeton University Press, 1958]), p. 5.

[8] Sanford Cohen, "The Supply Curve of Labor Re-examined," *Industrial and Labor Relations Review*, Vol. XIII (October, 1959), p. 66.

[9] See Glen G. Cain, "Unemployment and the Labor-Force Participation of Secondary Workers," *Industrial and Labor Relations Review*, Vol. XXI (January, 1967), pp. 275–97.

CHANGE IN EFFICIENCY

The supply of labor can also be varied by a change in efficiency of workers. Just as an increase in wage rates may increase the amount of labor supplied by inducing additional workers to enter the market, so an increase in wage rates may increase the efficiency of a given work force. When wages are at a very low level, an increase in wages will tend to improve efficiency by contributing to the physical well-being of the workers. Workers who are well fed and afforded proper housing facilities are capable of putting forth more effort than employees whose incomes are so low that they cannot properly provide for these basic needs. But once wage rates reach a level at which the worker can maintain a satisfactory standard of living, it is doubtful whether further wage increases have much effect on efficiency solely by reason of their reaction on physical well-being.

However, without regard to possible improvement in physical condition, a rise in wages may induce employees to work harder. A positive relation between wage increases and increased effort is more likely to be found in piece-rate industries than in industries where payment is by the hour. If the piece rate is raised, the worker can directly increase his take-home pay by producing more units of product, whereas in an industry where payment is by the hour, the worker is likely to feel that his increased effort would simply increase the employer's profit without any direct, immediate benefit to himself. Thus, it is principally in industries using incentive pay plans that variations in efficiency are likely to have any close relationship to changes in wage rates. Approximately 30% of the plant workers in manufacturing industries are paid on an incentive basis.

On the whole, under modern industrial conditions in a high-wage economy, wage changes probably have comparatively little effect upon worker efficiency. Because of the high degree of mechanization in American industry, the speed of the production line rather than individual worker effort is the controlling determinant of labor efficiency.

LONG-RUN SUPPLY OF LABOR

Long-run supply is affected by all the factors operative in the short run plus the additional element of population growth. Population growth involves the relationship between birth and death rates, on the one hand, and immigration and emigration rates, on the other.

The classical economists viewed the long-run supply of labor as highly flexible. They believed that labor supply adjusted itself to "the natural price of labor"—i.e., the level of real wages which was necessary "to enable laborers one with another to subsist and to perpetuate their race without increase or diminution."[10] This wage was conceived of as an equilibrium rate. If real wages rose above this subsistence level, births would increase, deaths would decrease, population would consequently expand, and, with an unchanged demand for labor, wage rates would necessarily fall. On the other hand, a fall in wage rates below the subsistence level would produce an increase in deaths and a decrease in births. Marriages would be postponed, and married persons would delay having children. Consequently, the supply of labor would decline below the equilibrium level, with the result that wage rates would be bid up to the "natural" wage.

The theory was phrased in terms of a subsistence wage because of the belief, then current, that population tended to increase faster than the means of subsistence. Population was thought to double itself every 25 years—thus increasing at a geometrical rate—while food production increased only in an arithmetical ratio. However, population was prevented from getting too far out of line with subsistence by certain "positive checks," such as vice, pestilence, war, and famine, and "preventive checks," such as postponement of marriage.

Modern population theorists look for no such geometrical increase in population growth. On the contrary, the experience of most of the older countries in Europe whose populations have neared stability indicates that the real problem may be one of stimulating population growth rather than retarding it.[11] It has been suggested that the rate of population growth can be represented by a logistic curve—that is, populations grow first at an increasing rate, then at a decreasing rate, finally approach an asymptote, and may eventually decline. One reason given for this phenomenon is that increasing density of population lessens fertility and therefore reduces the birth rate. This explanation, however, disregards the observed fact that the most densely populated sections of most cities also have the highest birth rates.

Population Projections for the United States

Because of the difficulty in estimating future behavior of fertility rates, the U.S. Bureau of Census customarily issues four projections of population growth based upon four different assumptions as to fertility. The latest figures available from the Bureau of Census[12] indicate a population from 215 million (Series D) to 228 million (Series A) in 1975 and

---

[10] David Ricardo, *Principles of Political Economy and Taxation* (Gonner [ed.]) (London: George Bell & Sons, 1913), p. 70.

[11] However, in certain countries such as India, for example, the rate of population growth is so great and the standard of living so low that the conditions described by subsistence wage theorists appear to exist.

[12] See U.S. Department of Commerce, Bureau of the Census, *Population Estimates* (Washington, D.C., December 18, 1967), Current Population Reports, Series P-25, p. 4.

from 256 million (Series D) to 300 million (Series A) in 1990. The total population is expected to grow by 19 million to 31 million, or by 9% to 16%, from 1966 to 1975; and by 59 million to 103 million, or by 30% to 52%, from 1966 to 1990.

While the prospect of the addition of possibly 100 million people to our population by 1990 is startling, this rate of population growth is considerably less than had been forecast some years ago. The reason for the scaling down of estimates is the sharp drop which has occurred in the birth rate. The birth rate in this country, which has been falling steadily for the past decade, reached a record low in 1967 of 17.9 births for every 1,000 Americans, a figure below the previous record low of 18.4 set in the Depression years of 1933 and 1936.[13] Figure 9–3 shows the relationship between the birth rate, the number of actual births, and changes in population.

The decline in the birth rate is all the more amazing in view of the fact that both the marriage rate per 1,000 population and the total number of marriages have been increasing. The decline is believed by some experts to reflect an increased emphasis on family planning and the desire of prospective parents for a smaller number of children than had formerly been fashionable. While "the pill" may have had some effect on the birth rate, population experts point out that there have been declines of a similar nature in earlier years before this type of contraceptive was perfected. The high cost of education and the desire of parents to give their children the benefit of a college education is undoubtedly a major factor in the current interest in controlling the size of families.

Even on the most conservative estimates, it is anticipated that the decline in births will soon reverse itself. The reason is that because of the great postwar baby boom there will be more than 42 million women in this country between the ages of 15 and 44 in 1970. So even if newlyweds do delay having babies, or have fewer babies, there will be such a high concentration of women in the population of childbearing age that births per year are expected to rise to about 4.6 million by 1975.[14]

Population Growth and the Labor Force

In Chapter 1, we considered the factors affecting the projected growth of the labor force in this country. It was there indicated that even though the rate of population growth was slackening, the labor force was growing at a faster rate because of the age composition of the population. Whereas over the past decade the labor force had been growing at a rate of 1.2%, between now and 1975 it is expected to grow at a rate of 1.8%.[15]

---

[13] *Time*, March 8, 1968, p. 25.

[14] *Business Week*, July 2, 1966, p. 19.

[15] National Industrial Conference Board, *Economic Potentials of the United States in the Next Decade* (New York, 1965), p. 6.

FIGURE 9–3

RELATIONSHIP BETWEEN BIRTH RATE, NUMBER OF BIRTHS,
AND CHANGES IN POPULATION, 1940–1975*

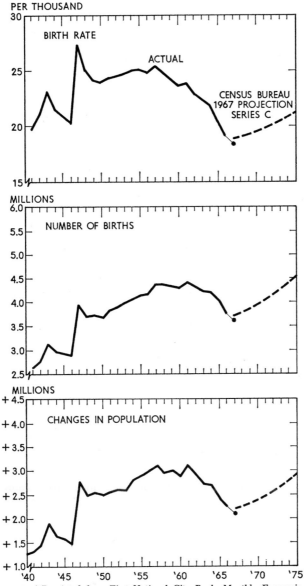

* Reprinted from First National City Bank, Monthly Economic
Letter, July, 1967, p. 77. Chart by First National City Bank.
SOURCE: U.S. Bureau of the Census. Projections are Series C, as
published February 20, 1967. Data are for fiscal years ended June 30;
estimates for fiscal 1967 by FNCB on basis of first nine months' data.

The growth of the labor force—and therefore of labor supply—reflects the influence of two factors—the labor participation rate and the actual number of persons in the population of working age. On the one hand, it is anticipated that between now and 1975 there will be some increase in the labor participation rate, particularly among women and, on the other hand, that there will be substantial additions to the population, particularly in the younger working ages.

The 18-through-24 age group will be growing at a rapid rate from now through the 1970's but may actually show some decline during the 1980's, as a reflection of the decline in the number of births during the 1960's. This group includes the young married couples and those seeking their first jobs. With a growing tendency for both husbands and wives to work, a high concentration of this age group in the population forecasts large additions to the supply of labor. The population in the prime working years, aged 25–64, will grow much more rapidly in the 1970's and 1980's than it has in the 1950's and the 1960's. Over 7 million persons will join this age group from 1970 to 1975—more than in the whole decade of the 1960's—and gains in subsequent years will be even greater.[16] This, too, will mean a rapidly expanding labor force.

Immigration

In considering the various factors which enter into the long-run supply of labor, mention must be made of net immigration. Because of our restrictive immigration policy, the effect of immigration on labor supply has been minimal. The annual volume of net civilian immigration to the United States averaged 306,000 between 1948 and 1956 and 342,000 between 1957 and 1965. These figures represent about 10% and 11% of the annual average population increase in the corresponding periods and only 0.1% and 0.2% of the corresponding midperiod populations.[17] Liberalization of the immigration law achieved through enactment of the October, 1965, amendments may result in a changed *character* of immigration with more skilled persons *admitted* as well as persons from different countries. However, as can be seen from the foregoing statistics, immigration is a relatively insignificant factor in the total labor supply of the economy.

SUMMARY

We have seen how supply is related to wage rates and have considered the meaning and content of labor supply from the point of view of the firm, the industry, and the economy. In the next chapter, we shall consider the other side of the picture—the demand for labor. After we

[16] *First National City Bank Monthly Economic Letter,* July, 1967, p. 78.
[17] *Population Estimates, op. cit.,* pp. 41–42.

have explored thoroughly both the demand and the supply for labor and their relationship to wage levels and employment, we shall be prepared in Chapter 11 to tackle the problem of wage determination as it occurs in the labor market.

QUESTIONS FOR DISCUSSION

1. Discuss how recent changes in population growth will affect labor supply in years to come.
2. Under what circumstances will the supply curve of labor to a firm be elastic? Inelastic? Draw a supply curve which is perfectly elastic. Draw a supply curve which is less than perfectly elastic.
3. Discuss the difference between a change in the supply of labor and a change in the amount of labor supplied. What circumstances are likely to cause a change of the former type? Of the latter?

SUGGESTIONS FOR FURTHER READING

HICKS, J. R. *The Theory of Wages*, chap. v, pp. 89–111. 2d ed. London: Macmillan & Co., Ltd., 1963.

An analysis of factors governing the individual supply of labor expounded from the classical point of view.

MINCER, JACOB. "Labor-Force Participation and Unemployment: A Review of Recent Evidence," in GORDON, R. A. (ed.), *Prosperity and Unemployment*, pp. 73–112. New York: John Wiley & Sons, Inc., 1966.

A discussion of the responsiveness of the labor force to economic factors in the labor market.

Population Estimates. Current Population Reports, Series P–25, No. 381. Washington, D.C.: U.S. Department of Commerce, Bureau of the Census, December 18, 1967.

A basic source of data on population growth detailed with respect to age, sex, color, etc.

ROSS, ARTHUR M. "Theory and Measurement of Labor Shortages," in HARBISON, F. H., and MOONEY, J. D. (eds.), *Critical Issues in Employment Policy*, pp. 2–34. Research Report Series No. 109. Princeton University, 1966.

A provocative discussion of the definition, meaning, and causes of labor shortages.

Chapter 10

THE DEMAND FOR LABOR

During the course of a year, at least 6 million enterprises —3 million farms and as many nonagricultural establishments—use some hired labor. How do these employers decide how much labor to employ and what price to pay for it? What determines whether the employer will hire more men or use machines to perform a particular job? These are problems relating to the demand for labor which we shall consider in the following discussion.

In examining the demand for labor, we shall consider in some detail a theory known as the marginal productivity theory, which attempts to explain the determination of the demand for labor. This theory is widely held by economic theoreticians; but in recent years, it has been attacked as unrealistic by a number of labor economists. Despite such criticism, the marginal productivity theory is still a doctrine to be reckoned with in any study of the functioning of the labor market. It has demonstrated remarkable flexibility, and as will be pointed out in the following discussion, its advocates claim that it is quite compatible with some of the newer theories of wage determination which emphasize the bargaining aspect in wage-employment relationships. In this chapter, we shall consider some of the merits and shortcomings of this theory and compare it with other theories which seek to explain the demand for labor.

THE WAGES FUND THEORY

One of the earliest theories which sought to explain the demand for labor was the so-called "wages fund" theory, which became popular in the latter part of the 18th century and the first part of the 19th century in England and France. Economists sought to explain the determination of the aggregate amount of funds which employers were prepared to expend in hiring labor. The amount of such funds available for paying wages and salaries was conceived of as substantially fixed at any given period of time. In some discussions, this fund was referred to as "capital."

The wages fund theory declared that the rate of wages is determined by the ratio between this "capital" and the working population. As explained by one famous exponent of the theory, "capital" meant circulating capital, and not even the whole of that but only the "part which is expended in the direct purchase of labor." "Wages not only depend upon the relative amount of capital and population, but cannot, under the rules of competition, be affected by anything else. Wages cannot rise but by an increase of the aggregate funds employed in hiring labourers, or a diminution in the number of competitors for hire; nor fall, except either by a diminution of the funds devoted to paying labour, or by an increase in the number of labourers to be paid."[1]

The wages fund theory was never clearly formulated, and there was much confusion as to the precise meaning of its terminology. Some formulations of the theory amounted to no more than a truism. To explain the rate of wages by saying that it is a result of the proportion between the number of employees and the amount expended upon their wages by employers is simply to state an arithmetical proposition, not an economic theory. On the other hand, to maintain that there is a definite and fixed fund which is available for payment of wages is clearly erroneous. Wages fund theorists believed that the fund could not be expanded at the expense of profits—that diminution in profits would also reduce the wages fund. But this conclusion rested on the implicit assumption that employers earned only "normal profits," that is, profits at the minimum level necessary to induce an employer to stay in business. As long as there are surplus profits, so that a reduction in profit will not force employers out of business, the wages fund can be expanded by diverting profits to wage and salary payments.

Wages fund theorists, in describing the fund as a "capital," frequently confused a capital composed of physical commodities with a money capital. Obviously, if the theory relies upon a fixed fund composed of so many dollars and cents available for expenditure upon labor, it can have no validity in a modern economy with an elastic credit system. The amount of funds available to pay the wages of labor can always be expanded by borrowing from banks if employers are willing to pay the market rate of interest.

But there is a sense in which the wages fund theory has some validity. In our modern economy, most products are produced by "roundabout" methods of production. That is, the various commodities which constitute the real wage of labor represent the result of a long "period of production." At any given moment, only a certain amount of finished products are emerging from the long production line represented by our entire productive process, just as on the production line at River Rouge, most of the cars are in an incomplete stage, with only a few ready to be driven off and purchased by consumers.

[1] J. S. Mill, *Principles of Political Economy* (Ashley [ed.]) (London: Longmans, Green & Co., Ltd., 1909), pp. 343–44.

If the flow of finished products cannot be substantially increased in the short run, an increase in money wages paid to employees may simply produce a rise in prices without augmenting workers' real wages. Thus, in the short run the rate of *real* wages is, to some extent, limited by the size of the "subsistence fund" representing the efforts of past labor which must support current labor until new products emerge from the productive process. However, such a wages fund is flexible over time. Contrary to the view of the proponents of the old wages fund doctrine, an increase in the working population need not reduce the wage rate. On the contrary, when time has permitted the larger number of workers to be better organized so as to achieve a more efficient division of labor, there may be an increase in current output of finished goods which will raise the level of real wages.

The wages fund theory was originally propounded as a means of explaining the determination of the level of real wages. In time, however, it was converted into a doctrine which could be used to prove that attempts by workers to raise their real wages were futile. This perversion of the doctrine ultimately led to its recantation by one of its famous proponents. He conceded that the wages fund was not fixed, that the whole of the capitalists' means was potentially capital (in the sense of advances to labor), and that the amount which actually became capital depended on capitalists' personal expenditures.[2]

THE MARGINAL PRODUCTIVITY THEORY

Following the demise of the wages fund doctrine, the marginal productivity theory became the theory generally applied by economists to explain the functioning of the market for labor. At first, marginal productivity attempted to encompass a theory of wages—that is, it sought to explain the determination of wage levels. This stage of the doctrine is closely associated with the work of John Bates Clark, who, in his influential treatise entitled *Distribution of Wealth*,[3] enunciated a theory which rested on three basic assumptions:

1. Rational employers, in an attempt to maximize profits, will be guided by the marginal productivity of a factor in determining the relationship between a factor's return and its utilization. This premise might be called the "marginal productivity principle" and explains employer demand for the factors of production.
2. Perfect competition exists, so that market forces tend to equalize rates of return for all factors over time.

[2] The recantation was made by John Stuart Mill. See Erich Roll, *A History of Economic Thought* (rev. ed.; New York: Prentice-Hall, Inc., 1942), p. 402.

[3] John Bates Clark, *Distribution of Wealth* (London: Macmillan & Co., Ltd., 1899).

3. Long-run general equilibrium exists in all markets—which implies a stationary state in which technological progress and changes in demand and supply are absent.[4]

Under the above-stated restrictive conditions, the aggregate labor supply is fixed; and assuming a homogeneous class of labor, it is true that the general level of wages for such labor will be determined by its marginal product.

However, in subsequent writings, other economists attacked the assumptions numbered 2 and 3 above as artificial and remote from the labor market of reality. In the writings of Alfred Marshall[5] and others, wage determination was explained by the interaction of supply and demand in the marketplace, with marginal productivity being used as a tool to explain the demand for labor. This is the sense in which we shall use the term "marginal productivity theory" in this text. It is *not* a theory of wages; it *is* a theory of demand for factors of production.

According to this theory, employers have a "demand for labor" just as they have a demand for coal, or electricity, or raw materials, or any other of the "means of production" which are required to manufacture a finished product. In considering labor as a means of production, these economists do not, of course, overlook the fact that labor is highly personalized and, therefore, for many problems in the field of labor economics, cannot be treated as the equivalent of so many hours of "energy" on the same level as a lifeless thing like a machine. However, they contend that from the point of view of an employer seeking to operate his plant in the most efficient manner possible, the outlay for labor is a cost of production in the same sense as the outlay for electricity or raw materials.

No matter how understanding an employer may be in dealing with his personnel, the exigencies of market competition compel him to attempt to obtain maximum output at minimum cost from available factors of production. In so doing, the employer will find it advantageous to consider whether or not he would be better off if he used a little less labor and more machinery, or perhaps employed more labor and wasted less material, and so on. Thus, in the employer's calculations, labor becomes merely one of the many factors which can be combined in various proportions to yield varying amounts of physical output.

What determines an employer's demand for labor, according to this theory? Marginal productivity theorists point out that an employer's demand for labor is obviously not determined simply by the physical requirements for production in a given plant. Most plants in our country could physically turn out a larger quantity of goods than they do and

[4] See Allan M. Cartter, *Theory of Wages and Employment* (Homewood, Ill.: Richard D. Irwin, Inc., 1959), chaps. i–iii, and especially pp. 18–19.

[5] Alfred Marshall, *Principles of Economics* (8th ed.; London: Macmillan & Co., Ltd., 1920).

could physically utilize larger work forces. The reason they do not do so must be because at some point it becomes unprofitable to produce a larger amount—either because costs rise or prices fall, or both. Therefore an employer's determination as to actual output must be made with an eye on revenue and costs. Likewise, an employer's utilization of labor must be determined by weighing the cost of employing additional labor against the contribution the added labor is expected to make to the revenue of the firm.

Of course, any such determination made by employers must of necessity be very rough and approximate. The average employer cannot estimate accurately the marginal contribution to revenue which will be made by employment of additional labor. Revenues depend not only upon output but also upon prices; and prices are, of course, subject to constant change and fluctuations in our economy. Nevertheless, these economists argue, as a general rule of economic conduct, it would seem logical to assume that if employers wish to maximize their profits, they will hire additional labor only if its cost is less than the anticipated marginal contribution of the labor to the revenue of the firm.

This principle of weighing marginal revenue contributed by a factor against the added cost incurred through its use is the heart of marginal productivity theory. The marginal productivity theory is generally stated in the form of two propositions: (1) Employers will not ordinarily pay labor (or any other factor of production) more than that factor adds to the revenue of the firm; and (2) the forces of competition tend to make employers pay labor (or any other factor) a wage (or price) approximately equal to the full value of its marginal contribution to the revenue of the firm, except in certain special circumstances which we shall consider at a later point in this discussion.

It is important to note that the theory states only a tendency. In a dynamic society such as ours, where prices are always changing, the contribution which employment of additional quantities of labor will make to the revenue of a firm is also subject to continual change. Employers, however, do not change wages or hire or fire workers every time they make a price change. Consequently, the most that can be expected is that whenever employers make adjustments in output, size of the plant, labor force, and capital equipment, they will do so with the objective in mind of attempting to secure as close an equivalence as possible between the "marginal cost" of a factor of production—that is, the additional cost incurred by employing an additional unit of a factor of production—and the marginal revenue product of the factor—that is, the addition to revenue of the firm attributable to employment of the additional unit of the factor.

The Role of Profit Maximization

The two propositions of the marginal productivity theory stated above are simply logical deductions from a premise basic to the theory, namely, that businessmen normally seek to maximize profits. As we shall see later in this chapter, a businessman who finds that with a given amount of labor, he is obtaining a marginal revenue product in excess of the marginal cost of labor, can actually increase his profit by employing more labor until the marginal cost and marginal revenue product of labor are equated. Therefore, if businessmen are interested in maximizing profits, and if they attempt to make estimates of cost and revenue of the marginal type we have considered, there would be some tendency for the wage of labor to approximate the marginal revenue product of labor in the particular firms in which it is employed.

Not all businessmen, however, are motivated by the desire to maximize profits. Recent studies have indicated that the desire for prestige, for power, and for security may be dominant motives in the minds of many employers. Such motives may frequently dictate a policy which is inconsistent with maximizing profit. For example, some businesses may expand and thereby add to their labor force, even though such additional expansion is unprofitable. The employer may recognize that such expansion is uneconomic but may be motivated by the desire to operate the biggest company in the field or to dominate a particular geographic area. Other employers may be unwilling to expand even though they could increase profits by such action. The reason may be that they prize security and liquidity, or perhaps they may simply have become satisfied that they have grown enough and are unwilling to assume the additional burdens and worries that are the concomitants of big business. Some employers may be interested only in "satisficing" profits, rather than in maximizing them. This means that they set a target level of profits based upon a "fair return on investment," which may be less than the maximum profit that can be earned.[6]

Sometimes, of course, the employer will pursue actions which from a short-run point of view do not maximize profits but which make good economic sense from a long-run point of view. For example, suppose there is a downturn in business and the employer must face the question whether or not to lay off certain employees. If prices for the employer's product have fallen, it is possible that the wage of these men will now exceed the marginal contribution their services make to the revenue of the firm. Therefore, from the point of view of maximizing short-run profits or minimizing losses, the employer would be expected to lay off these employees. If he chooses to keep them on the payroll, he may be motivated by personal relations with the employees or a sense of community responsibility. On the other hand, he may also figure that if he lays off the men and business later picks up again, he may need these particular men and may find it difficult to rehire them, since they may have found employment elsewhere.

---

[6] See Philip Kotler, *Marketing Management* (Englewood Cliffs, N.J.: Prentice-Hall, Inc., 1967), p. 131.

Employer motivation is complex. Marginal productivity theorists concede that motives and objectives other than profit maximization influence employer behavior, but they contend nevertheless that the behavior of most employers can best be explained in terms of long-run profit maximization. Critics of the theory, however, take issue with this assumption and argue that noneconomic motivation is so common that a realistic theory cannot be based on profit maximization. Here is the first of the major cleavages between this theory and other theories of labor demand.

Long-Run Adjustments

The marginal productivity theory is a theory of long-run tendencies. As we have already observed, employer behavior which appears uneconomic from the short-run point of view may actually be designed to maximize profits in the long run. Moreover, in the short run, employers cannot freely change the combination of the factors of production. Suppose an employer has been producing a product using 10 men and a machine. If the price of labor doubles, he may find that he would be better off using half as much labor and a larger, more complicated machine. But it may be impracticable for him to junk his existing machine immediately, or possibly the larger machine cannot be accommodated in his existing plant. Consequently, several years may elapse before he is able to make the adjustment which the marginal productivity theory states he should make if he wishes to maximize profit.

DEMAND FOR LABOR IN THE INDIVIDUAL FIRM

The marginal productivity theory may be considered from the point of view of the individual firm or of the economy as a whole; or stated another way, marginal productivity principles determine the nature of the demand curve for labor, and the demand curve for labor may be examined from the point of view of the individual employer or of the economy as a whole. In the following discussion, we shall be concerned only with the application of marginal productivity principles by the individual employer. At a later point in this chapter, we shall consider the problem of applying marginal productivity principles to the economy as a whole.

In the context of individual firm analysis the marginal contribution of a factor is determined by its effect on the *revenue* of the particular firm. If we say, as a paraphrase of the theory, that employers try to pay labor what it is worth, the term "worth" must be understood in a strictly economic sense, without any moral or social connotations. The advertising executive who thinks up new slogans for dog food has a high worth to his agency because his efforts add a lot to the revenue of the firm. The value of his "product" from the social point of view may be nil. The marginal productivity theory was originally enunciated in terms of a theoretical economy in which perfect competition prevailed. In such a system, factors of production would tend to be allocated in a manner such that the optimum aggregate national product would be obtained, and the value of the marginal product of particular employees would be some index of its social worth. This theoretical problem need not concern us, however, at this point. We know that our economy is not perfectly competitive, nor is there such a tendency in that direction to warrant using perfect competition as a norm in our discussion.

Significance of Monopolistic Competition

In the following analysis, we shall assume—what is a fact—that we have an economy characterized by "monopolistic competition." In such an economy, there is in each industry a number of firms, each selling a product which is slightly differentiated from the other. Each producer is in competition with other producers; but to some extent, he is a monopolist in his own little market. Hence the term "monopolistic competition." If the individual producer raises his price, he does not lose all his customers because some customers still prefer his product and will pay the higher price. In other words, while there are competitive products, they are not perfect substitutes in the minds of consumers; and to the extent that such substitution is imperfect, the individual producer is somewhat in the position of a monopolist who can raise his price without losing customers because he has a monopoly of the product. Similarly, when the individual producer lowers his price, he increases his business but does not take away all his competitors' business because some of their customers will remain loyal and buy their products despite this producer's price reduction.

We may assume, therefore, that the average employer with whom we shall be concerned will, in estimating his labor requirements, have in mind the fact that additional units of his product can be sold only at a lower price, which is required in order to take away some of the business from his monopolistic competitors and make it possible to market the larger volume. If additional output can be sold at a lower price, this will also mean that the marginal contribution to revenue made by additional employees will tend to decline. Therefore, the more workers the employer hires, the less he can afford to pay to each additional worker. In geometric terms, this means that the employer will have a downward-sloping demand curve for labor.

Geometry versus Reality

Of course, employers do not normally think in terms of geometrical curves. As a matter of fact, they usually would not even have sufficient data to plot a demand curve for labor if they wanted to! The concept of a demand curve for labor is simply an aid which helps economists to understand how employers make decisions involving the employment of labor. The employer must have some rough idea of the various wages he would be willing to pay for varying amounts of labor, based upon his estimates of the additional revenue which such labor could produce for him. The demand curve for labor is simply a geometric representation of this idea.

The demand curve for labor of a hypothetical employer is shown by line *DD* in Figure 10–1. The demand curve for labor shows the various

FIGURE 10–1

DEMAND CURVE FOR LABOR

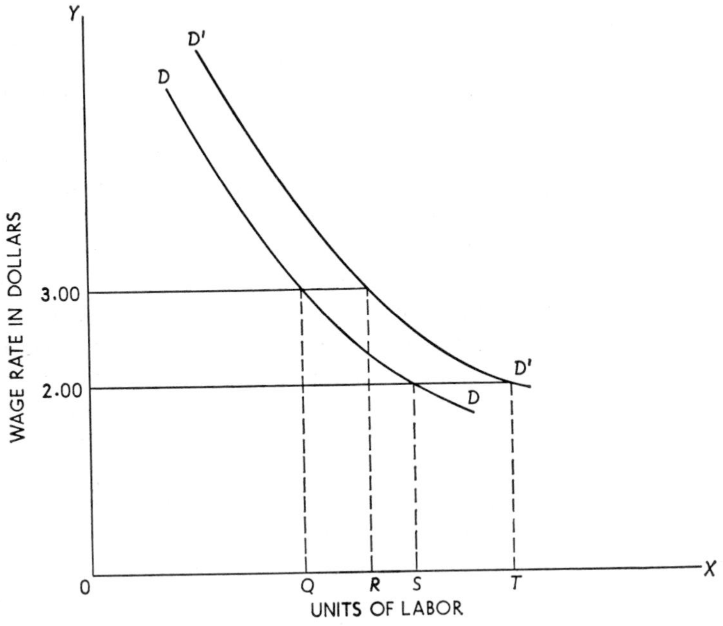

amounts of labor the employer would be willing to employ at various wage levels. As in the preceding chapter, we shall assume, for illustrative purposes, that labor is homogeneous so that we can talk about "units of labor" or "additional labor" without need for concern about personal differences. The lower the wage level, the more labor the individual employer feels he can profitably employ. Thus, at the wage of $3, this employer estimates he could employ only *OQ* units of labor, whereas if the wage rate falls to $2, he would employ *OS* units of labor. Such increases are referred to as changes in the quantity of labor demanded because they involve changes along a given demand curve. Sometimes, however, the entire demand curve for labor will shift. This may happen, for example, when there is an upturn in business, such as occurs during the business cycle. A shift in the demand curve for labor means that at every wage rate the employer is now willing to hire more labor than he was previously. For example, in Figure 10–1, if the demand curve shifts to position *D'D'*, then at the wage of $3 the employer will demand *OR* units of labor instead of the smaller amount *OQ* indicated by the previous position of the demand curve. This situation involves an *increase in the demand for labor*, whereas increased employment due to a reduction in wage rates is distinguished by economists as an *increase in the quantity of labor demanded*. A similar distinction in terminology was met in the last chapter in connection with changes in supply.

THE LAWS OF PRODUCTION

We have seen that in monopolistic competition the demand curve for labor is downward-sloping because of conditions in the market for the employer's product. There is also another and more fundamental reason why the demand curve for labor has this shape. This is found in the so-called "laws of production"—the law of diminishing returns and the law of scale. These two laws would have the effect of producing a downward-sloping demand curve for labor *even if the employer estimated that he could sell additional units* of his product with no reduction in price. These laws affect the amount of additional *physical* product which can be produced by adding additional amounts of one factor of production to other factors. They are laws of physical, not monetary returns.

The Law of Diminishing Returns

The law of diminishing returns is concerned with the effect on total output of adding successive amounts of one factor of production to another factor or group of factors which is held constant in amount. Thus, we may wish to know the effect on total product of adding additional workers to assist in the cultivation of one acre of corn. Or we may wish to know the behavior of total output of shoes as the amount of capital per worker is increased. The universal rule in such cases is that, with a given state of technology, the application of successive units of *any* variable factor to another fixed factor will, after a certain point is reached, yield diminishing returns. Or to put the proposition a little differently, additional units of labor added to another factor—say, capital—will, beyond a certain point (i.e., the point of diminishing returns), produce diminishing marginal increments in total physical product.

Significance for Marginal Productivity Theory. This law of diminishing returns is of fundamental importance to marginal productivity determination. Its relation to marginal productivity theory can best be illustrated if, for the moment, we direct our attention exclusively to physical product. Suppose that additional units of product can be sold at the same price, so that the employer is concerned primarily with the changes in total physical product attributable to employment of additional labor. Suppose, further, that labor itself is paid in physical product rather than in money. Under these conditions the marginal productivity theory would say that there is a tendency for the wage of labor to equal the marginal physical product it produces.

There could be no such tendency, however, if industry operated in a range of increasing rather than diminishing physical returns. This can be seen from the following example, which illustrates production under increasing returns. If increasing returns prevail, the addition of more labor to a fixed amount of another factor will produce more than proportionate increases in total product, with the result that the marginal physical product of labor will continually rise. The marginal physical product of labor is the increase in total product attributable to the addition of a unit of labor. Suppose that all workers are of equal ability (so that they have to be paid the same wage) and that employment of additional labor increases total product as follows:

Men	Total Product	Marginal Product
1...................	4	..
2...................	10	6
3...................	17	7
4...................	25	8

The addition of a fourth worker increases output by eight units. But the employer could not afford to pay a wage rate equivalent to 8 units of product, since all workers have to be paid the same wage, and payment of an hourly wage of 8 units of output would involve a wage bill of 32 units, which is in excess of total product.

In practice, employers operate within the range of diminishing returns. Therefore the marginal product of labor will be decreasing, not increasing, as in the above hypothetical example. In the following illustration, the addition of the fourth man increases total product from 14 to 17 units:

Men	Total Product	Marginal Product
1...................	4	..
2...................	10	6
3...................	14	4
4...................	17	3

The marginal physical product (i.e., the increase in total product attributable to the addition of the last unit of the variable factor) of the fourth man is three units, and the employer therefore can profitably pay up to three units as his wage. Because of diminishing returns, the wage bill will not exhaust total product—the wage bill would be only 12, while the total product would be 17. Moreover, there would be a limit to the output of the firm—there would be no incentive to expand output beyond the point at which the marginal product of labor equaled its wage. The demand curve for labor under these circumstances would be downward-sloping —even though prices were not affected by increasing output—simply because the marginal contribution to total physical product made by additional workers was declining, and therefore the wage which the employer could afford to pay for such additional labor would also decrease as employment rose.

The Law of Scale

The law of diminishing returns, as we have seen, is concerned with the effect upon total physical output of adding increasing amounts of variable factors to an unchanging amount of a fixed factor. The law of scale, on the other hand, concerns the effect upon total product of increasing *all* factors together. For example, if we double the amount of capital and the quantity of labor and the amount of land, will output likewise double? Will the increase in total product be greater or less than in proportion to the increase in the quantity of factors?

Significance for Marginal Productivity Theory. Why is this problem relevant to marginal productivity determination? The size of the marginal physical product contributed by a particular worker will depend upon the size of the establishment in which he is employed. Take the example of Jones the shoemaker. If Jones is employed in an establishment having only 10 employees, chances are that most of his work will be done by hand. Moreover, he will probably have to make the entire shoe himself, since the number of employees will be too small to permit efficient division of labor. However, as the size of the establishment grows, there will come a point—say, when 100 men are employed—at which it will pay the employer to utilize expensive machinery designed to perform individual operations such as lasting, cutting, and so on. Moreover, the workers can be arranged in a production line, each worker performing only a specialized operation at which he soon becomes highly proficient.

As a result of the introduction of machinery and division of labor, efficiency of operation will increase. Consequently, the physical productivity of a worker in the large factory will be greater than the physical productivity of a worker in the small plant. Here, we have a situation in which an increase in the amount of labor and capital produces a more than proportionate increase in total output. This consequence is fundamentally attributable to the fact that machinery can only be introduced in "chunks." A conveyor belt and production line cannot be advantageously used with only 10 employees, and the small firm cannot use half a machine. As the size of a firm grows, various "indivisible" chunks of other factors become profitable to use; and such utilization, impracticable in a smaller plant, may produce a substantial improvement in efficiency.

However, if such improvement were a continuing possibility as a function of increasing scale, there would be no limit to the size of firms. Our economy would be composed of giant monopolies, each supreme in its own field. Obviously, this eventuality has not occurred. The reason is that as a firm grows in size, the problems of organization, supervision, and coordination grow in complexity. Management becomes farther and farther removed from actual operations as the hierarchy of minor officialdom grows. As a consequence, beyond a certain size—which varies by industry —inefficiency develops, and the rate of increase in total product becomes less than proportionate to the increase in quantity of all factors used.

Another reason for the eventual decline in rate of growth of total output as size of firm grows is that beyond a certain point, it is not possible to increase entrepreneurship in the same proportion as other factors. Men who can efficiently manage million-dollar enterprises are few and far between. Consequently, as existing management finds it must itself coordinate larger quantities of labor and capital, inefficiency develops. This is simply a reflection of the operation of the law of diminishing returns—increasing amounts of labor and capital added to the unchanging factor of entrepreneurship result in diminishing returns in terms of total output.

Thus the law of scale and the law of diminishing returns set important limitations on the proportion and amount of factors which will be used in individual firms. Were it not for the law of diminishing returns, there would be no limit to the output of a firm; were it not for the law of scale, there would be no limit to the amount of all factors which could profitably be combined under one management. These laws, therefore, play an important role in determining the physical environment in which labor will work and thereby influence the size of physical product which will be attributable to the efforts of particular workers.

MARGINAL PRODUCTIVITY CALCULATIONS

Few employers have ever heard of marginal productivity; yet, they are called upon to apply the principles of this doctrine almost every day in the conduct of their business affairs. John Doe, a machine operator, applies to a broom factory for a job. Should the employer hire him or not? The mental calculation of the employer faced by this problem will in substance be no different from that which he would make in determining the desirability of undertaking any other type of acquisition for the plant. The question in each case is: Will purchase of the additional unit or units of the productive resource increase the revenue of the firm by an amount in excess of the addition to cost incidental to its employment? If the addition promises to augment profits so calculated, the resource will be acquired; if not, the opportunity to purchase will be forgone.

Approximate Nature of Calculation

Obviously, the calculation must ordinarily be approximate and often highly conjectural. Determination of Doe's anticipated marginal contribution to the firm would be facilitated if three conditions were satisfied: (1) if his employment did not require use of additional material or capital, so that his contribution would be net, without deduction for incidental expenses; (2) if the increment in output attributable to his employment could be measured in distinct, separable, completed physical units; and (3) if the price at which the increased output could be sold could be accurately forecast. In practice, these conditions are never realized, so that at best the employer's calculation of the marginal worth of an employee must remain in the realm of approximation.

In a Robinson Crusoe economy, where Crusoe had merely to evaluate the worth of the services of one man Friday, the marginal product of labor could be determined with fair precision. In a typical modern factory, however, where thousands of employees, aided by complex machinery, together pool their efforts to produce a joint product, the contribution of the individual employee becomes indistinct. Nevertheless, employers must make some estimate of the worth of additional employees. They do not go on hiring workers without limit.

Nature of Marginal Productivity Calculations

Table 10–1 is intended to clarify and elaborate the nature of shorthand calculation which the marginal productivity theory assumes employers make in determining the volume of employment in a firm. Few employers would have available such a detailed schedule as is here assumed, but the detailed figures will serve to illustrate more clearly the basic principles involved in marginal productivity determination.

Assume that our factory produces brooms and that the relationship between employment, physical product, and revenue is estimated by the employer to be as shown in Table 10–1. Consider first columns 1, 2, and 3 of Table 10–1. As additional units of labor are added to unchanging amounts of the other factors, the total physical product increases, at first more than in proportion to the increase in labor and subsequently less than in proportion to the increase in labor. Eventually, as more and more labor is hired, total product might actually decrease. This might be attributable to the fact that with, say, 10 men and a limited amount of machinery, the men would get in each other's way, with the result that total output would be curtailed. The variation in total product and marginal physical product shown in the table reflects the operation of the law of diminishing returns. If labor were paid in brooms and the rate of wages established in the market were 16 brooms, this employer could afford to hire only

TABLE 10-1

MARGINAL PRODUCTIVITY CALCULATIONS

(1) Units of Labor	(2) Total Product	(3) Marginal Physical Product	(4) Price per Unit (Dollars)	(5) Value of Marginal Physical Product (Dollars)	(6) Total Revenue (Dollars)	(7) Marginal Revenue Product (Dollars)
1.........	20	20	5.00	100	100	100
2.........	50	30	4.00	120	200	100
3.........	70	20	3.50	70	245	45
4.........	85	15	3.00	45	255	10
5.........	95	10	2.00	20	190	−65
6........	100	5	1.00	5	100	−90

three workers. With three workers on his force, the employer gets production of 70 brooms, the third employee having increased production by 20 brooms. But the addition of a fourth worker would increase output only to 85 brooms. Fifteen brooms is therefore the marginal physical product attributable to the fourth worker, i.e., it is the increment in total physical production attributable to the employment of an additional unit of the variable factor. If wages are paid in brooms, the employer cannot afford to pay this man 16 brooms when he adds only 15 brooms to the output of the firm.

Value of the Marginal Physical Product of Labor

Since, in a modern capitalistic economy, labor is paid in money wages and not in physical product, employers must estimate the money value of the physical contribution made by additional units of labor. The value of the marginal physical product of labor is obtained by multiplying marginal physical product (column 3) by price per unit of product (column 4). This figure would be a fair index of the value to an employer of the additional output produced by additional units of labor if the additional output could be sold without any reduction in price as compared with a smaller output. In other words, if an employer assumed that he could market additional units of product at a constant price, he could afford to pay labor a wage just a trifle less than the price per unit of such additional output and still make a profit. This is the situation which exists in what economists call "perfect competition." In perfect competition, each firm is small and produces only a minor portion of the output in a particular industry. Furthermore, unlike monopolistic competition, the product of each firm in the industry is indistinguishable from the product of any other producer. As a consequence, the individual employer assumes that if he produces a little more, the addition to the total output of the entire industry will be so slight that it will not affect market price. This situation may exist in the case of farmers producing wheat. Each farmer feels that his output is so small relative to the total output of the industry that he can produce and sell almost any amount of wheat at the same price. In geometric terms, this would mean that the farmer assumes that his demand curve for wheat is horizontal, if we were to plot price of product along the *Y* axis and quantities expected to be sold along the *X* axis. In perfect competition the individual employer would hire workers until the wage was approximately equal to the value of marginal physical product added by the last worker hired.

The Marginal Revenue Product of Labor

However, under monopolistic competition the value of the marginal physical product of labor is not a fair index of the value to an employer of the additional units produced by added labor because the additional output can be sold only at a lower price, and this lowers not only the price for the additional units but also the price for all other units of the firm's production. Therefore, we must determine what is the net amount added to the revenue of the firm by the employment of the additional labor. This figure is supplied by the marginal revenue product (column 7). The marginal revenue product of labor is calculated either by finding the difference between total revenue obtained with a given amount of labor and that obtained with a smaller amount of labor or by subtracting from the value of the marginal physical product the loss in revenue, if any, on units of product produced without use of the additional units of the factor, when the loss is caused by a fall in price because of the augmented output.

If the wage rate for broommakers were established in the market at $30, this firm could afford to employ only three men. The marginal revenue product (column 7) for the fourth man is only $10. It would not be profitable for this firm to employ the fourth man, since his employment would cost the firm more than he adds to revenue. The employment of the third worker results in production of 20 extra units, which can be sold only by taking a reduction in price from $4 to $3.50. The value of the marginal physical product is $70 (column 4 multiplied by column 3). But the reduced price is applicable as well to the 50 units which could have been produced without the extra man, and therefore the loss of revenue on these units of $25 (50 multiplied by $0.50 equals $25) must be subtracted from $70, leaving $45 as the marginal revenue attributable to the use of the third worker. Thus, it is apparent that in monopolistic competition a worker cannot be paid the value of his marginal physical product, since this would exceed the amount of his marginal revenue contribution to the firm. It is therefore with reference to the marginal revenue product of labor that the employer will make his employment decisions.

CONDITIONS OF PROFIT MAXIMIZATION IN THE INDIVIDUAL FIRM

The principles of marginal productivity determination elucidated in the foregoing computations are illustrated in geometric form in Figure 10–2. The line marked *MRP* represents the marginal revenue product obtained from employment of varying amounts of labor. This curve therefore indicates the value to the employer of varying amounts of labor and is identical with his demand curve for labor. For *OB* units of labor the

FIGURE 10–2

PROFIT MAXIMIZATION IN THE INDIVIDUAL FIRM

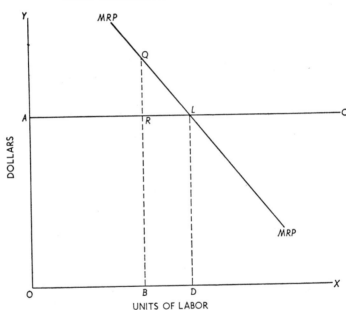

estimated marginal revenue product is *BQ;* as more labor is employed, marginal revenue product falls, so that for *OD* units of labor the marginal revenue product is equal to *DL*. Suppose, now, that a wage for this type of labor is established in the market of *OA* dollars. Suppose, further, that the employer can obtain any number of men he needs at this same wage level. The wage is therefore constant, regardless of the number of units of labor employed. This circumstance is shown by the horizontal line *AC*. This line is called the supply curve of labor because it indicates the amount of labor that will be supplied at a given wage. It also indicates the average cost to the employer of hiring additional units of labor. Since, in the present case, it has been assumed that each additional unit of labor can be obtained with no increase in price, the average cost and the marginal cost of each unit of labor are identical. The line *AC* therefore represents to the employer both the average cost and the marginal cost of hiring additional labor. At a later point in this discussion, we shall find that under different circumstances the average cost and marginal cost of labor may diverge.

Determination of Optimum Employment

With a demand curve and supply curve for labor as shown in Figure 10–2, what amount of labor will yield maximum profits for the employer? Suppose he employs only *OB* units. For this amount the marginal revenue product *BQ* is well above the cost *RB*, and it might therefore be thought that this amount would yield a maximum profit to the employer. But note that if the employer uses a little more labor, although marginal revenue product falls with each additional unit of labor utilized, he can neverthe-less increase profits as long as the marginal revenue product of labor remains above its cost. This will be so until we come to the point of intersection of the marginal revenue curve and the wage. For any amount of labor less than *OD* the employer can increase his profit by using more labor; and for any amount of labor greater than *OD* the employer will be losing money, since he will be paying labor in wages more than it produces for him in revenue.

The point in equality of marginal revenue product and wage is therefore the point of maximum profit for the employer. Under the assumed circumstances of a horizontal supply curve for labor, the em-ployer who is interested in obtaining the largest profit will seek to utilize that amount of labor for which the marginal revenue product of the last worker employed is approximately equal to his wage. If the employer follows this rule, ordinarily a reduction of wage rates will induce him to increase employment of labor, while an increase in wage rates will induce him to curtail employment of labor. This reaction is to be expected, however, only with a given marginal revenue product curve. If there should be an increase in wage rates concurrently with an increase in demand for labor (i.e., a shift to the right of the entire demand curve for labor), then it is quite possible that the wage increase will not produce any reduction in employment and, indeed, may even be associated with an increase in employment. This is frequently the case, as we shall see in our discussion in later chapters of wage changes during the business cycle. Increases in wage rates usually occur in periods when business is booming and the demand for labor is increasing. In such circumstances there is no immediate inducement for employers to curtail employment in response to the increased cost of labor. The marginal productivity theory, there-fore, is quite consistent with the observed pattern of wage-employment relationships which develops over the period of the business cycle.

We have seen that maximum profits are obtained by the employer if he attempts to hire an amount of labor such that the marginal revenue product of the last man hired will approximate his wage. This principle is applicable to all factors of production which the employer utilizes. The marginal productivity theory assumes that wherever possible the employer will attempt to obtain maximum output at minimum cost. If he can do this by using more of one factor of production rather than another, he will do so. The decisive consideration in each case is the contribution to revenues in comparison with costs. For maximum profits the employer should utilize the various factors of production so that the ratio of the marginal revenue product of each factor to its cost will equal the ratio of marginal revenue product to cost of other factors. Of course, if the employer is able to use an amount of each factor such that its marginal revenue product is equal to its cost, then the former condition of equality of ratios of respective marginal revenue products and costs will automatically be satisfied.

EXPLOITATION OF LABOR[7]

The marginal productivity theory assumes that there is a long-run tendency toward equality between the wage of labor and its marginal revenue product in the individual firm. Normally, the employer obtains his maximum profit by seeking to achieve this position. As we have seen, if the wage is below the marginal revenue product, it will pay him to increase output and employment to a point where this discrepancy is eliminated and the equality between wage and marginal revenue product is established. However, the marginal productivity theory recognizes that there may be certain situations in which a discrepancy can develop between marginal revenue product and wage which will be profitable for the employer to maintain, so that there will be no tendency to the normal equilibrium position of equality of wage and marginal revenue product. These exceptions from the general rule are referred to by economists as cases of exploitation of labor.

The term "exploitation" is used by economists simply to denote a condition in which labor will be paid a wage less than its marginal revenue product. It is a technical definition without social connotations. It has no necessary connection with the level of wage rates. The distressingly low rates paid to labor in some southern industries may present an acute labor problem, but the low rate is not itself any evidence of "exploitation" as the economist uses that term. Indeed, we shall see that exploitation of labor, as we have defined it, is as likely to be encountered where wages are high as where they are low.

---

[7] For a detailed discussion of this subject the reader is referred to Gordon F. Bloom, "A Reconsideration of the Theory of Exploitation," *Quarterly Journal of Economics*, Vol. LV (May, 1941), pp. 413–42.

Rising Supply Curve of Labor

Perhaps the most common source of exploitation is the lack of perfect elasticity in the supply curve for labor. In the preceding discussion, it was assumed that the supply curve for labor is horizontal (i.e., perfectly elastic); but frequently this will not be the case. For example, a firm may require such a substantial proportion of a particular type of labor in an area that it will have to offer higher wage rates when it wants additional labor, in order to attract workers away from other companies. This is particularly likely in cases of skilled labor which is in short supply. The type of exploitation here considered may therefore be more common where wage rates are high rather than low, as it is a result of scarcity in the labor market. In cases of such short supply a firm, in estimating its labor requirements, will take into account the fact that its demand for labor affects the market price of labor. The firm which is a large enough buyer of a particular class of labor so that its demand will affect the price of labor is termed a "monopsonist" by analogy to a monopolist who is a large enough seller of a commodity so that his supply will affect the price of a commodity. The monopsonist will assume that he is faced by a rising supply curve for labor, that is, that increasing amounts of labor can be obtained only at successively higher wage rates. This will affect his decision as to the amount of labor he will employ.

In our previous examples, we noted that if an employer can obtain additional workers at the same wage, the average cost of each additional worker and the marginal cost of each additional worker will be the same and will in each case be equal to the wage which is paid the worker. If, however, the employer has to pay higher wages to attract additional workers, the identity between average cost and marginal cost disappears. Suppose the prevailing wage paid by a firm has been $3 an hour, but in order to obtain additional workers, the employer finds he must increase the wage rate to $3.25 per hour. If he pays this rate to new workers, he will also be compelled to pay it to all other men of the same skill already in the firm, in order to avoid dissatisfaction among his employees. As a consequence, the addition to total wage cost (i.e., marginal cost) attributable to hiring an additional worker may under such circumstances be very great and considerably in excess of the wage, or average cost, of such a new man.

In Figure 10–3, units of labor hired by the firm are indicated along the X axis, while the cost of labor and its productivity in terms of dollars are indicated along the Y axis. The supply curve of labor (AC) is assumed to be rising to the firm. Each point on this line indicates the wage which will have to be paid to attract the amount of labor indicated along the X axis. The wage paid and the average cost of labor to the individual firm are therefore identical. However, when the average cost of labor is rising, the marginal cost will be greater, as has already been explained, since the marginal cost takes account not only of the higher wage paid to a particular employee but also of the addition to payroll resulting from paying the same higher rate to all employees already employed by the firm. Marginal cost is indicated in Figure 10–3 by the line *AF*. Obviously, the employer has to take account of the expensive consequences in terms of his total payroll of paying higher rates for new men; and for this reason, he employs that amount of labor for which the marginal cost of labor and its marginal revenue product are equal. This equality is achieved if *OD* units of labor are employed. It will be recalled that in our previous

FIGURE 10–3

EXPLOITATION: UPWARD SLOPING LABOR SUPPLY CURVE

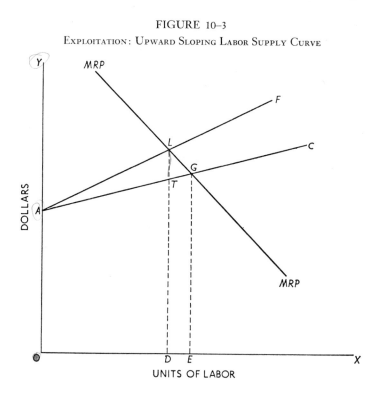

UNITS OF LABOR

example, where the supply curve of labor was constant, the employer also equated marginal cost of labor and marginal revenue product to maximize profits, since marginal cost of labor and the wage of labor were the same. However, in Figure 10–3, because the supply curve for labor is rising, for *OD* units of labor the marginal revenue product of labor (*DL*) will be above the wage paid to labor (*DT*). If the employer were to expand employment to *OE* units, which is the point where the wage and marginal revenue product are equal, he would, under the circumstances here set forth, reduce his profit. Here, then, is a case in which the wage will be less than marginal revenue product; therefore, exploitation will exist. Under the circumstances shown in Figure 10–3, the employer could not pay labor a wage equal to its marginal revenue product and still maximize profits.

Consequences of Exploitation

We have seen that if the wage of labor is approximately equated with its marginal revenue product, an increase in wage rates will lead the employer to reduce employment until at the smaller output the marginal revenue product of labor is raised to equal the now increased wage. In the case of exploitation attributable to a rising supply curve for labor, however, the effect of a wage increase upon employment will depend on whether there is a rise in the entire supply curve of labor or a change in its slope. If the entire marginal cost and average cost curves for labor shift upward but remain rising supply curves (as would be the case if there is a general increase in wage rates in the area), employment will be reduced in the individual firm, since there will have been a rise in the marginal cost of labor without a concomitant change in the marginal revenue productivity of labor. However, it is also possible that an increase in wage rates may be accompanied by a change in the shape of the supply curve of labor. For example, suppose a union enters the labor market and sets a uniform rate for labor, regardless of the number of workers required (within limits), which is equal to the former marginal cost of labor. In Figure 10–3, this would mean that the supply curve for labor would now be designated by a horizontal line drawn through point *L* on the marginal revenue product curve. If this were to occur, the employer would still find it profitable to employ the same number of employees (*OD*), since this amount would be indicated as most profitable by the intersection of the horizontal supply curve for labor and the demand curve for labor. The wage *DL* thus would be above the former wage *DT*, but because there would be no change in the marginal cost of labor, employment would be unaffected. All that would occur would be a reduction in profits of the firm. Here is a case in which workers would benefit from organization.

UNIONS AND MARGINAL PRODUCTIVITY THEORY

A rising supply curve for labor is most typical of skilled wage groups, but these are the very ones that are most likely to be highly unionized. When a trade-union sets a minimum wage rate for work of a particular kind, regardless of the number of workers the employer hires to do it, the effect is to make the supply curve for labor to the employer horizontal or "perfectly elastic," as the economists say. This has the effect of eliminating exploitation attributable to a rising supply curve for labor. But union organization, by reason of its multifarious rules and regulations and restrictions on employer freedom of action, may also make it more difficult for employers to utilize the optimum amount of labor and thus may produce a discrepancy between marginal revenue product and wage.

The correspondence of a worker's wage with his individual contribution to the revenues of the firm depends in some degree upon the ability of the employer to determine the amount of such contribution. This presupposes that the employer can hire and fire at will, rearrange job classifications, change men from one position to another, substitute machinery for labor, and in general freely alter the combinations of labor and capital within the firm. Unions, however, have restricted many of these former prerogatives of management. Consequently, in firms where unions are strongly entrenched, workers are not freely substitutable, and the task of marginal productivity determination is undoubtedly made more difficult.

Effect of Union Rules

Union rules which limit the employer's ability to substitute machinery for labor and restrict the freedom of the employer to measure the contribution of labor to output of the firm may produce a range of indeterminateness in wage-employment relations. For example, many unions are now interested in requiring employers to pay dismissal wages to employees who are displaced as a result of technological change. Suppose that as a result of a wage increase an employer finds it is profitable to introduce a new machine which will displace 10 workers. If the union now compels the employer to pay these displaced workers dismissal wages for some period of time after they are laid off, the employer may decide it is no longer profitable to introduce the machine. The union insistence on a dismissal wage has obviously not increased the marginal revenue product of the labor involved; yet, it has had the practical effect of enabling the union to raise the wage rates of these workers without producing immediate technological unemployment.

In effect, union rules have produced a range of indeterminateness within which some changes in wage rates may be effected without altering employment. The range of indeterminateness, however, is much narrower than the short-run repercussions of employment would indicate. Any wage adjustment, whether it immediately alters employment or not, does affect profits and the inducement to invest. If these are adversely influenced by union wage demands, wage increases even within the "range of indeterminateness" may cause unemployment in the long run.

DEMAND FOR LABOR IN THE ECONOMY

As we have observed earlier in this chapter, the marginal productivity theory in its original form purported to explain the determination of wages in the economy as a whole. It laid down a long list of assumptions and emerged with a conclusion that in equilibrium the wage of labor in the economy as a whole would be equal to the marginal productivity of labor in its least profitable use. This conclusion—and the highly artificial assumptions upon which it was based—did much to bring the theory into disrepute. Moreover, proponents of the theory erroneously reasoned from the existence of unemployment in the labor market to the conclusion that wages were too high and that if wages were only reduced, unemployment could be eliminated.

We have seen that present-day labor economists do not look upon marginal productivity as a theory of wages, but rather as a theory of demand. But even here, limitations must be recognized. As a result of the work of John Maynard Keynes[8] in the field of general equilibrium analysis, it is generally accepted that the marginal productivity theory cannot serve as a general theory of employment and that the theory does not adequately explain the demand for labor in the economy as a whole. The demand curve for labor in the economy as a whole is not simply the sum of demand curves of all individual firms. The reason is that each individual demand curve for labor is drawn up under the assumption that wages and prices in other firms remain constant. Thus, when the individual employer considers what effect a reduction in wage rates will have on his labor requirements, he assumes that sales of his product will be unaffected by the reduction in wages. However, when we consider the economy as a whole, a reduction in the wages paid to all labor will affect the demand curve for all labor because wage earners are the principal purchasers of the product of industry. Whereas, for the individual firm, the demand curve for labor may be assumed to be independent of the supply curve for labor, this assumption cannot be made when we are considering the economy as a whole. Therefore, it is possible that a reduction in wage rates might not increase employment at all when the reduction is nation-wide, even though increased employment would normally follow a wage reduction in the individual firm.

The demand for labor in the economy as a whole can only be understood by application of the aggregative analysis developed by Keynes, in which attention is given to changes in savings, investment, and national income. However, the fact that marginal productivity analysis has proved inadequate to deal with the demand for labor in the economy as a whole does not necessarily mean that it cannot be used to advantage to explain the demand for labor in the individual firm. Exponents of this theory still contend that it gives a logical explanation of employer behavior in the individual firm.

Furthermore, even from the point of view of the economy as a whole, the marginal productivity theory helps us to understand why the level of wages is high in a country such as the United States and low in a country like India. The average level of wages in a particular economy

---

[8] John Maynard Keynes, *The General Theory of Employment, Interest, and Money* (New York: Harcourt, Brace & Co., Inc., 1936).

will be determined by the scarcity of labor relative to other factors of production. In the United States, labor has always been in short supply relative to land and capital. As a consequence, the marginal product of labor has remained high. We have seen from previous examples in this chapter that as additional quantities of a factor of production are utilized, its marginal product declines. If labor were more plentiful in the United States, as it is in India, more labor would be used relative to capital, and its marginal product would be less. Employers have been ready to pay, and workers have been able to demand, a high level of wages in this country because the high ratio of land and labor to capital has made the incremental contribution of labor worth a high wage.

CRITIQUE OF THE MARGINAL PRODUCTIVITY THEORY

A number of criticisms have been leveled at the marginal productivity theory. Some of these have merit; others are based in part upon a lack of understanding of what the theory holds. The following are some of the major lines of attack against the marginal productivity theory.

1. Some economists object to the whole notion of marginality and marginal calculations on the ground that "businessmen don't think that way." It is all very well, they say, to draw up marginal revenue and marginal cost curves and sloping demand curves and rising supply curves, but the fact is that most employers have little or no idea of any points on these curves other than the point at which they are at the time. While businessmen know their existing prices, they do not know accurately how much their prices will have to be cut to sell additional units, or how much product can be sold at lower prices. Furthermore, factors of production are not easily divisible, so that, as a practical matter, businessmen cannot add one or two or three units of capital to determine how its marginal revenue productivity compares with that of labor. Capital is customarily embodied in "chunks" like machines and factories, and the employer cannot very well speculate on adding half a machine to his existing equipment. While this can be done to some extent in the long run when capital can be reinvested in various forms, the fact remains that in the short run the indivisibility of units of the factors adds to the difficulties of determining marginal contributions.

This means that there are inevitably large areas of indeterminateness inherent in practical application of marginal productivity principles, assuming that employers try to apply them at all. Some economists doubt whether employers are even interested in marginal calculations. They point out that when labor costs rise, many businessmen talk about increasing output to reduce *average costs* per unit, whereas according to marginal productivity principles, they should be thinking in terms of decreasing output because of increased *marginal* costs. If businessmen are, in fact, more interested in the behavior of average rather than marginal costs, a substantial revision would be necessitated in marginal productivity doctrine.

Despite these criticisms, advocates of the marginal productivity theory maintain that marginalism still exemplifies the typical economic calculations of the average businessman. They point out that marginal-type calculations are really very simple and are practiced by employers in every aspect of business. For example, if an employer is asked why he does not take on another bookkeeper or purchase a particular machine, his answer will usually be that the added return or revenue or service would not justify the additional expense. Here is an example of the weighing of marginal contributions and marginal costs which the employer does in a rough sort of way, despite the admitted difficulties in making such calculations. This same sort of rough approximation is all that marginal productivity theorists claim is necessary to make their theory workable in practice.

2. Some economists claim that the market for labor does not function like the ordinary product market and that therefore the marginal productivity theory, which runs in conventional terms of supply and demand for labor, does not give a realistic picture of the labor market. We have already had occasion to consider some of the peculiarities of the labor market. Thus there is typically no one price for a particular type of labor representing an equilibrium of supply and demand. On the contrary, many prices exist side by side, and there is little tendency for such differentials to disappear over time.

The contributions which have been made by labor economists in pointing out these characteristics of the labor market are important, but they do not invalidate supply and demand analysis. Both the volume of unemployment in a given labor market and the number of new job opportunities will have an effect on the whole structure of wage rates in a community, indicating that supply and demand considerations cannot be ignored. The fact that a union may set a wage in a particular market based upon a wage level established by some other union in a far distant city does not vitiate the usefulness of marginal productivity theory. Such a wage will probably differ from the wage which would be established in a free labor market; but whatever the wage which is established, it is still possible that the volume of employment at that wage will tend to be determined by the demand curve for labor, which reflects the marginal productivity of labor.

The marginal productivity theory, as applied to the demand for labor in the individual firm, is quite consistent with a diversity of wage rates for the same type of labor in a given labor market. It is true that marginal productivity theorists, in their attempt to explain the demand for labor in the economy as a whole, at one time made various artificial assumptions about the mobility of labor and a tendency toward the establishment of one rate for a given type of labor in the economy as a whole. But these assumptions and this aspect of the theory need not detain us, since, as has already been pointed out, it is now generally agreed that the marginal productivity theory is inadequate as an explanation of the demand for labor in the economy as a whole. Once we take a more limited view of the function of this theory, it can be integrated with recent developments in the field of labor market analysis. If, for example, two firms make different bargains for the same type of labor and pay such labor different rates, marginal productivity theory would simply indicate that the adaptation of the two firms in terms of price and output might differ but that both firms would attempt to apply marginal productivity principles in fixing the volume of employment at the different rates.

3. A major criticism directed against the marginal productivity theory stems from a fundamental disagreement as to the basic psychology and motivation of employers. Marginal productivity theorists, as we have seen, base their theory on the assumption that employers are motivated by a desire to *maximize* profits. But, as we have already observed, there is some evidence that management in certain companies may desire only a "fair return on investment,"[9] or may be motivated by considerations of community respect and other noneconomic objectives. It has even been suggested that the separation of management from ownership which typifies our large corporate business organizations may place management decisions in the hands of men who are more interested in such objectives as sales, power, prestige, and so forth, rather than maximum profits.[10] On the other hand, it can be argued that the increased professionalization of management and increased use by management of computers to obtain promptly the complex data necessary for accurate decision making will, if anything, tie business behavior closer to the theoretical goal of profit maximization.

Once the common denominator of maximizing profits is eliminated, a general principle governing employer hiring of labor becomes difficult to state. If businessmen are not interested in achieving maximum profits, it is difficult to see how a generalized theory of demand for labor can be evolved. The demand for labor would depend in each individual firm upon the psychological motivation of the particular employer, which might differ from that of other employers and might change from time to time. A theory, according to Webster, is a "general principle, formula, or ideal construction offered to explain phenomena and rendered more or less plausible by evidence in the facts." It would appear that if the assumption is made that businessmen are not generally interested in maxi-

---

[9] Among other possible goals are a predetermined rate of return on assets, and the highest profits that will not invite new entries. See William L. Baldwin, "The Motives of Managers, Environmental Restraints, and the Theory of Managerial Enterprise," *Quarterly Journal of Economics*, Vol. LXXVIII (May, 1964), pp. 238–56.

[10] Fritz Machlup, "Theories of the Firm: Marginalist, Behavioral, Managerial," *American Economic Review*, Vol. LVII (March, 1967), p. 5.

mizing profits and that other motives control their actions, economists will be led into a case-by-case analysis of individual employer reactions in the labor market rather than to statement of a general theory of labor demand.

Marginal productivity theorists, of course, recognize that all employers are not profit-minded to the same degree and that any decision in the labor market—as in any line of human endeavor—is the result of a complex of motivations, which may include considerations of prestige, family, security, power, and the like. However, they believe that most businessmen are normally concerned about how they are going to stay in business and that this involves keeping costs down and profits up. They contend, moreover, that managements in large corporations, whose balance sheets and profit and loss statements are made available to stockholders, are particularly interested in making a good showing relative to other large firms in the industry and in other industries. Management's reason for existing is to make profits for stockholder-owners, the usual measure of its success in earnings and dividends. Therefore, marginal productivity theorists state that as a general principle, it is fair to assume that maximization of profits is a dominant employer objective.

THE BARGAINING THEORY OF WAGES

Current interest in the peculiarities of the labor market and the dominant position of unions in shaping wage rates in many industries have led to a revival of interest in the bargaining theory of wages. The roots of this theory are found in the writings of early economists such as Adam Smith. Professor John Davidson published a treatise entitled *The Bargain Theory of Wages* in 1898, and Maurice Dobb further elucidated the theory in 1933.[11] Recently, a number of labor economists have espoused the theory as being a realistic substitute for the marginal productivity theory.

Basically, the bargaining theory holds that no single principle determines wage rates. In any labor market there may be a diversity of rates for the same type of labor. This diversity develops because of differences in the bargains made by various employers and their employees, or the unions representing the employees. Employers are conceived of as having upper limits above which they will not go in making a wage bargain. This upper limit will differ for various employers. Among the factors determining this upper limit are the productivity of the labor, the profitability of the business, the possibility of utilizing machinery as a substitute for labor, and the possibility that excessive labor costs might require the plant to shut down. The lower limit to the bargain is set by minimum wage rates established by state or federal governments, the possibility of labor

---

[11] See Maurice Dobb, *Wages* (London: Nesbet & Co., Ltd., 1933).

moving to other firms or areas, community standards of what is a just wage, and similar considerations.

If the foregoing propositions are all that is involved in the bargaining theory of wages, that theory is quite consistent with the marginal productivity theory. For the latter merely holds that whatever the wage which is set—whether by government, collective bargaining, or market forces—the employer will attempt to adapt to it by employing an amount of labor such that its marginal revenue productivity will be equal to the wage. Some exponents of the bargaining theory overlook this and assume that because the exact level of the wage is indeterminate and may fall anywhere between the upper and the lower level above referred to, therefore the adaptation in terms of employment must also be indeterminate. Marginal productivity theorists deny this and have attempted to integrate the bargaining aspect of wage determination into the general structure of the marginal productivity theory.

For some economists, however, the bargaining theory is much more than just a theory of determination of wage levels. These economists extend bargaining principles to the relationship between wages and employment in the individual firm. They believe that this relationship is much more tenuous and indeterminate than the marginal productivity theory would lead one to believe. Thus, bargaining theorists maintain that a union, by superior bargaining power, may squeeze out monopoly profits for the benefit of organized employees without affecting the volume of employment in the firm. Likewise, they argue that organized labor may achieve wage increases at the expense of the remuneration going to other factors of production which are immobile or lack the benefit of organization to protect their interests.

These conclusions are also not necessarily inconsistent with marginal productivity theory. The latter has always recognized that in the short run, bargaining pressures may squeeze out monopoly profits or increase remuneration of one group at the expense of another, without affecting employment. In the long run, however, marginal productivity theorists contend that there is a tendency for adjustments to be made which do affect the volume of employment. While it may be true that we live in a world consisting of a continuous series of "short runs" and never clearly see the long-run effects of particular actions, nevertheless it would seem that any theory of the demand for labor must take account of the fact that short-run reactions to bargaining pressures are not the last word and that changes in location, size, and number of plants, investment in labor-saving machinery, and similar actions are part of the adjustment of employers to changed cost conditions, which take time to work themselves out.

Probably the most complete exposition of a bargaining theory of wages is set forth by J. Pen in his volume entitled *The Wage Rate under*

Collective Bargaining.[12] Pen draws up so-called "ophelimity functions" for management and labor which are actually schemes of preferences of each for various wage rates.[13] He then expounds in considerable detail a theory of bargaining which sheds light upon the factors leading up to the selection of the wage rate finally agreed upon. However, Pen himself is quite cognizant of the fact that his theory relates to the determination of the wage rate and that marginal productivity principles still determine the wage-employment equilibrium. Thus, after remarking that employers react to various wage rates by quantity adjustment of labor utilized, he states:

In the theoretical explanation of this quantity adjustment the theory of marginal productivity can render good service. This theory, which for a long time has been considered as a principle helping to explain the wage rate, may definitely not be interpreted as such in modern society. If quantity adjustment leads to equality of wage and marginal value product of the labor, the wage rate is the determining factor, not the other way round. The marginal productivity theory only explains the wage rate if quantity adjustment of buyers and sellers determines the wage rate, in other words under perfect competition.[14]

Pen is quite right that the marginal productivity theory does not provide a satisfactory explanation of wage determination in our complex modern labor market. A strong union can maintain a high wage rate for a particular class of labor, despite the existence of a substantial pool of unemployed labor, which, on the basis of simple orthodox economics, might be expected to depress the wage rate. However, the marginal productivity theory still gives the best explanation of short-run and long-run adaptation of employment to given wage rates.

THE INVESTMENT THEORY OF WAGES

Dissatisfaction with the marginal productivity theory has led another economist, H. M. Gitelman, to advance a so-called "investment theory of wages,"[15] in which wages are seen as a return on investment in worker productivity influenced secondarily by a set of noninvestment factors centering around the type of job, structure of the firm, and area differences. On the demand side, Gitelman emphasizes the influence of the cost of labor turnover as a key factor in employer decisions as to what they can afford to pay for labor, while from the supply side the cost of

[12] J. Pen, *The Wage Rate under Collective Bargaining* (Cambridge, Mass.: Harvard University Press, 1959).

[13] *Ibid.,* p. 14.

[14] *Ibid.,* n. 17, p. 200.

[15] H. M. Gitelman, "An Investment Theory of Wages," *Industrial and Labor Relations Review,* Vol. XXI (April, 1968), pp. 323–52.

investment in training, education, and skill influences workers' readiness to accept job offers.

This theory is primarily short run in its outlook. The writer assumes that it is not feasible to draw up conventional demand curves for labor because "employers adjust their demand prices to the marketplace *prior* to their actual entry into it."[16] According to Gitelman, firms on entering the market do not have demand schedules, but rather effective demands determined by the demand for output filtered through the manpower requirements of production functions which presumably are deemed fixed. However, the whole point of the marginal productivity theory is that in the long run, production functions can be varied, both labor and capital become fluid, and it is at this time that the full effect of the theory can be seen at work. The investment theory adds to our knowledge concerning the factors influencing both demand and supply in the labor market, but it is doubtful that it will be accepted as a substitute for the marginal productivity theory.

SUMMARY

Theories of the demand for labor tend to evolve as our knowledge of the labor market improves and as the nature of the organization of industry and the labor market changes. The marginal productivity theory has held the center of the stage for many years as the accepted theory of labor demand, but recent criticisms indicate that it, too, is subject to revision and possible substitution by other theories. Whether its successor will be the bargaining theory or some other theory remains to be seen. At this point, no other theory has been elaborated in sufficient detail to constitute an adequate substitute.

In this and the preceding chapter, we have examined some of the factors which determine the supply and the demand of labor. We are now prepared to consider wage determination as it actually occurs in the labor market. This is the subject of the following chapter.

QUESTIONS FOR DISCUSSION

1. Explain what is meant by marginal productivity. What is the difference between the value of the marginal physical product of labor and the marginal revenue product of labor? Under what circumstances will they be the same?

2. Compare the marginal productivity theory with the bargaining theory of wages. What points of similarity are there in the two theories? What are the merits and shortcomings of each?

3. What conditions may produce a rising supply curve for labor? Will employers apply marginal productivity principles when faced by a rising supply curve of labor? Discuss.

[16] *Ibid.*, p. 348.

SUGGESTIONS FOR FURTHER READING

GITELMAN, H. M. "An Investment Theory of Wages," *Industrial and Labor Relations Review*, Vol. XXI (April, 1968), pp. 323–52.

An attempt to develop a so-called "investment theory of wages" as a substitute for the marginal productivity theory.

HICKS, J. R. *The Theory of Wages*, chap. i, pp. 1–22. 2nd ed. London: Macmillan & Co., Ltd., 1963. (See also review of Chapter I by G. F. Shore, *ibid.*, pp. 249–67 and commentary on same by J. R. Hicks, pp. 321–27.)

A classic discussion of the demand for labor from the marginalist point of view with current commentaries on the theory.

MACHLUP, FRITZ. "Theories of the Firm: Marginalist, Behavioral, Managerial," *American Economic Review*, Vol. LVII (March, 1967), pp. 1–33.

An excellent review and critique of various attacks which have been directed against marginal analysis, together with a bibliography of articles on this subject.

PEN, J. *The Wage Rate under Collective Bargaining*. Cambridge, Mass.: Harvard University Press, 1959.

A complete exposition of the bargaining theory of wages which nevertheless recognizes the role played by marginal productivity principles in wage determination.

PIERSON, FRANK C. "An Evaluation of Wage Theory," in ROWAN, RICHARD L., and NORTHRUP, HERBERT R. (eds.), *Readings in Labor Economics and Labor Relations*, pp. 403–20. Homewood, Ill.: Richard D. Irwin, Inc., 1968.

A broad review of various wage theories, with emphasis on recent approaches to understanding the operation of the labor market.

Chapter : WAGE DETERMINATION
11 : UNDER TRADE UNIONISM

In the three preceding chapters, we have considered the supply of labor, the demand for labor, and the labor market in which these forces operate. Wage determination in the individual firm reflects the various economic forces and circumstances we have examined. Thus, *ceteris paribus*, the wage level in a particular firm will ordinarily be lower if the demand for labor is decreasing than if it is increasing. Wages will be higher when labor is in short supply than where there is a large body of unemployed labor available. Rates will tend to be lower in the South than in the North.

When union business agents and management representatives sit down to the conference table to negotiate a new contract, the foregoing circumstances set some limit to the range within which wage rates will finally be set. In this chapter, we shall examine the conditions which cause a particular schedule of rates to be agreed upon by union and management representatives in the individual firm. How are wage rates adjusted in the collective bargaining process? What is the relationship between rates in different firms in the same industry? What are the criteria and pertinent economic circumstances which union and management consider in determining wage rates? In discussing wage determination, we shall concentrate our attention on changes in money wage rates, but this should not lead the reader to underestimate the importance of fringe benefits. As we have already observed in Chapter 5, the practice in union negotiations in recent years has been for so-called "package" settlements which include improvements in various forms of supplementary compensation as well as basic pay.

THE INTERNAL WAGE STRUCTURE

In the typical large industrial establishment today, literally hundreds of individual wage rates or wage classifications have to be adjusted as part of a wage negotiation. In our theoretical discussion in earlier chapters, we have talked about "the wage rate in the individual firm." This is obviously a simplification. It would be more correct to talk about a wage structure.

314

The wage structure is the whole complex of rates within the individual firm for all of the various jobs for which persons are employed. This wage structure does not necessarily move as a unit. There may be, of course, wage negotiations where a flat 10 cents an hour or a uniform percentage increase is given to all employees; but frequently, exceptions are made for particular groups of employees. There are always individual jobs which get out of line as a result of the passage of time and as a result of the impact of technological change. These require special treatment. Furthermore, there is the pressing problem of keeping a proper relationship between the skilled and the unskilled rates. As a result of these various factors, the wage structure may be compressed or stretched out from one negotiation to the next (viewing the wage structure in terms of the entire schedule of rates from the lowest to the highest paid employee).

While a great many rates must be altered in the course of a wage negotiation, labor and management do not normally make an issue of every individual rate. This would obviously take too much time. Instead, emphasis is placed upon the key rates in various job clusters. A job cluster may be defined as a stable group of job classifications or work assignments within a firm which are so linked together by technology, the administrative organization of the production process, or social custom that they have common wage-making characteristics.[1] Thus, in a factory, one job cluster may consist of various classes of lathe operators; another job cluster, of sweepers, janitors, etc.; another, of patternmakers, etc. Each cluster can be viewed as consisting of a key rate and associated rates. Key rates may be the highest rate in the particular cluster, the lowest, or sometimes the rate at which the greatest number of workers are employed. These are the rates on which union and management representatives focus in their bargaining negotiations, and once these rates are determined, the associated rates fall into line.

THE EXTERNAL WAGE STRUCTURE

Key rates in the individual firm are not determined in a vacuum. On the contrary, they are hammered out in a collective bargaining relationship where management attempts to safeguard its competitive position in the particular industry of which it is a part. Most company executives keep well informed as to the rates their competitors pay for comparable jobs. As one labor text puts it: "Wage level negotiation has been undertaken in the light of an increasingly refined and comprehensive knowledge of comparative wage rates."[2] Unless there are extenuating circum-

[1] John T. Dunlop, "The Task of Contemporary Wage Theory," in George W. Taylor and Frank C. Pierson (eds.), *New Concepts in Wage Determination* (New York: McGraw-Hill Book Co., 1957), p. 129.
[2] Sumner H. Slichter, J. J. Healy and E. R. Livernash, *The Impact of Collective Bargaining on Management* (Washington, D.C.: Brookings Institution, 1960), p. 592.

stances, management usually tries to keep its rates on a par with its competitors', on the theory that if its rates are lower, it will lose employees, and if its rates are higher, it will lose business because of the higher costs.

One writer uses the concept of a "wage contour" to elucidate the relationship between the key rates of various individual firms or establishments. "A wage contour is a stable group of wage-determining units which are so linked together by (1) similarity of product markets, (2) resort to similar sources for a labor source, or (3) common labor-market organization (custom) that they have common wage-making characteristics."[3] For example, the basic steel contour for production jobs consists of basic steel producers throughout the nation. By contrast, newspapers in New York City constitute a separate wage contour not directly affected by rates in other cities. The wage contour normally contains one or, in some instances, several key settlements. The contour is composed of rates for a key firm(s) and a group of associated firms. The key settlement may be set by the largest firm, the price leader, or the firm which customarily plays the role of wage relations leader. As we shall see later in this chapter, leader-follower relationships in wage determination are extremely important in our basic industries. Some firms within a wage contour will follow the key settlement closely; others will follow it in varying degree. But this external relationship will have an important bearing on the decision which is made with respect to changes in the key rates in the various job clusters of each establishment's internal wage structure.

The concept of the wage contour helps to explain differences which prevail in rates for similar jobs in different industries. For example, a comparison of rates paid to motor truck drivers in Boston in a variety of industries indicated that the rates paid for teamsters in these essentially substitutable jobs were twice as high in magazine distribution as in scrap iron and metal.[4] The reason for the variation is that each rate was a reflection of conditions in its own wage contour. Each is a reflection of the product market. Magazine distributors were more concerned about the rates that their competitors *in that industry* had to pay for truck drivers than what the rate was in the scrap-iron business. Of course, in a perfect labor market, these differences could not prevail because teamsters would tend to move to the higher paying industry, and the lower paying industries would have to raise their rates in order to hold their employees. In actuality, these differences persist over long periods of time because of the orientation of the wage rate determination process in terms of the product market and because of the differences in competitive conditions, profits, and demand conditions in the various industries using this similar type of labor.

[3] Dunlop, *op. cit.*, p. 131.
[4] *Ibid.*, p. 135.

GENERAL WAGE INCREASES

Much of the friction which develops in collective bargaining involves the issue of "wage increases." What precisely do we mean by this phrase? From time to time, an employer may review the performance of his employees and give merit increases to various employees. Where range systems are in effect, such a procedure is common, except in those companies where the progression from the minimum to the maximum rate is dependent solely on length of service. Decisions as to merit increases may involve considerable expenditures of money and may give rise to grievances which the union will process even to the point of arbitration. However, such increases are not of the type normally involved in general wage adjustments.

General wage increases normally have little or no relation to merit. They are usually given to all workers, whether or not the employer is satisfied with their individual performance. The justification for the increase may be an increase in the cost of living or the high profits made by the employer. The performance of the company as a whole is always a consideration, but the performance of the individual worker is not usually at issue in such negotiations. The increases are often but not always uniform for all employees. Many industrial unions prefer to have uniform adjustments for all employees in terms of so many cents per hour because this tends to give the lower paid workers—who represent the bulk of the union membership—a larger percentage increase than higher paid workers.

In the 1930's and the 1940's, when the advent of industrial unionism first made its impact felt on the wage structure, there was a strong trend for larger percentage wage adjustments for the lower paid employees. As a result, there was a definite narrowing of occupational differentials. By the early 1950's a slowing-down of this narrowing process was observable; and in recent years, there has been evidence of the maintenance of reasonably stable differentials. This has been partly attributable to an increasing tendency to grant special increases for skilled workers.

General increases may or may not affect minimum rates for particular jobs. For example, suppose the minimum hiring rate for a clerk in a department store is set by the collective bargaining agreement at $70 per week. If the union now wins a general wage increase for all employees of a uniform $2 per week, all clerks will now receive no less than $72 per week. The bargain may be, however, that the increase applies to all present employees of the company but does not apply to the minimum rates, so that new employees may still be hired at the $70-per-week figure. The employer may prefer such a deal, since it enables him to achieve some saving in labor cost through normal turnover of existing employees and hiring of new ones at the lower rate. Most unions, however, are interested in raising minimum rates as part of general wage adjustments.

What circumstances do unions and management take account of in determining the amount of a wage increase in an individual firm? Many arguments are used by ingenious union representatives to justify an increase in wage rates. Management representatives are equally adept at finding reasons why the increase cannot be made. In the following discussion, we shall consider some of the principal criteria which seem to play an important part in the determination of the size of general wage adjustments.

CRITERIA IN GENERAL WAGE ADJUSTMENTS

Intraindustry Comparative Standards

Perhaps the most common standard which is applied by both labor and management to determine whether a wage adjustment should be made in a particular firm is to compare its wage structure with those of other companies in the industry. Because of the importance of the standard of what the other fellow is doing, both union and management representatives usually come to the bargaining table armed with statistics, or at least a working knowledge, of what other firms in the industry are paying. In some industries, employers' associations make such data available; in others the employer may have to rely on telephone calls to the personnel directors of competing companies. Unions in many cases are able to obtain such data through their international office or through other locals.

Reliance on rates that other companies are paying would, at first glance, seem to put collective bargaining on a factual basis. "If a competitor can afford to pay given rates, why can't you?" is the question put by union agents to the employer. The trouble is that statistics—particularly when they are averages—may have little meaning because of shortcomings in their tabulation. Furthermore, job content of seemingly similar jobs varies considerably from firm to firm. The mere fact that a job classification calls for a stitcher, or a cutter, or a clerk, or a painter does not mean that the work or the skill required is identical or that the technical conditions will be similar for all employees having similar job descriptions. In the same industry or area the same job title may be used for dozens of dissimilar operations.

Actually, the criterion of intraindustry standards leaves ample room for bargaining. For example, the union may want to compare hourly rates in various plants, while the employer may want to compare weekly earnings. This is frequently the case where a company permits its employees to work some overtime each week at time and a half the regular rate, which gives its employees more take-home pay than workers in other plants. Nevertheless, the union will argue that hourly rates should be raised to bring them in line with rates in other plants in the industry. Frequently, the principle of "doing what the other fellow is doing" will be recognized by union and management representatives, but there will be disagreement as to whether the criterion should be the size of wage increases in other firms or the rates paid by other firms after such increases have been made.

Wage Leadership. In industries employing the most wage earners —steel, automotive bodies and parts, aircraft, rubber, baked goods, textiles, paper and paperboard, and others—the tendency is for the individual employer to keep his wage rates in line with rates paid by certain key firms in the industry, a policy which frequently results in an industrywide adjustment of wages whenever circumstances compel revision in such key companies.

The typical structure of an industry in the American economy is that four to eight companies will produce from one half to four fifths of the total output of the industry. Once wage scales have been set in the major companies, the pattern of wage adjustment for most employees in the industry has also been determined. Just as big companies influence small companies, so wage rates set in populous areas tend to affect rates in outlying areas. For example, building-trades negotiations in New York and Chicago are likely to be influential in local areas. The same situation will exist in printing industry negotiations in these two cities and in negotiations in the transit industry in Detroit and Boston.

Wage leadership does not depend upon the existence of national, regional, or other forms of industrywide bargaining. It is as important a phenomenon in the automobile industry, where company wages policies are set individually, as in the flat glass or Pacific Coast paper industry where companies bargain through joint committees or associations. Key wage bargains are important whether wages are determined by collective bargaining or by unilateral company decision in the case of unorganized employees. In some industries, wage leadership existed prior to the advent of unions. For example, other steel companies have historically adjusted their wages to patterns set by the United States Steel Corporation. In this and other industries, wage leadership has often gone hand in hand with price leadership.

Although wage leadership has existed in the absence of union organization, union wage pressure has tended to spread and to make explicit uniformity in wage rates as a cardinal basis of management wage policy. There is now double pressure for meeting the other fellow's wage rates: from competitors and from labor itself. Union contracts requiring payment of wages on a par with rates prevailing for work of a similar kind in other firms in the industry hasten the spread of wage increases through an industry. At the same time, however, such pressure may produce a feeling among company executives that upward adjustments should not be made unless other firms in the industry are making them, or the union demands them; and therefore, they make fewer, though larger, wage adjustments.

In some industries, there are not only wage leaders but also "high-wage firms." These companies try to pay more than the going rate for labor. Sometimes, such firms justify this policy on the ground that high wages attract better than average employees. In other cases the reason for the policy may be to keep out a union. In any case, unions use such differentials to their advantage. In bargaining with other companies in the industry, they will argue that competitors of the high-wage firm should pay wages equal to those paid by the high-wage company. Then, after obtaining such an increase from the other firms, they will go back to the high-wage firm (once it has been organized) and contend that it should maintain its historical differential. Companies which have adopted a higher than average wage policy as a means of keeping out a union may thus find that they are stuck with the policy when the union organizes their employees.

Unions typically use such a leveling approach in their bargaining strategy. Rates for a particular class of employees may be relatively high in one firm, perhaps because of the length of service of these employees, or perhaps because of unusual conditions under which they have to work. The union will cite the example of these high rates to other firms in the industry, which are likely to be unaware of the special circumstances creating them, and will argue that they should meet these high rates. In the same way a "bad settlement" made by one employer in an industry who could not risk a strike for financial reasons can be used by a union as a lever to raise the rates of every other firm in the industry.

Union Attitudes toward Wage Uniformity. Most unions want uniformity in wage rates for similar jobs throughout an area of competitive production. Unions are dynamic organizations; but paradoxically, one of their major objectives is stability. Frequently, achievement of this aim is dependent upon elimination of competition between firms in the sphere of wage rates. The more competitive the industry, the smaller the units in the industry; and the less responsible the employers, the greater is the likelihood that union wage policy will seek competitive parity in labor cost as a measure to relieve pressure on the wage structure. In an industry in which there is considerable variation in the size and efficiency of the individual firms, a union must decide whether the welfare of its members can best be served by equalization of hourly rates, piece rates, or labor costs per unit in the various plants under union jurisdiction. In some circumstances, the policy of equalization of wage rates or hourly earnings will provide the maximum incentive to industrial efficiency. It may be adopted in the form of uniform wage scales, as in the building and printing industries, where jobs are skilled and occupational rungs clearly defined; or it may take the form of uniformity in plant average hourly earnings, as in the carpet and rug industry, where rapid technology and lack of standardization of operations and product make this the most expedient policy. Such a plan attempts to stabilize earnings while leaving costs to management. Since backward companies must pay as high rates as the most efficient firms, a policy of uniformity in hourly or day wage rates provides the maximum incentive to adoption of improved machinery by the less efficient companies in an industry.

If, on the other hand, the union decides to equalize piece rates or unit labor cost, the incentive afforded to employers to improve efficiency is reduced unless the union agrees to adjust rates downward as improvements in technique permit greater output. For if piece rates are fixed, introduction of improved machinery serves merely to increase output per worker, so that labor's earnings, not employers' profits, are augmented by technical advance. In the men's clothing industry, for example, the Amalgamated Clothing Workers, through its Market Stabilization Department, has attempted to standardize labor costs on a national scale. Standard labor costs are established for various grades of clothing, and comformity with the standards of quality and labor costs is enforced by union representatives. Since the labor cost on a given grade of clothing is fixed and cannot be reduced, the employer is deprived of virtually all incentive to improve his method of production and the quality of his garments. Since the stabilization program substantially reduces the employer's incentive to make improvements in technique, if it were strictly enforced it would deter technological progress in the unionized portion of the industry and provide a major opportunity for expansion of production and employment in nonunion shops. In practice, of course, strict enforcement of the stabilization plan has been impossible. Furthermore, the program does not apply to high-quality garments. Consequently, an area is still left in which an incentive is offered to the employer to improve methods of production. In this connection, it is important to realize that even if employers cannot reduce labor costs through mechanization, technological progress may still hold forth the prospect of savings in other costs, such as material, electricity, etc.

The extent to which a strong union can introduce uniformity of wage rates in an industry is well illustrated by recent developments in the over-the-road trucking industry, where James R. Hoffa substantially achieved national contracts. While local differentials still remain to some extent, the union has used the device of the long-term contract and common termination dates to achieve its goal of eliminating the great dispersion of rates which formerly existed in this industry. The trend toward wage standardization in the trucking industry has already gone far and is likely to continue.

On the whole, it seems likely that equalization of wage rates will come to be the dominant form of union wage policy. Of course, there must necessarily be variations from this to suit the peculiarities of individual industries, but the policy of uniformity will probably come to prevail in those industries in which it is practicable because it is best adapted to the political necessities of unionism. It is simple, and its aim of equality in a particularly obvious and just form commends it as a slogan for the rank and file. Its reasonableness is convincing. As one union leader puts it: "If Joe Smith goes into a store to buy a hat, he has to pay the same price for it whether he happens to be an employee of General Motors or American Motors. Then why shouldn't he be paid the same rate for his work?"

Union preference for uniformity in wage rates has already made its impact felt on various aspects of the wage structure of American industry. Within individual firms, unionism has generally eliminated personal differentials in rates or brought them into a formalized, controlled wage scale. Likewise, union organization has tended to reduce or eliminate interfirm differentials in the same product and labor market.[5] As far as area differentials are concerned, there is evidence that suggests that within metropolitan or similar types of trading areas the existence of strong union organization is associated with a high degree of uniformity in rates. Thus, one study found a considerably lower dispersion of rates in the more highly unionized of two metropolitan areas; and the other concluded that within a single metropolitan area, unions reduced and even abolished interfirm differentials in the industries they organized.[6] As between various industries, however, union wage pressure may actually have increased wage differentials. As one writer puts it: "Unionism has penetrated most effectively into the relatively high-wage industries and has tended to 'make the rich richer.' "[7] The tendency to widen wage differentials is probably not evident, however, in the small groups of basic industries which closely follow key wage bargains.

Interindustry Comparative Standards

Wage determination in a particular firm may be affected not only by settlements made by key firms in the same industry but also by major companies in other industries. Some economists are of the opinion that "we have reached the stage where a limited number of key wage bargains effectively influence the whole wage structure of the American economy."[8] A study of wage changes made during the post–World War II period in 11 basic industries—steel, automotive, electrical, rubber, aluminum, aircraft, farm machinery, copper, petroleum refining, meat packing,

---

[5] Clark Kerr, "Wage Relationships—The Comparative Impact of Market and Power Forces," in John T. Dunlop (ed.), *The Theory of Wage Determination* (London: Macmillan & Co., Ltd., 1957), p. 181.

[6] *Ibid.*, p. 176.

[7] Lloyd G. Reynolds, "The Impact of Collective Bargaining on the Wage Structure in the United States," in Dunlop (ed.), *The Theory of Wage Determination, op. cit.*, p. 220.

[8] John T. Dunlop, "American Wage Determination: Its Trend and Significance," *Wage Determination and the Economics of Liberalism* (Washington, D.C.: Chamber of Commerce of the United States, 1947), p. 42.

and shipbuilding—found a high degree of uniformity in the size of wage adjustments in these industries.[9]

Two other researchers have found a "contour group" consisting of the following industries: rubber, stone clay and glass, primary metals, fabricated metals, nonelectrical machinery, electrical machinery, transportation equipment, and instruments.[10] Wages in these industries were found to have moved almost identically since 1948. In the words of the investigators,

All of these industries are high-wage industries, have strong industrial unions, typically consist of large corporations that possess considerable market power, and are geographically centered in the Midwestern industrial heartland of the continent.[11]

How are these key wage bargains transmitted from one industry to another? According to one economist who has studied this phenomenon in detail, there are four important circumstances which help produce this uniformity in wage movement:[12]

1. *The Input-Output Nexus.* Many of these industries have close ties with each other because of a buyer-seller relationship. For example, the automotive industry is the largest consumer of rubber and electrical products; aircraft is the largest consumer of aluminum. Buyers and sellers have an understandable interest in the wage policies of each other, since a rise in labor costs and in prices of the supplier will ultimately affect the costs and prices of the buyer industry.

2. *Similar Technology.* Most of these industries have a high capital-output and a high capital-labor ratio. Likewise, they are mass-production industries. Most produce capital goods or consumer durable goods. Therefore, they tend to react in similar fashion to current economic changes.

3. *Distribution of Participants.* Most of these industries are clustered in particular geographical areas. Furthermore, the employees in these industries are represented for the most part by a relatively few large national unions.

4. *Institutional Channels of Communication.* Most of the unions involved were originally CIO and are now part of the AFL–CIO. The leaders of the unions are important, nationally known figures in the labor movement, and there is considerable rivalry among them.

Such key wage bargains affect the thinking of unions and manage-

---

[9] John E. Maher, "The Wage Pattern in the United States, 1946–1957," *Industrial and Labor Relations Review*, Vol. XVI (October, 1961), p. 16.

[10] Otto Eckstein and Thomas A. Wilson, "The Determination of Money Wages in American Industry," *Quarterly Journal of Economics*, Vol. LXXVI (August, 1962), pp. 384–85.

[11] *Ibid.*

[12] Maher, *op. cit.*, pp. 5–6.

ment in a variety of industries. Both tend to look to these key agreements as a barometer of the labor market, indicating what workers expect in the way of wage adjustments. In a very real sense, a handful of key negotiators representing management and labor can set trends which will affect the compensation of millions of workers in other industries. Faced with the need of resolving differences, management and union leaders find in key wage bargains a convenient figure upon which they can rationalize a contract. Moreover, union leaders find they must meet the increase obtained by a union leader in another industry, or their personal popularity will be affected. The size of the wage increase obtained by various labor leaders is as assiduously studied by their constituents as the batting averages of baseball players, and if Walter P. Reuther wants to stay at the top of the league, he has to keep pace with his rivals in other unions. Union leaders are alert to capitalize on new types of benefits which may have been incorporated in contracts in other industries. Although there are an estimated 150,000 collective bargaining agreements in effect in the United States, about 20 unions are responsible for three quarters of them, and there is a constant exchange of information among them.

The variation in wage adjustments among firms and industries reflects differences in profitability, as well as in the ability of management to pass along wage increases in the form of higher prices. The variations may also reflect the effect of union rivalries. Leaders of competing unions—whether they are competing for prestige within the labor movement or actually competing for membership—have to avoid falling into a "me, too" policy of simply following another union's lead. "Each policy has to give its followers benefits equal to those obtained under the rival's policies and at the same time must appear to differ from the rival's policy. This leads to a preference for minimum differentiations."[13] Such differentiations may be in the form of varying (1) the amount of the wage adjustment while following the cost of the total package of benefits, (2) the timing of the adjustments, or (3) the nature and extent of fringe benefits. Furthermore, variations from the key wage pattern are more common the smaller the company and the fewer the employees on its payroll. Nevertheless, even with small companies, there tends to be some spill-over from the national trend.

Cost of Living

A criterion of major importance in wage negotiations—particularly during periods of rising prices such as we have experienced in recent years —is change in the cost of living. During periods of rising prices, wages typically lag behind prices. This lag is attributable in part to the fact that

---

[13] Benson Soffer, "On Union Rivalries and the Minimum Differentiation of Wage Patterns," *Review of Economics and Statistics*, Vol. XLI (February, 1959), p. 54.

wages are much more "sticky" than prices. In fact, most wages of organized employees are fixed by contract for a given period, frequently a year. During the contract period, price increases may rob wage adjustments of much of their value. The extent to which inflation can neutralize wage increases is clearly demonstrated in Figure 11–1. Despite large wage gains achieved by workers in the past three years, workers with three dependents have barely maintained the real purchasing power of their take-home

FIGURE 11–1

INCOME, EARNINGS, AND REAL TAKE-HOME PAY

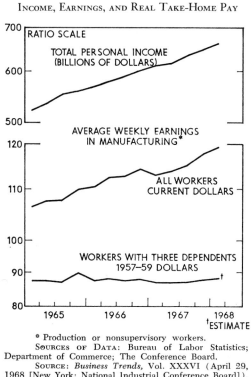

° Production or nonsupervisory workers.
SOURCES OF DATA: Bureau of Labor Statistics; Department of Commerce; The Conference Board.
SOURCE: *Business Trends,* Vol. XXXVI (April 29, 1968 [New York: National Industrial Conference Board]), p. 70.

pay (measured in 1957–59 dollars). It is understandable, then, that when union representatives sit down at the bargaining table, they naturally have in mind the cost-of-living increase since the last wage adjustment and tend to think in terms of a wage increase compensating for the rise in cost of living as a minimum demand. Management, too, is concerned in such times with retaining its employees and eliminating pay inequities, and usually recognizes the justice in a cost-of-living adjustment.

Union representatives place heavy reliance on increases in the cost of living as a justification for wage increases in times of rising prices. However, when the cost of living falls, they shift their arguments with great facility to some less vulnerable criterion. At such times, they will usually argue in terms of the need to maintain purchasing power.

The cost of living many enter into wage negotiations in several ways. In most cases, it is simply another one of the key criteria which unions and management consider in arriving at a wage adjustment. In other situations the cost of living may affect wage determinations in a much more specific manner. This will be the case where unions and management have already incorporated in their collective bargaining agreements automatic cost-of-living adjustments or escalator clauses. These clauses typically specify a precise relationship between changes in the cost of living and changes in the wage rates to be paid employees covered by the agreement. There is considerable variation in various contracts with respect to the ratio between cost-of-living changes and wage changes. Some contracts are adjustable only upward, but most make wages adjustable both upward and downward in response to changes in a specific cost-of-living index.

Whatever may be the cause, there is considerable evidence of correlation between wage increases and increases in the cost of living. Wages will normally rise by at least as much as workers' living costs, and with only a short lag. In an attempt to focus on the close relationship between increases in the cost of living, reductions in the unemployment rate, and wage adjustments, Figure 11–2 shows as wage adjustments only those increases actually decided upon in a given year, excluding those which are attributable to deferred arrangements under long-term labor contracts. As can be seen, since 1962 the contour of the Consumer Price Index curve and the wage adjustment curve are remarkably similar. Of course, it would be expected that wages and cost of living would show a positive correlation, since both tend to rise during the upturn stage of the business cycle when demand for goods as well as for labor is rising. At times, however, the trends will diverge; for example, during the 1958 recession, wages rose while the Consumer Price Index was relatively stable.

Development of Automatic Escalator Clauses. The development of automatic escalator clauses geared to changes in the cost of living may be said to have commenced with the General Motors contract of 1948. Prior to that time, cost-of-living provisions had been incorporated in various contracts; but in the aggregate, they covered relatively few workers. However, the General Motors settlement started a new trend. By 1950, approximately 2 million workers were covered by cost-of-living adjustments in labor contracts, and by 1960 the number had risen to 3.3 million.[14] However, as has been pointed out in Chapter 4, in recent years management has become wary about committing itself years in advance to open-end increases in wage costs dependent upon cost-of-living changes. Furthermore, since the increase in the Consumer Price Index was rela-

[14] *Monthly Labor Review*, Vol. LXXXII (December, 1959), pp. 1324, 1327.

FIGURE 11–2

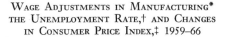

WAGE ADJUSTMENTS IN MANUFACTURING*
THE UNEMPLOYMENT RATE,† AND CHANGES
IN CONSUMER PRICE INDEX,‡ 1959–66

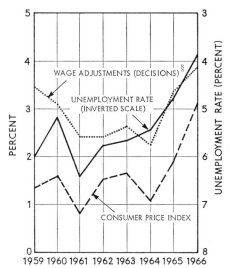

* Median percent wage adjustments where wage decisions were reached, i.e., includes only changes in wage rates decided upon during the year. Changes decided upon in earlier years and cost-of-living escalator adjustments are excluded.
† January of each year.
‡ Percent change during the year (January to January) in the Consumer Price Index (1957–59 equals 100).
§ Percent of estimated straight-time average hourly earnings.
SOURCE: *Monthly Labor Review,* Vol. XCI (February, 1968), p. 41.

tively modest from 1960 to 1965, cost of living was not a major factor in wage negotiations during this period. As a consequence, the number of production workers in manufacturing covered by escalation dropped from 29% in 1959 to 15% in 1965.[15] In 1968, however, as a result of the accelerated rate of increase in the cost of living, the AFL–CIO urged its member unions to negotiate cost-of-living escalator clauses to protect wage gains.[16] Some increase in the coverage of these clauses is therefore likely to occur as long as the increase in consumer prices continues unabated.

Ability to Pay

One of the most important considerations affecting wage determination is the basic economic situation in the firm and industry which for

[15] *Monthly Labor Review,* Vol. XCI (February, 1968), p. 47.
[16] *Business Week,* May 4, 1968, p. 54.

convenience we can denominate as "ability to pay." When profits and sales are increasing, when the employer needs to hold and attract labor in order to fill a backlog of orders, when prospects for the year ahead are bright, it is not surprising that the employer will favorably consider demands for an upward wage adjustment. On the other hand, if profits have fallen, sales are off, idle capacity exists, unemployment prevails, and there is no immediate prospect of a change for the better in the economic situation of the firm, employers are understandably loathe to increase their costs by agreeing to wage increases. A study of wage adjustments in the group of industries referred to on page 323 above during the period 1948 to 1960 found that profit and unemployment were the crucial variables in wage determination for the firms in these industries.[17]

Ability to pay, therefore, is undoubtedly a major consideration in wage negotiations for most firms in good times and bad. Determination of ability to pay is, however, a highly controversial subject. Management, while often pleading inability to pay, is reluctant to make this an issue of fact and permit union representatives to "have a look at the books." Management fears in this regard are based on the belief that such a move would be a prelude to union interference in business operations and encroachment on the whole sphere of managerial prerogatives. The U.S. Supreme Court has ruled in the case of a dispute between the Truitt Manufacturing Company and a steelworkers' union that refusal by an employer to substantiate a claim of inability to pay increased wages *may* support a finding of failure to bargain in good faith.[18]

Even if company financial records were to be opened as part of negotiations, the information contained in them would still be open to differences in interpretation. Furthermore, it is prospective earnings, not past earnings, which are the relevant consideration in wage determation, and the changing economic situation makes it difficult to estimate what the next year will bring in many industries. Ability to pay will ordinarily be more capable of accurate determination and will be more stable from year to year in the case of a company in a monopolistic market position than one in a highly competitive position.

There is considerable difference of opinion between unions and management, and among economists as well, as to the extent to which differences in ability to pay should be reflected in differences in wage rates. On the one hand, union representatives frequently argue that workers have to pay the same price for their necessities of life whether they work for a profitable firm or a less profitable one and, therefore, should be paid the same wage in all companies for similar work. Yet, unions have withdrawn from this position where it appeared that such a policy would

---

[17] Eckstein, *op. cit.*, p. 388.

[18] *National Labor Relations Board* v. *Truitt Manufacturing Co.*, 351 U.S. 149 (1956).

force marginal firms out of business and thus produce unemployment among union members.

Management representatives frequently use the ability-to-pay argument to obtain special concessions for their particular firms, particularly where for one reason or another, their cost of operation is higher than that of competitors. Obviously, the setting of different wage rates in an industry corresponding to the different level of profits in various firms would penalize initiative and good management, and would, in effect, offer a subsidy to the inefficient operators. On the other hand, a strict policy of wage uniformity based on the rates payable by the most efficient producer would force marginal firms out of business. Unions have had to choose between these two extremes and adapt their wage policies to the peculiar conditions existing in each industry. In most instances, they have made some concessions in the way of differentials for smaller, less profitable firms; but, as has already been stated, their preference is for wage uniformity.

Other Criteria in Wage Determination

There are a number of other criteria which are frequently applied by both management and labor in the process of wage determination. For example, when unions seek a reduction in the workweek, the important criterion frequently becomes maintenance of take-home pay despite the reduction in hours worked. In some cases, the new hourly wage rate is simply the arithmetical result obtained by dividing the take-home pay prior to the reduction in hours by the reduced number of hours worked. Improvement in productivity is another circumstance which is receiving greater emphasis from labor in negotiations, particularly so in recent years as a result of the publicity given to productivity gains by the so-called "wage guides" set forth by the President's Council of Economic Advisers. We shall have occasion to examine the subject of productivity and wages in greater detail in Chapter 14. It is worthy of note, however, that while unions talk a great deal about productivity gains where it suits their purposes, there is no correlation between interindustry differences in productivity gains and wage increases. As a matter of fact, industries with the largest long-run productivity gains, such as chemicals, tobacco, lumber, and textiles, have not been characterized by particularly large wage gains.[19]

The criteria explored in the foregoing discussion play an important role in narrowing the range of possibilities in wage determination. In many cases, however, the wage which is finally agreed upon is a reflection of sheer bargaining power, and talk of intraindustry standards or cost-of-living changes is mere rationalization pressed into service to support demands or concessions which need justification. Even arbitrators write

---

[19] Eckstein, *op. cit.*, p. 392.

these criteria into their opinions to support decisions already arrived at for other reasons.

It is also important to remember that wage changes are typically arrived at in a series of "rounds." These frequently provide for subsequent wage changes to be made during the term of the contract one, two, or even three years in the future. The relevant criteria and considerations are those that existed at the time of negotiation of the round, not when the agreed upon wage adjustment takes effect.

The Influence of the Product Market on Wage Adjustments

The demand for labor is a derived demand. This proposition simply means that the employer hires labor, not just to utilize its services, but because labor will produce a product for which there is a demand in the market place. As we shall see in Chapter 12, where this concept will be more fully discussed, the characteristics of the product market can affect the elasticity of the employer's demand curve for labor and therefore can influence his decision as to the amount of labor he will utilize and the wages he will be prepared to pay.

In recent years, numerous statistical investigations have been undertaken to determine whether monopoly power in the product market tends to be correlated with larger wage adjustments in the labor market. The criterion of monopoly power frequently used in such studies—which is acknowledged to be subject to many shortcomings—is the so-called concentration ratio—the proportion of the volume of shipments accounted for by the four largest firms in an industry. If this index of monopoly power is accepted, then, there is considerable evidence that throughout the 1950's workers in "monopolistic" industries enjoyed larger wage adjustments than those in competitive industries.[20] However, there is considerable disagreement as to whether this is a fortuitous or causal relationship.

Are there any reasons to expect, on an a priori theoretical basis, that such a positive correlation should exist?

1. In the first place, one might argue that since we are dealing with a derived demand curve for labor, the more inelastic the demand curve for the product, the more inelastic the demand curve for labor. However, this consideration has more relevance to the *level* of the wage rate than to the *size of adjustments* over time.[21]

2. One might argue that as productivity of labor increases over time, competitive industries are compelled to pass on such benefits in the form of lower prices, but in concentrated industries where administered prices

---

[20] See, for example, Bruce T. Allen, "Market Concentration and Wage Increases: U.S. Manufacturing, 1947–1964," *Industrial and Labor Relations Review*, Vol. XXI (April, 1968), pp. 353–65.

[21] *Ibid.*, p. 353.

are likely to exist, the gains of productivity may be reflected in higher profits which unions may be able to convert into higher wages.

3. Oligopolistic industries may have taken more time to adjust to postwar changes in demand than did competitive industries. This argument assumes that when World War II ended, competitive industries raised prices more sharply than monopolistic industries and therefore tended to be more aggressive in bidding for labor in the balance of the decade of the 1940's. The observed correlation during the 1950's of higher wage adjustments and a greater degree of market power would then simply be evidence of a "catching-up" phase by such industries.[22]

4. Monopolistic industries may offer a more favorable environment for union organizers than the competitive industries, so that a higher degree of union organization exists in the former than the latter. From this it can be argued that the conjunction of union power in the labor market and monopoly power in the product market produce the phenomenon of higher wage adjustments. It is probably true that such concentrated industries are more fully organized. The reasons are obvious. Companies tend to be larger, and therefore in terms of money and time expended by union organizers per potential union member, they afford a more inviting target than a small firm. Secondly, barriers to entry into the industry make it easier for the union to maintain its control without worrying about the effect of nonunion competition.[23]

While it may be true that the less competitive an industry, the easier it is for the companies in the industry to pass along wage increases, this does not necessarily mean that monopolistic industries are easier targets for unions seeking large wage adjustments. The competitive nature of the product market affects the employer's ability to resist.[24] Large companies in monopolistic industries are much readier to take a strike and to hold out for long periods against union demands than companies in more competitive industries. One would expect the highest wage adjustments to occur in relatively competitive industries with many small companies and a strong union, such as the trucking industry. Albert Rees has pointed out that in manufacturing it just so happens that almost all strong unions deal with concentrated industries, and so you get evidence of a correlation between "monopoly power" and size of wage adjustments, but in the economy as a whole, such correlation will not be apparent because there are many competitive industries—such as trucking, construction, and entertainment—which have very strong unions to deal with.[25]

[22] *Loc. cit.*

[23] Adrian W. Throop, "The Union-Nonunion Wage Differential and Cost-Push Inflation," *American Economic Review*, Vol. LVIII (March, 1968), p. 83.

[24] M. Segel, Union Wage Impact and Market Structure," *Quarterly Journal of Economics*, Vol. LXXVIII (February, 1964), p. 203.

[25] Albert Rees, "Union Wage Gains and Enterprise Monopoly," *Essays on Industrial Relations Research* (Ann Arbor and Detroit, Mich.: University of Michigan–Wayne University, Institute of Industrial Relations, 1961), p. 133.

Still another viewpoint is expressed by Leonard Weiss, who suggests that the higher rates found in the concentrated industries are fully explained by the personal qualifications of the labor obtained. Using a statistical analysis which takes account of a person's age, race, region, urban or rural residence, mobility, education, and similar factors, he concludes that monopolistic industries get superior quality for the wages they offer and there is no evidence of "monopoly rent" in the wages paid.[26]

UNION ATTITUDES IN WAGE DETERMINATION

Because strong unions dominate many of our major industries, union attitudes toward wage determination have a significant influence upon the structure of wages in our economy. Union attitudes, as transmitted to management at the bargaining table, are a mixture of basic union needs filtered through and molded by the personalities of the union bargaining representatives. It is up to them properly to assess which of the many possible objectives of union wage policy are in the best interests of the union. They have to weigh the needs of the various groups who make up the membership—the older men and the younger men, the full-time workers and the part-time workers—and try to arrive at a "package" to present to management which will satisfy the divergent needs of these various groups. In any negotiations on behalf of a union a primary responsibility of a union representative is to set policies which will hold the union together and perpetuate it in the face of stresses within and attacks from without.

Union officials sense these needs and coordinate them with their own. Most union officials have come up through the ranks the hard way, and they do not like the idea of going back to the workbench or donning the apron. They have usually risen to positions of power by being fighters, and they know that the continued loyalty of the membership and the continued existence of their positions as officials depend upon their belligerence toward management and their success in achieving substantial gains for their membership. Their job is to sense the pulse of the members and to give them what they want.

What does the membership want? Or to put it more realistically, what might the union representative believe that the membership wants? There are various possible objectives of union wage policy.[27]

1. The largest wage bill, regardless of whether or not all union members are employed.

[26] Leonard W. Weiss, "Concentration and Labor Earnings," *American Economic Review*, Vol. LVI (March, 1966), p. 115.

[27] John T. Dunlop, *Wage Determination under Trade Unions* (New York: Augustus M. Kelley, Inc., 1950), pp. 36–40.

2. The largest wage bill, including funds from the public support of unemployed union members.
3. The largest private payroll to employed members, deducting from
their wage income an amount to pay out-of-work benefits to unemployed members.
4. The largest possible amount of employment for union members.
5. The highest average wage income for each unit of labor affiliated with
the union.

While union leaders can hardly be expected to formulate objectives
in this precise fashion, they unquestionably take account of the alternatives of more money versus more unemployment, particularly in industries which are characterized by strong nonunion competition or the
competition of substitutable products of other industries. The final wage
adjustment which union leaders fall back on as the minimum acceptable
will be profoundly influenced by political influences within the union, by
government pressures, by personal rivalries with other union leaders, and
by similar noneconomic forces.

Union Attitudes toward Wage Cuts

Union leaders are elected to secure economic benefits for their
constituents. In depressed times, however, they may be faced with demands for wage decreases. Generally, unions oppose such demands or
only yield to them with the utmost reluctance when employer bargaining
power is obviously overwhelming. There are many reasons for this attitude, both economic and political.

A basic reason for union opposition to wage reductions is that there
is no assurance that a given change in wages will be associated with the
corresponding change in labor cost or with any predictable change in
costs or prices. Unit labor cost and wage rates or earnings do not necessarily move together; and in various industries, they have frequently moved
in opposite directions. The reason for this is that unit labor cost is a
function of productivity (output per man-hour) as well as hourly earnings. Since productivity may be affected by numerous changes in technology, organization, human efficiency, and intensity of labor utilization,
which unions can neither predict nor control, it is unreasonable to expect
union leaders to attempt to give as much weight to the effect of wage cuts
on labor costs as many economists and businessmen believe desirable.

Practically speaking, a union leader can ill afford the political repercussions of negotiating a wage cut avowedly to decrease or to prevent
further unemployment, when neither he nor the employer can be at all
certain that lower wages will have the hoped-for results. There is the
further fact that most union leaders and the rank-and-file employees do
not believe an employer when he pleads inability to pay. All too often,
they have heard this complaint raised year after year during contract
negotiations; yet, somehow, wage increases were granted, and the em-

ployer paid them. When a real crisis arises, the employer may have to take a strike to convince the union that this time he means business!

Unions resist employer demands for wage reductions in depressions because wage policy, by and large, is made by the employed rather than the unemployed union members. Even if there is reason on the part of the leadership to believe that the demand for the plant's labor is elastic, the employed members might prefer to pursue a wage policy of maximizing wage rates rather than employment. This is clearly the policy of the United Mine Workers and, generally, of most railway and building-trades unions.

Despite their firm opposition to wage cuts, unions have agreed to them on many occasions. There have been special reasons for such action in almost every case. Usually, the crucial factor is the presence of strong nonunion competition, which poses a threat to the continuance of plants under union contract. Another reason for unions accepting wage cuts is found in pressure from the unemployed. This makes itself felt in two ways. The unemployed members may believe that a wage reduction will increase their chances of employment. As their number grows, the pressure on the employed members to accede increases. In addition, the existence of unemployed reduces the union's bargaining power in negotiations. The fear that the unemployed will break a strike and that the employed will not hold out if a strike is called has impelled unions to agree to reductions.

Unemployment and Union Wage Policies

As has been pointed out, union leaders are extremely reluctant to accept a wage cut in the hope that it will increase employment. The wage cut means an immediate hardship to union members and to some extent constitutes a blot on the record of union leadership. The beneficial effects, if any, of the wage reduction may never become evident. Therefore, when a wage *cut* has to be weighed against the possibilities of increased unemployment at existing rates, most union leaders would argue in favor of maintenance of wages.

Is the same emphasis on wages and lack of recognition of employment reactions true when wage *increases* are under consideration? Under what circumstances is a limit set on wage increases by union recognition of the possibility that higher wages would endanger the competitive position of the firm and thereby create unemployment among union members?

There has been some controversy on this subject among economists in recent years. Some economists argue that the effect of a wage increase upon employment is unpredictable before the fact, and after the increase has been granted, it is impossible to determine what the effect of the increase has been on employment due to the constant fluctuation of business conditions. Therefore, it is argued, union leaders cannot normally take employment reactions into consideration in wage negotiations.[28]

There is some evidence to indicate that the impact of union organization has made wage adjustments less responsive to levels of unemployment. For example, one economist found that the relation of wage changes to varying levels of unemployment was stronger in the period prior to 1930 than in the last 20 years. He concludes that inasmuch as unionism has played a more important role since World War II than before 1930, "trade unions would appear to have made wage increases less sensitive to unemployment than under the essentially nonunion conditions during the first thirty years of the century."[29]

On the other hand, other economists contend that there are a number of industries where conditions exist which require that union leaders take account of possible employment reactions in making decisions as to wage policy. This is true where an industry is only partially unionized and imposition of excessive rates on organized firms will cause them to lose business to the nonunion sector of the industry. Similar concern with the employment effects of increased wage costs will also be found in industries characterized by strong competition in the product market and in industries where it is relatively easy for employers to move their plants to other areas.

Areas in which these conditions exist are by no means exceptional. About one out of every five workers in manufacturing is employed in five industries where there is clearly no single-firm control of the product market and where competition among firms is keen—textiles, apparel, leather goods, furniture, and lumber.[30] The textile and apparel industries have also been characterized by a movement of new capital into nonunion areas by reason of the high costs imposed by union wage pressure in organized areas. Industries in which union organization is only partial also are important in terms of workers employed. It is estimated that less than 50% of the workers in the following manufacturing industries are covered by union agreements: baking; chemicals, excluding rayon yarn; flour and other grain products; furniture; hosiery; jewelry and silverware; knit goods; leather luggage; handbags; novelties; lumber; paper products; pottery, including chinaware; shoes; cut stock and findings; stone and clay products; and silk and rayon yarn. Industries which are between 80% and 100% organized today account for less than half of all gainfully employed workers. Therefore, there are many industries in which unions must take

[28] Arthur M. Ross, *Trade Union Wage Policy* (Berkeley: University of California Press, 1948), p. 80.

[29] Kenneth M. McCaffree, "A Further Consideration of Wages, Unemployment, and Prices in the U.S., 1948–1958," *Industrial and Labor Relations Review*, Vol. XVII (October, 1963), p. 60.

[30] U.S. Department of Labor, Bureau of Labor Statistics, *Monthly Report on the Labor Force, January, 1964* (Washington, D.C.: U.S. Government Printing Office, February, 1964), p. 22.

account of employment reactions simply because such consideration is essential to the continued existence and strength of the union.

Effect of Unions on Wage Adjustments

In Chapter 13, in our discussion of inflation, we shall consider in detail the question of whether or not unions accelerate the rate of wage increases in the American economy. For the purposes of the present discussion, however, it is pertinent to observe that union organization affects the nature, size, and frequency of wage changes in unionized firms. Unions have profoundly affected the *form* of wage adjustments in American industry. Supplementary unemployment benefits, cost-of-living adjustments, guaranteed annual wages, pay for employee birthdays, and all sorts of welfare plans—these are some of the diverse ways in which employees have expressed their preferences for wage adjustments through collective bargaining.

Unions also affect the frequency of wage adjustments. Nonunion factory workers, for example, normally do not receive wage increases each year.[31] By contrast, most union factory workers do receive wage adjustments annually, either through annual negotiations or through deferred increases under contracts extending two or three years. Since nonunion workers are not tied by long-term labor contracts, it is understandable that when there are changes in the economic climate, nonunion plants will respond more quickly to such changes in terms of wage adjustments than organized firms. The nonunion response to an improvement in economic conditions is typically a change in the frequency of wage and benefit adjustments.[32]

The size of wage adjustments is also affected by the existence of collective bargaining agreements. Nonunion wage adjustments will vary more in amount from year to year because of the fact that nonunion plants are more sensitive to changes in economic conditions. This is likely to be true both in a slack and in a tight labor market.[33] On the average, however, a worker in a union factory is likely to receive in any one year a smaller percentage but a larger cents-per-hour increase than the nonunion worker, and since the union employee receives increases more frequently, there is some evidence that over a period of years he gains proportionately more than a nonunion worker. Thus, one study found that over the period from 1959–66, general wage adjustments totaled approximately 25.8% in union establishments compared to 23.6% in nonunion factories.[34]

[31] William Davis and Lily Mary David, "Pattern Wage and Benefit Changes in Manufacturing," *Monthly Labor Review*, Vol. XCI (February, 1968), p. 40.

[32] *Loc cit.*

[33] U.S. Department of Labor, Bureau of Labor Statistics, *Trends in Labor Compensation in the United States, 1946–1966* (Washington, D.C.; 1967), p. 9.

[34] Davis, *op. cit.*, p. 43.

POWER ASPECTS OF WAGE DETERMINATION

Wage determination in unionized firms involves a balancing of power. It reflects the union's power to strike and to inflict damage by a strike, and the company's ability to withstand a strike and impose loss of earnings on employees. Even when a strike is not threatened, the power of a union to strike makes itself felt at the bargaining table. As one writer puts it, unions regulate the wage rate "not by sustained control of supply, but by control of the buyer, who is the employer. The technique is the strike."[35]

Union bargaining power depends upon three basic elements: the right to strike, the ability to strike successfully, and the amount of loss which can be inflicted on the employer by a strike. The legal right to strike, of course, is a basic prerequisite to union power. If the union contract in question is a two-year contract with a wage reopening after one year and the contract contains a no-strike clause, the union may not be able to strike lawfully to enforce its wage demands during its term. A strike in violation of a contract may leave the union open to a suit by the employer for damages for breach of contract, or an injunction may be obtained to halt the unlawful work stoppage. Furthermore, when a union strike is unlawful, other unions frequently will not honor the picket line, and therefore the effectiveness of the strike is weakened. Obviously, when such circumstances exist, the union's bargaining power is limited.

If the union has the right to strike, the next consideration is its ability to strike successfully. This will depend upon such circumstances as the cohesiveness of the union, the degree of internal dissension, the possibility of raiding by rival unions, the amount of funds in the union treasury, the ability of the union to pay strike benefits, the extent to which strikers can obtain employment or compensation elsewhere, and, of course, the degree of support by the membership for the union demands. Even such circumstances as the time of year will affect a union's ability to strike successfully. Employees do not mind losing a few weeks' work on strike in the summertime, but they are loath to do so just before Christmas!

The third important factor which determines the bargaining power of the union is its ability to impose a substantial hardship on the employer by calling a strike. This will depend upon the nature of business of the employer, the position of the firm in the industry, its financial resources, and similar circumstances. If a company is engaged in retail trade, for example, it is extremely vulnerable to a strike because any business lost through a shutdown cannot be regained at a later date. People will not

[35] Charles E. Lindblom, *Unions and Capitalism* (New Haven, Conn.: Yale University Press, 1949), p. 58.

stop eating while a restaurant is on strike; they will simply eat their meals elsewhere. On the other hand, if an automobile company goes on strike, its permanent loss of business might be negligible. For a time, customers can be supplied out of inventory. Thereafter, many customers will wait for a particular make of car until production is resumed. Sometimes a strike may afford such companies a convenient excuse to curtail production and thus give dealers time to work down excessive inventories.

The power of the union to hurt the employer will depend upon the financial position and the profitability of the company. In some industries, companies work on narrow profit margins and have little working capital. They rely on continuing sales to enable them to meet their bills, and any interruption of production has to be avoided at all costs. In other cases, companies are financially strong and can stand a long strike. Frequently, large companies have a number of plants or branch operations, and if a strike shuts down only part of their operations, they can withstand a long strike by offsetting losses in one area with profits in another.

Just as a union's ability to strike successfully depends in part upon the time of year, so does its ability to impose losses on the employer. The threat of a strike is obviously most effective when the employer is going into his peak season. If contract negotiations break down during a slack season, the employer may not care about a strike, since he may have been thinking in terms of curtailing production and laying off employees anyhow. Both unions and management are keenly aware of the strategic importance of having contract negotiations occur at an advantageous time, and there is always a good deal of sparring over the issue of when a contract should expire or come up for renegotiation.

The loss which can be imposed upon a firm by a strike depends to some extent upon the class of labor involved and its importance in the entire scheme of production. It has long been recognized that the smaller the cost of a factor of production is relative to total costs, and the more essential it is to production, the higher its price can be pushed up without affecting the amount of the factor employers will utilize. In every plant or establishment, there are certain workers with relatively scarce skills who can paralyze production by a walkout. If their wages constitute only a small fraction of total costs of operation, it is understandable why an employer will frequently be willing to grant such workers large wage increases as the price of uninterrupted production. It was recognition of this principle which led the American Federation of Labor to organize skilled workers along craft lines.

Today, however, even a strike of unskilled workers can be as effective as a walkout of skilled craftsmen. This is the result of two developments: the refusal of other workers to cross a picket line and the decline in the use of strikebreakers. Today, a walkout of janitors and sweepers in a huge industrial establishment can, if it is a lawful strike, cause a complete shutdown and a forced layoff of thousands of workers. The right to strike has thus given great power even to unskilled groups who are ready to use this power militantly.

All of the foregoing considerations must be weighed by the union representatives in presenting union demands at the bargaining table. They must estimate, too, just how long a strike might result, what is the possibility of government intervention, and what the chances are that employee dissatisfaction resulting from a long strike might endanger their own positions. Management must likewise consider the strength and weaknesses of its own bargaining position. The wage which is ultimately arrived at will reflect a balancing of these power considerations, the profitability of the firm, general supply and demand conditions, and the personalities of management and union representatives.

SUMMARY

Wage determination in the American economy is a complex process. It reflects the influence of many forces. Thus if we were trying to explain why a production worker in a steel-fabricating company has a higher hourly wage rate than a production worker in a textile mill, the following are some of the major considerations which would require investigation: [36]

1. The monopoly power of the employer in the product market—Is it easy for the company to pass along to consumers the cost of higher wages?
2. The wage policy of the employer—Does it have a policy of paying wages equal to, or higher than, those of its competitors or of other firms in its local labor market area?
3. The state of union organization in the plant and industry—Is the employee a union member? What is the bargaining strength of the union, is its leadership aggressive, does it have to concern itself with nonunion competition? What is the extent of collective bargaining among firms with which the employer competes in the product market?
4. The trend of sales and employment in the respective industries— Are there unfilled job vacancies in the plant, is employment increasing and the demand for labor strong?
5. The supply of labor in the local labor market—Is there a large pool of qualified but unemployed labor available, or is labor in short supply?
6. The regularity of employment, both over the year and from year to year—Does the high wage rate in the steel company compensate in part for cyclical unemployment incident to the job?
7. The total package of compensation—What other benefits are received by the worker? To what extent can he expect overtime work?

[36] Derived in part from the discussion in Weiss, *op. cit.*, pp. 96–117.

How do the two jobs compare when we look at weekly earnings or annual income?

8. Size of firm—Is this a small or large firm, a public corporation or a small family business?
9. Size of labor market—Is the plant located in a large metropolitan area or in a small town?
10. The overall labor-force characteristics of the industry or firm—To what extent is the labor force in each firm composed of a high percentage of white, skilled, male workers?
11. Geographical location—Is the plant located in the South or in some other section of the country?
12. The personal characteristics of the employees in question—What is their respective age, race, education, health, etc.?
13. Profitability of the employer—How does profit of the employer compare with that of other firms in the particular industry? Was this a good year or a bad year? What is the trend in profits both in the firm and in the industry?
14. The job content—To what extent is a high degree of skill or training required to perform the particular job?

All of these considerations in varying degrees enter into the determination of wages. While we have placed considerable emphasis in this chapter on the role of unions in wage determination, it is important to recognize that the various factors enumerated above will shape and influence the impact which unions can exert upon the level and structure of wages.

QUESTIONS FOR DISCUSSION

1. Discuss the connection between the internal and external wage structure of a firm. What is the significance for collective bargaining of the concept of "wage clusters"?
2. Discuss the significance of key wage bargains in wage determination in the United States.
3. Discuss the interrelationship of monopoly power in the product market and union power in the labor market in terms of the effect of this interrelationship upon the wage level.

SUGGESTIONS FOR FURTHER READING

ALLEN, BRUCE T. "Market Concentration and Wage Increases: U.S. Manufacturing, 1947–1964," *Industrial and Labor Relations Review*, Vol. XXI (April, 1968), pp. 353–65.

    A discussion and empirical testing of the theory that those workers enjoy the most rapidly rising wages who are employed in partially monopolistic or oligopolistic industries.

ECKSTEIN, OTTO, and WILSON, THOMAS A. "The Determination of Money Wages in American Industry," *Quarterly Journal of Economics*, Vol. LXXVI (August, 1962), pp. 379–414.

A leading article on the factors determining money wages in American industry. Statistical analysis is used to test the hypothesis that the profit rate and unemployment rate are the primary determinants of money wages in a key group of industries.

LEVINSON, HAROLD M. "Unionism, Concentration, and Wage Changes: Toward A Unified Theory," *Industrial and Labor Relations Review*, Vol. XX (January, 1967), pp. 198–205.

A perceptive analysis of the relationship between union strength, competition in the product market, and the size of wage adjustments.

THROOP, ADRIAN W. "The Union-Nonunion Wage Differential and Cost-Push Inflation," *American Economic Review*, Vol. LVIII (March, 1968), pp. 79–99.

An attempt to measure the change in the nonunion-union wage differential during the 1950's and to estimate its impact on inflation.

WEISS, LEONARD. "Concentration and Labor Earnings," *American Economic Review*, Vol. LVI (March, 1966), pp. 96–117. See also, Leonard Weiss, "Concentration and Labor Earnings: Reply," *American Economic Review*, Vol. LVIII (March, 1968), pp. 181–84; and Frank P. Stafford, "Concentration and Labor Earnings, Comment," *American Economic Review*, Vol. LVIII (March, 1968), pp. 174–81.

A series of articles dealing with the findings made by Weiss that higher wages paid in so-called concentrated industries are fully explained by the personal qualifications of the employees involved.

| Chapter | WAGE CHANGES AND |
| 12 | EMPLOYMENT |

Union officials, in order to maintain their positions and retain the allegiance and interest of their membership, must constantly seek to obtain new benefits for their members. In view of the strength of organized labor in this country, it seems likely that over the long run the general trend of money wage rates in future years will be upward. What impact will such continuing wage pressure have upon employment?

The effect of wage changes upon employment constitutes one of the most controversial subjects in the field of labor economics. Most union leaders deny that there is any predictable relation between wage increases and employment in the *individual* firm in our dynamic economy. Orthodox economists generally take a contrary view. But when we come to the field of *general* wage adjustments occurring uniformly throughout the economy, we find that many economists argue that such wage adjustments need have no effect upon employment. What is the reason for this divergence in opinion? Under what circumstances will wage increases curtail employment? In this chapter, we shall inquire into the consequences of increases in wage rates upon employment, first from the point of view of the individual firm and secondly from the point of view of the economy at large. Finally, we shall examine some of the problems created by continuing union wage pressure.

WAGE CHANGES IN THE INDIVIDUAL FIRM

Short-Run Effect of Wage Increases

Assume that an increase occurs in the rate of wages which an employer is required to pay his labor force. This might be the result of a new union contract or of a minimum wage law or simply of increasing scarcity of labor in the labor market. Assume further that the demand for the product sold by the company remains unchanged, that there are no new inventions reducing costs of production in the firm, and that output in the company at the time the wage increase occurred was neither expanding nor contracting but was relatively stable. These various assumptions are generally taken care of by phrasing our inquiry in terms of the effect of a wage increase in the individual firm, "other things being equal."

Orthodox economists assume that the behavior of the employer under such circumstances will conform to the principles of marginal productivity determination, which we examined in Chapter 10. According to the marginal productivity theory, the employer endeavors to hire labor up to the point at which the marginal cost of labor is approximately equal to its marginal contribution to the revenue of the firm.

As we have seen in Chapter 10, if the supply of labor is perfectly elastic, the wage and marginal cost of labor are the same, and the employer will hire labor up to the point of approximate equality between marginal revenue product and wage. It will simplify our analysis if we ignore the complications produced by a rising supply curve for labor and, in the following discussion of employment policy in the individual firm, assume that the employer is faced by a perfectly elastic supply curve of labor so that marginal productivity determination will be made in terms of the wage of labor (which, under these conditions, will be equal to marginal cost of labor).

Under these circumstances, an employer who wishes to maximize profits will hire labor only up to the point where the last additional worker adds just enough revenue to compensate for the wage he receives. The lower the wage, the larger will be the size of the work force employed, since the employer can afford to keep on the payroll at such low wage rates those workers whose marginal contribution to the revenues of the firm is comparatively small. When wage costs rise, however, he will be compelled to lay off these men in order to achieve a new equilibrium in which the marginal revenue productivity of the least valuable man employed will be sufficiently great to equal the new higher wage level.

Wage Increases and Layoffs

The pressure on the employer to lay off workers when the wage rate rises comes about in two principal ways. In the first place, when wage costs rise, the employer generally finds it necessary to raise his price for his product in order to cover the increased labor costs. In some cases, he may find it inexpedient to raise prices but may achieve the same objective by lowering the quality of his product. In either case, whether the price be raised or quality impaired, he will ordinarily sell a smaller output, even though it is possible that his total sales receipts may increase or remain constant. With a smaller physical production, he will find that he needs fewer employees, and so he will be able to lay off some workers whose services are no longer required.

In the second place, when wage rates rise, the employer's profits will immediately be reduced. Therefore a strong incentive is provided for him to review his entire production setup in an effort to cut costs and save money. Even without a change in output, the employer may find it possible, by rescheduling output and rearranging work schedules, to eliminate some workers. Furthermore, if labor becomes more expensive, the employer may find that it is now economically profitable to utilize new laborsaving machinery in the plant which will also have the effect of displacing labor. Such substitution of machinery for labor usually takes some time to effect. The employer may have limited space in his plant, or perhaps he may have to defer substitution until his existing machinery is more fully depreciated. Substitution of machinery for labor, therefore, is ordinarily felt most as a long-run consequence of wage increases. It will be considered below in connection with our analysis of the long-run effects of wage pressure.

When labor becomes more expensive, employers are pressed to look over their labor force and decide whether certain jobs need to be performed at all, irrespective of whether they can be performed more cheaply by machines or automated devices. Thus, if labor is cheap, business establishments may employ a porter to clean floors and do odd jobs; but when this kind of labor becomes expensive, they may decide to eliminate this work and call in a contract cleaner on a periodic basis. This basic principle has important social implications. As we shall document in Chapter 16, with every rise in the minimum wage we have provided an incentive to employers to eliminate certain of the menial jobs at the lowest rung of the wage scale. This may be justified as part of a national effort to raise wage standards, yet it is quite probable that it is responsible for the creation of a substantial amount of hard-core unemployment. For in every society, there are persons whose education, training, and mental abilities are low, and these people can only find employment in jobs whose remuneration is low, corresponding to their low productivity.

Factors Affecting Elasticity of Demand for Labor

What determines the elasticity of the demand curve for labor in the short run? Or to put the question in another way: With a given increase in wage rates, what are the circumstances which determine whether the layoffs will be small (inelastic demand) or large (elastic demand)? Many years ago a famous economist, Alfred Marshall, formulated an answer to this question as part of his exposition of the laws of derived demand.[1] It was Marshall's theory that the demand for labor is a derived demand. Labor is not wanted for itself but for what it can produce. Therefore, if we want an explanation of the elasticity of demand for labor, we must look to the demand for the final product and the supply of other factors of production, from which the demand for labor is derived.

According to Marshall:

---

[1] Alfred Marshall, *Principles of Economics* (8th ed.; New York: Macmillan Co., 1920), pp. 383–86.

1. *The demand for labor will be the more inelastic the more essential the labor in question is in the production of the final product.* Obviously, the more skilled the worker is, the more likely that the employer will be highly dependent upon his services. Thus the demand for labor for skilled patternmakers is more likely to be less elastic than for common laborers; and the patternmakers, if they were to go out on strike, would be better able to extract a higher wage from management without layoffs than could the common laborers. With the latter class of employee an employer may find that he can operate temporarily with supervisory help, or he can bring in nonunion employees. In today's labor market, essentiality can be the result either of a high degree of skill or of a tight control over entrance into a trade exercised by a labor union.

2. *The demand for labor will be the more inelastic the more inelastic the demand for the final product.* The demand curve for the product will have a steep slope or be "inelastic" when increases in price of the product produce only a very small decrease in the quantity which consumers purchase of the product. A classic example of a product with an inelastic demand curve is salt. Even large increases in price would not materially affect sales of this product. If, however, the demand curve for the product is almost horizontal or "elastic," even a small increase in price will cause sales to fall off sharply, with the result that a large curtailment will be required in the labor force of the firm.

The range of possible reactions of employment to a wage increase may be crystallized by considering the difference in effect of wage increases under two extreme conditions of elasticity of demand for product—first, in a firm with a perfectly inelastic demand curve and, second, in a firm with a perfectly elastic demand curve. In the former case, the increase in costs resulting from a wage adjustment could be passed on completely to consumers in the form of a price rise without affecting sales volume at all. Therefore, there would be no unemployment caused by the price rise, although there could still be some unemployment resulting from substitution of factors within the firm. In the second case, at the other extreme, the firm with the elastic demand curve would be unable to pass any of the price increase on to consumers. The employer would find that to maximize profits, he would be better off selling a smaller volume at the same price and would therefore sharply curtail output and employment.

Firms in monopolistic positions are able to raise the price of their products without affecting sales materially, since consumers cannot shift easily to substitutes. On the basis of the foregoing theoretical analysis, therefore, we should expect that in firms which have an entrenched and protected position in the product market built up through advertising, patents, and sheer size and financial power, wage increases would produce relatively larger price increases and relatively less displacement of labor than in highly competitive companies.

When we are dealing with union wage adjustments on an industry-wide basis, and if the entire industry is well organized, then the demand curve for the product which is relevant is really the demand curve for the product of the entire industry. If, on the other hand, the union has organized only a part of the industry, then the demand curve which is significant is the demand curve for the product of the firms where wage adjustments are being made. The elasticity of demand for the product of these firms is likely to be greater than that for the product of the industry if there is a possibility that rates will not advance to the same extent in nonunion firms and that therefore nonunion product will be substituted by consumers for the product of the organized companies. As one writer points out, the union in the hosiery industry has all but disappeared because of the competition in the product market created by nonunion firms.[2]

3. *The demand for labor will be the more inelastic the smaller the ratio of the labor cost in question to the total cost of product.* In some firms, labor costs constitute a relatively small proportion of total costs—frequently less than 10 per cent of total costs. In such firms, if wage rates rise by, say, five per cent, total costs would rise by only one half of one per cent. If the full increase in total cost were reflected in a price increase, the rise in price would be so small that sales volume, and therefore employment, might not be affected to any significant degree.

But now, suppose that only a portion of the labor force is demanding an increase in wage rates. It is obvious that a small group of workers strategically placed in a company may be able to gain very large increases in rates for themselves, yet from the point of view of management the effect on overall costs may be minor. Of course, management must consider the effect of such wage changes upon the rates of other workers; but nevertheless, it still remains true that there are advantages to be gained in bargaining from being strong but small. From this point of view, small craft unions may well do a better job of wage bargaining for their membership than large industrial unions.

4. *The demand for labor will be the more inelastic the more inelastic the supply of other factors of production.* If the supply of other factors of production that are needed to work with the labor in question is inelastic, a small increase in demand will cause a large increase in the price of such factors. Conversely, a small reduction in demand will cause a sharp fall in the price of such factors. Two influences are seen at work in this relationship which can be illustrated by the following examples:

1. *The "substitution effect."* Suppose that a union of porters working for a company which cleans floors in various industrial and retail

---

[2] Albert Rees, *The Economics of Trade Unions* (Chicago: University of Chicago Press, 1962), p. 71. This book has an excellent discussion of Marshall's laws of derived demand on pages 70–73.

buildings demands a substantial wage increase. Management knows that if it purchases waxing and polishing machines it can speed up floor maintenance work and eliminate a number of porters. However, if there are a limited number of such machines available, so that any increase in demand will result in a sharp increase in the price asked for such machines, the bargaining power of the porters in demanding and obtaining wage increases will be improved. In other words, the inelasticity of the supply of this other factor of production will tend to make the demand for the porters' labor more inelastic. Management will then be prepared to pay more for this type of labor without substantially curtailing the amount of labor employed through increased mechanization.

2. *The "output effect."* The increase in costs resulting from the adjustment in wages given to the porters will necessitate an increase in price for services rendered by the floor-cleaning company. Therefore, it is likely that some of its customers will discontinue utilizing its services or will reduce their usage. Assume that the floor-cleaning company has been leasing polishing machines from another firm prior to the wage adjustment. Since the floor-cleaning company's business volume will be reduced as a result of the wage and price adjustments referred to above, it will have less need for polishing machines and may return some to the leasing firm. If the latter has no other place to use the machines and in effect is "stuck" with a fixed supply of them, it may be willing to accept a lower rental just to keep them busy. In other words, a relatively small reduction in demand for this factor of production might cause a substantial drop in its supply price. This is another way of saying that its supply curve is inelastic. If this were so, part of the wage increase gained by the porters could be achieved at the expense of the price paid for the other factor. In other words, an inelastic supply curve for a complementary factor of production would enable the porters to achieve a larger wage adjustment.

Circumstances in Which Wage Increases Do Not Reduce Employment

Suppose a union were to secure a substantial increase in wages from employers in a particular industry and the employers were then questioned as to the effect the wage adjustment would have on their employment policies. What would be the typical response? Chances are that most of the employers would say the wage increase would not cause them to cut their labor force; that, on the contrary, they intended to increase employment. They would explain that they had to give the wage increase in order to retain their present labor force and to attract additional workers.

Employers normally grant wage increases when times are good and prices are rising. They make wage changes in a dynamic business environment in which demand and supply conditions are in a continual state of flux. Against such a changing background, it is quite possible that wage increases will not be immediately associated with any diminution in employment. Let us consider briefly the various circumstances under which a wage increase need not have any adverse effect on employment.

1. *When output in the individual firm is increasing.* As we have already observed, one avenue by which wage increases affect employment is through the reduction in output which is caused by the increase in product price made to cover the higher wage costs. If, however, output is increasing in the firm at the time the wage increase is made, the effect of the wage adjustment upon employment is likely to be obscured, and employment in the firm may not be altered by the wage increase. Output may be increasing in a firm because of rising demand for its product attributable to a general business revival. During such a period, output, wages, profits, and prices all tend to rise together; and wage increases tend to be associated with increases, not decreases, in employment. Output may also be increasing in particular firms, even in periods of relative business stability, because the firm is growing, or the demand for the product of the industry is growing, or for similar reasons. Not only does expanding output normally carry with it additional job opportunities but also, in many industries—such as, for example, the steel industry—expanding output is associated with declining labor costs per unit of product. Therefore, if wage *rates* increase at a time when output is expanding in such industries, there may not even be any increase in unit labor costs, since the increase in wage rates may simply be offset by the decline in unit labor costs attributable to the expansion of output.

2. *When productivity is increasing.* As new and more productive machinery is introduced and changes are made in the organization of work, the productivity of labor tends to increase. This means that the employer will find that with a given number of workers, he can now produce a larger output than formerly. Such advance in productivity—which is a continuous process in our dynamic economy—has the effect of reducing labor costs per unit of product. Therefore, if money wage rates are raised at about the same rate that increasing productivity lowers unit labor costs, the two trends may offset each other; and on balance, there may be no net increase in unit labor costs. If the rate of increase in wage rates is no greater than the rate at which technological progress reduces unit labor costs, there will be no increase in unit labor cost, no increase in price, and no reduction in output and employment. However, although the wage increase under such circumstances does not produce unemployment, it may eliminate the possibility for any expansion of employment in the firm by preventing technological progress from being reflected in a reduction in price to consumers.

3. *When prices are inflexible.* There are certain situations in which a wage increase, even though it increases labor costs per unit, will not produce a change in the price charged by the individual firm. In such circumstances, the employer may calculate that even though his profits

are being squeezed by failure to adjust prices, he would lose more if he tried to alter his price.

This condition may exist when there are only a few sellers in an industry. Such a situation is known as "oligopoly," and the demand curve of the individual firm, as seen by the employer, will often have a "kink" at the prevailing price.[3] This is simply a geometric expression of the fact that each seller in the industry calculates that if he lowers his price, he will merely start a price war and therefore not appreciably increase his sales; whereas if he raises his price, his competitors may not follow suit, with the result that his sales will fall off sharply. Above the prevailing price the demand curve for the product of the individual firm approaches the horizontal, and below the prevailing price the demand curve approaches the vertical—thus producing the so-called "kink" at the prevailing price. Under such circumstances a rise in wage rates may not produce any change in prices or output. Consequently, employment will not be immediately affected. It must be borne in mind, however, that even when output remains constant, management may still find means of economizing on the use of labor which has become more expensive by reason of the wage increase. For example, in some industries, employers have sought to economize on the use of labor by resorting to the "stretch-out," i.e., a worker who formerly tended only one machine is required to operate two machines at the same rate of pay. Through this and similar devices a smaller labor force can be used more intensively, and some workers can be displaced, although output remains unchanged.

4. *When exploitation of labor exists.* As we have already observed in Chapter 10, a wage increase need not produce unemployment where a condition of exploitation of labor has previously existed. In other words, if an employer has been paying labor less than its marginal revenue product, and the effect of a wage adjustment is to increase the wage rate to the point of equivalence of marginal revenue product and wage, there will be no incentive for the employer to alter his price, output, and employment.

The foregoing analysis indicates that in the dynamic environment of the business world, the connection between wage changes and changes in employment is a very tenuous one. Wage increases do not necessarily produce increases in labor costs per unit of product—they may simply prevent reductions in labor costs attributable to technological change or increasing output from being reflected in price reductions to consumers. Even if the increase in wage rates increases labor costs per unit of product, it still may not affect prices where it is impracticable for the firm to raise prices because of competitive conditions; moreover, even if prices are

[3] For a detailed discussion of this situation, the technical reader is referred to P. M. Sweezy, "Demand under Conditions of Oligopoly," *Journal of Political Economy*, Vol. XLVII (August, 1939), p. 569.

raised, there need be no reduction in output or employment, if output was increasing anyway, or if the price increase is negligible because wages constitute such a small proportion of total costs.

Long-Run Effect of Wage Increases

As we have observed earlier in this chapter, the extent to which wage increases will produce unemployment in the individual firm in the long run can be summarized in the form of four laws:

If wages are raised, the resulting unemployment will be smaller in amount:

1. The less elastic the demand for the product.
2. The smaller the substitutability of labor in the process of production.
3. The smaller the portion which labor costs form of total costs.
4. The less elastic the supply schedules of the complementary factors.

These "laws" are applicable in both the short run and the long run, but it is only in the long run that factors 2 and 4 can exercise their full effect. In essence, these two tendencies reduce to the degree of fluidity of capital. It is machinery that is ordinarily the complement of labor, as well as its most important substitute. In the long run, capital not only can be substituted for labor (factor 2), but it also may be removed to other industries, or the supply may be altered (factor 4).

At any moment of time, employers, if they have acted rationally, will have pushed their use of labor and capital to the point where they have reached a margin of indifference, i.e., it is immaterial to them whether they utilize a unit of capital or a unit of labor at the margin. From this it follows that if the price of labor rises, employers will find two actions profitable: (1) to substitute capital for labor by introducing laborsaving machinery; and (2) to shift from less capitalistic to more capitalistic industries, i.e., to industries where the ratio of labor to capital is smaller. These reactions both take time. A full adaptation to an increase in the wage of labor may take years to work itself out. As a consequence, the full effect of wage increases upon the volume of employment can be observed only in the long run.

WAGE PRESSURE AND MECHANIZATION

A major means of improving efficiency and saving labor in our industrial economy has been the machine. Machines, however, are costly, and businessmen will normally invest in laborsaving machinery only if the investment gives promise of paying for itself in a reasonable period of time. A laborsaving machine pays for itself in terms of manpower saved, reduction in spoilage, and so forth. The higher the wage rate of the labor which can be displaced by the machine, the larger the savings which the machine will effect, and the more attractive its purchase becomes.

Businessmen are not uniformly alert to the advantages of using laborsaving machinery. There are many laborsaving machines which are known today and which may be in use in some companies but which are not utilized by others, either because their labor costs are not high enough to warrant the expenditure on machinery or because management is inefficient and has not sufficient initiative to look around and find out how its costs might be lowered. Undoubtedly, a substantial improvement in the level of industrial efficiency could be obtained if inefficient employers were induced to bring their production methods into line with the best in the industry.

Wage pressure may exert this influence in certain circumstances. Wage increases are likely to be most effective as a stimulus to substitution of machinery for labor in firms where wages, prior to the wage increase, were low, and management relied on low wages rather than efficient methods to compete. For example, one recent study based upon an examination of Census of Manufacturing data found that among low-wage industries, firms affected by increased wage costs resulting from a rise in governmental minimum wage rates showed the greatest tendency to substitute nonwage inputs in the production process.[4] Employers are most likely to be sensitive to wage increases in firms where labor costs constitute a large proportion of total costs and where competition is keen and profit margins are slim.

In this connection, it should be observed that although in companies operating on low profit margins, wage increases frequently provide a spur to improved efficiency, an increase in material costs, or insurance rates, or general overhead may have precisely the same effect. The increase in costs compels management to look around in the industry and bring its own plant up to date with others.

Not all machinery is introduced because of an increase in labor costs. As a matter of fact, it is possible that in our dynamic economy, only a small part of the substitution of machinery for labor which occurs is attributable to changes in wage rates. The reason is that invention is continuously bringing onto the market new machines and devices which have a high laborsaving potential and which, in many cases, would be profitable to use even at a much lower wage rate. For example, when the "semiautomatics" were introduced in the bottle industry, the Glass Bottle Blowers Association attempted to compete with the machine by accepting a 45% reduction in the hand price on fruit jars, but this substantial wage cut proved ineffective, and the machine continued to be introduced. Here is an example of a machine which would have been profitable to use even at a wage level 45% lower than that which prevailed when it was

---

[4] David E. Kaun, "Minimum Wages, Factor Substitution, and the Marginal Producer," *Quarterly Journal of Economics*, Vol. LXXIX (August, 1965), pp. 478–86.

introduced. Obviously, its introduction did not depend upon wage increases. Many other laborsaving machines fall in the same category. The point is that while wage increases accelerate the introduction of some machinery, a large part of the new machinery which is applied in industry depends upon research and invention which is not significantly influenced by changes in wage rates. The same is true of the modern development of automation, which has already been discussed in Chapter 6. The widespread application of automation in industry has depended upon our scientific know-how in the field of electronics and control mechanisms reaching a certain stage of development. On the other hand, a high wage level has been a factor in making application of automation practical.

Wage Pressure and Invention

We have seen that wage increases can affect the rate at which known mechanical improvements are applied by industry. Does the level of wages also affect the rate at which new methods are discovered? In other words, can wage pressure induce invention?

This is a subject upon which there is considerable theoretical discussion and controversy in the economic literature,[5] but very little substantiation in the form of empirical research. The theory of induced invention is usually associated with the name of J. R. Hicks,[6] who suggested that a rise in the rate of wages (the price of labor) relative to the rate of interest (the price of capital) would induce the discovery of methods of production which would save labor. This theory further postulates that the frequency of laborsaving inventions depends upon the rate of increase in wages relative to interest rates. Laborsaving inventions save labor, whereas capital-saving inventions save capital. According to this theory, if interest rates were to rise relative to wages, there would be a greater inducement to save capital; and as a result, the frequency of capital-saving inventions would increase.

Other economists, however, contend that because of the unpredictable nature of the process of invention, wage increases do not necessarily call forth any increase in the number of laborsaving discoveries. According to this view, most inventions will be laborsaving simply because of the continuing high cost of labor as an element of production and because

[5] See, for example, Syed Ahmad, "On the Theory of Induced Invention," *Economic Journal,* Vol. LXXVI (June, 1966), pp. 344–57; William Fellner, "Profit Maximization, Utility Minimization, and the Rate and Direction of Innovation," Papers and Proceedings of the Seventy-eighth Annual Meeting of the American Economic Association, *American Economic Review Supplement,* Vol. LVI (May, 1966), pp. 27–28.

[6] J. R. Hicks, *The Theory of Wages* (2d ed.; London: Macmillan & Co., Ltd. 1963), chap. vi, pp. 112–35. See also, for a critique of this theory, Gordon F. Bloom, "Note on Hicks' Theory of Invention," *American Economic Review,* Vol. XXXVI, (March, 1946), pp. 83–96.

most invention in our society is designed to lighten the arduousness of work.

Is the increase in research expenditure in this country related to continuing wage pressure? Funds spent on research and development performed by industry more than doubled from $7.7 billion in 1957 to $18 billion in 1968.[7] These were years characterized by a steady rise in money wages. On the other hand, research expenditures increased fivefold from 1920 to 1931, a period when wage rates were relatively stable. The great growth of research in this country cannot be attributed to wage pressure, although high wages, as one element of the cost-price structure, have undoubtedly produced an economic setting conducive to research and invention. One reason for the lack of any close relationship between wage levels and the amount of research expenditure is that the federal government finances over half of the research performed by private industry.[8]

Does wage pressure influence the direction of industrial research projects? One would expect to find major emphasis in research to reduce costs in view of the continuing upward pressure of unions on wages, particularly in large companies which support most of the research activity in this country. However, a study conducted by one of the authors suggests that most research funds are allocated to research on new products and improvement of present products, rather than to new-process research.

This emphasis on product improvement is not entirely inconsistent with major interest on the part of management in reducing labor costs. Very often, a need arises in one industry for a machine to cut costs, and this idea filters back to a supplier, who then devises a new product or a new machine to help fill this need. A new computer is a new-product development from the point of view of the industry making it, yet can be a significant cost-saving development in the industry utilizing it. From this point of view, much of the new-product development and product improvement which has characterized our technological progress has ultimately been reflected in reduced costs of production and a more efficient utilization of labor.

Of course, not all invention occurs in the industrial laboratory. Every employer, every foreman—indeed, every employee—is a potential inventor. Anyone who designs a new way of arranging the flow of production, devises a new attachment for a machine which increases man-hour output, adds to the stream of invention. Wage pressure—like any other pressure on profits—tends to make employers look around for new avenues to save money and thus may stimulate some invention. However, it is doubtful that there is any close relationship between the rate of wages and the frequency of invention, as suggested by Hicks.

[7] *Business Week*, May 18, 1968, pp. 72–73; *Economic Almanac, 1967–1968* (New York: Macmillan Co., 1967), p. 164.
[8] *Ibid.*

UNION WAGE MOVEMENTS AND INDUSTRIAL EFFICIENCY

In Chapter 5, we noted that union organization has tended to accelerate the adoption by management of two important wage practices. The first is uniformity in wage rates. This is the result of the spread of multiunit bargaining and of union interest in the stabilization on an industrywide basis of hourly earnings, piece rates, or labor costs. There is now double pressure for uniformity in rates—from competitors and from labor itself. The second practice is simultaneity in wage adjustments. This is a by-product not only of multiunit bargaining but also of the growing importance of leader-follower relationships in wage policies. Company executives tend to feel that wage adjustments should not be given unless other companies are making them at more or less the same time. As a result of these two practices, wage increases tend to occur more or less simultaneously and of a fairly uniform amount in a large number of industries. Obviously, the effect of a wage increase upon efficiency may be quite different when the wage increase takes place in only one firm in an industry and when it occurs throughout an industry. What, then, is the likely effect of these union wage practices on industrial efficiency?

Favorable Effects on Efficiency

The policy of uniformity in wage rates in an industry may hasten the spread of improved methods of production from the more progressive firms to those that are less efficient. In most industries, there are three or four large companies that do the majority of the business and set the pace for the technological development of the industry. According to a recent study, the larger firms in an industry are generally quicker to introduce new techniques than their smaller competitors.[9] If unions compel the smaller firms to pay the same rates as the larger firms, the small companies will have to keep abreast of the latest developments if they are to survive.

Unfavorable Effects on Efficiency

While uniformity in wage rates probably contributes to an improved standard of industrial efficiency, simultaneity in wage increases probably lessens the effectiveness of the stimulus which normally is forthcoming from wage pressure. If wage rates are raised generally in an industry, the individual employer, knowing that his competitors are faced by the same rise in costs as he, is much more likely to attempt to pass on the increased labor costs in the form of higher prices to consumers, in the expectation that competitors will follow a similar course, than if he alone

---

[9] Edwin Mansfield, "The Speed of Response of Firms to New Techniques," *Quarterly Journal of Economics*, Vol. LXXVII (May, 1963), p. 310.

had been compelled to grant a wage increase. Price increases are more likely to follow industrywide changes in wage levels than changes within a single firm, because the average businessman, although he has a fair conception of the demand curve for his individual product, either has no notion of a demand curve for the product of the industry or else assumes that it is inelastic within the relevant range. Thus, simultaneous union wage changes facilitate shifting the burden of higher labor costs to the consumer. To the extent that this is accomplished, the inducement afforded to management to increase its efficiency is lessened; and as a consequence, neither mechanization nor technological changes of other kinds may follow the wage increase. Profits may not be cut at all by the wage adjustment but merely be kept from rising as fast as they otherwise would have in good times.

WAGE CHANGES IN THE ECONOMY AS A WHOLE

We have seen that application of the marginal productivity theory to the problem of wage increases in the individual firm indicates that except in unusual cases of product demand and labor supply, cited on pages 348 and 349, the wage increase will result in a reduction of employment, *other things being equal*. The latter assumption is made to rule out the complications which might otherwise be produced by concurrent changes in the demand for the product or in the state of the arts. As. has already been mentioned, if a wage increase occurs in a firm at the same time as the demand for the product of the firm is growing and output is expanding, there need not be any immediate curtailment of employment. However, if other things remain equal—and if, in particular, we assume that the change in the supply curve for labor does not produce any change in the demand curve for labor—the wage increase will, according to orthodox economic theory, produce some reduction in employment in the individual firm.

When we come to analyze the effect of *general* changes in wage rates upon employment in the economy as a whole, we can no longer realistically assume that "other things will remain equal." The demand curve for labor in the economy as a whole is not independent of the supply curve for labor. Or to put the same proposition in a less technical way, changes in the amount of wages paid to labor as a whole are bound to affect the aggregate demand for labor. General wage adjustments affect the demand for labor because labor is industry's best customer, and if labor has more or less money to spend, the change in such expenditures may alter the total volume of employment in the economy. Furthermore, changes in wage levels throughout the economy will affect the profitability of investment, with the result that employers may increase or curtail their purchases of capital goods. This, too, will affect the total demand for labor in the economy.

Determinants of Aggregate Spending

What determines the volume of spending in the economy as a whole at any given time? Our understanding of this problem owes much to the theoretical analysis of John Maynard Keynes, a British economist, who developed a new approach to this problem in his famous work, *The General Theory of Employment, Interest, and Money*, which was published in 1936.[10] Keynes talks of total spending as "effective demand." Effective demand consists of two types of spending—spending by consumers, which is called consumption, and spending by businessmen for capital expenditures, which is called investment.

According to Keynes, as long as investment and consumption remain constant from one period of time to the next, output and employment also will be unchanged, and a stable level of income will be maintained from period to period, with no tendency to expand or contract. In order to maintain such a steady flow of income through the productive process, the amount of expenditure upon new investment must, according to Keynes, be equal to the amount which people are prepared to save out of their incomes.

For example, suppose that national income is $100 billion and that $80 billion of it is derived from the production of consumer goods, while $20 billion is derived from the production of capital goods. Assume further that consumers are prepared to spend annually $80 billion of their $100 billion income on consumer goods and to save the remainder. The total value of goods produced—both consumer goods and capital goods—is thus $100 billion, while consumers are ready to spend only $80 billion. Under such circumstances, in order to maintain national income at $100 billion in succeeding periods, businessmen must be prepared to spend $20 billion annually on new investment. If interest rates fall and make investment more attractive, businessmen would borrow money from the banks to undertake new investments; and as a result, incomes and employment would expand. The same reaction would occur if consumers were to increase their consumption. But if we assume that consumption and investment remain constant, then income and employment will remain constant from one period to the next.

Effect of a General Wage Adjustment: Special Case

Assume that unions obtain a general increase in wage rates throughout the economy. Assume further that the wage increase has no effect on interest rates or on businessmen's inclination to invest, and no effect on consumption. What effect would the wage increase have on employment? The answer is contained in the assumptions, for, as we have

---

[10] John Maynard Keynes, *The General Theory of Employment, Interest, and Money* (New York: Harcourt, Brace & Co., Inc., 1936).

already observed, if consumption or investment does not change, employment must also remain unchanged. Prices would rise, but output and employment would remain unchanged. A similar result would follow if there were a reduction in wage rates under these restrictive assumptions. In the latter case, there would be a fall in prices, with no alteration in output or employment.

Effect of General Wage Increase upon Aggregate Spending

The foregoing examples of possible reactions to a general wage increase and a general wage reduction are admittedly special cases in the general Keynesian theoretical framework. Keynesian theorists do not maintain that a wage increase will not reduce employment, nor do they contend that a wage reduction will not increase employment. They merely attempt to show by the use of the foregoing type of example that a general wage adjustment need not affect employment at all and that if employment is affected, it is because of the reaction of the wage change upon the real determinants of the volume of employment—namely, the volume of investment and the amount of consumption expenditures. If these variables are affected favorably, so that total spending is maintained or increased, a wage reduction will increase employment, for there will now be the same or a larger aggregate demand to purchase goods whose cost, and presumably price, has been reduced by the wage cut. On the other hand, in the case of a wage increase, employment will increase only if total spending increases more than proportionately to the increase in prices produced by the higher level of costs.

Four possible reactions of total spending may be distinguished as resulting from a general increase in wage rates:

1. The wage increase may expand total spending more than it increases prices. This might be the case if a wage increase were made in times of business depression. Both businessmen and workers might take the wage increase as a signal that business revival was under way and so increase their expenditures. As industry increased its output from very low levels, labor costs per unit of output would tend to decline, and the economies in labor costs resulting from such increase in output might offset the increase in labor costs produced by the wage increase, so that there would be, on balance, little or no increase in unit labor costs or in prices. Under such circumstances the increase in total spending would buy a larger volume of goods and services and thus support a larger volume of employment.

The late Professor Sumner H. Slichter believed that this same result might occur during the upswing phase of a business cycle when general "pattern" wage settlements were involved. It was his belief that when general wage adjustments are made in various key industries at more or less the same time, employers are prone to raise prices because they know their competitors have been saddled with similar increases in cost and are likely to follow suit. Slichter contended that when all or most of the firms in an industry increased their prices, the total amount spent on the product of the industry would ordinarily increase because the demand for the product of most basic industries is inelastic. Therefore, in the short run, expenditures would be increased by customers for the product of the industry; and at the same time, the firms in the industry would be paying out more funds for labor. The combined effect of increased spending from these two sources—given a flexible credit system—might well increase the total amount of spending in the economy more than enough to sustain or increase production at the new higher level of prices.[11]

2. The wage increase may increase total spending no more than it increases prices. Such a situation might develop if a general wage increase were made throughout the economy at a time when output was at high levels and a point of full employment had been attained. Under such circumstances the wage increase would produce a sharp increase in costs and prices, and there would be little or no effect upon employment. The increased spending would, in effect, be dissipated in the form of higher prices.

3. The wage increase may increase total spending, but not as much as it increases prices. When a wage increase occurs during a period of inflation, it frequently causes price adjustments which are greater than the amount which would be required to compensate for the rise in labor costs. Businesses which have been looking for a pretext to raise prices now do so and blame the price rise on "higher labor costs." As a result, even if total spending increases, the rise in the general price level may be so great that the total volume of spending will be insufficient to purchase all of the goods and services offered at the higher price level, and output and employment may therefore decline in particular industries.

4. The wage increase may not increase total spending and may actually diminish it. This could happen if businessmen become alarmed by the rise in costs and prices, and decide to postpone making new investments until prices come down to a more reasonable level. Consumers also may take a similar view. If this attitude of "wait and see" becomes prevalent, total spending may decline despite the higher level of wages, and employment will be reduced as a consequence.

Effect of Wage Increase on Borrowing, Investment, and Consumption

How does a general wage increase bring about a change in total spending? Of primary importance to the Keynesian theorists is the effect of the wage increase upon the rate of interest. When wages rise, businessmen are compelled to increase their working capital to meet larger cash

[11] Sumner H. Slichter, "Labor Costs and Prices," in American Assembly, *Wages, Prices, Profits, and Productivity* (New York: Columbia University Press, 1959), p. 173.

requirements for payment of wages. For a time, the banks will be willing to increase loans without raising the rate of interest; but as the volume of outstanding loans increases, banks will ultimately raise interest rates and tend to become more selective in the borrowers to whom they will lend funds. At this point, the volume of spending will be affected in two ways. In the first place, the rise in interest rates will make certain investments unprofitable. Businessmen will curtail purchase of capital goods, and this will be reflected in smaller wage disbursements to employees in these industries. In the second place, refusal by the banks to loan to particular prospective borrowers because of the general tightening of the credit situation will mean that these businessmen will have to revise their plans and curtail contemplated expansion; and this, too, will be felt in the volume of aggregate spending.

The increase in wage rates may also affect the anticipated profit rate on investment. If the rise in wages increases labor costs, it may increase the number of business failures and produce reduction of output and unemployment in marginal firms. This may have a depressing effect on the business community. On the other hand, if the wage increase is viewed by businessmen as the beginning of a general upswing in wages and prices, the profitability of present investment will be increased, since presumably capital equipment will, in the future, be produced at even higher costs. Thus, businessmen may be induced to expand current expenditures upon investment.

A third possibility is that the wage increase will stimulate consumption. The initial effect of the wage increase may be to increase the size of the wage bill for industry at large. Furthermore, the rise in prices may tend to shift real income from fixed-income groups to wage earners who obtain wage adjustments. Some economists believe that as a result of such a shift, a larger portion of incomes will now be spent and a smaller portion saved than under the former distribution. If so, the wage increase will be felt in a higher level of spending in the market for consumers' goods. On the other hand, some investigations indicate that consumption expenditures are not likely to be significantly affected by shifts in income between various groups. On the whole, it must be admitted that very little is known about the effect of shifts in income on consumption habits of various groups in the community; and therefore it is premature to predict what effect wage increases would have on this variable.

It can be seen from the foregoing analysis that the net result of a wage increase upon the volume of spending and the volume of employment depends in large measure on the psychological effect which the wage increase has on the economy. If it is viewed as the beginning of or part of a sustained upward trend in business, the outcome is likely to be favorable to employment. On the other hand, if businessmen and consumers feel that costs have gotten out of line and defer purchases, the consequences of the wage increase upon employment will be adverse.

Furthermore, the effect of the wage increase upon employment will be more favorable the earlier in a business upturn it occurs. As a boom wears on, the wage increase is more likely to be dissipated in the form of price increases and more likely to produce a rise in interest rates, with a consequent reduction in investment and employment.

Appraisal of Keynesian Approach

Although there is some feeling that the Keynesian theory and its advocates overemphasize the importance of changes in interest rates as a determinant of the volume of employment, there is no doubt that they have made an important contribution to clearer thinking in this field by directing attention to the effect of general wage adjustments upon the volume of total spending. Orthodox theorists tended tacitly to assume that aggregate demand would remain constant whether wage rates increased or decreased. Consequently, they were led to the conclusion that wage increases would produce price increases, reduced output, and contraction of employment. Keynes, however, demonstrated that aggregate demand is capable of expansion and that, as a consequence, it is possible that general wage increases will be reflected in a general increase in the price level, with no reduction in output or employment. Orthodox theorists tended to think in terms of an inelastic supply of money; Keynesian theorists reason in terms of an elastic money supply, which is the product of our modern credit system.

The Keynesian theory and the modern marginal productivity theory are not inconsistent. Each gives us valuable analytical tools to approach the wage-employment relationship from a different point of view and under different circumstances. When we are dealing with macroeconomic problems involving the level of employment in the entire economy, we will find the Keynesian approach more useful, even if we differ with Keynes in his estimate of the effectiveness of the interest rate as a means of stimulating or curtailing investment and employment. On the other hand, when we are concerned with problems in particular firms or even in particular areas—as, for example, in analyzing the effect of minimum wage regulations on southern firms—we shall find the marginal productivity approach more helpful.

WAGE INCREASES AS A RECOVERY MEASURE IN DEPRESSION

An increase in wage rates in one firm will not ordinarily provide a basis for more jobs, since the rise in wage rates simply increases costs without measurably altering the demand for the output of this particular employer. But when wage rates are increased generally throughout the economy, the effect of these increased disbursements upon general consumer demand cannot be ignored. If there are no leakages, and if the banking system expands the quantity of money sufficiently to maintain a higher level of prices without a rise in interest rates, then the rise in wage cost need not reduce employment and may even increase it if the rise in wages and prices is taken as an indication of the end of the deflationary downturn.

In a depression period the existence of unused plant and equipment and the widespread operation of industry at less than optimum capacity may make possible a rise in money wages and employment with a less than proportionate increase in prices. This consideration was one of the motivating factors in the National Recovery Administration program of 1933, which sought to achieve recovery by expanding wage earners' buying power. This program achieved a small increase in real wages from June, 1933, to June, 1935; the index of weekly industrial earnings rose from 70 to 80, while the cost of living index rose from 96 to 107.5. Real wages thus rose from 72.9 to 74.3.[12]

Wage increases will not significantly enlarge consumption expenditures if the employed workers who receive wage adjustments simply save the additional income or use it to pay off indebtedness to banks. Moreover, even if the wage increases increase consumption, they may merely improve the short-term outlook for business without affecting the views of the business community concerning the profitability of long-term investment in heavy plant and equipment. Because wage increases tend to affect short-term rather than long-term expectations, any favorable reaction upon business expenditures is likely to be reflected in increased inventory accumulation,[13] rather than in the purchase of fixed plant and equipment. Consequently, a recovery movement which is generated by increased wages is likely to be extremely susceptible to speculative influences. One reason that the speculative collapse of 1937 produced such a sharp curtailment in production and employment is the fact that long-term confidence had remained weak throughout the abortive boom, as evidenced by the tendency of businessmen to confine their buying of industrial equipment to replacement demands.

On the whole, relatively few economic theorists favor wage increases as a device to achieve recovery in depression. An exception is the school of underconsumptionists, who see in depression the cumulative effect of oversaving; in their view, wage increases are essential to eliminate the prime cause of the collapse of business, namely, the deficiency in consumer purchasing power. However, even granting their argument that it is desirable—and even necessary—to raise *consumption* during depression, this in itself is not enough to assume recovery. It is the propensity to

[12] C. F. Roos, *NRA Economic Planning* (Cowles Commission Monograph No. 2 [Bloomington, Ind.: Principia Press, 1937]), p. 444.

[13] This suggests the possibility that in a unionized economy, cycles in inventory accumulation may become of increased importance, thus giving more substance to the purely monetary theory of the cycle.

spend, not alone the propensity to *consume,* that is the crucial factor in the cyclical process. Spending must be stimulated by *all* groups in the community—by employers as well as by consumers. If every increase in expenditure by consumers were accompanied by a decrease in expenditure by employers, it is clear that no stimulus to business recovery would be imparted by wage increases.

Furthermore, in an economy which depends in part upon exporting to other countries, a general increase in labor costs at a time when other nations are undergoing the painful process of deflation may have a detrimental effect on employment in export industries. In our highly interrelated modern world, depressions tend to be worldwide, and recovery measures in one country must take account of conditions in other countries. If wages and prices are raised in this country at the same time as consumers in foreign countries find their incomes diminished and prices in their own countries reduced, our export industries will be less able to compete in foreign markets. The depressed condition of these industries will therefore be aggravated by the wage increase. In the absence of a concomitant increase in tariffs, our imports will be stimulated because domestic consumers will find that many articles can now be purchased cheaper abroad than at home. This may produce an unfavorable balance of payments and an outflow of gold, which may embarrass the central banking system and cause a tightening in the money supply at the very time when credit restrictions should be relaxed.

WAGE REDUCTIONS AS A RECOVERY MEASURE IN DEPRESSION

Can a reduction in the general level of wages act as a stimulant to start an upturn of employment and investment in depression? Theoretically, a reduction in wage rates might reduce the rate of interest by diminishing the needs of business for cash. The reduction in rate of interest might induce increased investment on the part of businessmen. But if it were believed that all that was needed to achieve an increase in investment was a reduction in interest rates, it would obviously be sound policy to change such rates directly rather than to seek to influence such rates indirectly through a reduction of wage rates.

A reduction in wage rates in key industries may stimulate investment and employment, particularly where rates have gotten out of line in export industries so that such industries have difficulty in competing in the world market. In 1931 in Australia, wage levels were reduced 10% by order of the Commonwealth Arbitration Board, and this wage cut is generally credited with having contributed to Australia's recovery from the depression. Australia's economy is, of course, heavily dependent upon the prosperity of its export industries. To some extent something of the same nature may have occurred in 1921 in the United States when recovery seems to have been materially aided by wage and price reductions which brought our high wartime price structure into alignment with world levels.

However, by and large, wage reductions are not an effective recovery measure because of their tendency to produce anticipations of a further fall in wages and prices and because of their adverse effect upon effective demand. Since the immediate effect of a wage reduction is likely to be a decline in wage payments and consumer expenditures, there must be an immediate compensatory increase in spending by business on inventories or capital goods to prevent a shrinkage in total purchasing power. In periods of depression, however, businessmen typically are in a cautious mood and are unlikely to rush into new investment merely because of a wage reduction. Any savings effected by them in production costs as a result of the wage reduction may simply be used to pay off debt or to build up bank balances. Thus, wage reductions are likely to reduce effective demand yet hold forth little promise of stimulating the rate of investment.

APPRAISAL OF WAGE POLICY AS A RECOVERY MEASURE

This brief discussion serves to indicate that wage policy is not a very effective or convenient recovery measure. In those special situations where wage policy can be utilized, its effectiveness will depend upon the nature of the particular depression and the basic causes of the maladjustments existing in the economic situation. In 1929, for example, wage reductions could not halt the deflation due to bank failures, nor could they raise the depressed level of long-term expectations. On the other hand, in 1920–21, wage reductions did contribute to recovery because the high wages left over from the war inflation were *themselves* a cause of the ensuing depression.

The fact that there is no certainty that employment will be increased if wage rates are reduced or increased in periods of business recession strengthens the case for wage rigidity. Maintenance of wages may be the best way to maintain consumption expenditures. It is important to maintain consumption during depression because experience has demonstrated that new investment is not likely to revive until inventories have been used up, and this process of depletion takes time. In the three years 1933–35, it is estimated that business inventories declined nearly $4 billion[14] (measured in 1929 prices). This represents a considerable disinvestment and indicates the large amount of slack which needs to be taken up before investment is likely to resume. During the intervening period of adjustment, maintenance of wages is desirable to prevent cumulative

[14] Simon Kuznets, *National Income and Capital Formation, 1919–1935* (New York: National Bureau of Economic Research, 1937), p. 40.

contraction. The policy of maintaining wages during depression which was adopted by Sweden in the early 1930's enabled that country to make a quick recovery from the depression. Wages fell less than 5% in Sweden in the worst year of the depression.[15] On the other hand, no country made such drastic cuts in wages and other costs from 1930 to 1933 as the United States, yet no country suffered more intensely from that depression. In the United States, total payrolls in manufacturing, mining, and steam railroads fell by over half from 1929 to 1932.[16]

The severe wage deflation of the Great Depression is not likely to be repeated in the future unless the pattern of our industrial relations undergoes a sharp reversal. Unions characteristically think of wages as income rather than as a cost and consequently have little sympathy for proposals that wages be rendered "flexible" to assist recovery from depression. The experience of the recession in 1938, as well as during the post–World War II period, suggests that the wage rigidity produced by such union attitudes may produce a cyclical pattern characterized by an extremely sharp fall in production and employment as declining demand impinges upon rigid wage costs. On the other hand, if consumer income is maintained by social security, relief, and supplementary unemployment benefit payments, a fairly rapid recovery can be achieved, since the relative stability of costs and prices attributable to maintenance of wage rates prevents the strengthening of deflationary forces.

QUESTIONS FOR DISCUSSION

1. Under what circumstances will a wage increase in a firm have little or no effect upon employment in that firm? Under what circumstances will a general increase throughout the economy have little or no effect on employment in the economy?

2. "The effect of a general wage increase upon employment in the economy as a whole is simply the sum of the effects of wage increases in all the individual firms in the economy." Discuss the validity of this statement.

3. Discuss the various possible effects of union wage pressure on the level of industrial efficiency. Are the consequences of union wage adjustments likely to differ from the effects of a wage increase in a single firm in an unorganized industry?

---

[15] A. Montgomery, *How Sweden Overcame the Depression, 1930–1933*, trans. L. B. Eyre (Stockholm: Alb. Bonniers Boktryckeri, 1938), p. 52.

[16] *Monthly Labor Review*, Vol. LVII (September, 1940), p. 538.

SUGGESTIONS FOR FURTHER READING

EDWARDS, EDGAR O. "Classical and Keynesian Employment Theories: A Reconciliation," *Quarterly Journal of Economics*, Vol. LXXIII (August, 1959), pp. 407–28.

An attempt to reduce Keynesian demand and supply functions to graphic form, and to compare classical and Keynesian theories.

HICKS, J. R. *The Theory of Wages*, chap. vi, pp. 112–35. 2d ed. London: Macmillan & Co., Ltd. 1963.

Statement of the theory which gives major importance to wage pressure as a stimulus to labor saving invention.

KEYNES, JOHN MAYNARD. *The General Theory of Employment, Interest and Money*, chap. xix, pp. 257–71. New York: Harcourt Brace & Co., Inc., 1936.

Statement of the Keynesian theory of the effect of general wage changes.

LESTER, RICHARD A. "Shortcomings of Marginal Analysis for Wage-Employment Problems," in PERLMAN, RICHARD (ed.), *Wage Determination: Market or Power Forces?* pp. 9–30. Boston: D. C. Heath & Co., 1964.

A critical view of marginal productivity analysis which minimizes the relative importance of wage changes on employment.

Chapter
13

WAGES, PRODUCTIVITY, AND INFLATION

According to the Council of Economic Advisers, "The only valid and noninflationary standard for wage advances is the productivity principle. If price stability is eventually to be restored and maintained in a high-employment U.S. economy, wage settlements must once again conform to that standard."[1] Union leaders, on the other hand, refuse to be bound by such a standard and have been successful in obtaining wage adjustments for their membership substantially in excess of the improvement in productivity.

The increase in labor productivity is no longer a matter of mere intellectual interest to economists. It has become a "hot" issue in almost every labor negotiation. It is important, therefore, to understand what is meant by labor productivity and how it is measured. In this chapter, we shall consider in detail the nature of productivity, its interrelationship with wages and prices, and the impact of union wage pressure on inflation.

CALCULATION OF PRODUCTIVITY INDEXES

Statistics of increased productivity are generally referred to as showing the increase in productivity of *labor*. This presentation tends to create the impression that in some way, labor is responsible for the increased output and so is entitled to a lion's share of the gains deriving from increased productivity. Actually, productivity could just as easily be stated in terms of any other factor used in production, such as dollar of capital invested. Productivity is simply a ratio between output measured in specific units and any input factor, also measured in specific units. For example, most drivers are concerned with the number of miles per gallon they get from their automobiles. This is a simple illustration of output—in this case, mileage—measured in terms of a specific input—in this case, gasoline. The same output could be measured in terms of input of tires, or battery, or any of the money, materials, and factors which jointly are responsible for the final output of pleasurable driving. As a matter of

[1] *Economic Report of the President*, February, 1968 (Washington, D.C.: U.S. Government Printing Office, 1968), p. 126.

custom and convenience, however, statistical series dealing with productivity are usually based upon a comparison over time of output in relation to labor input.[2] It is important to recognize that an index relating labor input and output, such as output per man-hour, reflects the combined influence of many variables, including changes in technology, capital investment, rate of plant utilization, managerial efficiency, and scale of operations as well as skill, quality, and effort of the labor force.

The most widely used statistics on productivity are those published by the Bureau of Labor Statistics of the U.S. Department of Labor. The Bureau makes available two series, one measuring productivity in terms of output per hour *paid* and the other in terms of output per hour *worked*. The hours-worked data are derived from a survey of households conducted each month by the Bureau of Census for the Bureau of Labor Statistics. The hours-paid data are based primarily on a monthly BLS survey of establishment payroll records. Theoretically, the difference between the two measures of labor input is equal to paid vacation time and other paid leave. Since the ratio of hours paid for relative to hours worked is continually rising as a result of the extension of fringe benefits, the productivity index based on hours paid will be lower than the index based on hours worked (i.e., the higher the hours input relative to output, the smaller will be the rise in the productivity index). Most economists maintain that hours worked is the proper statistic for purposes of productivity analysis.[3]

As a result of the difficulty in obtaining and combining outputs of varied plants and industries, practically all statistics of productivity depend upon production data derived either by construction of an index of output or by deflation of a value series. The BLS adopts the latter technique and measures output in terms of the *constant dollar value of the goods and services produced* in the private sector of the economy. This means that an estimate must be made of the value of final goods and services produced by the economy, and this figure is then deflated by a price index so as to eliminate the effect of changing prices. The net result, therefore, after such deflation is a figure which, in theory, represents the "real" product of the economy.

Although statistics of labor productivity are frequently carried out to decimal points, they are at best only rough estimates. As one expert puts it: "A reliable growth rate of two significant digits is impossible to establish. Even the first digit is in grave doubt. . . ."[4] Yet, great signifi-

[2] For a clear and concise explanation of the various concepts and terms used in productivity measurement, it is recommended that the student read John W. Kendrick, "Productivity, Costs, and Prices: Concepts and Measurements," in Richard L. Rowan and Herbert R. Northrup (eds.), *Readings in Labor Economics and Labor Relations* (Homewood, Ill.: Richard D. Irwin, Inc., 1968), pp. 473–83.

[3] *Ibid.*, p. 477.

[4] Oskar Morgenstern, "Qui Numerare Incipit Errare Incipit," *Fortune*, Vol. LXVIII (October, 1963), p. 173.

cance is attached in public discussion to the first decimal point in productivity figures, which may indicate that the growth rate is, say, 3.5% rather than 3.1%. It is important to recognize that because of the complexity of our economy and the paucity of accurate statistical data concerning its operation, productivity calculations are from beginning to end based upon estimates, imputation, and intelligent guesswork.

First, the output and man-hour data provide only partial coverage for some industries or categories and require imputations of one sort or another. Second, existing data and techniques do not fully account for changes in quality of goods and services produced. Since price indexes are used to eliminate the effect of price changes during the period studied, the results reflect all of the inadequacies of the price index. Third, there are problems of maintaining consistency between methods of estimating output and labor input as well as between the output per man-hour measures and other economic variables. Fourth, the choice of a particular base year for the weights may have an effect upon the trend. Furthermore, in selecting a time period for study, it is important that the opening and closing dates be at comparable stages of the business clycle, or else the changes sought to be measured may reflect the difference between trough and peak, rather than a meaningful long-term trend. Fifth, there is considerable variation in trends of individual component factors and industries, many differing from the sector trend and the trend for the private economy. Sixth, year-to-year changes in output per man-hour are irregular and therefore not necessarily indicative of long-term trends; similarly, long-term trends are not necessarily applicable to any one year, to any particular group of years, or any period in the future.[5]

The most commonly used statistics of productivity change measure output per unweighted man-hour in the private sector of the economy. These figures are subject to a major distortion resulting from the shift of employment from the agricultural sector of the economy. As was noted in Chapter 1, there has been a long-term trend in the shift of jobs from farm to factory in the United States. This had the effect of increasing the growth in productivity recorded for the total economy, since the nonagricultural sector, with a higher level of productivity than agriculture (though a slower rate of increase), became more important.

According to U.S. Department of Labor calculations, this man-hour shift contributed about one half of a percentage point to the annual rate of increase in productivity.[6] The difficulty with unweighted man-hour output figures, which do not adjust for such interindustry shifts, is that

---

[5] For a description of the difficulties in measuring changes in productivity, see Solomon Fabricant, "Meaning and Measurement of Productivity," in J. T. Dunlop and Vassilii P. Diatchenko (eds.), *Labor Productivity* (New York: McGraw-Hill Book Co., 1964), pp. 12–26.

[6] U.S. Department of Labor, *Manpower Report of the President, 1963* (Washington, D.C.: U.S. Government Printing Office, March, 1963), p. 72.

they have a built-in inflationary bias. For workers normally receive a wage increase when they shift from a low-productivity industry such as farming to a high-productivity industry such as manufacturing. Yet the statistical result of the shift is to raise the average rate of productivity. And if this figure is now used as a guide for future wage increases, the shift itself is used as a justification for another wage increase to all employees in the entire economy!

It is evident that productivity statistics are subject to a whole range of distortions, so much so that they really do not lend themselves to formulations of national wage policy. Productivity has increased, but we really do not know how much, certainly not with the degree of accuracy to determine whether a 3% wage increase is inflationary and a 2.5% adjustment is not.

PRODUCTIVITY TRENDS

If we take a long look back over the past 150 years, it appears that there has been a continuing acceleration in the rate of productivity

FIGURE 13–1

OUTPUT PER MAN-HOUR IN PRIVATE ECONOMY
(1957–59 = 100)

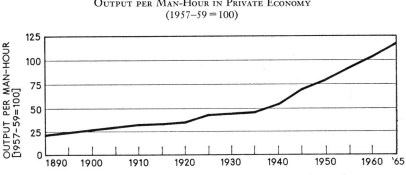

Data: Bureau of Labor Statistics; National Bureau of Economic Research.
SOURCE: Chart by *Business Week*, October 15, 1966, p. 87. By permission of McGraw-Hill, Inc.

improvement in our economy. It has been estimated that during the first half of the 19th century, productivity per man-hour increased about 25%. In the second half of the century, it may have doubled; and in the first half of the 20th century, it almost trebled.[7] Figure 13–1 shows the increasing rate of growth of output per man-hour from 1890 to 1965.

Over the entire postwar period, productivity in the private economy —as measured by output per man-hour—rose at an annual average rate of

[7] Sumner H. Slichter, *Economic Growth in the United States*, ed. John T. Dunlop (Baltimore, Md.: J. H. Furst Co., 1961), p. 44.

3.2%.[8] However, in 1965 and 1966, the increase was only 2.8%[9] while in 1967, the improvement seems to have been only 1.4%.[10] The significance of these percentages can be better appreciated when it is recognized that a growth rate of 2% per year means that output would double in 36 years, while a 3% rate results in a doubling of output in about 24 years.

In manufacturing, the rate of growth of man-hour output has been less than for the entire private economy, primarily because the latter figure reflects the high rate of growth in the agricultural sector. For the postwar period, the annual average rate of growth in productivity for manufacturing was 2.9%, while the rate for the nonfarm sector was 2.6%.[11] Between 1947 and 1966, the volume of production (in constant dollars) in manufacturing more than doubled—it increased by 120%—while the man-hours required to produce these goods increased by less than 25%! Yet, though improved methods of production were saving labor, employment in the nation's factories increased during this entire period by over 21%, about the same as the increase in the entire private sector of the economy.[12]

Growth in output per man-hour varies significantly from year to year. Typically, high rates of productivity gains are registered in the early stages of cyclical recovery when unused human and capital resources are put into use. Thus, in the postwar period, productivity gains were greatest in the recovery years of 1950 (8.2%), 1955 (4.4%), and 1962 (4.7%).[13] The relationship between year-to-year changes in output per man-hour and in capacity utilization (in manufacturing only) is illustrated by the two charts in Figure 13–2.

The annual rate of productivity improvement represents an amalgam of many divergent component changes reflecting the different experience of various sectors and industries in the economy. The pace of productivity advance has been most rapid in agriculture, averaging 5.9% per year, or more than double the rate for the nonfarm sector.[14] Output per production worker man-hour has nearly tripled since 1947 in the synthetic fiber industry, doubled in both the anthracite and bituminous coal-mining industries, increased by approximately 50% in the confectionery, canning, preserving, and freezing, paper and pulp, and basic steel industries, but gained very little in the coke and glass containers industries.[15]

[8] *Manpower Report of the President, April, 1967* (Washington, D.C.: U.S. Government Printing Office, 1967), p. 32.

[9] *Ibid.*, p. 32.

[10] *Economic Report of the President, February, 1968, op. cit.*, p. 51.

[11] Martin Ziegler, "Productivity in Manufacturing," *Monthly Labor Review*, Vol. XC (October, 1967), p. 1.

[12] *Ibid.*

[13] *Manpower Report of the President, April, 1967, op. cit.*, p. 32.

[14] *Ibid.*, p. 33.

[15] Leon Greenberg, "Productivity Measurement for Economic Analysis," in Dunlop and Diatchenko, *op. cit.*, pp. 49–50.

FIGURE 13–2

Output per Man-Hour and Capacity Utilization
(Year-to-Year Percent Changes)

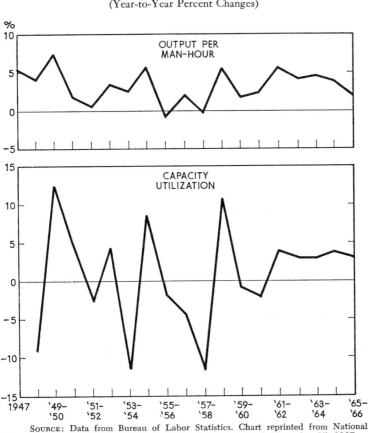

Source: Data from Bureau of Labor Statistics. Chart reprinted from National Industrial Conference Board, Road Maps of Industry, No. 1582, November 15, 1967.

Since the rate of man-hour output increase varies among industries, changes in the industry mix can affect the overall rate of productivity change. In 1967, for example, productivity in the agricultural sector jumped by an amazing 10.5%, while the increase in output per man-hour in manufacturing was only 1%.[16] It is obvious that the low rate of productivity increase scored for the overall private economy in 1967 of 1.4% would have been even lower if agriculture were a smaller part of the total output and employment picture.

Likewise, we have noted that the service industries are growing in importance relative to goods-producing industries. Will this change affect the overall rate of improvement in productivity? Figure 13–3 shows the

[16] *Manpower Report of the President, April, 1968* (Washington, D.C.: U.S. Government Printing Office, 1968), p. 187.

FIGURE 13-3

Postwar Productivity Growth by Industry

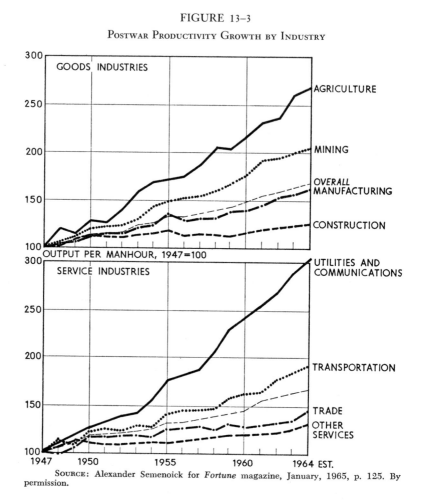

Source: Alexander Semenoick for *Fortune* magazine, January, 1965, p. 125. By permission.

trend in productivity in various goods-producing industries as contrasted with the service industries. It is obvious that one cannot generalize about rates of man-hour output change in either sector. Some service industries show rapid improvement in productivity. Nevertheless, the *Manpower Report of the President, April, 1968* concludes that:

Since these . . . [service-producing] . . . industries generally had low rates of productivity growth and have usually been less amenable to technological change, concentration of employment growth in the service-producing industries has made it that much more difficult to achieve rapid rates of productivity growth for the economy as a whole.[17]

[17] *Ibid.*

The Relation of Productivity and Employment

Increasing productivity is, of course, a manifestation of the dynamic influence of technological change in our economy which over the long run has created more jobs than it has displaced. On the other hand, the year-to-year improvement in productivity has a definite relation to employment which has important implications for governmental policy.

The volume of unemployment in our economy depends upon three major factors:

a) The growth in the labor force.
b) The increase in output per man-hour.
c) The growth of total demand for goods and services.

Changes in the average hours of work are also relevant, though quantitatively less important than the three factors enumerated above. As productivity rises, less labor is required per dollar of total output, or more goods and services can be produced with the same number of man-hours. Consequently, if output does not grow, employment will decline; if output increases more rapidly than productivity (less any decline in average hours worked), employment will rise. But we must also take account of the fact that the labor force is growing each year too. So unless gross national product (the total expenditure for goods and services in the economy, corrected for price changes) rises more rapidly than the sum of productivity increases and labor force growth (modified by the change in hours of work), the increase in employment will be inadequate to absorb the growth in the labor force, and the rate of unemployment will increase. Only when total production expands faster than the rate of labor force growth *plus* the rate of productivity increase and *minus* the rate at which average annual hours fall will the rate of unemployment be reduced.[18]

What does all this mean in concrete terms? The challenge is well stated by Garth L. Mangum:

For the next 15 years the average annual growth of the labor force will be about 1¾ percent. The average annual rate of increase in output per manhour has been 2.8 percent over the postwar period. Leaving aside any question of acceleration in the latter rate, the sum is 4½ percent per year, the rate at which jobs must be created just to keep unemployment from rising above the already excessive level of unemployment. These numbers represent an unprecedented challenge. An economy with a 3 percent historical growth rate

[18] *Technology and the American Economy* (Report of the National Commission on Technology, Automation, and Economic Progress [Washington, D.C.: U.S. Government Printing Office, 1966]), Vol. I, p. 10.

and a 3.5 percent record for the past two decades must suddenly and permanently begin creating jobs at a rate of 4½ percent and above.[19]

In the following chapter, in our discussion of unemployment, we shall consider further the implications of this quotation.

FACTORS AFFECTING GROWTH IN OUTPUT PER MANHOUR

In the long run, improvement in output per man-hour comes primarily from three sources: (1) an increase in the amount of capital per worker; (2) an improvement in the quality of the labor force; and (3) the impact of research and invention. Let us examine each of these factors in turn so as to understand more clearly the manner in which increases in man-hour output are generated in our economy.

Capital per Worker

Contrary to popular conception, productivity does not depend primarily on human effort. The main reason for increased productivity in the United States is the increased efficiency of machine technology. Not only is the machinery which a worker uses today far more efficient than the machinery in use 50 or 100 years ago, but also the amount of capital used per worker has increased tremendously over the years. Capital per production worker in manufacturing rose from $5,188 in 1939 to $21,498 in 1963.[20] Equipment, plant, and total capital stock have risen even faster *per man-hour*—as compared with *per worker*—as a result of the decline in average hours worked by employees.

The ways in which this increased capital investment has manifested itself in our economy are varied and widespread. Since 1947, the number of tractors on farms has almost doubled; dial telephones have increased in our nation from 65% to 98% of all Bell System telephones; diesel locomotives have increased from 15% of total locomotives to 97%; and mechanical loading has taken over all but a minor portion of production in bituminous coal mining.[21] In recent years the wider use of instrumentation and automatic controls and the more extensive use of electronic data processing, as phases of the new and much discussed cycle of automation, have represented a major portion of business capital equipment purchases. First used commercially in 1951, there were over 35,000 general-purpose computers in use by late 1966.[22]

[19] Garth L. Mangum, "The Role of 'Job Creation' Programs," in *Unemployment in a Prosperous Economy*, ed. William G. Bowen and Frederick H. Harbison (Princeton University Research Report Series No. 108 [Princeton, N.J., 1965]), p. 107.

[20] *Economic Almanac, 1967–1968* (New York: National Industrial Conference Board, 1967), p. 276.

[21] *Manpower Report of the President, 1963, op. cit.*, p. 73.

[22] Edgar Weinberg and Robert L. Ball, "The Many Faces of Technology," *Occupational Outlook Quarterly*, Vol. XI (May, 1967), p. 1.

The Quality of Labor

We have seen that there has been a marked reduction in the utilization of unskilled common labor in our modern economy, and, on the other hand, a sharp increase in semiskilled, skilled, and professional and technical jobs. Employment of professional, technical, and kindred workers, who have been by far the fastest growing occupational group during the past decade, may increase at more than twice the average rate for all fields of work between 1960 and 1975.[23] Furthermore, as can be seen from Table 13–1, there has been a continuing improvement in the educational level attained by the average worker. Obviously, better education and higher skills have contributed materially to the increase in manhour output.

TABLE 13–1

PERCENT OF EMPLOYED MEN WHO HAVE COMPLETED FOUR YEARS OR MORE
OF HIGH SCHOOL
October, 1952–March, 1966

	October 1952*	March 1966	Change, 1952–66
All occupations.......................40.1	56.8	16.7
Professional and managerial workers...........71.1	84.1	13.0
Clerical and sales workers....................65.8	74.7	8.9
Craftsmen, foremen and kindred workers........34.0	48.7	14.7
Operatives and kindred workers...............24.3	39.5	15.2
Service workers†............................27.3	44.3	17.0
Laborers, except farm and mine..............16.6	28.4	11.8
Farm workers............................20.7	29.2	8.5

° Excludes persons not reporting years of school completed.
† Includes private household workers.
SOURCE: *Monthly Labor Review*, Vol. XC (June, 1967), p. 42.

Equally significant is the tremendous increase in what one economist calls "brainpower"—or "high-level manpower."[24] For example, in 1965, 539,000 Bachelor's and first professional degrees were awarded—a gain of over 100,000 in just three years and more than 250,000 above the number awarded just 10 years earlier. By 1975, the number of such degrees awarded is expected to reach 900,000![25] These graduates gravitate into positions as engineers, architects, scientists, executives, technicians, teachers, and professional personnel. Over the past 50 years, the increase in such

[23] U.S. Department of Labor, *Employment Projections by Industry and Occupation, 1960–75* (Special Labor Force Report No. 28 [Washington, D.C.: U.S. Government Printing Office, March, 1963]), p. 244.

[24] Frederick Harbison, "High-Level Manpower, Productivity, and Economic Progress," *Labor Productivity, op. cit.*, pp. 322–335.

[25] *Manpower Report of the President, April, 1967, op. cit.*, pp. 167–8.

"high-level manpower" has been about twice as great as the increase in the labor force as a whole.[26] The increase in industry's utilization of such personnel may be due to the high rate of technological innovation in our economy which has created the need for staff and specialized personnel. By the same token, the availability of such "brainpower" has made it possible for industry to utilize more fully the potential created by research and technological change and has therefore contributed to maintenance of a high level of improvement in productivity in our economy.

Research and Development

As we observed in the previous chapter, expenditures for research and development performed by industry have more than doubled over the past 10 years. The number of scientists and engineers engaged in R.&D. work also nearly doubled in the past decade and now stands at more than 450,000.[27] Much of the work performed in research laboratories will not make its influence felt for many years in the future, since a considerable amount of research is basic and theoretical, rather than applied. The expansion of research in recent years is a further guarantee that the improvement in productivity we have witnessed in the past will continue in the future.

ALTERNATE MEANS OF DISTRIBUTING PRODUCTIVITY BENEFITS

Should the gains of increasing productivity be distributed through falling prices or rising money wages? On the whole, reduction in commodity prices would seem by all odds to be the *fairest* method of distributing the benefits of increasing productivity. In large measure, the increasing productivity of labor reflects the combined efforts of the whole community—of savers who contribute the capital equipment, of scientists who pioneer new methods, of entrepreneurs who combine the factors into new and more efficient working teams, and of workers who contribute the skill and brawn to make the technological advances a physical reality. Therefore, if these groups are all to be treated equitably, the increase in productivity representing their joint efforts should be reflected in falling prices, since only in this way can all groups share alike.

Does labor as a group have any special claim to the gains of technological advance that its needs should be given precedence over those of the rest of the community? Labor, as a group, may bear the major share of the inconveniences and dislocations produced by technological change, so

[26] Harbison, *op. cit.*, p. 333.
[27] Leon Greenberg, "Technological Change, Productivity and Employment in the United States," paper read at Conference on the Manpower Implications of Automation, Washington, D.C., December, 8–10, 1964, p. 19.

that a preferential right to the benefits might be claimed as compensation. However, the particular workers who would get preferential treatment would be those who remain employed at the higher wages, while the ones who actually suffer the "inconveniences and dislocations" would find that the buying power of their relief checks would be reduced by the preferential treatment accorded their more fortunate employed brethren. Moreover, labor is not the only group affected by the incidence of technological change. Innovation in one firm may produce bankruptcy in competitors, compelling entrepreneurs to move to other areas to seek new businesses. Similarly, stockholders and bondholders may suffer losses as a result of improved processes in competing firms. Are savers and entrepreneurs also entitled to compensation for the dislocations caused by technological change?

While it is difficult to prove that labor has any special right to the gains of productivity, some defense of distribution in the form of higher money wages is possible on the ground that unless this method is adopted, the full potentialities of technological progress will not be realized. Some economists believe that the greatest stimulus is afforded to new investment, and adjustment to technological progress is facilitated, when the price level remains relatively stable. Such stability of prices could be achieved by raising money wages as productivity increases. Union leaders recommend this policy, arguing that increased wage payments are necessary to stimulate effective demand and to provide a market for the increased abundance of industrial production.

On the other hand, other economists maintain that a slowly falling price level is best designed to increase employment and production. They stress the distinction between *productivity* and *production*. Productivity may increase in an industry, yet production can decrease. This has been the pattern in the coal industry, for example, where labor costs have been driven up so high as to act as a deterrent to increased production, and employment, as a consequence, has been sharply curtailed. Some economists fear that this pattern can be—and, indeed, is presently being—duplicated in our economy, with the result that production is not increasing fast enough to absorb the workers displaced by technological advance.

Actually, when the problem of distributing the gains of increased productivity is viewed as part of the larger problem of maintaining full employment, there may not be a "best way" of distributing the gains of technological progress. A policy that worked well during the decade of the twenties may not produce the same result during the sixties, account being taken of the rigidities in our labor market resulting from union organization and a possible increase in the importance of administered pricing. In this complex area of economic analysis, it must be recognized that the effect of reduction in prices or of rising wages upon production and employment will depend upon the stage of the business cycle, businessmen's anticipations, and other circumstances which vary from time to time.

It should also be mentioned that from the practical point of view, little enthusiasm is generated for the policy of falling prices among the general public. Employees, of course, prefer more money in their pay envelope. To trade this for an expectation that prices may fall in the future is to trade a real and present benefit for something which is conjectural and of indeterminate magnitude. Employers also prefer to do business in an economy which has a slight inflationary bias. Such an economic environment is much more propitious for expansion and for taking risks; falling prices have too often been associated with periods of recession and therefore unconsciously dampen business expectations.

HOW GAINS OF INCREASING PRODUCTIVITY HAVE BEEN DISTRIBUTED

Over the last hundred years the typical adjustment of the American economy to technological advance reflected in rising man-hour output has been in the form of rising money wages rather than through a falling price level. No other price series has risen as rapidly as hourly earnings of labor.

The Long-Term Trend in Real Wages

Real wages have risen more or less continuously in this country for over one hundred years; during most of this time, union organization was either nonexistent or of negligible importance. As Table 13–2 indicates, in the 57 years from 1909 to 1966, average hourly earnings in manufacturing rose from 19 cents to $2.71 while real average hourly earnings almost quadrupled. Real average hourly earnings are money average hourly earnings corrected by an index of the cost of living to take account of price changes.

Table 13–2 shows the trend in hourly earnings and weekly earnings of production workers in manufacturing industries from 1909 to 1966 in terms of "1957–59 dollars." Despite the fact that the price index was more than three times as high in 1966 as in 1909, real hourly earnings had almost quadrupled, with a somewhat smaller gain occurring in real weekly earnings. The fact that real weekly earnings have not risen as fast as real hourly earnings undoubtedly reflects the influence of a shorter workweek and the fact that workers have chosen to take some of the gains of increasing productivity in the form of more leisure time.

Since 1900, real hourly compensation of production workers in manufacturing (average hourly earnings plus fringe benefits deflated by the change in consumer prices) has risen at approximately the same average rate as the average hourly productivity of manufacturing labor. However, the gains of labor extend beyond the increase in purchasing

TABLE 13–2

"REAL" AND GROSS AVERAGE HOURLY AND WEEKLY EARNINGS
OF PRODUCTION WORKERS IN MANUFACTURING INDUSTRIES,
SELECTED YEARS, 1909–66

| | In Current Dollars | | CPI* | In 1957–59 Dollars | |
Monthly Average	Hourly Earnings	Weekly Earnings	1957–59 =100	Hourly Earnings	Weekly Earnings
1909........0.19	9.74	31.3	0.61	31.12	
1914........0.22	10.92	35.0	0.63	31.20	
1919........0.47	21.84	60.3	0.78	36.22	
1929........0.56	24.76	59.7	0.94	41.47	
1933........0.44	16.65	45.1	0.94	36.92	
1939........0.63	23.64	48.4	1.29	48.84	
1947........1.22	49.17	77.8	1.56	63.20	
1948........1.33	53.12	83.8	1.58	63.39	
1949........1.34	53.88	83.0	1.66	64.92	
1950........1.44	58.32	83.8	1.72	69.59	
1951........1.56	63.34	90.5	1.72	69.99	
1952........1.65	67.16	92.5	1.78	72.61	
1953........1.74	70.47	93.2	1.87	75.61	
1954........1.78	70.49	93.6	1.90	75.31	
1955........1.86	75.70	93.3	1.99	81.14	
1956........1.95	78.78	94.7	2.06	83.19	
1957........2.05	81.59	98.0	2.09	83.26	
1958........2.11	82.71	100.7	2.10	82.14	
1959........2.19	88.26	101.5	2.16	86.96	
1960........2.26	89.72	103.1	2.19	87.02	
1961........2.32	92.34	104.2	2.23	88.62	
1962........2.39	96.56	105.4	2.27	91.61	
1963........2.46	99.63	106.7	2.31	93.37	
1964........2.53	102.97	108.1	2.34	95.25	
1965........2.61	107.53	109.9	2.37	97.84	
1966........2.71	112.20	113.1	2.39	99.20	

NOTE: "Real" earnings, represented by gross earnings expressed in 1957–59 dollars, provide a rough indication of the changes in the purchasing ability of money earnings resulting from changes in the prices of consumers' goods and services since 1957–59. Since many of the families have two or more workers, average family incomes exceed average individual earnings.
* Consumer price index of the Bureau of Labor Statistics.
SOURCE: Adapted from National Industrial Conference Board, *Economic Almanac, 1967–1968* (New York: Macmillan Co., 1967), p. 53.

power of hourly earnings; for, concomitant with the rise in earnings, there has been a substantial reduction in working time. Between 1909 and 1967, for example, average annual hours per employee were reduced about 25%. In manufacturing, the average workweek of production workers fell from 51 hours in 1909 to 40.6 hours in 1967. Furthermore, the average number of days worked in a year has declined substantially through longer vacations and more frequent holidays.

Labor's Relative Share in National Income

Has the rise in the price of labor given labor as a group a larger share than other groups in the increased national income? Some economists answer in the negative. They claim that the percentage of national income going to labor has remained relatively constant over a long period of years, except in deep depression. This statistical record has led some economists to conclude that for the material prosperity of labor as a whole, it makes no great difference whether money wages rise swiftly or slowly, or whether labor is organized or unorganized; for—according to these economists—without regard to these factors, labor's distributive share tends to remain fairly constant over time.[28]

Presumably, the mechanism that would produce this result would follow one or the other of the following avenues: (1) Money wages are pushed up and are followed by price increases, with the result that labor does not succeed in improving its position relative to other factors of production. (2) Money wages are pushed up; other prices are not raised correspondingly; and employers suffer a reduction in profits, curtail the use of labor, and substitute capital, with the same result as in (1) above.

Upon analysis, however, it will be found that the statement that labor's distributive share has remained fairly constant is both ambiguous and inaccurate. In the first place, what is meant by "labor's distributive share"? We can compare the share of compensation of employees as a percentage of national income, as a percentage of privately produced income, as a percentage of income originating in corporate business, or as a percentage of income originating in manufacturing, to cite only a few possibilities. It is unfortunately true that an economist starting out with a premise can—in this field, at least—find some series of statistics to support his contentions. As can be seen from Table 13–3, the results shown by the various series are not the same.[29] In the second place, analysis of the two most comprehensive series—relating employee compensation to national income and to privately produced income—indicates that there has been a definite shift in distribution of income to labor over the period studied.

One writer explains this shift as follows:

One important factor has been the change in the relative supplies of labor and capital. The number of man-hours worked has not expanded as fast as population despite the great rise in real hourly earnings, while reproducible capital (in constant prices) has nearly doubled in relation to manhours. The greater responsiveness of the supply of capital to the demands of a growing economy has led to price-induced substitution with existing techniques and probably also to capital-using innovations. The opportunity for factor substitution in this historical rather than in a static sense has been of great practical importance as a built-in stabilizer of relative shares. Aside from relative factor

---

[28] For example, in an article appropriately called "A Law That Cannot Be Repealed," Professor Sidney Weintraub presents statistics purporting to prove that since 1900, American business enterprises have spent roughly 50 cents of each dollar of sales revenue on wages and the remainder on interest, rent, profits, and taxes. See *Challenge*, April, 1962, p. 18.

[29] Robert M. Solow, "A Skeptical Note on the Constancy of Relative Shares," *American Economic Review*, Vol. XLVIII (September, 1958), pp. 618–31.

TABLE 13-3

Share of Compensation of Employees in Various
Income Totals, 1929–63

Year	As Percent of National Income	As Percent of Income Originating in Corporate Business	As Percent of Income Originating in Private Industry	As Percent of Income Originating in Manufacturing
1929..........58.2	74.2	55.6	74.2
1930..........61.9	78.5	59.0	76.7
1931..........66.6	87.9	63.2	88.0
1932..........73.0	101.1	69.3	108.0
1933..........73.6	101.6	69.5	104.7
1934..........70.0	88.1	65.6	89.4
1935..........65.4	83.3	60.8	82.6
1936..........66.1	79.7	61.3	78.3
1937..........65.1	79.7	61.0	78.7
1938..........66.6	82.3	61.8	83.3
1939..........66.1	80.5	61.6	79.9
1940..........63.9	75.8	59.5	73.4
1941..........61.9	72.4	57.6	69.0
1942..........61.9	71.5	56.8	71.1
1943..........64.3	72.0	57.6	73.4
1944..........66.4	73.6	58.8	74.8
1945..........68.0	76.8	59.8	77.3
1946..........65.1	79.5	60.1	78.8
1947..........65.0	77.0	61.3	75.9
1948..........63.1	74.3	59.5	72.8
1949..........64.7	75.4	60.7	73.6
1950..........63.7	73.1	59.8	70.6
1951..........64.6	73.3	60.3	70.5
1952..........66.7	76.2	62.3	74.7
1953..........68.3	77.9	64.2	76.4
1954..........68.8	79.2	64.6	78.1
1955..........67.8	76.5	63.6	74.6
1956..........69.1	78.5	65.1	77.0
1957..........69.6	79.4	65.6	78.1
1958..........70.0	80.7	65.6	80.6
1959..........69.5	78.4	65.3	77.5
1960..........70.8	80.2	66.6	79.6
1961..........70.9	80.6	66.5	80.3
1962..........71.2	80.5	66.7	80.0
1963*..........71.2	80.1	n.a.	n.a.

* Preliminary.
Source: Gertrude Deutsch, *Relative National Accounts* (Technical Paper No. 4 [New York: National Conference Board, 1964]), pp. 19–22.

supplies, shifts in the structure of industry, particularly those involving a diminution in the relative importance of agriculture,[30] have probably operated to

[30] The shift from agriculture to industry has been reflected primarily in a reduction in the number of farm proprietors, rather than hired farm labor. The compensation of owners of unincorporated businesses in agriculture shows up as profits in national accounts. However, when these persons move to jobs in industry as employees of corporations, their compensation becomes part of wages and salaries.

favor the labor share. Rising prices, by adversely affecting the income of rentiers, may also have contributed to the increase in the relative share of labor.[31]

It should also be observed that even if labor received only a constant share in national income, it would be gaining materially relative to other groups, for no other group has achieved greater gains in leisure time than has labor in the past 50 years. It is possible that union organization has proved effective in accelerating the rate at which increasing productivity is converted into leisure as well as in securing for employees various benefits, such as paid vacations, which are not fully reflected in statistics of national income payments.

Effect of Union Organization upon Income Shares

While labor as a group may have increased its share in national income, this does not mean that all groups within labor have fared equally well. If strong unions such as the Steelworkers and the Automobile Workers win large wage increases which set off an inflationary spiral while bank clerks, for example, obtain only small wage increases, the effect may be to redistribute real income from the latter to the former. However, some recent investigations suggest that labor's share of income, industry by industry, has fared no more favorably in unionized industries than in nonunion industries.[32] As a matter of fact, there is some evidence that labor's share of income originating in manufacturing, mining, and public utility industries, where union organization is very strong, has tended to decline over the past 25 years, while the labor share of income originating in finance and services, where unions have made few inroads, has risen.[33] However, the evidence on impact of unions on labor's relative share is inconclusive. Very often, results depend upon the base year used, the selection of industries studied, and similar statistical conditions.

WAGE POLICY AND PRODUCTIVITY CHANGES

What is the "best" relationship between wages and productivity, taking account of the institutional rigidities in our economic system and the objective of avoiding inflation? In 1962, the Council of Economic Advisers adopted so-called "wage-price guideposts" as a standard for the public to use in judging the extent to which private price and wage decisions were consistent with the public interest in a noninflationary econ-

---

[31] Irving B. Kravis, "Relative Income Shares in Fact and Theory," *American Economic Review*, Vol. XLIX (December, 1959), p. 918.

[32] These investigations relate to the share of income, *by industry*. The conclusions do not necessarily apply to the experience of individual members of the labor force.

[33] See Allan M. Cartter, *Theory of Wages and Employment* (Homewood, Ill.: Richard D. Irwin, Inc., 1959), p. 167.

omy. From 1962 to 1967—when the Council ceased recommending a specific percentage figure and simply called for "restraint" in wage changes—the Council suggested a norm for wage adjustments approximating the trend rate for productivity in the economy as a whole, or about 3.2% per annum. The Council recognized that productivity changes vary substantially from year to year and therefore recommended that the trend rate over a number of years be used as the guide for labor and business to follow in their wage negotiations.

In the words of the President's Council of Economic Advisers:

The general guide for noninflationary wage behavior is that the rate of increase in wage rates (including fringe benefits) in each industry be equal to the trend rate of overall productivity increase. . . . The general guide for noninflationary price behavior calls for price reduction if the industry's rate of productivity increase exceeds the overall rate, for this would mean declining unit labor costs; it calls for an appropriate increase in price if the opposite relationship prevails; and it calls for stable prices if the two rates of productivity increase are equal.[34]

Any guide to wage policy, however, must recognize that wages are not only a cost and therefore a determinant of prices, but also a price reflecting the influence of supply and demand in the labor market. The Council of Economic Advisers recognizes this ambivalent role of wages and spells out two circumstances in which variations should be permitted in the general guide in order to permit adjustments in the labor market:

1. Wage rate increases should exceed the general guide rate in an industry which would otherwise be unable to attract sufficient labor or where wage rates have been exceptionally low.
2. Wage rate increases should be less than the general guide rate in an industry which could not provide jobs for its entire labor force even in times of generally full employment, or where wage rates have been exceptionally high.[35]

The rate of productivity change does not bear any necessary relationship to the rate of expansion or contraction in an industry. Therefore a further modification of the general guide is suggested by the Council to take account of movements of capital into or out of an industry:

1. Prices should rise more rapidly or fall more slowly than indicated by the general wage guide in an industry where the level of profits has been insufficient to attract capital required to finance a needed expansion in capacity, or in which costs other than labor costs have risen.
2. Prices should rise more slowly or fall more rapidly than indicated by the general guide in an industry in which the relation of productive

---

[34] *Economic Report of the President, January, 1962* (Washington, D.C.: U.S. Government Printing Office, 1962), p. 189. The "trend rate" is the annual average percentage change in output per man-hour during the latest five years.

[35] *Ibid.*

capacity to full-employment demand shows the desirability of an out-flow of capital, or in which costs other than labor costs have fallen, or where excessive market power created a higher rate of profit than can be earned elsewhere on an investment of comparable risk.[36]

It should perhaps be observed that the statement that wage rates should rise at the same pace as man-hour output does not mean that the entire increase in man-hour output should go to labor. If this result were to follow, nothing would be left over to pay a return on the increased amount of capital used to produce the increased output. An example will make this clear. Suppose that employee compensation for the economy as a whole averages $2 per hour and that the value of output per hour averages $3. Suppose that over a period of years, average output per hour rises to $4. If wages are to rise at the same rate as man-hour output, they should rise by one third—from $2 to $2.67 per hour. If wages rose by $1 an hour, equal to the full value of the increase in output per hour, the dollar amount of profits and interest per hour's work would be unchanged. This would mean that the return of capital per unit would actually fall, since the amount of capital used per hour has tended to increase over time and is perhaps the major factor responsible for increasing productivity. It is obvious, therefore, that if labor were to attempt to appropriate for itself the entire increase in man-hour output, there would be little point in investing additional capital in business. Capital formation would be dis-couraged, and the ultimate result would be a decline in investment and a diminution in job opportunities.[37]

The experience with the wage-price guideposts indicate the diffi-culty in controlling wages through voluntary restraints as pressures build up in the latter part of a boom period. From 1962 to 1964, unemployment in the nation averaged close to 4 million persons. Against this backdrop, the guideposts, together with White House pressure, had some success in holding down the rate of advance in wage rates. Thus, in 1965 the United Steelworkers, after a call from the President, settled their wage dispute for about 3.5%, or very close to the wage-price guideline. In 1966, however, unemployment dropped below 3 million, and the pressures in the labor market blew the lid off voluntary restraints. A succession of strikes resulted in settlements substantially in excess of the guidelines, with the railroad shopcrafts, for example, winning adjustments of 5.6%. By 1967, the Council of Economic Advisers ceased recommending any specific figure and merely called for restraint, but the plea fell on deaf ears. In that year the United Auto Workers scored a 6% gain in wages, and in 1968 the

---

[36] *Ibid.*

[37] Committee for Economic Development, *Defense Against Inflation*, A State-ment on National Policy by the Research and Policy Committee (New York, 1958), p. 59.

target was even higher, with the Communication Workers of America gaining wage increases averaging about 6.5% over three years.

The value of the wage-price guideposts is a much debated issue among economists, labor leaders, and businessmen.[38] Some believe that popularization of the notion that wages should advance in line with productivity simply established a minimum for wage demands, while strong unions were able to build upon this and bargain additional amounts above the minimum to which they felt their membership was entitled. Others feel that the guideposts focused public attention and discussion on a crucial issue and may have led both labor and management to temper wage and price decisions made during this period. Still others contend that the guideposts were never expressed in terms that were meaningful to negotiators at the bargaining table and that the complexities of "package" bargaining cannot be contained in a single overall percentage figure.

Wage Guideposts and Foreign Trade

Even if it were determined that, say, 3% wage increases per year were noninflationary in our domestic economy, the merit of such upward adjustments would still have to be appraised in the light of our position in foreign trade. The United States has had a balance-of-payments deficit almost continuously since 1950. The result has been a massive drain on our gold supply, which from a high of some $23 billion in the early 1950's has dwindled to about $12 billion today. This loss of gold together with other unfavorable factors in our fiscal policy has led to a loss of confidence in the dollar, which precipitated a major crisis in the international monetary community in early 1968.

If we are to stop the alarming drain on our gold, we must make it more attractive for foreign nations to buy our product, and we must enable our manufacturers to compete more effectively in world markets. Since early 1967, it appears that our unit labor costs have been rising at a rate probably exceeding that of most European countries.[39] If this trend continues, it will further aggravate our balance-of-payments problem.[40] As can be seen from Figure 13–4, the trend in our net export balance has been steadily downward since 1965.

---

[38] See, for example, John Sheahan, *Have Guideposts Helped to Stabilize the Economy?* (Brookings Institution Research Report No. 75 [Washington, D.C., 1967]); Robert M. Solow, "The Wage-Price Issue and the Guideposts," in F. H. Harbison and J. D. Mooney (eds.), *Critical Issues in Employment Policy* (Princeton University Research Report No. 109 [Princeton, N.J., 1966]), pp. 57–74.

[39] *Economic Report of the President, February, 1968, op. cit.,* p. 177.

[40] Obviously, the problem of exports versus imports is only one part of the overall problem of the balance of payments deficit. The Vietnam war, investment abroad by U.S. Corporations, travel abroad by U.S. citizens—all of these factors have also contributed to the present crisis. See *Economic Report of the President, February 1968,* Table 26, p. 167, for a breakdown of the various elements entering into the overall deficit in balance of payments.

FIGURE 13-4

U.S. NET EXPORTS 1964-67*
(In Billions of Current Dollars at Seasonally Adjusted Annual Rates)

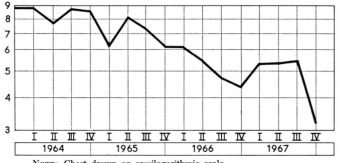

NOTE: Chart drawn on semilogarithmic scale.
* Reprinted from *The National Economy and the Vietnam War* (New York: Committee for Economic Development, 1968), p. 22.
SOURCE: U.S. Department of Commerce, Office of Business Economics, *Survey of Current Business.*

THE LABOR DILEMMA

If money wage rates generally rise at the same rate as man-hour output in the economy as a whole, prices will tend to be stable. A corollary of this policy would be the freezing of the shares of the various factors of production in their present ratios. Organized labor in this country has clearly stated its opposition to any such restriction on labor's future progress. In the words of Walter P. Reuther: "A healthy balance between capacity and demand requires a shift in the present distribution as between labor income—wages and salaries—and non-labor income—profits, interest, and the like. Wages and salaries, at least in the immediate future, must increase faster than our normal potential for increasing productivity."[41]

In other words, the wage guides are not acceptable to organized labor. Nor does business and labor generally seem ready to live by these rules. Major union settlements in 1967 provided wage and benefit increases averaging about 5½% a year over the life of the contracts, while average hourly compensation in the entire private economy increased by 6%.[42] Even if new collective bargaining settlements reached in 1968 should again average 5½% (which now appears too conservative in view of recent settlements), the rise in average hourly compensation for the

[41] Report to the United Automobile Workers' convention, Atlantic City, N.J., May 6, 1962.
[42] *Economic Report of the President, February, 1968, op. cit.,* p. 125. The two rates of increase are not strictly comparable. Average compensation reflects new and continuing contracts in organized sectors as well as all compensation in non-union areas; it also reflects changes in employers' contributions for social insurance. Moreover, it is influenced by shifts in the composition of the labor force.

economy as a whole would be appreciably larger than in 1967. One reason is that the second- and third-year provisions of contracts negotiated in 1966 and 1967 will provide larger increases on the average, in 1968, than were inherited in 1967 from similar provisions of earlier contracts. The tempo of wage adjustments in the economy will also be affected by the 14% increase in the minimum wage which went into effect in 1968. The latest minimum wage adjustment will probably have an even greater impact than did the 1967 increases, which mainly restored the minimum wage to a more typical relationship with the average wage level in the economy.

We have seen from our earlier discussion in this chapter that current increases in man-hour output are well below the trend rate and in 1967 amounted to only 1.4%. If wages continue to rise by about 6% per year while productivity advances at only 1.5% to 2.0%, we can expect prices to rise in the neighborhood of 4% per year—substantially more than the rate of price inflation we experienced in the first part of the 1960's. Figure 13–5 shows the trend in the Consumer Price Index from 1960 to 1967. Of equal significance is the fact that the Industrial Price Index, which remained relatively level from 1961 to 1965, rose sharply in the following three years.

The inflationary impact of large wage adjustments is augmented by the fact that our economy is operating at a high level of employment and at the upper reaches of its capacity. Industrial operating rates have climbed to the highest peak since 1953 suggesting that some firms have been compelled to start using antiquated and high-cost plant and equipment. Unemployment also continues at a low rate for the economy as a whole which inevitably means that labor shortages, particularly of skilled and technically trained personnel, and the employment of less qualified workers will add a further impetus to the upward movement of costs. Figure 13–6 indicates dramatically how unit labor costs have sharply risen in 1966 and 1967. The significance of this rise is highlighted by the fact that from 1960 to 1966 unit labor costs in manufacturing had been relatively stable.

Our economy, therefore, faces a dilemma. As a nation we have as objectives two goals which may not be compatible: full employment and price stability. In 1967, there were almost 3 million persons unemployed in our country. Furthermore, millions more were underemployed and were denied the benefits of full-time employment. Any massive governmental efforts to reduce hard-core unemployment, to cut down the idleness of our teen-agers and the poverty and despair in our ghettoes, can only be accomplished through the expenditures of vast sums of money which will add fuel to the fires of inflation. On the other hand, if through price regulation (without wage regulation) our government were to attempt to set a ceiling on prices, or if governmental fiscal and monetary policy drastically curbs consumer, business, and government expenditures, we

FIGURE 13–5
CONSUMER PRICE INDEX 1960–67*
(1957–1959 = 100)

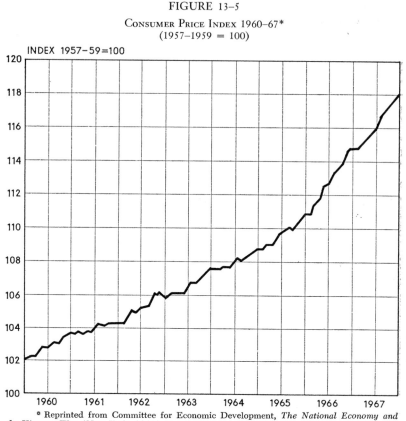

* Reprinted from Committee for Economic Development, *The National Economy and the Vietnam War* (New York, 1968), p. 18.

SOURCE: U.S. Department of Labor, Bureau of Labor Statistics, *Monthly Labor Review;* U.S. Department of Commerce, Office of Business Economics, *Business Statistics,* 1967.

may be able to stabilize prices but will probably put an end to the present boom. The result may well be a downturn in production and employment.

Theoretically there is a "trade-off" relationship between a given rate of price increase and the rate of unemployment. To quantify what must be given up in price stability to achieve a given reduction in unemployment, economists have devised what has come to be called the "Phillips curve." This curve is named for Professor A. W. Phillips, who about 10 years ago attempted to trace the relationship between price changes and unemployment rates in Great Britain. Figure 13–7 shows a theoretical Phillips curve for the American economy together with an attempt to fit actual data for the years 1954 to 1966 to the theoretical curve. As can be seen from the figure, the actual correlation is not very close.

The curve on the left—which was drawn by the Commerce Department's Office of Business Economics—suggests that if we want price

FIGURE 13-6

AVERAGE HOURLY EARNINGS, OUTPUT PER MAN-HOUR,
AND UNIT LABOR COSTS IN MANUFACTURING*

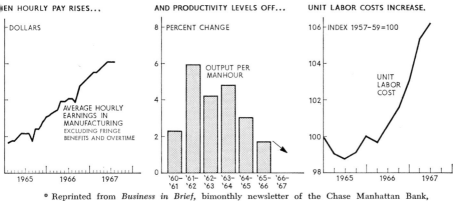

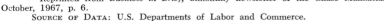

° Reprinted from *Business in Brief,* bimonthly newsletter of the Chase Manhattan Bank, October, 1967, p. 6.

SOURCE OF DATA: U.S. Departments of Labor and Commerce.

increases which would inflate real gross national product by only 1%, we would have to accept an unemployment rate of 6%. On the other hand, a 3% jobless rate would generate inflation, as measured by the so-called Gross National Product Deflator—of about 3.1% per year.[43] It should be emphasized that the so-called curve is purely a conceptual tool. To the

FIGURE 13-7

PHILLIPS CURVE: THEORETICAL AND IN RELATION
TO DATA FOR YEARS 1954–66*

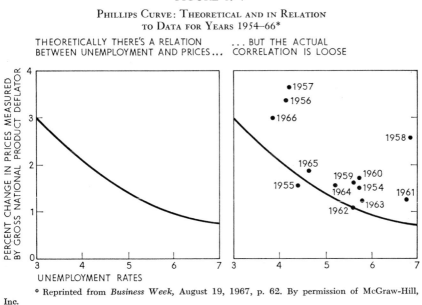

° Reprinted from *Business Week,* August 19, 1967, p. 62. By permission of McGraw-Hill, Inc.

SOURCE OF DATA: Commerce Department; Labor Department.

[43] *Business Week,* August 19, 1967, p. 67 .

extent that such a relationship exists, it is not immutable and can be changed. The objective of our national policy should be to reduce the job-price trade-off so that more progress can be made in reducing unemployment with a minimum increase in prices. This calls for elimination of structural imperfections in the labor market, improving the mobility of labor, providing better training for new additions to the labor force and for the hard-core unemployed, and similar constructive measures.

UNIONS AND WAGE INFLATION

Much of the discussion on the wage-price-inflation issue tends to cast unions as villains of the piece. The reasoning is that if it were not for union bargaining strength and their "exorbitant" wage demands, wage rates would not be pushed up as fast, and therefore the dilemma with its unpalatable consequences would never have to be faced. There are really two logical steps in this reasoning which require examination. First, is it true that unions make wage rates higher than they would otherwise be? Second, to what extent is price inflation the result primarily of cost-push or of demand-pull factors?

Do Unions Accelerate the Rise in Wage Levels? Negative View

Those who contend that unions have not caused wage rates generally to rise any faster than they would have in the absence of union organization emphasize that changes in wage rates, like changes in prices, are simply the reflection of more fundamental developments in the underlying forces which determine supply and demand in the marketplace. They claim that the sharp increases in money wage rates which occurred in the post–World War II period and are recurring now are the result of the increase in the supply and velocity of money which made itself felt through an expanding demand for goods of all kinds. The growth of consumer credit, large expenditures upon plant and equipment, high farm incomes, rising governmental expenditures, and similar circumstances contributed to the inflation, which in turn produced a shortage of labor and high wage rates.

Exponents of this "demand-pull" theory of inflation concede that the wage-price spiral was a contributing cause of the inflation in the post–World War II era, but they also maintain that it was not the sole cause or even a sufficient cause to explain the degree of price inflation that occurred. Furthermore, they contend that unions were not necessarily responsible for the behavior of wages during this period. Thus, Walter A. Morton, speaking of the immediate post–World War II period, concludes that "there is no reason to believe that prices would have risen less even if labor unions had been weak or nonexistent."[44] In the postwar setting,

[44] Walter A. Morton, "Trade Unionism, Full Employment and Inflation," *American Economic Review*, Vol. XL (March, 1950), p. 26.

unions were, in this view, "simply thermometers registering the heat, rather than furnaces producing the heat."[45]

Factors Inflating Demand in the post–World War II Era

The years following the end of World War II were unquestionably years of expanding demand. An important reason for the upsurge in demand was the backlog of needs which could not be satisfied during the war years. With the end of restrictions on supply, consumers rushed to purchase automobiles, television sets, houses, and other things which they had been unable to obtain during the war years. Most consumers and businesses came out of the war with relatively large balances of liquid assets and relatively small debts, so that there was enough money in the economic system to finance the increased expenditures which both consumers and businessmen wished to make. As liquid assets were used up, debt increased in order to maintain the high rate of expenditures. There was a rise of $324 billion, or nearly 75%, in the total net public and private debt between 1948 and 1958. Furthermore, the velocity and the supply of money rose rapidly during this period. Another major factor stimulating demand was government spending which, after a temporary decline at the end of World War II, rose steadily during most of this period. From 1947 to 1957, government purchases of goods and services rose 203% while private expenditures rose only 71%. State and local government expenditures increased by almost as much as federal purchases.[46]

Since the immediate postwar decade, the growth in money supply has continued—in the past two years at an accelerated rate (see Figure 13–8). Government programs, whether they be in the form of aid to disadvantaged groups or simply an increase in the statutory minimum wage, have been creating new consumers whose purchasing power has added to the inflationary spiral. Consumer income went up from $228 billion in 1950 to $497 billion in 1964, an increase of 118% or a little more than 5% per year compounded. In 1964, the rate of increase was almost 7%; in 1965, 8%; in 1966, 8.4%; and in 1967, almost 11%.[47] In view of the fact that output in the private economy has been increasing only at an annual rate of 5.7%, it is apparent that a continuation of the current rate of increase in consumer purchasing power will add further impetus to the upward movement of prices. It is understandable, therefore, why many economists and most union leaders minimize the importance of wage

---

[45] Milton Friedman, "Some Comments on the Significance of Labor Unions for Economic Policy," in David McCord Wright (ed.), *The Impact of the Union* (New York: Harcourt Brace & Co., Inc., 1951), p. 39.

[46] Committee For Economic Development, *Defense Against Inflation, op. cit.,* p. 23.

[47] Hayden Stone, Inc., *Monthly Investment Letter,* February, 1968, p. 3.

FIGURE 13-8

U.S. CURRENCY AND DEMAND DEPOSITS, 1960–67*

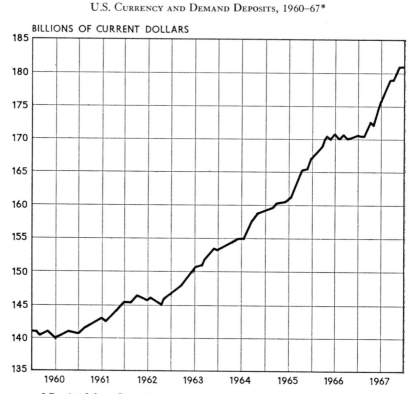

BILLIONS OF CURRENT DOLLARS

* Reprinted from Committee for Economic Development, *The National Economy and the Vietnam War* (New York, 1968), p. 19.

SOURCE: Board of Governors of the Federal Reserve System, *Federal Reserve Bulletin;* U.S. Department of Commerce, Office of Business Economics, *Business Statistics,* 1967.

pressure as a cause of inflation and point instead to the "demand-pull" aspect of the economic situation.

Wage Gains among Unorganized Workers

We have spoken earlier of unions being mere avenues through which inflationary forces transmit their impact to wages and prices. In support of this position, it may be observed that money wage rates seem to have risen as fast, if not faster, in previous periods of inflation, when union organization was a negligible factor in the labor market. For example, in the period from 1917 to 1921, organized labor represented less than 12% of the labor force, as contrasted with 25% in the post–World War II period. Yet increases in money wage rates generally in these two postwar periods of inflation were strikingly similar.

Another illuminating comparison is provided by the steel industry. Workers in this industry actually made larger percentage gains in money and real hourly earnings during the period 1914–20, when union organization was negligible, than during the period 1939–48, when the CIO United Steelworkers spearheaded a drive for wage increases in the industry.[48]

That union organization is not necessary to give workers large increases in money wages if the necessary basic factors are present—high demand for labor and/or shortage of labor supply—is illustrated by a comparison of the gains in the form of wage and salary payments received on an annual basis by employees in largely organized, as compared with employees in largely unorganized, sectors of the economy. Annual wage and salary payments received per full-time employee in manufacturing in 1965 were 119% of the 1960 level; the comparable figure for health services was 120%; for retail trade, 117%; and for banking, 118%.[49] Examination of occupational averages of nonmanufacturing industries for February, 1961, to February, 1967, indicates that wages have risen most rapidly in the relatively low-paying, largely unorganized service industry group.[50] Those who have sought to acquire a maid, or anyone, male or female, to perform housework, can attest to the fact that without the aid of union organization domestic servants have probably achieved greater gains in hourly wages than Reuther's automobile workers!

Indeed, it can be argued that rather than accelerating increases in the wage level, union organization has inhibited such increases, primarily through the lag produced by the term of existing union contracts. Union wage adjustments, as a consequence, tend to follow rather than lead nonunion wage adjustments in the upturn of the cycle.

DO UNIONS ACCELERATE WAGE INCREASES?
AFFIRMATIVE VIEW

A number of economists have concluded that unions do push up money wages to a level higher than that which would exist in a nonunion economy. H. Gregg Lewis, for example, concludes that in recent years the average union/nonunion relative wage was approximately 10%–15% higher than it would have been in the absence of union organization.[51] Albert Rees concludes that "strong American unions seem to be able to raise the relative earnings of their members by 15 to 25 per cent."[52] These and other economists argue that it would be surprising if unions did not have this effect in view of the fact that the principal purpose of the trade-

---

[48] Albert Rees, "Postwar Wage Determination in the Basic Steel Industry," *American Economics Review*, Vol. XLI (June, 1951), p. 400.

[49] *Economic Almanac, 1967–1968, op. cit.*, pp. 80–81.

[50] *Monthly Labor Review*, Vol. XCI (April, 1968), p. 48.

[51] H. Gregg Lewis, *Unionism and Relative Wages in the United States* (Chicago: University of Chicago Press, 1963), p. 5.

[52] Albert Rees, *The Economics of Trade Unions* (Chicago: University of Chicago Press, 1962), p. 77.

union movement is to influence the level of money wage rates. Unions have compelled many companies to accept conditions which management opposed, such as the union shop and the closed shop. It would seem strange if their bargaining power could not also compel management to accept wage levels above those that management would voluntarily establish for nonunion employees.[53] Evidence of the ability of unions to force such high wage levels on employers is found in the history of the many employers in the coal, hosiery, cotton textile, garment, and shoe industries who were forced out of business because the union compelled them to pay wages above the nonunion scale.

Have wages simply been chasing prices up, or have wages been pushing prices up? A number of economists contend that given conditions in the market favorable to the exercise of union bargaining power, union organization results in a greater inflation in wages and prices than would occur in a nonunion economy. The following are some of the reasons advanced in support of this contention:

1. First and foremost is the dominant position of labor unions in our key industries. Between 80% and 100% of employees are under union contracts in the aluminum, steel, coal and metal-mining, automobile and automobile parts, agricultural equipment, rubber products, shipbuilding, building construction, longshoring, railroad, and trucking industries. With such complete control of the labor force in these industries, unions are in a position to exact higher rates than would be the case in a free labor market. Furthermore, since bargaining tends to be on a multiunit basis, all or most of the employers of the industry have their labor costs raised more or less simultaneously. As a result, there is a natural inclination to raise prices, since each producer knows that his competitor "is in the same boat" and will welcome a chance to pass on increased costs to consumers.

It is significant, too, that the industries in which unions are strongest are key industries from which wage and price changes fan out rapidly in the entire economy. As one writer has put it: "Strong textile unionism and weak auto unionism would produce a different wage atmosphere."[54] Economists who believe that unions create an inflationary bias in wage changes stress the fact that a comparison of the size of wage changes in union and nonunion companies will not reveal a significant differential, because it is well known that nonunion companies, in order to avoid union organization, keep their wages abreast of, and frequently exceed, wage adjustments being made in organized firms in their particular industry.

[53] Sumner H. Slichter, "Do the Wage-Fixing Arrangements in the American Labor Market Have an Inflationary Bias?" in Richard L. Rowan and Herbert R. Northrup (eds.), Readings in Labor Economics and Labor Relations (Homewood, Ill.: Richard D. Irwin, Inc., 1968), p. 460.

[54] Lloyd G. Reynolds, "Structural Determinants of Cost Inflation and Remedial Measures," Monthly Labor Review, Vol. LXXXII (August, 1959), p. 873.

2. In the second place, in a highly unionized economy, key wage bargains are spread rapidly from one industry to another, even though supply and demand conditions within the "follower" industries may not justify the same increase as that granted in the "leader" industry. Union workers are strong believers in uniformity of wages—that is, uniformity with the highest wage rate paid. This is particularly true where members of one international union may be employed in a number of industries. If a profitable firm in one industry employing members of a particular union gives a large wage adjustment, the cry immediately goes up from the membership to obtain the same increase for all members of the union. Whereas, in a nonunion economy, wage adjustments are likely to spread gradually by affecting local supply and demand conditions, and to vary in size depending upon the profitability of the particular firm and local conditions, in a unionized economy key wage adjustments jump rapidly from one industry to another. Union business agents learn of increases won by other unions and incorporate the same size demands in their own wage negotiations, regardless of the differences in cost and demand conditions which may prevail in the particular firms with which they bargain. Thus, it is possible that wage increases may spread more rapidly and may be more likely to produce price increases in a unionized economy than in a free labor market.

3. Events indicate that unions will press for further advances in wage rates even when profits are declining and unemployment is growing in the economy or in an industry. Wages rose in each of the years 1949, 1954, and 1958, despite falling demand for labor and relatively high unemployment. There is considerable evidence that wage increases under trade-unions are less sensitive to the existence of high unemployment than under nonunion conditions.[55] One investigator found that the relation of wage changes to varying levels of unemployment was stronger in the period prior to 1930 than in the last 20 years. Inasmuch as unionism has played a more important role since World War II than before 1930, "trade unions would appear to have made wage increases less sensitive to unemployment than under the essentially nonunion conditions during the first 30 years of the century."[56] While there is room for disagreement as to the influence of unions on the level of money wage rates in periods of rapid expansion, there seems to be little doubt that unions hold up wages in periods of severe contraction and, in fact, tend to push up wages in the early stages of business contractions.

4. The existence of union contractual arrangements with employers

---

[55] See, for example, Robert R. France, "Wages, Unemployment and Prices in the United States, 1890–1932, 1947–1957," *Industrial and Labor Relations Review*, Vol. XV (January, 1962), pp. 171–90; and Kenneth M. McCaffree, "A Further Consideration of Wages, Unemployment, and Prices in the U.S., 1948–1958," *Industrial and Labor Relations Review*, Vol. XVII (October, 1963), pp. 60–74.

[56] McCaffree, *op. cit.*, p. 60.

was until recently a factor which on the whole retarded the wage-price spiral by producing a minimum time lag during which wage rates could not be negotiated. The stabilizing effect of such contracts has, however, been offset by two developments. The first is the inclusion in union contracts of cost-of-living escalator provisions. Whereas, previously, the cost of living had been merely one of the many factors which entered into wage negotiations, under escalator provisions, there is a direct and automatic relationship between wage rates and the cost of living. The second is incorporation of an "annual improvement factor" in union contracts, guaranteeing the members of the bargaining unit a minimum increase based upon supposed increases in productivity. The combined effect of these two developments tends to make union contracts into inflation-producing documents.

The Effect of Cost-of-Living Provisions in Union Contracts

Do escalator clauses in union contracts *cause* inflation? The answer would seem to be no. Considered alone, cost-of-living adjustment clauses do not initiate inflation, but they can *intensify* an inflationary trend attributable to other factors. As one economist puts it: "Escalator clauses appear more likely to feed a monetary or fiscal inflation than to initiate one. There seems to be little question, however, that wage escalation would act to aggravate an existing inflation due to these forces. By reducing or eliminating the normal time lag in making wage adjustments, a barrier to spiraling incomes and labor costs would be lowered."[57] Whereas wage rates are most commonly negotiated annually in the absence of long-term agreements, wages are frequently adjusted quarterly pursuant to cost-of-living clauses in long-term contracts. Furthermore, the very existence of escalator clauses in labor contracts in key industries may increase the inflationary expectations of employers and labor in other sectors of the economy, and thus result in larger wage settlements than might otherwise be arrived at.

Assume, for example, that the cost-of-living index goes up as a result of an increase in farm prices. The result may be a wage increase for a million workers. This wage increase can, in turn, result in widespread price increases. Then, by the time the next quarter comes around again, a sufficient round of price increases may have been created so that another cost-of-living wage adjustment will be justified under the contract. This cumulative relationship proceeds on a quarterly basis and offsets the tendency of many businesses to let prices alone except when they are jolted by large increases in cost, such as may be produced by a large wage adjustment. To put the matter another way, frequent cost-of-living adjustments jar industry into frequent price increases, which intensify the upward wage-price spiral.

[57] Jules Backman, "Wage Escalation and Inflation," *Industrial and Labor Relations Review*, Vol. XIII (April, 1960), p. 405.

Wage increases resulting from escalator clauses generally take place in manufacturing industries and therefore affect the prices of manufactured goods. When such prices rise, the cost of goods purchased by the farmer tends to rise, which in turn produces an increase in the price for farm products. To the extent that farm prices rise as a result, there will be a tendency for the consumer price index to rise, since food accounts for about one third of the index. And once the consumer price index rises, the stage has been set for another increase in wages under escalator provisions in industry.

The inflationary potential of escalator clauses has been recognized by many foreign countries since the end of World War II, and many governments—among them Chile, France, Australia, Austria, Belgium, Norway, Denmark, Sweden, and Finland—have taken steps either to prohibit this type of automatic wage adjustment or to restrict it in order to lessen its tendency to feed inflationary forces. In this country, limitations on escalator clauses have been introduced primarily at the insistence of management in collective bargaining agreements. Business must have known costs in order to project prices and production for the future. An open-end escalator clause introduces an element of uncertainty into management planning which businessmen have been trying to avoid by placing ceilings or other limitations on cost-of-living adjustments in labor contracts.

Unions and Cost-Push Inflation

Even if we assume that unions do accelerate the rate of increase in wage levels in our economy, does this necessarily mean that they are a primary moving factor in causing inflation. Is the inflation cost induced?

Many economists and businessmen stress this point of view. For example, in a recent address Roger M. Blough, chairman of the board of the United States Steel Corporation stated:

. . . since employment costs—direct and indirect—account for three-quarters of all costs in the economy as a whole, they have been a major force in pushing consumer prices up at an annual rate of 4 per cent since last spring. . . . So today we find ourselves caught in another serious round of wage-push inflation—a phenomenon that has been with us almost continually ever since the Wagner Act—passed more than 30 years ago—conferred upon labor what Arthur Krock has described as the "unique statutory power to raise the costs of production virtually at will."[58]

How do wage increases affect prices? Wages have two dimensions. In the first place, they are the principal component of the income stream. Therefore, a rise in wage rates usually adds additional dollars to demand in the marketplace without an immediate offset in terms of an increase in the

---

[58] Address before Student Legal Forum, University of Virginia Law School, December 4, 1967.

supply of goods and services. As a matter of fact, some proponents of the cost-push theory maintain that the *only* way an expansionist monetary policy can materially affect prices is through increasing the dollars in pay envelopes, for the pay envelopes of employees are the major circuit which can transmit injections of money and credit into the income stream.

In the second place, wages are the major cost of production in industry. To the extent that the rate of increase in wages exceeds the rate of advance in productivity, unit labor costs rise and price increases are likely to follow. Many industrial products are priced by the manufacturer even before they are produced; an increase in *anticipated* costs of production can therefore lead to an immediate increase in prices even before the higher wages have had an effect upon the income stream. Finally, the knowledge on the part of businessmen and workers that wages are likely to increase year after year at a substantial rate builds an inflationary bias into business planning and consumer purchasing behavior in the marketplace.

APPRAISAL OF THE DILEMMA

In April, 1968, William McChesney Martin, Jr., Chairman of the Federal Reserve Board, deplored the continuing inflation in prices, the mounting governmental deficit, and the alarming deficit in our balance of payments and stated that the United States is "in the midst of the worst financial crisis we have had since 1931."[59] Whether Mr. Martin's appraisal of the situation is overly pessimistic, only time will tell. The fact is that the nation is struggling with a problem of inflation with no ready or acceptable solution available.

Continuing inflation—particularly at an accelerated rate—is intolerable, since it would endanger the value of savings, erode the standard of living of fixed-income groups, and further jeopardize the stability of the dollar in international commerce. It is also a policy packed with political dynamite; for if the middle-class citizens of America should rightly or wrongly come to conclude that wage pressure by organized labor is responsible for the inflation, then they might be led to sponsor and support restrictive measures which could spell the end of a free labor market as we know it.

But while inflation is both dangerous and undesirable, it seems unlikely that this nation is prepared to take the extreme measures required to curb the upward movement of prices, if such action would curtail employment and necessitate a drastic cutback in many of the social programs which now appear so urgently necessary. The dangers posed by a policy of inaction in our city slums loom larger in the minds of most Americans today than the dangers inherent in inflation. Likewise, it is doubtful that

[59] *New York Times*, April 28, 1968, p. E 3.

labor will exercise "restraint" in demanding wage increases unless similar action is forthcoming from business with respect to profits. Government, labor, and business alike are in agreement that wage and price controls should only be adopted as a last resort.

For the immediate future, therefore, it appears likely that governmental monetary and tax policy will be used to slow up the inflationary process, but the rise in prices will continue to be fed, on the one hand, by continuing wage increases and, on the other hand, by rising expenditures of governments, federal, state, and local. In the present economic milieu, where wages are increasing faster than productivity and government expenditures continue to mount, it seems idle to argue whether the inflation is wage-push or demand-pull. The health of our economy requires a damper on both aspects of the price mechanism which together are contributing to a dangerous inflationary spiral.

QUESTIONS FOR DISCUSSION

1. How have the gains of increased productivity been distributed in the postwar years? From the point of view of achieving maximum employment in our economy, what is the "best" method of distributing such gains?
2. What is meant by "labor productivity"? How does this concept differ from "labor efficiency"? What are the factors which have produced the increase in output per manhour in American industry?
3. Are union organization, full employment, and price stability compatible in a free labor market? Discuss the economic and political implications of this question.
4. Union leaders maintain that cost-of-living escalator clauses in union contracts are beneficial to the economy because they help to maintain the real purchasing power of the workingman's dollar. Discuss the validity of this statement with particular relation to the problem of inflation.

SUGGESTIONS FOR FURTHER READING

Burck, Gilbert. "Must Full Employment Mean Inflation?" *Fortune,* Vol. LXXIV (October, 1966), pp. 120 *et seq.*
   An analysis of the current problem of inflation with particular emphasis on the monetary factors which have fed the inflation.
Denison, Edward F. *The Sources of Economic Growth in the United States and the Alternatives before Us.* Supplementary Paper No. 13, New York: Committee for Economic Development, 1962.
   A major analytical and statistical treatise on the various sources of economic growth including an appraisal of the contribution made by the various factors of production.
Dunlop, John T., and Diatchenko, Vasilii P. (eds.). *Labor Productivity.* New York: McGraw-Hill Book Co., 1964.
   A collection of articles on various aspects of the problem of productivity by economists from various countries, including the United States.

KENDRICK, JOHN W. "Productivity, Costs and Prices: Concepts and Measures," in ROWAN, RICHARD L., and NORTHRUP, HERBERT R. (eds.), *Readings in Labor Economics and Labor Relations*, pp. 473–83. Homewood, Ill.: Richard D. Irwin, Inc., 1968.

A concise discussion of the problem of defining and measuring productivity.

SOLOW, ROBERT M. "The Wage-Price Issue and the Guideposts," in HARBISON, F. H., and MOONEY, J. D. (eds.), *Critical Issues in Employment Policy*, pp. 57–74. Princeton University Research Report Series No. 109. Princeton, N.J., 1966.

An appraisal of the contribution made by the wage-price guideposts in damping down the inflationary spiral.

Technology and the American Economy. Report of the National Commission on Technology, Automation, and Economic Progress, Vol. I. Washington, D.C.: U.S. Government Printing Office, 1966.

A fact-filled report on various aspects of technological progress in the United States, representing findings of a select committee appointed by the President in December 1964 to investigate this problem.

UNEMPLOYMENT AND POVERTY IN A HIGH-EMPLOYMENT ECONOMY

In the previous and earlier chapters of this text, we have referred to the paradoxical problem which faces this nation, namely, that at the same time as we are experiencing an unprecedented prosperity with total employment and gross national product at all-time record heights we are also faced with continuing unemployment and poverty in our midst affecting millions of our citizens. In this chapter, we shall examine these two problems—unemployment and poverty—and shall consider their probable causes and the programs presently being applied in a massive attempt to reduce their impact on our population.

THE EXTENT OF UNEMPLOYMENT

Unemployment of some amount is a normal concomitant of a free labor market. Irregularity of employment is, in a sense, one of the costs which a system of free enterprise exacts in return for the privileges it bestows. Thus, the American worker has greater liberty than a worker anywhere else in the world to shift his place of employment in order to benefit his economic welfare. This is no idle gift—indeed, as we have seen from our discussion of the labor market, it is a privilege frequently exercised by the American worker. But the freedom of the worker to quit and to move is balanced by the freedom of the employer to fire, with the result that the individual employee is subjected to the vicissitudes of his current employer's business fortunes. Similarly, the absence of a central planning board integrating the production and employment policies of various firms means that in certain industries, there may be a temporary surplus of labor while, at the same time, there can be shortages of labor in others.

Thus, employment and unemployment typically fluctuate over time. A major determinant of the volume of unemployment is the level of business activity. At the depth of the Great Depression in 1933, one in every four persons was unemployed. On the other hand, in 1953, only about 1,602,000 persons were unemployed out of a total civilian labor force of 63,815,000 persons, or about 2.5% of the labor force. This is considered by economists to be close to the minimum amount of unemployment possible in peacetime in a dynamic economy such as ours, where some workers are always in process of changing jobs at any given time. Generally speaking, economists until very recently were accustomed to speak of the economy as being in "full employment" when unemployment of 2 to 3 million persons existed. This unemployment was considered to be in part frictional and in part the hard-core joblessness of those "misfits" who cannot adapt themselves to permanent jobs in our society.

In the last few years, however, there has been a revolution in thinking on this problem, not only by economists but also by business, government, and the public at large. There is now an awareness and recognition that we as a nation have a social responsibility to reduce and eliminate unemployment, regardless of the classification we may apply to it. We have come to understand that hard-core unemployment is not as hard-core as we once thought; that its persistence is a reflection of the indifference of society, rather than of some immutable law; and that with time, money, and the cooperation of government and the business community many of the unfortunate persons who have been a permanent part of the unemployed can be trained and given productive employment in industry.

In 1967, on the average about 3.8% of the civilian labor force, or 2,975,000 persons were classified as unemployed each month.[1] The number of persons who experience unemployment in a given year is roughly three to four times the average number unemployed over the year. Over 11 million American workers were jobless and looking for work at some time during 1966, and the figure was probably somewhat larger in 1967.[2] Over 45% of the workers who experienced some unemployment in 1966 were out of work for only one to four weeks. Presumably unemployment for this group results largely from voluntary job changes, some delay in finding new jobs, and the usual seasonal layoffs. In view of the briefness of the jobless period, members of this group are not likely to have serious financial problems nor is this degree of unemployment a serious problem for the economy.

We can distinguish a second group among the unemployed—about 3.4 million workers who at some time during the year were out of work for a period from 5 to 14 weeks. For many of these workers, too, unemployment may have been a transitional experience cushioned to some extent by unemployment insurance and other benefits, but for many of the workers involved—particularly those with the longer period of joblessness—serious financial consequences may have resulted from such involuntary idleness.

[1] *Manpower Report of the President, April, 1968* (Washington, D.C.: U.S. Government Printing Office, 1968), p. 221. This excellent annual report is replete with timely statistics on employment and unemployment. The authors have drawn widely on the Report for basic statistical data in this chapter.

[2] *Ibid.*, p. 18.

Finally, we come to the 2.7 million workers who were out of work for 15 or more weeks. Of these, more than 1 million were out of work for more than six months.[3] Most of these workers will fall in the hard-core unemployed category. Many of them have only brief periods when they are at work. For example, of the men out of work 15 or more weeks in 1966, 7 out of every 10 were unemployed at least twice during the year.[4] It is obvious from these figures that finding a job for the long-term unemployed is not necessarily a solution. There is an obvious need for training the chronically unemployed so that they can qualify for up-graded jobs with more promise of continuity of employment.

FIGURE 14–1

MAJOR UNEMPLOYMENT INDICATORS, 1953 TO 1968
(Seasonally Adjusted)

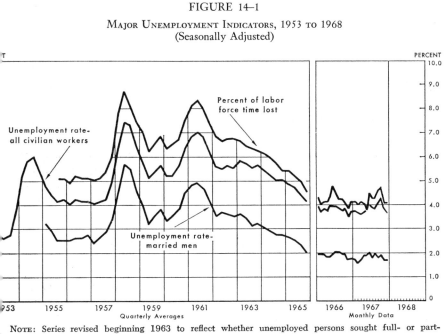

NOTE: Series revised beginning 1963 to reflect whether unemployed persons sought full- or part-jobs.

SOURCE: U.S. Department of Labor, Bureau of Labor Statistics, *Employment and Earnings,* Vol. XIV ary, 1968), p. 26.

While much remains to be done in reducing the volume of unemployment, some major gains have been made in recent years in reducing long-term unemployment. Despite large additions to the work force between 1961 and 1966, the proportion of workers unemployed for 5 weeks or more of the year was cut nearly in half—from 11.6% to 6.4%, while the proportion of workers unemployed 15 weeks or more dropped from 6.3% in 1961 to 2.8% in 1966.[5] Figure 14–1 shows clearly the sharp

[3] *Loc. cit.*
[4] *Ibid.,* p. 19.
[5] *Loc. cit.*

reduction in unemployment which has been achieved since 1961. Note that the unemployment rate for married men—the principal breadwinners in our economy—has averaged less than 2% for the years 1966 and 1967—a rate many observers feel may be close to a practical minimum.

MEASUREMENT OF UNEMPLOYMENT[6]

Although unemployment is still a serious problem facing our economy, particularly in our central cities, our knowledge of the actual dimensions of the problem leave much to be desired. As was pointed out in Chapter 1, our statistics on unemployment are based upon a monthly survey of 35,000 households, the results of which are extrapolated for the economy as a whole. Some economists contend that such sample-based statistics are inadequate and that they should be supplemented with a biennial Census of Unemployment.

A further criticism directed at the statistics is that the particular definitions adopted in the survey understate the true volume of unemployment in the nation by failing to take account of the so-called "invisible unemployed" who are not counted in official unemployment statistics. The invisible unemployed fall into four[7] major categories:

1. Persons who are working part-time but would like full-time work if they could find it. The extra hours these men and women would work if they could find full-time employment represent a surplus of labor which is not reflected in official statistics. The reason is that the government figures include in the "employed" category anyone who has worked at least one hour for pay in the week preceding the survey. The U.S. Department of Labor estimates that about 1 million to 1.5 million part-time workers actually want full-time employment.[8]
2. Seasonal workers who would like year-round employment if they could get it. The Bureau of the Census does not even include in the labor force seasonal workers who were neither working nor seeking work in the survey week. While many in this group may desire employment only on a seasonal basis, there are undoubtedly many others who would prefer year-round employment but do not even bother to look for it because of their belief, based on past experience, that there are no job opportunities for their particular skills.
3. Members of the "reserve labor force," who come onto the labor market only when there is a shortage of labor and jobs are readily avail-

---

[6] It is recommended that the reader refer back to the definition of employment and unemployment in Chapter 1, pages 7–8.

[7] It is possible to distinguish a fifth category of persons who are kept occupied on a full-time basis at a job where they are really not needed. This is frequently true of young men and women on the farm. The U.S. Department of Agriculture has estimated that there is a considerable amount of "disguised unemployment" on the farm amounting to the equivalent of more than 1 million workers who are not needed for farm work. See *Survey of Current Business*, December, 1962, p. 27.

[8] *Manpower Report of the President, April, 1968, op. cit.*, p. 22.

able. Since members of this group would answer in a survey that they are not working and not looking for a job, they are ordinarily excluded from the labor force statistics.

Who are the people who make up the "reserve labor force"?

a) Men below normal retirement age who are out of the work force—numbers in this category have been rising in recent years, particularly among nonwhites.
b) Youth in slum areas who have dropped out of school and are neither working nor seeking work.
c) Older persons, many receiving retirement benefits, who would like to work if jobs were available.
d) Women who want to work either to support themselves and their families or to supplement their husband's income but cannot do so because of lack of child-care facilities.
e) Persons in school who would take part-time or full-time employment if jobs were available.
f) Persons with limited education or skills who come into the labor market only when jobs are so abundant that their handicaps are overlooked.

The U.S. Department of Labor estimates that in September, 1966, 5.3 million men and women—1 out of every 10 persons outside the labor force—wanted a job. About ¾ million—over 250,000 men and 500,000 women—were not looking for jobs simply because they thought it would be impossible to find one for which they would qualify.[9] Obviously, this group is of major concern from the point of view of manpower policy.

4. Persons with physical handicaps. These persons are treated as unemployable rather than unemployed and are excluded from the labor force figure. Experience during World War II, however, taught employers that there is a definite place in industry for the blind, the maimed, and the crippled. The U.S. Department of Labor has estimated that there are about 5 to 7 million handicapped workers who could be placed in industrial occupations. In considering statistics of unemployment, it is important to bear in mind that concepts of employability alter with the changing needs of the economy and that tomorrow we may consider persons to be unemployed who today are deemed unemployable.

It is apparent that inclusion of some or all of the so-called "invisible unemployed" in unemployment statistics would give an entirely different picture of our needs for the future in terms of providing new jobs. To this number we could also add those who are "unemployed" on a *qualitative* basis—i.e., a Negro with a college degree who because of discrimination is compelled to take a job which does not utilize his skills. Undoubt-

---

[9] *Ibid.*, p. 23.

edly there are great numbers of our workers—white and nonwhite—who fall in this category which might better be called "underemployment". The existence of the invisible unemployed complicates the problem of devising a policy to reduce unemployment. As we have already mentioned, in 1967 somewhat less than 3 million persons were classified as unemployed under the official statistics. As government moves through appropriate monetary, fiscal, and manpower policy to reduce this figure, it finds that it is to some extent on a treadmill. For the more successful it is in expanding the demand for jobs and reducing the supply of unemployed labor, the more likely are the members of the invisible unemployed to seek jobs in the labor market. Another way of saying this is that the labor participation rate tends to increase when jobs are plentiful and wages are high. Furthermore, employment of the invisible unemployed may further accelerate the rise in unit labor costs which currently faces the economy, since it is likely that members of this group, because of lack of training and job experience, are less productive than members of the regular labor force [10]

WHO ARE THE UNEMPLOYED

Statistics of unemployment are made by individuals. Who are the unemployed? Who is the typical unemployed person? What are the conditions or circumstances which typify the bulk of our unemployment?

Unskilled Workers

The unemployed person is likely to be unskilled. As can be seen from Figure 14–2, the unemployment rate for laborers is greater than for any other group in the labor market. This is true year after year without variation. The second highest unemployment rate is that of operatives and kindred semiskilled workers. By contrast, the rate for professional, technical, and managerial personnel has averaged about 1.2% for several years, attesting to an acute shortage in the marketplace for qualified persons in these categories.

Youth

Unemployment has always been substantially higher among young persons than among adults (see Figure 14–3). Teen-agers, for example, include a large proportion of new entrants into the labor market, and they customarily have a period of unemployment associated with "shopping around" for a satisfactory position. Frequently, they begin their working careers by taking part-time jobs which may be temporary or seasonal. Young people, since they have fewer family commitments than older

[10] Jacob Mincer, "Labor Force Participation and Unemployment: A Review of the Evidence," in R. A. Gordon and M. S. Gordon (eds.), *Prosperity and Unemployment* (New York: John Wiley & Sons, Inc., 1966), pp. 73–112.

FIGURE 14–2

UNEMPLOYMENT RATES ARE LOWEST FOR
PROFESSIONAL AND MANAGERIAL WORKERS
—HIGHEST FOR NONFARM LABORERS

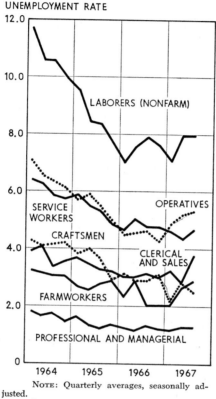

NOTE: Quarterly averages, seasonally adjusted.

SOURCE: U.S. Department of Labor, *Manpower Report of the President, April, 1968* (Washington, D.C.: U.S. Government Printing Office, 1968), p. 74.

workers, change their jobs more frequently in a search for the "right" job. Furthermore, they tend to be more vulnerable to layoffs because of inexperience and lack of seniority.

In the past few years, however, the sharp increase in the incidence of unemployment among this group has created a problem of grave concern to our nation. The rate of unemployment among men and women aged 16 to 19 is approximately three times the average rate for all unemployed. It is paradoxical that the United States keeps larger proportions of its children in school longer than does any other nation to insure their preparation for productive lifetime activity, yet the unemployment rate among youth is far higher in the United States than in any other industrial nation.

FIGURE 14–3

UNEMPLOYMENT RATES BY AGE AND SEX, 1953 TO DATE
(Seasonally Adjusted)

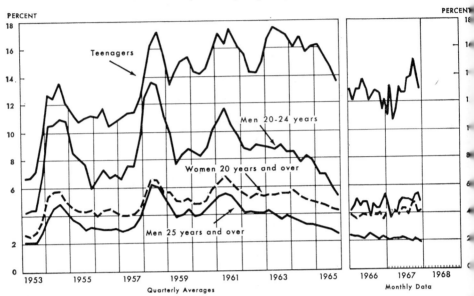

SOURCE: U.S. Department of Labor, Bureau of Labor Statistics, *Employment and Earnings*, Vol. XIV (January, 1968), p. 28.

Moreover, it had been rising sharply until the introduction of various government-sponsored youth programs in the last few years.[11]

The overall unemployment rate for youth has remained high primarily because of the experience of nonwhite teen-agers. The jobless rate for white youth aged 16 to 19 has declined steadily—from 14.8% in 1964 to 11.0% in 1967. For Negro teen-agers, however, the unemployment rate has remained discouragingly high for the past four years and in 1967 stood at 26.5%.[12]

The problem of providing jobs for our youth is given additional urgency by the momentous changes which are taking place in our economy. In the first place, as a result of the sharp increase in the birth rate after World War II, there will be a tremendous increase in the number of young men and women who enter the labor market during the balance of the decade. Between 1950 and 1960 the labor force aged 14 to 24 increased by less than 400,000. By contrast, between 1960 and 1970, this group will increase by more than 6 million. Whereas, in the early 1950's, less than 2

---

[11] *Manpower Report of the President, April, 1968, op. cit.,* p. 111.

[12] U.S. Department of Labor, Bureau of Labor Statistics, *Employment and Earnings,* Vol. XIV (January, 1968), p. 11.

million persons turned 18 annually, in the years ahead the number will exceed 4 million. In the second place, the labor force will be augmented by a continuing exodus from the farm. It has been estimated that about 9 out of every 10 of the youngsters now on the farm will eventually have to find work in the nonagricultural sector.[13] Third, if the pace of hostilities in Vietnam should diminish so that the requirements of the armed services lessen, the surplus of youth in the civilian labor market will become even more acute.

Teen-agers today comprise nearly 30% of the approximately 3 million Americans out of work. Unless productive employment can be found for these youths, we shall reap a bitter social harvest of unrest and delinquency. Alleviation of this problem requires not only the availability of more jobs but also an extensive training program which can fit these young men and women for the new jobs that technology is producing in our dynamic economy.

The Uneducated

Recent studies have indicated a close relationship between education and unemployment. As can be seen from Table 14–1, in general the more years of schooling completed, the lower the unemployment rate of the worker. A notable exception occurs for the high school dropout who does not finish four years of high school. The reason that Table 14–1 shows a higher rate of unemployment for persons with some high school education than for those with no high school education at all is that persons in the latter category tend to be mature workers who completed their formal education 10 years or more ago and have since acquired the skills and experience necessary to maintain relatively stable jobs. High school dropouts, on the other hand, tend to be relatively young and are new entrants to the labor market with few acceptable skills.

The higher rate of unemployment for workers with less education reflects the fact that a higher proportion of such workers are employed as blue-collar workers, as laborers, and in various occupations which, while providing jobs requiring little formal training, are also most exposed to the vicissitudes of the business cycle.

The kinds of jobs that are available today and will become available in the future require trained, educated persons to fill them. Between 1965 and 1975, professional, technical, and kindred workers are expected to increase by 45% while laborers will decrease by 3%.[14] The need is apparent for programs to train the uneducated and dropouts for better jobs and at the same time to make it possible for qualified young people to continue their education despite lack of funds.

---

[13] Eli Ginzberg, "Youth Without a Future," *Challenge*, October, 1963, p. 33.

[14] *Manpower Report of the President, April, 1967* (Washington, D.C.: U.S. Government Printing Office, 1967), Table E–8, p. 274.

TABLE 14–1

Unemployment Rates, by Age, Sex, and Years of School Completed, March, 1966

Years of School Completed and Sex	Percent of Labor Force Unemployed							
	Total, 18 Years and Over	18 and 19 Years	20 to 24 Years	25 to 34 Years	35 to 44 Years	45 to 54 Years	55 to 64 Years	65 Years and Over
BOTH SEXES								
Total	3.7	10.5	5.9	3.7	2.7	2.6	3.1	3.0
Elementary: Less than 5 years*	5.9	.....	(†)	11.2	7.2	6.0	4.0	3.9
5 to 7 years	5.0	(†)	9.4	8.5	4.0	3.4	5.3	3.0
8 years	4.7	23.4	14.3	5.0	4.5	3.8	4.1	2.5
High school: 1 to 3 years	5.3	15.1	8.6	6.4	3.4	3.6	2.8	3.1
4 years	3.1	7.7	5.2	2.6	2.3	1.7	2.4	3.5
College: 1 to 3 years	3.0	6.3	5.2	3.7	1.5	1.2	2.0	3.3
4 years or more	1.1	.....	1.8	1.2	0.9	1.0	.4	2.2
MALE								
Total	3.4	10.5	6.0	3.4	2.2	2.3	3.4	3.6
Elementary: Less than 5 years*	6.3	.....	(†)	13.1	6.6	5.9	4.6	4.8
5 to 7 years	5.5	(†)	10.6	8.4	4.3	3.7	6.0	2.8
8 years	4.3	(†)	13.4	3.7	4.2	3.4	4.0	2.6
High school: 1 to 3 years	4.8	15.2	8.6	5.5	2.5	2.9	2.9	5.3
4 years	2.6	6.8	5.0	2.1	1.7	1.2	2.9	4.0
College: 1 to 3 years	2.8	3.9	4.8	3.7	1.8	1.0	1.8	2.8
4 years or more	1.0	.....	2.3	1.4	0.4	0.7	0.6	3.2
FEMALE								
Total	4.1	10.5	5.6	4.4	3.7	3.1	2.5	2.0
Elementary: Less than 5 years*	4.4	.....	.....	.....	(†)	6.4	2.0	1.9
5 to 7 years	3.9	(†)	(†)	8.9	3.4	2.6	3.6	3.5
8 years	5.6	(†)	8.6	8.4	5.2	4.5	4.5	2.1
High school: 1 to 3 years	6.1	14.8	8.6	8.3	5.2	4.8	2.6	
4 years	3.8	8.5	5.5	3.5	3.2	2.3	1.7	2.7
College: 1 to 3 years	3.3	9.2	5.6	3.7	1.0	1.5	2.2	(†)
4 years or more	1.3	.....	1.3	0.3	3.2	1.8	.....	.....

* Includes persons reporting no school years completed.
† Percent not shown where base is less than 100,000.

SOURCE: "Educational Attainment of Workers, March 1966" (Special Labor Force Report No. 83 [Washington, D.C.: U.S. Department of Labor, 1967]) p. A 15.

Older Workers

Unemployment among older workers poses a special problem. The difficulty is not so much in the rate of unemployment as in its duration once it occurs. In 1967, the unemployment rate for males 55–64 years of age was only 2.4%. This was considerably above the rate for the age group 35–44 (1.7%), but below the average rate of unemployment for all workers (3.8%).[15] Older workers are less likely to lose their jobs than younger employees because they are protected by seniority rights, but when they do become unemployed, they find it extremely difficult to obtain reemployment. Frequently, they are the victims of a plant shutdown and find that their only skill has become obsolete. Long-time ties to family and community render them less mobile than younger workers, so they often stay on in depressed areas, even though there is little likelihood of finding a new job there. Many older workers, still short of retirement age, may simply stop looking for work after a time and therefore do not even get counted as unemployed under the Bureau of the Census definition. In 1967, males 45 to 64 years of age represented 12.2% of the unemployed, but 25.7% of those out of work for 27 weeks or more.[16]

Negro Workers

Unemployment has been much heavier among Negro than among white workers. As Figure 14–4 indicates, although the unemployment rates for nonwhites[17] declined by more than half between 1962 and 1967, it was still twice as high as for whites. However, for nonwhite married men, who are the chief providers in nearly three fourths of the nonwhite homes, the unemployment rate dropped at a faster rate than for white married men during the last five years and now stands at about 3 ½ %.[18] Nonwhite workers are not only twice as likely to be unemployed as white workers but also they are twice as likely to be among the long-term unemployed. About 1 ½ % of the total nonwhite labor force is among the long-term unemployed—i.e., out of a job for 15 weeks or more.[19]

In attempting to determine the full incidence of unemployment on the Negro population, it is important to remember, as we have already indicated in our earlier discussion in this chapter, that conventional definitions and surveys used for measurement of unemployment may tend to

---

[15] *Manpower Report of the President, April, 1968, op. cit.,* Table A–12, p. 236.

[16] *Manpower Report of the President, April, 1968, op. cit.,* Table A–18, pp. 241–42.

[17] About 92% of the nonwhite population is Negro; statistics of nonwhites therefore generally reflect the condition of the Negro population.

[18] U.S. Department of Labor, Bureau of Labor Statistics, *Social and Economic Conditions of Negroes in the United States* (B.L.S. Report No. 332 [Washington, D.C., October, 1967]), p. ix.

[19] *Ibid.,* p. 37.

FIGURE 14–4

UNEMPLOYMENT RATES FOR MARRIED MEN, WHITE
AND NONWHITE, 1962–67

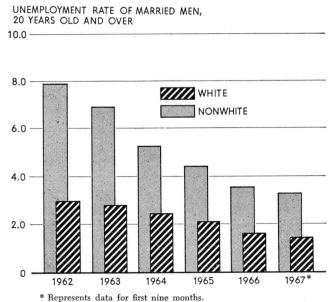

UNEMPLOYMENT RATE OF MARRIED MEN,
20 YEARS OLD AND OVER

* Represents data for first nine months.
SOURCE: U.S. Department of Labor, *Manpower Report of the
President, April, 1968* (Washington, D.C.: U.S. Government Printing
Office, 1968), p. 62.

underestimate the true amount of Negro unemployment. As a matter of
fact, the Census Bureau estimates that its Current Population Survey
misses about 13% of the nonwhite population of working age compared
with about 2% of the white. The Bureau estimates that the undercount is
greatest among nonwhite men in the prime working years. If unemployment rates for the undercounted are twice those for the counted, the
undercount could change the total unemployment rate for nonwhites by
about one half of 1%.[20] Likewise, since the Census Survey lists anyone
who worked *at all* during the survey week as being "employed," official
estimates undoubtedly understate the real impact of underemployment on
Negroes, many of whom are compelled to take part-time work even
though they would prefer full-time employment.

The proportion of men of working age who neither work nor look
for work is another indication of inequality of opportunity, since discouragement in finding jobs is an important reason given by Negroes for being
outside the labor force. Nonwhite men are much less likely to be participants in the labor force than white men, except in age groups under 24

[20] *Ibid.*, p. 38.

where longer school attendance of white youth outweighs other facts affecting labor participation. Between 1960 and 1967, the proportion of nonwhite men 25 to 64 years of age not in the labor force rose from 75 to 91 per 1,000 people; among white men the increase was less—from 47 to 55.[21]

A number of reasons have been advanced for the high unemployment rate among nonwhite workers. It has been estimated, for example, that about half the racial difference in unemployment rates is due to the heavy concentration of nonwhites in occupations such as unskilled farm and nonfarm labor, semiskilled production jobs, and service work where there is typically a great deal of unemployment.[22] Today Negroes still hold 25% of all nonfarm laboring jobs but only 5% of white-collar jobs.[23] Despite six years of occupational advances, over two fifths of nonwhite men and three fifths of all nonwhite women workers are still employed in service, laboring, or farm jobs—substantially more than twice the proportion among whites. Furthermore, within each broad occupational group, unemployment is substantially higher for nonwhite workers because they tend to be near the bottom of the skill ladder in each occupational group, partly because of discriminatory hiring and layoff practices.

Lack of education is another major cause for the high incidence of unemployment among nonwhites. The nonwhite worker frequently comes from a poor family and is compelled to leave school early in order to supplement family income. Lack of skills plus discriminatory hiring practices then force him into unskilled, low-paying jobs which fluctuate most with the business cycle. Fortunately, substantial improvement has been made in educational attainments of nonwhite workers in recent years. Six years ago, nonwhite young men averaged two years less schooling than white young men. Today the gap is only one-half year. Nonwhite teenage boys are completing high school and going into college in increasing numbers. For the first time the typical nonwhite young man can be said to be a high school graduate.[24]

The continuing high level of Negro unemployment reflects the net effect of two opposing trends. On the one hand, the lessening of racial discrimination in hiring practices has tended to improve Negro employment opportunities. On the other hand, the shift in the job mix in the economy to jobs requiring a higher level of skill and educational attainment has made it more difficult for Negroes to find employment. There is no simple answer to the problem of Negro unemployment.

---

[21] *Manpower Report of the President, April, 1968, op. cit.,* p. 62.

[22] *Manpower Report of the President, 1963* (Washington, D.C.: U.S. Government Printing Office, 1963), p. 43.

[23] U.S. Department of Labor, Bureau of Labor Statistics, *Employment and Earnings,* Vol. XIV (September, 1967), p. 14.

[24] *Social and Economic Conditions of Negroes in the United States, op. cit.,* p. x.

It must be attacked on a broad front. Success in reducing the rate of unemployment depends upon the degree of cooperation forthcoming from both business and organized labor, both of whom have been guilty of discriminatory practices. It is apparent that even if all Negroes who want to work were given jobs, their rate of unemployment would be disproportionately high as long as they are concentrated in industries and occupations which have the least stability over the business cycle. Better education and improved training, therefore, are essential to any real solution of this problem.

OCCUPATIONAL CHARACTERISTICS OF THE UNEMPLOYED

In some occupations, unemployment is part of the normal routine of the ebb and flow of work. Take, for example, the construction industry, which has an unemployment rate almost twice the rate for all workers. Construction is subject to sharp seasonal swings; projects are short term, and the worker has only a passing attachment to any particular employer. The high hourly rates paid in this industry are intended to compensate workers—in part, at least—for the loss of income they regularly suffer in the intervals between jobs.

On the other hand, the high rate of unemployment among mine workers reflects a long-term reduction in jobs attributable to mechanization and competition from other products. Many mine workers are reluctant to leave their communities when they lose their jobs; as a result, they become part of a long-term unemployed hard core clustered in depressed areas.

In manufacturing, fluctuations in employment are closely tied to the level of activity in the particular industry and to the stage of the general business cycle. The automobile industry is an example of an industry which is subject to major swings in demand by consumers and in which employment fluctuates from month to month and from year to year.

In Chapter 1, we commented on the shift in employment that is occurring between goods-producing and service-producing industries. As service-oriented employment grows in our economy, it will tend to introduce a greater degree of employment stability over the cycle than formerly existed when a greater proportion of persons were employed as production workers in goods-producing industries. Industries such as construction, mining, and nondurable goods manufacturing had unemployment rates in 1967 higher than the average for the entire private economy.

Furthermore, as can be seen from Figure 14–5, white-collar workers have unemployment rates about half that of blue-collar workers. The shift in employment from blue- to white-collar workers should also tend to stabilize employment.

FIGURE 14–5

UNEMPLOYMENT RATES BY MAJOR OCCUPATION GROUPS, 1957 TO DATE
(Seasonally Adjusted)

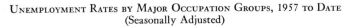

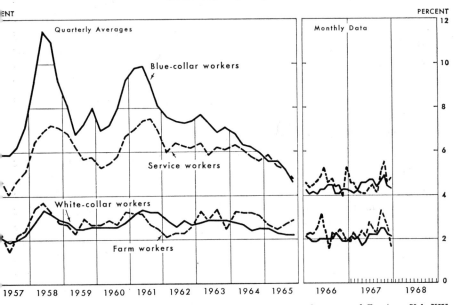

SOURCE: U.S. Department of Labor, Bureau of Labor Statistics, *Employment and Earnings,* Vol. XIV
nuary, 1968), p. 30.

THE LOCATION OF UNEMPLOYMENT

One of the characteristics of our unemployment problem is pockets
of unemployment that persists in various depressed areas of the country.
Appalachia—a region which contains part of 12 states and all of West
Virginia—continues to have a persistent unemployment problem reflecting the effects of the migration from the area of coal-mining, steel-manu-
facture, and similar industries and the lack of any other industry to take
up the slack in manpower. While Appalachia is more than half rural,
many urban areas are also trouble spots. In December, 1967, the U.S.
Department of Labor classified nine major areas as "areas of substantial or
persistent unemployment." The cities of Newark, New Jersey, and Oakland and San Diego, California, have also been added to this list. This
classification makes areas eligible for some assistance under the Public
Works and Economic Development Act of 1965.

The geographic distribution of these high-unemployment areas
was as follows: three additional areas in California (Fresno, San
Bernardino–Riverside–Ontario, and Stockton), plus the cities of San
Diego and Oakland; two areas in Massachusetts; one in Pennsylvania; two

in Puerto Rico; and one in Wisconsin. Examination of the economic situation in each of these areas indicates the wide variety of factors which can contribute to produce a serious unemployment condition. Most people think of California as a growth area, and so it is. But the problems of the California distressed areas stem from a large influx of migrants plus localized cutbacks in certain industries, largely defense oriented. On the other hand, the situation in Massachusetts, Pennsylvania, and Puerto Rico reflects longstanding economic and technological problems. By further contrast, the Wisconsin area suffered primarily because of the shutdown of one major company.[25]

Unemployment in the Cities

In the last few years, Americans have suddenly become aware that their large central cities are literally decaying. Poverty, crime, disease, inadequate housing, and unemployment—all of these seem to have crowded into the central cities, creating problems of such magnitude that only a massive aid program financed by the federal government can hope to make any progress in curing these ills. The problem of the central cities was further complicated by the gravitation of large numbers of Negroes to these areas, while white workers and their families moved to the suburbs. In 1967, 60% of the white labor force in 20 Standard Metropolitan Statistical Areas (SMSA's)[26] lived outside the central cities, while only 20% of the nonwhite labor force lived in the suburbs.[27]

Superficial examination of statistics of unemployment in urban areas gives a false impression that all is well. The overall unemployment rate in 1967 for the 20 metropolitan areas referred to above was 3.9%, which was about the same as the national rate in that year.[28] However, the rate for the central cities was 4.7%,[29] and in the slum areas of 10 cities was actually 10% or more, with two city slum areas recording unemployment rates above 15%.[30] This is the stuff of which human misery culminating in riots is made.

Nonwhite unemployment is much more concentrated in urban centers than white joblessness. The 270,000 unemployed nonwhites in 20 metropolitan areas accounted for 42% of total nonwhite unemployment.[31] Moreover, the unemployment rate for nonwhites in these areas is more

---

[25] *Manpower Report of the President, April, 1968, op. cit.,* pp. 142–43.

[26] Standard Metropolitan Statistical Areas consist of large cities and their adjacent suburban counties. Central cities include the corporate limits of the city or cities named in the particular SMSA title.

[27] Paul O. Flaim, "Jobless Trends in 20 Large Metropolitan Areas," *Monthly Labor Review,* Vol. XCI (May, 1968), p. 17.

[28] *Ibid.,* p. 16.

[29] *Loc. cit.*

[30] *Manpower Report of the President, April, 1968, op. cit.,* p. 84.

[31] Flaim, *op. cit.,* p. 17.

than twice that for whites—7.5% versus 3.3%.[32] The SMSA jobless rate for nonwhite teen-agers of 33% was three times as high as for SMSA white teen-agers (11%) and about 45% above the rate for nonwhite youth residing outside the 20 SMSA's (23%).[33]

In 1967, about 550,000 unemployed lived in central cities, and 40% of them were nonwhite. Why is the central city rate of unemployment higher than for the SMSA area? A number of diverse factors contribute to produce this result:

1. The central city has a heavy concentration of nonwhite workers who traditionally have higher unemployment rates for reasons discussed earlier in this chapter.
2. Workers living in suburbs are by and large better educated than workers in the central cities and are more likely to be employed in white-collar jobs which offer more stable employment.
3. The central city has more newcomers—frequently migrants from other areas of the country—who usually experience difficulty in obtaining a job in the new area.
4. A smaller proportion of the suburban labor force is over 55 years of age than in the central city. We have already observed that older workers suffer from longer periods of unemployment once they lose a job.
5. The exodus of many manufacturing plants from the central city to outlying areas and the lack of public transportation facilities to transport urban residents to these outlying areas has left many unskilled and semiskilled workers in the cities with no nearby employer available to use their labor.
6. Nearly two fifths of all households in 10 slum areas surveyed by the U.S. Department of Labor had women heads—almost twice the national figure.[34] Many of these women could only work part time because of family responsibilities.
7. Close to 7% of central city slum residents are employed only part time, although they would prefer full-time work. The comparable figure for the nation as a whole is about 2.3%.[35]

Besides having high rates of unemployment, the workers living in the slum areas of central cities were much more likely than others to be out of work for long periods. Furthermore, above-average proportions of the men of normal working age were neither employed nor looking for work. Many slum residents could find only part-time work of an unskilled, low-paying type. The usual measures of unemployment—based on the concept of persons who have no work at all and are actively looking for work—are really inadequate to deal with the economic situation of

---

[32] *Loc. cit.*

[33] *Ibid.*, p. 16.

[34] *Manpower Report of the President, April, 1967, op. cit.*, p. 77.

[35] *Ibid.*, p. 74.

disadvantaged workers in slum and rural areas. The U.S. Department of Labor has therefore adopted the concept of "subemployment" to deal with the problem of our "employed poor," many of whom work a few hours a week and subsist at a poverty level. The Labor Department has decided to measure subemployment on an annual basis, including in this category two specific groups of workers—those who were unemployed 15 or more weeks during the year and those who made less than $3,000 for year-round full-time employment.[36]

Obviously, the figures for subemployment are substantially greater than for unemployment as usually measured. In 1966, the rate of subemployment was 10%, and approximately 9 million persons fell in this category. The subemployment rate for nonwhite men was 22% as compared with 8% for white men.[37] A high percentage of slum residents fall in the category of workers whose annual incomes are less than $3,000. The Department of Labor estimates that while about half a million persons are unemployed in the slum areas of large SMSA's, the number who would be classified as subemployed would probably exceed 1.5 million.[38] In a survey of slum areas in 13 major cities in 1966, the Department of Labor found that the rate of subemployment was 34%! In other words, one out of every three slum residents who was already a worker, or should and could become one with suitable help, was either jobless or not earning enough for living above the poverty level.[39]

POVERTY AND UNEMPLOYMENT

In his 1964 message on the State of the Union, President Lyndon B. Johnson declared all-out war on poverty in America and pointed out the close link which exists between poverty and unemployment. Although it is fortunately not true—if we look at long-term trends—that "the poor are always with us," the fact remains that poverty, illness, and lack of education can create bonds which can bind one generation after another to low incomes and high unemployment.

How shall we define poverty? This is no easy task, yet the type of definition adopted can well have a major influence upon public policy designed to reduce poverty in America. The Council of Economic Advisers defines poverty in absolute terms, using as a measure annual family income from all sources of less than $3,000. For single persons the applicable standard is $1,500 annual income. If we use this measure, we find

[36] For a discussion of this concept, see *Manpower Report of the President, April, 1968, op. cit.*, pp. 34–35. The rate of subemployment represents the number of persons falling in the above-mentioned two groups taken as a proportion of the entire labor force with a week or more of work experience during the year.

[37] *Ibid.*, p. 35.

[38] *Ibid.*, p. 85.

[39] *Manpower Report of the President, April, 1967, op. cit.*, p. 75.

that today about one seventh of our total population has not shared in the nation's prosperity and remains in poverty, as so defined.[40]

The difficulty with an absolute figure as a measure of poverty is that its adequacy changes from year to year. Back in the Great Depression, President Franklin D. Roosevelt spoke of "one third of a nation" as being in poverty, but if he had then used the $3,000 figure, the proportion in poverty would have been closer to two thirds! Furthermore, there is always the problem of how to deal with the retired couple who have a net income of less than $3,000 but are not impoverished because they own their own home and automobile and have securities or other assets. On the other hand, some people whose incomes exceed $3,000 may, because of large families, repeated illness, or just poor financial management, be literally poverty-stricken. It is well to remember that the measure used by the Council of Economic Advisers looks only at income—not assets—and therefore must necessarily give only a partial picture of a family's economic condition.

Some economists believe that a more meaningful definition of poverty can be given in relative terms. In other words, in any given society at any given point of time, the "poor" are those at the bottom of the income distribution pattern. These economists would focus attention on how far those at the bottom are from the median income group. For example, Victor R. Fuchs suggests defining as poor any family with an income less than one half that of the median family at the time.[41] As was mentioned above, the choice of definition is more than semantics. If we define poverty in absolute terms, we can observe a sharp reduction over the years (see Figure 14–6). By contrast, in relative terms there has been no change. "Continued increases in real per capita income are likely to lead to continued decreases in absolute poverty, but a decrease in poverty defined relatively can only be achieved by a shift in the distribution of income."[42] The question therefore presents itself whether or not we as a nation should establish a goal for income distribution just as we aim for other goals such as full employment, price stability, and so on.

Who are the poor? Where do they reside? The South remains the major region afflicted by poverty. Approximately 30% of American families live in the South, but 46% of the poor live in the South. Both southern whites and southern Negroes are disproportionately represented in the poverty class.[43]

[40] *Economic Report of the President, 1968* (Washington, D.C.: U.S. Government Printing Office, 1968), p. 129.

[41] Victor R. Fuchs, "Toward a Theory of Poverty," in *The Concept of Poverty* (Washington, D.C.: U.S. Chamber of Commerce, Task Force on Economic Growth and Opportunity, 1965), p. 74.

[42] *Ibid.*, p. 89.

[43] Eugene Smolensky, "The Past and Present Poor," in *The Concept of Poverty, op. cit.*, p. 50.

FIGURE 14–6

FEDERAL SPENDING FOR THE POOR AND NUMBER OF POOR, 1964–68

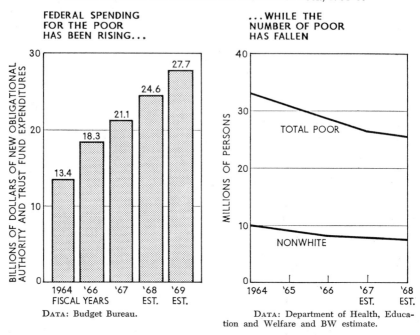

FEDERAL SPENDING
FOR THE POOR
HAS BEEN RISING...

...WHILE THE
NUMBER OF POOR
HAS FALLEN

DATA: Budget Bureau.

DATA: Department of Health, Education and Welfare and BW estimate.

SOURCE: *Business Week*, May 4, 1968, p. 76. By permission of McGraw-Hill, Inc.

Although it has become almost axiomatic to equate poverty with urban slums, poverty is relatively more prevalent on our farms and in rural nonfarm areas than in urban areas. In 1965, over 5.5 million people were living in rural areas, of whom an estimated 27% were poor.[44] Two factors contribute to the low incomes of rural people. First, the mix of the elements which affect earning capacity—education, age, sex, work availability—is less favorable than in other areas of the country. Second, income opportunities are poorer in rural areas, so that rural residents earn substantially less than they might reasonably expect on the basis of their earning capacity. Among the poorest of the poor nationally are the hired farmworkers of our country. In 1965, approximately 3.1 million individuals did some wage farmwork during the year. On the average, these workers were employed 123 days on all jobs, farm and nonfarm, and earned the total of only $1,054 during the year.[45]

Poverty is not evenly distributed throughout the population. The aged, nonwhites, and members of households headed by a woman constitute larger fractions of the poor than of the general population. Moreover,

[44] *Manpower Report of the President, April, 1967, op. cit.*, p. 106.
[45] *Ibid.*, p. 108.

the rate of progress in reducing poverty has varied widely among these and other groups. Between 1959 and 1966, the number of poor nonfarm households headed by a man declined 20%, while the poor nonfarm households headed by a woman increased by 2%. As a result, households headed by a woman constitute a growing proportion—now nearly half—of all poor households.[46] In 1966, nearly two out of three of these women had two or more children. This was a key factor in keeping 53% of poor women out of the work force.[47]

Of the 6 million families with less than minimal incomes in 1966, as defined by the Social Security Administration,[48] 70% were headed by males, nearly a third of whom were 65 or over. Disability, family responsibilities, and related factors precluded employment for nearly three quarters of this age group. Low-paying jobs rather than inability to work were the major reason for low income for other male-headed households. Over half the males under 55 worked the year round, but most held jobs as laborers or semiskilled craftsmen.[49] Here again we see that the problem of poverty is closely associated with substandard employment.

As might be expected, Negroes share more than their proportionate burden of poverty. Negroes make up 11% of all households, but 29% of poor households. In March, 1967, two thirds of Negro male household heads classified as poor were employed, but nearly a third worked as unskilled laborers and over one fourth in low-skilled factory jobs. Four out of every 10 poor Negro households had women heads, over half of whom cared for three or more children.[50]

Although Negroes bear more than their share of poverty, most of the poor in this country are white. Furthermore, the same characteristics are found regardless of color of the family breadwinner. Lack of skill spells marginal income; lack of facilities or help to take care of young children means that the woman head of the household cannot work or may only work on a part-time basis.

Poverty breeds poverty. Low incomes mean that parents cannot give their children the opportunities for better health and education which are needed to improve their lot. Furthermore, chronic unemployment can create such exhaustion of financial assets and incurrence of debt that families may withdraw from the private labor market and become dependent upon public welfare. The persistence of unemployment and

[46] *Economic Report of the President, 1968, op. cit.,* p. 142.

[47] *Business Trends,* Vol. XXXVI (New York: National Industrial Conference Board, March 18, 1968), p. 47.

[48] A household is considered poor by the Social Security Administration if its income falls below the level deemed necessary to maintain minimal living standards. These vary according to family size, age, and sex. For a typical family of four, the minimal annual income would be $3,300.

[49] *Ibid.,* p. 47.

[50] *Loc. cit.*

poverty in families and communities can crush initiative, result in loss of skills, and curtail interest in acquiring new skills needed to compete for jobs in the labor market.

Since in this affluent nation poverty affects a relatively small minority of our families, it is at least possible to contemplate its total elimination if our citizens deem it socially desirable to do so. One economist has estimated that it would be possible to eliminate extreme poverty through a redistribution involving less than 2% of the gross national product.[51] In the next few years, there will be much public debate about the best method to utilize to reduce or eliminate poverty in this country. Some advocate the so-called "negative income tax"; others favor an income subsidy. Meanwhile, the federal government in 1968 will spend approximately $28 billion dealing with various aspects of the poverty problem. Table 14–2 shows the breakdown of the major federal programs presently in effect.

How can we win the battle against poverty? As Figure 14–5 shows, substantial progress has already been made in reducing the number of poor, both white and nonwhite. But more work and effort is needed, not only from the government but also from business, labor, and various social and philanthropic agencies. Fortunately, we are not dealing with a problem of mass poverty, such as that which typifies many underdeveloped countries, nor are we faced by poverty resulting from large-scale unemployment. Poverty in this country is a problem of certain specific people whose personal, social, demographic, and environmental characteristics must be changed in order to enable them to escape from poverty.

It is obvious that mere financial assistance to needy families is not enough. We must improve the "employability" of these underprivileged groups so that they can raise their incomes through productive work. This calls for expansion of employment opportunities in depressed areas and strengthening of federal, state, and local programs of training. These same programs are also necessary to reduce hard-core unemployment and upgrade the skills of our substandard employed. A number of federal programs have made an encouraging start in these directions.

THE AREA REDEVELOPMENT ACT

In 1961, Congress passed the Area Redevelopment Act with the objective of stimulating the expansion of employment opportunities in economically distressed areas through a variety of programs, including:

1. Loans payable to the Treasury at low interest rates which would help create new jobs in expanding industries.

[51] W. H. Locke Anderson, "Trickling Down: The Relationship Between Economic Growth and the Extent of Poverty among American Families," *Quarterly Journal of Economics*, Vol. LXXVIII (November, 1964), p. 1.

TABLE 14-2 How Washington Helps the Poor

Major Programs	Spending $000,000 Fiscal 1968	Where the Money Goes
Training and education		
Pre-college education [HEW]	$1,200	9.5-million students, 30% Negro
Head Start [OEO]	325	Pre-school help for 616,533 children
Job Corps [OEO]	285	Training, education for 98,000 school dropouts, 58% Negro
Neighborhood Youth Corps [OEO]	281	Jobs, training, education for 389,200 youths, 42% Negro
Manpower Development [Labor Dept.]	251	Classroom and job training for 179,000, 48% and 32% Negro
CollegeWork-Study grants [HEW]	102	Subsidizes part-time work for 226,300 needy students
Educational Opportunity Grants [HEW]	95	Grants to 170,412 poor college students
Concentrated Employment [Labor Dept., OEO]	55	Helps 94,000 hard-core unemployed, 85% Negro in 76 slums
Work Incentive & Training [HEW]	40	Trains or educates 32,000 welfare recipients for work
Upward Bound [OEO]	30	Pre-college help for 23,000
Vista [OEO]	30	Trains, pays 5,000 volunteers to work on 450 projects among poor
Migrants [OEO]	25	Education, housing, day care for 148,500 seasonal workers
Follow Through [OEO]	15	Extra care in first school years
Health		
Health insurance for aged [HEW]	1,700	Medicare coverage for 6.3-million poor
Medical care [HEW]	1,400	Medicaid for 6.9-million welfare recipients and other poor
Vocational Rehabilitation [HEW]	280	Diagnoses, treatment, services and facilities for 697,500 poor
Indian health [HEW]	99	Furnishes health care, education to 390,000 Indians, Eskimos
Child and infant health [HEW]	56	Furnishes care for 170,000 children, 75,000 mothers
Comprehensive Health Services [OEO]	33	Neighborhood centers help 223,000
Housing		
Low-Rent Public Housing [HUD]	184	Helps finance 1.2-million poor people in 477,119 housing units
Neighborhood Facilities [HUD]	27	Grants to build or rehabilitate about 100 community centers
Rent Supplement [HUD]	4	Subsidizes 12,000 poor families or individuals in 3,350 units
Cash benefits		
Social Security [HEW]	7,900	Old-age and disability payments to an estimated 7.3-million poor
Public Assistance [HEW]	3,500	Grants to 8.2-million under state welfare programs

DATA: Budget Bureau and BW estimates of amounts going to persons fitting official definition of poverty.
SOURCE: *Business Week*, May 4, 1968, p. 78. By permission of McGraw-Hill, Inc.

2. Creation of new community facilities, such as industrial parks, access roads, and rail lines, to help communities attract new industry.
3. Technical assistance to industries which lack the money to utilize the latest industrial techniques.
4. Retraining displaced workers so that they are better able to qualify for new job opportunities.

The retraining provisions of the ARA, as it is called, are particularly significant because they represent a breakthrough of the federal government into an area in which most economists agree massive efforts will be required in the next few years if we are to fit our labor force for the jobs that will become available. The fact is that in many areas of the country, shortages of skilled machinists and technicians of various kinds exist side by side with large pools of unemployed labor. The ARA delegates to the Secretary of Labor the responsibility for determining area and individual training needs, determining whether training facilities and services are available to meet these needs, selecting and referring individuals for training, and paying retraining subsistence allowances to eligible trainees. These responsibilities are carried out by the federal-state employment security system. The training period is limited to 16 weeks.

While experience under the ARA is still too limited to permit proper appraisal of its effectiveness, the act has been widely criticized for being faulty both in administration and in basic concept. Some critics maintain that the ARA has spread its meager tools too thin by designating too many areas as eligible for relief. More than one third of all the counties in the United States have been put on the list of eligibility for ARA benefits. Other critics believe that the entire ARA program is unsound in principle because it encourages people to remain in depressed regions, whereas a more effective solution might result from migration of workers to other areas where better economic opportunities exist.

Finally, many businessmen maintain that retraining can be more efficiently performed and supervised by private industry than by governmental agencies. Whether or not the government's ARA program is sound in principle, it is apparent that the funds available are quite inadequate to achieve the announced purposes of the act, in view of the immensity of the problem. President Johnson's recently enacted Antipoverty Act will enable additional funds and increased governmental attention to be directed to these depressed areas.

THE MANPOWER DEVELOPMENT AND TRAINING ACT OF 1962

In 1962, Congress, recognizing that millions of unemployed persons lacked marketable skills and that the retraining problem was a general one not confined to specific depressed areas, enacted legislation to promote training programs. The act provides a program of occupational training, with priority given to unemployed persons and to persons in farm families which net less than $1,200 per year. Courses of training are offered to employed persons in order to update and upgrade skills. The U.S. Department of Labor has also placed high priority on the initiation of special training programs for youth.

Training programs under the MDTA are much more extensive than under the ARA and can last as long as 52 weeks. For unemployed persons receiving training, the act permits the payment of training allowances equal to the average unemployment compensation benefits in the respective states. These training allowances are financed 100% by federal funds for the first two years and by 50–50 matching funds thereafter. All training projects must be supported by a survey of local training needs to determine those occupations for which specific demand exists and in which training appears indicated. The training is conducted principally through existing state vocational agencies in classes, but on-the-job training opportunities are also offered. Thus, in 1968, about 186,000 persons will participate in on-the-job training and the 1969 budget anticipates 281,000.[52] In 1966, institutional training programs were also added to the list of approved training programs under the act, and in 1967, about 109,000 persons completed institutional training courses.[53]

THE ECONOMIC OPPORTUNITY ACT OF 1964

In August, 1964, Congress passed the Economic Opportunity Act of 1964, more popularly known as the "Antipoverty Act." This law represents the first attempt by our federal government, through one comprehensive piece of legislation, to attack the major bases of poverty in our nation. Title I of the act establishes a Job Corps to increase the employability of young men and young women age 16–21 by providing them with education, vocational training, and useful work experience, including work directed toward the conservation of natural resources. Title II authorizes a system of grants to assist community action programs designed to combat poverty. Title III includes special programs to combat poverty in rural areas, such as assistance to migrant and seasonal workers. Other parts of the act extend aid to small businesses and provide for work experience programs similar to those authorized under the MDTA. A new bureau—the Office of Economic Opportunity—has been established under the law to administer its broad provisions and has undertaken a wide variety of programs to help the disadvantaged groups in our nation. Among these are the Neighborhood Youth Corps, Project Head Start, Jobs Corps, and others.

---

[52] *Manpower Report of the President, April, 1968, op. cit.,* p. 206.

[53] *Ibid.,* p. 205

Industry Cooperative Programs

One of the most encouraging developments in the last few years has been the increasing involvement by business groups in training programs aimed at making productive workers out of residents in slum areas. For example, in Chicago, major industries are cooperating with government and community agencies to provide employment and training for 3,000 problem youth. In the steel industry, seven major steel companies and the Steelworkers' Union and government have cooperated in developing a series of training projects.

In 1968, President Johnson launched a new program to be called "Job Opportunities in Business Sector" (JOBS). The idea behind it is that industry should pay the normal costs of training and hiring the jobless and that government should pay the extra costs involving the hard-core unemployed, including extra training, transportation, health, counseling, and the like. A "National Alliance of Businessmen," headed by Henry Ford II, will attempt to get 500,000 hard-core unemployed into productive jobs over a period of three years. In almost every city of the nation, programs with similar objectives enlisting the cooperation of government, business, unions, and community agencies are underway in a vast attempt to make a major impact on hard-core unemployment.

TYPES OF UNEMPLOYMENT

Unemployment can be classified into various types, either from the point of view of the individuals concerned or from the point of view of economists who look at the phenomenon of unemployment as it affects the economy as a whole.

Why the Unemployed Look for Work

When individuals are asked why they are unemployed and looking for work, their responses tend to follow a particular pattern. Based on six separate studies made by the U.S. Department of Labor, the following average breakdown results:

40% of the unemployed had lost their previous jobs.
15% had quit their last jobs.
25% were reentering the labor force after a period of absence.
20% were new entrants who had never held a full-time job.

These proportions will vary over the year. For example, job losers ranged from one fourth of the unemployed in June, 1966, to about half of the total in December, 1964, and January, 1966. On the other hand, more than one fourth of the unemployed were new entrants in June, when school was out of session, but less than one sixth were in this category in the winter months.[54]

Persons on layoff, whether temporary or indefinite, as well as those who lose their jobs permanently are classed as "job losers." Although most people think of this classification when the term unemployment is mentioned, actually unemployment from this source represents only about one fourth of total unemployment. As can be seen from Table 14–3, job losers are a more important component of total unemployment for Negroes than for whites. The higher job-loser rate for Negro men, for example, is probably attributable to their concentration in semiskilled and unskilled jobs in industries where seasonal and economic cutbacks are common. In addition, discrimination results in Negro workers being the first ones fired and the last ones recalled.[55]

Persons who voluntarily leave their job and immediately start to look for work are termed "job leavers." Obviously, the line between this group and the job losers is not entirely clear, since some workers may leave in anticipation of a job loss which seems imminent. The job-leaver rate is high among teen-agers and young adults, who change jobs frequently before deciding to settle in one. This is the least important group numerically in the overall class of unemployed persons.

Labor-force entrants are either new entrants or those who for one reason or another have not been in the labor force for some time. As might be expected, most persons entering the labor force for the first time are teen-agers who are still in school. The entrant rate causes most of the seasonal variation in the overall unemployment rate. In June, 1966, over 30% of the unemployed were new entrants to the labor force.

Economic Classifications of Unemployment

Economists customarily classify unemployment into various types, such as cyclical, technological, seasonal, and other categories, which we shall consider in the following discussion. Obviously, any such categorization is arbitrary. For example, technological unemployment—the displacement of labor attributable to mechanization and automation—is frequently distinguished from cyclical unemployment—the unemployment associated with the rise and fall of business activity over the cycle. In actuality, it is almost impossible to separate these two kinds of unemployment, for the typical unemployment problem is the complex result of a number of diverse factors. Nevertheless, such classification is useful in pointing out a direction for public policy and in enabling economists, trade-union officials, and other persons concerned with the problem of

[54] Kathryn D. Hoyle, *Why the Unemployed Look for Work* (Special Labor Force Report No. 78 [Washington, D.C.: U.S. Department of Labor, January, 1967]), p. 32.

[55] *Ibid.*, p. 36.

TABLE 14–3

UNEMPLOYMENT RATES, BY REASON FOR LOOKING FOR WORK, COLOR, AGE, AND SEX,
SELECTED MONTHS' 1964, 1965, AND 1966

Age, Sex, Month, and Year	Total Unemployment Rate		Job-Loser Rate		Job-Leaver Rate		Entrant Rate	
	White	Non-white	White	Non-white	White	Non-white	White	Non-white
BOTH SEXES, 14 YEARS AND OVER								
June, 1964..........	5.5	10.8	1.9	4.8	0.6	1.2	3.0	4.8
December, 1964.....	4.2	8.8	2.0	4.9	.5	1.1	1.7	2.8
June, 1965..........	5.0	9.3	1.6	3.6	.6	1.1	2.8	4.6
November, 1965.....	3.5	7.5	1.4	3.1	.7	1.3	1.4	3.1
January, 1966.......	3.9	8.2	2.0	3.9	.6	1.3	1.3	3.0
June, 1966..........	4.3	9.0	1.0	2.7	.6	1.1	2.7	5.2
14–19 YEARS OLD, BOTH SEXES								
June, 1964..........20.5		33.2	1.7	5.1	1.0	1.9	17.8	26.2
December, 1964.....12.7		23.2	2.8	6.3	0.8	2.3	9.1	14.6
June, 1965..........19.4		30.4	1.4	2.8	0.9	1.3	17.1	26.3
November, 1965.....10.0		26.6	1.6	4.9	1.6	4.5	6.8	17.2
January, 1966.......10.1		26.9	2.6	7.2	1.7	3.0	5.8	16.7
June, 1966..........16.8		31.6	1.0	3.2	0.9	1.5	14.9	26.9
MALES, 20 YEARS AND OVER								
June, 1964..........	3.2	7.0	1.9	5.2	0.5	0.9	0.8	0.9
December, 1964.....	3.4	7.5	2.1	6.1	.4	.5	.9	0.9
June, 1965..........	2.6	5.4	1.5	4.0	.4	.7	.7	0.7
November, 1965.....	2.2	4.7	1.4	3.1	.4	.8	.4	0.8
January, 1966.......	3.2	5.7	2.2	4.0	.5	.6	.5	1.1
June, 1966..........	2.0	5.0	1.0	3.2	.4	.8	.6	1.0
FEMALES, 20 YEARS AND OVER								
June, 1964..........	4.6	8.9	1.9	4.1	0.8	1.6	1.9	3.2
December, 1964.....	3.6	7.8	1.6	3.0	.7	1.8	1.3	3.0
June, 1965..........	4.4	7.7	1.9	3.4	.8	1.7	1.7	2.6
November, 1965.....	3.9	6.9	1.2	2.8	.9	1.3	1.8	2.8
January, 1966.......	3.7	7.8	1.4	3.1	.6	1.8	1.7	2.9
June, 1966..........	3.4	6.6	0.9	1.9	.9	1.6	1.6	3.1

SOURCE: Kathryn D. Hoyle, *Why the Unemployed Look for Work* (Special Labor Force
Report No. 78 [Washington, D.C.: U.S. Department of Labor, January, 1967]), p. 37.

unemployment to attack this complex phenomenon in an orderly
manner.

CYCLICAL UNEMPLOYMENT

The outstanding source of unemployment in our modern economy
is the recurrent fluctuation in business which has been called the business

cycle. While the business cycle has characterized American industrial development almost since its inception, mass unemployment of a cyclical nature is a comparatively recent problem. Prior to 1929, the number of unemployed in industry did not exceed 5 million per annum. Yet, in 1933, it is estimated that approximately 13 million workers were unemployed. The figure of 13 million understates the tragedy of unemployment, for another 25 million persons were directly or indirectly dependent upon these unemployed.

Various theories have been advanced by economists to explain the recurrent fluctuations in business activity which we call the business cycle. Some economists believe that in a capitalistic system, progress characteristically proceeds in fits and starts. They argue that the primary force impelling fluctuations in economic activity is the impact of inventions, wars, and new discoveries. These factors raise the rate of profit which businessmen expect to make on new investment and induce them to risk capital in new ventures. But when the new investment has caught up with the developments of science and technology and has exploited to the limit what is economically feasible, all that remains for a while is mere upkeep and replacement. As a consequence, new investment contracts; output and employment recede; and depression sets in. Other economists, while conceding that the profitability of investment may fluctuate from time to time due to the impact of such outside influences, contend that the great fluctuations which actually occur in production and employment are attributable to the instability of our credit system. Were it not for the great expansion of credit which occurs during the upswing of the cycle, the boom would never run to excess, and presumably the resulting downward adjustment would be less severe.

Characteristics of Cyclical Unemployment

The causes of the business cycle constitute a separate field of study which is outside the scope of our immediate inquiry in this book. It is pertinent to this discussion, however, to observe certain definite characteristics in the fluctuation of employment which customarily develop in boom and depression. Thus, for example, it is well established that the durable-goods-producing industries experience more extreme variations in output and employment over the cycle than those producing nondurable goods. The construction industry is particularly hard hit during depression, the reason being that investment in homes or business plants is the type of expenditure which can easily be postponed when income declines.

The burden of cyclical unemployment is not spread evenly. Some industries and occupations fare reasonably well, while others are subject to extreme variations in demand. Employment in manufacturing has proved to be one of the most volatile in the nonagricultural group. Since employment in the service industries is much more stable over the cycle than in manufacturing, the shift in employment from the latter to the former will have a stabilizing effect upon employment over the cycle. While the economy has seemed less susceptible in recent years to the extreme depression-boom cycle of the 1920's and 1930's, nevertheless a glance at Figure 14–1 clearly reveals that a cyclical pattern in employment and unemployment still persists.

SECULAR TRENDS IN EMPLOYMENT

Secular trends are long-term trends which may perhaps take 50 years to run their course. They are distinguishable from cyclical movements, which on the average do not exceed 10 years in duration.[56] Secular trends in employment within an industry are due to the influence of technological change, population growth, and competition from other industries. Perhaps these trends are also due to some fundamental "law" in the development of an industry. For example, the typical development of an industry might be represented by a logistic curve—that is, production and employment rise first as an increasing rate, then at a decreasing rate, finally reach a maximum as demand becomes stabilized, and eventually decline.

Secular trends are at work not only in particular industries but also in the economy as a whole, and perhaps also in the world at large. Thus, changes in gold supply, wars, changes in the pattern of consumer demand, and population shift will all affect employment trends. According to one theory—associated with the name Kondratieff—there are "long waves" in economic development reflecting such underlying causes and averaging in the neighborhood of 50 years in duration. On the other hand, Simon Kuznets has evolved a theory of a long cycle lasting about 20 years. Both theories would agree that if the low point of a long wave or long cycle happens to coincide with the low point of a business cycle—as may have been the case in 1933—a very serious and deep depression will result, with a corresponding sharp reduction in the volume of employment.

TECHNOLOGICAL UNEMPLOYMENT

Technical unemployment is that displacement of labor by machinery and improved methods of production which is attributable to advances of the arts and sciences or to improvements in the technique of management. This definition does not make technological unemployment synonymous with all kinds of displacement of labor by machinery. For example, suppose that a minimum wage is imposed on an industry, dou-

---

[56] Business cycles are normally considered to be of two types—the so-called "40-month cycle" and the so-called "Juglar cycle," which lasts about 10 years. The so-called "Kondratieff cycle," which lasts about 50 years, is, for the purpose of this discussion, included in the category of secular trends.

bling the wage rates it has to pay. Employers would now find it profitable to introduce machines already known and in use in other industries but which hitherto had not been profitable to utilize in this particular industry operating at a low wage rate. Some labor will be displaced by the introduction of the machines, but it would be misleading to attribute this to technological change. The unemployment in this case is attributable to the rise in the price of labor and would have occurred even in a stationary state where technological progress was absent. Thus, for the purpose of precise analytical reasoning, it is important to distinguish "substitution" unemployment from "technological" unemployment. In actual practice, however, it is usually impossible to separate the two, so that any figures for technological unemployment are likely to contain a substantial amount of substitution unemployment as well.

Possibility of Permanent Technological Unemployment

Can laborsaving machinery produce permanent technological unemployment? The answer to this question will depend upon whether we are considering a particular firm or industry, on the one hand, or the economy as a whole, on the other. In a particular firm or industry, the effect of a laborsaving machine upon employment will depend upon the rate of introduction of the machine, the laborsaving capacity of the machine, the extent to which the skills of the old workers are still useful under the new method of production, and the elasticity of demand for the product.

Whether laborsaving machinery can produce permanent technological unemployment in the economy as a whole has long been the subject of controversy in the literature. According to economic theory, the effect of a laborsaving invention is to raise the marginal product of capital relative to labor and thus reduce the relative share of labor in the national income. Some writers have seized on this possibility to argue that a decline in the relative share of labor in the national income will mean a shift of income from those classes which save little to those which save more, with the result that consumer purchasing power will be diminished, a deflationary influence will be exerted on the consumption goods industries, and the equilibrium level of employment will therefore be reduced.[57] This conclusion, however, rests on an erroneous major premise and is not borne out by historical evidence. While most inventions are laborsaving, there has been no long-run trend toward a reduced share for labor in the national income. The effect of a laborsaving invention in reducing the relative share of labor in the national income is only temporary. Since the invention also increases the marginal productivity of capital, and therefore the expectation of profits, investment will increase and thereby raise the marginal productivity of labor and the level of employment.

[57] Joan Robinson, *Essays in the Theory of Employment* (New York: Macmillan Co., 1937), p. 135

Technological Progress and Employment Opportunities

The kind of technological progress we have experienced in the past has expanded employment opportunities for two reasons. In the first place, the production of laborsaving machinery has itself constituted a major form of new investment and has contributed directly to a rise in employment in the durable goods industries. In the second place, the invention of a laborsaving device such as the gasoline engine ushering in the automobile age has created a tremendous tide of secondary investment in road construction, gas stations, tire plants, motels, etc. Therefore, even though technological change as we have known it has produced serious problems of dislocation of communities, obsolescence of skills, and large-scale unemployment, it also has at the same time opened up extensive new job opportunities.

What about automation? Is this just a new version of laborsaving invention—or is it something different which may therefore have quite different repercussions upon employment?

Automation and Unemployment

In order to answer this question, let us first consider what is meant by the term "automation." Automation is something definite and distinguishable from merely improved mechanization or general technological progress. Automation means *continuous automatic production,* linking together more than one already mechanized operation, with the product automatically transferred between two or among several operations. Most of the ideas and equipment that make automation possible have been with us for a long time. If there is anything new about automation, it is the widespread and systematic application of its principles today.[58]

As was noted earlier, in Chapter 6, although organized labor has in the past generally recognized that it was not in its best interests to attempt to stem the march of technological progress, recently labor leaders have become more outspoken about the possible depressing effects of automation upon employment. AFL–CIO's President George Meany, speaking at that organization's fifth convention, expressed his view as follows:

Automation can be a blessing or it can be a curse. . . . I say this with deep sincerity—there is no longer any question in my mind as to the direction in which automation is going today. There is no element of blessing in it. It is rapidly becoming a real curse to this society. When you study what's happening, you realize that this is a real threat. This could bring us to a national catastrophe.[59]

---

[58] According to a recent study, a growing proportion of investment is being allocated to purchases of automated equipment: 11% in 1955, 12% in 1959, and 19% in 1963. See U.S. Department of Labor, *Automation, Productivity and Manpower Problems* (Washington, D.C.: U.S. Government Printing Office, 1964), p. 7.

[59] National Industrial Conference Board, *Conference Board Record,* March, 1964, pp. 55–56.

Is Meany's concern justified? There is no question that the labor-saving capacity of automation is tremendous. Automation not only substitutes mechanical power for human power but also mechanical judgment for human judgment. Automation will reduce the number of workers required in many offices and plants. On the other hand, it will create many new jobs in industries which manufacture and assemble the intricate machines and complicated controls which make automation possible. Likewise, skilled personnel will be required to maintain the automated equipment. In these respects the impact of automation is much like that of other forms of technological change which over the years have provided more jobs and a rising standard of living for American labor.

However, there are three aspects of automation which can create major problems for labor and which should not be ignored.

In the first place, it is possible that automation will not create as much secondary investment as some of the earlier developments in technology. This is because automation involves not so much a substitution of machinery for labor—which requires large amounts of new investment—as a linking and integration of already mechanized operations and the application of electronic controls. While the spread of automation has resulted in the construction of many new plants designed to produce the new electronic equipment which automation requires, it is by no means clear that such investment will be sufficient to offset the loss of purchasing power resulting from a reduced wage bill in the automated plants.

In the second place, while other forms of technological change have created problems through displacement of individual workers in existing organizations, automation may create problems of wholesale displacement of labor by rendering plants obsolete and inducing a change in plant location. The new flow concept of production has made many multistory plants inefficient and required a move to one-story structures. The development of automation techniques has reduced the attractiveness of location in low-labor-cost areas. Instead, many companies adopting such techniques will now gravitate to other areas. Such plant abandonment may create additional distressed areas with surplus labor available.

In the third place, it is not clear that the effect of automation upon skill requirements of our labor force will be the same as for other types of technological change. As we have observed in earlier chapters of this text, technological progress in this country has created a need for a more skilled labor force. Automation also falls in this trend. For example, thousands of jobs have been created in the electronic data processing industry for programmers, systems analysts, operators, and other technical personnel. Automation has also created a demand for hydraulic and pneumatic repairmen, electricians, and machinists qualified to handle and repair the complicated control systems and servomechanisms. On the other hand, there is also some disquieting evidence that operating skill requirements are more often reduced or unchanged by automation in those establishments where a high degree of technological advancement short of automation has already been achieved. The increase in operating skills appears to be required by the prior change from manual to machine operation rather than by the change from machine to automation.

Despite the fact that automation presents acute and peculiar problems with respect to the level of employment, it seems likely that in the long run—as one aspect of the stream of technological progress—automation will provide a net benefit to the economy both in terms of employment and in terms of standard of living. It is well to remember that 25 years ago, nuclear fission was an abstract theory; today, several hundred thousand workers are employed in the production and application of nuclear products. Who is to say what new products, what new avenues of production and distribution, the new frontier of automation will open up?

SEASONAL UNEMPLOYMENT

Seasonal unemployment is due to variations in business during the year caused by climatic or other seasonal changes in supply and by changing seasonal demands reflecting custom, habit, and style factors. On the supply side, seasonal variations result in a fluctuating flow of materials or seasonal alteration in production techniques. Agriculture, for example, reflects the direct influence of the weather and therefore is peculiarly susceptible to seasonal variation in output and employment. Moreover, the various industries which process agricultural products are likewise subject to seasonal fluctuation in employment due to the availability or nonavailability of the raw material upon which their operation depends. On the demand side, seasonal variations are particularly marked in those industries which produce unstandardized consumption goods with relatively elastic demands. The Easter bonnet and the Christmas card are two illustrations of commodities in the demand for which seasonality plays a dominant role. To a lesser extent, seasonal variations attributable to either supply or demand conditions characterize the manufacture of agricultural equipment and the fertilizer, construction, and mining industries.

The seasonal variation in employment in particular industries takes on such a definite pattern that it can be forecast with considerable exactitude. Within any large state or area—if industry is diversified—opposite seasonal variations tend to counteract one another, so that the net seasonal fluctuations in total employment may be relatively small in consequence. For the country as a whole, such a balancing will always occur; but because of the distance involved and the insufficient mobility of labor, a substantial amount of seasonal unemployment may remain. Statistical techniques have been developed to eliminate the influence of seasonality from data of employment, production, and sales, so as to permit analysis of such statistics free from the distortion of seasonal variations, which tend to obscure long-term trends.

In agriculture, the problem of seasonal unemployment is even more acute. The seasonality of the pattern of demand for labor has given rise to a migratory labor force, moving from one area to another, following the cycle of the crops. These people, generally in the very low income brackets, unable to form fixed associations or community ties, present a serious political and sociological problem with which no relief agency has been able to cope.

FRICTIONAL UNEMPLOYMENT

Frictional unemployment is attributable to time lost in changing jobs rather than to a lack of job opportunities. Frictional unemployment, defined broadly enough, could encompass almost all types of unemployment, since the cyclical unemployed, the seasonal worker, and the victim of declining demand in a particular industry must all take time to find new jobs. Frictional unemployment, however, can be distinguished as that type which would not be significantly reduced by a general increase in demand. Even during World War II, when unemployment of other types was practically nonexistent, frictional unemployment persisted, for the shifting of labor from areas of relative surplus to areas of relative scarcity could not be accomplished without a lapse of time.

The concept of frictional unemployment also involves the notion of unemployment of relatively short duration. Thus a constantly changing pool of workers aggregating, say, 2 million, most of whom find new jobs in three or four months, would be considered normal frictional unemployment with a labor force of 75 million. But if examination indicated that there was a stagnant pool of 1 million men who remained unemployed for long periods of time, it would be evident that there was a problem not of transition from one job to another but of serious dislocation, attributable perhaps to major technological innovation rendering useless the skills of a particular trade, or the depressed condition of a particular industry or geographical area. It is important to recognize, therefore, that it is not the *amount* but the *nature* of the unemployment which characterizes it as frictional.

The volume of frictional unemployment in a large country such as the United States is substantial because of the multitude of workers who make job changes. For example, a Bureau of Labor Statistics study revealed that about 5.5 million of the almost 70 million Americans employed in January, 1966, were working in an occupation different from the one they were in January, 1965. Of this number, about 80% also changed their employer during the year, and about 75% changed the industry in which they were working.[60]

[60] Samuel Saben, *Occupational Mobility of Employed Workers* (Special Labor Force Report No. 84 [Washington, D.C.: U.S. Department of Labor, June, 1967]), pp. 31, 36, 37.

The volume of frictional unemployment to some extent reflects the ability of workers to withstand some unemployment while they are looking around for a job. The high wages earned by our employees while they are at work and the unemployment compensation benefits those involuntarily unemployed receive while out of work enable them to take more time while looking for a new job and to find an opening which will improve their ultimate income, rather than being compelled to take the first job opening that is available.

Frictional unemployment is a reflection of freedom of movement in the labor market coupled with some degree of immobility. John Doe quits his job in Cleveland to go to work in Detroit, but it may be several months at the earliest before he can move his family and start work in the new location. Such friction exists even with regard to changes of jobs within a given city or state. Public employment exchanges tend to reduce time lost by giving better publicity to job openings. Unions may also perform the same function. As we noted in our discussion of labor mobility in Chapter 8, the search for work is still pursued on a rather haphazard basis by most workers. There is much that can be done in this area by government and business to improve information about job vacancies. Any such improvement would tend to lower frictional unemployment.

Wage-Distortion Unemployment

If we look at the labor market, we find a heavy concentration of unemployment among teen-agers, unskilled and inexperienced workers, and poorly educated persons, and among Negroes. In a free labor market, one would expect that this surplus of labor would tend to bring down rates in relatively unskilled jobs so that more of these people could find work at rates which made their employment profitable to employers. In actuality, however, the labor market has not functioned in this manner, primarily because of the effect of government-imposed minimum wage rates and high entrance rates in unskilled jobs maintained by labor unions. As one economist puts it, "Relative spreads between high and low wage occupations and high and low wage industries have not been widening to the extent that one might expect, given the persistence of excess supplies of unskilled and inexperienced labor in this period."[61] Other economists have noted that there has been a persistent lack of so-called "ports of entry" or "vestibule jobs" at low rates where inexperienced workers could achieve entry into firms with a minimum of difficulty.

Recognition of this problem does not mean that minimum wage laws are "bad." Employment at substandard wages is an evil which society has a right to eliminate. At the same time, however, it may be necessary to

---

[61] G. H. Hildebrand and G. E. Delehanty, "Wage Levels and Differentials," in Gordon and Gordon (eds.), *op. cit.*, p. 295.

find a way to make it possible for workers whose marginal productivity is very low to obtain and hold employment. One suggestion is to have the federal government subsidize part of the wage—based upon the difference between the government minimum and what the labor would bring in the free market—until through adequate training and experience the employee is worth the minimum established by law.

Demand versus Structural Unemployment

Definition and classification of types of unemployment constitute more than a useful exercise in orderly thinking. The classification of unemployment as one type or another can have important ramifications in terms of policy decisions, for a remedy which is applicable to one type of unemployment may not be satisfactory if the unemployment is actually attributable to other causes. If we consider seasonal and frictional unemployment as "normal" types of unemployment which would prevail even if the economy were operating at an extremely high level of activity, then we are left with the other categories of unemployment to be solved. Cyclical unemployment is generally considered as a type by itself; it can be categorized as unemployment which occurs during a recession and is caused by a temporary drop in aggregate demand. But at this writing, the economy is in a strong upswing. In the words of the Council of Economic Advisers,

> With the virtual elimination of cyclical unemployment in 1966, most of that which remains can usefully be described as either "frictional" or "structural." But these terms are not entirely precise; often a particular worker who is without a job cannot easily be classified as either frictionally or structurally unemployed. Moreover, whenever there is also unemployment that is due to inadequate demand, it becomes impossible in many cases to say which particular workers are unemployed for frictional, structural, or cyclical reasons.[62]

Because of the difficulty in classifying the unemployment which exists from time to time, discussions have proceeded primarily on the basis of the comparative effectiveness of reducing total unemployment by (1) measures to raise aggregate demand, via tax policy, expenditure increase, or monetary expansion; or (2) measures to improve the employability of the unemployed via retraining, education, placement, and other labor market policies.[63] Those emphasizing the former represent the "inadequate aggregate demand" school; those stressing the latter represent the "structural" point of view. It should be emphasized that adherents of these various points of view recognize that this is not an all-black–all-white

[62] *Economic Report of the President, 1967* (Washington, D.C.: U.S. Government Printing Office, 1967), pp. 103–4.

[63] Richard A. Musgrave, "Demand versus Structural Unemployment," in William G. Bowen and Frederick H. Harbison (eds.), *Unemployment in a Prosperous Economy* (Princeton University Research Report Series No. 108 [Princeton, N.J., 1965]), p. 93.

situation and that there must be a judicious mixture of the two policies. The debate really concerns the matter of emphasis in public policy.

The President's Council of Economic Advisers has, on the whole, championed the inadequate-demand point of view. Thus, Walter W. Heller, former Chairman of the Council, contended that hard-core unemployment is only an insignificant fraction of the total and that a large part of it—due to such factors as obsolescence, automation, changes in demand, and the like—would disappear if proper tax, spending, and credit policies produced an expansion of demand.[64] Other economists, while not discounting the worth of retraining programs, emphasize that jobs are created only by the spending of money. As one writer puts it: "Education does not create jobs; retraining does not create jobs; placement does not create jobs. . . . jobs are created only by the purchase of goods and services."[65]

In this view, practically any desired employment level could be attained by aggregative means alone if we would or could accept the consequences in terms of inflation.[66] The choice of an unemployment target, then, depends upon the trade-off which the economy is willing to accept between price inflation on the one hand and unused resources on the other, and as experience has demonstrated, it is extremely difficult to avoid inflation once unemployment drops below the 4% level. This school of thought further maintains that the improvements which have occurred in employment in recent years were spread over all groups—both the disadvantaged and the advantaged workers. As Arthur Okun, a member of the Council of Economic Advisers puts it, ". . . the teenage worker and Negro worker pose a hard problem, but not a hard-core problem. Quite the contrary, their job opportunities are especially sensitive to over-all economic conditions."[67]

The opposing view, propounded by such diverse public figures as William McChesney Martin, Jr., chairman of the Federal Reserve Board, and Stanley H. Ruttenberg, economic adviser to the Secretary of Labor, holds that structural unemployment has become indefinitely persistent even in periods of unprecedented general prosperity and that even a substantial improvement in business conditions will leave structural unemployment at an abnormally high level. Martin, as a banker, adds an additional warning that if we try to solve structural unemployment by a massive monetary and fiscal stimulation of overall demand, we shall have to carry this program to such lengths as to create serious new problems of an inflationary character.

[64] *Economic Report of the President, 1964* (Washington, D.C.: U.S. Government Printing Office, 1964), pp. 166–90.

[65] Garth Mangum, "The Role of 'Job Creation' Programs," in Bowen and Harbison (eds.), *op. cit.*, p. 108.

[66] *Ibid.*, p. 110.

[67] Arthur M. Okun, "The Role of Aggregate Demand in Alleviating Unemployment," in Bowen and Harbison (eds.), *op. cit.*, p. 76.

Structuralists tend to emphasize that the position of the hard-core unemployed groups has deteriorated rather than improved as overall employment moved to record highs. There is some evidence to bear out this contention. For example, whereas in 1961 the overall teen-age unemployment rate was 2.3 times the national unemployment rate, in February, 1966, it was 2.9 times the national rate.[68] Similar concern is voiced by structuralists concerning the alarming rate of unemployment among non-white residents of the ghettos. Structuralists maintain that the governmental policy advocated by demand theorists—such as a tax cut in 1964—produced the largest relative decline in unemployment rates among the workers who were best off before the tax cut: adult workers, white workers, and more skilled workers,[69] so that the position of the disadvantaged groups relatively deteriorated. Likewise, they doubt the efficacy of merely pumping funds into the economy as a means of reducing unemployment, and stress the need for programs tailored to the particular groups who constitute the long-term unemployed in our economy.

THE CHALLENGE OF A HIGH-EMPLOYMENT ECONOMY

In 1946, Congress enacted the Employment Act of 1946. This statute provides:

It is the continuing policy and responsibility of the federal government to use all practicable means consistent with its needs and obligations and other essential considerations of national policy, with the assistance and cooperation of industry, agriculture, labor and state and local governments, to coordinate and utilize all its plans, functions, and resources, for the purpose of creating and maintaining, in a manner calculated to foster and promote free competitive enterprise and the general welfare, conditions under which there will be afforded useful employment opportunities including self-employment, for those able, willing and seeking to work and to promote maximum employment, production and purchasing power.

Under this act the President is charged with the responsibility of formulating a program to achieve the objectives stated in the statute. To assist the President in carrying out this responsibility, a Council of Economic Advisers was created in the Executive Office of the President. The Council prepares for the President annually, for submission by him to Congress, an Economic Report, which includes relevant data on current levels of employment, purchasing power, and production, and recommendations for such legislative actions as may best effectuate the purposes of the act.

---

[68] Joseph D. Mooney, "Teenage Labor Problems and the Neighborhood Youth Corps," in Frederick H. Harbison and Joseph D. Mooney (eds.), *Critical Issues in Employment Policy* (Princeton University Research Report Series No. 109, [Princeton, N.J., 1966]), p. 97.

[69] Charles C. Killingsworth. "Unemployment after the Tax Cut," in *Unemployment in a Prosperous Economy, op. cit.,* p. 84.

The Employment Act of 1946 is not a "full-employment" act. Its aim has been interpreted to be high-level employment, and the content of this concept has evolved over time. For a number of years, the Council of Economic Advisers adopted as a "reasonable interim objective" the reduction of unemployment to a 4% figure. At this writing, unemployment is averaging below that amount, and increasing attention is now being directed to improvement of employability of various disadvantaged groups in the labor market.

However, the problem of maintaining even a 4% level of unemployment is no easy task in view of the changes which are occurring in the American economy. In the previous chapter, we observed that when account is taken of the rate of growth of the labor force and the rate of increase in man-hour output, we must find a way to increase the number of jobs at a rate of 4½% per annum just to keep unemployment from rising. This task is further complicated by a number of trends which are tending to raise the unemployment rate in our economy. First, the self-employed have been a continually declining fraction of the labor force; since they are not subject to significant unemployment, their declining importance should raise unemployment rates. Second, women have become an ever increasing portion of the labor force, and they have a higher unemployment rate than men. Third, the shift from farm and rural to urban pursuits tends to convert what may have been underemployment to unemployment visible in the official statistics. One trend operating in the opposite direction has been mentioned in previous discussions, that is, the decreasing importance of goods-producing industries and blue-collar jobs and the increasing importance of service industries and white-collar jobs, which have been characterized by greater stability in employment.[70]

Because unemployment is a complex problem arising from a variety of causes, it must be attacked on many fronts at once. Structural elements and lack of sufficient demand jointly contribute to our present unemployment problems, and any successful policy must attack both aspects. Any sound solution to the unemployment problem must recognize that a job in our modern society is more than a source of income—it is a symbol of status, a symbol of identity with the social environment. Whatever may be the merits of a negative income tax or other outright subsidies, we must find productive work for our unemployed and our poor if they are to feel an identity with the bulk of the citizens in our nation.

QUESTIONS FOR DISCUSSION

1. Discuss the characteristics of the typical unemployed person. Of what significance is the shift in employment from goods-producing to service industries?

[70] Okun, *op. cit.*, p. 73.

2. "Hard-core unemployment is not made of rock, but of ice, and melts when total demand expands." Discuss the validity of this quotation.

3. Discuss the merits and deficiencies of the definition of unemployment used by the Bureau of the Census. In your opinion, what groups are excluded by this definition who should be counted among the unemployed?

4. What is meant by the "trade-off" between unemployment and price inflation? What factors in the labor market will influence this relationship?

5. Discuss the meaning of the following concepts: poverty; subemployment; invisible unemployment.

SUGGESTIONS FOR FURTHER READING

FLAIM, PAUL O. "Jobless Trends in 20 Large Metropolitan Areas," *Monthly Labor Review*, Vol. XCI (May, 1968), pp. 16–28.

    A timely discussion of the extent and causes of unemployment in major metropolitan areas of the United States.

FORTUNE MAGAZINE. A Special Issue on Business and the Urban Crisis, January, 1968.

    A current analysis, liberally illustrated by charts and figures, of the problems facing Negroes on the nation's ghettos.

LEVY, MICHAEL E. "Full Employment and Inflation: A 'Trade-Off' Analysis," *The Conference Board Record*, Vol. III (December, 1966), pp. 17–27.

    An excellent discussion and summary of the literature on structural and hidden unemployment and their relationship to price stability and full employment.

NORTHRUP, HERBERT H., and ROWAN, RICHARD L. (eds.). *The Negro and Employment Opportunity*. Ann Arbor, Mich.: University of Michigan, Bureau of Industrial Relations, 1965.

    A series of articles on various aspects of the Negro employment problem in American industry.

Report of the President's National Advisory Commission on Civil Disorders. Washington, D.C.: U.S. Government Printing Office, 1968.

    An up-to-date study of poverty and unemployment in the slums and how these factors contribute to riots, crime, and unrest.

PART V

*Governmental Wage Regulation
and the Shorter Workweek*

GOVERNMENTAL
REGULATION OF WAGES

Governmental wage regulation in the United States has been largely confined to the establishment of minimum wages and maximum hours, except in times of emergency. In such times, as during World War II and the Korean War, the government has regulated the terms of compensation of the vast majority of the labor force. More recently, the government has tried a system of wage restraint through the publication of wage "guidelines." This chapter examines the various types of wage regulation and their economic effects.

THE FEDERAL FAIR LABOR STANDARDS ACT

The basic minimum wage law of the land is the Fair Labor Standards Act, or Wage and Hour Law. It was first passed in 1938 and substantially amended in 1949, 1956, 1961, and 1965. The original 1938 act required that employees within its jurisdiction were to receive a minimum wage of not less than 25 cents an hour beginning October 24, 1938; 30 cents an hour beginning October 24, 1939; and 40 cents an hour beginning October 24, 1945. The act also provided machinery whereby the 40-cent objective could be achieved prior to 1945 through recommendations of industry committees composed of labor, management, and the public. Because of wartime wage increases, nearly all workers covered by the act were receiving 40 cents per hour or more before the statutory requirement took effect. In 1949 the statutory minimum wage was raised to 75 cents an hour, in 1956 to $1, in 1961 to $1.15, and in 1963 to $1.25, except that occupations which were newly covered by the 1961 amendments had their minimum set first at $1 for 1961, then $1.15 as of September 1, 1965 and $1.25 as of September 1, 1966. The 1965 amendments, like those of 1961, differentiated between those already covered by the act and those brought under its purview for the first time. The minimum of the former was set at $1.40 per hour as of February 1, 1967, and raised to $1.60 one year later. The latter group's minimum was established at only $1 per hour for 1967, and is to reach $1.60 per hour in four annual steps, or as of February 1, 1971. The minimum wage for farm workers who were first covered by the 1965 amendments was, however, limited to $1.30 per hour pending further action by Congress. The history of the Fair Labor Standards Act is summarized in Figure 15–1.

The Fair Labor Standards Act also regulated hours of work by requiring that time and one half be paid for all work over a standard workweek, set since 1940 at 40 hours.

FIGURE 15–1

FEDERAL MINIMUM WAGE HISTORY

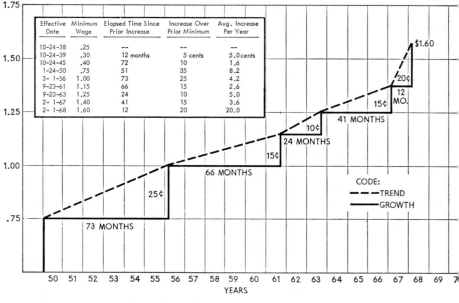

Effective Date	Minimum Wage	Elapsed Time Since Prior Increase	Increase Over Prior Minimum	Avg. Increase Per Year
10-24-38	.25	--	--	--
10-24-39	.30	12 months	5 cents	5.0 cents
10-24-45	.40	72	10	1.6
1-24-50	.75	51	35	8.2
3- 1-56	1.00	73	25	4.2
9-23-61	1.15	66	15	2.6
9-23-63	1.25	24	10	5.0
2- 1-67	1.40	41	15	3.6
2- 1-68	1.60	12	20	20.0

Chart by Retail Trade Board, Boston, Mass.

The act has never covered all employees, but coverage has greatly been expanded in recent years. The U.S. Department of Labor estimates that approximately 42.8 million workers are now covered by the act, almost triple the number originally under its protection. The increased coverage reflects both the expansion of the law's breadth and the growth of the labor force. Those outside the law's purview include principally employees of small farms and small or intrastate businesses; some government employees largely covered by other and often more generous laws; and managerial, supervisory, professional, and outside sales personnel whose compensation generally would in any case be unaffected by minimum wage legislation. Table 15–1 summarizes the coverage of the Fair Labor Standards Act by industrial groups.

TABLE 15–1

STATUS OF NONSUPERVISORY EMPLOYEES UNDER THE MINIMUM WAGE PROVISIONS OF THE FAIR LABOR STANDARDS ACT AND UNDER STATE MINIMUM WAGE LAWS AND ORDERS, BY INDUSTRY, AS OF FEBRUARY 1, 1968[a]

(In Thousands)

Industry	Total Number of Nonsupervisory Employees[c]	Employees Covered by the FLSA[b]			Number of Nonsupervisory Employees Not Covered by FLSA[c]	Number of Nonsupervisory Employees Covered by State Laws Only[c,e]	Number of Nonsupervisory Employees Not Covered by FLSA or State Laws[e]
		Total Number Covered[d]	Number Covered Prior to 1966 Amendments	Number Covered by the 1966 Amendments[d]			
United States	51,866	42,778	33,052	9,726	11,769	3,484	8,285
Agriculture, forestry and fisheries[f]	1,513	466	15	451	1,047	102	945
Mining	533	529	529	—	4	3	1
Contract construction	3,292	3,257	2,640	617	35	6	29
Manufacturing	17,517	16,942	16,871	71	575	93	482
Transportation, communications, utilities	3,917	3,842	3,738	104	75	31	44
Wholesale trade	3,275	2,487	2,360	127	788	67	721
Retail trade	9,150	5,372	3,051	2,321	3,778	1,814	1,964
Finance, insurance, real estate	2,857	2,133	2,133	—	724	141	583
Services (excluding domestic service)	7,589	5,069	1,715	3,354	2,520	1,227	1,293
Domestic service	2,223	—	—	—	2,223	—	2,223
Government	—	2,681	—	2,681	—	—	—

a Estimates are based on employment data for 1967. All employees are included except executive, administrative, and professional employees and academic administrative personnel and teachers in elementary and secondary schools.

b Employees added to coverage by the 1966 amendments include those who will be covered in 1969.

c Estimates relate to the private sector only.

d Includes the estimated 2,681,000 government employees added to coverage by the 1966 amendments.

e Estimates of employees covered by state minimum wage laws only are for those states having minimum wage laws or orders enacted or revised from 1961 to December 1, 1967.

f Total nonsupervisory employment based on data representing 1967 annual average. Coverage estimates include data on agricultural workers obtained from a survey conducted by the Department of Agriculture as of May, 1967. May data does not vary markedly from annual average data.

SOURCE: Wage and Hour and Public Contracts Divisions, U.S. Department of Labor.

Large numbers of workers originally covered by this law's wage provisions were not covered by its overtime and hours provisions until the 1965 amendments. There remain about 5 million fewer employees covered by the hours provisions than by the wage minimums. Employees in restaurants, hotels and motels, and agriculture are exempt from the overtime provisions, and those in hospitals and nursing homes and seasonal labor have less restrictive overtime requirements.

Superminimum and Prevailing Wages

In some areas, federal minimum wage legislation has gone beyond the Fair Labor Standards Act. The most extraordinary law of this character applies to pilots and copilots employed on airlines, holding certificates entitling them to make regularly scheduled flights. This law went into effect in 1934 and is now contained in Section 401 (L) of the Civil Aeronautics Act of 1938. It provides that pilots shall receive not less than a rate based upon a formula composed of base pay of $1,000–$3,000 per year, plus hourly pay, plus mileage pay, with bonuses for night flying and for flying over certain terrain; that copilots shall not receive less than their October 1, 1933, rates, which averaged about $190 monthly; and that no pilots or copilots shall fly more than 85 hours in one month. Since the introduction of faster planes automatically increases mileage pay, a pilot with eight years' experience, flying a Boeing 707 Jet plane, 85 hours per month, one half day and one half night, must by law be paid in excess of $15,000 per year and actually now receive two or three times that amount!

A second superminimum wage law, known as the Davis-Bacon Act, was first passed in 1931. As later amended, it requires contractors engaged in construction work valued at $2,000 or more, and paid for by federal funds, to pay at least the prevailing minimum wages to all construction employees. In 1965, by the O'Hara-McNamara Services Act, the Davis-Bacon type of regulation was extended to government-contract on-site services other than construction—for example, machinery installation.[1]

The Secretary of Labor determines prevailing minimum rates for the various crafts under the Davis-Bacon Act procedure. As interpreted by Secretaries since 1931, "prevailing" is usually synonymous with "union." Building-trades unions have found the Davis-Bacon Act a valuable tool to prevent undercutting of their wages and to assist the extension of the union rate. For, not infrequently, the union rate has been determined to be prevailing in a locality not even unionized but in addition paying considerably less than the union rate which actually prevails in a large city some miles away.

A third superminimum wage law is the Public Contracts or Walsh-Healey Act, which was enacted in 1936, two years prior to the passage of

---

[1] Some 35 states have laws similar to the Davis-Bacon Act.

the Fair Labor Standards Act, as a means of filling part of the gap left by the demise of the NRA. The Walsh-Healey Act provided, among other things, that for all government in-plant contracts in excess of $10,000, wages should not be less than the "prevailing minimum" as established by the Secretary of Labor. This law became inactive after the Fair Labor Standards Act of 1938 became law, but it was revived in 1948 by the then Secretary of Labor and over the next 16 years about 50 determinations of prevailing minimum wage laws were promulgated, each covering a whole industry. In 1964, the courts ruled that the Secretary of Labor's procedure in setting prevailing minima was denying due process to interested employers and other parties.[2] Since then, the Walsh-Healey Act has been in a state of suspension. In view of the broad coverage of the Fair Labor Standards Act and the high minimum rates now called for by that law, it is difficult to justify the existence of the Walsh-Healey Act.

As in the case of the Davis-Bacon Act, the Secretary of Labor historically interpreted "prevailing" wage rates under the Walsh-Healey Act to mean the union rate where a union rate existed at all. The purpose was apparently to reduce the effect of nonunion competition on unionized plants. The most obvious action of this type was the establishment of the United Mine Workers' wage structure as the prevailing Walsh-Healey rate in 1956 for the apparent purpose of eliminating the nonunion and strip mines as serious competitors for sale of coal to the Tennessee Valley Authority.[3]

State Minimum Wage Legislation

State minimum wage legislation was originally intended as protection for women and children. Seventeen such laws were in existence in 1923, when the U.S. Supreme Court ruled that the states had no power to enact wage protective laws.[4] In the early 1930's, state legislators again began to enact minimum wage laws, and again the Supreme Court ruled them unconstitutional, but this time quickly reversed itself.[5] As of March, 1968, 39 states, Puerto Rico, and the District of Columbia had enacted minimum wage laws, but those in 3 states were inactive or the rates were

---

[2] The Secretary used data collected by the U.S. Bureau of Labor Statistics to determine prevailing wages. Since these data were gathered for other BLS purposes on promise to cooperating employers that no individual company would be identified, their source could not be given to those who wanted to check them, thus denying due process in a proceeding. See *Wirtz* v. *Baldor Electric Co.*, 16 WH Cases 551 (1964).

[3] Two studies shed much light on the Walsh-Healey Act and its procedure. Herbert C. Morton, *Public Contracts and Private Wages: Experience under the Walsh-Healey Act* (Washington, D.C.: Brookings Institution, 1965); and Carroll L. Christensen and Richard A. Myren, *Wage Policy under the Walsh-Healey Public Contracts Act: A Critical Review* (Bloomington, Ind.: University of Indiana Press, 1966).

[4] *Adkins* v. *Children's Hospital*, 261 U.S. 525 (1923).

[5] *West Coast Hotel Company* v. *Parrish*, 300 U.S. 379 (1937).

established so low as to be meaningless.[6] Thus, 36 states, Puerto Rico, and the District of Columbia have effective minimum wage laws,[7] 36 of which cover both men and women. The balance of the effective state laws apply to women and minors only.[8] The data in Table 15-1 show that approximately 3.4 million persons in private employment are covered by state laws which have been adjusted since 1961, and 8.3 million are under both federal and state laws. In the latter case, the higher of the two minima applies.

Procedure for Setting State Minimum Wages

Laws in states, like the FLSA, expressly fix the amount payable as the minimum wage (see Table 15-2). In six states the laws also authorize rate fixing under the wage board procedure, which is the method generally utilized in the other states, the District of Columbia, and Puerto Rico.

Briefly, the wage board procedure involves the following steps: (1) survey of the occupation by the administrative agency to ascertain whether a substantial number of women and minors are paid "oppressive" or "unreasonable" wages, (2) appointment of a wage board, (3) transmission of the wage board's recommendations to the administrative agency, (4) public hearings, and (5) issuance of the wage order.

A wage order may be revised on the labor commissioner's initiative or on petition of citizens in the state. The procedure for revising it is usually the same as for issuance of the original order.

The advantage of a statutory rate is that it establishes immediate, widespread protection. But this method has been characterized as "inflexible," since legislative action is required to adjust the rate to changing economic conditions, and it is impossible for one blanket rate to take account of individual industry conditions. A quicker response to movements in the cost of living and a greater sensitivity to problems of a particular industry have caused the wage board laws to be designated as "flexible."

Flexibility, combined with wide coverage, appears to be the goal in the states which provide for both a statutory minimum and the wage board procedure. As an additional safeguard against a static rate the Massachusetts law was amended in 1952 to require the commissioner of labor to make a biennial review of all wage orders.

[6] The Illinois, Kansas, and Louisiana laws are totally inactive.

[7] The 36 states with active minimum wage laws are Alaska, Arizona, Arkansas, California, Colorado, Connecticut, Delaware, Hawaii, Idaho, Indiana, Kentucky, Maine, Maryland, Massachusetts, Michigan, Minnesota, Nebraska, Nevada, New Hampshire, New Jersey, New Mexico, New York, North Carolina, North Dakota, Ohio, Oklahoma, Oregon, Pennsylvania, Rhode Island, South Dakota, Utah, Vermont, Washington, West Virginia, Wisconsin, and Wyoming.

[8] The effective laws applying only to minors are those in Arizona, Arkansas, California, Colorado, Minnesota, Ohio, Oregon, Utah, and Wisconsin.

TABLE 15–2

STATE STATUTORY MINIMUM RATES[1]

Jurisdiction	Statutory Minimum Rate (Hourly Rate unless Otherwise Indicated)
Alaska...........................	$2.10[2]
Arkansas........................	$1.00 eff. 1/1/69 ($1.10 eff. 1/1/70; $1.20 eff. 1/1/71)
Connecticut.....................	$1.40 ($1.60 eff. 7/1/68) $1.10 for the first 200 hours for persons under 18 and $1.40 thereafter ($1.25 for the first 200 hours and and $1.60 thereafter, eff. 7/1/68)
Delaware........................	$1.25
District of Columbia.............	$1.40 ($1.60 eff. 2/1/69) $1.25 ($1.40 eff. 8/1/68; $1.60 eff. 8/1/69) for employees in hotel, restaurant, and allied occupations
Hawaii..........................	$1.25
Idaho...........................	$1.15 ($1.25 eff. 2/1/69)
Indiana.........................	$1.15 ($1.25 eff. 7/1/68)
(Applies to men and women 18 years of age and over.)	
Maine...........................	$1.40 ($1.50 eff. 10/15/68) $1.25 ($1.40 eff. 10/15/68; $1.50 eff. 10/15/69) for employees in nursing homes and hospitals
Maryland[3].....................	$1.15 ($1.30 eff. 2/1/69) for previously covered employees $1 ($1.15 eff. 6/1/68; $1.30 eff. 6/1/69) for employees newly covered
Massachusetts...................	$1.60 Wage boards may not recommend a lower rate except: $36 *a week* for janitors and caretakers of residential property when furnished living quarters $1 for ushers, ticket takers, and ticket sellers $1.35 ($1.50 eff. 2/1/69) for farmworkers
Michigan........................	$1.25
(Applies to men and women between 18 and 65 years of age.)	
Nebraska........................	$1.00
Nevada..........................	$1.25 for men and women 18 years of age and over $1.10 for girls under 18; $1 for boys under 18
New Hampshire..................	$1.40 ($1.60 eff. 2/1/69) $1.25 ($1.30 eff. 2/1/69; $1.45 eff. 2/1/70; $1.60 eff. 2/1/71) for employees in nursing homes $1.15 ($1.30 eff. 2/1/69; $1.45 eff. 2/1/70; $1.60 eff. 2/1/71) for employees in nonprofit hospitals, orphanages, or homes for the aged 75% of minimum wage for persons 18 years of age or under, or persons with less than 6 months' experience
New Jersey[4]...................	$1.40 ($1.50 eff. 1/1/69)
(Applies to men and women 18 years of age and over.)	
New Mexico.....................	$1.40 ($1.60 eff. 2/1/69) for previously covered employees $1.15 ($1.30 eff. 2/1/69) for "service employees," as defined, and newly covered employees, including agriculture

TABLE 15-2—*Continued*

Jurisdiction	Statutory Minimum Rate (Hourly Rate unless Otherwise Indicated)
New York	$1.60
North Carolina (Applies to men and women between 16 and 64 years of age.)	$1
Oklahoma (Applies to men and women between 16 and 64 years of age.)	$1
Oregon[4] (Applies to men and women 18 years of age and over.)	$1.25
Pennsylvania	$1.15 ($1.30 eff. 2/1/69; $1.45 eff. 2/1/70; $1.60 eff. 2/1/71)
Puerto Rico[5]	Rates ranging from 25 cents to $1 for over 75 specified classes or subclasses of occupations.
Rhode Island	$1.40 ($1.60 eff. 7/1/68) $1.25 ($1.40 eff. 7/1/68) for employees of nonprofit religious, charitable, civic, literary, or educational organizations, except nonprofit hospitals.
South Dakota (Applies to persons 14 years of age and over.)	$20 *a week* for workers in cities with a population of 2,500 or more. $17 *a week* for workers in cities with a population of less than 2,500.
Vermont	$1.40
Washington[4] (Applies to men and women 18 years of age and over.)	$1.60
West Virginia	$1
Wyoming (Applies to men and women 18 years of age and over.)	$1.20 ($1.30 eff. 1/1/69)

[1] Applies to men, women, and minors unless otherwise specified in the first column.
[2] The Alaska law provides that the rate shall be 50 cents above the federal minimum rate.
[3] A 1965 ordinance set $1 an hour for men, women, and minors with certain exceptions in Baltimore, Md.
[4] Under wage board laws or provisions, New Jersey, Oregon, and Washington may by wage order set minimum rates for minors under 18.
[5] Sets higher rates by wage order.
NOTE. Rates as of January 1, 1968, unless otherwise specified.
SOURCE: U.S. Department of Labor.

MINIMUM WAGES AND EMPLOYMENT

Minimum wage legislation is generally advocated on four grounds:

1. To eliminate poverty caused by the existence of substandard wages which do not afford workers a minimum decent standard of living.
2. To eliminate unfair competition based upon substandard wages which drags down the wages paid by other firms.
3. To increase the purchasing power of lower income workers.
4. To provide a floor for maintaining a high wage structure in depressed periods.

These arguments ran through the hearings preceding the enactment of the original Fair Labor Standards Act of 1938 as well as those pertaining to the subsequent amendments. The fourth, a quite different point from the first three, is especially prominent in trade-union arguments. The first was a strong factor in the rationale behind the 1965 amendments which both raised the minimum wage and expanded the coverage of the law.

Theoretical Effects of the Minimum Wage

Minimum wage legislation means higher wage costs to the individual employer affected by such legislation. Economic theory tells us that if an employer finds that labor has become more expensive, he will try to economize in its use or to get more work out of his labor force. There may be some workers who can be dropped from the payroll simply by rescheduling work or changing assignment of duties. In some cases, it may be possible to eliminate jobs which no longer "pay" at the higher wage rate. The most effective way of reducing labor costs is, of course, through substituting machinery for labor. The lower the wage paid prior to the establishment of the minimum wage, and the greater the increase in costs imposed by such legislation, the greater the incentive to the employer to introduce laborsaving machinery.

In many cases the process of mechanization will involve purchase of machinery which was already known and in use in the industry, but which was not adopted at the low-wage level. Sometimes, however, the wage increase will cause employers to introduce machinery which would have been profitable to introduce even at a lower wage level, but which management failed to adopt because of inefficiency and reliance on payment of substandard wages as a means of competition. In other words, imposition of a minimum wage may provide the "shock" which compels inefficient management to look around in the industry and bring its production methods in line with more efficient firms in order to survive. This will involve not only adoption of laborsaving machinery but also methods and layouts which will reduce overhead, material costs, insurance expense, and other expenditures. It should be remembered that introduction of laborsaving machinery is sometimes a long-term process. Some employers may not be able to utilize the newest machinery in an antiquated plant and may have to delay purchase of machinery until they can move to a new location; other employers may try to get a few more years out of old equipment before making the large capital expenditure required for modern machinery. As a result, the displacement of labor through the introduction of laborsaving machinery may not occur until several years after the imposition of the minimum wage; and if business meanwhile increases, there may be no unemployment observable at all.

Another avenue by which a minimum wage may react upon employment is through the effect of the wage increase on price. Large companies frequently have big advertising budgets and are able to obtain a higher price for their products by building up the idea of quality in consumers' minds. Small companies, on the other hand, must often compete primarily on the basis of price. If a minimum wage raises the labor costs of smaller concerns, it puts them at a substantial competitive disadvantage. If they raise prices to compensate for the increase in costs, some part of their business will tend to shift to their larger competitors, and they may eventually be forced out of business. If this result occurs, the total volume of employment in the industry may be lowered after the shift of business is effected, even though some labor displaced in small companies will find employment in the large companies, for the larger companies are likely to be more mechanized, and a dollar's sales in such companies will require employment of a smaller amount of labor than in the low-wage plants.

It should be noted that if a minimum wage law produces unemployment, the incidence of unemployment may be expected to fall most heavily upon those with the least skills—that is, upon those employees whose wages have been below the legal minimum and who have the most difficulty in finding jobs. It will be recalled that in our analysis of unemployment in Chapter 14, it was pointed out that a disproportionate share of the persistent unemployment since 1958 has fallen upon the unskilled group. Our succeeding analysis will attempt to determine whether this unemployment has been partially a result of minimum wage legislation.

Minimum wage legislation affects not only employer efficiency but employee efficiency as well. Workers who in 1938 received less than the minimum of 25 cents per hour obviously had difficulties in making ends meet. Similarly, in 1968, workers who earned less than the $1.60-cent-an-hour minimum, or $64, for a 40-hour week, had difficulty in providing adequate food, clothing, shelter, and medical care for themselves and their families. Establishment of a minimum wage which eliminates substandard wages is likely to have some beneficial effect on the health, efficiency, and morale of workers which may be reflected in improved man-hour production. Also, the higher cost of labor makes employers more labor-conscious and is likely to cause management to devote more time and effort to training workers and selecting new employees more carefully. The net result may be better productivity, which will tend, in part, to offset the higher wage costs, so that the rise in unit labor costs will be less than the rise in wage rates. To the extent that this is true, the effect of the wage increase on employment will be lessened.

In general, economic theorists conclude that imposition of a minimum wage will tend to produce some unemployment in the individual firm affected by such legislation. The amount of the unemployment will vary from firm to firm, depending upon the magnitude of the wage increase, the importance of labor costs relative to total costs, the ability of the employer to reduce costs other than labor costs, the extent to which business of the firm falls off if it increases prices, the effect of the wage increase on man-hour output, and the extent to which the company introduces laborsaving machinery. As has already been mentioned, however, the tendency to reduction of employment may not be observable because of counteracting changes in the business scene.

Empirical Studies—The 25-Cent Minimum of 1938

Fortunately, we can do more than theorize about the imposition of a minimum wage. We have empirical studies which shed light on what actually occurred when minimum wage laws were imposed, starting with the imposition of the 25-cent-per-hour minimum in 1938.

Two weeks after the 25-cent-an-hour minimum went into effect (this was the initial requirement of the Fair Labor Standards Act of 1938), the administrator of the act reported to the President that, in all, between 30,000 and 50,000 persons, or less than 0.05% of the workers affected by the law, lost their employment for reasons probably traceable to the act. Of these workers, about 90% were concentrated in a few industries in the South, such as pecan shelling, tobacco stemming, lumbering, and bagging. Other industries which were seriously affected by the minimum wage included cottonseed crushing, seamless hosiery, and cotton garment manufacture.[9]

Many firms in these industries reacted to the wage increase by substituting machinery for labor, but other reactions included:

1. Narrowing differentials between the high-paid and the low-paid workers by not granting increases to high-paid workers equal to those required to bring the lowest paid within the law.
2. Carefully weeding out inefficient employees.
3. Establishing higher standards of efficiency for new personnel and improving selection techniques to put these standards into effect.
4. Increasing attention to working conditions and other personnel problems in order to improve the general efficiency of the labor force.

Management had almost complete freedom to make these adjustments, since in industries which were directly affected by the 1938 legislation, unionization was largely absent.

The net effect of these adjustments upon employment is not entirely clear, but it appears that in a few industries the substitution of machinery for low-paid hand labor created substantial technological unemployment. In such industries as tobacco stemming and cottonseed crushing, an aver-

[9] See, for example, U.S. Bureau of Labor Statistics, *Hours and Earnings of Employees of Independent Tobacco Stemmeries* (Serial No. 1388 [Washington, D.C.: U.S. Government Printing Office, 1941]); and J. F. Moloney, "Some Effects of the Fair Labor Standards Act upon Southern Industry," *Southern Economic Journal*, Vol. IX (July, 1942), pp. 5–23.

age of from 3 to 10 workers were displaced by a single machine. In these industries, extremely low wages made labor so cheap that basic mechanical improvements had previously never been seriously considered.

Hardship engendered by this technological unemployment was, however, offset by the fact that the Fair Labor Standards Act of 1938 was inaugurated at the depth of the 1937–38 recession, and business conditions and employment generally improved immediately thereafter. Moreover, in 1940 the defense boom inaugurated a period of prosperity which more than took up any slack in employment caused by technological developments.

Besides creating some technological unemployment, the Fair Labor Standards Act also upset the competitive equilibrium in many industries. High-wage firms often were required to make little or no adjustment in order to conform with the act; low-wage firms, on the other hand, faced a serious situation. A study of 26 plants in the seamless hosiery industry indicated that the 12 high-wage plants made few wage adjustments between 1938 and 1939, while the 11 low-wage plants were forced to raise wages 35%. In many instances, these low-wage companies also made large expenditures in capital equipment in order to maintain a sound cost position. In this same industry, employment in the high-wage firms increased between 1938 and 1940 by 7.5%, while employment in the low-wage group decreased 12.8%.[10]

The Effects of the 75-Cent Minimum

The 75-cent minimum established in 1949 affected substantially the same industries and the same areas as did the original act of 1938. Thus, of the 1.5 million workers covered by the act who the Bureau of Labor Statistics estimated were receiving less than 75 cents per hour prior to January 25, 1950 (the effective date of the 1949 amendments), 840,000 were employed in the South or Southwest. These areas were, of course, the principal concentrations of subminimum wages in 1938. Again, as in 1938, the cottonseed-crushing, tobacco-stemming, seamless hosiery, cotton garment, fertilizer, and lumber industries were the southern industries most directly affected.

In some other respects the situation at the time of the establishment of the 75-cent minimum in 1950 was similar to that in 1938 when the initial 25-cent minimum became effective. Unionization was still largely absent from the industries directly affected, so that management had pretty much of a free hand to adjust to the higher minimum. And once again, the effect of the higher minimum was obscured by an economic

---

[10] A. F. Hinrichs, "Effects of the 25 Cent Minimum Wage on Employment in the Seamless Hosiery Industry," *Journal of the American Statistical Association*, Vol. XXXV (March, 1940), pp. 13–23; and H. M. Douty, "Minimum Wage Regulation in the Seamless Hosiery Industry," *Southern Economic Journal*, Vol. XV (October, 1948), pp. 176–89.

upswing resulting from military action—this time the Korean War, which began six months after the 75-cent minimum went into effect.

The Effects of the $1 Minimum

The $1 minimum which went into effect in 1956 generally affected the same industries, principally southern industry, as did its predecessor minima. However, the $1 minimum affected these industries more severely, and having been through the adjustment mill several times, these industries had less capacity to mechanize and otherwise offset the increases than in past instances.

The Bureau of Labor Statistics estimated that approximately 2 million workers were directly affected by the $1 minimum, and that an average increase of 15 cents per hour was needed to bring these workers up to the $1-per-hour rate. Studies of the Bureau of Labor Statistics after the rate went into effect indicated that most industries reacted to the new minimum by compressing their wage structures, reducing overtime, laying off inefficient workers, and raising prices. Mechanization played a lesser role, although materials handling equipment was introduced or its use expanded to eliminate common labor. The principal emphasis, however, was on cutting labor costs directly by eliminating personnel, extra shifts and overtime.

The $1 minimum wage had a more severe and direct effect on employment than did previous legislation. Employment in industries which had substantial employment at rates under $1 declined even in 1956–57 when the economy was strong. Sixteen of the so-called "high-impact" industries suffered a drop in employment from 10% to 25%, with unskilled workers especially hard hit.[11] Because lower rated employees received increases required by law, but lesser or no increases were granted to higher rated jobs, wage schedules were compressed.[12]

The 1961 Amendments

In 1961, Congress raised the minimum for previously covered workers to $1.15 as of September 1, 1961, and $1.25 as of September 1, 1963. In addition, the act was extended to 3.6 million additional workers, mostly in retail trade. For those newly covered, overtime payments were waived for three years, and minima were set at $1 as of September 1, 1961; $1.15 four

---

[11] U.S. Department of Labor, Wage and Public Contracts Division, *Studies of the Effects of the $1.00 Minimum Wage* (Washington, D.C.: U.S. Government Printing Office, 1959). See also, Harry M. Douty, "Some Effects of the $1.00 Minimum Wage in the United States," *Economica*, Vol. XXVII (May, 1960), pp. 137–47. A critique of the Department of Labor studies is George Macesich and Charles T. Stewart, Jr., "Recent Department of Labor Studies of Minimum Wage Effects," *Southern Economic Journal*, Vol. XXVI (April, 1960), pp. 281–90.

[12] *Ibid.*, and David E. Kaun, "Economics of the Minimum Wage: The Effects of the Fair Labor Standards Act, 1945–1960" (unpublished doctoral dissertation, Stanford University, 1963).

years later; and $1.25 as of September 1, 1966. As a result, approximately 15% of those covered in 1961 received wage increases, but this included nearly 67% of those in the 15 southern industries which have been affected by every change in the Fair Labor Standards Act since 1938. In 1963, the increase in the minimum to $1.25 affected directly an estimated additional 2.6 million workers, again including those in these 15 southern industries. In October, 1960, for example, average hourly earnings in the southern lumber industry were $1.18 per hour; by June, 1962, these earnings had risen to $1.27 under the impact of the minimum, with 63% of the employees receiving wage increases. Employment in this industry continued on a downward trend, dropping from 173,000 to 141,000 between October, 1960, and June, 1962.[13]

The 1961 and 1963 increases in the minimum wage law brought under the act low-wage retail employees who had not been covered since the 1949 amendments. Employment in retailing continued its expansion; but in nonmetropolitan areas of the South, employment in covered retail trade declined from 160,000 in June, 1961, to 143,000 in June, 1962, while employment in retail trade in these areas in establishments *not* covered by the FLSA rose from 549,000 to 574,000.[14]

The 1965 Amendments

The 1965 amendments, which raised the minimum wage to $1.60 per hour in two steps for those already within the purview of the law and in several steps for those newly brought within its coverage, was enacted in a period of great prosperity and rising employment. Government sponsors of higher minimum wage laws hailed the results as contributing to the fight against poverty without substantially affecting employment. A more careful examination of the available data indicate that the effects of the 1965 amendments are those which one might expect in a period of economic expansion:

—employment in some of the newly covered sectors, such as laundries and agriculture declined, with the latter continuing, and perhaps accelerating a long-term trend;[15]
—some industries, such as motels and hotels, restaurants and hospitals continued to expand, but these sectors of the economy also experienced considerable price increases

[13] U.S. Department of Labor, *Report Submitted to the Congress in Accordance with the Requirements of Section 4(d) of the Fair Labor Standards Act* (*Washington, D.C.*: U.S. Government Printing Office, January, 1963), pp. vii, 35, and 40.

[14] U.S. Department of Labor, *Effects of Minimum Wage Rates Established under the Fair Labor Standards Act in Retail Trade in the United States and Puerto Rico: A Study of Changes in Wage Structure of a Matched Sample of Retail Establishments, 1961–1962* (Washington, D.C.: U.S. Government Printing Office, November, 1963), p. 5.

[15] Agricultural employment was also affected by the cutting-off of "Bracero" or imported Mexican labor. Reducing supply is, of course, another way to raise minimum wages.

—the same industries in the South, which have been directly affected by every rise in the minimum wage were again affected, but as during World War II and the Korean War, the impact was obscured by the rising level of sales and prosperity.[16]

The impact of a minimum wage in a period such as the one in the mid-1960's may indeed not be felt until the business cycle turns downward. Then the higher costs have their sharpest repercussions on marginal firms and employment; and it is at this time that marginal employees, whose value to the firm may be barely equal to, or less than, the ever higher minimum wage, are displaced, or never hired. In view of the fact that even in times of great prosperity, hard-core unemployment exists among untrained, young, and minority group persons—often one and the same—the arguments for minimum wages as a cure for poverty deserve examination.

Minimum Wages and Poverty

The U.S. Department of Labor reported that the $1.60 minimum wage meant that "for the first time in the history of the Fair Labor Standards Act, the statutory minimum wage will yield an above-poverty wage."[17] This is perhaps a correct statement for those who receive the wage, but it ignores the possible impact on employment, not only of the marginal employees already on industry's rolls, but perhaps of a more important group, the submarginal population which even in prosperity finds great difficulty in obtaining work. Not only will the members of the latter group find it more difficult to obtain work if the price of their labor is raised, but their numbers can be increased by those whom industry can no longer afford as the minimum wage is raised.

An objective analysis of the wealth of data on the impact of minimum wages on employment seems to confirm the theoretical economic expectation—that increased unemployment is a likely result of raising minimum wages. The effect may be offset by other factors, such as rising demand, or inflation, or it may be obscured by such events as a recession and the difficulty of distinguishing between the results of a general employment decline and a decline attributable to the higher minimums. Nevertheless, the studies of empirical results, as well as those of the effects of state or local laws, tend to confirm the unemployment effects.[18]

---

[16] The only studies available at this writing of the 1965 amendments are the official ones by the U.S. Department of Labor, Wage and Hour and Public Contracts Divisions. Our conclusions are based upon a careful reading of these studies, and differ from the official conclusions.

[17] U.S. Department of Labor, Wage and Hour and Public Contracts Divisions, *Minimum Wages and Maximum Hours Standards under the Fair Labor Standards Act* (Washington, D.C.: 1968), p. 2.

[18] For a confirmation of these studies by an examination of state experience and a theoretical analysis of city experience, see John M. Peterson, "Employment Effects of State Minimum Wages for Women: Three Historical Cases Re-examined," *Industrial and Labor Relations Review*, Vol. XII (April, 1959), pp. 406–22; and a

This apparent effect of minimum wages assumed great importance after 1957, when unemployment rose substantially and remained thereafter above five per cent of the labor force. But unskilled workers have had a persistent unemployment rate since 1958 of more than twice the national rate. Many of these unskilled workers have little education beyond the primary grades. An increasing proportion are high school dropouts, whose unemployment rate has hovered around 20 per cent. Many are also Negroes, who suffer the added disadvantage of discrimination by color.

In future years, as we have noted throughout this text, the greatest employment opportunities will occur among professional and technical occupations. Among the manual occupations, the need for skilled mechanics will also increase. But the number of unskilled jobs will remain relatively stationary, despite a tremendous increase in unskilled additions to the labor market. It seems, therefore, ever more apparent that the higher the wage minimum, the greater will be the effort to substitute machinery for unskilled work or to recast methods somehow so as to make the unskilled increasingly unnecessary, particularly in manufacturing enterprises. To push for ever higher minimums is likely to make unemployed victims of those who are supposed to become higher paid beneficiaries of a minimum wage law.

There is another concern about raising the minimum wage which is of great significance. Although the imposition of a higher minimum does tend to narrow differentials, it also tends to exert an upward pressure on wages above the minimum, both in industries directly affected and in all other industries competing for labor. This adds still another inflationary push to the economy, in which inflationary tendencies are already so strong. To the extent that an upward revision in the minimum wage results in price increases, it will again hurt most the low-wage groups for whom the minimum is urged as a benefit.

Our concern with poverty may therefore be in conflict with the policy of a steadily rising minimum wage. Perhaps minimum wages should continue to rise and the resulting unemployment should be tolerated. In such case, it should be understood that one of the costs of minimum wage legislation is increased public welfare, training, rehabilitation, and subsidy payments to those who are priced out of the labor market.

---

criticism by Richard A. Lester, and Peterson's rebuttal, *Industrial and Labor Relations Review*, Vol. XIII (January, 1960), pp. 254–73. See also Maurice Benewitz and R. E. Weintraub, "Employment Effects of a Local Minimum Wage," *Industrial and Labor Relations Review*, Vol. XVII (January, 1964), pp. 276–88. As one observer has noted also: "The actual statistics of Labor Department industry studies have, in the great bulk of postwar cases, shown declines in employment in the wake of minimum wage increase—though the *stated conclusion* of these same studies has usually been that there is no evidence of unemployment caused by the minimum wage." Thomas Sowell, "Discussion, the Shorter Workweek Controversy," *Industrial and Labor Relations Review*, Vol. XVIII (January, 1965), p. 243.

Minimum Wages and the North-South Differential

Because the minimum wage laws have directly affected the South considerably more than other areas, southern manufacturers have argued for a lower minimum in the South than elsewhere. Northern manufacturers, anxious to reduce the North-South differential, have successfully opposed this request. Is maintenance of a North-South wage differential justified?

The argument has been advanced that imposition of a uniform minimum wage on the South and North alike would slow down the rate of southern industrialization. Indeed, it has been suggested that northern manufacturers desire a high minimum for the South as a form of internal protective tariff to halt the migration of capital to the South and export of goods to the North. However, other investigations indicate that the wage differential has not been as important a factor in interregional migration of industry as might at first have been suspected. Within the South, employment in manufacturing has expanded no more rapidly in the low-wage sections than in the higher wage sections. Indeed, the greatest rate of expansion has occurred in the relatively high-wage state of North Carolina. Capital has been attracted to the South because of climatic advantages, tractable labor supply, low taxes, access to cheap power, and raw material. Presumably, these attractions would still induce capital to move even if wage rates were higher.

A somewhat similar argument stresses the fact that variation in wage rates is the means by which a free labor market brings about an adjustment between areas of relative surplus and areas of relative scarcity of labor. Thus, if there is a surplus of labor in small towns, and in the South generally, wage rates will be lower in those areas compared to the cities of the North. Consequently, an inducement is afforded to capital to seek out the areas of surplus population. Not only is such a relocation of capital socially desirable; but also, the regional dispersion of industry is of strategic importance to our national defense. Imposition of a uniform minimum wage, it is contended, will concentrate unemployment precisely in those areas where the need for job opportunities is greatest and will impede the migration of capital.

The difficulty with this argument is that lower wages in the South did not attract sufficient capital to erase the North-South differential prior to the establishment of minimum wages. But our analysis in Chapter 8 did point out that this differential is primarily the result of the historic shortage of capital in the South and, further, that the migration of industry to the South in recent years may eventually reduce that differential. Therefore, as capital has migrated to the South in larger amounts since the minimum wage has been in effect, the case for a North-South minimum wage differential is now weaker than heretofore. If, on the other hand, the minimum wage encourages labor to remain in the South rather than to migrate, the oversupply of labor relative to capital in that area will not be lessened at as fast a pace as would otherwise be the case. Such a development, not yet discernible, would be the best argument in favor of a lower southern minimum.

Actually, the case against the minimum wage in the South is not best put in terms of a differential. Rather, one can question the wisdom, on a national scale, of pricing the uneducated and unskilled out of the market before they can be educated to fill standards upon which the minimum wage forces industry to insist. Heavy labor migration from the South to the North, particularly of uneducated and unskilled whites and Negroes from southern rural areas, has peopled northern cities with groups of citizens who have little to offer industry today. Meanwhile, industry has moved many of its plants away from the high-cost city locations to suburban and rural areas. Special treatment for a region is difficult to justify; raising the price of the unskilled while the demand for the unskilled remains stagnant is at least subject to debate.

EMERGENCY WAGE REGULATION

Government control of all wage rates in our democracy has been a phenomenon which occurs only in wartime or similar grave national emergency. The government moves to take wages out of control of individual unions and managements as part of a program to curb runaway prices. Recently, however, the United States, like other democracies, has attempted to "guide" wage and price adjustments in order to avoid disruption of international trade and inflation at home. An examination of attempts to control wages in war and peace—something quite different from setting minimum wages—is the subject of the balance of this chapter.

WORLD WAR II WAGE STABILIZATION

In 1939, the United States possessed a relatively large volume of unused resources. The Bureau of Labor Statistics estimated unemployment in 1939 at almost 9.5 million. The steel industry was operating at only about five-eighths capacity, the textile industry at three-quarters capacity. This unused capacity was typical of potential war industry in general.

Under these circumstances, the country was able to commence war production without serious inflation at the outset. Nevertheless, new purchasing power created by increased employment in war industry caused purchasing power to expand at a more rapid rate than output of civilian goods. This, plus shortages of key skills, products, and equipment, tended to push prices up before unused resources of men and machines were fully employed.

At the time of the Japanese attack on Pearl Harbor on December 7, 1941, there had already been established an agency, the National Defense Mediation Board, to deal with strikes which interfered with defense production. This agency, however, was threatening to fall apart. President Franklin D. Roosevelt therefore convened a special Labor-Management Conference, which resulted in the establishment of the National War Labor Board (WLB).

Until October, 1942, the WLB had no authority over voluntary wage adjustments. During the first nine months of its existence, however, when its sole concern was with cases involving disputes between labor and management, the WLB developed its basic stabilization program, which was later applied both to voluntary requests for wage adjustments (submitted either from management alone in nonunion plants or jointly from union and management in union plants) and to cases in which the WLB decided disputes between unions and management.

The core of this program was the so-called "Little Steel Formula." Basically, this formula provided that establishments which had not had an increase of 15% in average straight-time hourly earnings since January, 1941 (equivalent to the rise in living costs between January, 1941, and May, 1942), should be permitted to increase wages to this amount. It is noteworthy that wages were thus stabilized at this level without regard to increases in the cost of living which followed after May, 1942.

Wages are, however, almost never, in the strict sense of the word, stabilized. Rather, wages are restrained. Thus, although the WLB stabilized basic wage rates in accordance with the Little Steel Formula, wages continued to rise throughout the World War II period. This happened because workers received wage increases on account of promotions, by changing jobs, by receiving merit or length-of-service increases, or by alteration of piece rates. Then, too, workers increased their earnings (without altering wage rates) by working overtime and by working evening or night shifts, for which a bonus or "shift differential" was paid. Finally, although wage rates were stabilized, the WLB permitted the institution and liberalization of fringe benefits, such as vacations, holidays, or health and welfare plans; and the WLB granted wage adjustments to eliminate inequities and substandards, and to aid in war production.

Dispute Cases versus Stabilization

To stabilize wages and settle labor disputes at the same time is both conflicting and complementary. It is conflicting in that frequently a dispute could most easily be settled by ignoring stabilization. "Quickie" strikes during World War II frequently were strikes against stabilization rather than against the employer, who was often willing to pay higher wages but was not permitted to do so. If, however, stabilization is ignored in order to settle a dispute, obviously the way would be clear to circumvent stabilization simply by invoking a dispute.

Effects of World War II Stabilization

The rise in the cost of living between January, 1941, and July, 1945, was approximately 33.3%. During the same period, basic wage rates increased about 24%; straight-time hourly earnings, adjusted for employment shifts, 40.5%; gross hourly earnings, 51.2%; and gross weekly earnings, 70.5%.[19]

In terms of spendable earnings, the increases were much less. Inflation control involves use of taxes and credit controls as well as of wage and price controls. The average worker supporting a wife and two children had increases in spendable earnings (real earnings less federal taxes) between January, 1941, and July, 1945, of 24%; the average single worker saw his spendable earnings increase only 11.6%.

On the basis of these data, a good case can be made that wages during World War II were stabilized about as well as could be expected. Partially, perhaps, because wages and prices were controlled well and decontrolled too fast, a dramatic wage-price spiral featured the immediate postwar years, pushing consumer prices up at a rapid rate. When it appeared that wages and prices were approaching stability, the Korean War began, and a new wage-price spiral commenced.

WAGE STABILIZATION DURING THE KOREAN WAR

When the Korean War started in June, 1950, the United States had been experiencing a decade of war and postwar prosperity of unprecedented magnitude, and full employment of manpower and equipment. The inflationary impact of the Korean War was immediate—but immediate more because of psychological rather than basic economic factors. For despite full employment, war expenditures in bulk did not occur until *after* the greatest price increases.

Immediately, everyone—consumer and producer alike—seemed to act as if he had played the role before. Goods were snapped up off the shelves, labor agreements were voluntarily reopened to grant wage increases, factories worked overtime trying to fill the accelerated demands, and prices shot up. Here was inflation resulting not from a shortage of supply relative to demand but because people *expected* shortages to occur and because they *expected* prices and wages to be stabilized. Everyone seemed busy buying against a shortage which never occurred, and raising

---

[19] National War Labor Board, *Termination Report* (Washington, D.C.: U.S. Government Printing Office, n.d.), Vol. I, p. 55.

wages and prices to get ahead of wage and price control which came too late. Although wage and price control legislation was enacted soon after the Communists invaded South Korea, President Harry S Truman's administration did not invoke it until a serious wage-price spiral had already occurred. Once price and wage controls were invoked, the inflation halted its runaway course. In view of the psychological character of the inflation and the lack of any genuine supply shortage relative to demand, it is logical to assume that the slowness to invoke controls was a costly mistake. Once controls were invoked, however, they worked quite differently from those of World War II.

The Wage Stabilization Board

Wage stabilization during the Korean War was administered by the Wage Stabilization Board. Whereas the War Labor Board of World War II was created as an agency with power to act only in dispute cases and then later was granted authority over voluntary wage adjustments, the Wage Stabilization Board was created to control voluntary wage adjustments and then later was given limited control over dispute cases. Although a dispute case—the Steelworkers–Big Steel controversy—just about put the finishing touches on the work of the Wage Stabilization Board, most of the controversies before the WSB were cases in which employers and unions joined forces in an endeavor to obtain special consideration.

The approach of the War Labor Board of World War II, in general, was to set policy on the basis of its decision in individual cases, particularly dispute cases. Thus, we have already noted that the basic stabilization doctrine—the Little Steel Formula—was arrived at in that fashion. The approach of the Wage Stabilization Board was quite different. After wages and prices were temporarily frozen on January 25, 1951, the WSB began promulgating regulations governing the conditions under which such increases as merit, length of service, promotion, inequity, etc., could be granted without specific WSB approval. Unions and managements which wanted permission for larger increases than allowed by the general regulations then had to request specific permission from the WSB. As requests were granted, general regulations were changed, so that although *initial* policy was set by general regulation, specific cases modified the regulations and resulted in new ones.

In a real sense, the wage stabilization picture during the Korean War resembled a game of leapfrog. A general regulation, which set a permissive wage increase ceiling, was laid down. A special case came up, and the increase permitted jumping the ceiling. Soon after the price-wage freeze on January 25, 1951, these "leaps" proceeded rapidly; then, for a while, they slowed down. In the end, they took one big leap—the steel case—and then, wage stabilization virtually collapsed. Wage controls were anything but a conspicuous success during the Korean War.

ANALYSIS OF WAGE CONTROLS OF WORLD WAR II AND OF THE KOREAN WAR

Why did wage controls work quite differently during World War II than during the Korean War? There are several reasons, grounded in the different character of the times, and of unions and employers during those times.

Different Economic and Psychological Conditions

We have already noted some of the different economic and psychological conditions of the two periods. The slow start of the defense program in 1939, the background of a depression decade, and the lack of personal and business income savings and borrowing capacity all prevented inflation from getting a running start. In contrast was the Korean War period: a background of a prosperity decade, with plenty of personal and business income savings and borrowing capacity, all of which could (and seemingly was) put to use to bid prices up.

Equally as important as, if not more important than, economic conditions were the different psychological conditions of the two periods. World War II was an all-out effort psychologically. Contributing to inflation was unpatriotic. Nearly everyone was involved emotionally in the war effort.

The Korean War was a partial effort, psychologically and emotionally as well as economically and militarily, especially as soon as the hopes for easy victory faded. Under those conditions, concern with the general problem of inflation was decidedly secondary in most peoples' minds. The psychological reaction to the outbreak of the Korean War—buying and bidding up prices and wages so as to be in the best possible economic position when controls were imposed—is the best indicator of the public's (including businesses' and unions') reaction to controls at that time.

The Changing Character of Labor and Management

As different as were economic and psychological conditions during World War II and the Korean War, they were no more different than were the attitudes of management and labor. During World War II, management still fought unions on the prime issues of wages, fringes, and union security. Indeed, management of the early 1940's can truly be said not to have accepted unions as a permanent institution. Consequently, management fought unions hard on the crucial issues of wages. *It appears quite clear in retrospect that wage stabilization succeeded so well during World War II because employers feared that wage increases would be ruinous to them and therefore supported stabilization.*

Management's fight on the wage front during World War II was strengthened by the belief among employers that they could not expect to obtain a fair profit from a price control agency and the Democratic administration. Consequently, if they yielded on wages, employers expected that price lids would be maintained, and they would be caught in a price-wage squeeze.

By the time the Korean War broke out, managements, especially of large companies, had found that they could live with unions, even with large wage increases, fringes, and the granting of union security. Consequently, these employers were more interested in labor peace than in wage stabilization. The president of General Motors argued before the Wage Stabilization Board against freezing the cost-of-living and annual improvement increases in his agreement with the United Automobile Workers at least as vehemently as did the president of the UAW.

Moreover, experience had convinced employers that the government would give them a square deal on prices, even if the government was not of their political choice. By the time of the Korean War, there was little fear of a price-wage squeeze in business circles.

The unions of the Korean War had changed since the beginning of World War II as much as employers. At the start of World War II, unions were new in most industries, insecure and unaccepted. They gladly accepted union security in place of wage increases, and then fringes to keep wage rates stable. During World War II, unions were feeling their way and gaining acceptance.

By the time the Korean War began, unions had gained acceptance, security, fringes, and large wage increases after surviving the postwar labor strife rather handily. Being responsive to their membership, unions saw no answer but wage increases to offset the effects of rising prices on union members. With management anxious to co-operate, the unions obtained what they wanted.

"Stabilization" by Big Bargains

During World War II the government, acting through the War Labor Board, a tripartite agency, composed equally of labor, management, and public representatives, established its stabilization norm—the Little Steel Formula—and stuck to it, with some yielding on the fringes. The then current war, the economic and psychological situations, and the prevailing character of labor and management relations made that possible.

During the Korean War the government adopted no such independent position. Essentially, what the Wage Stabilization Board did was "to take the top national bargains [especially the UAW–General Motors agreement] and turn them into governmental policy."[20] When a bargain

---

[20] Clark Kerr, "Governmental Wage Restraints: Their Limitations and Uses in a Mobilized Economy," *Proceedings of the Fourth Annual Meeting,* Industrial

exceeded such policy, it was sometimes turned down; but often, it was approved as a special case. The then current war, the economic and psychological situations, and the prevailing character of labor and management relations again made that possible.

The effect of stabilizing at "big bargain" levels, as the Korean War WSB did, is undoubtedly to push wages of some companies higher than would otherwise have occurred. For once the top limits are set, unions, in response to the membership, push for the limit. It would probably be accurate to state that the Korean War stabilization program was not only started too late but was also maintained too late. For after the institution of controls stopped the psychological inflation, they tended more, in the absence of serious supply-demand disequilibria, to push wages up to the big bargains than to keep them stabilized.

WAGE RESTRAINT IN PEACETIME

The comparative experience of wage controls during World War II and the Korean War sheds much light on the difficulties faced by an economy which attempts to control wages. Without the economic similarity of World War II conditions and lacking also the patriotic and psychological factors therein involved, one could predict great problems in any attempt to control—or, more accurately, to restrain—wages. As we have more fully discussed in Chapter 13, the Kennedy and Johnson administrations' attempts to utilize the so-called "guideline" approach emphasized the lessons learned during the Korean War. Without the country being in real and obvious danger, a guideline admonition was certain to have only a passing impact once the labor market became really tight.

QUESTIONS FOR DISCUSSION

1. Discuss the theoretical effects of a minimum wage upon unemployment. How would the actual results of the 25-cent minimum in 1938 and the $1.10 and $1.60 minima in 1967 and 1968 compare with the consequences predicted by economic theory? If Congress enacts a higher minimum, what would you expect would be the effect on employment in those industries which have been affected each time the minimum wage has been increased?

2. Compare wage stabilization policies of World War II, of the Korean War period, and of the early 1960's. What were the basic reasons for the differences in approach and results?

3. Discuss the pros and cons of a differential for the South under the minimum

---

Relations Research Association, Boston, 1951, pp. 14–30. Our discussion owes much to Dr. Kerr's excellent analysis, based upon his service both with the World War II WLB and the Wage Stabilization Board of the Korean War period.

wage law. If Congress enacts a higher minimum wage law, do you think there should be a southern minimum wage differential?

SUGGESTIONS FOR FURTHER READING

KAUFMAN, JACOB J., and FORAN, TERRY G. "The Minimum Wage and Poverty," in LEVITAN, SAR A. *et al.* (eds.), *Towards Freedom from Want,* pp. 189–218. New York: Harper & Row, Publishers, 1968. Industrial Relations Research Association Series.

An attempt to assess the contribution of minimum wages to reducing poverty, this study is more favorable to the minimum wage approach than is the analysis in most of the literature.

KERR, CLARK. "Governmental Wage Restraints: Their Limits and Uses in a Mobilized Economy," *Proceedings of the Fourth Annual Meeting,* Industrial Relations Research Association, Boston, 1951, pp. 14–30.

Although written several years ago, this remains the outstanding analysis of wage control in total and limited war.

SHEEHAN, JOHN. *The Wage-Price Guideposts.* Washington, D.C.: Brookings Institution, 1967.

A thorough analysis of the guideposts, which is more favorably disposed toward their contribution to stabilization than are the writers of this textbook.

U.S. DEPARTMENT OF LABOR, WAGE AND HOUR AND PUBLIC CONTRACTS DIVISIONS. *Economic Effects Studies,* various dates.

A continuing series of studies of the economic effects of minimum wages regularly issued and available from the Department. These studies are essential for the basic data for analysis of the impact of minimum wages, but the conclusions need to be examined in the light of the criticisms voiced by such comments as those by Macesich and Stewart, cited in note 11 above, and by Sowell, in note 18.

Chapter
16

THE SHORTER WORKWEEK

For over one hundred years prior to 1950, American labor saw working hours decline and opportunities for leisure (or additional work) increase. Since 1950, regular hours of work have stabilized at 40 per week and 8 per day. Why this has occurred and what are the economic implications of proposed shorter workweeks and workdays are discussed in this chapter.

HISTORY OF THE SHORTER-HOUR MOVEMENT

Just as capital accumulation has made possible the raising of wages, so it has permitted the shortening of hours. Competitive tendencies, however, have been more evident in the former than in the latter. The level of real wages rose substantially from 1910 to 1930, a period in which there was little welfare legislation and trade-union power, but hours reduction moved much slowly. Despite such pathbreaking acts as Henry Ford's introduction of the five-day week in the 1920's, most employers, not under pressure from government or unions, have apparently historically been more willing to raise wages than to reduce hours in order to attract more or superior employees. Nor should this be surprising. Higher earnings are more attractive to employees than opportunities for more leisure, and higher wages can mean more hours worked and more total production, sales, and profits. The historical development of the shorter-hour movement emphasizes the outside pressures which have moved society to the 8-hour day and 40-hour week.

One of the earliest manifestations of the shorter-hour movement was in the form of a resolution adopted by the journeymen carpenters of Philadelphia, who, in 1791, declared that a day's work should last only from 6 A.M. to 6 P.M. But the mores of an agricultural society accustomed to labor from dawn to dusk—and believing that idle time was an invitation to the devil—had too strong a grip on the young industrial community. As a consequence, the 14- to 16-hour workday remained commonplace. The various trade-union societies, however, continued to agitate for shorter hours; and in 1840, as a result of their successful lobbying, President Martin Van Buren signed the bill establishing the 10-hour day in government navy yards. This lead, however, was not quickly followed by industry. In some localities the building trades and other craftsmen secured the 10-hour day in 1845; but with the exception of these skilled trades and child labor legislation in certain states, the 12-hour day continued to be the rule until the Civil War.

The period following the Civil War was marked by special interest in shortening the hours of work. The postwar depression had produced unemployment, which was further aggravated by the return of soldiers to their civilian occupations. The growth of the national unions during this period provided a medium by which labor's fears could be made articulate. In the 1880's, the shorter-hour movement received a strong impetus from the sponsorship of the Knights of Labor, which, at the peak of its power, succeeded in obtaining the eight-hour day for more than 200,000 men. However, the gain was only temporary. With the demise of the Knights, the 10-hour day again became customary, except for certain strategically situated workers who were able to use their bargaining power to secure shorter hours. Thus, not long after the formation of the American Federation of Labor, the carpenters and bricklayers won the eight-hour day in many cities; and in 1916 the Big Four railroad brotherhoods, by threatening a nationwide tie-up, secured passage of the Adamson Act guaranteeing the eight-hour day for operating crews of railroads.

The high demand for labor during and immediately following World War I was reflected in reduced hours as well as in higher money wages. Average hours in all manufacturing fell from 55 in 1916 to 51 in 1920, the most rapid gain secured in the shorter-hour movement up to that time. In 1919, the spectacular strike against the 12-hour day in the steel industry mobilized public opinion behind the shorter-hour movement, but it was not until 1923 that the steel industry finally succumbed to this pressure and introduced three eight-hour shifts. In 1926, the American Federation of Labor adopted a resolution in favor of the five-day workweek; and in 1927, Henry Ford inaugurated the five-day workweek in all his plants. By 1929, the eight-hour day was firmly established in American industry, although the average workweek continued to be six days.

The mass unemployment of the Great Depression brought new urgency to the shorter-hour movement. Labor viewed the shorter workweek as a means of spreading available jobs over more persons and thus reducing the volume of unemployment. In some industries the larger manufacturers were interested in finding a means of compelling small competitors to go along in a program of shorter hours and curtailed output. The result was the National Recovery Administration with its industry codes. Under these codes the 44-hour week was established in most industries. It is estimated that as a result of these provisions, most employees covered by the codes received reductions in hours ranging from 8 to 10 hours a week. With the passage of the Public Contracts (Walsh-Healey) Act in 1936 and the Fair Labor Standards Act in 1938, the effect, as noted in the previous chapter, was to make the 40-hour-week standard by October, 1940, for most workers engaged in interstate commerce. Hours worked above the maximum of 40 hours were required to be remunerated at time and a half.

The requirements of war production forced the first upward shift in the trend of hours. In contrast to the period of World War I, which saw hours reduced, the period of World War II was marked by a sharp increase, but only a temporary one. Throughout the war the overtime provisions of the Fair Labor Standards Act were kept in effect, so that time and one half was paid for all work in excess of 40 hours per week. When hostilities ended, the 40-hour week again became standard (see Figure 16–1). Moreover, industries which were not covered by the hours

FIGURE 16–1

AVERAGE WEEKLY HOURS, 1850–1967

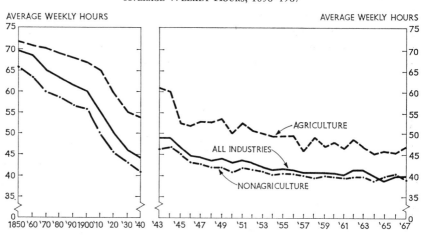

SOURCE: U.S. Bureau of Labor Statistics.

provisions of the FLSA, such as air transport, railroads (nonoperating employees), and some units of retail trade, went on the 40-hour week for the first time.

Several groups regularly work less than the 40-hour standard. The largest among these is the big-city office workers, nearly all of whom are nonunion. They suffer the rigors of commuting, which extends their period away from home; but once they arrive at the office, they are usually detained only seven hours per day, five days per week.

Among unionized groups, scheduled hours of less than 40 are found most commonly in building constructing, needle trades, printing trades, breweries, coal mining, and longshoring. The rubber industry in Akron, Ohio, and in several other cities, as well, went on a six-day, 36-hour week in 1936. During World War II, these plants changed over to a 40- or 48-hour week, and many of them remained on this basis, although the

Akron plants reverted to the 36-hour pattern. Recently, at least one major Akron plant, and the large Uniroyal plant in Detroit, have gone on a 40-hour week. The return of rubber plants to the 40-hour standard has been facilitated by the fact that time and one half has not been paid until 40 hours have been worked; and it has been furthered by the desire of employees to increase their earnings by working the extra four hours.

Shorter Workyear

But if unions cannot be credited with much success in reducing the scheduled workweek below 40 hours, they have certainly scored in reducing the workyear by obtaining the benefits of paid leisure for their members. A majority of unionized employees (and many nonunion ones as well) in nonagricultural jobs enjoy at least 6 to 8 paid holidays per year with 10 and 12 becoming increasingly common. Two-week vacations are now general, with the seniority requirements for three- and four-week vacations being steadily lowered from 15 to 5 and 25 to 10 years' service, respectively. In 1963, the United Steelworkers negotiated the first "sabbaticals"—13 weeks off every five years for long-service employees in the steel, can, and aluminum industries. If the net effect of holiday and vacation programs is averaged out on an hours basis, the average workweek per year of American workers is certainly well below the 40-hour standard.

Other Hours Legislation

Besides the Public Contracts and Fair Labor Standards Act, there are a number of federal and state laws limiting hours of work. Most of the former pertain to public employment or transportation and are the result either of early legislation when general legislation did not exist or of concern for safety of passengers or crew of common carriers. State laws predominantly affect women and minors and hazardous jobs. Special protective laws for women may have been preempted by the Civil Rights Act of 1964, Title VII of which forbids discrimination by reason of sex as well as of race. As will be noted in our detailed discussion of this law in Chapter 24, the courts have not come to grips as yet with the apparent conflict of laws which on the one hand are designed to give women equal employment opportunity, but which on the other hand provide special protection to women, and thereby, for example, prohibit their employment in mining or other hazardous jobs or industries.

BASIC FACTORS AFFECTING THE TREND TOWARD SHORTER HOURS

This brief historical survey suggests that three classes of factors have influenced the movement toward shorter hours of work in American industry. The first may be called "social," including the impact of habit and custom. The mores inherited from a primarily agricultural pioneering community undoubtedly contributed to the view, so prevalent during the early years of the struggle for shorter hours, that work was a blessing and that long factory hours were a virtue rather than a vice. Similarly, the mixing in the labor market of immigrants with habits of work inherited from industrially backward nations rendered large masses of the working population relatively indifferent to the shorter-hour movement.

The second factor has been the influence of governmental legislation, both state and federal. Legislative regulation of hours has been of importance, particularly in recent years, with NRA, Walsh-Healey, and the Fair Labor Standards Act all contributing substantially to hours reduction. State legislation has been an important factor in reducing the hours of work of women and children.

The third type of factor which has affected the shorter-hour movement is the economic, which may be classified further into four components: (1) the bargaining strength of labor, (2) the bargaining strength of employers, (3) the type of employment, and (4) the general level of economic activity. Thus, we have seen that labor in the skilled building trades, by virtue of its strategic bargaining power, has constantly been able to win shorter hours well in advance of the national trend.

The record of particular industries in the movement toward shorter hours is, of course, in large part a reflection of peculiar technological and demand conditions associated with certain types of employment. Thus, one might expect that seasonal industries, where spoilage and other factors require peak production during a relatively short period, would encounter greater difficulty in reducing hours of work than the building industry. And finally, the recurrence in our industrial development of depression periods with large-scale unemployment has probably tended to organize public opinion behind the shorter-hour movement as a means of reducing unemployment.

The Role of Unions

Prior to 1932, the role of unions in winning shorter hours was limited. Nevertheless, unions did win shorter hours for certain key groups more rapidly than for workers generally, and unions certainly must be given credit for dramatizing the hours issue. But it appears that the competitive market mechanism deserves the prime credit for hours reduction prior to the New Deal era.

After 1932, unions played an increasingly important role in affecting the trends in hours worked, not only directly but indirectly through their lobbying in behalf of the Fair Labor Standards Act of 1938 and other more specialized legislation. Moreover, in most industries, unions now require premium pay for weekend work, whether or not the number of hours exceeds 40 per week. Most union contracts also require payment of time and one half in excess of eight hours' work per day, again regardless of the number of hours worked per week. And despite the fact that the nonunion city office workers are the largest group regularly working less than 40-hour schedules, unions are today the leading force behind moves to reduce the scheduled workweek or to increase the penalty pay for overtime. The reason for this is found in the changing character of the arguments for shorter hours.

THE ARGUMENTS FOR SHORTER HOURS

At various times the proponents of shorter hours have based their arguments on four principal contentions: (1) The health of the population will be improved by a shorter workweek; (2) shorter hours mean increased leisure, which is not only good in itself but also will permit workers to purchase and enjoy the products of industry; (3) shorter hours will increase worker efficiency enough to offset the loss in work time; and (4) shorter hours are necessary to insure full employment. Today, only the last is argued in depth, with the second point utilized as a support for the employment argument.

Health and Leisure

Shorter hours have frequently been advocated as a health measure. It is on this basis, for example, that the regulation of hours for women and the regulation of hours in dangerous trades primarily rest. Regulation of hours in transportation is also partly based on this argument, although here it is the health and safety of the consumer as well as that of the worker which is protected.

The arguments based on health are more applicable to a longer workweek than 40 hours. Consequently, the proponents of a workweek shorter than 40 hours do not use the health argument much except in cases of particularly dangerous or strenuous trades or occupations.

Purchasing Power Theory

Organized labor has traditionally put forth the argument that increased leisure with earnings maintained would permit workers the time to spend more as consumers and thus would bolster the economy. It has also been maintained that more leisure would be helpful in encouraging citizens to participate in political and civil affairs, but this argument is not used as often today as in former years when hours of work exceeded 40.

During recent years, it has been customary for union leadership to overemphasize the purchasing power theory of the business cycle. Obviously, if workers were employed 12 hours a day, they would not have much time to do anything else besides eat and sleep, and they would not make very good customers for that part of the industry which does not produce absolute necessities. Since only a very small portion of industry produces these absolute necessities, it is also obvious that demand must exist for the miscellaneous luxuries, semiluxuries, and other things which make up America's high living standard. Shortening the working day, so long as it does not impair earnings, may make workers better customers for these essentials and nonessentials of modern capitalistic production.

Certainly, the five-day week and shorter working hours have greatly expanded spending for leisure. Moreover, the employee who works shorter hours receives a greater saturation of advertising over radio, television, and other media, and this may make him more desirous of spending to "keep up" or to enjoy the latest conveniences or luxuries.

But how much more the average worker's family will spend on consumption goods if his hours are reduced below 40 is not easy to determine. Since the worker's family spends the bulk of his income on consumption goods, it may well be that he is about as good a customer for the nonessential items of industrial production as can be expected. Moreover, this leisure argument assumes, first, that the increased costs resulting from decreasing the hours will not adversely affect employment and therefore, in turn, adversely affect consumer expenditures, which, as we shall point out, is likely to occur; and second, it also assumes the shorter-hour movement will not be simply a device to increase overtime pay. Where actual hours are not reduced but merely made more expensive by penalty overtime payments, the increased leisure argument is irrelevant; for here, the workers' take-home pay, not the workers' leisure, is increased.

Efficiency and Productivity

Historically, the reduction in hours of work has been accompanied by increases in productivity. As a result, the increased costs occasioned by shorter hours have not led to higher prices—at least over long periods of time.

The fact that shorter hours and increased productivity have marched hand in hand has given birth to the argument that reduced hours increase efficiency and/or productivity and hence absorb the increased costs of shorter hours, even if the shorter hours are accompanied by wage adjustments sufficient to maintain weekly earnings.

Productivity and worker efficiency are not necessarily synonymous terms. Productivity is not a measurement of the man alone but of the man and his equipment. It is a statistic commonly measured by dividing output by man-hours worked. As already noted, rising labor productivity is largely a manifestation of the joint contribution of increasing capital, improved managerial technique, and scientific advance.

On the other hand, labor efficiency, as defined here, refers to changes in output resulting solely from changes in labor effort or input, other factors being held constant. Hence an increase in labor efficiency will result in an increase in productivity, but an increase in productivity does not necessarily mean that labor efficiency has increased.

Shorter Hours and Efficiency. Unfortunately, there have been few studies made of the effect of hours on labor efficiency, and those which are available deal mainly with increases in hours above rather than reductions below 40. In addition, most of the more important studies which attempt to relate efficiency and hours of work were made during World War II, when conditions were quite abnormal. Nevertheless, the studies revealed significant, if not perfectly conclusive, relationships between hours of work and output as regards (1) the seven-day and 60-hour week, (2) the five- versus the six-day week, and (3) hours reduction below 40.

The Seven-Day Week. In the early stages of World War II, a number of plants in the United States and a larger percentage in Great Britain went on the seven-day week, with hours ranging from 44 to 72. The prewar standard in the United States was a five-day, 40-hour week; in Britain, a six-day, 48-hour week. Nevertheless, the experience with the seven-day week in both countries was very similar. For a time after the longer schedule was adopted, output increased. Then, as fatigue accumulated, weekly output fell to levels existing before the change, or even below. Workers were found to have a tendency to pace themselves under different work schedules in order to avoid extreme fatigue. Where workers had no control of the speed of work, output increased under the seven-day week, but so did spoilage, sickness, and absenteeism. The unanimous conclusion of all studies was that the seven-day week and hours of 60 or more a week reduced the efficiency of labor and were uneconomical for business.[1]

The Five- versus the Six-Day Week. The effect on worker efficiency of an increase from a five- to a six-day week and the effect of a decrease from the six- to the five-day week were also able to be examined as a result of the adjustments during and following World War II.

In a majority of cases the shift from the 40-hour, five-day week to the 48-hour, six-day week was accompanied by an increase in output directly proportional to the increase in hours; and in all cases, output increased to some extent.[2] However, the war emergency, the existence of wage incentives in a number of the plants, and in some instances the fact that production was at a moderate pace prior to the increase in hours prevented resentment on the part of the workers as well as excessive fatigue and the consequent lowering of efficiency.

On the other hand, the rate of absenteeism increased in the great majority of the cases after the addition of the sixth day, particularly in the plants where female labor was used. The lack of time for shopping and household chores was undoubtedly the main reason for the increase in absenteeism. If stores and other services had not inaugurated special

---

[1] U.S. Department of Labor, Bureau of Labor Statistics, *Hours of Work and Output* (Bulletin No. 917 [Washington, D.C.: U.S. Government Printing Office, 1947]).

[2] *Ibid.,* pp. 12–14.

evening hours for war workers, undoubtedly the rate of absenteeism would have been still higher under six-day operations.

The general conclusion of the Bureau of Labor Statistics report was that "the addition of the sixth day had no disadvantageous effect on output, provided daily hours were held to eight."[3] Other studies support the conclusion that the 48-hour week was best for war production and that adding the sixth day had no ill effect unless the daily hours were excessive.[4] It should be noted again, however, that different results might occur if the six-day week were inaugurated in peacetime.

After the war, many of the plants covered by the BLS survey resumed a normal five-day week. Although the increase in hours by the addition of a sixth day had resulted in an almost proportionate increase in weekly output in most cases, a decrease in hours was accompanied by a less than proportionate decrease in production. As in the increase of the workweek, so, too, in the decrease—absenteeism among men was little affected by the shift. Women's absences increased after both changes, in the latter instance probably because they lost interest in the work and were preparing for a resumption of household duties.

The most logical explanation advanced for the observed improvement in efficiency as hours of work were reduced was that workers who were paid on an incentive basis wished to make up lost take-home pay brought about by the elimination of time and a half for the sixth day.

Hours below 40—the Kellogg Experiment. A number of plants cut hours below 40 during the Great Depression and then continued at the shorter hours after employment conditions improved. One of the most publicized of these cases occurred at the Battle Creek, Michigan, plant of the Kellogg Company, where four six-hour shifts were substituted for three eight-hour ones as of December 1, 1930.

As a depression palliative, the six-hour day proved beneficial to workers and the company. But as experience with this work schedule accumulated under varying degrees of utilization of plant and output, certain weaknesses became evident. The company's plants operate around the clock, and its operations are largely machine-paced, so the short shifts provide little opportunity to reduce overhead costs. Furthermore, in order to avoid Saturday and Sunday work, hours were generally held to 30 a week during a substantial part of the year. Despite the relatively high hourly rates of pay, the 30-hour week meant that employees received lower pay than that of workers in similar industries. On a 40-hour schedule, even at lower hourly rates, the take-home pay would be enhanced—but the work force would be cut.

After World War II, the Kellogg employees found that they were

---

[3] *Ibid.,* p. 14.

[4] See Herbert R. Northrup and H. R. Brinberg, *Economics of the Work Week* (New York: National Industrial Conference Board, 1950), for supporting data.

earning less with their 30-hour week than were other workers in the area. In addition, many were "moonlighting"—working at a second job or business by employees who prefer more income to leisure. The Kellogg Company therefore agreed to let employees vote by department whether they wanted an eight-hour or a six-hour day. By 1959, all but a few of the 2,500 male employees had chosen the eight-hour day, 40-hour week. On the other hand, the 1,200 women employees at Kellogg still adhere to the short workweek. They point out that this enables them to earn money and still take care of home and family.

Management at Kellogg's no longer believes that the short workweek improves efficiency. It notes also that modern employee-based fringes—hospitalization, pensions, and government social security—increase costs when work is divided and more than offset minor efficiency improvements which might have occurred.[5]

Akron Rubber Tire Industry

As we have already noted, large segments of the rubber tire industry, especially in Akron, Ohio, have worked on a six-hour day, six-day week schedule since the 1930's. The results have been relatively unsatisfactory to both employees and companies, both in terms of earnings and productivity, so that only a few plants are left operating these hours. Moreover, tire manufacturing is now no longer concentrated in Akron, but rather often in newer plants, particularly in the South, where the eight-hour day persists.

One of the authors has been interviewing a company official over the last 20 years on the effects of the six-hour day. His company has always been disappointed with results of the six-hour day insofar as improved efficiency is concerned; but he also noted that wage rates are higher and plants are older in Akron than in other areas, and that therefore comparisons between the six-hour day in Akron and the eight-hour day in other rubber tire plants are difficult to make. The last plant of this company which was on the six-hour schedule converted to eight hours in 1967.

A striking development of short work schedules, such as have existed in Akron, is their propensity to encourage moonlighting. According to one study: "In Akron the best guesses hold that 16 to 20 percent of the rubber workers hold a second job, not a *part*-time job but a *full*-time job. About another 40 percent hold down a second, merely part-time employment."[6]

A second study found that "the incidence of dual wage or job holding is significantly higher for . . . 36-hour Akron rubber workers

---

[5] "Operation of the 6-Hour Day in Plants of the Kellogg Co.," *Monthly Labor Review*, Vol. XXXIII (June, 1931), pp. 148–55; and R. F. Janssen, "The Short Work Week," *Wall Street Journal*, January 10, 1962.

[6] Sebastian de Grazia, *Of Time, Work and Leisure*. (New York: Twentieth Century Fund, 1962), p. 71.

than for . . . 40-hour rubber workers located outside of Akron," and that "total multijobholding is significantly related to the length of the primary job workweek."[7] Actually, the desire of members of the United Rubber Workers to hold on to the 36-hour week has been a direct function of moonlighting. The leaders of the United Rubber Workers made a determined attempt at the 1956 convention to eliminate the six-hour day and go back to the 40-hour week. They were defeated precisely because the Akron workers did not want to give up the extra income they gained from holding two jobs and working many hours over 40 per week. In the last several years, however, the plants have hired thousands of young employees who desire more opportunity for earnings on their primary job and who have not as yet developed outside income interests. The votes of these new employees are tipping the balance in favor of the eight-hour day, 40-hour week.

New York City Electricians

In July, 1962, after a strike had shut down the construction industry of New York City, members of Local No. 3, International Brotherhood of Electrical Workers, won the five-hour day, 25-hour week. Previously, this local had been on a six-hour day. What the union won was a basic 25-hour week at $4.96 per hour, with overtime at $7.44 per hour for another five hours—weekly take-home pay of $161.20 at a time when no unemployment existed in this craft. Since then, these wages have been substantially increased.

Despite the "breakthrough" of the New York City's electricians, the seven-hour day remains the standard in the building trades. The position of Local No. 3 of the electricians' union is enhanced by its monopoly control of the electrical industry's labor force in the area, as well as by its tight hold on the construction electricians.[8] In addition, Local No. 3 made its demand more palatable by opening up its apprentice rolls. It agreed to the addition of 1,000 apprentices to the annual quota of 250 and liberalized the rules for their utilization as well. A significant number of the new apprentices were recruited from the Negro and Puerto Rican communities—a breakthrough for these minorities.

It is extremely doubtful if New York City's high-paid electricians are more efficient today than they formerly were. Initially, at least, the principal effect was more overtime. To what extent, also, moonlighting was generated is not known. One of the authors does, however, have personal knowledge that members of Local No. 3 worked Saturday on

[7] John C. Deiter, *MultiJobHolding and the Short Workweek Issue.* (Ann Arbor, Mich.: University Microfilms, Inc., 1965), p. 81.

[8] See *Business Week,* July 6, 1963, pp. 90–92; and for background, see *Allen Bradley Co.* v. *Local 3, International Brotherhood of Electrical Workers,* 325 U.S. 797 (1945).

many occasions in the City's suburbs at rates substantially below the union scale when they were still on a 35-hour week.[9]

Moonlighting

From the three cases cited, it is apparent that hours shorter than 40 per week do not yield discernible improvements in efficiency. They do seem to encourage people to make productive use of their time by seeking other work. Such moonlighting is not new, but it seems to be a regular phenomenon. In May, 1966, a total of 3.6 million persons were counted as moonlighters—that is, they held two jobs or more.[10] Since, however, in order to avoid taxes, union, or employer censure, many moonlighters do not report their second activity, the actual number of moonlighters is probably considerably greater.[11] A majority of moonlighters is found among professional, self-employed, government-employed, education, and farming groups, but more recently the number of those from blue-collar workers has been increasing.

In times of unemployment, moonlighting is often attacked as a contributor to that unemployment. The studies of moonlighters which have been made, however, do not bear this out. The largest segment of moonlighters are those with a special skill which is in demand or those who have a strong desire to enhance their incomes. Their moonlighting activity supplements their basic income from the primary job but is usually insufficient as a primary means of support.

Moonlighting is a further indication of the preference of many persons for additional income rather than additional leisure. The grievances in nearly any company inevitably include complaints from some workers that they did not receive a fair share of overtime work—"the golden hours" at time and one half or double time. The following comment of a then union research director is every bit as true today as it was when delivered more than a decade ago:

Aside from the workers' desire for their paid holidays and paid vacations there is no evidence in recent experience that workers want shorter *daily* or *weekly* hours. The evidence is all on the other side. Hundreds of local and national officials have testified that the most numerous and persistent grievances are disputes over the sharing of overtime work. The issue usually is not that someone has been made to work, but that he has been deprived of a chance to make overtime pay. Workers are eager to increase their income, not to work fewer hours.[12]

[9] Based on several contacts with moonlighting electricians during 17 years' residence in Westchester County, New York.

[10] Harvey R. Hamel, "Moonlighting—An Economic Phenomenon," *Monthly Labor Review*, Vol. XC (October, 1967), p. 17.

[11] *Ibid.*; and de Grazia, *op. cit.*, pp. 71–72.

[12] George Brooks, "The History of Organized Labor's Drive for Shorter Hours of Work," *AFL–CIO Conference on Shorter Hours of Work*, published in Special Report No. 1, *Daily Labor Report*, No. 177, September 11, 1956, p. 13.

Nevertheless, whenever the specter of unemployment appears on the horizon, union officials will probably, as they have always in the past, demand shorter working hours as a palliative. This raises the question of whether shorter hours will reduce unemployment.

HOURS REDUCTION AND EMPLOYMENT

There are two points of view from which reduction in hours of work per day or per week can be examined as a remedy for unemployment. The first is a reduction in hours without a change in the basic wage rate, so that the workers previously employed now receive fewer hours of work and correspondingly reduced earnings. The second is the effect of a shortening of hours with compensatory increases in basic rates, so that earnings for the shorter working time remain undiminished. No one now seriously advocates the first approach. Nevertheless, a short analysis of the possible effects on unemployment of a reduction in hours without compensatory overtime will point up the economic relationships between hours reduction and employment, and will also help to clarify those relationships where compensatory wage adjustments are involved.

Shorter Hours with Unchanged Basic Wage Rates

It is not unusual for persons to assume logic and correctness in the statement attributed to Samuel Gompers that "if anyone is out of work, the hours of work are too long." The idea is that if hours are only reduced sufficiently, unemployment can be automatically eliminated.

A realistic look at the supply factors shows that the effect of shortening hours, even without the compensatory adjustments in wage rates which unions demand, cannot be assessed by a mere arithmetical calculation. For example, it might be thought that as long as basic rates are unchanged, unit labor costs should likewise remain constant. But employers will have to add new workers who will require training and who may be less skilled than those already employed, so that the immediate effect of the plan is probably to produce some decline in the efficiency of labor. Moreover, in some industries, work sharing produces technical difficulties. The balance of operations may not be workable with two six-hour shifts instead of one eight-hour shift—or, for that matter, there just might not be enough demand for two shifts of 32 or 35 hours where one of 40 hours now suffices.

Even if unit labor costs do not change, capital costs per unit of output will be increased in those plants which operate fewer hours per week after the shorter-hour program is inaugurated. The rise in fixed costs per unit will force marginal firms out of business and thus add to the amount of unemployment. Moreover, the reduction in profits in all plants will make entrepreneurs somewhat more reluctant to invest; and therefore, in the long run the level of employment may be further reduced.

On the demand side the shortening of hours of work of employed labor may provide job opportunities for persons formerly on relief or receiving unemployment benefits. Where there are no compensatory wage adjustments, the earnings of those formerly employed full time will be reduced, and therefore an increase in consumer demand can only follow if the newly employed workers greatly expand purchases over what they had consumed while receiving unemployment benefits or on relief to an extent greater than the drop in expenditures by those formerly employed 40 hours and now working and earning less.

Reduction in Hours with Compensatory Wage Increases

On the whole, a program of shorter hours is unacceptable to labor unless it is accompanied by compensatory wage adjustments, so that labor income is maintained. In advocating such a policy to reduce unemployment, organized labor has shown its customary bias in emphasizing the role of demand conditions and ignoring the more immediate repercussions of the increased hourly price of labor on costs and business profits.

Employers, by and large, can be expected to react to a program of reduced hours with compensatory hourly wage increases as they would react to any increase in marginal cost. Prices will tend to rise; a smaller output will be demanded; and ultimately, a new equilibrium will be established at a lower level of output. In order to think this through, let us assume that the demand for labor under these circumstances in a particular firm has an elasticity of unity. If the union raises hourly rates 5% and reduces hours of work by 5%, it will have duplicated the readjustment that the employer himself would have made to the changed cost conditions. But since a new equilibrium has been established at the higher unit price of labor, there is no incentive to hire any additional labor. It is therefore clear that if the demand curve for labor in a particular firm has an elasticity of unity or greater, the reemployment objective of the shorter-hour movement must fail of accomplishment.

The precise value to be assigned to the elasticity of demand for labor has been the subject of some controversy among economists. On the whole, it seems likely that in depression periods, when management is extremely sensitive to cost increases of any kind, the demand for labor is elastic, at least in an upward direction. That is, a given percentage increase in wage rates will produce a more than proportional reduction in employment. Although there is room for disagreement as to the precise value of the elasticity of demand for labor, it seems likely that the reduction in hours must be substantially greater than the percentage increase in hourly wage rates if the immediate effect of the institution of the shorter working week is not to increase the volume of employment. The effect of the shorter hours of work with compensatory wage adjustments will depend upon the relation between three factors: (1) the percentage decrease in the hours of work, (2) the percentage increase in hourly rates, and (3) the elasticity of demand for labor. Thus, if the elasticity of demand for labor were equal to minus two (i.e., the volume of employment diminishes 2% with each increase of 1% in wage rates), and if the increase in hourly rates were 5%, then the percentage reduction in hours would have to be more than 10% if more workers are to be hired.

Effect of Increasing the Number of Shifts

More promising as a means of converting unemployment into leisure is the six-hour shift, provided that the six-hour shift means the use of two or more shifts per day. Suppose, for example, that a plant in a continuous-process industry has been accustomed to run continuously for five days a week, using three eight-hour shifts. If this plant were to change to four shifts of six hours each, it would appear that employment would be increased. However, if each worker, now employed a shorter number of hours, wishes to keep his pay undiminished, it is evident that there will be a rise in labor cost per unit, despite the fact that the number of shifts has increased. The increased labor costs will be reflected in higher prices and a reduced total output, so that ultimately no permanent increase in employment may result from this change-over.

But there are circumstances in which the addition of another shift may tend to increase employment. The substitution of two six-hour shifts for a previous eight-hour day, or perhaps for a longer day including some employment at overtime, will tend to reduce capital costs per unit by allowing management to work capital longer while labor works shorter hours. The decrease in total unit costs attributable to this influence will tend to offset the increase in unit labor costs occasioned by shortening the hours of work with compensatory wage increases, so that, on balance, profits may be unimpaired.

While it may be conceded that the more intensive use of capital is a favorable factor, it should be recognized that if the increase in the number of shifts does increase employment, it will have this effect only after a series of highly complicated long-run influences are set in motion. The spreading of overhead will not affect marginal costs, while the reduction of hours with increases in basic hourly rates will raise marginal costs. Hence, as far as immediate price and output reactions are concerned, the change in the number of shifts does not alter the picture. Some plants will be forced out of business, while other plants, in which the proportion of labor costs is relatively low and overhead costs relatively high, will find their profits increased by the changeover to additional shifts. Ultimately, the number of plants in the industry undergoing the change will diminish, with a larger volume of business concentrated in a smaller number of firms, each using capital more intensively than was true before the shorter-hour program was inaugurated.

The ability to inaugurate an additional shift will vary considerably from industry to industry; and in those firms attempting it, the benefits obtained will vary, depending upon the importance of overhead costs. In some plants where equipment is antiquated, working additional shifts may mean increasingly frequent breakdowns without adequate time for repairs. In industries which do not operate continuously, the amount of reemployment which can be provided by a shortening of hours of work will depend in part upon the availability of unused machinery and equipment. To the extent that less efficient equipment is brought into use, the upward pressure on costs is intensified.

Interindustry Shifts

A program of shorter hours with undiminished take-home pay would produce important changes in the demand for particular industries. The increased availability of leisure would probably be reflected in an increased demand for sporting goods and other recreational goods by which leisure can be made more enjoyable. Likewise, the effect of the increased wage disbursements—assuming that there were some initial reemployment—would operate to stimulate the consumer goods industries. At the same time, however, the nondurable consumer goods industries would experience the greatest increases of cost relative to the rest of the economy, since it appears that the nondurable consumer goods industries have higher ratios of wages to value added than do the capital goods industries. Thus, insofar as the effect on costs is concerned, the former industries would be hardest hit by the combination of shorter hours and increased wage rates; while the capital goods industries, having a higher ratio of capital costs, would be the ones to benefit most from the addition of extra shifts.

This combination of altered cost and demand positions would ultimately produce some readjustment in the disposition of the total labor force among the various industries in the economy. The net effect upon employment can only be conjectural. If wage disbursements increase initially as a result of the shorter hours of work with compensatory wage rate increases, it appears that a larger proportion of the national income would be spent on nondurable consumer goods than before the hours program was instituted. Two factors will contribute to this result. On the one hand, the total income of wage earners will increase if there is some reemployment; and the income of workingpeople, particularly during periods of large-scale unemployment, is likely to be spent upon nondurable consumer goods. But as we have seen, these are the very industries which will feel most of the impact of the shorter-hour program. Therefore, prices will rise in these industries relative to the general price level; but because of the relatively inelastic demand typical of these industries, the total receipts of the nondurable consumer goods industries will probably increase. This augmented volume of expenditure concentrated in these industries will probably support a larger volume of employment than it would under its previous distribution, since the nondurable consumer goods are likely to be more labor-employing than other industries. At the same time, since the proportion of labor costs to total costs is less in the capital goods industries than in the nondurable consumer goods industries, and since the adjustments resulting from the changeover to more shifts with shorter hours per employee may lead to a more efficient allocation of output concentrated in fewer plants, prices of machines should rise less than in proportion to consumer goods. This would stimulate the demand for laborsaving machinery and thus increase the volume of investment and employment.

Shortages of Skilled Labor

Any general uniform reduction in hours per week is likely to increase the number of bottlenecks which develop in production and therefore raise a barrier to full employment. A shortage of skilled workers in a key industry can have repercussions which produce unemployment throughout the economy. If the shorter-hour program is applied to skilled workers, management is faced by three alternatives, all of which are likely to react unfavorably upon employment generally. Management can, of course, employ the same skilled workers as before, but now pay them additional overtime because of the shortening of the basic workweek. This would have the same effect as a wage increase and would therefore raise costs and prices. On the other hand, management can attempt to hire other workers and train them to fill these jobs; but these men will, on the average, be less experienced and make more mistakes, so that labor cost per unit will tend to rise through their employment. Lastly, if management is unwilling or unable to find additional skilled help, bottlenecks and shortages will develop which will cause stoppages, depriving even the unskilled of their jobs.

The shortage of skilled labor is often a regional or local problem. It can be especially severe in small towns having available only a limited pool of labor. Thus a program of shorter hours must be undertaken with caution. On the other hand, in some industries, it is conceivable that a reasonable shortening of hours, even if it does produce some rise in costs, could be accomplished without too difficult a readjustment. An appreciation of the various possible repercussions of a shorter-hour program indicates the danger of any general uniform shortening of hours accomplished by legislative decree.

NATURE OF UNEMPLOYMENT

Any attempt to utilize shortening of hours as a means of curbing unemployment must also consider the nature of the unemployment. That of the latter part of the 1960's has been overwhelmingly structural—the young, the unskilled, and the Negro, disabilities often found in one person. Certainly, merely reducing hours of work cannot accomplish the miracle of finding jobs for those who do not have the background, education, training, means, or motivation to accept even unskilled jobs in industry. Nor will reducing hours transfer people from the high unemployment inner cores of the cities to the new manufacturing plants in the suburbs and rural areas.

To the extent, therefore, that unemployment is structural, a decrease in hours will not solve such unemployment problems unless it is accompanied by an extraordinarily successful retraining and integration program, together with greater improvement in the mobility of labor. But the costs of such programs, combined with the burden imposed by the shorter workweek (as noted below) could easily discourage rather than encourage employment. Dividing up work—and raising its costs—is not likely to improve the matching of jobs and men.

COSTS OF THE SHORTER-HOUR PROGRAM

Figure 16–2 shows the hourly increases required to maintain weekly pay as a 40-hour schedule drops to 32. Approximately a 14% increase is needed to offset a five-hour decline, and more than a 25% increase to accomplish an eight-hour decline.

Even this is not the whole story. Suppose the workweek is reduced to 35 hours, but the business requires 40 hours of work to meet its commitments. Then, five hours must be worked at time and one half. As calculated in Table 16–1, this would mean an increase not of 14% but of

FIGURE 16–2

RISING COST OF A SHORTER WORKWEEK

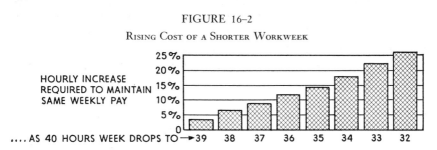

SOURCE: Reprinted by special permission from *Business Week*, October 20, 1962. Copyright, 1962, by McGraw-Hill, Inc.

TABLE 16–1

COST OF REDUCTION IN WORKWEEK

Cost of reduction in workweek:
1. No loss of pay for employee
2. No loss of production for employer
Assume rate of pay = $3 per hour; for 40-hour week, weekly pay = $120
1. If workweek is lowered to 35 hours:
No loss of pay for employee; hourly rate now raised to $3.43 to equal $120 weekly take-home pay
Increase in weekly rate 14.3%.
2. If employer requires 40-hour week:
Five hours must be worked overtime; time and one half of $3.43 = $5.15; 35 hours @ $3.43 plus 5 hours @ $5.15 = $145.80.
Increase in weekly rate 21.5%.

21.5%! Obviously, such wage increases cannot be borne by a significant segment of American industry—and equally obviously, such wage increases therefore would be likely to create unemployment, not employment.

AUTOMATION AND HOURS

In the early 1960's, when unemployment ranged from 5% to 7.5% of the labor force, union officials particularly, but many other persons as well, argued that automation was rapidly reducing the number of jobs, so that hours reduction would be necessary to offset resultant unemployment, while on the other hand, increased productivity gained from automation would permit the increased costs of the hours reductions to be absorbed by industry.

Actually, this has proved both an incorrect analysis and an oversimplification. Automation has actually tended to increase overall the number of jobs. To be sure, changes effected by automation have helped to create or accentuate unemployment problems in some areas and among some labor force groups while creating industries and jobs for other areas and groups. The effects of automation thus vary considerably from industry to industry, from area to area, and from one labor force group to another.

Moreover, the advent of technological progress and automation does not proceed smoothly throughout industry, but rather varies widely from industry to industry in its extent and character. A general hours reduction would therefore fall on both heavily and lightly automated industries, on the industries for which technological unemployment is a problem, and on those growing as a result of changing technology. It would give a bonus to the fully employed—or threaten their employment. It would seek, against heavy economic odds, to help those not fully employed.

To succeed in creating employment, a reduction in hours from 40 to 35, with pay maintained, would require a minimum productivity increase of 15%—a most unlikely development. But even if such an increase in productivity occurred, it would probably be insufficient because the substantial investment in expensive equipment required by automation greatly increases fixed costs. To the extent that a shorter workweek keeps this equipment idle, fixed costs per unit during operating periods increase and tend to offset decreases in costs resulting from increases in productivity.

A shorter workweek, with take-home pay maintained, would so increase costs that automation could well be discouraged except for the larger, wealthier firms. This could accelerate a trend toward economic concentration and possibly increase rather than diminish technological unemployment.

The most desirable manner of attaining full employment is by high-volume production, so that labor is fully employed 40 hours a week and the community benefits from technological progress in the form of a rising level of real income. From the point of view of maximizing national welfare, increasing leisure for labor, obtained by reducing hours of work below 40 a week, can hardly be preferred to rising real income for the whole community. Moreover, it must be reiterated again that there is no guarantee that a reduction in the workweek will increase employment. The crux of the problem is whether full employment could in fact be attained at the 35-hour level or whether the rise in costs attributable to the program of shorter hours with less work would not so depress business confidence that investment would be discouraged and unemployment would prevail even with the shorter workweek.

LONG VACATIONS AND EMPLOYMENT

Negotiation in 1963 by the United Steelworkers with steel, can, and aluminum companies of 13-week vacations every five years for long-service employees was an attempt to spread the work by a related but different approach than the shortening of the week. The program became effective in 1964, just as employment in the industry began a substantial improvement from a recession low point. Hence, any evaluation of the program is difficult.

Discussions by one of the authors with steel industry executives do indicate that some replacements have been necessary for those on sabbaticals, but not on a one for one basis. In addition, such summer replacements have received good training for future promotions. On the other hand, the sabbaticals have added another cost to an industry already suffering from severe foreign and substitute product competition. Whether business—and thus jobs—have been lost because of these additional costs cannot be determined.

OVERTIME AND EMPLOYMENT

From time to time, when unemployment has been serious, proposals have been made to increase overtime pay under the Fair Labor Standards Act from time and one half to double time. The rationale is that it is sometimes cheaper to pay workers time and one half than to employ additional workers, and therefore by making overtime more expensive, unemployment would be reduced. In 1964, President Lyndon B. Johnson proposed this to Congress. The idea had the strong backing of organized labor, but did not reach a Congressional vote.

Fringes, Overtime, and Turnover Costs

We noted in Chapter 5 that fringe benefit costs have risen rapidly and substantially. Moreover, fringe benefits such as hospitalization, and many governmental benefits such as social security, are employee-related, not hours-related. In addition, state unemployment benefit systems, as will be explained in Chapter 18, penalize companies with excessive turnover and hence favor long hours, not more employees.[13]

On the other hand, overtime costs have risen, too, because the base by which time and one half is figured has risen sharply. In other words, if a wage is increased from $2 to $2.50 per hour, overtime increases from $3 to $3.75. Overtime's expense has therefore tended to keep pace with the rise in fringe costs in many industries.

Such an analysis is, however, unrealistic because (1) it assumes the employer is certain that he knows how long he will need a new employee (or overtime), and (2) it ignores training and layoff costs. The average employer often hesitates to add to the labor force until he feels reasonable assurance that he has need of an employee for a longer period. In the meantime, he will usually use overtime work to fill his needs.

The basic reason for the hesitation to hire is not only the high cost of fringes, but also the high cost of employing and laying off workers. Finding, interviewing, processing, and training people can often cost several hundred dollars per employee. Then, if a layoff occurs, new expenses mount. In a large New England plant studied by one of the authors, each time one person was laid off, three to five "bumps" occurred as a result of the working of the plant seniority system. The plant management estimated that each layoff cost $600–$900 because of the upset, retraining, and lost time involved! Naturally, in such a situation, management will prefer to utilize overtime rather than hire new employees if it is uncertain as to the length of time for which additional work hours are needed.

There is evidence that the amount of overtime utilized in industry has been increasing.[14] Whether this is a function of increased fringe benefit costs is not known. If, however, it is related to the increased costs of hiring and laying off employees, making it more expensive to utilize overtime is a dubious remedy. The net effect would be an increase in labor cost, either because of utilizing the more expensive overtime, or because of hiring more employees instead of using overtime, which, if our assumptions are correct, would be an additional cost over the former use of overtime at time and one half. This, of course, assumes that the company or industry would not offset the new costs by a decrease in labor utilization, which is by far the most likely impact. Obviously, the relation of fringe benefits, overtime, and employment is complex, and employment would not easily be generated by altering this relationship.

---

[13] On this subject, in general, see Joseph W. Garbarino, "Fringe Benefits and Overtime as Barriers to Expanding Employment," *Industrial and Labor Relations Review*, Vol. XVII (April, 1964), pp. 426–42; and particularly the comment thereon by Robert M. MacDonald and reply by Professor Garbarino, *ibid.*, Vol. XIX (July, 1966), pp. 562–72.

[14] See MacDonald, *loc. cit.*, for details of this point.

CONCLUDING REMARKS

Whenever unemployment becomes a serious problem, the question of shorter hours will come to the fore. Nevertheless, a reduction of the workweek seems at best a poor remedy for the problem of unemployment, and certainly no solution for the disadvantaged in our society who are without jobs. If our society decides to take improvement in productivity in the form of reduced hours of work rather than in disposable income, economic growth can be impaired. Hence a further reduction in hours could well curtail rather than expand employment.

QUESTIONS FOR DISCUSSION

1. Is there a competitive tendency toward reduction of hours of work? Evaluate the importance of governmental legislation and union organization in shortening hours of work.
2. Discuss the relationship of hours reduction and efficiency. What are the advantages and disadvantages of a six-hour shift?
3. Discuss the possible effects on employment (*a*) of raising the penalty on overtime to double time and (*b*) of establishing a national program of three months' vacation every five years.

SUGGESTIONS FOR FURTHER READING

DANKERT, CLYDE E.; MANN, FLOYD C.; and NORTHRUP, HERBERT R. (eds). *Hours of Work.* Industrial Relations Research Association, Publication No. 32. New York: Harper & Row, Publishers, 1965.

    A series of articles by 12 social scientists on various aspects of the workweek and hours controversy.

GARBARINO, JOSEPH W. "Fringe Benefits and Overtime as Barriers to Expanding Employment," *Industrial and Labor Relations Review*, Vol. XVII (April, 1964), pp. 426–42; and comment and reply thereon by Robert M. MacDonald and Professor Garbarino, *ibid.*, Vol. XIX (July, 1966), pp. 562–72.

    An analysis and discussion of the impact of fringe benefits, overtime pay, and employment and layoff costs on the propensity to employ additional persons as against working existing employees overtime hours.

PART VI

Economics of the Search
for Security

Chapter	SECURITY FOR OLD AGE
17	AND PREMATURE DEATH

In this chapter, we shall examine the primary methods and issues involved in providing security for the aged and for the survivors of those who die prematurely; in Chapter 18 the methods and issues of providing security against unemployment will come under scrutiny; and in Chapter 19, we shall discuss security measures for the sick and injured. The search for security has led to both governmental and private attempts at mitigation of the problems involved. In this and the ensuing two chapters, the relative merits of the governmental and the private solutions will be examined.

THE ECONOMIC PROBLEMS OF OLD AGE AND PREMATURE DEATH

Old Age

The economic problems of the older worker have become more serious in recent years because of the aging of the population. The number of the aged (those 65 and over) has increased both actually and relative to the number of persons of working age (20–64) years, and this increase is expected to continue throughout most of the 20th century. In 1900, there were almost 13 persons in the working group to 1 over 65; by 1950, this ratio had declined to 7 to 1; and by 1967, 5 to 1. In addition, with compulsory retirement at 65 in many industries and a trend toward earlier retirement with subsidized private plan retirement benefits, a smaller percentage of those over 65 are now working than was formerly the case. In terms of real numbers, the increase in the aging population is equally significant. In 1900, there were 3 million over 65; in 1950, 12 million; in 1960, 16.6 million; in 1967, 18.8 million; and by the year 2000, there are expected to be 28 million in this category.[1] The old-age group, aided by advancing medical science, is an ever increasing one.

[1] U.S. Department of Health, Education, and Welfare, Social Security Administration Office of the Actuary, Actuarial Study No. 62, *United States Population Projections for OASDHI Cost Estimates,* December, 1966.

Apart from the older individual's desire to work, there is the practical problem of his being able to find employment. Rightly, or not, employers usually prefer younger workers to older ones. It is generally believed that efficiency and the capacity to work decline with age, but opinion differs as to the precise age at which this occurs, the magnitude of the decline, and how it varies between occupation and industry. Table 17–1 shows how labor-force participation declines with age. The man out

TABLE 17–1

DISTRIBUTION OF LABOR FORCE, 1965

Age	Number (000 omitted)	Percentage
14 and 15 years	1,180	1.5
16 to 19 years	6,350	8.1
20 to 24 years	9,301	11.9
25 to 34 years	14,989	19.1
35 to 44 years	17,228	22.0
45 to 54 years	15,845	20.2
55 to 64 years	10,355	13.2
65 years and over	3,107	4.0
Total	78,358	100.0

SOURCE: Bureau of Census Population Estimates, *Summary of Demographic Projections,* No. 388 (March, 1968), p. 75.

of work and in his late 40's or 50's can testify to the difficulty of finding a new job.

Another factor which has accentuated the problem of old age is the increased urbanization of the population. Although we were once a predominantly agricultural nation, more than two thirds of our population now resides in urban communities. There is less room for aged grandparents in the smaller city dwelling than there once was in the farmhouse; and it is more difficult and costly to provide necessities for the aged in the city than in the rural areas, where food is grown on the farm.

When workers reach an age when they can no longer produce efficiently, it is certainly inhuman just to discharge them. Progressive employers of generations ago established the first pensions for this reason. To be sure, the worker was supposed to make provision for himself through savings. But farsighted employers realized that worker morale was improved, and the employer's reputation as a fair manager enhanced, if a pension plan was established. By 1968, about one out of every two employees in private nonfarm establishments was covered by a private pension plan, and in the aggregate, these plans were paying 3.6 billion annually in benefits to over 3 million beneficiaries. It is estimated that by 1980, three out of five nonfarm employees will be covered by private pension plans; that plan benefits will grow to 9 billion annually; and that the number of plan beneficiaries will be 6.5 million.

Along with the growth of private pension plans, the need to provide for the aged worker became recognized as a community need. Because the worker who was not provided for became a public charge, it was considered desirable, through compulsory government insurance, to see to it that old-age needs were at least partially cared for.

Despite the relief provided for the aged through their own savings, private pension plans, and government insurance, another factor has emerged which has, and will continue to have, a significant impact on their security. Since the mid-1930's, the cost of living in the United States has increased at an average annual rate of 1½% to 2½%. The impact on the purchasing power of a fixed pension income has been quite severe. For example, by the year 1967, the employee who retired on a fixed pension in 1962 had experienced a 9% decrease in the purchasing power of that pension; the 1957 retiree, a 16% decrease; the 1952 retiree, a 21% decrease; and the 1947 retiree, a 33% decrease. The periodic increases in government-provided benefits during this period has, for lower income employees, substantially offset the results of continued inflation. However, employees in the middle to upper income levels have not fared as well.

Loss of Breadwinner

Closely allied with the problem of old age is that of the family which loses its principal breadwinner. Advances in medical science which have strengthened life expectancy have been made primarily by successful attack on causes of death before the age of 40. Maladies such as cancer and heart disease, which strike persons at the peak of their earning power, have increased the number of their victims since 1900. In addition, accident hazards resulting from such conveniences as the automobile have also increased. Few heads of families have sufficient life insurance (both private and employer-provided) to do more than tide their survivors over a relatively short period. The problem of taking care of survivors, therefore, has been of significant public interest.

The extent of the problem created by the loss of the breadwinner is demonstrated by these data. In 1967, there were 9.2 million widows, of whom 5.8 million were over age 65.[2] Even young, able-bodied widows who have dependents are handicapped in their search for work because of the difficulty of caring for children and trying to earn a living at the same time.

---

[2] Data from U.S. Department of Commerce, Bureau of the Census, "Marital Status and Family Status: March, 1967," *Population Characteristics* (Washington, D.C.: U.S. Government Printing Office, 1967), Series P–20, No. 170.

PUBLIC AND PRIVATE APPROACHES TO THE ECONOMIC PROBLEMS OF OLD AGE AND PREMATURE DEATH

The depression which began in 1929 forcefully called attention to the need for an overall, national, or social approach to the problems caused by loss of income to the family. To be sure, some attack had already been begun prior to 1929 on the need to supply an income to the family when the breadwinner no longer could produce a paycheck, but the pre-1929 approach was confined largely to compensating the worker for loss sustained in accidents suffered at the place of work—workmen's compensation. It was not until 1935, with the passage of the Social Security Act, that an overall program was begun to deal with loss of income because of old age, death of the breadwinner, or unemployment. The 1935 law was modified and expanded in 1939. And in almost every election year beginning with 1950, significant amendments have been enacted. Despite the many changes, the double-pronged "insurance-assistance" approach to the alleviation of economic security which was originally adopted is still in effect today.

Public Approaches

The essential difference between social insurance and general public assistance or relief measures is, first, that under social insurance "the law specifies with precision the conditions governing eligibility, and the nature and amount of the benefit. Second, the specific conditions do not include a requirement to undergo a test of means or need."[3] Thus, benefits under social insurance are predictable, while those under public assistance are not, since the discretion of the program administrator in determining whether or not to grant assistance—and if so, how much—must be very great. In other words, persons who meet specified eligibility requirements under the law have a right to social insurance; but they must establish a need or prove that they are worthy in order to secure public assistance. As a practical matter, the borderline between insurance and public assistance is not always precise.[4] For example, the receipt of unemployment compensation insurance is sometimes dependent upon lack of opportunity for "suitable work" which, in turn, permits administrative discretion which can be used to deny benefits to those who might otherwise be eligible.

It should be noted that social insurance and other forms of social security are not necessarily antagonistic but rather can and should be complementary.

[3] Eveline M. Burns, *The American Social Security System* (Boston: Houghton Mifflin Co., 1949), p. 31.

[4] For an exploration of the differences, see Herbert S. Denenberg, "The Right to Income: Social Insurance versus Public Assistance," *Journal of Risk and Insurance,* Vol. XXIX (March, 1962), pp. 87–98.

Social insurance deals with *presumptive* rather than with *demonstrated* need, and is a social institution dominated by a concept of *average* rather than *individual* need. This characteristic of social insurance limits the extent to which this form of social security can deal with the total problem of family economic insecurity. A program dealing with average conditions and needs will always have to be supplemented by a system of public assistance to provide for emergencies and special needs.[5]

In addition to insurance and public assistance, two other types of benefits are utilized in the American social security system: status benefits to veterans, which World War II and the Korean War have made very important; and work relief, such as was used by the Works Progress Administration (WPA) during the 1930's but which has not been an important factor since that time.[6]

Tables 17–2 and 17–3 summarize the American social security program in terms of beneficiaries and benefits for selected years. Examining these tables, we find that *social insurance* is used as a means of protecting a majority of the labor force against the risks of old age and loss of the breadwinner; against the risks of unemployment; against loss of earnings because of occupational accidents or diseases (workmen's compensation); against the risks of permanent and total disability; and in four states, against loss of earnings because of nonoccupational temporary disability.

The public assistance programs are of two kinds: (1) *special public assistance*, which attempts to meet the needs of specific groups, that is, aged persons not covered or covered inadequately by old-age, survivors, and disability insurance; families with dependent children; the blind; and the permanently and totally disabled; and (2) *general public assistance*, which is a last-resort measure given to those who are not eligible for other programs and are in need. The social security type in use besides social insurance and special and general public assistance is the veterans' security program, designed to provide for veterans and their families in the event of death, disablement, or incapacity, or unemployment following discharge.

The material in Tables 17–2 and 17–3 also emphasizes the variety of programs which are included in the American social security system. For example, a person who suffers loss of income because of age may be eligible for old-age insurance under the old-age, survivors, and disability insurance program, either in his own right or as the aged dependent or survivor of a beneficiary; if a railroad man, he may be entitled to a pension under the Railroad Retirement Act; or he may apply for old-age assistance (OAA). In addition, veterans drawing disability payments continue, of course, to receive these benefits when they are old.

---

[5] Burns, *op. cit.*, p. 36.

[6] Social Security Administration, Bureau of Family Services (Public Assistance Report No. 52 [Washington, D.C.: U.S. Government Printing Office, March, 1962]).

TABLE 17-2. SOCIAL INSURANCE AND VETERANS' PROGRAMS: CASH BENEFITS AND BENEFICIARIES, BY RISK AND PROGRAM, 1940-65 [In Thousands]

Risk and Program	1940	1945	1950	1955	1960	1962	1963	1964	1965[1]
AMOUNT OF BENEFITS									
Total[2]	$1,540,259	$2,604,095	$6,321,473	$12,166,803	$22,615,138	$27,050,822	$28,723,389	$29,973,289	$32,565,495
Retirement[2]	330,819	591,701	1,423,471	5,157,390	10,759,614	13,138,785	14,238,044	15,122,225	16,791,861
OASDHI	17,150	148,107	651,409	3,747,742	8,196,131	10,161,892	10,794,622	11,281,479	12,541,519
Railroad retirement	83,342	106,240	176,925	335,880	594,446	638,350	653,739	667,490	705,311
Public employee retirement[3]	206,210	283,974	536,929	998,028	1,926,382	2,306,816	2,762,815	3,150,989	3,525,132
Federal civil service	49,069	64,816	135,267	260,388	547,367	659,664	756,901	829,569	896,649
Other Federal employees[4]	54,141	76,158	151,662	277,641	529,015	636,092	870,914	1,061,420	1,233,483
State and local government	103,000	143,000	250,000	460,000	850,000	1,011,060	1,135,000	1,260,000	1,395,000
Veterans' program[5]	24,117	53,380	58,208	75,740	42,655	31,727	26,868	22,267	19,899
Disability[6]	476,508	954,449	2,441,922	3,185,181	4,859,643	5,851,283	6,187,333	6,466,129	7,024,060
OASDHI					568,167	1,105,050	1,210,208	1,308,825	1,573,237
Railroad retirement	30,824	30,900	77,315	103,089	146,748	156,079	158,952	161,668	149,431
Public employee retirement[3]	22,950	33,430	213,250	334,699	491,857	570,601	624,863	692,777	751,314
Federal civil service	12,950	18,930	40,520	71,131	152,466	193,983	223,960	250,543	278,806
Other Federal employees[4]			148,730	208,568	244,392	262,571	275,903	302,234	317,508
State and local government	10,000	14,500	24,000	55,000	95,000	114,048	125,000	140,000	155,000
Veterans' program[5]	293,734	644,450	1,674,000	1,981,775	2,529,673	2,724,285	2,819,083	2,846,041	3,026,384
Workmen's compensation	129,000	241,000	360,000	521,000	755,000	879,000	932,000	1,001,000	1,057,000
State temporary disability insurance[7]			89,258	192,673	311,324	364,893	392,764	409,894	425,948
Railroad temporary disability insurance[8]		4,669	28,099	51,945	56,874	51,375	49,463	45,924	40,755
Survivor:									
Monthly benefits	161,515	417,789	901,817	2,068,435	3,671,637	4,565,294	4,869,099	5,176,449	5,876,517
OASDHI	6,371	99,651	276,945	1,107,541	2,316,211	3,011,101	3,216,009	3,416,403	3,978,990
Railroad retirement	1,448	1,772	43,884	121,847	201,251	233,906	244,215	255,041	278,442
Public employee retirement	16,000	20,128	34,409	80,621	184,620	228,619	265,569	295,782	324,406
Federal civil service			8,409	38,851	104,707	130,489	153,514	172,873	190,575
Other Federal employees[4]				1,770	4,913	6,330	7,055	7,908	8,831
State and local government	16,000	20,128	26,000	40,000	75,000	91,800	105,000	115,000	125,000
Veterans' programs[5]	105,696	254,238	491,579	688,426	864,555	976,669	1,018,306	1,074,223	1,149,679
Workmen's compensation[9]	32,000	42,000	55,000	70,000	105,000	115,000	125,000	135,000	145,000
Lump-sum payments	36,756	65,301	86,693	195,622	299,503	346,474	381,347	407,467	420,490
OASDHI	11,833	26,127	32,740	112,871	164,286	183,418	205,936	216,371	216,930
Railroad retirement	2,497	8,138	12,722	16,088	19,989	21,987	24,090	24,352	22,158
Public employee retirement	18,466	25,987	28,522	49,836	75,713	96,925	100,671	113,109	124,555
Federal civil service	5,810	10,244	8,147	9,197	11,586	15,676	14,291	16,794	18,106
Other Federal employees	156	243	375	639	1,127	1,249	1,379	1,314	1,450
State and local government	12,500	15,500	20,000	40,000	63,000	80,000	85,000	95,000	105,000
Veterans' program[5]	3,960	5,049	12,709	16,827	39,515	44,144	50,650	53,635	56,847
Unemployment	534,661	574,855	1,467,570	1,560,175	3,024,741	3,148,986	3,047,566	2,801,017	2,451,558
State unemployment insurance[10]	518,700	445,866	1,373,114	1,379,219	2,866,650	3,012,610	2,926,490	2,670,754	2,283,433
Railroad unemployment insurance	15,961	2,359	59,804	93,284	157,690	132,685	99,430	78,428	60,493
Veterans' unemployment allowances[11]		126,630	34,652	87,672					
Training and related allowances[12]					401	3,691	21,646	51,835	107,632
BENEFICIARIES[13]									
Retirement:[2]									
OASDHI	77.2	591.8	1,918.1	5,443.2	10,309.7	12,248.2	13,038.1	13,588.8	13,918.2
Railroad retirement	102.0	129.1	174.8	329.2	444.0	474.1	489.2	495.0	498.4
Public employee retirement	193.8	256.1	406.3	606.1	977.2	1,149.1	1,268.4	1,377.4	1,482.4
Federal civil service	37.1	110.9	111.0	164.9	263.3	304.0	323.1	342.6	359.4

State and local government...................	113.0	155.0	73.5	106.2	178.0	245.4	295.2	344.8	388.0
Veterans' program[5]........................	33.8	60.4	222.0	335.0	535.0	600.0	650.0	690.0	735.0
			54.1	59.8	33.2	24.3	20.5	16.9	14.0
Disability:[2]									
OASDHI.......					542.6	1,161.0	1,380.0	1,518.5	1,653.9
Railroad retirement......................	39.3	39.0	76.0	87.1	96.6	99.6	100.9	102.2	102.5
Public employee retirement...............	29.8	44.7	131.0	188.8	247.2	279.9	295.7	314.3	332.1
Federal civil service..................	15.5	23.7	43.0	61.3	102.1	122.0	130.0	139.5	149.3
Other Federal employees[4].............			56.0	85.5	90.1	96.9	100.7	104.7	107.8
State and local government............	14.3	21.0	32.0	42.0	55.0	61.0	65.0	70.0	75.0
Veterans' program[5]....................	576.3	1,083.8	2,314.1	2,609.0	2,976.0	3,125.9	3,160.2	3,180.2	3,202.9
State temporary disability insurance[7]...		5.4	55.2	96.5	121.0	135.7	144.6	146.5	150.2
Railroad temporary disability insurance[8]..			31.2	31.9	29.7	28.2	27.4	25.8	23.1
Survivor:									
OASDHI..................	35.7	533.5	1,093.9	2,096.6	3,446.0	3,965.7	4,226.8	4,458.7	4,680.9
Railroad retirement......................	3.0	4.4	136.3	196.5	251.0	265.2	275.0	282.5	288.4
Public employee retirement[14].............	25.0	32.3	58.3	121.9	223.4	258.8	280.4	302.0	321.8
Federal civil service..................		.3	18.3	70.2	149.5	175.7	190.0	205.9	220.2
Other Federal employees[4].............				1.7	3.9	5.1	5.6	6.1	6.7
State and local government............	25.0	32.0	40.0	50.0	70.0	78.0	85.0	90.0	95.0
Veterans' program[5]....................	323.2	537.3	991.2	1,154.2	1,262.0	1,595.5	1,706.7	1,814.5	1,899.7
Unemployment:									
State unemployment insurance[10].........	982.4	465.0	1,323.5	1,099.5	1,723.0	1,728.6	1,622.9	1,439.7	1,187.4
Railroad unemployment insurance........	41.5	3.3	76.8	63.1	69.9	65.8	49.6	39.4	31.1
Veterans' unemployment allowances[11]....		88.9	32.1	72.4	1.6				
Training and related allowances[12]......						2.9	21.2	50.7	74.8

[1] For some programs, 1965 data are preliminary.

[2] Includes benefits to dependents where applicable.

[3] Excludes refunds of contributions to employees who leave service.

[4] Included under retirement are a significant amount and number of disability payments for 1940 and a small but unknown amount and number of disability and survivor payments for 1945 and 1950.

[5] Retirement data are for veterans of the Civil War, the Indian Wars, the Spanish-American War, the Boxer Rebellion, and the Philippine Insurrection; beginning October 1951, includes all service pensions. Disability data include pensions and compensation, and subsistence payments to disabled veterans undergoing training. Survivor data include special allowances for survivors of veterans who did not qualify under OASDHI (Servicemen's and Veterans' Survivor Benefit Act of 1956). Lump-sum payments are for burial of deceased veterans.

[6] Excludes payments for medical care.

[7] Benefits payable in California, New Jersey, New York, and Rhode Island. Includes maternity data for Rhode Island and private-plan beneficiaries in California and New York; data for private-plan beneficiaries in New Jersey not available.

[8] Includes maternity data.

[9] Small but unknown amount of lump-sum death payments included with monthly survivor payments.

[10] Includes payments made by the states as agents of the federal government under the federal employee's unemployment compensation program and the Ex-Servicemen's Compensation Act of 1958 and payments under the temporary extended unemployment insurance programs; beginning 1961, includes program in Puerto Rico.

[11] Under the Servicemen's Readjustment Act of 1944 (terminated July, 1949) and the Veterans' Readjustment Assistance Act of 1952 (terminated January, 1960). Amount (but not number) includes self-employment allowances—for 1945, $11,675,000 to 12,100 veterans (average monthly number); for 1950, $1,606,000 to 1,500 veterans; and a negligible amount thereafter.

[12] Under the Area Redevelopment Act of 1961 and the Manpower Development and Training Act of 1962, training allowances based on unemployment insurance in the state of training and allowances for transportation and maintenance when training is away from home.

[13] For OASDHI, average monthly number; for railroad retirement program, public employee retirement systems, and the veterans' programs, number on rolls June 30; for state unemployment and temporary disability insurance and for veterans' unemployment allowances, average weekly number; for railroad unemployment and temporary disability insurance, average number during 14-day registration period; for Area Redevelopment Act and Manpower Development and Training Act, number on rolls December 31. Beneficiary data for workmen's compensation not available.

[14] For federal programs under Uniformed Services Contingency Option Act of 1953 and for state and local government retirement systems, number represents families.

SOURCE: Based on reports of administrative agencies. Statistical Supplement, 1965, *Social Security Bulletin.*

TABLE 17–3

VETERANS' PROGRAMS: VETERANS RECEIVING COMPENSATION OR PENSION, BY TYPE OF PAYMENT AND AGE, 1940–65
[In Thousands]

June 20[1]	Total[2]	Disability Compensation or Pension										Service Pensions[4]
		Service-Connected							Nonservice-Connected			
		All Ages	Under Age 65			Age 65 and over			All Ages	Under Age 65	Aged 65 and Over	
			Total	Disability rating[3]		Total	Disability Rating[3]					
				Under 70%	70%–100%		Under 70%	70%–100%				
1940	610	385	...	...	...	...	...	...	189	...	...	34
1945	1,144	912	...	...	...	...	...	...	159	...	...	60
1950	2,368	1,990	...	...	...	...	...	...	290	...	...	54
1955	2,669	2,076	2,026	1,841	185	57	43	14	531	319	278	60
1956	2,739	2,083	2,004	1,825	179	70	53	17	597	304	366	56
1957	2,797	2,074	1,980	1,807	173	84	65	19	670	279	462	50
1958	2,850	2,064	1,980	1,807	173	84	65	19	741	279	462	44
1959	2,934	2,053	1,952	1,781	171	101	78	23	841	257	584	39
1960	3,009	2,027	1,908	1,746	162	119	93	26	947	219	728	33
1961	3,107	2,000	1,868	1,711	158	131	104	27	1,077	182	895	29
1962	3,150	1,987	1,849	1,693	156	138	109	29	1,138	166	972	24
1963	3,181	1,989	1,844	1,686	158	145	115	30	1,170	165	1,005	21
1964	3,197	1,993	1,846	1,684	162	147	117	30	1,186	176	1,010	17
1965	3,217	1,992	1,846	1,679	167	146	117	29	1,210	197	1,013	14

1 For 1940–57, as of June 30.
2 Persons receiving payments under special acts and as retired emergency and reserve officers included in total but excluded from distribution.
3 Disability is rated by the Veterans Administration according to average impairment of earning capacity, graduated in intervals from 10% to 100%.
4 Payments to aged veterans of the Civil War, the Indian Wars, the Spanish-American War, the Boxer Rebellion, and the Philippine Insurrection.
SOURCE: Veterans Administration, Department of Veterans Benefits, published and unpublished data. Statistical Supplement, 1965, *Social Security Bulletin.*

Benefits payable to those who have lost a breadwinner are equally varied, with the OASDHI, railroad retirement, assistance, and veterans' programs all having a role. Insecurity because of unemployment is less involved (and less adequately provided for) but is covered by three programs: state unemployment compensation, a railroad plan, and status benefits for veterans. Loss of earning power because of accidents on the job is handled largely by state workmen's compensation programs, which vary greatly in coverage and protection. In addition, four states have benefits designed primarily for loss of earning power due to nonoccupational temporary disability. The railroad program also includes both temporary and permanent disability insurance that applies to occupational as well as nonoccupational disability. As already noted, OASDHI provides such benefits, too. Aid for a specific disability—blindness—is available in all jurisdictions, and aid for permanent and total disability is given in 49 states. Dependent children have special provisions made for them if the breadwinner cannot support them because of mental or physical incapacitation or if the breadwinner deserts them.

Another feature of the American social security program is the variety of governments involved. Old-age, survivors, and disability insurance is wholly a federal program; old-age assistance and other special assistances involve both the federal and the state governments, as does unemployment compensation. Workmen's compensation is wholly a program of the states, except for small segments of employees covered by federal laws. General assistance involves local governments, but the states are parties to these programs in varying degrees. Finally, even when the federal government alone is involved, there is no unity of administration. Thus, by virtue of their political power the railroad unions have secured separate and superior social security arrangements for themselves, and civil service employees also have a special program exclusive of the general system.

Private Approaches

Despite the fact that the United States is the richest country in the world, and despite the high repute which our folklore accords to the person who saves, the fact remains that Americans cannot save enough to care for all contingencies of loss of income because of old age, death of the breadwinner, unemployment, or illness or accident. More than one third of American families do not save at all, and the 20% with the highest incomes account for 60% of all savings.[7] Moreover, many of those who do save spend their savings later for better housing, sending their children to college, etc.

For this reason, employer-provided benefits have taken on a significant role in providing a measure of economic security for the American

---

[7] Data from Federal Reserve surveys or income and saving.

public. Reference has already been made to the rapid growth of private pension plans and the number of beneficiaries receiving benefits under these programs. But equally important in protecting the survivors of a deceased employee is the group life insurance provided by his employer. At the end of 1966, group life insurance in force totaled more than $343 billion and accounted for more than 35% of all life insurance in force in the United States. The average amount of insurance per employee was approximately $6,780. These data include insurance on executives and other highly paid personnel. In plans administered by unions or jointly by unions and employers, the average amount of insurance per employee was approximately $2,140. Moreover, from 1956 to 1966, group life insurance in force increased 193%.[8] It is expected that this trend of providing greater death benefits for employees will continue in the future, with particular reference to providing for the employee's survivors in the form of income payments, either through life insurance or in conjunction with the employer's pension plan.

THE OLD-AGE, SURVIVORS, DISABILITY, AND HEALTH INSURANCE PROGRAM (OASDHI)

When the original Social Security Act was passed in 1935, a significant percentage of our population was not covered or was not able to meet eligibility requirements for benefits. Through a series of amendments, however, coverage has been extended to the point that of every 100 persons in paid employment in the United States during 1967, about 90 were earning credits toward OASDHI. And almost half of those not covered consist of civilian employees of the federal government who are covered by their own retirement system.

Benefits

The types of benefits provided under OASDHI are as follows:

Retirement benefits:
Primary monthly benefit to retired worker (reduced benefit, ages 62–64; full benefit, age 65)
Monthly benefit to his wife if 62 or older (reduced if claimed before age 65)
Monthly benefit to his dependent children under 18 or disabled
Monthly benefit to wife, whatever age, if caring for child
Monthly benefit to dependent husband, if 62 or over (reduced if claimed before age 65)
Survivors' benefits
Monthly benefit to widow, 62 or older
Monthly benefit to widow or divorced wife, whatever age, if caring for dependent children

---

[8] Institute of Insurance, *Life Insurance Fact Book* (New York, 1967), pp. 26–27.

Monthly benefit to child under 18 or disabled
Monthly benefit to dependent widower 62 or older
Monthly benefit to dependent parent 62 or over
Burial benefit in lump sum to widow or widower, or to person who
  paid burial expenses
Disability benefits
Monthly benefit to worker if totally disabled for work
Monthly benefits for same dependents as under retirement benefits
Monthly benefit to disabled widows and widowers between ages 50
  and 62
Medical benefits
Hospital, nursing, and outpatient service
Voluntary supplementary coverage

All benefits are based upon the monthly payment to the worker who retires at age 65 or over, which is called the primary insurance amount. This, in turn, is determined by the worker's average monthly wage. While there is more than one method of computing the average monthly wage, it will usually be figured as follows: The total of creditable earnings in covered employment and self-employment after 1950, or age 21 if later, and until age 65 (62, if a woman) is divided by the number of months elasping in this period, except that the five years of lowest earnings are omitted, as well as any years for which a disability freeze was in effect.

As already mentioned, the monthly retirement benefit payable to a retired worker is the same as his primary insurance amount, but with the proviso that benefits are first drawn at or after age 65. Retired workers who start collecting benefits at 62, 63, or 64 receive less than the primary insurance amount. The full amount, however, is payable to eligible disabled workers, regardless of age.

The monthly benefits for dependents of a retired or disabled worker, the survivors of a deceased worker, or the disabled widow or widower of a deceased worker are equal to specified fractions of the primary insurance amount. For example, a wife who starts drawing benefits at 65 or who has a child in her care receives one half; an eligible widow receives 82.5%; a child of a retired worker receives one half; a child of a deceased worker receives three fourths. However, the total family benefit is subject to a maximum of 80% of the average wage or a specified dollar amount, whichever is less. The dollar amount will increase each year until it reaches its maximum of $434.40 in the year 2006.

Examples of what benefits are payable at various levels of average monthly wages are given in Table 17–4. The minimum monthly payment to a worker retiring at age 65 is $55; the maximum is $218. However, the figures in this table represent the ultimate benefits that will become payable under the 1967 amendments to the Social Security Act. Since it was not possible for earnings up to $650 per month ($7,800 per year) to be covered before 1968, it will not be until the year 2006 that a male

TABLE 17-4

SOCIAL SECURITY ACT AS AMENDED IN 1967
WORKER AND FAMILY MONTHLY BENEFITS
EFFECTIVE FEBRUARY, 1968

Average Monthly Wage	Retired Worker (Age 65) or Disabled Worker	Retired Worker, Wife, Age 65	Retired Worker, Wife, Eligible Child	Widow (Age 62)	Widow (under Age 62) Eligible Child	Maximum Family Benefits
$300	$127.10 (42%)	$190.70 (64%)	$240.00 (80%)	$104.90 (35%)	$190.80 (64%)	$240.00 (80%)
$325	134.30 (41%)	201.50 (62%)	262.40 (81%)	110.80 (34%)	201.60 (62%)	262.40 (81%)
$350	140.40 (40%)	210.60 (60%)	280.80 (80%)	115.90 (33%)	210.60 (60%)	280.80 (80%)
$375	146.40 (39%)	219.60 (59%)	292.80 (78%)	120.80 (32%)	219.60 (59%)	300.00 (80%)
$400	153.60 (38%)	230.40 (58%)	307.20 (77%)	126.80 (32%)	230.40 (58%)	322.40 (81%)
$450	165.00 (37%)	247.50 (55%)	330.00 (73%)	136.20 (30%)	247.60 (55%)	354.40 (79%)
$500	177.50 (36%)	266.30 (53%)	355.10 (71%)	146.50 (29%)	266.40 (53%)	374.80 (75%)
$550	189.90 (35%)	284.90 (52%)	379.90 (69%)	156.70 (28%)	285.00 (52%)	395.60 (72%)
$600	204.00 (34%)	306.00 (51%)	408.00 (68%)	168.30 (28%)	306.00 (51%)	415.20 (69%)
$650	218.00 (34%)	323.00 (50%)	432.00 (66%)	179.90 (28%)	327.00 (50%)	434.40 (67%)

NOTES:
1. Average monthly wage of more than $450 is not generally possible for males retiring before 1971.
2. The minimum monthly benefit (prior to actuarial reduction) payable to a worker who retires at age 65 or to a sole surviving beneficiary is $55.
3. Percentage figures represent monthly benefit as percent of corresponding average monthly wage.
4. Retired worker may elect benefit as early as age 62; in such case, his primary insurance amount is reduced permanently by 5/9ths of 1% for each month by which early retirement age precedes age 65. Thus, for example, worker who elects retirement benefit at 62 will receive 80% of the primary insurance amount payable at age 65 on the basis of his average monthly wage. Workers eligible for disability benefits receive the full primary insurance amount regardless of disability retirement age.
5. Wife's benefit equals 50% of employee's benefit but is subject to a maximum of $105 monthly. Wife's benefit can be claimed as early as age 62; in such case, her benefit is reduced permanently by 25/36ths of 1% for each month by which early retirement age precedes age 65. Thus, for example, if wife's benefit is claimed at age 62, she will receive 75% of the amount payable at her age 65.
6. The wife of a retired or disabled worker is entitled to one-half of the primary insurance amount if she has not reached age 65 but has in her care the worker's eligible child, who also is entitled to a benefit of one half of the primary amount.
7. Benefit payable to widow age 62 or over is 82.5% of deceased husband's primary insurance amount. Widow under age 62 without an eligible child in her care may elect a benefit as early as age 60; in such case, her benefit is reduced permanently by 5/9ths of 1% for each month by which initial payment date precedes her age 62. A disabled widow may elect a reduced widow's benefit as early as age 50; at age 50, the benefit would be 50% of the deceased spouse's primary insurance amount.
8. Monthly benefit payable to a widowed mother with one child is three quarters of the primary insurance amount of the deceased husband for the mother and an equal amount for the child. Generally, the mother's benefit is paid until she remarries or the child attains age 18 or marries.
9. Monthly benefit payable to a widow and two or more children is three quarters of the primary insurance amount of the deceased husband for the mother, and a like amount for each child. For all average monthly wages shown above, the Maximum Family Benefit is payable in these cases.
10. Maximum Family Benefits sometimes exceed amounts shown above due to rounding of individual benefits to next higher multiple of $0.10.
11. The lump-sum death benefit payable under the Social Security Act is the lesser of (a) three times the primary insurance amount, or (b) $255.

SOURCE: Social Security Administration.

worker can achieve an average monthly wage of $650 and thus qualify for maximum benefits (2004 for a female worker). Table 17–5 shows the maximum benefits that can become payable to male workers in the years prior to 2006.

The average monthly benefit received by retired workers in November, 1967, was $91.48. In that month, all OASDHI benefits totaled

TABLE 17–5

1967 AMENDMENTS TO SOCIAL SECURITY ACT
EFFECTS ON PRIMARY INSURANCE AMOUNTS
PAYABLE TO FUTURE RETIREES

Age 65 on January 1	Primary Insurance Amount
1968	156.00
1969	160.50
1970	165.00
1971	168.40
1972	170.70
1973	172.90
1974	175.20
1975	177.50
1976	179.70
1977	180.80
1978	182.00
1979	184.20
1980	185.40
1981	186.50
1982	187.60
1983	188.80
1984	188.80
1985	189.90
1986	191.00
1987	192.00
1988	192.00
1989	193.00
1990	194.00
1991	195.00
1992	195.00
1993	196.00
1994	197.00
1995	199.00
1996	201.00
1997	203.00
1998	205.00
1999	207.00
2000	209.00
2001	211.00
2002	213.00
2003	215.00
2004	216.00
2005	217.00
2006	218.00

Note: Figures are for male workers and assume maximum Social Security wages for all years since 1950. Primary Insurance Amounts for females are higher until maximum benefit levels are reached.
SOURCE: Social Security Administration.

$1.7 billion. This amount was divided among 23.6 million recipients, of whom 12.0 million were retired workers, 2.6 million spouses, 2.8 million children, 3.2 million widows and widowers, 1.2 million disabled workers, 0.9 million dependents of disabled workers, and 0.9 million aged parents and persons with special age-72 benefits. The 1967 amendments will, of course, increase these totals.

Eligibility

Insured Status. Eligibility for benefits is based upon the extent and the time a person spends in employment covered by OASDHI. The yardstick for measuring whether one is insured is the "quarter of coverage"—a three-month period beginning January 1, April 1, July 1, or October 1, in which one was paid $50 in wages, provided such earnings or income was in occupations or industries covered by OASDHI. Self-employed persons receive four quarters of coverage for every year in which they net $400 of self-employment income.

A man is fully insured when he reaches age 65 (62 for women) or dies, if at that time he has one quarter of coverage (earned any time after 1936) for each four calendar quarters that have elapsed since December 31, 1950, or after age 21, if later. At least 6 quarters of coverage are necessary in any case; 40 quarters of coverage entitle one to a fully insured status for life. One is currently insured at any time if he has at least 6 quarters of coverage within the preceding 13 quarters. In counting the number of calendar quarters that have elapsed since 1950, the following should be omitted: any quarters before age 21, and any quarters in which the earnings record was frozen owing to disability.

To be eligible for retirement benefits for himself and his dependents, and for his surviving aged widow and parents to be eligible for survivor benefits, the worker must be fully insured. (For dependent husband and widower's benefits, the working wife must be *both* fully and currently insured.) Currently insured status provides benefit eligibility for surviving children, widows with children, and lump-sum death payments. Payment of the disability benefits is contingent on fully insured status *and* social security credit for 5 years of work in the 10 years before the beginning date of the disability (for those disabled before age 31, there must have been coverage in one half the quarters between age 21 and the time disabled or, for persons becoming disabled before age 24, there must have been coverage in six out of the last 12 quarters).

The Retirement Test. An eligible retired worker, dependent, or survivor who does not earn more than $1,680 in a year can receive benefit checks for all 12 months of the year. But such beneficiaries earning more than $1,680 in a year may receive benefit checks for less than full benefits. One dollar of benefits is lost for each $2 earned between $1,680 and $2,880. An additional dollar of benefits is lost for each dollar earned over $2,880. Moreover, regardless of how much is earned in a year, the beneficiary may qualify for benefits in any month in which he does not earn more than $140 in wages or does not do substantial work if self-employed. This so-called "retirement test" is not applicable to individuals who reach age 72.

Financing

The OASDHI program is paid for by equal contributions from both employer and employee in covered employment. Self-employed persons

TABLE 17–6

HISTORY OF SOCIAL SECURITY TAXES

Year	Tax Rates			Tax Base	Maximum Annual Tax Employer-Employee Each
	Pension Rate	Hospital Insurance Rate	Combined Rate		
1937–49	1.0%			$3,000	$ 30.00
1950	1.5			3,000	45.00
1951–53	1.5			3,600	54.00
1954	2.0			3,600	72.00
1955–56	2.0			4,200	84.00
1957–58	2.25			4,200	94.00
1959	2.5			4,800	120.00
1960–61	3.0			4,800	144.00
1962	3.125			4,800	150.00
1963–65	3.625			4,800	174.00
1966	3.85	0.35%	4.2%	6,600	277.20
1967	3.9	.5	4.4	6,600	290.40
1968	3.8	.6	4.4	7,800	343.20
1969–70	4.2	.6	4.8	7,800	374.40
1971–72	4.6	.6	5.2	7,800	405.60
1973–75	5.0	.65	5.65	7,800	440.70
1976–79	5.0	.7	5.7	7,800	444.60
1980–86	5.0	.8	5.8	7,800	452.40
1987 and after	5.0	.9	5.9	7,800	460.20

NOTES:
1. Tax rates for self-employed differ from those shown above.
2. Taxes shown are those provided for under the Social Security Act as amended in 1967.
SOURCE: Social Security Administration.

covered by the program pay three quarters as much as the total of employer and employee contributions on the same amount of earnings. Initially, the employee tax was 1% on the first $3,000 of earnings in covered employment. Table 17–6 shows the changes that have occurred in both the base and the tax rate since that time, as well as the changes scheduled for the future.

The OASDHI taxes are collected by the payroll deduction method for the employed, and with income taxes for the self-employed, under the administration of the Internal Revenue Service. The bulk of the taxes collected are deposited in the OASI Trust Fund of the U.S. Treasury.

The balance goes into separate Disability Insurance and Health Insurance Trust funds. All expenses and benefits of the program come from these tax receipts. The reserve portions of the trust funds are invested in interest-bearing U.S. government securities.

As of November, 1967, reserves in the OASI Trust Fund amounted to $24.3 billion, the Disability Trust Fund had assets of $2.1 billion, and the Health Insurance Trust fund had assets of $1.6 billion.

Administration

The OASDHI is a wholly federal government–administered program, with the exception that initial determinations of disability are made by state agencies and that medical expense benefits are administered through fiscal intermediaries such as Blue Cross and private insurance carriers. Two departments of the federal government share these administrative functions—the Treasury and the Department of Health, Education, and Welfare. The Internal Revenue Service of the Treasury collects the taxes, and the Secretary of the Treasury is the managing trustee of the trust funds. The Treasury also issues benefit checks, and appropriations are made from the fund to cover administrative expenses.

All other administrative functions are handled by the Social Security Administration, which is now a division of the Department of Health, Education, and Welfare. Centralized records are kept in Baltimore, Maryland, and field offices are located throughout the United States. In addition, research and actuarial divisions are attached to the Social Security Administration in Washington as is an appeals council which hears cases involving claimants who are dissatisfied with interpretations of eligibility or amount of benefits due.

OLD-AGE ASSISTANCE

That OASDHI could not cover all persons was recognized at the inception of the social security program. Those already past age 65 in 1937 were left out of the program. However, under the 1939 amendments, coverage after age 65 was possible, and so those who were over that age in 1937 could qualify with 1½ years of work. But the writers of the Social Security Act recognized that some of the excluded oldsters did not have the resources to get along without public assistance, and they also realized that for some persons receiving relatively low insurance benefits, supplementation would be necessary. So they provided a system of grants-in-aid to the states for payments to the *needy* aged. Old-age assistance (OAA) is one of the three original categories of relief programs provided by the Social Security Act. The other two were aid to families with dependent children (AFDC) and aid to the blind (AB). A fourth category—aid to the permanently and totally disabled (APTD)—was added in 1950. The fifth category, medical assistance for the aged (MAA), was added in 1960. It is designed to provide aid to those aged who are not eligible for OAA but are medically indigent.

Old-age assistance was actually received by more persons than OASDHI until the 1950 amendments broadened the coverage of the OASDHI program. Moreover, OAA payments have, on average, been kept better adjusted to the cost-of-living increases than have OASDHI payments. In November, 1967, the highest average OAA payment was New Hampshire's $108.05 per month; the lowest, Mississippi's $38.55. The reason for the variation is that although the federal government foots a good portion of the bill, OAA, unlike OASDHI, is mainly a state-administered program.

The 1958 amendments to the Social Security Act made two important changes in the matching formula, which determines how much the federal government contributes toward OAA payments: (1) substitution of average for individual maximums and (2) provision of some variability in the share of OAA payments that will be met—i.e., while matching for the first $30 remained at four fifths, matching for that part of the average payment that exceeded $30 but was no more than $65 varied from 50% to 65%, depending on the average per capita income in the state for the most recent three years. Unlike past formulas, which related to cash payments only, both money payments to recipients and payments to vendors for medical care qualified (see Table 17–7.)

Subsequent amendments to the formula further liberalized the federal matching proportion by allowing extra amounts for vendor payments and by extending the four-fifths matching provision as shown in Table 17–7.

The Social Security Act makes these grants-in-aid for old-age assistance contingent on an age requirement no higher than 65 years, a residence requirement which does not exclude persons who have resided in the state for five of the nine years immediately preceding application and for one year continuously immediately preceding application, and a citizenship requirement which does not exclude any citizen of the United States. State laws in existence prior to 1935 frequently contained more exacting eligibility requirements, particularly as to residence.

Federal aid is limited to needy persons, but the states are permitted wide latitude in defining need, subject only to the requirement (effective July 1, 1941) that any income or resources of the applicant must be taken into consideration and (effective August, 1943) to an annual review of the recipient's eligibility for assistance. Such review, however, varies from a thorough one in some states to a perfunctory one in others.

The proportion of aged persons on the old-age assistance rolls varies widely across the country: from fewer than 1 out of 20 in 12 jurisdictions

TABLE 17–7

Maximum Matchable Amounts and Federal Matching Proportions
for Public Assistance under Various Laws

| | Old-Age Assistance, Aid to Blind, and Aid to Disabled | |
Law	Maximum Matchable Individual Payment (per Month)	Federal Matching Proportion
1935 Act.....................	$30	One half
1939 Act.....................	40	One half
1946 Act.....................	45	Two thirds of first $15 plus one half of remainder
1948 and 1950 acts...........	50	Three quarters of first $20 plus one half of remainder
1952 and 1954 acts...........	55	Four fifths of first $25 plus one half of remainder
1956 Act.....................	60	Four fifths of first $30 plus one half of remainder
1958 Act.....................	None	Four fifths of first $30 plus variable grant (ranging between 50 and 65 per cent) on next $35
1960 Act.....................	None	Same as 1958 Act, plus—for OAA only—an additional amount on vendor medical payment
1961 Act.....................	None	Maximum for average vendor medical payment raised to $15, and first bracket of formula extended to $31
1962 Act.....................	None	Fraction in first part of formula increased to 29/35, and bracket extended to $35
1965 Act.....................	None	3/137 of the first $37 plus variable grant or next $38

Source: Social Security Administration.

to more than 1 out of 4 in 7. For the United States as a whole, 1 out of 19 persons 65 or over was receiving OAA in December, 1966.

EMPLOYER-PROVIDED RETIREMENT BENEFITS

Although the origin of private pension plans dates back to the 1870's, the significant growth in these plans has come since the 1940's. To some extent, their growth is attributable to a recognition of the economic security problems of old age. However, the more specific factors that have influenced this growth include tax advantages and increased demands of collective bargaining. The tax advantages are that an employer's contributions to such a plan are a deductible business expense (particularly significant during World War II and the Korean War when excess profits taxes were levied), while employees are not taxed on these contributions until benefits are distributed or made available. Moreover, funds in such a plan accumulate free of tax, and when benefits are paid, they may qualify for additional tax benefits. The increased demands of labor have followed a recognition, in the late 1940's, that pensions were a proper subject for collective bargaining.[9] Other factors contributing to this growth have been a recognition on the part of business management that pension plans are an efficient and socially acceptable method of handling the situation of a superannuated employee whose efficiency is declining, as well as an efficient method of attracting and retaining competent personnel.

Types of Plans

Broadly speaking, retirement benefits are provided under either of two programs—pension plans and deferred profit-sharing plans. Under a pension plan, the employer agrees either to provide a fixed amount of benefit (and will contribute whatever this costs), or to make a fixed contribution (which will provide a variable benefit depending upon factors such as the employee's age and the length of time he participates in the plan). A deferred profit-sharing plan operates in a fashion similar to the latter type of pension plan with the notable exception that the employer's contribution, instead of being a fixed amount, depends upon profits and may vary from year to year.

Pension plans may be established as the result of collective bargaining or, as is the case with respect to many plans, as a result of unilateral action on the part of the employer. While profit-sharing plans could also come about as a result of collective bargaining, this has not, as a practical matter, been the case in the past. The vast majority of profit-sharing plans have been established by unilateral action of the employer.

Although a great many of the collectively bargained plans are established with a single employer, a significant number of union employees are covered under multiemployer or the so-called area plans. Under this type of program, a group of employers, usually in the same industry or in the same geographic area, contribute to a single fund. Employees are free to move from employer to employer, within the plan, without losing pension credits.

Benefit Levels

The retirement benefits provided by private pension plans vary a great deal from employer to employer. The amount and type of pension benefit provided in collectively bargained plans is usually a fixed dollar amount, regardless of the employee's earnings. A formula frequently used to determine the employee's benefit is one which provides a dollar amount (such as $3 or $4) of monthly pension for each year of service the employee has completed at retirement. The basic auto agreements negotiated in 1967 provide a benefit of as much as $6 a month per year of service.

In plans covering nonunion employees, the benefit is usually related to the employee's earnings and frequently reflects his length of service.

[9] *Inland Steel Company* v. *United Steelworkers of America,* 170 F. (2d) 247, 251 (1949).

Moreover, it is common, in unilaterally established plans, to reflect OASDHI benefits in the formula. Thus, for example, the plan might provide a lower pension benefit with respect to earnings under the OASDHI wage base than it does for earnings over this amount, or the plan benefit might be reduced by all or part of the employee's OASDHI benefit.

Another observation concerns the range of benefit levels generally found in private pension plans. Many pension planners develop a program which, when OASDHI benefits are taken into account, produces total retirement benefits which range from 40% to 60% of the employee's earnings. Generally, the higher percentages apply to lower paid employees (due to the relative value of OASDHI benefits at their earnings levels).

A great many private pension plans also provide benefits in the event of death, termination of employment, or total and permanent disability. These benefits are discussed later in this chapter and in the following chapters.

Eligibility for Retirement Benefits

In some plans, particularly those where employees make contributions, participation is not permitted until the employee has attained some minimum age or has completed some minimum period of service. Some plans also have a maximum age for participation (either expressed directly as such or in the form of a requirement that the employee must have completed some minimum period of service by normal retirement age).

To be eligible for full retirement benefits, the employee must have attained the normal age specified by the plan. This is age 65 in the great majority of plans. As previously mentioned, many plans also require that to be eligible for benefits, the employee must have completed some minimum period of service (for example, 15 years) by normal retirement age. Also, most plans permit early retirement, usually at age 55 or 60 (with or without some minimum service requirement), but at a considerably reduced pension. Many plans also permit earlier retirement in the case of total and permanent disability but without as much of a reduction in benefits as is generally the case with a regular early retirement. The distinction is that in a regular early retirement, the benefit is reduced for two reasons: (1) the employee's accrued pension is less than it would have been at normal retirement; and (2) the benefit is actuarially reduced to reflect the fact that benefits will be paid over a longer period. In disability retirements, it is customary for the "actuarially equivalent" reduction not to be made. It should be noted, however, that some plans, particularly those that are collectively bargained, provide for a "subsidized" early retirement benefit if the employee retires before he is eligible for OASDHI benefits. In essence, these plans provide for a supplemental benefit (over and above the regular early retirement benefit) until the employee is eligible for OASDHI benefits.

While retirement policies among companies with pension plans are quite varied, many firms require retirement at a specified age, with few or no exceptions allowed. The general trend is in this direction, and unions, which have often opposed compulsory retirement, have actually pushed for early rather than late retirement in recent years because of unemployment problems. Where late retirement is permitted, it is frequently subject to management approval and does not carry with it any increase in benefits over what would have been payable at normal retirement.

Termination of Employment Benefits

If, under certain conditions, an employee retains rights to a pension even if he leaves a company, that pension plan gives "vested rights." (Vesting does not mean merely the return of the employee's contribution; it entails rights to the employer's share, usually in the form of retirement income.) Generally, vested rights accrue only after a certain number of years of service, with additional requirements of age also being common.

The general trend in recent years has been toward the increased adoption of vesting provisions as well as the liberalization of existing vesting provisions. Moreover, there is an increasing interest on the part of the federal government in this type of benefit. Evidence of this is found in the January, 1965, report of the President's Committee on Corporate Pension Funds. This Committee observed that vesting is necessary if private pension plans are to serve the broad social purpose which justifies their favored tax status.[10]

From an employer's viewpoint, vesting represents an additional cost —not only because of the additional benefit provided but because of the administrative work and records that vesting entails. And, to the extent that his plan provides vested benefits, it does not encourage employees to stay with his firm. From a broad social viewpoint, vesting protects the retirement income of employees who are forced to leave the company because of disability or unfavorable business conditions. Furthermore, vesting allows an employee to leave a company voluntarily without fear of losing his retirement income, thus encouraging labor mobility.

A question related to that of vesting is the portability of vested pension rights—the ability of the employee, in effect, to carry the value of his vested pension rights to his new employment. More will be said about this subject later in this chapter. At this point, however, it should be observed that the multiemployer or area plans provide for portability to a limited extent in that an employee may shift from one participating employer to another without losing his accrued pension rights.

Funding Private Pension Plans

Some pension plans are not funded. The employer simply pays the cost of the pension as it is incurred, with the pension thus being on a

[10] President's Committee on Corporate Pension Funds and other Private Retirement and Welfare Programs, *Public Policy and Private Pension Programs* (Washington, D.C.: U.S. Government Printing Office, January, 1965), pp. 39–40.

pay-as-you-go basis. Such plans have the disadvantage of incurring major costs in one year which should be spread over a number of years. Moreover, the employer loses flexibility in terms of when he makes contributions (unless benefits are terminated or suspended, contributions must be made when benefits are due), and loses the cost-reducing impact achieved by investment income on the assets accumulating free of federal tax in a funded plan or the cost reduction that could be achieved by having employees contribute. In addition, there is no guarantee that promised pensions can be paid if the business either becomes hard-pressed or goes bankrupt. Still another disadvantage is that these plans do not reap the full tax advantages to the employer which the Internal Revenue Code grants to plans that are funded in advance. Perhaps the most significant disadvantage, from the employee's viewpoint, is the lack of benefit security.

Despite these disadvantages, some employers and unions have established pension funds on a pay-as-you-go basis. A notable example of such a plan is the United Mine Workers of America Welfare and Retirement Plan. Welfare and pension benefits are financed solely by employer contributions based on coal production. The financial adversities experienced under this plan have necessitated occasional reductions in the monthly pension paid to retired workers.

A much sounder way to handle pension financing is by funding—accumulating funds for future payment. Under this approach, funds are set aside on some systematic basis prior to the employee's retirement date. An actuary determines the amount to be set aside, basing his estimate on such things as the age distribution of the work force, labor turnover, mortality rates, expected investment income, etc. The funds contributed are either paid to an insurance company or are given to a trustee. In either event, the amounts are contributed on an irrevocable basis and must be used to provide plan benefits. Thus, if the employer should go out of business or if the plan should be terminated for any reason, assets in the plan will be used to the extent possible to provide benefits.

Employee Contributions. One of the advantages of a funded pension plan, from the employer's viewpoint, is that it permits employee contributions. Such contributions will reduce the cost of benefits (or, alternately, permit a higher level of benefits than could be supported by employer contributions only). Additionally, there is the principle that it is salutary for those who benefit to participate in the cost so that they understand and appreciate that nothing is free. On the other hand, there is the practical aspect that the employer's contribution to a pension plan is a deductible income tax expense, but the employee's contribution is not. Hence the employer can pay the cost at a smaller net expense than the employee. Moreover, the administrative cost of a contributory plan is higher, since additional records must be kept and additional disbursements must be made.

While a great many pension plans have been established on a contributory basis, there is a definite trend toward noncontributory plans. Almost all of the plans which have been collectively bargained are on a noncontributory basis. Unions also take the position that workers forgo a wage increase when they bargain for pensions and thus, in effect, are "contributing."

Investment of Pension Funds. An additional aspect of funded pension plans involves the investment of employer and employee contributions. Broadly speaking, there are two methods—the use of a trust fund or the use of an insurance company contract. Under a trust fund approach, all contributions are turned over to a trustee (generally a bank or a trust company) who invests and reinvests these contributions, plus investment income, and who disburses benefits. A great many of these plans utilize the "pooled" trust fund of a corporate trustee, and as a result, contributions are invested in a diversified portfolio of fixed-income and equity-type investments. In other situations, a separate trust fund is maintained with the employer and/or union retaining varying degrees of control over investment policy. At the one extreme, the trustee may be given full control over investment policy; at the other, the employer and/or union retains this control, often employing investment counsel for this purpose.

In an insured plan, all contributions are turned over to the insurance company, which assumes complete control over the policy pursued with respect to the investment of such contributions. Generally speaking, insurance companies are required by law to invest their assets predominantly in fixed-income investments; only a small percentage of its assets (such as 5%) may be invested in equities. The bulk of the contributions made to date under insured plans have been invested in this fashion. However, legislation passed in a large number of states in recent years permits insurance companies to segregate the *employer* contributions made under qualified pension plans and to invest these contributions in common stocks and other equity-type investments in much the same fashion as in trust fund plans. Many insured pension plans have already shifted over to this new type of investment facility, and it is expected that this trend will continue in the future.

Although the greatest percentage of qualified pension plans are insured, the greatest percentage of employees covered by private pension plans are under the trust fund approach. At the end of 1966, 60% of the total number of private pension plans were insured; 73% of the employees covered were under trust fund plans. These statistics lead to the conclusion that up until this time, the insured plan has had its greatest popularity with smaller employers, and the trust fund plan, with its greater flexibility, has been more attractive to larger employee groups.

The Cost of Private Pension Plans

Although actuaries are capable of estimating the annual and ultimate costs of a pension plan with reasonable accuracy, it is a fact of pension life that the ultimate cost of a pension plan cannot be known with precision until the last pensioner covered under the plan has died. In the long run, the cost of a pension plan will equal the sum of the benefits actually paid to covered workers and the cost of administering the program, less the investment return on plan assets. The actuary will make periodic estimates with respect to the factors that might influence this cost. He will, for example, make assumptions as to the number of employees who will work and survive until retirement, the age at which they will retire, and the length of time they will live and collect benefits. If the plan benefit is based on earnings, he may also make assumptions as to future salary levels. He will also take into account the expected investment return on plan assets. Periodically, the actual experience of the plan is checked against the assumed experience, and any necessary adjustments in the contribution pattern are made.

The net result of these repeated actuarial valuations of a pension plan is that it is possible to predict its cost with reasonable accuracy. It must be kept in mind, however, that these estimates are subject to the instabilities which are not at all unusual in our dynamic capitalistic economy.

The Real Cost of Pensions. Regardless of actuarial estimates as to the cost of a pension plan, there remains the question of who ultimately bears its cost. A basic law of economics is that the real cost of anything is what one forgoes in order to secure it. If business spends a certain amount on pensions, other things being equal, less will be spent on wages or other items of costs, or less will be allocated to profits, unless a business can pass the whole burden of the pension cost on to the consumers. To the extent that the products the workers buy are increased in price by the costs of pensions, the workers contribute to these costs as consumers. There is no such thing as a free pension. It must be paid for, either directly or indirectly, in the form of higher prices, unless the pension cost is offset by increased productivity.

Pensions, moreover, introduce into cost calculations an item that is less flexible than wages, even granting the rigidities of the present wage structure. Employees can be laid off—pensioners cannot.

Finally, it should be noted that increased productivity does not decrease the cost of paying pensions, except insofar as it permits the business to operate with less workers and, therefore, fewer future pensioners. Pensioners involve a cost without any direct return, since they do not contribute to production. On the other hand, an indirect return may accrue from the fact that pensions sometimes permit younger and more efficient workers to take over jobs.

EMPLOYER-PROVIDED DEATH BENEFITS

As previously noted, group life insurance in force totaled $343 billion at the end of 1966. This contrasts with the $48 billion in force in 1950 and the $175 billion in force in 1960. Employer-provided death benefits are the major source of income for the survivors of many employees.

The group life insurance benefits for employees in collective bargaining units are often lower than the benefits being provided for nonunion employees. However, in recent years, several unions have negotiated for supplemental death benefits payable in the form of income to the surviving spouse and/or children of the employee. These benefits, called "bridge" and "transition" benefits, were part of the 1964 contract of the Auto Workers and were improved in their 1967 contract. Similar benefits can be found in other industries. The transition benefit in the 1967 Auto Workers Contract provides for monthly payments of $150 to the eligible survivor (if not eligible for unreduced social security benefits; otherwise, the benefit is $100) for a period of up to 24 months. Eligible dependents include the employee's spouse (if married at least one year), children, and dependent parents. After 24 months, the bridge benefit takes effect, but only with respect to a surviving spouse who was at least age 50 at the employee's death. This benefit is payable until the earlier of remarriage, attainment of age 62, or such earlier age at which full spouse benefits are payable under social security. In no event is the bridge benefit payable during a month in which the spouse is eligible for mother's benefits under social security.

Employer-provided death benefits may also come from sources other than group life insurance plans. Many pension plans, for example, provide for a death benefit (in addition to the employer's group life insurance plan) either in the form of life insurance benefits or in the form of income benefits to a surviving spouse and/or children. Interest in spouse benefits (which have long been popular in other countries) is rapidly growing in the United States.

One further source of employer-provided death benefits which can often be of significance to an employee's survivors is his employer's profit-sharing plan. These plans usually provide that an employee's account is fully vested in the event of his death and that it will be paid to his beneficiaries. Approximately 6 million employees were covered by such plans at the end of 1967.

CURRENT OASDHI ISSUES

Most students of social security favor, in principle, the widest possible coverage of an insurance program and the narrowest possible coverage of an assistance program. This preference is based upon both social and economic grounds. The social reasons are grounded in the democratic belief that older persons have a right to spend their final years in dignity, with an income based upon right rather than an income secured on the basis of demonstrated need. Under an insurance system, the worker and his employer, or the self-employed person, contribute during his working life a given amount of earnings, which is then used to finance an income after retirement. By complying with the published rules of the insurance system, the retirement income is earned. Need is not a factor.

In contrast, assistance is based upon need, which means that need has to be defined. Even with the best of intentions, different administrators will define need differently. In other instances, favoritism or political pressure may determine who receives assistance and who does not. In Louisiana, a change in administrations brought with it a twofold increase in the number of old-age assistance recipients. The aged are a significant group worth pleasing to the ambitious politician, sometimes without proper consideration for the general welfare. Under such circumstances, need can be redefined in terms of political regularity, with consequent degradation of the older person in real need.

The economic grounds for preferring an insurance program to an assistance program are closely related to the social ones. Insurance is paid for by the beneficiaries or their employers under a system of taxation that is clearly earmarked for a specific purpose. Assistance comes out of general taxation, which permits liberality without tying costs to benefits, or costs to responsibilities. In the long run, assistance is likely to be found to be less efficient and more expensive, with those employed burdened with the care of an increasing older population that has not provided for its own retirement by insurance.

Too Much OAA?

Under present arrangements, OAA will continue to provide income for needy older persons who cannot qualify for OASDHI benefits, but this group may be expected to become small in the future. More and more, OAA will play a supplementary role to OASDHI, providing additional income for the small proportion of insured oldsters who cannot make ends meet on their benefits and personal resources.

This will be true, however, only if the purchasing power of benefits remains relatively stable. Should prices rise sharply and OASDHI benefits not keep pace with them, many more aged persons may find it necessary to supplement benefits with OAA payments.

Reduction in the amount of dependency among the aged, moreover, may not be translated into smaller relief rolls and lower assistance payments if we are not alert to distortions that have already cropped up in the popular concept of the purpose of old-age assistance. There is widespread confusion in the public mind between the assistance and insurance programs for the aged. It is too often not clearly understood that OAA payments are intended only for the "needy" who do not have sufficient means to get along decently without such aid.

Public Pension Protection for All

Problems of omission, coordination, and duplication remain among public retirement systems, although legislation since 1950 went a long way toward eliminating them. Logically, the various government systems should combine to guarantee all persons who have worked in their productive years a basic monthly pension when they are too old to work. In the past, the gaps in coverage of OASDHI and nontransferability of wage credits among the individual systems, however, have prevented attainment of this ideal. The extension of OASDHI to most nongovernmental employment and self-employment, the joint protection provided by OASDHI and the railroad retirement system, and the procedure for bringing state and local government employees into the OASDHI system are all steps in the direction of correcting these shortcomings. Still to be achieved is some integration of civil service and other federal retirement systems with OASDHI—at least to the extent of preventing loss of protection for people moving between private and public employment.

Perhaps of more concern to future generations are the double benefit rights which have been earned by veterans and their families under OASDHI and the veterans' programs. Nonservice-connected pensions were provided before this country embarked on a general program of income insurance for retirement. In a way, they can be viewed as a pioneer social security program for the segment of the population distinguished by having served in the Armed Forces.

The argument for continuing to provide such benefits loses its force, however, when citizens generally have OASDHI protection. Besides, veterans no longer account for a small portion of the population that we can afford to treat with extra generosity. In 1940, veterans and their families represented only 11% of the whole population. By 1967, they numbered an estimated 90 million and constituted 45% of the total population.

Adopting as a guiding principle the attitude that military service in time of war or peace should be regarded as an obligation of citizenship and should not be considered inherently a basis for future benefits, the President's Commission on Veteran's Pensions, headed by General Omar Bradley, indicated:

> Our society has developed more equitable means of meeting most of the same needs and big strides are being made in closing remaining gaps. The nonservice-connected benefits should be limited to a minimum level and retained only as a reserve line of honorable protection for veterans whose means are shown to be inadequate and who fail to qualify for basic protection under the general old-age and survivors insurance system.[11]

"Pay as You Go" versus Reserve Financing

In discussing how the insurance program is financed, it is necessary to separate old-age and survivors benefits from the disability benefits.

[11] President's Commission on Veterans' Pensions, *Veterans' Benefits in the United States: Finance and Recommendations, Report to the President* (Washington, D.C.: U.S. Government Printing Office, April, 1956), p. 138.

When the latter were adopted in 1956, a special trust fund was set up as an answer to the argument that disability benefit costs might bankrupt the OASI system. As has already been pointed out, an additional one half of 1% was added to the combined employer-employee rate (and three eighths of 1% to the self-employed rate) in all future years to finance the disability benefits. Increases in the OASDHI tax schedule are all attributable to increased contributions to the OASI Trust Fund.

The present method of financing old-age and survivor benefits is actually a practical compromise between two extremes: pay as you go and level premium. The latter would require a uniform contribution rate at all times, much higher to meet current outlays in earlier years and lower than necessary for the same purposes in later years. Because of the enormous reserve fund which level-premium financing would require building up, it has not been adopted. Rather, the plan has been to set taxes on a modestly increasing basis which will divide costs over the years and build up a large but not enormous (for the job to be done) reserve. The Fund can then absorb short-term fluctuations in benefits and at the same time grow to such a size that its interest earnings can be a significant aid in overall financing. Figure 17–1 depicts the history of the Fund from 1951 to 1966, and projections to the year 2025.

Proponents of the pay-as-you-go method argue that we are actually paying as we go now, since, when current contributions are exceeded by costs, we shall have to convert the government securities in the Trust Fund into cash by taxation or borrowing. Hence, they believe that it would be better to meet benefit costs as they arise.

There are several objections to this viewpoint. One very practical one is that it jumps costs too high at a later date after keeping them low initially, so that employees and employers become conditioned to a large benefit for a low cost and resist future increases which must become effective if pay as you go is not to be dropped in favor of meeting costs either from general taxation or by deficit financing. Another objection along these same lines is that short-term fluctuations in benefits can occur and thus cause erratic and uncertain tax changes if strict pay-as-you-go financing is to be maintained.

The contention that we are already on a pay-as-you-go plan, since the assets of the Trust Fund are invested in government securities, is open to serious question. The securities purchased for the Trust Fund are not created for that purpose. If they were not sold to the Trust Fund, they would be sold elsewhere to permit the government to borrow the funds it needs. So long as there are government bonds or securities outstanding, it makes no difference whether they are in the hands of private banks or public trust funds insofar as costs are concerned. It therefore follows that we are not now on a pay-as-you-go plan because government taxation or borrowing to redeem the securities in the Trust Fund pays the cost of the services or projects for which the bonds were issued, not the costs of

FIGURE 17–1

Projecting the Rising Trust Fund to Year 2025

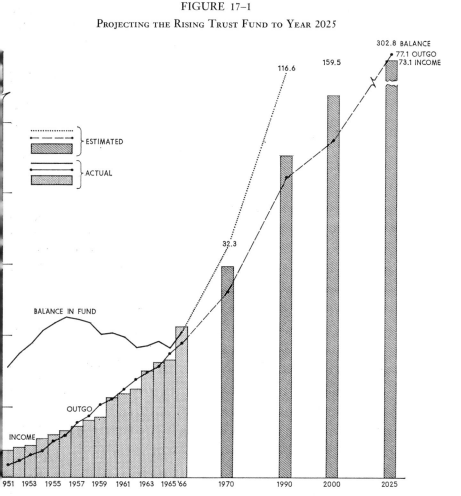

Source: U.S. Department of Health, Education, and Welfare, *Social Security Bulletin,* February, 1968.

old-age and survivor benefits. It is no more an unusual procedure for the OASI Trust Fund to invest in government securities than for a private insurance company's reserve fund to do the same with its current surpluses.

Pay as you go is based upon a very dangerous assumption, for it assumes that future generations and Congresses will be willing to levy special taxes at a much higher rate than present ones. The cost of retirement is both a present one and a future one. By levying all the cost of those retired at the time of retirement, pay-as-you-go adherents would have us, in effect, live off our depreciation. What we would be doing would be analogous to the factory owner who takes no heed of machine depreciation until the machine wears out. Then he must charge the cost of a new machine against the profits of a single year, instead of spreading the cost over many years. Proper provision for the aged requires that the costs of retirement be divided between the future and the present.

In January, 1959, the Advisory Council on Social Security Financing (which was appointed in accordance with the 1956 amendments) made a report based on over a year of careful study. Its major finding was: "The method of financing the old-age, survivors and disability insurance program is sound, and based on the best estimates available, the contribution schedule now in the law makes adequate provision for meeting both short-range and long-range costs."

"Earmarked" Taxes versus General Revenues

Another element of financing social security benefits which has received considerable attention in recent years is the question of whether or not some portion of these benefits should be financed from general revenues rather than by means of an "earmarked" tax as is presently the situation. Those who favor the use of general revenues point out that the present OASDHI tax is regressive in nature in that lower income and middle-income families pay a higher proportion of their incomes than do families with higher incomes. They also point out that the use of general revenues would permit a greater degree of fiscal flexibility in that taxes or benefits could be raised or lowered independently. On a more immediate and short-term basis, this could permit the financing of substantial increases in benefits that have been contemplated by several members of Congress.

On the other hand, proponents of our present system of an earmarked tax argue that the use of general revenues would remove the restraints inherent in a program where taxes and benefits are directly tied together. Removal of these restraints could permit an escalation of benefits and taxes. Moreover, proponents argue that it would be difficult to draw a logical line as to how much of the program should be financed from general revenues; that pressures would mount for the increased use of general revenues; and that ultimately, the entire program would be financed on this basis.

Compulsory Retirement

The cost of a retirement program now and in the future is going to depend considerably on how many persons past 65 continue to work. The more that do work, the less will be the cost. In 1966, of the 18.5 million people aged 65 or over in the United States, 62% were eligible for OASDHI benefits, but only 55% were receiving benefits. If all eligible persons were to retire and take benefits at age 65, or if limits on income were removed as a condition of receiving benefits, long-range costs of OASDHI would greatly increase.

Because many persons over 65 prefer work to retirement, forced retirement increases the cost of an adequate retirement program. To combat the trend to compulsory retirement, the late Professor Sumner H. Slichter proposed a small OASDHI tax rebate to the employer who keeps older workers on the job. The employer and the community would benefit, while the worker involved would be happier, since only those over 65 who wanted to work would participate in the plan. A contribution which will buy a pension at age 65 will buy a one third larger pension at age 68 and a one half larger pension at age 70. That is because fewer people would receive the benefits at the higher ages, and pensioners who retire at the more advanced ages would live fewer years supported by pensions.

If this proposal is adopted, it should also include provisions for unlimited earnings after age 70. At present, a person can earn an unlimited amount after age 72 and still receive his pension. It would seem reasonable that if this were changed to age 70, more people might wait until then to retire; but 72 may be too long after 65 to be worth waiting for. In this connection, the limit on earnings in covered employment between ages 62 and 72 was increased to $1,680 by the 1967 Social Security Amendments. Care must be taken, however, to prevent retirement from becoming too financially worthwhile and thus upping too high the cost of retirement by inducing those to retire who at 62 might otherwise be inclined to stay in the labor force. The trend in private industry is already toward liberal early retirement.

MEDICARE

In 1965, Congress enacted a liberal and comprehensive medicare law. The law became effective on July 1, 1966, and was amended in 1967. Its basic provisions are set forth in Figure 17–2. The so-called "basic coverage" is financed by payroll taxes varying from 0.5% of the first $7,800 earned for both employee and employer (and the same for self-employed) in 1967 to 0.9% in 1987. The "supplementary coverage" is paid for by contributions from benefits and from federal funds as noted in Figure 17–2. Eligibility is basically the same as for the social security system. The payroll taxes for the medicare program are included in the tabulations in Table 17–6, page 509.

Considering the magnitude of this program at its inception (19 million people became covered on July 1, 1966), medicare got off to a surprisingly smooth start. There have been, of course, a number of administrative problems—notably delays in processing bills from hospitals and doctors. However, when one considers that the program involved some 6,500 hospitals, 250,000 physicians, 1,200 home health agencies, 74 Blue Cross organizations, 33 Blue Shield plans, 15 insurance companies, 100 group practice prepayment plans, and numerous other agencies, the early administration problems seem relatively inconsequential.

One of the most important issues of the medicare program involves

FIGURE 17–2

MEDICARE—WHAT IT MEANS

BASIC COVERAGE	SUPPLEMENTARY COVERAGE
(To be financed by increased Social Security taxes)	(Voluntary insurance to be financed by individual monthly premiums of $4 and Federal funds; individual pays first $50 of his total annual costs and 20% of the costs of all services totaling more than $50).

HOSPITAL CARE

Full coverage after the first $40 for up to 60 days in each period of illness*; coverage for up to 30 additional days, for which patient pays $10 a day. "Lifetime reserve" of 60 days toward which patient pays $20 a day. Psychiatric care is included for up to 60 days in each period of illness, with a lifetime limit of 190 days.

PHYSICIANS' CARE

Physicians' and surgeons' (including certain dental surgeons') fees. (100% reimbursement for radiological or pathological services by physicians to patients in hospitals.)

HOME NURSING CARE

NURSING HOME CARE

Post-hospital care for 20 days in each period of illness at no cost to patient, plus 80 additional days, for which patient pays $5 per day.

Up to 100 nursing visits each year in addition to those allowed under the basic plan, without any requirement for prior hospitalization.

OTHER HEALTH SERVICES AND SUPPLIES

Coverage includes costs of out-patient charges, X-rays and other diagnostic tests, radiological treatments, casts, splints, artificial limbs and ambulance service.

HOME NURSING CARE

Up to 100 visits by nurses or technicians in each period of illness at no cost to patient.

OUT-OF-HOSPITAL

Yearly limits for mental, psychoneurotic and personality disorders is $250 or 50% of expenses, whichever is smaller.

* A period of illness, as defined by the bill, normally starts with the first day of hospitalization and ends whenever the patient has spent 60 consecutive days without hospital or nursing home care.

SOURCE: Adapted from *The New York Times,* July 25, 1965.

its cost. It is estimated that the first 12 months of benefit payments amounted to $2.4 billion for inpatient hospital services; $640 million for physicians and other services; $75 million for extended care facilities; $16 million for home health agencies; and $13 million for outpatient hospital services. The cost of this program is already in excess of that originally

estimated and will undoubtedly become higher. Overutilization and malingering undoubtedly have contributed to this problem, but the most
significant item has been the rising cost of medical services. The cost of
medical care has been advancing faster than other elements of living
expense and, with the advent of medicare, rose quite sharply. One possible
result of this might be federal control over medical fees—a course of
action which will undoubtedly receive strong opposition from the medical profession.

Another major issue of the medicare program is the frequently
voiced concern that it will lead to government health insurance. Most
likely, if it follows the social security system, it will grow in both
coverage and benefits—and the costs will far exceed the sponsors' claims.

Still another issue of the federal government's program for providing health care is the cost of medicaid—provided for under Title 19 of the
Social Security Act. Under this program, the federal government provides
financial assistance to the states that provide medical assistance for individuals who are on welfare or who are "medically needy." By 1967, 21 states
had fully implemented their programs for medicaid, and 12 had partially
implemented their programs by providing benefits only for those individuals on welfare. Five other states were in the process of establishing their
programs. The cost of medicaid was originally expected to involve a federal outlay of under $1 billion a year, during its early years, but has already
exceeded this amount. It is expected that the cost of medicaid for the
government's fiscal year ending in 1972 will be in excess of $3 billion. Part
of the difficulty is due to the fact that the states were allowed to establish
their own standards as to who would be considered as "medically needy."
Liberal standards have greatly expanded the number of potential beneficiaries. As a result, it is quite likely that Congress will establish some limit
on the definition of "medically needy" and will not provide federal funds
if a state sets a standard which is more liberal than this federal limit.

CURRENT PRIVATE PENSION PLAN ISSUES

The economic and social impacts of private pension plans and their
funds have caused a great deal of interest in Congress and in the executive
branch of the federal government. There has been a growing debate over
certain issues, and as a result, a number of legislative proposals have been
made in Congress. The major issues involve the desirability (or lack of
desirability) of federal requirements concerning vesting, minimum funding, the reinsurance of private plans, and the portability of pensions.[12]
Additionally, there is growing concern over the size that pension funds

---

[12] For an excellent discussion of these issues and this program, pro and con,
see *The Debate on Private Pensions* (Washington, D.C.: American Enterprise
Association, 1968).

have reached and are expected to reach, and the fact that economic power thus created is concentrated in a limited area.

Vesting

At the present time, vesting is not required in a private pension plan. Even so, a great majority of these plans do provide for some form of vesting, and the trend is toward the adoption of vesting or the liberalization of existing vesting provisions. Despite this, there are many who advocate that vesting be required for all private pension plans. The major arguments advanced for this position are that vesting (after a reasonable period of service) is a matter of equity and fair treatment and that vesting should be required to ensure that private plans achieve their broad social purpose. It is also pointed out, in support of requiring vesting, that such would strengthen the nation's program for retirement protection and would enhance the mobility of the nation's work force.

Those who oppose compulsory vesting point out that private plans have already made major strides toward providing this form of benefit on a voluntary basis and challenge the need and desirability of governmental intervention. They also point out that compulsory vesting will increase the cost of private pension plans, will greatly reduce their flexibility, and may well retard rather than encourage the development of new plans. An additional argument is that if other resources are limited, the inclusion of vesting will reduce the benefits that might otherwise be payable to long-service retirees, with the result that individuals at or near retirement will suffer to the benefit of younger, short-service employees. Also, it is pointed out that the evidence that lack of vesting inhibits labor mobility is inconclusive.

As a matter of fact, the vesting demand runs directly counter to a prime purpose for which employers established pension plans—that is, to decrease turnover. It was to reduce mobility, not to contribute to it, that pensions were historically advocated. Compulsory vesting would make pensions more expensive and at the same time alter the purpose and reduce the incentives for employers to establish them.

Minimum Funding

Present Internal Revenue Service rulings do not require private pension plans to reduce prior unfunded plan liabilities. The only requirement is that liabilities being created currently must be funded and that prior unfunded liabilities cannot increase. Despite this latitude, the great majority of private pension plans are being funded on a basis which involves the amortization of prior liabilities over some stipulated period of time.

The advocates of requiring that all plans adhere to some minimum funding standard point out that in the absence of adequate funding, a pension plan may turn out to be an empty or only partially fulfilled promise. Moreover, the requirement of some minimum funding will make more possible the meeting of pension obligations in case of plan termination and permit workers with vested rights to have their expectations fulfilled.

Those who oppose minimum funding maintain that such requirements could slow down pension plan improvements and discourage new plans from coming into existence. They point out that a plan may be actuarially sound, even though it is not fully funded, and that such requirements might result in plans which provide smaller benefits or no credit for past service.

Reinsurance of Private Pensions

Allied to the issue of minimum funding is the question of reinsuring private pension plans. Interest in this particular subject has arisen out of the fact that a pension plan, if it is terminated, may not have sufficient assets to meet all accrued pension obligations. When this happens, some employees will receive little or none of their accrued benefits. For this reason, there is a growing interest in some system which would reinsure private pension plans against this contingency. Proposals that have been made suggest that each private plan with unfunded liabilities be assessed with some form of premium or charge in order to create a fund with which to provide any needed benefits when a plan is terminated due to business reasons. These proposals contemplate that the reinsurance would be provided through a federal agency.

The arguments advanced in favor of such a system center around the fact that a pension plan may prove to be an empty promise to an employee if the plan is terminated and assets are insufficient to provide all accrued benefits. It is also observed that such a reinsurance system is comparable to the Federal Deposit Insurance system.

One of the real questions posed by the reinsurance concept is whether or not the possibility that a business operation will come to an end is a properly insurable risk. The opponents of such a system point out that such reinsurance would tend to discourage adequate funding of prior liabilities, and in plans where prior liabilities have been fully or partially funded, there might be a tendency to reduce future funding levels. Additional arguments include the fact that the reinsurance premiums would be an additional plan cost and that pension reinsurance would invite subsequent federal regulation and possible control of pension fund investments.

Portability of Pensions

Portability of pensions involves the worker's right to transfer his vested pension rights from employer to employer, probably through some form of central clearinghouse, so that he receives a single combined pension at retirement. Limited forms of portability already exist in multiemployer plans where, within a given industry or geographic location, members of a particular union may move from employer to employer without losing pension credits.

Those who favor portability maintain that this would produce greater benefits, that more small employers would be encouraged to provide pensions, that early vesting would be encouraged, and that such is necessary to achieve optimum performance of the private pension system. Those who oppose portability feel that it would result in greater regulation of private plans, that portability is, in effect, being provided by private plans, since vested benefits are being held for the benefit of individuals after they leave employment, and that the complexities and costs of a clearinghouse system outweigh its advantages.

Investment of Pension Funds

At the end of 1967, reserves held in connection with private pension plans amounted to $103.4 billion. Approximately 69% of this amount was held in conjunction with noninsured or trust fund plans. Of this amount, about 48% was invested in preferred or common stock. Table 17–8

TABLE 17–8

ASSETS OF PRIVATE NON-INSURED* PENSION FUNDS

(Millions of Dollars†)

	Book Value 1962	End of Year 1967
Cash and deposits	707	1,180
U.S. government obligations	2,925	2,250
Other debt	18,101	25,530
Preferred stock	749	980
Common stock	15,729	33,850
Mortgages on real estate	1,876	3,940
Other assets	1,805	4,100
Total Assets	41,890	71,820

* Includes funds of nonprofit organizations and multiemployer plans.
† Figures may not add to total because of rounding.
SOURCE: U.S. Securities and Exchange Commission, Statistical Releases Nos. 2219, 2278.

indicates the way in which noninsured pension funds were distributed from 1962 to 1967. While corporate bonds still represent a significant share of the total portfolio, common stocks have increased proportionately over this period of time. The advantages of equity investment are obvious. In this connection, it has been estimated that by increasing earnings by 1%, benefits can be increased by 20%.

Increasing equity investment is not without its problems. A few large New York banks, through their holdings of stocks for pension funds, are in a position to exert considerable control over many large corporations. As a result, one authority has stated: "It may not be too much to say that the center of influence in our economy, having left the Wall Street of the 1920's and migrated in the 1930's and 1940's to the provincial centers of corporate power, has now returned to New York financial circles."[13]

How this resulting investment power is to be exercised poses delicate problems for both banks and insurance companies, and is quite likely to come under some form of federal regulation.

QUESTIONS FOR DISCUSSION

1. Discuss the differences between the old-age, survivors, and disability insurance program and the old-age assistance program from the point of view of administration, coverage, benefits, financing, and basic approach.
2. What are the principal arguments for and against a pay-as-you-go system of financing OASDHI?
3. What are some of the problems raised by bargained pension plans? Discuss the effect of such plans on the functioning of the labor market.
4. What is the future of Medicare? Explain your answer.

SUGGESTIONS FOR FURTHER READING

BERNSTEIN, MERTON C. *The Future of Private Pensions*. New York: Free Press of Glencoe, Inc., 1964.

    A critical survey of the present and future system of private pensions.

McGILL, DAN M. *Fundamentals of Private Pensions*. 2d ed. Homewood, Ill.: Richard D. Irwin, Inc., 1964.

    An authoritative work on the private pension movement.

MELONE, JOSEPH J. *Collectively Bargained Multi-Employer Pension Plans*. Homewood, Ill.: Richard D. Irwin, Inc., 1964.

    An analysis of all aspects of multiemployer pension plans.

MYERS, ROBERT J. *Social Insurance and Allied Government Programs*. Homewood, Ill.: Richard D. Irwin, Inc., 1964.

    An authoritative discussion of social insurance and public assistance, with special emphasis on OASDHI.

[13] Paul B. Harbrecht, *Pension Funds and Economic Power* (New York: Twentieth Century Fund, 1959), p. 249.

| Chapter | SECURITY AGAINST |
| 18 | UNEMPLOYMENT |

In a progressive society the constant process of growth, innovation, and change may lead to wide fluctuations of business activity. One important result of such movements is periodic fluctuation in the volume of unemployment. Unemployment is not only associated with the depressed portions of the business cycle but also with seasonal changes in our society, with technological innovation, and with the restlessness and search for better jobs and homes which is usual within at least some segments of our labor force.

It was the incidence of mass unemployment during the 1930's, when approximately one fourth of the labor force experienced unemployment during some years, and when millions of persons were out of work for very long periods, which brought federal and state legislation into being to compensate workers for loss of income as a result of unemployment. The unemployment provisions of the Social Security Act and the state laws related to them were intended to deal with short-term unemployment problems; but recently, efforts have been made to extend the duration of compensation payments in order to afford protection during prolonged periods of joblessness.

Since some of our largest unions were formed at a time when mass unemployment existed, they have always been interested in measures designed to mitigate the hardship and insecurity associated with loss of employment. In Chapter 6, we noted the widespread interest in seniority and subcontracting as aspects of such union concern. More recently, unions have developed increased interest in dismissal compensation and supplementary unemployment compensation benefits as additional measures to lessen the burden of unemployment. In this chapter, we shall review the governmental unemployment insurance program and then consider dismissal wages and supplementary unemployment compensation benefit plans.

UNEMPLOYMENT INSURANCE

Unemployment insurance is a federal-state program providing for partial maintenance of income during temporary periods of unemployment. As with OASDHI, this program pays benefits as a matter of right to qualifying workers regardless of whether they have other assets to fall back upon, for the right to benefits is established by employer payment of taxes on wages earned during periods of employment.

Unemployment insurance must of necessity be government administered. While private companies can sell retirement policies, disability insurance, health and accident insurance, or workmen's compensation, no private insurance company can afford to sell unemployment insurance because of the unpredictable risks involved.

Under our unemployment insurance laws the risk or cost of such insurance is spread over all the geographical areas and industries of a state. But to the extent that unemployment is national or regional in origin, this state-by-state program fails to achieve the full advantage of spreading the costs among all who may be affected by, or contribute to, the same event and the risks arising from it. The costs are, however, spread over time, in that taxes are collected in both good years and bad, and benefits are paid as needed, but obviously in larger amounts in years of greater unemployment.

Development of the Unemployment Insurance Program

Unlike old-age and survivors insurance, which is entirely a federal program, the field of unemployment compensation was left primarily to the states by the Social Security Act of 1935. This was done apparently for fear of a constitutional challenge and because one state, Wisconsin, had already adopted an unemployment compensation law and others were seriously considering such legislation. The role of the federal government in unemployment compensation was thus restricted, although it saw to it that the states followed certain procedures set forth in the Social Security Act of 1935. This act originally provided for a 3% tax on the payroll of all employers who employed eight or more workers during 20 weeks of one year in all except certain excluded employments. The act further provided that employers who were paying taxes in their own states for the financing of an unemployment insurance law could offset that state tax against the federal tax up to 90%. The inducement afforded by this offset provision resulted in the passage of unemployment compensation legislation by all the states in a very short time.

The Social Security Act laid down certain conditions which state unemployment compensation laws were required to meet if employers of that state were to be made eligible for the tax offset. All funds collected by the state had to be used entirely for the payment of unemployment benefits through state public employment offices or a similar state agency approved by the Social Security Administration. Taxes had to be deposited immediately upon receipt in the Unemployment Trust Fund, of which the Secretary of the Treasury is the administrator. No state law could deny benefits to a person otherwise eligible if that person refused to accept new work because the position offered was vacant on account of a

FIGURE 18-1

Unemployment Benefits as of January, 1967

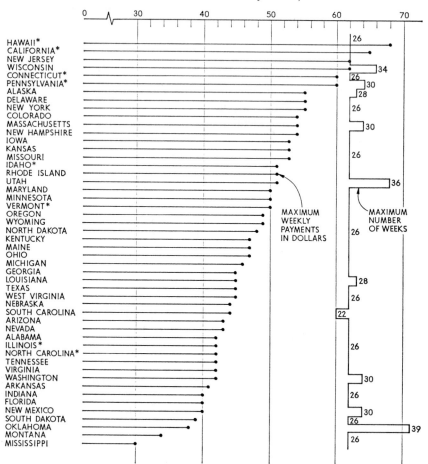

° These states extend benefits when unemployment reaches a specified level.
Source: U.S. Department of Labor, Bureau of Employment Security.

labor dispute; if the wages and conditions of work were substantially less favorable than those of similar jobs in the area; or if, as a condition of employment, the person would be required to join a company union or to sign a "yellow-dog" contract. Finally, states were required to meet certain administrative standards established by the Social Security Administration to qualify for the tax offset. Figure 18-1 and Table 18-1 provide summary information on the state laws.

Coverage of Unemployment Insurance Laws

At the time the Social Security Act was adopted, there was general acceptance of the idea that for administrative reasons, some size-of-firm

TABLE 18–1

MAXIMUM WEEKLY UNEMPLOYMENT INSURANCE PAYMENTS

Higher maximum benefits are paid to claimants with dependents in the 10 states listed below:

State	Basic Maximum Payment	Maximum Dependents' Allowance	Combined Maximum Payment
Alaska................	$55	$25	$80
Connecticut............	60	25	85
Illinois................	42	28	70
Indiana................	40	12	52
Maryland*..............	50	—*	50
Massachusetts...........	54	Difference between average weekly wage and basic payment	Average weekly wage
Michigan...............	46	30	76
Nevada................	43	20	63
Ohio..................	47	11	58
Rhode Island...........	51	12	63

* Dependent allowance at lower weekly benefit amounts only.

Alaska, Ohio, and Wyoming further limit the amount payable to interstate claimants.

Nineteen states make automatic adjustments of maximum weekly payments based on average wages.

Maximum Number of Weeks

The following states pay unemployment benefits for a specified length of time: Hawaii, Maryland, New Hampshire, New York, North Carolina, Vermont, and West Virginia. The remaining states have variable duration provisions based upon the claimant's earnings and/or employment.

California, Connecticut, Idaho, Illinois, and Vermont extend the weeks of benefit by 50% and North Carolina by eight weeks when unemployment reaches specified levels. In Pennsylvania, with a variable duration and maximum of 30 weeks, potential benefits may be extended by 50% but may not exceed 39 weeks. Hawaii has a separate law under which benefits may be extended up to 13 weeks.

SOURCE: U.S. Department of Labor, Bureau of Economic Security.

restrictions were necessary for the federal-state system of unemployment insurance. Therefore, the federal unemployment tax provisions applied only to firms which employed eight or more individuals in the United States at least one day of each of 20 or more different weeks in a year. In addition, the Social Security Act of 1935 excluded certain classes of service from coverage. Agricultural and domestic workers—and to some extent, family workers—were exempted, chiefly for administrative reasons. State and local governments were exempted because the application of the federal unemployment tax to such government units was believed to be unconstitutional. Federal and maritime workers were not covered because they were exclusively under federal jurisdiction. Religious and other nonprofit institutions were excluded on the precedent of earlier tax laws. The self-employed are generally excluded under the unemployment insurance program because of the difficulty in determining whether, in a given week, a self-employed worker is unemployed. The states can, and sometimes do, liberalize their coverage beyond the requirements of federal law.

The most significant addition to the coverage of the federal law was made in 1954. Coverage was extended to firms that employed four or more workers at least one day of each of 10 or more weeks of a year, effective January 1, 1956. At the same time, unemployment protection was added for federal civilian employees unemployed after December 31, 1954. Nonetheless, coverage still remains restricted to a significant degree. In 1964, 48.9 million individuals were covered by unemployment insurance. Almost 15 million wage earners were not covered by any form of unemployment insurance.

TABLE 18–2

MINIMUM FIRM SIZE FOR COVERAGE UNDER STATE
UNEMPLOYMENT INSURANCE PROGRAMS,
JANUARY, 1967

Number of Employees	States[1]
One or more	22
Three or more	3
Four or more	26

1. Requirements usually specify a given number of weeks in which the employer hires the cited number of employees and/or a given size payroll.
2. As of January 1, 1960, Minnesota required coverage of one or more employees in cities of 10,000 or more. Domestics continue to be covered in New York only if they work for employers of four or more. Data include District of Columbia.

SOURCE: U.S. Department of Labor, Bureau of Employment Security.
1 Includes District of Columbia.

Although the federal statute sets minimum standards for coverage (and other aspects of the laws) which the states must meet, it does not prevent the states from providing wider coverage than the specified minimums. Thus, as Table 18–2 indicates, some 25 jurisdictions cover firms employing fewer than four employees for some specified period.

By 1967, 34 states provided some form of coverage for some or all state government employees. Analysis of applicable legislation reveals that states have experimented with coverage of other special groups, such as domestics—and in California, even self-employed persons.

Despite the extensions of unemployment insurance, the failure to provide protection for a substantial portion of the work force shows that the need to provide even greater coverage is a very real one. Many persons have suggested that this problem arises because of the divided responsibility under the federal-state system. It was hoped that allowing the states to pass their own laws would encourage experimentation and diversity, but those who raise the point of divided responsibility contend that the fear of putting their own businesses at a cost disadvantage has prevented the states from improving their own systems. This is one major reason why, throughout the life of the unemployment insurance system, many have advocated either more extensive federal standards or even complete federalization of the system. We shall later examine arguments for and against federalization.

Eligibility

Workers cannot draw unemployment insurance unless they have been employed by a firm in covered industry. But even a covered worker is not automatically entitled to benefits when he is out of work. Whether or not he will receive them depends upon a number of factors, some of which relate to the period prior to termination of his employment, and some to the date when he goes to seek unemployment compensation benefits.

He must have worked for some specified number of weeks in covered industry in the year before applying for benefits and/or earned an amount of wages specified in the law. He must also have left his last employment without creating reasons for disqualification and is subject to a waiting period of a week in almost every jurisdiction. He must register with the state employment service; be ready, willing, and able to work; and accept suitable employment if it is offered to him.

As already noted, the "labor standard" of the Social Security Act forbids states from excluding otherwise eligible persons from benefits under the program if they refuse work in struck plants, substandard job offers, or work which would require them to refrain from joining a union or to join a company union. Other than these labor standard provisions, the federal act contains no requirements concerning eligibility and disqualification provisions. These are left to the states and vary widely from one jurisdiction to another.

But in every jurisdiction, eligibility conditions are set, and for very compelling reasons. Unemployment insurance is meant to protect persons who are genuinely attached to the labor force from the hardships occurring when unemployed for a temporary period and seeking other work. For this reason, all the laws require that persons who receive benefits must have had some minimum employment experience in the base period, must register for work and be able to accept it, and must take available work when offered on reasonable terms. These provisions are administered by a state board or administrator who interprets and applies the law.

Eligibility requirements became less stringent during the early history of the unemployment compensation law. Waiting periods were reduced, and earnings and employment requirements became more flexible. Within the last few years, however, there has been some tightening of eligibility requirements. One study has recommended that this should be done in some states "to confine eligibility to workers with 'substantial attachment to the labor market.' "[1]

The problem arises because we are witnessing two parallel revolutions which affect unemployment insurance. There is steady pressure and a noticeable trend toward payment of higher benefits for longer periods of more uniform duration. At the same time, as noted in Chapter 1, an extraordinary growth in part-time secondary workers in the labor force has occurred. For persons with only marginal attachment to the labor force, the temptation presented by larger benefits paid for as long as 39 weeks can lead to an increase in malingering and other undesirable practices which, in the past, have never been problems of any magnitude in the system. The federal-state system will have to balance protection against fraud and malingering against requirements of fairness.

Since eligibility is related to employment within a particular state, workers would lose rights by moving from one state to another if it were not for the existence of an Interstate Benefit Plan whereby workers who qualify for benefits in one state may draw their benefits in another. The original home state pays the benefits, and the state in which the worker then dwells acts as the agent for the transaction. All 50 states cooperate in this plan. The Interstate Benefit Plan, however, does not help a worker who would qualify for benefits only if his credits in both states were totaled. As a result, a "basic plan for combining wages" has been subscribed to by 48 states, as of August, 1966. This plan provides for the totaling of credits where that is necessary to make determinations for eligibility. Still another problem arises when a worker is eligible for benefits but would be eligible for the maximum benefits only by combining wages in the states. The Extended Interstate Benefit Plan for Combining Wages, adopted by 45 states, is specifically designed to handle this problem.

Unemployed persons may be denied benefits even after they meet the eligibility requirements, if the reasons why they leave work "disqualify" them under the various state laws. For example, all state laws disqualify a worker from benefits, either wholly or partially, if he has voluntarily left his job, if he is discharged for misconduct, or if he has refused suitable work without good cause. Other states disqualify workers who leave jobs to get married, or because they become pregnant, or because they retire from the labor market to take care of home duties. Disqualifications include leaving a job to go into business for oneself or to return to school

[1] Richard A. Lester, *The Economics of Unemployment Compensation* (Princeton, N.J.: Princeton University, Industrial Relations Section, 1962), p. 126.

or college. In addition, workers may be denied benefits in many states if they are not "actually seeking" work, which means taking certain job-seeking activity measures set by the state boards.

Three of the most troublesome problems arise in connection with benefits for workers whose "unemployment is due to a strike, a vacation, or retirement." All states disqualify a worker from benefits, either wholly or partially, if he is unemployed because of a stoppage of work caused by a labor dispute in which he is directly involved. Two states have provisions, however, which specify a definite period of disqualification, after which the worker may collect benefits. In New York, the period is seven weeks plus a waiting period; in Rhode Island, six weeks plus the waiting period. In these two states, the unemployment compensation law provides what is, in effect, a "supplemental strike fund" and obviously increases the union's "staying ability."

Vacation pay may be treated as a form of disqualifying income, but several states permit benefit payments if the worker is on vacation without pay, through no fault of his own. On the other hand, a state may refuse payment on the ground that the employment relation still continues during vacation or that the worker on vacation is not available for work.

A final abuse affects those who retire but claim they are looking for work. In many states, workers and executives collect 26 weeks of unemployment insurance after retirement—and never return to the labor market.

In some states, persons falling within many of these ineligible classes are denied benefits for a specific number of weeks, after which they may receive benefits. But in an increasing number of states, workers falling in certain of these classes find that their rights to benefits are not merely postponed but canceled for a specific number of weeks for the current benefit year, and they may find that their rights to benefits are canceled until they have met some employment criterion. For example, one state requires that some classes of disqualified workers must work for three days in each of four weeks or earn $200 before they may receive benefits again.

Benefit Amounts

The unemployment insurance system was intended to pay recipients of benefits about 50% of their regular earnings. Since the inception of the unemployment insurance program, there has been continuous progress in liberalization of the benefits payable to workers who are unemployed. At first, most of the state laws provided for payment of benefits based upon a percentage of full-time weekly wages or average weekly wages. Later, the full-time weekly wage, with an alternative of the weekly wage determined by the highest quarterly earnings, was extensively utilized. Today, most of the states compute the weekly unemployment compensation benefit as a fraction of the highest quarterly earnings in the base period.

This change in the basis of computing benefits has obviously increased the actual benefits received by unemployed workers.

Nevertheless, there has been a general failure under the system to provide half of regular earnings. As shown by Figure 18–2, no state provided as much as 50% of average weekly wages in the year 1965.

On the other hand, since take-home pay today is a smaller percentage of earnings than in 1939, the worker may receive a larger percentage of his actual living expenses today than in 1939. Although benefits do not now approach the 50% standard in most states, there is growing interest in automatic adjustment of benefits as wages rise, now practiced in a number of states.

Duration of Benefits

The period over which benefits are paid has steadily lengthened. In 1968, the maximum duration varied from 22 weeks in South Carolina to 39 weeks in Oklahoma (and in eight other states when unemployment reaches a specified rate). Only one state had a maximum duration of less than 26 weeks. And 11 states provided that any person eligible for benefits could receive them, if necessary, for the maximum period.

Despite the lengthening of duration of benefit payments which has occurred, many workers exhaust their benefits during recession periods before finding another job. This circumstance, as well as the relatively low level of benefits, explains why workers must fall back on other resources.

In 1958, Congress enacted a Temporary Unemployment Compensation (TUC) Act for the period until June, 1959. Under this act, states wishing to extend their benefits by half the original period for workers who would otherwise exhaust benefits could borrow money from the federal government. Although only 16 states and the District of Columbia entered the program, over 2 million persons were paid something over $600 million under it between June, 1958, and July, 1959 ($3.9 billion was paid in regular benefits in 1958 and $2.9 billion in 1959). So severe was the effect of the 1958 recession on employment that 60% of those receiving TUC benefits exhausted them before finding work.[2]

Again, in 1961, in response to the 1960–61 recession, Congress temporarily extended unemployment benefits, this time under the title Temporary Extended Unemployment Compensation (TEUC). As with TUC, benefits could be extended for up to one half the duration provided by state law. However, this period was subject to two other limits: (1) TEUC benefits could not exceed 13 weeks in a benefit year; (2) TEUC benefits plus state benefits could not exceed 39 weeks in a benefit year. TEUC benefits in the amount of $769 million were paid to 2.8 million persons.

[2] U.S. Department of Labor, Bureau of Employment Security, *Labor Market and Employment Security*, September, 1959.

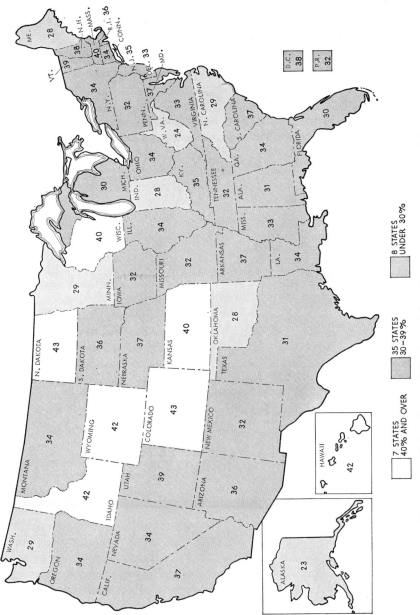

D.C. 38   P.R. 32

ME. 28
N.H. 38
MASS. 40
R.I. 36
CONN. 34
VT. 39
N.Y. 32
N.J. 35
PENN. 37
DEL. 33
MD. 37
W. VA. 24
VIRGINIA 33
N. CAROLINA 29
S. CAROLINA 37
GA. 34
FLORIDA 30
OHIO 34
KY. 35
TENNESSEE 32
ALA. 31
MISS. 33
LA. 34
MICH. 30
IND. 28
ILL. 34
WISC. 40
MINN. 29
IOWA 32
MISSOURI 32
ARKANSAS 37
N. DAKOTA 43
S. DAKOTA 36
NEBRASKA 37
KANSAS 40
OKLAHOMA 28
TEXAS 31
MONTANA 34
WYOMING 42
COLORADO 43
NEW MEXICO 32
IDAHO 42
UTAH 39
ARIZONA 36
WASH. 29
OREGON 34
CALIF. 37
NEVADA 34

HAWAII 42

ALASKA 23

7 STATES
40% AND OVER

35 STATES
30–39%

8 STATES
UNDER 30%

SOURCE: U.S. Department of Labor, Bureau of Employment Security.

Unlike in the earlier program, TEUC benefits were financed by a temporary increase in the payroll tax. Hence, whether or not a state participated in the program, its employers were still subject to the extra tax. This no doubt accounts for the fact that every state participated in TEUC, which expired in 1962.

Financing

As already noted, the original Social Security Act of 1935 provided that states could offset the 3% payroll tax up to 2.7% by enacting unemployment compensation legislation and complying with the other rules set forth in the Social Security Act. In 1961, the tax was raised to 3.1%, but the offset was continued at 2.7%.[3] In most states, the standard rate of contribution is 2.7%; only in a few does the standard rate exceed this level. The majority of the states have a $3,000 tax base, like the federal tax itself. In 1967, however, 18 states had increased the tax base, usually to $3,600.

The Social Security Act requires that all money received in a state unemployment fund must be paid to the Secretary of the Treasury, who deposits it in a Treasury fund known as the Federal Unemployment Trust Fund. Withdrawals from a state's account may be made only for unemployment benefits, or for unemployment benefits because of temporary disability; but in the latter event, withdrawals may be made only to the extent of employees' contributions in such state. As will be pointed out in Chapter 19, four states have adopted temporary disability laws.

The initial 3% rate, chargeable to employers only, was based upon anticipated unemployment of a more severe nature than actually occurred once the law began to operate fully. Moreover, the costs of administration have been less than anticipated. As a result, reserve funds developed rapidly. Even during the sharp recession of 1938, most of the states then paying benefits collected more money than they paid out. As reserves grew, pressures became persistent for a reduction in tax rates. Since, under the provisions of the Unemployment Tax law, experience rating was the only method by which states could reduce tax rates, all of the states were led to adopt experience-rating plans.

Aggregate state withdrawals from the trust funds have exceeded aggregate state deposits in a number of years with the result that many funds have been underfinanced from time to time. Some states have been forced to seek interest-free loans from the federal government, made available, on certain conditions, to states with depleted reserves.

States with inadequate reserves could raise them in one of three ways. Tax rates could be raised above 2.7%, and this has been done in an increasing number of states. Minimum tax rates (under the state's experi-

---

[3] For example, the tax on $3,000 of wages would be $93 (3.1% times $3,000); the maximum offset permitted would be $81 (2.7% times $3,000); the $12 difference ($93 minus $81) would go to the federal government's account, rather than the state's.

ence-rating system, to be discussed in the next section) could be raised, so that the most stable employers could subsidize more of the system. The taxable base could be raised, in which case all employers would pay more. Still another approach was to restrict eligibility requirements. As already noted, this approach is also being taken in many states.

The reduction in average tax rates which has occurred presents dangers in recessions. It also creates pressure against lengthening durations or increasing benefits further. It may lead to increasingly stringent disqualification provisions. Many experts feel that an average tax of 2% of covered total wages would probably provide a system which would meet all reasonable demands placed upon it.

The federal share of the unemployment compensation tax (0.4%) is first used for annual appropriations to the states to cover the costs of administration of the unemployment compensation laws. The entire cost of administration is covered by these grants because all funds collected from taxes on employers or employees must be used for payment of benefits. Federal grants are also made to the states for the cost of administering the state employment offices, through which unemployment compensation benefits are handled. Since the costs of administration prior to the 1950's proved to be less than anticipated, the federal government developed a substantial surplus from its tax share. The Administrative Financing Act of 1954 utilized these surpluses to protect the solvency of the insurance funds. It provides for the automatic appropriation to the Federal Unemployment Trust Fund of the annual excess of federal unemployment tax collections over employment security administrative expenses. These excess collections were used first to establish and maintain a $550 million fund[4] in the federal unemployment account available for noninterest-bearing loans to state agencies with depleted reserves. The excess collections beyond $550 million are used to establish a $250 million reserve for administrative expenses. Finally, any excess tax collections are returned to the states.

During the recession of 1958, the federal funds were insufficient to provide adequate loan facilities when unemployment severely drained state reserves. As a result, several states were eligible for loans for which there were no funds.[5] Furthermore, the 0.4% federal tax may not yield enough funds to pay even for administration in the future.

Although the employer pays the complete cost of the program in most states, three states—Alabama, Alaska, and New Jersey—presently collect employee contributions.

Those favoring employee contributions believe that employees as well as employers should contribute to their security against unemploy-

---

[4] The fund was first set at $200 million.

[5] *Hearings before the Committee on Wages and Means on Unemployment Compensation* (House of Representatives, 86th Cong., 1st sess. [Washington, D.C.: U.S. Government Printing Office, April, 1959]), pp. 8–9.

ment and that more liberal benefits could be paid if employees were also taxed. Organized labor, however, has generally been opposed to employee taxes, and many employers fear that if employees contribute, the pressure for more liberal benefits will be so much greater that employer taxes will be higher, not lower.

In 1946, Congress amended the Social Security Act to provide that an amount equal to the total of employee payments paid into a state unemployment fund, less administrative costs, could be used in the payment of cash benefits to individuals for temporary disability. Three states —California, New Jersey, and Rhode Island—require employee contributions to provide disability benefits in accordance with this provision.

Experience Rating

The Federal Unemployment Tax Act provided that employers can get credit against the federal tax not only for the contribution which they pay under a state law but also for the contributions which they are excused from paying under the state experience-rating system. As a result of this incentive, all states had adopted experience-rating plans by 1948. In general, these plans provide for rates substantially lower than 2.7% for employers with good experience in maintaining stable employment and higher rates for the employers who are least successful in accomplishing this objective. In 1967, 16 states had a zero rate in their most favorable schedule; 36 states provided for rates above 2.7%. Because of this tax variation, the average tax rate for the country as a whole has been consistently lower than the 3% provided in the Social Security Act. For example, in 1967, it was 1.6% of the aggregate state taxable wages. As a result of these low tax rates, there is some danger, as previously noted, that the revenues to finance unemployment compensation may be inadequate in times of crises.

Experience rating was based on the presumption that employers who were given an incentive would control unemployment more carefully and would police claims of former employees to prevent fraud. Furthermore, the system was thought to be a fair way of apportioning cost by requiring higher percentage payments from employers and industries with higher unemployment experience. Experience rating was also meant to adjust fund income to outgo and to prevent unnecessary taxation and accumulation of funds.

Many arguments have been raised against experience rating. Unemployment is more often the result of market and technological conditions than employer action; and, therefore, it may be unfair to allocate the cost to the employer affected. Experience rating may discourage employment during recessions because at that time unemployment compensation taxes are likely to be the highest. A tax on payrolls affects the marginal costs of the firm. To increase such costs in recessions, which appears inevitable for most firms under experience rating, is to add to marginal costs at a time when such costs are most sensitive and when increased marginal costs can most easily and adversely affect employment.

One of the most unfortunate economic results of experience rating is that taxes are likely to be reduced in times of prosperity and raised in times of depression. Experience rating makes insufficient provision for the fact that most good employment records are made when general economic conditions are good, and bad ones when general economic conditions are bad. Consequently, the costs of unemployment insurance taxes are low when industry is best able to pay them, and high when industry is least able to pay them.

It is unlikely, as long as the state-federal system exists, that experience rating will disappear. However, it is possible that some changes of a more limited nature may occur. Congress may limit the amount of rate reduction which may be permitted if the federal offset is to be allowed or if the state is to qualify for federal loans. Alternatively, Congress may give the states the right to use uniform rate reductions in the future, as opposed to the present employer-by-employer experience-rating methods. This would reduce discrimination in rates between employers in the same state but would not eliminate interstate competitive reductions.

Some Future Prospects

Important questions remain for the future. What role should be assigned to unemployment insurance? How much more should it accomplish than it does at present? How are changes to be brought about in the unemployment compensation program?

Any uniform changes in the system are likely to require a greater degree of federal control than at present. Voluntary uniform action among the 52 jurisdictions (which include the District of Columbia and Puerto Rico) is unlikely. From the very beginning, some degree of federal control has existed. The tax offset method compelled the states to adopt laws which met minimum federal requirements concerning financing and administration, and the states were also required to adopt the so-called "labor standard" relative to payment of benefits.

The middle ground of revised federal standards for continuing state programs might leave administration in local hands while obtaining the advantages of more uniform financing rules (though choice of method might still be available), of higher benefits relative to wages, of better duration and disqualification provisions, and of broader coverage. Such a program need not set a single dollar benefit standard but rather could set a percentage-of-wages standard. This would allow benefits to vary with wages while providing the same given proportion of income loss everywhere.

Is the concept of a system designed to meet only short-term unemployment attributable to the employer a satisfactory one? A study cited above concludes that as a consequence of low benefits, limited coverage, and short duration of payment, only about 20% of all wages were compensated by unemployment insurance during the period involved in the study.[6] Furthermore, the large number of benefit exhaustions led Congress to provide aid in extending durations through TUC in 1958 and through TEUC in 1961.

If such insurance is to provide greater assistance when unemployment is most widespread, the duration of payments will have to be lengthened to 39 weeks or longer, and benefits will have to be increased. The more widespread use of dependents' allowances will have to be considered in order to relate benefits to needs, and insurance may have to be better coordinated with relocation and retraining of workers. Some progress has already been made by the Area Redevelopment Act and the Manpower Development and Training Act, which utilize unemployment insurance machinery for providing financial assistance to workers being retrained. Such broader social goals will require more federal leadership and might make integration of all social insurances more attractive.

Longer durations and higher benefits, which assure regularly attached labor-force members greater and more realistic protection in periods of recession, would also provide windfall temptations to marginal workers, as earlier noted. If working 20 weeks might entitle one to 39 weeks of benefits at 60% of wages, malingering might well become serious. Variable benefits and durations may be required in order to cope with this problem.

THE DISMISSAL WAGE

As noted in Chapter 6, the dismissal wage is a payment, usually in the form of a lump sum, made by an employer to a worker who has been laid off permanently from his job. It is frequently based on length of service and compensation received during the period of employment. For example, a common formula for determining the size of a dismissal wage is one week's pay for each year of service. This dismissal wage has become an important part of organized labor's program to provide security against loss of earnings because of unemployment.

The number of companies having severance plans has greatly increased in recent years. A 1964 study showed that of the 427 companies surveyed, 44% had a severance pay program.[7] By size of firm, 34% of those employing between 250 and 499 employees had such a plan; 42% of those firms employing between 500 and 999 employees; 50% of those employing between 1,000 and 4,999 employees; and 67% of those employing 5,000 or more.

---

[6] Lester, *op. cit.*, p. 38.

[7] National Industrial Conference Board, *Personnel Practices in Factories and Offices: Manufacturing* (S.P.P. No. 194 [New York, 1964]).

Management's Attitude toward Dismissal Wages

As noted in Chapter 6, dismissal wages are not a union idea. Managements in many progressive companies have made such payments voluntarily for many years. Some companies look on dismissal wages as a sort of supplement to a pension plan. Increasingly, companies are utilizing the early retirement provisions of their pension plans in this regard. Union interest in early retirement has now reached significant proportions and is likely to spread.

On the whole, management often recognizes the need for dismissal wage payments in the case of long-service employees who will find it difficult to obtain employment elsewhere. However, management is opposed to the idea of general payment of dismissal wages to all employees who are laid off, on the ground that ups and downs of employment are not within the control of the employer and requiring the payment of dismissal wages would simply add to the cost of doing business and, in the end, discourage investment and reduce employment. Although the payments may be most justified in the case of technological unemployment which renders obsolete the skills of particular workers displaced by machines, management contends that the requirement of paying large dismissal sums to workers displaced by laborsaving machinery might make it so expensive that investment in such machinery would be discouraged. If this were to happen, technological displacement of labor in particular firms might be lessened, but employment and income in the economy as a whole would suffer by reason of the reduced expenditures on new plant and equipment.

Labor's View of Dismissal Wages

Labor spokesmen view the dismissal wage not only as a crutch to assist the displaced worker during a period of unemployment but also as a club to compel management to minimize displacement of labor. The idea is to make employers think twice about laying off employees when they put in new machinery by making such layoffs costly. As stated by the late Philip Murray: "The objective, of course, primarily is not to provide dismissal wages to displaced workers, but to compel industry to keep workers on the payroll by planning the introduction of technology, so that industry will not have to pay the dismissal wages and workers are not displaced."[8]

In other words, from the viewpoint of the union, the dismissal wage is a means of making unemployment costly to the employer. Unions would use dismissal wages to restrain employers from introducing new machinery in times of depression and falling demand when it was difficult

---

[8] Philip Murray, *Technological Unemployment* (United Steelworkers Publications, No. 3 [Pittsburgh: United Steelworkers of America, 1940]), p. 39.

for them to utilize the displaced labor elsewhere in their plants. Unions believe that the dismissal wage would make employers reappraise their hiring and layoff policies. In an establishment where a dismissal wage plan was in effect, the employer, in hiring new workers, would have to take into account the chance that he might ultimately have to lay them off and pay them dismissal wages. Similarly, whenever he considered firing workers, he would take into account the amount of the dismissal wage and the chance that the size of the labor force might have to be increased in the future. Obviously, it would not pay the employer to lay off workers and give them dismissal compensation if he anticipated that he might have to rehire them in the near future. The possibility of saving payment of dismissal wages can be thought of as reducing the cost of keeping men on the payroll during the intervening period of slack demand. Thus, dismissal compensation, according to union spokesmen, would not only encourage employers to plan their technological changes in such a way as to produce a minimum of dislocation to labor but also would have some tendency to iron out short-term fluctuations in employment.

The Dismissal Wage and Wage-Employment Equilibrium

If an employer has a broad dismissal wage plan in force and the union secures a large wage increase, the employer is confronted with a situation in which maintenance of the same volume of employment has become more costly; but reduction in the size of the work force, while cutting one kind of wage cost, would add another. This dilemma may encourage the employer to seek other ways of reducing costs rather than to take the course of reducing the payroll through a reduction in the work force. Thus, it may be found possible to eliminate waste in use of materials, plant space, and other factors, so that it will not be necessary to raise prices at all. However, this presupposes a backlog of inefficiency which may not exist. In the normal case, the union wage increase will produce an increase in prices; but because of the dismissal wage requirement, employment will not be reduced by the full amount which might otherwise have occurred had there been no such plan in effect.

Thus, the existence of a dismissal wage requirement can produce a range of indeterminateness in wage-employment determination. In effect, it raises the upper limit to which, in given circumstances in the short run, the wage can be increased without altering the volume of employment. The number of layoffs which will result from a wage increase will depend upon the size of the wage adjustment, the elasticity of demand for the product, the degree to which capital can be substituted for this form of labor, the relation of labor costs to total costs, the size of the dismissal wage, and the length of time for which the changed cost-price situation is expected to prevail. Assuming that anticipated future cost-price changes will be such as to require an expansion of the work force, the larger the dismissal wage and the shorter the period for which the changed cost-price situation is expected to prevail, the greater will be the inducement to the employer to retain employees on his payroll. Since the men have become more expensive to the employer whether they are employed or unemployed, it is only logical that the employer should choose to get some work performed for the increased cost. Thus, from the viewpoint of the individual workers concerned, the dismissal wage has the effect of making the short-run demand for labor more inelastic.

Appraisal of Dismissal Wage

The dismissal wage has some merit as a means of controlling the rate of technological change. When the social cost of lost skills, abandoned towns, poverty, and unemployment is taken into account in the balance sheet of technological progress, it is possible that the unrestricted substitution of machinery for labor will be found to have produced a rate of progress in excess of what might be regarded as the optimum rate for the community. Insofar as a dismissal wage compels employers to adopt a rational plan of technological improvement with a view to minimizing the disturbance to employment, and further compels them to assist the men displaced during the transition period, it simply distributes to management a share of the burden of the social cost of change. But where, as in the case just examined, the dismissal wage is associated not with technological progress but simply with a union wage increase, the same justification for the dismissal wage is not applicable. In the latter case, the effect of the dismissal wage is to make it costly for the employer to discharge workers and to adjust his operations to the new high level of costs imposed by the union.

Even in the case of technological change, however, the desirability of dismissal wage payment is debatable. As has been mentioned, requiring the payment of dismissal wages would make management hesitate to introduce laborsaving machinery in times of depression and falling demand; yet, these are the very times when, from the viewpoint of the economy as a whole, investment expenditures by industry should be encouraged, not penalized. Furthermore, it is not easy, in practice, to distinguish unemployment which is attributable to laborsaving machinery from unemployment due to the ups and downs of the business cycle. If employers introduce new laborsaving machinery in times of expanding demand, they often can use the displaced workers elsewhere in the plant. Then, when recession sets in, these men and others are laid off. Should managements in individual companies assume the burden of paying dismissal compensation at such times for these men, or should unemployment compensation be handled exclusively by the state or federal government? One drawback of leaving dismissal compensation to decisions of individual companies and unions is that the amount a worker will receive will vary from company to company, depending upon the size of the firm, the generosity of the employer, the strength of the union, and similar considerations. A liberalized program of government unemployment compensation would probably provide a more equitable distribution of benefits and have a less depressing effect on investment in new technology than a union-sponsored program of dismissal compensation. It must be borne in mind, however, that the ultimate union objective may be further liberalization of state unemployment compensation benefits and that pressure for dismissal wages may simply be a means of letting employers know that unless they support legislation to achieve this objective, they are going to bear the cost of unemployment just the same.

Relation to Unemployment Compensation

At the present time, the dismissal wage fills a need which is not met by unemployment compensation or by supplementary unemployment benefits. Unemployment compensation, as we have seen, is aimed at temporary unemployment on the part of workers who have been laid off and are looking for a new job. Supplementary unemployment benefits, as will be pointed out in more detail in the final section of this chapter, are designed to take care of temporary layoffs, due to seasonal and other variations in business, of workers who remain attached to the labor force of a particular company. The dismissal wage, however, is particularly designed for long-service employees who find that their jobs have ended because of a contraction in demand for the product or because of the introduction of laborsaving machinery. Where the latter cause is involved, skills which these employees have built up over a long period of years may be rendered useless. Skilled workers can be transformed into relatively unskilled workers almost overnight by drastic change in the technology of an industry. If the workers affected are well along in years, the result may be permanent unemployment. Dismissal wages represent an attempt to compensate such workers for this permanent loss of their employment. Union leaders argue that such compensation is particularly justified when technological change is the cause of the layoff, because technological improvement in industry generally results in effecting some savings for the employer.

Now that some unemployment insurance programs contain provisions encouraging vocational rehabilitation, a further connection between the programs may be noted. Workers who lose work because their skill becomes obsolete must be retrained. The dismissal wage is a partial cushion during the retraining period. But now, under a few state programs, workers who lose their skills may draw unemployment benefits for the entire period that they are in an approved retraining program. Thus, if the severance pay cannot provide enough cushion until new skills are acquired, unemployment insurance will lengthen the period in which retraining with some income is possible.

But this raises the question of dual payment and may run into legal barriers. At the present time, the receipt of dismissal wages either reduces or bars unemployment compensation in more than 20 states. In these situations, dismissal compensation is deemed to be a form of wages, and while a worker is receiving the benefit of such payments, he is not considered eligible for unemployment compensation. Thus, if he received 10 weeks' pay as a dismissal wage, he would have to wait 10 weeks to become eligible for unemployment compensation. Of course, from the viewpoint of the unemployed worker, the dismissal wage is more desirable than unemployment compensation because the former is usually equal to his previous full weekly pay, while this is not true of the latter.

Should an unemployed worker be entitled to receive both unemployment compensation and dismissal wage? Union men would answer yes. They view the dismissal wage as a payment for past services and as a sum intended to reimburse the worker for the loss of earnings he may suffer in the future even if he obtains a new job because, in effect, he has to start his working career all over again. On the other hand, management argues that in many states the tax it pays under unemployment compensation laws is based on the unemployment experience of the particular company. Therefore, if the company takes care of unemployed workers by paying them dismissal wages, it would have to pay twice if the worker desires unemployment compensation. Moreover, while there is some merit to the "past-service argument" when long-service employees are involved, this does not hold when younger employees, who can obtain other jobs more readily, are laid off.

SUPPLEMENTAL UNEMPLOYMENT BENEFITS

At its convention in March, 1954, the United Automobile Workers unanimously went on record in favor of a new collective bargaining objective—a guaranteed annual wage. In June, 1955, the United Automobile Workers and the Ford Motor Company signed a historic contract which was hailed by union officials as containing the first major step toward the much-heralded labor goal of a guaranteed annual wage.

Examination of the initial Ford-UAW contract reveals, however, that the union did not gain a guaranteed annual wage. Rather, what Ford proposed as the accepted alternative was a supplement to state unemployment compensation. Subsequent contracts, particularly in the automobile industry, have moved these supplemental benefits closer to the annual wage concept. Hence, an examination of both guaranteed wages and supplemental benefits is appropriate.

The Guaranteed Annual Wage

An annual wage guarantee is a guarantee by an employer to his employees of a weekly paycheck of a constant amount for a given number of weeks of the year, usually 40 or more, without a guarantee that the employee will be remunerated at his usual rate. The federal Social Security Act of 1935 included a specific provision to encourage the spread of guaranteed annual wage plans by permitting states to offer reduced unemployment compensation taxes to guaranteeing employers. The Fair Labor Standards Act of 1938 also sought to encourage these plans by permitting exemptions from the overtime pay requirements of the law where employment was provided on an annual basis. Very few companies, however, have availed themselves of these provisions. Only a few of these plans are operative, with a relatively small number of covered employees. These plans are concentrated primarily in the consumer goods and service industries in companies with a record of fairly steady production and employment. By and large, eligibility requirements sharply limit the number of workers covered by such plans, and there is no tie-in with state unemployment insurance systems.

The announcement by the UAW leadership that the union was going to seek guaranteed annual wage plans from the automobile companies brought forth a torrent of speeches, articles, and assorted literature either for or against the GAW.

The union argument had a number of facets:

1. If executives and office personnel are paid on an annual basis, why should the production worker be paid by the piece, hour, or day? Biologically, a worker has the same regularity in satisfying his physical needs as his boss. Why, then, should he be paid any differently?
2. Management can, if it tries, do much to eliminate fluctuations in employment over the year. The annual wage cannot and does not attempt to cope with long-term cyclical unemployment—it is aimed at short-term layoffs. If the annual wage made it expensive for management to lay off workers, there would be an incentive to diversify production and adopt better scheduling practices, so that year-round regular work could be provided.
3. Annual wages would increase and stabilize employment. Employers could finance the annual wage by making payments in to a trust fund in good times and by drawing on the fund when layoffs are made. This would tend to stabilize purchasing power and make workers more willing to commit themselves to installment purchases of homes, appliances, etc.
4. The annual wage would achieve savings in labor cost by reducing labor turnover and the loss of skills which result from such layoffs.

The following basic arguments were advanced against the GAW by employers:

1. To adopt GAW before stability in production has been achieved in an industry would put the cart before the horse. The steel industry and the automobile industry, both of which manufacture products characterized by extreme fluctuations in demand, cannot by themselves regularize employment and production. They cannot produce for inventory to any appreciable extent, nor can blast furnaces be used in

off seasons for production of baby cereals. The GAW would simply add another cost without stabilizing employment.

2. The GAW would reduce investment and employment because employers would be hesitant about making new investments, since, in addition to the normal risks of business, there would be added the burden of paying annual wages to employees who might have to be laid off if the investment proved unprofitable.

3. The GAW would run counter to a basic principle in unemployment compensation, namely, that a worker's salary should be reduced when he is not working, so that he will have an incentive to seek other work while his regular job is unavailable. If the GAW means full or almost full pay for those laid off, the senior workers might actually vie to be laid off first in order to get what amounts to a paid vacation.

4. The GAW would be used as an entering wedge by unions to attempt to control production schedules and would ultimately lead to unions having a voice in pricing, production planning, employment, and other management prerogatives.

While the UAW did not succeed in obtaining a GAW plan, many of the arguments listed above, both pro and con, are applicable to SUB. Furthermore, since the union spokesmen have been able to move SUB closer to their GAW goal at each successive negotiation, the arguments surrounding the GAW are still very much evident in both management and union pronouncements on SUB.

Supplemental Unemployment Benefit Plans

The main union drive for guaranteed annual wages and for supplemental unemployment benefits came from former CIO organizations involved in broad industrial coverage and representing workers over wide geographic areas. Spearheading the movement were the Steelworkers and the Automobile Workers. Today, most of the workers covered by SUB plans are in the automobile, steel, can-manufacturing, rubber, and glass industries.

SUB plans have been of two types—insurance fund and individual account plans.

Insurance Fund Plans. This type of plan is by far the most common today. The Ford plan falls in this class, as do the other plans in the automobile industry, and in can manufacturing, steel, and rubber. Although insurance fund plans differ in provisions among companies, they have these common characteristics:

1. Company contributions are based on payroll, being limited to a fixed charge in accordance with employee hours worked.

2. Company contributions are paid into a trust fund established for the benefit of the employees covered. A maximum funding position is specified, and once it is attained, no further contributions by the employer are required (or employer contributions are applied to provide a bonus).

3. State unemployment insurance benefits are included in the computation of total benefit awards.
4. Up to an established maximum, benefit amounts are related to a percentage of wages.
5. Generally, eligibility for the state benefits is a prerequisite for benefits under the company plan.
6. While company costs remain fixed, total benefits vary in accordance with trust fund position.

The plans vary from industry to industry. For example, the Ford plan, as amended in various negotiations, pays benefits up to 52 weeks. It is designed to pay, together with any unemployment compensation that is due, 95% of take-home pay, minus a $7.50 weekly deduction for work-related expenses. Certain maximums may apply when state unemployment compensation benefits are not paid and when the employee refuses to accept work. Under the Rubber Workers' current contracts, SUB benefits are 80% of straight-time weekly earnings. The duration of benefits under the Rubber Workers' plan is 52 weeks of compensation for employees with less than 5 years of seniority up to 4 years of benefits for those with 25 or more years of service. In both the Ford and Rubber Workers' plans, employer contributions in excess of the amount needed in the trust fund are applied to provide a bonus for employees.

Individual Account Plans. Individual account plans are primarily found in the glass industry, although they have also been adopted by other groups. These plans provide for establishment of individual vested accounts for all employees, much like savings accounts. Plans of this nature have the following common characteristics:

1. Individual accounts are established for each employee, and contributions are paid into the account by the employer, based upon employee hours worked.
2. The accounts are vested—that is, they belong to the individual employee, and he may draw from the account when he is laid off, is ill, retires, or leaves the company. When he dies, any balance is paid to his estate. The plan is, therefore, considerably broader than a mere supplement to unemployment compensation.
3. There is no integration with state systems of unemployment compensation. Since the particular account belongs to the individual employee, he can draw from it whether or not he is eligible for state unemployment compensation benefits.

Comparison of Insurance Fund and Individual Account Plans

Both plans have certain common characteristics. On the whole, they represent "reserve financing" rather than "pay as you go." In both cases, the liability of the employer is limited to a fixed cents-per-hour labor charge. Both adopt the plan of supplementing income rather than guaranteeing employment or annual wages.

Insurance plans, by pooling the risk of unemployment, can pay higher benefits to laid-off workers during the initial stages of the plan than are available from individual accounts. Insurance plans tend to maintain pay differentials among workers except for the highly rated employees, since benefits are computed as a proportion of income. This is not true of the individual account plans, where payments are dependent upon the balance in the particular worker's account and the size of the benefit he chooses to draw. Insurance plans tend to equalize total jobless benefits, as workers from the low-benefit states will receive more in supplementation from the company fund than co-workers in states where state unemployment benefits are more liberal. Individual account plans, as already observed, have no relation to state benefits. From the tax viewpoint, contributions of the employer to the insurance fund are not deemed taxable income to the employees, and no income tax is paid by an employee until funds are actually paid to him. On the other hand, company contributions to individual accounts represent additional income to the employee immediately, and the employer is required to withhold income taxes on such amounts when they are credited to the respective accounts.

SUB and State Unemployment Compensation Laws

The supplementary unemployment benefit plans negotiated by UAW with Ford, General Motors, and Chrysler contained a provision making their introduction contingent upon the issuance of rulings by states in which two thirds of the employees of each company reside to the effect that payments to unemployed workers could be made by these companies concurrently with state unemployment benefits. In many states, a laid-off worker who receives vacation pay is not entitled to receive unemployment compensation because the vacation pay is treated as "wages." There was considerable question at the time the UAW contracts were signed as to whether the SUB plans could be put into effect without amendment of state unemployment compensation laws. However, practically all states have allowed integration of SUB with state unemployment laws. No state expressly prohibits such integration, and only a few states have made no ruling either way.

Appraisal of Supplementary Unemployment Benefit Plans

Under the Ford SUB plan, the typical laid-off employee who earns about $167 a week before taxes and around $150 after taxes (if he has two or three dependents) could receive total benefits of about $135 per week. With payments at this level, the employee is losing only about $15 a week by reason of being unemployed. If the employee prefers to live on this reduced sum while waiting to return to his regular job, rather than taking employment elsewhere, this can hardly be called malingering. Most employees in this industry have built up skills, associations, and seniority which are valuable, and they can hardly be condemned for preferring to return to their regular jobs. In order to get employment elsewhere, most of these laid-off workers would probably have to conceal the fact that they intended to return to their former jobs.

Likewise, the burden of costs imposed by SUB is not so great as has been pictured by some critics. Employer contributions have been limited to a fixed rate, with benefits varying (if necessary) according to the trust fund position. Contributions to date have been in the neighborhood of 5 or 6 cents per hour worked.

It is not likely that there will be a very great expansion of SUB plans in the immediate future. In general, long-service employees control union policies. Since seniority protects long-service employees against layoff except in the most severe downturns, these employees have evidenced little interest in SUB plans.

As noted in Chapter 6, the combination of state and SUB benefits have now reached a state where in some industries, notably rubber tire, senior employees have the right to take layoffs instead of working. How high these benefits may reach before they become general impediments to working is something which society must consider.

Also, it is not likely that SUB plans will spread as fast as pension plans. Nonunion employers are much more likely to install pension plans than SUB plans. The latter are, as noted, pretty much confined to former CIO unions in a few mass-production industries.

SUB plans did not have material effects on employment swings in the 1958 recession and may be expected to have a very slight effect as economy stabilizers during other recessions, because—with relatively limited coverage—the total payments involved are not sufficiently large. On the other hand, the fact that these payments are concentrated in a few communities will be helpful in maintaining purchasing power in these areas.

But the claim that SUB plans would encourage industry to stabilize employment seems to have had some effect in the automobile industry. It would appear, however, that it was not SUB, per se, as originally conceived, but new rules and payments for short workweeks and continued high employment which brought about declines in the monthly swings in automobile employment.

Prior to 1962, automobile companies traditionally scheduled short workweeks as a means of adjusting production to demand. This was not penalized by SUB rules until the changes made in the 1961 negotiations. Then, commencing in 1962, an automobile worker on a short workweek received (*a*) 65% and, after 1964, 75%, of his base pay for hours not worked up to 40 if his hours were reduced to adjust production to demand or (*b*) 50% of his base pay if the cause of the short workweek was a breakdown or similar unavoidable delay. In 1967, short workweek benefits were increased to 80% of gross pay for both scheduled and unscheduled short workweeks. Because of these changes, the practice of scheduling short workweeks has been substantially curtailed.

But the UAW's very success in blocking the use of the short workweek has resulted in greater use of overtime. For employers prefer to pay a considerable amount of overtime compensation in order to forego the costs and risks of adding more employees to the payroll if such employees are likely to be laid off or put on short workweeks. This is another aspect of the fringe benefit story and its effect on employment, as was discussed in Chapters 5 and 15, and explains why the demand for an overtime rate that is higher than time and one half originated with the UAW.

Thus, the UAW has moved SUB toward its original goal of the guaranteed annual wage. Automobile companies now pay 95% of take-home pay to automobile workers for a full week and 80% of gross pay to those laid off for parts of weeks. The incentive for employers to produce more with less workers is likewise enhanced.

But whether Walter P. Reuther or other labor leaders achieve the goal of the guaranteed annual wage, the fact remains that union-negotiated SUB or GAW plans are an unsatisfactory and incomplete method of meeting the real problem which requires attention—that is, the inadequacy of our state unemployment compensation laws. At best, union-negotiated SUB plans can cover only a portion of union members and an even smaller percentage of the total labor force. Moreover, it will be difficult for unions to negotiate such plans where they are needed most—in smaller, weaker firms with fluctuating employment records and in companies faced by declining demand. Furthermore, such negotiated plans do not provide for the pooling of unemployment risks, which is possible under a statewide plan. It is to be hoped that union pressure for supplementary unemployment benefits will lead management, labor, and legislators alike to reappraise and attempt to improve our present inadequate unemployment compensation system.

QUESTIONS FOR DISCUSSION

1. What are some of the major differences between "insurance fund" and "individual account" SUB plans? Which is best for the employee? For the employer?

2. Discuss the adequacy of the present system of unemployment compensation. To what extent are union demands for dismissal wages and supplemental unemployment benefits associated with inadequacies in unemployment compensation laws?

3. Discuss the advantages and disadvantages of experience rating an employer's contributions under a state unemployment compensation law. Is experience rating equitable for all employers?

SUGGESTIONS FOR FURTHER READING

CARLSON, VALDEMAR. *Economic Security in the United States,* chap. vii. New York: McGraw-Hill Book Co., 1962.

An excellent statement of the rationale and economics of unemployment compensation.

GORDON, MARGARET S. *The Economics of Welfare Policies.* New York: Columbia University Press, 1963.

A view of the economics of unemployment insurance as well as OASDHI.

LESTER, RICHARD A. *The Economics of Unemployment Compensation.* Princeton, N.J.: Princeton University, Industrial Relations Section, 1962.

An analysis of the unemployment insurance system, with recommendations for improvement.

TURNBULL, J. G.; WILLIAMS, C. A., JR.; and CHEIT, EARL F. *Economic and Social Security.* 3d. ed. New York: Ronald Press Co., 1967.

A scholarly discussion of unemployment insurance and SUB as well as other social insurances.

Chapter	SECURITY FOR THE SICK
19	AND THE INJURED

Loss of income because of sickness and injury, together with the costs incurred by illness, reaches staggering proportions. The Social Security Administration has estimated that nonoccupational short-term sickness alone cost American families $12.2 billion in income loss during 1966, while consumer spending for medical care in that year exceeded $30 billion. Table 19–1 shows how the medical care dollar was

TABLE 19–1

PERSONAL CONSUMPTION EXPENDITURES FOR MEDICAL CARE*
IN THE UNITED STATES, 1948–66
(Billions of Dollars)

Year	Total Medical Care†	Hospital Services	Physicians' Services‡	Medicines and Supplies	Dentists	All Other Medical Care§
1948	7.5	1.6	2.4	1.9	0.9	0.4
1949	7.8	1.7	2.5	2.0	0.9	0.5
1950	8.5	2.0	2.6	2.2	1.0	0.5
1951	9.2	2.2	2.7	2.5	1.0	0.5
1952	9.9	2.4	2.8	2.6	1.1	0.5
1953	10.7	2.6	3.1	2.7	1.2	0.6
1954	11.6	2.9	3.4	2.8	1.4	0.6
1955	12.3	3.1	3.5	3.0	1.5	0.6
1956	13.4	3.4	3.8	3.3	1.6	0.7
1957	14.7	3.8	4.1	3.7	1.8	0.7
1958	16.0	4.2	4.6	3.9	1.9	0.8
1959	17.4	4.6	5.0	4.2	1.9	0.9
1960	18.6	5.1	5.3	4.4	2.0	1.0
1961	19.7	5.6	5.5	4.6	2.1	1.0
1962	21.4	6.1	6.0	4.9	2.3	1.0
1963	22.8	6.8	6.4	5.1	2.3	1.2
1964	25.0	7.7	7.0	5.4	2.6	1.3
1965	27.6	8.5	7.8	5.9	2.8	1.3
1966	30.6	9.7	8.3	6.6	3.0	1.5

* Includes expenses for health insurance, but not private expenditures in federal, state, city, and other government hospitals and nursing homes.
† Income cases will not add to total, due to rounding.
‡ Includes osteopathic physicians' services.
§ Includes other professional services and nursing home care.
SOURCE: Health Insurance Institute, 1967 Source Book of Health Insurance Data.

distributed in 1966 and how the shares taken by the different items have changed since 1948, when the total spent was $7.5 billion. These estimates point to the seriousness of the financial burden caused by sickness and injury, and they explain why there is so much interest in programs that alleviate this burden.

In this chapter, we shall discuss governmental and employer-provided programs designed to furnish income security for those who are unable to work by reason of illness or accident. In addition, we shall also discuss the issues involved in proposals to provide various types of health insurance to the employed population. However, for convenience of organization, medical care for the aged and disability benefits under OASDHI were discussed in Chapter 17 and will not be reconsidered here.

WORKMEN'S COMPENSATION

Workmen's compensation was the first type of social insurance to be developed extensively in the United States. It is designed to assure prompt payment of benefits to employees injured on the job or afflicted by occupational diseases; or in the case of a fatality in industry, to pay benefits to dependents. Workmen's compensation does not cover accident or injury outside of working hours, but only such accidents as occur on or pertain to the job.

The Development of Workmen's Compensation

Before workmen's compensation laws were passed, an employee injured on the job had little recourse. To be sure, under the common law the employer was required to provide a reasonably safe place for his employees to work. If, however, an employee was injured and the employer did not voluntarily pay some compensation, then the employee had to take his case to court for redress.

Besides the fact that employees rarely had the funds to hire sufficient legal assistance to pursue a case of this character in court, the employer had certain defenses which made it difficult for the employee to collect damages. In the first place, an employer might plead contributory negligence: that is, that the victim was also at fault to some degree. Or the employer might attempt to prove that the real fault was lodged with a fellow worker. This was known as the "doctrine of common employment" or the "fellow-servant doctrine." If these defenses were not available, the employer might plead a third one—the "doctrine of assumption of risk." Under this doctrine the employee was assumed to have had knowledge that he was engaged in a dangerous occupation and, therefore, if he still chose to work in that occupation, he had to assume the known risks of being injured.

In the latter part of the 19th and the early 20th centuries, the federal government and several states passed legislation designed to modify some of these common-law doctrines. It was not, however, until the lawmakers ruled out the question of blame in industrial accidents by passing workmen's compensation laws that progress was really made in providing compensation for injuries incurred on the job. These laws made the employer liable for work injuries, without regard to who was at fault. Hence, the injured employee could be compensated (1) even if the employer's negligence did not cause the accident and (2) even if the employee himself was negligent. Compensation laws were based on the theory that work injuries were inevitable and that the problem was to provide restitution rather than fix blame.

The Nature of Workmen's Compensation Laws

The first state workmen's compensation law was passed in New York in 1909. By 1948, workmen's compensation legislation had been enacted by all of the states, as well as by Puerto Rico. Special federal compensation laws cover civilian government employees, longshoremen and harbor workers, and private employees in the District of Columbia.

Workmen's compensation legislation, however, does not completely cover the American work force. In the first place, some states fail to provide coverage for certain types of accidents or diseases; and agricultural, domestic, and certain other workers are usually excluded from coverage of these laws. Then, in 24 jurisdictions, workmen's compensation acts are elective rather than compulsory. In such states, employers may refuse to operate under the compensation act if they prefer to risk suit for damages by injured workers. In a few states, the laws are compulsory as to some employments and elective in others. When employers elect not to come under a compensation act, employees are remitted to their old remedies at common law, and must prove that the employer was negligent. In such circumstances, however, the employer loses his common-law defenses—contributory negligence, the fellow-servant doctrine, and assumption of the risk.

Besides agricultural and domestic workers, compensation laws usually exclude casual employment. In addition, railway employees come under the Federal Employers' Liability Act (FELA) rather than under workmen's compensation. And maritime employees come under the Jones Act, which gives them the same rights that railroad workers have under the FELA. These two employee groups claim that they are able to collect more compensation by negligence suits than by compensation laws because of the fact that juries are generally sympathetic to them and unsympathetic to railroad and shipping concerns. As of January, 1968, in 25 jurisdictions, private employers who have less than a specified number of employees, varying from 2 to 15, are excluded from compulsory coverage of compensation legislation.[1]

---

[1] Most basic data on workmen's compensation in this chapter is taken from U.S. Chamber of Commerce, *Analysis of Workmen's Compensation Laws* (1968 ed.; Washington, D.C.).

Compensation laws are limited not only as to persons and employers included but also as to injuries covered. For example, some states exclude coverage if the injury is due to the employee's intoxication, willful misconduct, or gross negligence. In addition, a large number of states restrict coverage, to some extent, for occupational disease.

Nature of Benefits

Workmen's compensation laws provide two basic types of benefits: (1) cash payments for loss of income or death and (2) medical services, including rehabilitation, or cash payments for these services.

Most of the acts provide cash benefits based upon a percentage of the worker's wage up to a specified maximum. A few states vary the payments with the worker's marital status and number of dependents. The periods during which the compensation is paid vary tremendously, and the maximum weekly payments range from $35 to $150. In 22 jurisdictions, the weekly maximum for temporary total disability is $60 or more; another 19 pay between $45 and $60, while 10 pay less than $45.

Death benefits also vary considerably. In 9 states, in the District of Columbia, and under the two federal compensation acts, payments are made to the widow for life or until remarriage, and to children until they reach a specified age. In 29 jurisdictions, death benefits are limited to payments for periods ranging from 300 to 1,000 weeks, but 5 of these states continue to pay to children until they reach a specified age. Thirteen states limit the maximum amount but not the number of weeks during which compensation is payable. Death benefits are usually based upon a percentage of the average weekly wage of the deceased workman; but Oklahoma pays a lump sum, and Kansas pays a flat pension. The total maximums stated in the laws range from $12,000 to $64,000 in those jurisdictions with limits.

Twenty-seven states, the District of Columbia, and the two federal acts make permanent total disability payments for life or for the entire period of the disability. The remaining jurisdictions limit the time from 330 weeks to 550 weeks or the total amount of payments from $12,500 to $35,000 as of January, 1968. Payments also vary in some states according to the number of dependents.

Fifteen states, the District of Columbia, and the two federal acts make temporary total disability payments for life or the entire period of disability. In the other states, the payments are limited from 208 to 1,000 weeks and from $9,976 to $65,000. In 11 states, persons who are compensated for temporary total disability receive additional benefits for dependent children.

Most compensation laws provide payments for permanent partial disability. Two categories of such injuries are generally recognized— scheduled and nonscheduled. The former includes specific injuries such as the loss of use of an arm or a leg; the latter includes more general injuries such as an injury to the head or back. Most states provide specific payments for scheduled injuries, and the maximum payable for such injuries varies considerably. For example, in 1968, for the loss of an arm at the shoulder, the maximum amount payable in several states was approximately $7,000, whereas the maximum amount payable under the federal act was $107,640. Payments for nonscheduled injuries are generally related to the loss of earning power; and, in many cases, they exceed payments for scheduled injuries.

In all the compensation acts, medical aid is required to be furnished to the injured employee. However, in January, 1968, approximately half of the states confined medical benefits for occupational diseases and accidents as to duration or cost, or both. In addition, all acts require the employer to furnish artificial limbs and other necessary appliances.

Before any cash payments are made, nearly all states require a waiting period of one week after the injury. Medical benefits begin immediately, however, and compensation may be retroactive to the date of injury if the disability continues beyond the waiting period.

Administration

To make certain that benefit payments will be paid when due, the states require that the covered employer obtain insurance or give proof of his qualifications to carry his own risk, which is known as self-insurance. In most of the states, the employer is permitted to insure with private insurance companies. State insurance systems exist in 18 states and Puerto Rico. In six of these states and in Puerto Rico, the system is called "exclusive," because employers are required to insure in the monopolistic state fund. Competitive state funds exist in 12 states, where employers may choose whether they will insure their risks in the state fund or with private insurance companies, or qualify as "self-insurers" with the privilege of carrying their own risks.

In most states, a specific agency has been established to administer the act. In five states, however, there is no administrative agency empowered to supervise the compensation law, and injured workers can look only to the courts to enforce their claims. In states where the law is administered by a commission or board, the state agency usually has exclusive jurisdiction over the determination of facts, with appeals to the courts limited to questions of law. In a few states, however, the courts can consider the issues anew.

Second-Injury Funds and Special Provisions

A second injury to an employee who has already sustained an injury —such as the loss of a limb—may cause an employee to be totally disabled. If an employer were held responsible for the resulting total disability, this would encourage hiring discrimination against the handicapped. Therefore, as of January, 1968, all but four states had second-injury funds which limit the employer's liability to the disability caused by the second injury alone. The difference between the disability for the loss as a whole, and what the loss would have been in the absence of a prior injury, is made up from the fund.

Many states limit the application of the fund to cases where the prior injury resulted in the loss of use of a member of the body. Most of the funds are supported by a charge made against the employer or his insurer when a worker who has been killed on the job leaves no dependents.

Because workmen's compensation is basically a state matter, jurisdictional problems arise when an employee employed by a company located in one state is injured in another. In some cases, he is covered by the state where he is hired; in some, where he is injured; and in many cases, the jurisdiction is in doubt.

All the compensation laws cover legally employed minors. Twenty-one of the acts provide additional compensation in the case of injury to minors who are illegally employed. In 25 states, the District of Columbia, and under the Longshoremen's and Harbor Workers' Act, compensation is paid to minors illegally employed on the same basis as if they were legally employed. Five states do not cover minors illegally employed. In those states, the minor would have his common-law right of action for negligence.

Twelve of the 21 jurisdictions which, in January, 1968, provided extra compensation in the case of injury to illegally employed minors, require the payment of double compensation. The other nine impose penalties ranging up to 300% of the benefit otherwise payable.

Financing

For 1966, the Social Security Administration estimated that $1.98 billion was paid in workmen's compensation benefits, including medical benefits. Unlike the situation for other social insurances, the funds for workmen's compensation are not provided for by specific taxes levied upon employer or employee, or both. There is no central fund from which compensation is payable to eligible injured workers. Rather, the employee's compensation claim is against his employer, who must insure the risk. In nearly all jurisdictions, workers make no direct contributions to costs.

Analysis of Workmen's Compensation

A careful scholar of the social insurances has pointed out that workmen's compensation

. . . bears the scars of the fact that it was a pioneer social insurance program. . . . Restricted coverage, limitation of risks recognized . . . dollar limitations to amounts payable, the presence of private insurance techniques and self-insurance—all stem from the early and understandable desire to proceed with caution and to hedge the program with various safeguards designed to secure public acceptance and to allay misgivings on the part of employers.[2]

In the same vein is the comment of another authority who has worked in the workmen's compensation field for over two decades: "If, in the field of our mechanical contrivances, the same adherence to old models had prevailed as that which is found in respect to social arrangements, we should now be driving around in ox carts."[3]

Undoubtedly, workmen's compensation is inadequate in the three essentials of coverage, benefits, and administration. The large numbers of excluded categories, the failure to make provision for all occupational diseases, and the number of laws which are elective reduce the coverage of this legislation.

The complicated benefit system is very inadequate. In 1940, no jurisdiction provided benefits that averaged 50% of wages lost for all classes of injuries. Since then, benefits, despite increases in most states, have steadily fallen behind increases in the level of wages. At the same time, there is some costly and inefficient overlapping between compensation and other social insurance programs.

Administration is perhaps the weakest phase of workmen's compensation. There is tremendous variation from state to state in the caliber of administration. Some states make an excellent effort to see that claims are promptly paid, that workers know their rights, and that final reports are received from insurance companies on benefits paid, how benefits were computed, and the nature of the injury for which benefits were paid.

Unfortunately, good administration of workmen's compensation is apparently relatively uncommon. Many states collect little pertinent information. The majority of employed workers apparently do not know their rights, and state administrators make no real effort to correct this lack of information. Only a few states attempt to find out how promptly workers are paid, how much is paid for medical expenses, how adequate benefits are to take the place of lost wages, and for what purpose benefits are paid.

Along with poor administration, inordinately expensive administration is the rule rather than the exception. It has been estimated that a large percentage of the cost of workmen's compensation goes for administration.

Methods of financing are both questionable and geared to keep benefits at a minimum. Self-insured employers and poorly run insurance companies have become insolvent and thus denied injured workers' bene-

---

[2] Eveline M. Burns, *The American Social Security System* (Boston: Houghton Mifflin Co., 1949), p. 186.

[3] Marshall Dawson, *The Development of Workmen's Compensation Claims Administration in the United States and Canada* (International Association of Accident Boards and Commissions, 1951), p. 39.

fits, and some employers fail to seek coverage at all. Since both insurance companies and employers have an interest in keeping costs at a minimum, and since most workers are not too well-informed of their rights, the pressure to keep benefits down, to avoid expansion of coverage, and to pay the very least allowable in compensation is dominant in most state legislatures and most state administrative agencies. Moreover, since the individual is usually left to obtain his own benefits, he frequently becomes involved in litigation and lawyers' fees, if he is to protect his rights, or else faces loss of benefits because of ignorance of his rights. In other instances, benefits have been held up by attempts of insurance companies to transfer doubtful jurisdictional cases to the state jurisdiction which pays the least benefit. On the other hand, sometimes compensation costs can get out of line because of excessive liberality of state administrations.

Accident Prevention and Rehabilitation

The prime objective of workmen's compensation legislation is, of course, the payment of benefits to those injured on the job. If, however, the social purpose of workmen's compensation is to be achieved, it should encourage safe working practices which will prevent injuries before they occur; and it must provide the means to rehabilitate workers who have been injured so that they can, insofar as possible, become self-supporting once more.

There can be no doubt that workmen's compensation has encouraged safe working practices. The insurance rate which is charged to the employer is often determined by the accident frequency and severity record of his factory. Substantial savings in insurance costs accrue to the employer whose plant safety record is of high quality. The larger insurance companies in the compensation field provide safety counseling as part of their services. In addition, most states provide for safety inspections. Many employers have found that they can regain all of their costs spent on safety by reduced costs in compensation through fewer work injuries.

Unfortunately, however, relatively few plants have adequate safety programs. Estimates of the Bureau of Labor Statistics indicate that only one third of all workers are subject to planned, organized safety efforts. Consequently, American industry had, in 1966, 2.2 million disabling injuries and 14,500 deaths, with an estimated direct economic loss of 255 million man-days of work—representing full-time employment of about 1 million persons for one year. However, the severity and the frequency of injuries per man-hour worked have, for the most part declined over the years. This is illustrated in Figure 19–1.

Although accident prevention is obviously socially more desirable than compensation after injury, most workmen's compensation administrators either have no authority to enforce safety regulations or have no funds to spend on safety, or no interest in the subject. In some states, industrial health and safety programs and law enforcement are assigned to one department, workmen's compensation administration to another.

Workmen's compensation legislation has been less a stimulation to rehabilitation than to accident prevention. Only about one third of the state laws contain specific provisions for tiding permanently impaired workers over a period of vocational rehabilitation. A few other states make liberal provisions for the same purpose, although not unlimited ones. Usually, however, the awards for rehabilitation are meager, and insufficient to accomplish the task.

In two thirds of the states, the permanently disabled worker must look to a private or public agency for assistance in rehabilitation. In some states, disabled workers are referred to such agencies as a matter of

FIGURE 19–1

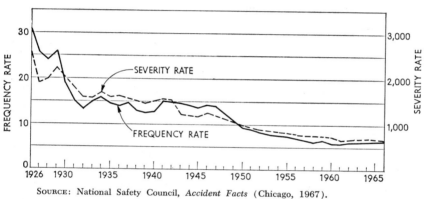

SOURCE: National Safety Council, *Accident Facts* (Chicago, 1967).

routine. In many, however, it is up to the disabled worker—or a charitable agency to which he has gone for financial assistance—to make such a referral. Having "compensated" the worker for a disabling injury, the state under these circumstances feels no obligation to return him to useful employment.

STATE TEMPORARY DISABILITY LEGISLATION

Temporary disability insurance is designed to compensate workers for time lost from work as a result of a nonoccupational illness or accident. In contrast to permanent and total disability legislation, as discussed in Chapter 17, temporary disability legislation limits payments to a fixed period, usually from 12 to 26 weeks. And whereas workmen's compensation pays compensation for occupational injuries and illnesses, temporary disability insurance is designed to provide compensation for injuries and illnesses contracted away from, and not related to, the job. Finally, although every state has a compensation law, only four states have enacted temporary disability insurance laws—California, New Jersey, New York, and Rhode Island. The Railroad Unemployment Insurance Act also provides temporary disability benefits for nonoccupational as well as occupational disability.

Development of Disability Insurance

In 1942, Rhode Island enacted the first disability insurance law. At that time, Rhode Island imposed a tax of 1.5% of payroll on employees, in addition to taxes upon employers, for support of unemployment compensation. This employee payroll tax was reduced to 0.5% in 1942, but the 1% reduction in employee payroll tax on the first $3,000 of wages was shifted to support the disability legislation.

In 1946, Congress amended the Social Security Act to permit states which had levied taxes upon employees in support of unemployment compensation to use an amount equal to the total employee contributions to the unemployment trust fund for cash disability payments. On the basis of this legislation, which affected nine states, Rhode Island discontinued its 0.5% tax on employees for unemployment compensation but continued its 1% disability tax, and California and New Jersey enacted a disability insurance law wholly separate and distinct from unemployment compensation.

Analysis of State Disability Legislation

The four state disability insurance laws are of three distinct kinds. The oldest of the state laws, that of Rhode Island, provides for a single state fund which collects all contributions and pays all benefits. No private plans can be substituted for the Rhode Island state fund, nor is any cognizance taken of any benefits that may be provided under a private plan. Like the other states, Rhode Island and New Jersey provide a seven-day waiting period before benefits are paid; but whereas the other three states require a waiting period before each separate disability is compensated, Rhode Island requires only one waiting period each benefit year.

The laws of Rhode Island, California, and New Jersey are administered by the state unemployment compensation agencies in these states. These three disability laws follow the unemployment compensation system in regard to eligibility requirements. Temporary disability is defined, in general, to mean physical or mental illness incapacitating a person so that he cannot perform his work. By administering the disability legislation with existing unemployment compensation agencies, the records of unemployment insurance can be utilized and administrative savings effected.

In California, New Jersey, and New York, employers may self-insure or insure with a private carrier or the state fund. In California and

New Jersey, workers are automatically covered by the state plan unless the employer takes affirmative action to institute a private plan. Both California and New Jersey attempt to safeguard the state funds against adverse selection of risks, for example, by requiring that private plans do not discriminate against any class of risks, such as plants which hire a large portion of women (since women generally lose more time because of illness than men). In California, the requirements have been such that most private insurers have withdrawn from this market, thus leaving the state plan as the primary method by which most workers are covered.

The New York law differs radically from the other three, in that it is wholly divorced from unemployment compensation and in that there is no limitation upon rights to establish private plans. New York's law is administered by the State Workmen's Compensation Commission, and the administration of the law is modeled upon the state workmen's compensation administration. New York's law, like those of the other three states, has a 26-week benefit duration.

The Social Security Administration estimates that in 1966, the state temporary disability legislation resulted in the payment of over $443.1 million in benefits. Private plans accounted for $208.7 million in benefits; state funds, for $234.4 million.

The failure of temporary disability legislation to spread beyond the four state and railroad jurisdictions is not a result of a political deadlock on the merits of providing protection against nonoccupational disabilities. Rather, it is a result of a conflict over methods, particularly the following: (1) the degree of federal versus state participation; (2) private insurance versus public financing; and (3) administrative tie-up with unemployment compensation versus administrative tie-up with workmen's compensation. Until these issues are resolved or compromises are reached, temporary disability legislation is not likely to spread. In the state of Washington, for example, an act of the legislature was nullified in a state referendum because opponents of any law were joined by opponents of the type of law enacted. Since this occurred, in 1950, no new law has been enacted by any state.

In the meantime, private plans are attempting to fill the void. Union welfare plans often include temporary disability provisions, and a number of employers have unilaterally established plans of this type.

HEALTH AND WELFARE PLANS

Privately organized protection against the cost of sickness has grown at a tremendous rate in recent years. Hospitalization insurance has become so popular that by 1966, 158 million people had such protection. Other types of medical care insurance have also become increasingly important, though not so prevalent as hospitalization benefits. In 1966, surgical expense contracts covered approximately 144 million persons, and regular medical expense contracts over 116 million.[4] The rapid overall growth of health insurance is pictured in Figure 19–2.

FIGURE 19–2

Growth of Hospital, Surgical, and Regular Medical Expense Protection in the United States, 1940–66

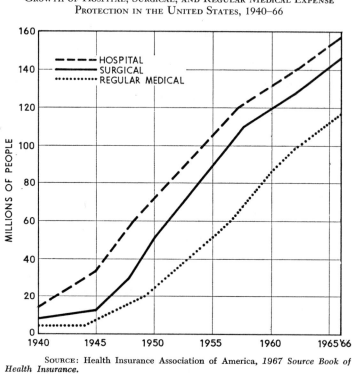

SOURCE: Health Insurance Association of America, *1967 Source Book of Health Insurance.*

The major suppliers of medical expense protection are the commercial insurance companies and the Blue Cross–Blue Shield organizations, with the commercial companies covering the largest portion of the public. Other sources of medical expense protection are the so-called "independent" plans such as New York City's Health Insurance Plan (HIP) and the Kaiser Foundation Health Plan which Henry Kaiser, the industrialist, inaugurated on the West Coast.

HIP had an enrollment of 700,000 subscribers in metropolitan New York during 1966. These subscribers have a very complete medical and surgical program and are divided into groups in the metropolitan area. Each subscriber may join any group in his county, and he may change groups if he so desires. When ill, a subscriber is attended by one of the

[4] Health Insurance Association of America, *1967 Source Book of Health Insurance*, pp. 12–14. A regular medical expense contract provides benefits for doctors fees for nonsurgical care.

physicians who is participating in the program and who is caring for the subscriber's group. The Kaiser Plan provides comprehensive medical care and hospitalization to over 1.1 million persons. It offers both individual and group membership, the latter usually organized on a union or company basis. The plan operates a number of modern hospitals to service its

FIGURE 19–3

GROWTH OF MAJOR MEDICAL EXPENSE COVERAGE
IN THE UNITED STATES, 1951–66

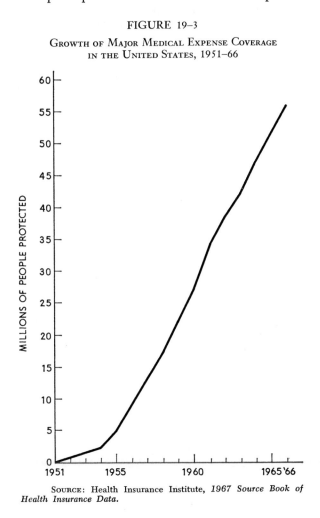

SOURCE: Health Insurance Institute, *1967 Source Book of
Health Insurance Data.*

members. Kaiser's plans can be tailor-made to meet the needs of each group.

The newest and broadest form of protection—major medical insurance—has grown very rapidly in the last decade, as shown by Figure 19–3. This form of coverage is designed to help absorb the cost of serious or catastrophic illness. Usually, major medical plans provide for a deductible amount which is equivalent to the benefits paid under a basic hospitalization-surgical-medical insurance plan, plus a "corridor" cash amount of from $100 to $300. After bills up to that amount have been incurred, the major medical plan takes over and pays for a specified percentage (usually 80%) of all medical bills up to a maximum of $10,000, $15,000, or even higher. Sometimes the deductible and maximum are applied to a specific injury or sickness; sometimes the deductible applies each calendar year but to all expenses from all causes, and the maximum is a lifetime amount for all expenses due to all causes.

Unions and Welfare Funds

Unions have been active in the welfare and benefit field since the latter part of the 19th century. At that time, several of the railroad unions were organized as fraternal and beneficial societies. The life insurance programs of these organizations are still operating. For the most part, however, the union welfare programs were union financed and union administered prior to World War II.

The wage stabilization program of World War II brought about a radical change in union welfare concepts. Whereas, in 1942, the Bureau of Labor Statistics could report that "there are relatively few formal sickness-insurance plans in effect at the present time and reference to them occurs very rarely in union agreements," that agency found that "more than 3 million workers . . . were covered by some type of health, welfare, and/or retirement benefit plan under collective bargaining agreements by mid-1948."[5] Unions concentrated their efforts during World War II where the law permitted. The National War Labor Board declined as a rule to order the institution of a welfare plan, but it would approve such plans if voluntarily arrived at. With employers anxious to hold their manpower, and with the costs to the employer of a welfare program deductible as an expense against taxes (including excess profits taxes), agreements for welfare programs were relatively easy to secure during the war.

After the war, unions pushed hard for benefits. In 1946, John L. Lewis won his Health and Welfare fund for the miners; during the next two years, benefit plans were adopted through collective bargaining in the steel, automobile, rubber, and other industries. Meanwhile, benefits similar to those won by unions have been rapidly adopted throughout industry for office, professional, and various nonunion groups. The U.S. Department of Labor estimates that in each of the years from 1959 to 1966, from 20% to 30% of all workers (22% to 33% of union and 11% to 25% of nonunion workers) benefited from the establishment or improvement of health and welfare plans.

When health and welfare plans were first introduced, the trend was

---

[5] E. K. Rowe and A. Weiss, "Benefit Plans under Collective Bargaining," *Monthly Labor Review*, Vol. LXVII (1948), p. 229.

for joint employee-employer contributions. Since then, union pressure has pushed more and more plans into a solely employer-financed system. A 1965 study of 163,500 welfare and pension plans showed "employer pay all" contributions in 43.8% of all plans (36.0% of welfare plans, 72.9% of pension plans, and 40.0% of combination welfare pension plans).[6]

Analysis of Health and Welfare Plans

Are health and welfare and the various group insurance programs adequate protection against loss of income and/or savings because of injuries and illness? What are some of the social and economic effects of the increasingly important role of unions in providing for the medical, hospital, and related disability care of union members?

First, it should be emphasized that health, welfare, and insurance programs provide a very important and practical service. This fact need not be labored to anyone who has received disability payments from an insurance company or who has seen his hospital and doctor bills materially reduced by Blue Cross and Blue Shield memberships. To millions of Americans, the economic ravages of illness and injury have been substantially reduced by coverage of health, welfare, and insurance plans.

On the other hand, the typical health, welfare, and insurance plan fails in several respects to provide security against major disasters resulting from sickness and injury. Some of the areas most frequently neglected in the past are the cost of drugs, mental illness, and dental care. Recently, however, there has been growing interest in providing more adequate coverage in these areas. In the 1967 Ford–UAW agreement, for example, prescription drugs were included for coverage.

In cases of chronic illness or injuries, health, welfare, and insurance plans are a great help in meeting initial expenses; but once the period of coverage ends, the patient is financially on his own. Many health, welfare, and insurance plans are devised to care for the routine accident or illness: a broken leg, or an appendectomy, or—in a happier vein—a maternity confinement. Costs over and above that covered by welfare plans in such cases do not usually represent a serious financial strain on the employed worker. And, as already noted, the phenomenal growth of major medical insurance is now providing more workers protection against even catastrophic losses. Figure 19–3 shows this growth. In 1966, over 56 million people were protected by major medical coverage. Of these, over 52 million had received their protection through employee benefit plans.

Even with major medical insurance added to the typical health, welfare, and insurance plan, there remain objections to complete reliance on such plans for economic security against sickness and accident. One such objection is the fact that coverage of such plans is still incomplete.

---

[6] U.S. Department of Labor, Labor-Management Services Administration, *Welfare and Pension Plan Statistics: Characteristics of 163,500 Plans Filed as of July 1, 1965* (Washington, D.C.: U.S. Government Printing Office, 1965), p. 17.

Although over 82% of the population has some form of health insurance, much of the protection is inadequate. Moreover, those who are not covered include those least able financially to withstand the costs of hospital and medical care—the unorganized, the unemployed, the casually employed, and other marginal and low-income population groups. The middle-income classes and the unionized workers are undoubtedly the most completely covered by health, welfare, and insurance plans.

Closely allied to this point is the fact that most welfare plans are contingent upon employment at a particular company or membership in a particular union. This fact is not so serious with respect to welfare plans as it is with respect to pension plans. Despite some variation in benefits, one welfare plan is not likely to differ too greatly from another in the same area or industry. Except for fulfilling the requirements of a waiting period (which is usually less than a year) and the restrictions that might apply to preexisting conditions, no loss of accrued welfare benefits is likely to result from changing employment. A health and welfare plan provides a current benefit—unlike a pension plan, which provides benefits which will be received in the future.

Employers have been conscious of the influence of welfare plans since they were introduced in the 1920's as a part of a program aimed at reducing turnover. Now, unions are looking at welfare plans in the same light. This accounts for a good deal of union insistence that employers use a plan which the unions have developed and which the unions control.

The desire to hold their members is as natural for union leaders as is the desire of employers to hold their employees. Unfortunately, welfare plans have also been used as instruments of coercion and racketeering. When loss of union membership means loss of union-controlled benefits, the average worker is likely to give additional pause before joining an attempt to unseat a dictatorial or otherwise unsatisfactory union leadership.

As for racketeering, we have already noted earlier in the book that congressional investigations have revealed abuses of important magnitude. The large amounts accumulated in welfare and pension funds, and the importance of these funds to the economic security of the workers, underscores the importance and need of their effective regulation.

QUESTIONS FOR DISCUSSION

1. What is the primary purpose of workmen's compensation laws? How effectively has the actual legislation accomplished this purpose?

2. How does the state disability legislation differ from workmen's compensation? What are the reasons why this type of legislation has not yet been passed in other states?

3. What role can union health and welfare plans play in a national health program?

SUGGESTIONS FOR FURTHER READING

CHEIT, EARL F., and GORDON, MARGARET S. (eds.). *Occupational Disability and Public Policy*. New York: John Wiley & Sons, Inc., 1963.

A survey of workmen's compensation problems and proposals by a group of experts.

DICKERSON, O. D. *Health Insurance*. Rev. ed. Homewood, Ill.: Richard D. Irwin, Inc., 1963.

An authoritative study of the issues involved in health insurance in the United States.

HEALTH INSURANCE ASSOCIATION OF AMERICA. *1967 Source Book of Health Insurance*. New York, 1967.

A source book of basic data and other factual material pertaining to voluntary medical and hospital insurance in the United States.

MUNTS, RAYMOND. *Bargaining for Health. Labor Unions, Health Insurance and Medical Care*. Madison, Wisc.: University of Wisconsin Press, 1967.

A study of the role of unions in bargaining for health care.

U.S. CHAMBER OF COMMERCE. *Analysis of Workmen's Compensation Laws*. 1968 ed. Washington, D.C.

A source book of basic data and other factual material pertaining to the workmen's compensation laws in effect in the United States.

PART VII

*Government Control of
Labor Relations*

| Chapter 20 | GOVERNMENTAL CONTROL OF THE WEAPONS OF CONFLICT |

Americans pride themselves on having maintained free collective bargaining and a free labor market in a world which is becoming increasingly regimented and collectivized. But the degree of freedom in our collective bargaining is relative. It is relatively unrestricted when compared with labor relations in the Soviet Union and other countries in the Communist bloc. On the other hand, an appraisal of the development of labor relations in this country reveals a patchwork of judicial decisions, laws, and regulations which have continually eroded and narrowed the field of individual action. In this chapter, we shall examine in detail some of the major weapons of conflict in the struggle for power between unions and management and shall consider how governmental and judicial controls have attempted to curtail their use.

LABOR AND THE COURTS IN EARLY AMERICA

The basic economic and social environment in the United States has, on the whole, been hostile to the development of union organization. In a land of opportunity, rich in natural resources and capable of providing a high standard of living to its wage earners, trade-unions have been unable to draw their membership from a proletariat with strong class allegiance, as in most European nations. On the contrary, class lines have been fluid; and even among wage earners, there has been continuing respect and support for the institution of private property. Union leaders have come to recognize this difference in outlook among our workers and have had to adopt a new kind of unionism—antisocialistic and business oriented—in order to attract and retain membership.

This same strength of private property rights which is a product of the free enterprise of the American environment is reflected in the attitude of both employers and courts toward union organization. In their struggle for recognition of the right to organize, unions have had to combat not only antagonistic employers, vehemently committed to defend their right to run their own businesses without interference from their employees, but also an unfriendly judiciary and an inimical common law. Members of the judiciary tended to be selected from the propertied classes of the community and therefore reflected a conservative attitude in their opinion in labor disputes. But even had their personal predilections been liberal, the fact remains that the controlling precedents of common law were generally restrictive of organized labor's actions.

Our common law, which is based upon the customs of the land as reflected in the accumulated decisions of the judiciary, has its roots in English history. In the 18th century, English courts outlawed labor combinations which exerted pressure to increase wages or to secure the closed shop as a means toward that end. British courts and statesmen considered such combinations among workmen to be inimical to the public interest because they interfered with the free working of market forces. In the famous *Philadelphia Cordwainers* case of 1806, and in numerous others during the next 30 years, American state courts adopted this same viewpoint and held that concerted action by combinations of workmen to better their wages and working conditions represented an illegal conspiracy against the public and against employers.

Then, in 1842, in the case of *Commonwealth* v. *Hunt*,[1] the Supreme Judicial Court of Massachusetts decided that a strike in support of a closed shop was not, per se, illegal; and that unless it could also be shown that the workers' objectives were bad, the conspiracy doctrine did not apply. Although the conspiracy doctrine continued to be utilized occasionally for some years to break up strikes, the decision in *Commonwealth* v. *Hunt* dealt it a blow from which it never recovered.

Judicial Tests of Legality

After the decision in *Commonwealth* v. *Hunt*, many courts tended to judge the legality of union activity on the basis of "motive" and "intent." This proved to be a highly subjective standard, which frequently reflected the prejudices of the individual judge rather than the facts of the case. Equally unsatisfactory was the so-called "means" test, which attempted to draw the line between permissible and unlawful union activity on the basis of whether or not the union action involved peaceful persuasion or unlawful intimidation. A further theory utilized by courts in labor cases in these early years was the doctrine of restraint of trade. This doctrine assumed much greater importance in judicial decisions with the subsequent enactment of the Sherman Antitrust Act, which will be discussed below. The doctrine of restraint of trade, however, also existed in common law. In general, the common-law doctrine was based on the premise that everyone should have equal access to the market and that when two or more persons combined to block access to the market and thereby inflicted injury upon the public, a conspiracy in restraint of trade existed. All restraints, whether inspired by labor or industry, were not considered illegal per se. The legality of such restraints was held to depend upon their "reasonableness," which was determined by the courts

---

[1] *Commonwealth* v. *Hunt*, 4 Metcalf 111 (1842).

by weighing the extent of coercion exercised, if any, and the effect of the restraint on the volume of business and access to the market.

The Injunction

By the late part of the 19th century, the courts had generally recognized the right of employees to organize in unions without civil or criminal liability. However, the use of concerted economic weapons—the strike, the boycott, and picketing—was generally held unlawful on the basis of one of the theories referred to above. The most effective weapon management was able to utilize to restrain such action by unions was the injunction.

The major objective of organized labor in the latter part of the 19th and the early part of the 20th century was to free itself from the shackles of the injunction. The injunction is a legal technique developed in equity courts to provide relief against continuing injury where recovery in the form of monetary damages does not suffice. Upon a showing that "irreparable damage" might occur to the party requesting the relief unless certain acts of the defendant are stopped, the judge may issue an order forbidding the defendant to do such acts. If the defendant disobeys the court order, he may be fined or imprisoned for contempt of court.

The effectiveness of the injunction was based upon the speed with which it could be secured and the manner in which it could be applied. An employer could go into court and secure what is known as an ex parte injunction by alleging that grave and irreparable damage would occur to his business or property if the injunction were not granted. Such an ex parte injunction could be obtained by the employer or his attorney appearing before a single judge, without notice to the union and giving the judge only his side of the story. If the judge granted the request for an injunction—as he usually did—he would issue an order of the court forbidding the union officers and members to do a long list of prohibited acts. Such an order would completely tie up union organizational activities, and at the same time leave the employer free to discharge union members and otherwise act to destroy union organization in his plant before the union could be heard in court. By the time the case was brought to a hearing to determine whether the injunction should be dissolved or made permanent, the employer could often whip the union. If union officials violated any part of the injunction, they could be held in contempt of court and fined or jailed by the court, without trial by jury. This was true whether or not the injunction was made permanent.

The application of injunctions to labor disputes developed rapidly after the *Debs* case of 1895.[2] In that case, Eugene Debs, leader of the Pullman strike,[3] was enjoined by an order obtained by the U.S. govern-

---

[2] *In re Debs,* 158 U.S. 654, 15 S. Ct. 900 (1895).

[3] The strike involved an abortive attempt to establish industrial unionism on the railroads.

ment from continuing a boycott of Pullman cars which, the government alleged, interfered with interstate commerce and the transportation of the mail. Although injunctions had been used in labor disputes prior to this time, the case focused nationwide attention on the injunction technique as a weapon against union organizational activities.

A further development which contributed to the popularity of the injunction as a management tool in labor disputes was the so-called "yellow-dog" contract. This is a contract which an employer requires a worker to sign, stating that as a condition of employment, he agrees not to join a union. The phrase "yellow dog" was applied by unionists at an early date to workers who signed such contracts, and the contracts have been known by that appellation ever since.

In practice, employers made no real attempt to enforce such contracts against the individual workers who signed them. The importance of the contracts was that if they were legal, then attempts by union organizers to compel workers who had signed such contracts to join a union were deliberate efforts to cause a breach of such contracts, and such action could be enjoined by the courts. Unionists maintained that because workers had no choice but to sign such agreements, they were without force or effect. The majority of state courts rejected this view, holding that inequality of bargaining power did not preclude enforcement of contracts. The New York courts, however, accepted labor's point of view.

Because of the general antagonistic attitude of the courts, labor unions attempted at an early date to secure passage of legislation which would outlaw yellow-dog contracts and thus curb the use of this effective antiunion organization weapon. Between 1890 and 1914, no less than 14 states enacted legislation making it a misdemeanor or otherwise unlawful for employers (1) to exact yellow-dog contracts from their employees and (2) to interfere with the right of the employees to join or otherwise belong to a legitimate union. In addition, in 1898, Congress passed the Erdman Act, which contained similar provisions for the benefit of operating employees of the railroads.

The courts, however, declined to view with favor this legislation, which contained the principles of the Wagner Act 40 years before that law was conceived. The Supreme Court found that both the state laws and the pertinent section of the Erdman Act were unconstitutional because the 5th and 14th amendments to the Constitution guarantee freedom of contract as a property right.[4] According to the courts, an employer had a constitutional right to request his employees to sign yellow-dog contracts and to enforce such contracts, and also to discharge his employees

---

[4] *Coppage v. Kansas*, 236 U.S. 1, 35 S. Ct. 240 (1915), which nullified the state laws; and *Adair v. United States*, 208 U.S. 161, 28 S. Ct. 277 (1908), which nullified Section 10 of the Erdman Act.

because of union activities. In short, the courts held that furthering union activities or even preventing interference therewith was not a sufficient promotion of the general welfare to permit interference with the sanctity of contracts, not even if they were yellow-dog contracts. Furthermore, in 1917, in the *Hitchman Coal and Coke* case,[5] the U.S. Supreme Court completely supported the enforceability of yellow-dog contracts. It ruled that a court of equity could issue an injunction restraining attempts to organize employees bound by contracts with their employer not to join a labor union. Needless to say, these decisions caused unionists to take an extremely jaundiced view of the judiciary and to redouble their efforts to curb judicial interference in labor-management relations.

THE APPLICATION OF THE ANTITRUST LAWS TO ORGANIZED LABOR

Section I of the Sherman Act of 1890 states: "Every contract, combination in the form of trust, or otherwise, or conspiracy in restraint of trade or commerce among the several States, or with foreign nations, is hereby declared to be illegal." For some years after this act was passed, there was speculation as to whether or not this broad statutory language applied to labor. Finally, in 1908, in the case of *Loewe* v. *Lawlor*,[6] commonly known as the *Danbury Hatters* case, the U.S. Supreme Court ruled that a nationwide boycott organized by the union to persuade wholesalers and retailers to refrain from buying the company's products was an illegal restraint on commerce. The Court interpreted the statutory phrase, "restraint of trade or commerce," to apply to interference by a union with the interstate shipment of goods. The Court ordered the union to pay treble damages amounting to over half a million dollars, and individual members of the union were held responsible for their share of such damages.

Labor leaders were justifiably concerned about this result and immediately commenced pressure for exemption of labor from the antitrust laws. This drive culminated in the passage of the Clayton Act of 1914. Section 6 of that act declared:

. . . nothing contained in the antitrust laws shall be construed to forbid the existence and operation of labor . . . organizations, instituted for the purposes of mutual help, and not having capital stock or conducted for profits, or to forbid or restrain individual members of such organizations from lawfully carrying out the legitimate objects thereof; nor shall such organizations, or the members thereof, be held or construed to be illegal combinations or conspiracies in restraint of trade under the antitrust laws.

[5] *Hitchman Coal and Coke Co.* v. *Mitchell*, 245 U.S. 229, 38 S. Ct. 65 (1917).
[6] 208 U.S. 274, 28 S. Ct. 301 (1908).

Section 20 of the Clayton Act barred issuance of federal injunctions prohibiting activities such as strikes, boycotts, or picketing "in any case between an employer and employees, or between employers and employees, or between employees, or between persons employed and persons seeking employment, involving or growing out of, a dispute concerning terms or conditions of employment." This same section concludes with a broad statement that none of the acts specified in this paragraph shall be considered violations "of any law of the United States."

Despite this broad language, the U.S. Supreme Court in 1921 in the case of *Duplex Printing Company* v. *Deering*[7] held that the Clayton Act did not give labor unions a complete exemption from the antitrust laws. The case involved a secondary boycott of products of Duplex carried out for the most part by persons who did not stand in a direct employment relationship with Duplex. Construing the language of Section 20 of the Clayton Act narrowly, the Court held that the defendants were not "employees" within the meaning of the Clayton Act and therefore were not entitled to exemption from the Sherman Act. As a result of this decision, which appeared to nullify congressional intent, employers stepped up their use of the injunction as a weapon to curb labor's organizing efforts.

OTHER LEGAL IMPEDIMENTS TO ORGANIZATION

Another major impediment to organization provided by the common law was the freedom of an employer to refuse employment to workers because of union activity. Employers thus could maintain what might be called an "antiunion closed shop." In furtherance of antiunion activities, employers were, in the absence of legislation, free to engage in blacklisting of union members and to utilize labor spies to ferret out union sympathizers. The common law did provide that a worker may not be hounded or libeled in order to prevent him from seeking security or maintaining employment, but this protection proved of little value because the employer also had the right to advise other employers that he had discharged a man because of his union or "radical" sympathies or activities.

More than one half of the states now have laws which outlaw the blacklist, and six states require employers, upon demand, to give discharged employees a truthful statement of the reasons for discharge. These state laws against blacklisting, however, have not been easily enforced, although in at least one case, such a law was used by workers to secure an injunction against the use of the blacklist.[8] It was almost impossi-

---

[7] 254 U.S. 443, 41 S. Ct. 172 (1921).

[8] E. E. Witte, *The Government in Labor Disputes* (New York: McGraw-Hill Book Co., 1932), pp. 212–20.

ble to prevent one employer from telling another over the telephone that Jones, Smith, and Brown were "radical unionists," so that when these three applied for employment to the second employer, they were refused a job on the ground that no vacancies were available. It was not until the passage of the National Labor Relations Act in 1935 that effective protection against blacklisting was finally achieved.

STRIKES, BOYCOTTS, AND PICKETING AND THE COURTS BEFORE 1932

As has been pointed out in the discussion thus far, the courts (in years prior to 1932) tended to interpret both the common law and the statutory law in a manner unfavorable to the development of organized labor. The practical effect of such an antagonistic attitude on the part of the judiciary can best be appreciated by examining its impact on the major weapons a union can utilize to achieve its objectives—the strike, the boycott, and picketing. From the point of view of federal law, it is convenient to consider judicial interpretation prior to 1932 and after 1932, since in that year the Congress enacted the Norris–La Guardia Act, which drastically altered the power of federal courts to intervene in labor disputes.

Strikes

Workers on strike do not ordinarily regard themselves as having terminated their employment relationship. They have left their work temporarily, and in concert, in order to secure more favorable terms of employment. But they regard themselves as having a vested or property right in their jobs. The courts, however, have not recognized this right until very recently—and then only in a modified form. On the whole, courts have been more ready to accept ideas concerning employer property rights than employee property rights—at least until recently.

As was pointed out at the beginning of this chapter, after the courts abandoned the theory of conspiracy, they continued to regulate union conduct by looking into the motives or intent of union conduct. In the case of strikes, this involved an analysis of the purpose or objective of the walkout.

Courts have frequently enjoined the continuance of a strike where the purpose of the strike was to force the employer to cooperate in committing an illegal act. They have also taken similar action in cases where, after weighing the damage done by a strike against the objective sought to be accomplished, they have concluded that the strike was "unjustified." This is, of course, a highly subjective criterion, but it has been widely applied in a variety of circumstances. For example, prior to 1932, judges frequently found sympathetic strikes unlawful. These are strikes by one group of workers in support of another, such as a strike of plumbers out of sympathy for striking gravediggers. Judges have found no possible justification for inflicting loss on the employers of plumbers merely because of a dispute between gravediggers and their employers. Likewise, despite the pathbreaking case of *Commonwealth* v. *Hunt*, many state courts, if not the majority, have condemned strikes to obtain a closed shop. The reason is that the closed shop is regarded as monopolistic and attaching a condition to the right of a worker to obtain employment.

On the other hand, in the case of strikes against technological change and jurisdictional strikes, courts have usually adopted a "hands off" attitude. Although most courts have indicated that they regard strikes aimed at preventing technological advance as harmful to society, they have recognized the problem that such progress often creates for workers and have usually not interfered, in the absence of legislative enactment, with the attempts of unions to retard technological change. Likewise, in the case of jurisdictional strikes—which are contests between unions over which group of workers shall perform a specified piece of work—most courts have declined to enjoin strikes per se. They have regarded jurisdictional strikes as a matter for regulation by the legislative branch of the government.

Lockouts

A lockout is an act by an employer or employers locking out employees from their jobs in an effort to compel them to accede to the terms of employment desired by management. In contrast to the strike, where numbers and relationships may under the conspiracy doctrine make a difference, a lockout under common law may be practiced without legal restriction, whether by a single employer or by employers in combination. What one employer may do, all may do. There is, however, one exception to this common-law principle, and that is that a lockout in violation of a collective agreement may be enjoined. On the other hand, an employer who is a member of an association and obligated thereby to cooperate with his fellow employers may be sued if he fails to cooperate in the lockout activities.

Boycotts

Economic pressure by unions can be exerted in other ways than by strikes. One of the most familiar of labor's weapons has always been the boycott. In a certain sense, all strikes are boycotts. For when workers are on strike, they are "boycotting" their employer and urging all others to do likewise. Such a strike would thus qualify as a "primary" boycott—primary because the strikers are exerting pressure directly on the employer on whom they are making their demands.

Generally, however, strikes are not considered as coming within the meaning of boycotts. In public discussions, the term "boycott" is used almost exclusively to mean an organized refusal to deal with someone in order to induce him to change some practice he follows. Such a boycott may be in the form of a "we do not patronize" list or in other forms of pressure designed to prevent sales of particular products, or it may be a refusal to handle certain goods.

Examples of such pressures are readily found in everyday union activity. Recently, the United Automobile Workers resorted to a nation-wide boycott of Kohler products in its bitter battle against this manufacturer of plumbing wares. In another case, this same union asked its members not to use fishing tackle manufactured by a firm which allegedly had locked out members of the United Steelworkers. Union building-trades men have usually refused to handle materials manufactured under nonunion conditions.

Boycotts of these types are not as simple as strikes because they can involve pressure on third parties. For example, if the United Automobile Workers picketed a store which was selling fishing tackle purchased from the aforementioned firm, it would be engaging in a "secondary boycott" —that is, it would be applying pressure on a third party in order to aid the Steelworkers' fight against the manufacturer directly involved in the dispute.

Before 1932 a majority of American courts held secondary boycotts unlawful per se—"as if it were in a separate category of tort liability."[9] Other courts, however, recognized that labor had an interest in maintaining standards and therefore had a right to engage in boycotts for this purpose. For example, some courts have upheld labor's rights to boycott nonunion products on the ground that the distribution of goods produced under nonunion conditions will depress standards won by the union.

Picketing before the Norris–La Guardia Act

One of the most controversial questions of public policy in the field of labor relations today concerns the extent to which picketing by labor unions should be regulated. A companion question upon which conflicting views are found in the field of labor law involves the extent to which such limitations on the right to picket are constitutionally permissible.

Picketing is a familiar form of pressure utilized by unions which has become an indispensable adjunct of the strike. Picketing usually involves the patrolling of a struck establishment by one or more persons bearing signs or placards stating that the workers are on strike or that the employer is unfair to organized labor, or words of similar effect. The average worker will not pass a picket line. This is based partly on the fear of social ostracism; partly on the feeling that unless he supports the group on strike, they may not support him some day when his union is out on the

---

[9] Charles O. Gregory, *Labor and the Law* (2d rev. ed.; New York: W. W. Norton & Co., Inc., 1961), p. 122.

street; partly on fear of physical violence; sometimes because of fear of sanctions contained in the constitution of his own union. Whatever the motivations, it is clear that the picket line is a most effective weapon. In our highly unionized economy a picket line, manned even by a small group in a large company, can completely paralyze a plant or establishment because other union men who work in the plant, or deliver it supplies, will not cross the picket line.

Picketing may be thought of in two ways. It is a form of expression, letting the public and labor supporters know that a controversy exists and giving labor's side of that controversy. It is also a form of pressure intended to dissuade persons from patronizing or entering a place of business.

At first, the courts took the view that picketing per se was illegal. Later, they grudgingly conceded that picketing was legal as long as it was peacefully conducted and did not bar entrance to and exit from the plant, and as long as it did not obstruct traffic on a public thoroughfare. But while the courts conceded the legality of picketing, they also severely regulated it, often limiting the number of pickets permitted and generally outlawing "stranger picketing"—that is, picketing by persons not employees of the plant. The attitude of the courts on stranger picketing was conditioned by their belief that workers had no interest in a labor controversy unless they were employees of the plant itself, a theory which ignores the relation of labor conditions in one plant with those in another.

Those who believed in labor's right to picket freely did not generally support picketing which prevented entrance and exit into a plant, or picketing which obstructed ordinary commerce on a public thoroughfare. They took the view, however, that picketing was a form of expression and hence, if peacefully conducted, was protected by the first amendment, as are other forms of communication. That viewpoint, however, was almost unanimously rejected by the courts prior to 1932. Indeed, the tendency right up to the passage of the Norris–La Guardia Act was to limit rather than to expand the right of labor to picket in support of its interests.

THE NORRIS–LA GUARDIA ACT

In 1932, when the membership of the American Federation of Labor was the lowest in 20 years, the AFL achieved its greatest legislative triumph to date. After almost 50 years of sustained effort, the AFL succeeded in making the federal judiciary "neutral" in labor disputes. The law which accomplished this result was the Norris–La Guardia Anti-injunction Act, passed by a Democratic-controlled House of Representatives and a Republican Senate, and signed by the then Republican President, Herbert Hoover.

We have seen how labor had been frustrated in its aim to secure passage of legislation which would effectively make lawful the use of union tactics deemed necessary by labor for its survival and successful growth. The Norris–La Guardia Act represented a new approach to this problem. It did not legalize union action; it simply deprived the federal courts of jurisdiction in most situations involving labor disputes. It reflected essentially a laissez-faire philosophy. The law should intervene only to prevent damage to tangible property and to preserve public order; otherwise, the disputants should be left to their own resources to work out their problems. Both labor and business would now be free to promote their own interests in the field of labor policy through self-help, without interference from the courts. The act thus represented a reaction to judicial policy making, which had produced the anomalous result of the same action being enjoinable in one state and not in another. Henceforth, all federal courts were barred from passing judgment as to the lawfulness or unlawfulness of the objectives of labor's actions. This same principle was soon extended to many state courts, for the federal act was immediately copied by a dozen or more state legislatures.

The Norris–La Guardia Act commences with a statement of public policy which affirms the right of workers to engage in collective bargaining through unions of their own choosing. Yellow-dog contracts are declared to be against this public policy, and the federal courts are instructed not to enforce such contracts. Then, Section 4 of the act establishes the following rules for the courts:

> No court of the United States shall have jurisdiction to issue any restraining order or temporary or permanent injunction in any case involving or growing out of any labor dispute to prohibit any person or persons participating or interested in such dispute as these terms are herein defined from doing, whether singly or in concert, any of the following acts:
>
> *a*) Ceasing or refusing to perform any work or to remain in any relation of employment; . . .
>
> .   .   .   .
>
> *e*) Giving publicity to the existence of, or the facts involved in, any labor dispute, whether by advertising, speaking, patrolling, or by any other method not involving fraud or violence.
>
> *f*) Assembling peaceably to act or to organize to act in promotion of their interests in a labor dispute;
>
> *g*) Advising or notifying any person of an intention to do any of the acts heretofore specified;
>
> *h*) Agreeing with other persons to do or not to do any of the acts heretofore specified; and
>
> *i*) Advising, urging, or otherwise causing or inducing without fraud or violence the acts heretofore specified. . . .

The Norris–La Guardia Act has been aptly called "the last monument to the spirit of complete free enterprise for unions."[10] It left unions pretty much free to use their tactical weapons without judicial interfer-

---

[10] Gregory, *op. cit.*, p. 197.

ence. As we shall see, a "liberalized" Supreme Court interpreted the statute broadly so as to confer almost complete immunity on labor leaders in labor disputes. As long as violence was not used, unions could resort to threats, coercion, boycotts, picketing, strikes, and so on without fear of federal court action. Some labor critics say that the act went too far in this direction and that the problems we face today in terms of abuse of union tactics would not have resulted had the Norris–La Guardia Act attempted to make a distinction between lawful and unlawful union objectives, as did the Clayton Act. This is a debatable issue which we shall better understand after discussing the Norris–La Guardia Act and its aftermath.

The act defines "labor dispute" in the broadest possible way so as to preclude judicial constructions, such as occurred in the Clayton Act, which whittled away the effect of the latter law: "The term 'labor dispute' includes any controversy concerning terms or conditions of employment, or concerning the association or representation of persons in negotiating, fixing, maintaining, changing or seeking to arrange terms or conditions of employment, regardless of whether or not the disputants stand in the proximate relation of employer and employee." It will be observed that Congress specifically took account of the fact that organized labor had a valid interest in conditions of employment even where it did not represent a single employee and that although such a situation did not involve a dispute technically between "an employer" and its "employees," nevertheless the protection afforded by the Norris–La Guardia Act was applicable.

The act, in effect, outlawed injunctions in labor disputes except where violence is involved. Even in such cases, the granting of injunctions is severely restricted. The act provides that except for a five-day restraining order, no injunction may be granted restraining unlawful activities of a union in labor disputes cases except on a full hearing in open court. Furthermore, before the court can issue an injunction, it must find that unlawful acts have been and will be committed unless restrained; that the plaintiff will suffer substantial and irreparable injury; that as to each item of relief sought, greater injury will be inflicted upon the plaintiff by the denial of relief than will be inflicted upon the defendants by granting it; that the plaintiff has no adequate remedy at law; and that the police officers of the community are unwilling or unable to furnish adequate protection. Moreover, even if the above findings are made, the act provides that no relief shall be granted a plaintiff involved in the labor dispute who has failed to comply with any obligation imposed by law or who has failed to make every reasonable effort to settle the dispute by negotiation or any available governmental machinery of mediation or voluntary arbitration. It is understandable after reading this long catalog of conditions that union attorneys are generally able to frustrate the attempt of management attorneys to secure injunctions even in cases where the union may have engaged in violence, intimidation, and other unlawful acts which were not intended to be protected by the act.

The Norris–La Guardia Act and the Courts

With a single piece of legislation, Congress thus repealed a century of judicial interpretation and created laissez-faire, or economic free enterprise, for organized labor as well as for business. Henceforth the courts were not to interfere with strikes, boycotts, and picketing which were conducted peacefully and otherwise within the law. Moreover, by defining "labor dispute" in a broad fashion, Congress insured labor's right to engage in sympathy strikes, secondary boycotts, stranger picketing, and other activities where nonemployees of a concern come to the aid of the concern's employees in labor disputes directly or by applying pressure upon third parties.

Reversal of Sherman Act Decisions

The combined effect of the Norris–La Guardia Act and the liberalized view of labor disputes which the Supreme Court adopted after 1937 resulted in a revision of precedents on the application of the Sherman Act to organized labor. Commencing in 1940, the Supreme Court handed down a group of landmark decisions which seemed to delineate the legal status of unions under the antitrust laws. Three leading cases—*Apex Hosiery Co.* v. *Leader*,[11] *United States* v. *Hutcheson*,[12] and *Allen-Bradley Co.* v. *Local 3, International Brotherhood of Electrical Workers*[13]— broadly defined the permissible limits of concerted union activity, and suggested that unions are subject to the antitrust laws under existing legislation only:[14]

1. Where the union intends to achieve some commercial restraint primarily and not as a by-product of its essential intent to advance its own cause.
2. Where union activity is not in the course of a labor dispute as broadly defined by the Norris-La Guardia Act.
3. Where a union combines with some nonlabor group to achieve some direct commercial restraint.

The extended immunity granted to labor from the antitrust laws and the injunction was followed to its logical conclusion in other decisions, to which we have already referred in Chapter 7. Their combined effect was to permit unions to perform many acts which the law classifies as illegal when done by other groups or organizations within the community. It is

---

[11] 310 U.S. 469, 60 S. Ct. 982 (1940).

[12] 312 U.S. 219, 61 S. Ct. 463 (1941).

[13] 325 U.S. 797, 65 S. Ct. 1533 (1945).

[14] See "Should Labor Unions Be Subject to Antitrust Laws?" *Congressional Digest*, October, 1961, p. 231.

not surprising, therefore, that this line of decisions, together with the tremendous growth in economic power of organized labor in the past few decades, produced a demand in some circles for new legislation which would "subject labor to the antitrust laws."

Then on June 7, 1965, the U.S. Supreme Court handed down two landmark decisions which seemed to indicate that unions might not be as immune from antitrust liability as was generally thought. Both of these cases were brought by employers against unions alleging violations of Sections 1 and 2 of the Sherman Antitrust Act. In the so-called *Pennington* case,[15] the employer alleged that the United Mine Workers had conspired with large coal operators to force smaller operators, including the plaintiff, out of business by raising wage rates and fringe benefits in the big companies and then forcing these rates on the smaller companies with the knowledge that the latter would have to close down. Although the case was remanded for a new trial because of an error in the instruction given to the jury by the trial judge, the Supreme Court held that if the United Mine Workers had in fact conspired with the major coal operators to drive the smaller operators out of business by requiring them to sign wage agreements which they could not afford, they would be guilty of a violation of the Sherman Act.

The *Pennington* case is of paramount importance for two reasons. In the first place, it reversed the generally accepted assumption which prevailed until that time that any union action relating to wage agreements with employers was exempt from the antitrust laws. The *Pennington* decision indicates that a union agreement with one employer or group of employers with respect to wages, hours, or working conditions that the union will seek to negotiate with *other* employers is not exempt from prosecution. In the second place, the trial court left it to the jury to determine as a *question of fact* whether there was a purpose among the alleged conspirators to impose a national contract upon the small producers with the intent of restraining trade and driving them out of business or whether the purpose was to improve working conditions, compensation, and other legitimate union objectives. This sounds very much like the old judicial tests of legality of union action which sought to determine "motive" and "intent."

In the *Jewel Tea* case,[16] decided on the same day, the company claimed that the Meat Cutters Union had violated the Sherman Act by negotiating agreements with Chicago food stores which provided that meat could not be sold before 9 A.M. or after 6 P.M., even if there were no butchers in the store. Jewel maintained that the union's insistence on the marketing-hours provision was part of a conspiracy between the union

[15] *United Mine Workers* v. *Pennington*, S. Ct. 59 LRRM 2369, 381 U.S. 657 (1965).

[16] *Local 189, Amalgamated Meat Cutters* v. *Jewel Tea Company*, 59 LRRM 2376, 381 U.S. 674 (1965).

and the Associated Food Retailers of Greater Chicago, which represents the independent food stores and meat dealers. Although the company lost its case before the High Court, the actual decision represented a loss for organized labor; for the Court's opinion made it clear that if the trial judge had not found, as a question of fact, that there was an intimate connection between hours of work and hours of sale, the agreement negotiated by the union might well have been a violation of the Sherman Act. Here again, as in the *Pennington* case, the Supreme Court has indicated that findings of fact arrived at in a courtroom by a jury or by a trial judge sitting without a jury can impose liability on unions under the antitrust laws, even though the subject matter involves an issue which unions can reasonably believe is a proper subject for collective bargaining.

While critics of organized labor may draw comfort from these cases, the decisions will do little to curb the abuses of which most businessmen complain, yet will add an additional element of uncertainty into the collective bargaining process. "Bringing labor under the antitrust laws" is not really a satisfactory solution for labor problems. Our existing antitrust laws have not been particularly successful in preventing monopoly in industry, and court decisions have been notably unsuccessful in clarifying in businessmen's minds what is lawful and unlawful in this complicated field of law. To inject the courts into this area would simply add confusion rather than solve the problem. What is needed is specific legislation aimed at eliminating particular abuses upon which there is general agreement that governmental action must be taken. For example, consideration should be given to a comprehensive review of the Norris–La Guardia Act to adapt it to the current labor scene. It should be remembered that when that act was passed, there was no Wagner Act or Taft-Hartley Act; and furthermore, organized labor had not achieved its present position of strength in industry at large. Many labor experts agree that the original purpose of the Norris–La Guardia Act has long since been fulfilled and that the statute is in many respects obsolete.

PICKETING AFTER THE NORRIS–LA GUARDIA ACT

As we have seen, the enactment of the Norris–La Guardia Act in 1932 substantially limited the power of the federal courts to issue injunctions in labor disputes. State courts, however, continued to enjoin picketing under a variety of circumstances and for a variety of reasons, except where the power of state courts had been circumscribed by the enactment of state "little Norris–La Guardia acts," modeled after the federal statute.

In passing judgment on the legality of strikes, courts sometimes made a distinction between organizational picketing and recognition picketing. The former is said to involve picketing by a minority union directed to the employees of an employer in order to persuade them to become union members or to win their adherence to the union cause. The latter is directed to the employer in order to compel him to recognize the minority union; in effect, it brings pressure on the employer to force the employees to join the picketing union. In practice, it is difficult to make a valid distinction between the two forms of picketing, for either type, if effective, will bring economic pressure to bear upon both employer and employees, with the objective of compelling recognition of the minority union as the bargaining representative for the employees.

Before considering the attitude of the courts toward picketing since enactment of the Norris–La Guardia Act, it may be helpful to explore the conflicting arguments, pro and con, advanced by union and management spokesmen on the subject of picketing. Should recognition picketing be permitted, prohibited, or restricted, and under what circumstances? For the purpose of this discussion, we shall consider organizational and recognition picketing as being substantially the same, since the same arguments are in general applicable to the two types of picketing.

Arguments Favoring Unrestricted Recognition Picketing

Union spokesmen argue that the picket line is labor's most effective organizing device. They contend that many employers are still extremely hostile to labor and can prevent employees from really expressing their desires unless the union can apply economic pressure. They argue further that unions must have the right to picket even after dismissal of a representation case or loss of an election because employers sometimes maneuver unions into an election proceeding before the union is really ready, and therefore the union must be able to continue to try to get its message across to employees. Finally, union spokesmen contend that they have a basic right to try to cure conditions which threaten the maintenance of wages and other working conditions in organized companies. If most of an industry is organized, for example, but a few employers are nonunion, pay low rates, and cut prices, they can demoralize the entire industry. Unions maintain that under such circumstances, they must have the right to continue to picket and bring pressure on the nonunion employer until he has been organized. If attaining this objective requires some employees to join the union against their will, union spokesmen feel that this is still in accord with democratic procedures because the union must look to the wishes of the majority of workers in the industry, not in an individual plant.

Arguments Favoring Restriction of Recognition Picketing

Management spokesmen who contend that recognition picketing should be prohibited usually begin with the Taft-Hartley Act itself (or similar state labor relations acts) as the basis for their argument. That act and its predecessor (the Wagner Act) were intended to reduce the many industrial disputes arising out of the problem of selection of a collective bargaining representative. Furthermore, it was made clear in the Taft-Hartley Act that employees were to be free *not* to join a union if they did

not want to. In view of these acts, the argument runs, recognition picketing should be prohibited. Union organizers can still distribute literature at
plant gates and hold meetings to explain their position to employees.
Beyond that, the peaceful machinery of the National Labor Relations
Board and state labor relations boards should be substituted for the
economic pressure and violence generated by the picket line. This argument is particularly forceful when the peaceful machinery has been used
and the union has lost. The management viewpoint is put cogently by
former NLRB member, Joseph A. Jenkins, who, in his concurring opinion in the *Curtis* case, said: "I do not believe that Congress intended to or
did write a statute providing for elections conducted at public expense
which are to be considered binding if the union wins, but not binding if
the union loses."[17]

If recognition picketing can continue indefinitely even after a union
has been decisively rejected by employees in an NLRB election, a small
employer cannot possibly withstand the pressures which can be applied
by a powerful union. Opponents of unrestricted picketing emphasize the
coercive aspects in picketing and the tremendous power this weapon
confers on union leaders, who can break many businesses at their whim.
They question whether the picket line, as an organizing device, is entitled
to the same protection today, when organized labor numbers 18 million, as
when its membership was a weak 3 million.

Picketing and Free Speech

Commencing in 1937, a series of cases was brought before the U.S.
Supreme Court involving the question whether picketing could be restricted by state legislatures and courts or whether it was protected from
such regulation as a form of free speech guaranteed by the first amendment of the federal Constitution. These cases are of major interest to
students of labor problems not only because they concern a major union
weapon—picketing—but also because they indicate how the changing
views of the Supreme Court may influence the pattern of state legislative
and judicial control of labor relations and thus profoundly affect the
evolution of collective bargaining in our society. As will appear more
fully in the following discussion, it seems in retrospect that the Supreme
Court first became intrigued with the idea of treating picketing as a form
of free speech entitled to constitutional protection and then retreated
from this position when it recognized the coercive elements present in
picketing and the legitimate right of the states to limit picketing in certain
instances to protect the public interest.

In 1937, in a case which affirmed the right of a state to enact a "little
Norris–La Guardia Act," Justice Louis D. Brandeis remarked: "Members
of a union might without special statutory authorization by a State make
known the facts of a labor dispute, for freedom of speech is guaranteed by

---

[17] *Curtis Brothers, Inc.*, 41 LRRM 1025, 1033.

the Federal Constitution."[18] This statement was misconstrued by many lawyers and judges to mean that picketing was a form of free speech guaranteed by the Constitution. Actually, Justice Brandeis merely said that union members might make known the facts of a dispute, without stating what means they might use for this purpose. He did not say that union members had a constitutional right to make known facts by means of a picket line. Nevertheless, three years later, in the case of *Thornhill* v. *Alabama*,[19] the Supreme Court completely accepted the doctrine that picketing was a form of free speech. An Alabama law, which termed picketing a form of loitering and made it a misdemeanor, was held unconstitutional on the ground that picketing is a form of speech protected by the first amendment and that a penal statute which makes picketing a misdemeanor without regard to the manner in which it is conducted is unconstitutional on its face. In the companion case of *Carlson* v. *California*[20] the Supreme Court elaborated the doctrine of picketing as a form of speech in the following words: "Publicizing the facts of a labor dispute in a peaceful way through appropriate means, whether by pamphlet, by word of mouth or by banner, must now be regarded as within that liberty of communication which is secured to every person by the Fourteenth Amendment against abridgement by a State." And in 1941, in *American Federation of Labor* v. *Swing*,[21] the U.S. Supreme Court held unconstitutional the decision of the Illinois Supreme Court enjoining peaceful stranger picketing of a beauty parlor when none of the employees of the beauty parlor were members of the union conducting the picketing.

However, the notion that picketing is merely a form of free speech did not prove very satisfactory, in view of the coercive elements usually present in picketing. As a result, the U.S. Supreme Court slowly began to modify its views. In 1941, the Supreme Court refused to set aside an Illinois injunction which forbade all picketing by a milk drivers' union where there had been a background of previous violence.[22] In three important cases handed down in 1950, the Supreme Court held that the state courts could constitutionally restrict picketing which had as its objective action which violated a state statute or was deemed contrary to public policy.[23]

---

[18] *Senn.* v. *Tile Layers' Protective Union*, 301 U.S. 468, 57 S. Ct. 857 (1937).

[19] 310 U.S. 88, 60 S. Ct. 736 (1940).

[20] 310 U.S. 106, 113; 60 S. Ct. 746, 749 (1940).

[21] 312 U.S. 321, 61 S. Ct. 568 (1941).

[22] *Milk Wagon Drivers* v. *Meadowmoor Dairies, Inc.*, 312 U.S. 287, 61 S. Ct. 552 (1941).

[23] *Building Service International Union* v. *Gazzam*, 339 U.S. 532, 70 S. Ct. 784 (1950); *Hughes* v. *Superior Court of State of California*, 339 U.S. 460, 70 S. Ct. 718 (1950); *International Brotherhood of Teamsters* v. *Hanke*, 339 U.S. 470, 70 S. Ct. 773 (1950).

Finally, in *Vogt* v. *Teamsters*,[24] the Supreme Court upheld the action of a Wisconsin court in enjoining simple stranger picketing, thus fully acknowledging the retreat from the Thornhill doctrine and amounting, as the dissenters observed, to "formal surrender." Speaking for a majority of the Supreme Court, Justice Felix Frankfurter stated that picketing is fully subject to the right of the states to balance the social interests between employers and unions, provided only that the states' policies are rational. Although Justice Frankfurter noted that the states could not, under the Thornhill doctrine, proscribe all picketing per se, he made it clear that state courts and legislatures are free to decide whether to permit or suppress any particular picket line for any reason other than a blanket policy against picketing.[25] One commentator concludes that this decision "sounded the death knell for organizational picketing in intrastate commerce, as far as the federal Constitution is concerned."[26]

In May, 1968, in the *Logan Valley Plaza* case,[27] the Supreme Court, again expressly equating picketing with the right of free speech under the first amendment, voided an injunction by a state court against picketing carried on in a shopping center on private property. In this case, a union which was attempting to organize a supermarket located in a shopping center carried on peaceful picketing in the parking lot and on the sidewalk and parcel pickup area of the market. The state court had issued an injunction against such picketing and compelled the union to picket out on the highway which was obviously much less effective. In a divided opinion, the Court held that because the shopping center serves as the community business block and is freely accessible and open to people in the area, the state court could not, through the use of the doctrine of trespass, infringe on the privilege of persons to exercise their rights of free speech. The Court went on to say, however, that the fact that it was invalidating a blanket injunction against *all* picketing in the center did not mean that the owners could not prescribe reasonable regulations as to where the picketing could be carried on within the shopping center.

This decision not only frees unions from what had been a major handicap in carrying out effective picketing as part of organizing drives in the retail business but also raises some disturbing questions as to how far

---

[24] 354 U.S. 284, 77 S. Ct. 31 (1956).

[25] However, states cannot enact laws restricting peaceful picketing in a manner which deprives workers of rights guaranteed under the Taft-Hartley Act. Thus, for example, the U.S. Supreme Court has held unlawful a Virginia statute which imposed a fine on any person participating in picketing who was not a "bona fide" employee of the business or industry being picketed. Such a law against stranger picketing would be inconsistent with the Taft-Hartley Act, which makes no distinction as to whether a person picketing is an employee or not. See *Waxman* v. *Commonwealth of Virginia*, 51 LRRM 2221 (October 8, 1962).

[26] T. L. Bornstein, "Organizational Picketing in American Law," *Kentucky Law Review*, Fall, 1957, pp. 25 and 56.

[27] *Amalgamated Food Employees Local 590* v. *Logan Valley Plaza*, 68 LRRM 2209, 88 Sup. Ct. 1601 (1968).

the right of free speech can be exercised at the expense of the equally protected constitutional right of private property.

The cases referred to above all arose as the result of efforts of state courts and legislatures to prohibit or restrict picketing. The federal government has also passed legislation restricting labor's right to picket. These restrictions are embodied in the Taft-Hartley Act and in the Landrum-Griffin Act, which we shall consider in detail in Chapters 21 and 22. In 1951, the Supreme Court, in a decision consistent with its changed viewpoint toward picketing, held that the provisions of the Taft-Hartley Act banning certain types of picketing in connection with secondary boycotts did not violate constitutional guarantees of free speech.[28]

Present Status of Picketing

As far as federal law is concerned, picketing by unions for either organizational or recognitional purposes is now subject to major limitations imposed by the Landrum-Griffin Act in 1959. We shall examine these provisions in detail in Chapter 22. The Congress, in adopting these restrictive provisions, attempted to make a distinction between picketing which is coercive in effect and that which is designed solely to inform the public of a labor dispute and does not have the effect of interfering with deliveries to a business establishment. As we shall learn from our analysis of these statutory provisions, such a distinction is extremely difficult to apply in practice. Decisions of the NLRB on this subject have been so confusing that neither labor nor management today can be wholly certain as to the legality of a picket line.

BOYCOTTS AFTER THE NORRIS–LA GUARDIA ACT

We have seen that the Norris–La Guardia Act deprived the federal courts of jurisdiction in most cases involving labor disputes. However, its effect upon such union tactics as boycotts was even broader, for the U.S. Supreme Court interpreted the Norris–La Guardia Act as not only depriving the federal courts of jurisdiction to enjoin labor tactics enumerated in Section 4 of that act, but also as making such acts lawful for all purposes under federal law. This momentous decision was enunciated by the Court in the *Hutcheson* case,[29] which involved a secondary boycott organized by a carpenters' union against the Anheuser-Busch Brewing Company. The Court held that because of the intervention of the Norris–La Guardia Act, which had "infused new spirit" into the Clayton Act, such union conduct did not violate the Sherman Act, even though in 1908 it had reached a contrary conclusion on similar facts in the *Danbury Hatters* case.

[28] *International Brotherhood of Electrical Workers* v. *National Labor Relations Board*, 341 U.S. 694, 71 S. Ct. 954 (1951).

[29] *United States* v. *Hutcheson*, 312 U.S. 219, 61 S. Ct. 463 (1941).

As a result of a more liberal judicial attitude reflecting the spirit of the Norris–La Guardia and Wagner acts, by the late 1930's and early 1940's union boycotts were no longer repressed by federal courts. The result was a major expansion in the use of the secondary boycott by organized labor. Strategically placed unions, particularly in the field of distribution, were able to expand their sphere of organization by bringing pressure on persons whose only relation to the dispute was that they did business with the particular employer involved. The Teamsters exerted additional pressure on nonunion employers by obtaining "hot cargo" agreements, in which employers agreed not to deal with nonunion employers.

The abuses which arose from the widespread use of such tactics by organized labor, together with the rash of strikes in 1947, led to a demand for restrictive labor legislation. The Taft-Hartley Act, passed in that year, had as one of its prime objectives the outlawing of all secondary boycotts. As we shall observe in our discussion of this act in Chapter 21, the provisions directed against secondary boycotts were poorly drawn and left many loopholes. Additional statutory restrictions aimed at closing these loopholes were incorporated in the Landrum-Griffin Act, which will be analyzed in Chapter 22.

LIMITATIONS ON THE RIGHT TO STRIKE

Writers are often prone to equate the right to strike with democracy and a free labor market. It has been said that preservation of the right to strike is what distinguishes our economy from those of Communist nations and that if this right is compromised, then other individual rights will also suffer. Actually, however, the right to strike has been limited in a number of important respects by the Taft-Hartley and Landrum-Griffin Acts, and yet economic democracy still flourishes in our country. The change from the era of uninhibited union action under the Norris–La Guardia Act is a rather remarkable one and is deserving of closer scrutiny.

Strike action can be divided into two general categories—primary and secondary. A primary strike is a strike which occurs in connection with a labor dispute and directly involves the employer of the striking workers. A secondary strike is a strike which is aimed at an employer other than the employer of the striking workers. Suppose the carpenters on a construction job strike for higher wages. This is a primary strike directed against their employer, who, let us say, is the general contractor on the job. Now, a nonunion flooring subcontractor brings in nonunion men to put down asphalt tile flooring in the building. The carpenters go on strike in protest against the use of nonunion workers on the job. This is a secondary strike.

While it is difficult to generalize in such a complicated field, it can be said that the law generally permits primary strike activity and prohibits secondary strike activity. A similar rule applies to picketing. There are, however, important exceptions. All secondary strike activity is not unlawful; and on the other hand, there are many kinds of primary strike activity which are either prohibited or subject to limitations under our statutes. Let us examine some of the major types of primary strike activity which are restricted by federal law.

Strikes against Public Policy as Set Forth in Federal Statutes

In this category would fall strikes which directly violate or compel an employer to violate restrictive provisions contained in labor laws such as the Taft-Hartley law. Thus, for example, it is unlawful for a union to strike to compel an employer to recognize one union when another union has already been certified as the collective bargaining agency by the NLRB. The NLRB has held that it is unlawful for a union to strike to compel an employer to sign a "hot cargo" contract in the construction industry, even though the statute expressly permits such contracts if voluntarily made. A strike for a closed shop is unlawful under the Taft-Hartley Act, and it is also unlawful in many states under common law.

Strikes Arising out of Jurisdictional Disputes

The Taft-Hartley Act makes it an unfair labor practice for a union to engage in a strike to force or require any employer to assign particular work to employees in a particular labor organization or in a particular trade, craft, or class rather than to employees in another labor organization or in another trade, craft, or class, unless such employer is failing to conform to an order or certification of the Board determining the bargaining representative for employees performing such work. The law further provides that whenever it is charged that there has been a violation of this section, "the Board is empowered and directed to hear and determine the dispute out of which such unfair labor practice shall have arisen." The U.S. Supreme Court has held that this provision means that the Board must inquire into the merits of the dispute and then make a binding award of the work.[30] The Board has discretionary authority to seek an injunction against jurisdictional strikes in violation of the statute. As a result of these statutory provisions, the NLRB is now required to determine jurisdictional disputes by what amounts to compulsory arbitration.

Strikes during the Term of a Valid Collective Bargaining Agreement

A strike to compel a change in the terms of a contract prior to the expiration date of the contract has been held to be unlawful under the Taft-Hartley Act. This is true whether or not the contract contains a

[30] *National Labor Relations Board* v. *Radio Engineers Union,* 47 LRRM 2332, 364 U.S. 578 (1961).

no-strike agreement. A strike in violation of a collective bargaining agreement is not protected concerted activity under the Taft-Hartley Act, and may constitute an unfair labor practice.[31] A strike during the term of a contract over grievances or in protest over employer unfair labor practices is not, however, unlawful (unless in violation of a no-strike clause).

Section 301 of the Taft-Hartley Act provides that suits for violation of contracts between an employer and a union may be brought in any district court of the United States. The remedy of the employer would normally be damages for breach of contract, for the U.S. Supreme Court has held that the Norris–La Guardia Act bars issuance of an injunction in such cases.

The Taft-Hartley Act specifically prohibits strikes called before the end of a 60-day notice period prior to the expiration of collective bargaining agreements. This provision was included in the law in order to give conciliation agencies sufficent time to meet with the parties and attempt to resolve disputes before a walkout occurs.

Strikes against the Government as Employer

Most governmental bodies—federal, state, and municipal—forbid strikes by employees on the ground that such strikes are against the sovereign and therefore against the public interest. Section 305 of the Taft-Hartley Act makes it unlawful for any individual employed by the United States or any agency thereof, including wholly owned government corporations, to participate in any strike. The problem of government employees and the right to strike will be more fully explored in Chapter 23.

National Emergency Strikes

The Taft-Hartley Act contains provisions enabling the government to obtain a temporary injunction in cases involving strikes which imperil or threaten to endanger the national health or safety. After such an injunction is obtained, the strike action becomes unlawful. These provisions will be discussed in Chapter 23.

The foregoing brief outline describes the status of strikes in interstate commerce where federal labor laws are applicable. Where state law is applicable to a local dispute, the results will depend upon the provisions of the state statute, or upon common law in the absence of an applicable statute. Basically, courts, in the absence of statutes to guide them, still apply the old rule of ends and means. If the ends are illegal, the court is likely to enjoin the strike, no matter how peaceful the means used may be. This result reflects the historical judicial attitude that a strike is fundamentally an intentional tortious interference with an advantageous business

---

[31] *United Mine Workers of America* (Boone County Coal Corp.), 117 NLRB 1095 (1957); enforcement denied, 257 F. (2d) 211 (D.C. Cir. 1958). Cf. *Boeing Airplane Co.* v. *National Labor Relations Board*, 174 F. (2d) 988 (D.C. Cir. 1949).

relationship and therefore should only be permitted if it is carried on for a proper purpose. Strikes to improve working conditions are generally held to be a valid purpose, but a strike for a closed shop may still be held lawful in one state and illegal in another.

LIMITATIONS ON THE RIGHT TO LOCK OUT

Labor legislation in this country has gradually deprived employers of most of the effective tactical weapons which they used in the past to combat efforts of unions to organize their employees. We have seen how the Norris–La Guardia Act outlawed the yellow-dog contract and barred injunctions against unions in federal court—thus eliminating two devices which had been widely used to discourage union organizing efforts. Likewise, the unfair labor practice provisions of the Wagner and Taft-Hartley laws restricted other tactics frequently utilized by antiunion employers, such as discriminatory hiring and firing practices, spying on employees, antiunion speeches, and so forth. While this restrictive legislation was primarily intended to prevent employers from obstructing the efforts of employees to organize and bargain through representatives of their own choosing, it also had the effect of weakening the tactical position of employers who reach an impasse in bargaining with unions over economic issues. For example, the Norris–La Guardia Act and the state statutes patterned after it have made it extremely difficult—and sometimes impossible—to halt mass picketing, vandalism, and other violence which sometimes results from efforts of management to bring employees through a picket line into a struck plant. As a consequence, most employers are reluctant to run a plant with strikebreakers, even though they have a legal right to do so. The Norris–La Guardia Act, therefore, tends to make the picket line a more effective weapon for imposing economic losses upon the employer and consequently gives the union a strategic advantage in collective bargaining.

There is another effective employer tactical weapon which is relatively little used and about which little has been written. That is the right to lock out. In some respects, the employer's right to lock out his employees may be thought of as paralleling the employees' right to withhold their services through strike action. Just as the right to strike has been subjected to restrictions where it contravenes certain purposes, so the employer's right to shut down operations has been held to be a limited managerial prerogative. Although, with minor exceptions,[32] there are no

---

[32] The Taft-Hartley Act prohibits lockouts (and strikes) for a period of 60 days after notice is given of a proposed modification or expiration of a collective bargaining agreement (Section 8 [*d*] [4]). In addition, lockouts (and strikes) which imperil the national health and safety are subject to injunction for a limited period of time during the fact-finding procedure prescribed by Section 206 of the Taft-Hartley Act.

statutory prohibitions against use of the lockout, nevertheless, as a result of decisions of the NLRB and the courts, the lockout has been so circumscribed by restrictions that an employer involved in a labor dispute would be ill advised to shut down his plant without first obtaining competent legal advice.

In the first place, it is clear that an employer cannot use the lockout as a device to avoid union organization. The Taft-Hartley Act prohibits discharges of employees where the purpose is to discourage membership in a labor organization. Since an employer cannot discharge individual employees in order to deter unionization, it is not surprising that both the NLRB and the courts have held that he cannot shut down an entire plant and lay off all employees in order to accomplish the same result. Of course, employers will generally point to some economic reason for the shutdown, while union spokesmen will claim that the action was taken to break the union. Cases which come before the NLRB on this issue usually involve complex factual situations susceptible of either interpretation, which tends to complicate the problem presented to the Board for determination.

In the second place, the rule has been established that an employer cannot seek to avoid his commitment under an existing union contract or to wrest bargaining concessions from a union by shutting down his plant and moving to another area. In such cases, the NLRB has usually required the employer to offer employment to the former employees at the new location, to pay their moving expenses to such new location, and, in addition, to make the employees whole for the loss they may have suffered by reason of the unlawful discharge.

In the third place, the NLRB for many years looked upon the lockout as a lawful employer weapon only where unusual economic circumstances justified it as a *defensive* measure against a threatened strike. The Board condemned lockouts by individual employers undertaken in the course of collective bargaining negotiations to bring pressure on the union for a satisfactory settlement. Although the union can strike to enforce its demands, the NLRB had generally taken the position that a lockout in such circumstances would interfere with the protected concerted activities of the employees. For example, in the *American Brake Shoe*[33] case, the Board said that if an anticipatory lockout were to be permitted as lawful, the employer would be immunized from effective strike action and the employees' right to strike would be rendered virtually meaningless.

However, in 1965, in the *American Shipbuilding*[34] case, the U.S. Supreme Court held that a company did not violate the Taft-Hartley Act when, after an impasse had been reached in contract negotiations, it shut

[33] 116 NLRB 832.
[34] 58 LRRM 2672, 380 U.S. 300 (1965).

down its plant and laid off the employees for the purpose of bringing pressure to bear on the union which was threatening to strike during the company's busiest season. Although in subsequent decisions, the Board has indicated it views this decision as obliterating any distinction between offensive and defensive lockouts, the Board is still unwilling to place the right to lockout on the same basis as the right to strike.

Both the NLRB and the courts have permitted so-called "defensive" multiemployer lockouts in situations where a number of employers in an industry bargain jointly with a union. If during the course of negotiations, a union should strike one company, the other companies can lock out their employees in retaliation for the union's selective strike and as a defensive measure against the union's whipsaw technique. On the basis of the Court's reasoning in *American Shipbuilding*, an offensive lockout by an employer or employers in a multiunit bargaining situation would also appear to be legal, at least if it is deferred until an impasse has been reached in negotiations.

Much of the fear of the NLRB about the effects of an unrestricted lockout policy seems to be unwarranted; for a lockout still deprives the employer of the opportunity to carry on business. It precipitates what the employer normally hopes to avoid and therefore is not likely to be widely used regardless of a more liberal trend in the decisions. It is most likely to be resorted to in multiemployer bargaining situations and in cases where an individual employer wishes to forestall a union which is prone to resort to quickie strikes and violence.[35]

QUESTIONS FOR DISCUSSION

1. What is meant by the term "injunction"? Discuss the manner in which the injunction has been used to impede labor's organizational efforts. To what extent can employers still use the injunction in labor disputes?

2. Should all picketing be treated as a form of free speech? Discuss the changing attitude of the U.S. Supreme Court on this issue.

3. What are the points of similarity between the strike and the lockout? In what way do the two actions differ? Should employers have the same freedom to lockout as unions have to strike?

4. Should unions be subject to the antitrust laws? Discuss the validity of the tests established by the *Pennington* and *Jewel Tea* cases as criteria for determining whether or not the Sherman Act prohibitions are applicable to concerted action by employees.

[35] Edward R. Lev, "Suggestions to Management: The Lockout," *Labor Law Journal*, Vol. XIX (February, 1968), p. 107.

SUGGESTIONS FOR FURTHER READING

Lev, Edward R. "Suggestions to Management: The Lockout," *Labor Law Journal,* Vol. XIX (February, 1968), pp. 80–111.

A review of cases on employer lockouts at the NLRB and court level by a writer critical of the Board's approach.

"Should Labor Unions Be Subject to Antitrust Laws?" *Congressional Digest,* October, 1961.

An entire issue devoted to a discussion of the pros and cons of application of the antitrust laws to organized labor.

Stewart, Frank H., and Townsend, Robert J. "Strike Violence: The Need for Federal Injunctions," *University of Pennsylvania Law Review,* Vol. CXIV (1966), pp. 459–486.

An article contending that the Norris–La Guardia Act should be amended so that federal courts can enjoin violence in labor disputes.

"Union-Employer Agreements and the Antitrust Laws: The Pennington and Jewel Tea Cases," *University of Pennsylvania Law Review,* Vol. CXIV (1966), pp. 901 ff.

A concise analysis of the significance of the Pennington and Jewel Tea cases.

Chapter 21

THE TAFT-HARTLEY ACT

Since its enactment in 1947, the Labor-Management Relations Act of 1947—more popularly known as the Taft-Hartley Act—has been the subject of controversy. Although at its inception it was most criticized by labor leaders, who characterized it as a "slave labor law," it is now widely condemned by businessmen, who argue that the NLRB has interpreted the act in a manner inconsistent with the intent of Congress. In this chapter, we shall consider in detail various provisions of this act and its effect upon employers, unions, individual employees, and the general public. Since the Taft-Hartley Act is, in form, an amendment of the earlier National Labor Relations Act, or Wagner Act, as it is commonly known, we shall commence our discussion with a brief consideration of the Wagner Act.

THE WAGNER ACT

Legislative Background and Statutory Policy

The Wagner Act was enacted largely because of the failure on the part of American employers to modernize their concepts of industrial relations by giving employees an opportunity to participate in the determination of wages, hours, and working conditions. The failure of industry to alter its long-standing policies and voluntarily to recognize unions of its employees was all the more remarkable in view of the ample warnings that if industry did not act, government would be compelled to do so. Commencing in 1885, a long list of government commissions, agencies, and (in later years) statutes contained governmental endorsement of the principle of collective bargaining. In 1898, Congress passed the Erdman Act, which contained provisions making discrimination against union activity on the railroads a misdemeanor. Although this provision was declared unconstitutional, later railway legislation, including the Railway Labor Act of 1926, endorsed unionism and collective bargaining. Between 1890 and 1914, no less than 14 states enacted legislation similar to the Erdman Act, only to have the courts declare such laws unconstitutional. Both the

Norris–La Guardia Act of 1932 and the National Industrial Recovery Act of 1933 contained statements of policy endorsing the right of employees to bargain through representatives of their own choosing, but neither act contained effective penalties in case of employer disinclination to conform to these statutory purposes.

In 1935, Congress passed the Wagner Act, which, in retrospect, appears to be the most significant labor law ever enacted in the United States. Congress virtually ordered employers to stop interfering with the efforts of unions to organize their employees. It put the power of the federal government behind the union organizer, assuring him that employees could make the choice whether or not to join a union without fear of employer interference. Moreover, in contrast to earlier legislation, the Wagner Act provided an effective mechanism to secure compliance by employers. The Wagner Act, therefore, required a completely new orientation of employer industrial relations policies.

The heart of the substantive provisions of the Wagner Act is contained in Section 7, which states the statutory policy in these words: "Employees shall have the right to self-organization, to form, join, or assist labor organizations, to bargain collectively through representatives of their own choosing, and to engage in concerted activities, for the purpose of collective bargaining or other mutual aid or protection."

The administration of the Wagner Act was given to a three-man National Labor Relations Board. The NLRB developed a large staff to enable it to carry on its work, including attorneys, investigators, hearing officers, review officers, and the many clerical personnel required to perform the detailed work in a nationwide administrative agency. The NLRB had jurisdiction only over employers engaged in interstate commerce. The Supreme Court has given the phrase "interstate commerce" an elastic definition, so that the jurisdiction of the Board has been held to apply not only to companies actively engaged in shipping products across state lines, but also to intrastate businesses which use a substantial quantity of raw materials shipped across state lines or sell products a substantial portion of which are destined for shipment across state lines.

UNFAIR LABOR PRACTICES

Enactment of the Wagner Act occurred at a time when the labor market was vastly different from that which exists in industry today. Organized labor numbered only 4 million union members, primarily concentrated in the construction trades, transportation, mining, and needle trades. The great basic industries of the country were either unorganized or were characterized by bargaining with company unions dominated by management. In 1935, for example, industries such as basic steel, agricultural implements, petroleum refining, rubber products, electrical machinery, and meat packing had from 50% to 80% of their employees covered by company unions.[1] Employers were openly hostile to unions and used every weapon at their command to prevent union organization. Lockouts, intimidation, blacklists, yellow-dog contracts, spying, and discrimination were commonplace.

In drafting the Wagner Act, Congress recognized that business hostility to unions was a fact to be reckoned with and that pious pronouncements of policy in favor of union organization, unbuttressed by sanctions against violators of congressional policy, would achieve nothing. The act therefore enumerated so-called "employer unfair practices" and made such conduct unlawful. Furthermore, it empowered the NLRB to issue cease and desist orders against such illegal conduct, and to enforce such orders in the courts. During the 12 years of the Wagner Act administration until its amendment in 1947, employees and their representatives filed more than 45,000 charges of unfair labor practices against employers with the NLRB. It is therefore apparent that protection of employees against management unfair labor practices constituted a major function of the Board.

The unfair labor practices prohibited by the Wagner Act (in each case directed against employers) are the following:

1. *To interfere with, restrain, or coerce employees in the exercise of rights guaranteed in Section 7.* This is an all-inclusive provision which actually covers all of the more specific unfair labor practices enumerated below. However, it was aimed at such employer practices as spying on unions, questioning employees about their union affiliation, using blacklists or yellow-dog contracts, or favoring one union over another.

A major problem which arose under this section involved the question of freedom of speech. Since unions were weak during the early years of the Wagner Act, the NLRB considered the effect of antiunion speeches by employers as an important part of a totality of conduct which might interfere with the rights of employees under the act. Employers complained that the NLRB went too far in its zeal to protect employees and actually deprived employers of rights of free speech guaranteed by the Constitution.

2. *To dominate or interfere with the formation or administration of any labor organization or contribute financial or other support to it.* This section was designed to prevent the formation or use of company unions which were supported by and subservient to the employer. As has already been mentioned, company unions were commonly used by employers in the early 1930's as a device to deter legitimate independent unionism; but as a result of the effective enforcement of this provision, employer-controlled company unions gradually disappeared from the labor scene.

3. *By discrimination in regard to hire or tenure of employment or*

---

[1] H. A. Millis and E. C. Brown, *From the Wagner Act to Taft-Hartley* (Chicago: University of Chicago Press, 1950), p. 110.

any term or condition of employment to encourage or discourage membership in any labor organization. This section was designed to make it unlawful for employers to use blacklists, yellow-dog contracts, or other devices to discourage membership in unions. Employers were forbidden to inquire of job applicants whether they were union members or favored unions, and employers could not fire employees because of union membership or lawful concerted activities protected under the act.

A proviso was included in this section permitting an employer who had entered into an agreement with a union duly representing his employees to require membership in the union as a condition of employment. This was the so-called "closed-shop" proviso, which was amended by the Taft-Hartley Act.

4. *To discharge or otherwise discriminate against an employee because he has filed charges or given testimony under the act.* This section was deemed necessary by Congress in order to assure protection to employees who invoked the provisions of the act against employers.

5. *To refuse to bargain collectively with the representatives of his employees duly chosen pursuant to other provisions of the act.* This section of the law was inserted to require employers to meet and negotiate with representatives of their employees. It is clear from the legislative history of the act that Congress did not intend to compel employers to agree to anything; it did want to assure that they would at least sit down and bargain. The language of this section aroused violent criticism from management spokesmen, who objected to the fact that the obligation to bargain was imposed only on them and not on unions. Furthermore, they criticized the manner in which the NLRB established criteria as to what was "good-faith" bargaining, claiming that such rules, in effect, required employers to come to an agreement contrary to the original statutory purpose.

The prohibition of specific unfair labor practices in the Wagner Act ushered in a new era in labor relations. Whereas, in earlier years labor leaders found the power of the courts interfering with their organizing activities, with the advent of the Wagner Act the courts, in effect, became an ally of labor, standing ready to enforce valid orders of the NLRB in cases where the Board found am employer guilty of unfair labor practices and the employer ignored the Board's cease and desist order. Despite its shortcomings, and despite the delays attendant upon its enforcement, the unfair labor practice procedure contained in the act represented such an improvement from organized labor's point of view over pre–Wagner Act conditions that organizing activity was greatly enhanced.

In a typical unfair labor practice case under the Wagner Act, the NLRB received a complaint from the union in behalf of an individual worker alleging some violation of the act. A field examiner of the Board investigated the case, and if the Board found that there was sufficient evidence to warrant a hearing, it set down the case for hearing and, if necessary, issued such subpoenas as were needed for the appearances of records and persons. In more than three quarters of the cases, however, settlement was achieved by informal methods before the hearing actually took place.

Hearings under the Wagner Act were conducted under the best accepted methods of administrative process. The NLRB was always careful to give all interested parties due notice and the right of hearing. However, the Board did act as both judge and prosecutor, which to some critics seemed unfair. Criticism of this feature of administration of the law ultimately led to establishment of the position of independent General Counsel under the Taft-Hartley Act, whose job it is to initiate complaints and bring them before the Board.

In enforcing unfair labor practice cases, the Board could issue certain orders. For example, it might require the employer to "cease and desist" from activities which it found in violation of the law. More important, it might require the employer to take affirmative action—for example, the reinstatement with back pay of employees who had been discharged or discriminated against because of union activity, or even the employment of workers who were never hired but who were refused employment because of their union affiliation. In addition, the Board could order the employer to disestablish a company union and withdraw recognition from any union which was recognized or with which he bargained if that union had been aided by the employer. Finally, in cases in which the employer was found to have refused to bargain with a union which was the duly chosen representative of his employees, the NLRB would order him to bargain upon request of that union.

REPRESENTATION CASES

Equally as important as unfair labor practice cases in the work of the NLRB, and every bit as controversial as a result of the split in the American labor movement which existed until 1955, have been representation cases. Section 9(a) of the Wagner Act provided that "Representatives . . . selected for the purposes of collective bargaining by the majority of the employees in a unit appropriate for such purposes, shall be the exclusive representatives of all the employees in such unit for the purposes of collective bargaining. . . ." This provision, with important additions which we shall consider at a later point in this discussion, was carried over into the Taft-Hartley Act.

Congress adopted the majority rule principle basically because experience had shown that it was the only practical method. The representative of the majority is thus the representative of all the employees in the bargaining unit, whether or not they are union members, just as a congressman represents all persons in his district regardless of whether they are members of his party or whether they voted for him or his opponent in the last election. If minority representation were permitted in collective bargaining, the employer would be constantly faced with demands from one group or another desirous of attracting support. Obviously, under such a setup, neither collective bargaining nor a business would stand much chance of survival. The NLRB has further determined that majority means a majority of the employees voting, not a majority of those eligible. This compels all interested groups to vie in getting out the vote. As a result, votes cast in NLRB elections averaged 80%–90% of those eligible, as compared with the average of 50%–65% of those eligible who vote in national elections.

In order to determine whether or not a particular union was the representative of workers in a plant, the NLRB held elections by secret ballot among the employees. The names of the union or unions seeking certification were placed on the ballot along with "no union." If a union won a majority of the votes cast, it was certified as the collective bargaining agent with which the employer had to bargain as the exclusive representative of the employees involved. If "no union" received a majority, no certification was made.

BARGAINING UNIT PROBLEMS

One of the most difficult kinds of problems faced by the NLRB involved deciding which employees were eligible to vote in an election to determine the bargaining agent and which groups of employees should have the right to separate choice of bargaining agents. Congress delegated these problems, known as questions of the "appropriate bargaining unit," to the NLRB, giving it almost unlimited authority[2] in Section 9(b) of the Wagner Act, which stated that "the Board shall decide in each case whether, in order to insure to employees the full benefit of their right to self-organization and to collective bargaining, and otherwise to effectuate the policies of this Act, the unit appropriate for the purposes of collective bargaining shall be the employer unit, craft unit, plant unit, or subdivision thereof." This wide authority was given to the NLRB in the belief, based on experience of the National Recovery Administration labor boards, that the various problems which arose were not foreseeable and could best be determined by the NLRB.

Although the Board decided each case on the merits, it grouped the facts determining its bargaining unit decisions around two basic criteria —the history of collective bargaining, if any, and the mutuality of interests of the employees. A typical bargaining unit was composed of production and maintenance employees in a single plant. Foremen and super-

---

[2] This authority has been restricted to some extent in the Taft-Hartley Act with respect to craft units, guards, and professional employees. See subsequent discussion in this chapter.

visors were excluded from the production workers' unit because of their peculiar relation to management. Likewise, office, clerical, and white-collar workers were separated from production and maintenance employees, as were professional employees. In addition, guards and watchmen were placed in separate units because of their unique position, and temporary employees were often deemed outside the bargaining unit because they had no permanent status in the plant. All these decisions were based on the fact that production and maintenance employees have a basic common denominator which was lacking among other plant groups, especially since many of the latter have a special and different relation to the employer.

Effect of AFL–CIO Rivalry

Determination of the bargaining unit was complicated by the rivalry between the AFL and the CIO. The struggle between these two groups was bitterly fought in cases involving the question whether employees should be represented on a craft or on an industrial basis. During the early years of the Wagner Act, the CIO concentrated organizing drives in the great basic industries of the country—steel, automobile, electrical, chemical, oil, etc.—and sought to organize companies on an industrial basis. This drive brought it into conflict with the AFL, which frequently represented strategically placed craft groups in such industries. In resolving the issue of the appropriate bargaining unit, where both an industrial union and a craft union claimed the right to represent a particular group of workers, the NLRB would consider the claims of both parties; and if it found, upon the basis of all the circumstances, that the craft could logically lay claim to consideration as a separate bargaining unit, and if there was reasonable doubt as to whether the majority of this craft preferred representation by the craft union or the industrial union, the Board permitted the workers in the craft to determine the issue for themselves. The Board accomplished this by providing that the workers in the craft would have a choice in an election of voting for the craft union, the industrial union, or no union, whereas the other production workers could vote only for the industrial union or no union.

When Congress passed the Wagner Act, it did not, of course, foresee the split in the labor movement. Therefore, it anticipated that in those situations where employees wanted to be represented by a union, a petition for an election would be filed with the Board by the union (normally an AFL affiliate), and a prompt, peaceful determination of the question of the representation would be made through the administrative procedures of the Board.

This procedure broke down when AFL and CIO unions engaged in a bitter struggle with each other over the right to represent employees in given bargaining units. Instead, the plant became a battleground, with both employer and employees as casualties. If one union felt confident enough to move for an early election, the other union would use all sorts of pressures to defer it. If it appeared that one union was successfully signing up members in a plant, the other might institute a boycott of the products of the company, picket the premises, threaten workers, or use similar pressures to weaken the hold of the rival union. The employer could do nothing to protect his business or employees against such tactics, for the Norris–La Guardia Act had deprived employers of their most effective weapon—the injunction. Since the Wagner Act imposed no prohibition on the activities of unions similar to the unfair labor practices proscribed for employers, employees had no way to protect themselves against such union pressures.

Even after one union was certified as the exclusive bargaining agent, there was nothing in the Wagner Act which prohibited a rival union from continuing its organizing and harassing activities, including picketing and boycotting. Employers were bound by the results of an NLRB election; but a rival union which lost an election was not bound by such results as a practical matter, since it could still attempt to achieve through economic pressure what it could not accomplish through peaceful procedures under the act.

WAGNER ACT, UNION GROWTH, AND STRIKES

That the Wagner Act achieved its basic purpose in compelling a change in employer policy toward unions cannot be doubted. In 1935, when the act became law, union membership stood at 3.9 million. In 1947, when the Wagner Act was amended, union membership exceeded 15 million. Although this union growth must be attributed to many factors, it was without a doubt substantially hastened by the Wagner Act. If the Wagner Act is judged in terms of fulfillment of its stated policy of "encouraging the practice and procedure of collective bargaining," it was eminently successful.

On the other hand, the Wagner Act cannot be said to have minimized the causes of industrial disputes except in one important respect. The representation procedure of the act provided a peaceful and democratic means of determining whether a union had the right to represent a group of employees. The substitution of NLRB procedure for the use of force in determining this question was one of the great contributions of the act.

Insofar as strikes generally are concerned, however, the Wagner Act had little contribution to make. Congress gave the NLRB no authority to interfere in disputes over terms and conditions of employment. Once the union was certified as bargaining agent and the employer's conduct was purged of unfair labor practices, the Wagner Act left matters to the parties themselves. But since the protection of the act spurred union activity, the period 1935–41 saw a great surge of union growth. A combination of immature unions and management inexperienced in industrial relations resulted in numerous strikes which more mature and experienced parties might have avoided. Critics of the Wagner Act blamed either the act or its administration by the NLRB as the cause of the strife. Proponents of the act blamed management opposition to both the act and unions as the cause. Perhaps a more accurate analysis would place the blame mainly on the growing pains of unions and the learning pains of management.

THE TAFT-HARTLEY ACT

The Wagner Act was under severe public criticism from its enactment in 1935 until its amendment 12 years later. Repeated attempts to modify the Wagner Act were bottled up in congressional committees, but finally, in 1946, the stage was set for new labor legislation by an unprecedented wave of strikes. In that year, time lost through strikes reached an all-time high of 116 million man-days—a figure three times higher than in the previous year or in 1937, the two worst years up to that time for which such statistics are available. Then followed the congressional elections of November, 1946, which reflected strong public dissatisfaction with current labor policies and which were interpreted by Congress as a mandate for corrective labor legislation. On June 23, 1947, the Labor-Management Relations Act—more popularly known as the Taft-Hartley Act—was passed by Congress over President Truman's veto.

Thus ended an important stage in the development of national labor policy in this country. The attitude of government toward collective bargaining by employees had passed through a succession of stages from active hostility in the early 1800's, when labor organizations were prosecuted as conspiracies, to active encouragement of union organization under the Wagner Act. Enactment of the Taft-Hartley law represented a new stage in government treatment of both management and labor. The metamorphosis which had occurred in public thinking on the subject of collective bargaining is well exemplified by a comparison of the original phraseology of Section 7 of the Wagner Act with its revised wording in the Taft-Hartley Act: "Employees shall have the right to self-organization . . . for the purpose of collective bargaining or other mutual aid or protection, *and shall also have the right to refrain from any or all of such activities.* . . ." Whereas, formerly, the weight of government influence had been placed behind union organization activities, the Taft-Hartley Act appeared to place the government in the position of a neutral, recognizing the right of employees to organize or not to organize. In theory, the government was to be not a partisan but a policeman, protecting both management and labor from unfair labor practices. However, as we shall observe in the later discussion, critics have alleged that the actual administration of the act has deviated from this apparent statutory policy.

The Taft-Hartley Act also qualified the principle that organized labor should be free to use its economic weapons without restriction. Secondary boycotts, strikes, and picketing for certain purposes were all subjected to regulation by the act. In this and other respects which will be discussed in the text, the Taft-Hartley Act established the principle that law, protecting the interest of management, labor, and the public, plays a necessary role in labor relations.

Scope and Administration of the Act

The Labor-Management Relations Act of 1947 was, in form, an amendment of the Wagner Act. Title I incorporated the text of the Wagner Act—with, however, a number of major modifications and additions. Title II, which dealt with conciliation of labor disputes and national emergency strikes, is discussed in Chapter 23. Title III authorized suits by and against unions, and Title IV created a joint committee to study and report on basic problems affecting friendly labor relations and productivity. Administration of the act remained under the National Labor Relations Board, but a number of important changes were made in the composition and power of the NLRB. Section 3 of the act enlarged the Board from three to five members. To remedy the oft-repeated charge made against the Board under the Wagner Act that it was both judge and prosecutor, the prosecuting function was removed from the Board and vested in a General Counsel who in this respect was made completely independent of the Board. In the handling of cases the General Counsel has final authority, subject neither to appeal to the Board nor to appeal to the courts, both as to institution of formal unfair labor practice proceedings and as to dismissal of charges. However, the General Counsel is subject to the Board's direction in matters of basic policy, such as determination of what categories of employers and employees are subject to coverage of the act. The General Counsel is responsible for the administration of the Board's field offices and field personnel, but not the staff of trial examiners who hear unfair practice cases.

The case intake of the Board has continuously risen in every fiscal year since 1958. In the fiscal year ended June 30, 1967, a record 30,425 unfair labor practice and representation cases were filed. This represents about a 5% increase over the previous year and an 82% increase over fiscal 1958.[3] Although one might think that as the basic provisions of the Wagner and Taft-Hartley Acts became better known and understood, there would be a diminution of cases charging violations of the act, the actual experience has been to the contrary. As a matter of fact, the number and percentage of alleged employer refusal-to-bargain violations have mounted year by year.

[3] 67 LRR 302.

Ten years ago, in fiscal 1958, 1,039 Section 8(*a*) (5) refusal-to-bargain charges were filed with the Board against employers, constituting 17.1% of all charges filed against employers. By fiscal 1967, the number of such charges had more than tripled, totaling some 3,819 charges and rising to 34% of all charges filed with the Board. Furthermore, during this same period, the proportion of all unfair labor practice charges found to have merit by the Board climbed from 20.7% in fiscal 1958 to 36.2% in 1967.[4] In 1936, the first full year of the Board's operation under the Wagner Act, allegations of unlawful discrimination brought by unions against employers under Section 8 (3) of the act accounted for 69% of all charges, while 30 years later such charges still account for about 66% of all complaints.[5]

The significance of these statistics is subject to two interpretations. On the one hand, they may indicate an increasing disregard by employers for the rights of employees in violation of the provisions of the act. This is possible but rather doubtful when account is taken of the kinds of charges filed and the circumstances under which they are filed. A more likely explanation is that unions have found in recent years that the filing of such charges is a useful bargaining tactic, and that in view of the alleged prolabor bias of the Board, they are more likely to gain by filing such charges than lose. Employers, too, have found that it sometimes suits their bargaining strategy to file charges against unions, and indeed in almost any long-drawn-out bargaining negotiation or strike, it has become almost a customary practice for both parties to file charges with the Board.

The villain in labor relations disputes is delay, which frequently works to the benefit of the employer. The Board has sought to speed up its handling of cases by delegating decision-making authority to the Board's 31 regional directors in representation election cases, pursuant to authority given the Board by Congress in the 1959 amendments to the act. Congress has refused, however, to authorize such delegation of authority in the handling of unfair labor practice cases. The Board has attempted to speed up settlement of these cases through voluntary processes. For example, in fiscal 1967, nearly 80% of all unfair labor practice cases were settled or adjusted, and about 78% of this number were settled or adjusted in a median of 43 days.[6]

Extent of Coverage of the Act

Under both the original Wagner Act and the Taft-Hartley Act, the NLRB was granted jurisdiction extending to any business "affecting commerce." Because of its limited budget, however, the Board has never exercised fully the powers granted to it by Congress. In 1950, 1954, and

---

[4] 67 LRR 184–85.

[5] Gerald A. Brown, "Exploring the World of Remedies," 66 LRR 177.

[6] 67 LRR 192 (February 19, 1968).

1958,[7] the Board laid down general standards intended to exclude "local businesses" from the Board's jurisdiction. These standards, based upon sales volume and similar criteria, were intended to keep the Board from being inundated with a flood of cases involving small companies with relatively few employees. For example, under the present standards the Board will not take jurisdiction of cases involving retail concerns unless they do a gross volume of business in excess of $500,000. Nonretail concerns must show at least $50,000 "outflow or inflow, direct or indirect."[8] Other standards are established for office buildings, public utilities, radio stations, and other enterprises.

The action of the Board in thus limiting its jurisdiction nullified in practice certain aspects of the protection which the act attempted to afford to small employers. For example, the Taft-Hartley Act makes it an unfair labor practice to coerce an employer or self-employed person to join a union. Obviously, this provision is most meaningful in the case of small employers or self-employed persons working without hired help; yet the Board would not ordinarily take jurisdiction of such cases because the business involved would not normally meet the Board's jurisdictional requirements. To make matters worse, the U.S. Supreme Court held in a series of decisions that state labor relations boards had no power to act in cases involving interstate commerce where the National Labor Relations Board had refused to assert jurisdiction. The High Court reasoned that Congress, by vesting in the NLRB jurisdiction over labor relations matters affecting interstate commerce, had completely displaced state power to act. The net result of NLRB policy and the Supreme Court's interpretation of the law was the creation of a no-man's land in the field of labor relations where the small employer was without a forum to hear his case. This serious defect in the administration of the Taft-Hartley Act was not remedied until enactment of the Landrum-Griffin Act in 1959.

The Taft-Hartley Act made important changes in the definition of the word "employee," as this term was used in the Wagner Act, with the result that supervisors were excluded from the protective coverage of the

---

[7] Under Section 701 of the Landrum-Griffin Act, which limits the discretion of the Board in declining jurisdiction, reference is made to "standards prevailing upon August 1, 1959." These standards incorporate the general standards announced on October 2, 1958, referred to in part above in the text, and standards affecting the hotel and motel industry set forth in the *Floridan Hotel* case (44 LRRM 1345) on July 30, 1959.

[8] Direct outflow refers to goods shipped or services furnished by the employer outside the state. Indirect outflow includes sales within the state to users meeting any standard except solely an indirect inflow or indirect outflow standard. Direct inflow refers to goods or services furnished directly to the employer from outside the state in which the employer is located. Indirect inflow refers to the purchase of goods or services which originated outside the employer's state but which he purchased from a seller within the state. Direct and indirect outflow may be combined, and direct and indirect inflow may also be combined to meet the $50,000 requirement. However, outflow and inflow may *not* be combined.

act. Under the Wagner Act the NLRB vacillated as to whether or not that act protected the right of supervisors to form unions and engage in collective bargaining, but it consistently held that the act protected supervisors as employees from discriminatory practices by employers. Under the Taft-Hartley Act, however, supervisors were deprived of both of these protections and were therefore compelled to rely solely on economic weapons to achieve their objectives. Supervisors could still join unions, but employers were free to use any means to intimidate and forestall such organization. In practice, the Taft-Hartley Act dealt unions of supervisors a hard blow. After its enactment, contracts of the Foreman's Association of America with Ford Motor Company and other important firms were not renewed. However, the act has had little effect in printing and other industries in which it was customary to include foremen in unions of employees.

HOW THE EMPLOYER WAS AFFECTED

In form, the Taft-Hartley Act retained the five unfair labor practices specified in the Wagner Act; and therefore, to a casual reader, it might appear that the employer is still subject to the same restrictions as under the Wagner Act. Actually, however, newly added provisions in the law were intended to afford the employer important new freedoms.

Free Speech

The Taft-Hartley Act accepted in principle employers' complaints on the "free speech" issue. Under the original Wagner Act the employer was prohibited from interfering with employee organization activities. This was so construed that practically any opinion expressed by an employer against union organization was held to be an unfair labor practice. In the years immediately prior to enactment of the Taft-Hartley Act, however, the Board modified its views so as to permit some employer opinions to be stated in the interest of preserving the right of free speech. During the time of the Wagner Act, NLRB policy toward employer free speech went through three distinct phases:

The first was characterized by the requirement that the employer maintain strict neutrality by remaining silent; the second, by the concession that the employer could express his antiunion views, so long as they were not accompanied by threats or promises, and so long as employees were not required to listen; and the third, by the refinement that the employer could make noncoercive antiunion speeches to compulsory audiences of his employees, provided that similar opportunities were afforded union representatives to express their views.[9]

[9] Joseph Shister, Benjamin Aaron, and C. W. Summers (eds.), *Public Policy and Collective Bargaining* (Industrial Relations Research Association Publication No. 27 [New York: Harper & Row, Publishers, 1962]), p. 35.

The Taft-Hartley Act attempted to clarify employer rights of free speech by specifically providing in Section 8(c) that the expression of any views, arguments, or opinions could not be considered evidence of an unfair labor practice unless there was an actual threat of reprisal or force or promise of benefit.

The protection afforded by this provision would seem capable of acting as a serious deterrent to union organizing activity in those areas, such as parts of the South, where unions are not yet entrenched. Literal acceptance of the language of the free speech amendment would seem to imply that an employer is not required to remain neutral in his utterances and can actively campaign against unionization as long as he is careful to avoid language which contains a threat of reprisal or force or promise of benefit. In actual practice the benefit derived by employers from this particular provision has depended upon whether or not the majority of the NLRB members represented the views of a Republican administration or a Democratic administration. The Eisenhower Board tended to broaden the scope of the free speech privilege and held, for example, that up to 24 hours before a representation election the employer could address his employees on the subject of union organization without giving the union the same privilege. The Board questioned whether the union would permit the employer to take over a meeting in the union hall to present his views!

The Kennedy and Johnson Boards, however, have moved in the direction of restricting employer statements, even though they are technically permissible under the free speech amendment of the act. The Board has restricted the application of Section 8(c) by holding that it applies only to unfair labor practice cases and not to representation elections. In the latter type of case, the Board has reasserted the early Wagner Act viewpoint that "laboratory conditions" must prevail in an election, with the corollary result that employers are restricted from arguing effectively against acceptance of the union by their employees.

Designation of Union as Bargaining Agent through Authorization Cards

One of the most controversial issues of the Board's administration of the act involves its use of union authorization cards as a means of determining the collective bargaining representative. Under the Wagner Act the Board was authorized to hold secret ballot elections "or utilize any other suitable method" to determine the representative of the employees. The Taft-Hartley amendments deleted the quoted phrase, which led most management spokesmen to believe that the secret ballot election was the only permissible method of determining the bargaining representative. However, the Board maintains that in cases where the employer's unfair conduct has made the secret ballot a nullity, it is useless to hold a runoff election, since presumably the same unfair conduct will have vitiated the results of this election.[10] Therefore, the Board relies on authorization cards solicited by the union from employees in which employees are to indicate their consent to the union acting as their bargaining representative.

In theory the Board is correct, since it would seem that Congress must have intended that the Board have some alternative method of determining the wishes of employees in cases of flagrant violations of the act by an employer. The problem lies in the great number of cases where the conduct of the employer does not go this far, but simply represents a doubt as to the majority status of the union and opposition to the union being designated as bargaining agent. Under these circumstances union agents have now found a procedure whereby they can get two chances to win representation. First, the organizing union solicits signatures from employees. Sometimes threats, misrepresentations, and arm-twisting of various sorts will be involved, and frequently employees may think they are simply authorizing a secret election at which they can then vote against the union without fear of reprisal. Once the union agents have a majority of signatures, they notify the employer of this fact and request formal bargaining. The union usually offers to prove its majority status by submitting the cards to an independent third party. The union petitions the Board for an election either at the same time or within a short time thereafter.

If the employer voluntarily bargains with the union, the petition for the election is withdrawn and the plant has been organized. If the employer refuses recognition, the union may still succeed in organizing the plant without an election. This depends upon whether the Board finds that the employer had a "good-faith" doubt as to the majority status of the union as evidenced by the authorization cards. If the Board finds that the employer did not have such doubt but simply sought to delay action by seeking an election, it may deny him an election and order him to bargain with the union. Even if the Board finds that there was good-faith doubt, the election may never be held if the employer commits an unfair labor practice before the election. The union can then withdraw the election petition, alleging that the unfair practice eliminates the possibility of a fair election, and under appropriate circumstances, the Board may then order the employer to bargain with the union. Finally, even if the union loses the election, it may then allege that employer preelection conduct constituted an unfair labor practice, and again the Board may compel the employer to bargain.

The Board's present policy has been criticized by union spokesmen as "too restrictive" and by management spokesmen as "going too far." Under the Board's rule, if an employer refuses to accept the authorization

---

[10] In fiscal 1966, unions lost 104 out of a total of 171 rerun elections held by the Board. See *Thirty-First Annual Report of the National Labor Relations Board for Fiscal Year Ended June 30, 1966.* (Washington, D.C.: U.S. Government Printing Office, 1967), p. 204, Table 11 C.

cards without giving any reason for so doing, it is up to the General Counsel affirmatively to show lack of good faith on the part of the employer. Union attorneys argue that this misplaces the burden of proof and that the Board should require that the employer affirmatively prove his good-faith doubt as to the validity of the union's proof of majority status by card check.[11] Employers, of course, are upset by the fact that the card check procedure enables unions to use all sorts of persuasion to obtain the signatures, while the employer never has an opportunity to get his message across. In a sense, therefore, the use of the card check procedure further restricts the right of free speech of the employer and his opportunity to communicate his views concerning union organization to his employees. Finally, there are the rights of the employees to consider in this whole controversial field. It is somewhat ironic that the Board purports to deny the employer a rerun election—or an original election —because allegedly employer misconduct has made employee free choice impossible, and yet the remedy—namely ordering bargaining based upon card checks—may afford employees even less protection against the very kind of undue persuasion for which the employer was condemned.

Are authorization cards a valid indication of employee preference? The Fourth Circuit has declared that they are "inherently unreliable" and that "an employer could not help but doubt the results of a card check."[12] The Board prides itself on maintaining "laboratory conditions" in an election; yet with respect to authorization cards it will not consider the subjective intent of the individuals at the time that they signed, if on its face there is no ambiguity in the card itself. There seems to be little doubt that signature cards are inferior to a secret ballot election, but what is the Board to do when, in its determination, a secret ballot election no longer can reflect employee free choice because of unfair conduct of the employer?

Despite the heated argument on this subject, it is important to remember that bargaining orders based on authorization cards represent only a minority of cases handled by the Board. During fiscal 1967, the Board conducted 8,183 elections and issued only 107 bargaining orders based on a card-count majority. According to NLRB Associate General Counsel H. Stephen Gordon, "of these 107, a total of 102 orders involved employers whose commission of unfair labor practices had made a fair election impossible or nullified an election already held."[13] Nevertheless, the minor importance of such cases in the overall case load of the NLRB is no consolation to the employer who finds himself faced with an order to

---

[11] Donald W. Fisher (Counsel Sheet Metal Workers International Association), "Recognition of Noncertified Unions," in D. R. Sheriff and U. M. Kuebler (eds.), *NLRB in a Changing Industrial Society* (Iowa City, Iowa: Center for Labor and Management, University of Iowa, 1967), p. 36.

[12] *Logan Packing*, 66 LRRM 2596.

[13] 67 LRR 166.

bargain with a union which, rightly or wrongly, he believes does not represent a majority of workers in the bargaining unit. Nor is it any consolation to employees who find themselves represented by a union that was opposed by a majority vote of the bargaining unit.

Reinstatement

Section 10(*c*) of the act prohibited the Board from ordering reinstatement or back pay in any case where the discharge was made "for cause." This provision was included, according to the majority report of the House Labor Committee, in order to "put an end to the belief, now widely held and certainly justified by the Board's decisions, that engaging in union activities carries with it a license to loaf, wander about the plant, refuse to work, waste time, break rules and engage in incivilities and other disorders and misconduct." The basis for this charge does not appear to have been factual.

The NLRB has continued to order reinstatement where circumstances warrant this remedy for workers illegally discharged. In September, 1962, for the first time in 27 years, the NLRB commenced adding 6% interest to back-pay awards granted to employees who were illegally discharged. While there is no specific authorization in the Taft-Hartley Act for such action, the Board relied on "accepted legal and equitable principles" as justification for adding interest to back-pay awards.[14] In 1966, back pay ordered by the Board amounted to $8,911,040 compared with $2,782,360 in 1965. Included within the large total for 1966 was one case which by itself required payment of $3 million in back pay and $1.5 million in pension adjustments. However, even when this case is excluded, the remaining back-pay awards of $4,411,040 set an all-time record.[15]

Procedural Privileges

Employers were also granted important procedural rights. Whereas, previously, employers could petition for an election only when confronted with demands for bargaining rights by two or more competing unions, they could now seek an election whenever a union made a demand for recognition. The grant of this privilege to the employer restrained premature claims of representation by unions attempting to organize a plant; for if the union failed to secure a majority vote in an election called by the employer, the act prohibited the holding of another election for 12 months. The right to request an election has been frequently utilized by employers. During the fiscal year ended June 30, 1966, employers petitioned for elections in 466 cases.[16]

Another important right provided in the Taft-Hartley Act is the

---

[14] NLRB Press Release, September 21, 1962.

[15] *Thirty-First Annual Report, op. cit.,* p. 16.

[16] *Ibid.,* p. 19.

privilege to sue unions in federal court for breach of contract. Section 301(*a*) of the act provides:

Suits for violation of contracts between an employer and a labor organization representing employees in an industry affecting commerce as defined in this Act, or between any such labor organizations, may be brought in any district court of the United States having jurisdiction of the parties without respect to the amount in controversy or without regard to the citizenship of the parties.[17]

Furthermore, Section 303 of the act provides that whoever is injured in his business or property by reason of certain enumerated unfair labor practices of a labor organization may sue in federal district court "and shall recover the damages by him sustained and the cost of the suit." Although contrary to the grim prognostications of union leaders, there has been no rush by employers to sue unions[18] in federal court, nevertheless, this section of the act carries with it implications of great significance for the development of labor relations in this country.

One direct result of the inclusion of Section 301(*a*) in the Taft-Hartley Act has been an increase in frequency of clauses in labor contracts protecting the union against financial liability in the event of unauthorized strikes. Contrary to expectations, however, there appears to have been no reduction in the frequency of no-strike clauses in labor agreements negotiated since enactment of the Taft-Hartley amendments.

Suppose a collective bargaining contract contains a no-strike clause and an agreement to arbitrate disputes. The union strikes in violation of its contractual agreement. Can an employer require the union to desist from such action by bringing suit in federal court under Section 301(*a*) for specific performance of the agreement not to strike?

Enforcement would, of course, require a court order equivalent to an injunction, which would seem to be prohibited by the Norris–La Guardia Act. However, it can be argued that an exception should be made in order to carry out the statutory purpose of the Taft-Hartley Act. Since a major statutory purpose of the Taft-Hartley Act was to reduce the number of strikes, and since the U.S. Supreme Court has already ruled that Section 301 of the Taft-Hartley Act enables a union to bring a suit in federal court against an employer for specific performance of an agreement to arbitrate,[19] should not the employer be held to have the same right against the union?

[17] While Section 301(*a*) is considered above in connection with employer procedural rights, it should be noted that equal rights are accorded to unions to bring suits against employers.

[18] The Landrum-Griffin Act amendments to the Taft-Hartley Act broadened this provision so that today an employer can sue a union for damages sustained as the result of any activity or conduct defined as an unfair labor practice in Section 8(*b*)(4) of the Taft-Hartley Act, as amended.

[19] *Textile Workers' Union* v. *Lincoln Mills*, 353 U.S. 448, 77 S. Ct. 912 (1957).

Whatever the logic or justice in this argument, the Supreme Court has seen fit to disagree with it. In *Sinclair Refining Co. v. Atkinson,*[20] decided in June, 1962, the Court held that the Norris–La Guardia Act barred a suit by an employer under Section 301 of the Taft-Hartley Act for an injunction against a union's breach of a no-strike pledge contained in an agreement requiring arbitration of disputes. The Court held that the case involved a labor dispute within the meaning of the Norris–La Guardia Act, and therefore the federal courts were deprived of jurisdiction. The Court intimated that it was up to Congress to resolve the discriminatory pattern of law which has resulted from the conflict between the Taft-Hartley and Norris–La Guardia Acts.

Justice Brennan, speaking for the dissenting three justices, argued that the Taft-Hartley Act should be accommodated to the Norris–La Guardia Act by permitting injunctions against unions for breach of contract. In his words, the decision of the majority

. . . deals a crippling blow to the cause of grievance arbitration itself. Arbitration is so highly regarded as a proved technique for industrial peace that even the Norris–La Guardia Act fosters its use. But since unions cannot be enjoined by a federal court from striking in open defiance of their undertakings to arbitrate, employers will pause long before committing themselves to obligations enforceable against them but not against their unions.[21]

The Sinclair decision poses the basic question whether the Norris–La Guardia Act is out of date and requires modification to conform to governmental policy embodied in labor laws enacted since its passage. As a practical matter, amendment or repeal of the Norris–La Guardia Act seems remote because of the emotional attachment which labor has to this particular law. One possibility of strengthening the employer's position in collective bargaining contracts requiring arbitration of disputes would be to make a failure to abide by such an agreement an unfair labor practice and give the NLRB the power to obtain injunctive relief, as it does in other unfair labor practice cases.

Good-Faith Bargaining

It will be recalled that the Wagner Act provided that it was an unfair labor practice for an employer to refuse to bargain collectively with representatives of his employees. The statute did not set forth the requirements of bargaining in good faith, but the NLRB gradually developed a series of rules which, in the eyes of employers, erroneously interpreted the statute and required the employer to make counterproposals and thereby accede to union demands. The Taft-Hartley amendments added a new provision, Section 8(d), which defined the obli-

---

[20] 82 S. Ct. 1328 (1962).
[21] 82 S. Ct. 1328, 1345 (1962).

gation to bargain and stated further that the obligation "does not compel either party to agree to a proposal or require the making of a concession." Despite this statutory instruction, the NLRB has nevertheless tended to view a refusal to make a counterproposal as evidence of bad faith.

A classic test of the meaning of the statutory language was posed by the 1960 case involving negotiations between the International Union of Electrical Workers and the General Electric Company. The company, in accordance with a long-standing policy which has become known as "Boulwarism,"[22] offered a complete package of benefits to the union and then, except for minor modifications, sought to stand by this offer. IUE, after a short strike, finally signed a contract with GE, but then filed a charge with the NLRB alleging that the company had not bargained in good faith. Four and one-half years after the 1960 three-year agreement was signed and 18 months after GE, the IUE, and 100 other unions had peacefully arrived at successor three-year contracts, the NLRB ruled that GE was guilty of bargaining in bad faith![23]

In finding a violation of Section $8(a)(5)$ of the Taft-Hartley Act, the NLRB rested its conclusion upon an alleged "totality of conduct" by the company which in its opinion tended to "freeze" its bargaining stance, even though admittedly the company had made certain concessions from its first offer and even though the Board found that the company was at all times willing and anxious to sign a new contract. This case raised serious questions in the minds of employers, management consultants, and lawyers as to whether it is any longer possible for employers to engage in so-called "tough" bargaining with unions.

The confusion created by this decision has been further compounded by the *H. K. Porter*[24] case in which the Circuit Court for the District of Columbia sustained a finding by the Board that an employer had failed to bargain in good faith when it refused to sign a contract containing a union dues checkoff. Significantly, the union had insisted just as adamantly that it would not sign a contract *unless* it contained a checkoff; yet this apparently did not constitute a violation of the good-faith bargaining requirements. In a subsequent hearing on this case before the circuit court,[25] the issue was raised as to whether or not the company could be forced to grant the checkoff clause, and the court held that the Board had the authority to order the company to do so. The NLRB then ordered the company to grant the checkoff. Such action brings us very close to compulsory arbitration with the Board and the courts actually

[22] See Herbert R. Northrup, *Boulwarism* (Ann Arbor, Mich.: Bureau of Industrial Relations, University of Michigan, 1964).

[23] *General Electric Company*, 150 NLRB 192 (1964). This case will probably be appealed to the U.S. Supreme Court.

[24] *NLRB* v. *H. K. Porter Company, Inc.*, 153 NLRB 1370 (1965), *enf.* 363 F. 2d 272 (D.C. Circuit, 1966).

[25] *Steelworkers* v. *NLRB*, 66 LRRM 2761 (D.C. Circuit, December, 1967).

writing the contract which labor and management must live by. This would seem to be the very thing that Congress wished to avoid when it wrote into Section 8(*d*) the express provision that a party was not required to make concessions.

The NLRB not only tells employers and unions when they must make concessions but also has set up a complicated set of rules as to what they can and cannot bargain about. First, the parties have a mandatory obligation to bargain about rates of pay, wages, hours, or other conditions of employment. This language has been broadly construed by the Board and the courts to include such matters as Christmas bonuses,[26] employee-stock purchase plans,[27] and employee discounts on purchase of the employer's product.[28] Perhaps most significant is the fact that the U.S. Supreme Court supported the contention of the Board that a company has a mandatory obligation under the Taft-Hartley Act to bargain with union representatives concerning an economically motivated decision to subcontract out work which had theretofore been performed by the employees in the bargaining unit. In the now-famous *Fibreboard Paper Products* case,[29] the Court affirmed the order of the Board requiring the company to resume the subcontracted operation and to reinstate the displaced employees with back pay. This decision was greeted with dismay by employers on the grounds that the requirement to bargain about what they considered to be vital management decisions with respect to operation of the business would result in endless delays and deprive business of flexibility in an era when change and prompt reaction to change are the keynotes of business. On the other hand, the Board contends that where subcontracting impinges upon work which the bargaining unit is qualified to do, the union should have an opportunity to discuss with the employer the proposed decision to give this work to others.

A second class of bargaining subjects falls in a prohibited category. These are items, such as the closed shop, which Congress has declared contrary to public policy. Finally, there are matters which may be classified as "nonmandatory subjects," such as, for example, an employer demand that the union contract contain a clause calling for a prestrike secret vote of the employees as to the employer's last offer. The Supreme Court has held that the parties can talk about such subjects, but if either party insists upon inclusion of such matters in a contract, it violates the good-faith bargaining requirement of the law![30]

---

[26] *General Telephone*, 54 LRRM 1055, *aff'd.* CA 5 (1964), 57 LRRM 1055.

[27] *NLRB* v. *Richford Oil Corp.*, CA D.C. (1956), 37 LRRM 2327; *cert. denied* S. Ct. (1956), 37 LRRM 2837.

[28] *Central Illinois Public Service Co.*, 51 LRRM 1508, *aff'd.* CA 7 (1963), 54 LRRM 2586.

[29] *Fibreboard Paper Products Corp.* v. *NLRB*, 57 LRRM 2609, 379 U.S. 203 (1964).

[30] *National Labor Relations Board* v. *Wooster Division of Borg-Warner Corp.*, 356 U.S. 342, 78 S. Ct. 718 (1958).

The good-faith bargaining requirement of the Taft-Hartley Act has been the subject of so much litigation, has resulted in so many unrealistic decisions, and has caused so much delay in collective bargaining negotiations that employers, unions, and the Board alike agree that a change is desirable. As to what that change should be, however, there is no agreement. Many economists believe that the distinctions between mandatory and nonmandatory bargaining are satisfactory for the courtroom but not for the smoke-filled conference room, and that collective bargaining would benefit if the Section $8(a)(5)$ provision were scrapped. Employers would like to eliminate the power of the Board in this area, which they believe infringes on the right to manage their business. Employer opposition also stems from the fact that the Board has used this section of the law to require bargaining with a union even where it may have lost an election, as we observed in our earlier discussion.

On the other hand, unions and the Board are concerned by the fact that the simple order to bargain is not effective in compelling a truly recalcitrant employer to deal with the union, except after what may be years of litigation. Numerous study commissions, beginning with the Senate Advisory Panel on Labor-Management Relations Law in 1960, have taken note of the inadequacy of the Board's power under Section $8(a)(5)$ and have observed that the resultant delays have frequently been injurious to the rights of employees. Some labor experts believe that new remedies need to be fashioned, such as, for example, making the benefits of a contract retroactive to the date of the first refusal by the employer to bargain in good faith. This, however, would be an extreme remedy which, again, would take us a long way down the road to compulsory arbitration; for it would put the Board in the position of writing a contract for labor and management which the parties had never mutually agreed to. Thus far, the Board has declined to take such drastic action and has relied primarily on cease and desist orders.

HOW UNIONS WERE AFFECTED

Unfair Labor Practices

The Wagner Act sought to overcome the disparity of bargaining power between employers and employees which existed at the time of its enactment. Therefore, its restrictive provisions were all directed at employers, while unions were left free to engage in strikes, picketing, and various forms of coercion short of violence, in order to achieve organization of the workers. For this reason the Wagner Act was criticized as being a one-sided law. The Taft-Hartley Act was designed to remedy this one-sidedness. It proceeded on the assumption that substantial equality of bargaining power had been achieved and that therefore both union and management should be subject to similar prohibitions regarding unfair practices.[31] The bulk of unfair labor practice cases handled by the Board continue to be brought against employers, but a substantial number now involve complaints against unions. In the fiscal year ended June 30, 1966, a total of 4,941 unfair labor practice charges were filed against unions. Of this amount, 52% were filed by employers, 42% by individuals, and the balance by other unions.[32]

The unfair labor practices to which unions are subject are six in number, enumerated in Section 8(*b*) of the act:

1. *Restraint or Coercion.* It was made an unfair labor practice for a union to restrain or coerce employees in the exercise of the rights guaranteed them in Section 7. The latter guarantees the right to bargain collectively through representatives of the employees' own choosing and also the right to refrain from such activity (except where a union shop has been authorized by law). Most of the unfair labor practice charges filed against unions involve alleged violation of this section of the law. Union activities which have been found violative of the provisions of this section include mass picketing, the blocking of ingress to and egress from struck plants, and threatened physical violence toward employees. Recently, the statutory language has been construed to impose an obligation upon a labor organization, when acting as exclusive bargaining agent, to refrain from taking any "unfair" action against employees in matters affecting their employment. The NLRB has held that a union was guilty of an unfair labor practice where it unfairly reduced an employee's seniority classification.[33] On the other hand, the Supreme Court, by a divided vote, sustained the Board's holding that a union did not violate this section of the act when it imposed and subsequently instituted court proceedings to enforce fines against members who crossed a lawful picket line in support of the union's authorized strike.[34]

2. *Illegal Demands for Union Security.* It was made an unfair labor practice for a union to cause an employer to discriminate against an employee for nonmembership in a union unless there was a union security contract with the employer which was recognized under the act. The closed shop was prohibited, even though both employer and employees were satisfied with its operation. This prohibition, if enforced, could have had far-reaching effects upon labor relations in view of the fact that prior to enactment of the Taft-Hartley law, in the neighborhood of 4.8 million employees worked under closed-shop arrangements.[35] However, on the whole, closed-shop industries have either ignored the prohibition or cir-

---

[31] Despite this change in emphasis, more than 80% of the Board's time under the Taft-Hartley Act has been spent in handling cases submitted by unions, not employers.

[32] *Thirty-First Annual Report, op. cit.,* pp. 6, 8.

[33] *Miranda Fuel Company, Inc.,* 51 LRRM 1585.

[34] *NLRB* v. *Allis Chalmers Manufacturing Company,* 338 U.S. 175.

[35] *Monthly Labor Review,* Vol. LXIV (May, 1947), p. 766.

cumvented it. This part of the law imposes no penalties and therefore is not brought into operation unless an individual employee charges an unfair labor practice.

A union-shop provision in a collective agreement was recognized under the act if it allowed at least 30 days after hiring before new employees were required to become members of the union. However, before a union could negotiate such a security provision, it was required to fulfill a number of conditions: (*a*) file all required reports and affidavits, (*b*) receive designation as bargaining representative by a majority of the employees, (*c*) show that at least 30% of the employees in the bargaining unit wish to authorize the union to make a union security agreement, and (*d*) secure a majority vote of all employees in the unit in favor of such a clause, in a specially conducted NLRB election. The requirement of a special election proved to be a time-consuming and costly formality. In October, 1951, after a period of four years in which the NLRB held 46,146 union-shop elections, of which 97% authorized the union shop, the act was amended by the so-called "Taft-Humphrey amendments" so as to permit voluntary union-shop contracts without elections.

Even if a union satisfied all the requirements enumerated above and even if an employer engaged in interstate commerce was willing to grant the union shop, its inclusion in a collective bargaining contract was prohibited under the act if the particular state in which the business was located imposed more drastic conditions on union security clauses or forbade them entirely. Despite dire predictions by labor leaders, there is no evidence that this latter provision seriously weakened the labor movement, although it did accelerate enactment of "right-to-work" laws by a number of states. As of January, 1968, the union shop was prohibited in 19 states.

As has already been pointed out in Chapter 6, the Taft-Hartley Act makes it illegal for a union or an employer to enforce a union security clause against anyone for any reason other than nonpayment of dues or initiation fees. The inclusion of this clause in the act is evidence of the concern of Congress that the union shop, by giving the union a monopoly of job opportunities in the particular establishment, might be used as a club to intimidate workers who disagreed with the policies of union officials.

3. *Refusal to Bargain.* It was made an unfair practice for a union to refuse to bargain collectively with an employer. This provision was apparently directed at those unions which had become so powerful that their "bargaining" activities consisted of presenting demands with a "take it or leave it" attitude. It is doubtful, however, that this provision has brought about any change of attitude by unions in negotiations, since the act makes it clear that the obligation to bargain in good faith does not

compel a union (or an employer) to "agree to a proposal or require the making of a concession." Furthermore, bargaining by ultimatum by unions has been sanctioned by the NLRB under certain circumstances, yet denied to employers. (See *GE* case, *supra.*)

For example, in one recent case[36] the Board held that the unions involved did not refuse to bargain in good faith by giving the employer an ultimatum backed by a strike threat to sign certain contract proposals immediately, without any further opportunity to consult with its bargaining agent. The ultimatum was the culmination of protracted bargaining which had extended over a period of five months and resulted in an impasse.

4. *Illegal Strikes and Boycotts.* Section 8(b)(4) of the act made it an unfair labor practice for a union to engage in or to encourage any strike[37] or refusal by employees to use, manufacture, transport, work, or handle goods if an object of such action was one of the following:

a) To require an employer or self-employed person to join a union or an employer organization. The purpose of this clause was to prevent unions from forcing independent businessmen, such as plumbers, bakery deliverymen, and others, to join a union. Congress believed that the economic independence of these groups should be protected, even though their hours of work and earnings might affect the standard of employees who work for hire in the same occupation.

b) To force the employer or any other person to cease dealing in the products of another employer or to cease doing business with any other person. This clause was directed at the so-called "secondary boycott." If employees in plant A strike to compel employer A to grant higher wages or to grant a union shop, this involves direct action against the employer primarily involved in the dispute; but if the employees, having a grievance against employer A, picket or induce a strike in company B, which uses the products of plant A, then a secondary boycott or secondary action is involved. Congress not only made the secondary boycott an unfair labor practice but it also directed the NLRB to seek federal court injunctions against its continuance under certain circumstances and, furthermore, authorized damage suits to be brought in federal court by employers against unions which engage in secondary boycotts. Congress thus condemned secondary boycotts because they unduly widen the area of industrial disputes by interrupting the operations of employers only remotely connected with the chief cause of the controversy.

Congress may also have been concerned about the secondary boycott because it had become a potent weapon in the hands of strong labor unions to force union membership on unwilling employees. Since the

---

[36] *Lumber and Sawmill Workers' Union,* 47 LRRM 1287.

[37] The act defined "strike" to include a concerted stoppage or slowdown.

national labor policy now stated that employees should have the right to join or to refrain from joining a union (unless there was a compulsory union-shop provision in effect), it is not surprising that Congress found it necessary to restrict boycotts in order to make employee rights of self-determination effective.

Union leaders objected vehemently to these provisions of the act. They pointed out that the act even outlawed such traditional union action as a concerted refusal to handle "scab" products made in a nonunion shop or in a shop in which a strike was in progress. Even where one nonunion employer threatened the working standards of an otherwise fully organized industry, a refusal on the part of employees in the organized plants to handle or process goods intended for or coming from the nonunion plant would violate the act.

While it is clear from the foregoing discussion that the Taft-Hartley Act effectively curtailed many forms of union secondary boycott activity, nevertheless, it also left major loopholes. Thus, if a Teamster business agent attempted to persuade X's employees not to handle the goods manufactured by Y, this was unlawful; yet the act did not prohibit the business agent from warning X directly that he had better not handle Y's product! Likewise, the act permitted boycott action applied through inducement of employees individually, instead of in concert, and inducement of employees of railroads, municipalities, and governmental agencies. Inducement of supervisors was also not barred by the original Taft-Hartley language, because the statute referred to inducements to the "employees of any employer," and the definition of "employee" in the act excluded supervisory personnel. One other loophole resulted from NLRB rulings on "hot cargo" agreements. After some vacillation the Board held that "hot cargo" agreements could validly be included in collective bargaining agreements and presumably could be enforced by appropriate court action. The fact that they were sanctioned as a subject of collective bargaining and were included in contracts enforceable in law strengthened the hands of unions in making secondary boycott action effective.

One of the most difficult problems arising in connection with the ban on secondary boycotts was the determination as to where primary action ended and secondary action began. For example, if a picket line around plant A in which a labor dispute existed prevented drivers from employer B from entering and picking up merchandise, was the picket line unlawful because of its effect on employees of employer B? The NLRB has answered no, since the strike against A is privileged activity, and the repercussions on B are only incidental. But suppose the primary dispute is with a trucking company. Can the employees of that company picket the trucks they are loading and unloading on the premises of employer A? This raises the question of the so-called "ambulatory situs" —the trucks are in a sense an extension of the employer's business site. The Board has ruled that such picketing is permissible where it is confined to one employer and conducted at the only place where the union could picket effectively.[38]

Another situation in which the line between primary and secondary action is blurred is the so-called "common situs" problem, which has been a major source of friction in the construction industry, where it is customary for a general contractor and various subcontractors to work on the same premises. Suppose employees of the general contractor or union subcontractors picket the premises in protest over another subcontractor using nonunion labor. Under the Board and court interpretations of Section 8(*b*)(4)(*A*), such action has been held to be a secondary boycott. It is not surprising that the building-trades unions are the most frequent users of the secondary boycott technique. For the fiscal year 1966, NLRB records show that 1,692 secondary boycott charges were filed with the Board.[39] Unions in the building and construction field were involved in a large number of such complaints. The building-trades unions contend there is no secondary boycott action involved because there is really only one employer—the general contractor—and all of the subcontractors are so related to him by the nature of the work that they cannot be considered to be "neutrals" so far as picketing is concerned. The Supreme Court, however, has held that the subcontractors are to be treated as independent employers in considering the applicability of Section 8(*b*)(4)(*A*).

c) *To force or require an employer* (*including the employer of the strikers*) *to recognize or bargain with one union if another union is the certified bargaining agent, or to force another employer* (*not the employer of the strikers*) *to recognize an uncertified union.* This clause was intended to protect employers from strikes by an uncertified union, aimed at compelling the employer to deal with it rather than with another union already certified. Under the Wagner Act, many companies found themselves in a disastrous dilemma as a result of rivalry between CIO and AFL unions. If the employer yielded to the pressure of the uncertified union, he violated the Wagner Act and was subject to sanctions for so doing. If he did not yield, his business could be destroyed. He could get no injunction or court relief against the picketing because of the anti-injunction provisions of the Norris–La Guardia Act. The dilemma to the employees was as real. Because they had exercised their right of free choice, they stood to lose their jobs through the efforts of the union which they had rejected.

The attempts on the part of unions to nullify the right of workers to join unions of their own choosing were indefensible and completely at variance with the basic principles of the Wagner Act. Such activities were also, of course, part of the basic conflict between the principle of exclu-

---

[38] *Schultz Refrigerated Service, Inc.*, 87 NLRB 502 (1949).
[39] *Thirty-First Annual Report, op. cit.*, p. 8.

sive jurisdiction upon which American unionism had been built and the principle of self-determined organization which the Wagner Act made law.

The Taft-Hartley Act made such strikes illegal and made it mandatory for the NLRB to seek injunctive relief in the courts, if, after a preliminary investigation, there was reason to believe that the union was engaging in a strike prohibited by this section.

d) To force or require an employer to assign particular work to employees in one union or craft rather than to employees in another union or craft. This clause was intended to outlaw the so-called "jurisdictional" strike. Such strikes, growing out of controversies as to which craft has the right to perform a particular job, were particularly common in the construction industry and evoked widespread public criticism. As a direct result of the enactment of the Taft-Hartley law, the building-trades unions set up machinery to adjust jurisdictional disputes among the various crafts.

A union which engaged in any of the activities banned in the above four situations committed an unfair labor practice and rendered itself liable in damages to anyone whose business or property was injured as a result of the strike. Moreover, when a charge was filed alleging that a union was engaging in activities under (*a*), (*b*), or (*c*) above, it was made mandatory that the Board seek an injunction against the union, if the Board had reasonable cause to believe the charge was true. In the case of jurisdictional disputes, however, the Board had to hear and decide such cases itself unless, within 10 days after the charge was filed, the parties agreed to voluntary adjustment. The mandatory injunction provision mentioned above did not apply to jurisdictional disputes, but the NLRB could seek an injunction in situations where such relief was appropriate.

In the fiscal year ended June 30, 1966, injunctions were granted in 25 cases involving jurisdictional disputes, most of them in the building and construction industry.[40] It is obvious from this record that the machinery set up by the building trades to handle their disputes is not fully effective.

Although the Board has often been attacked for injecting itself into the substance of collective bargaining, it religiously refrained from making determinations of work assignments in jurisdictional dispute cases coming before it. In 1961, however, in the *Columbia Broadcasting* case,[41] which involved a dispute between a union of television technicians and a union of stage employees over which union would control the work of providing electric lighting for television shows, the Supreme Court held that the NLRB could not "duck" this responsibility imposed upon it by

---

[40] *Ibid.*, p. 155.

[41] *National Labor Relations Board* v. *Radio and Television Broadcast Engineers' Union*, 364 U.S. 573, 81 S. Ct. 330 (1961).

Congress and that it must make an affirmative award of disputed work in such cases. The assumption by the Board of the role of arbiter in such disputes will add pressure on unions to settle such controversies through their own dispute machinery.

5. *Excessive Initiation Fees.* It was made an unfair labor practice for a union which had a union-shop agreement to charge membership fees in an amount which the Board found excessive or discriminatory under all the circumstances. In a number of cases, the Board has ordered a union to reduce its admission fees, but the total effect of this provision has been minor.

6. *Featherbedding.* It was made an unfair labor practice for a union to "cause or attempt to cause an employer to pay or deliver or agree to pay or deliver any money or other thing of value, in the nature of an exaction, for services which are not performed or not to be performed." This clause is sometimes referred to as the "antifeatherbedding" provision; but actually, its scope is much more limited than the practice of make-work rules which is ordinarily encompassed within the term "featherbedding." If some work is performed in return for the compensation—even though it is mere standing around during a recorded broadcast—then the statutory requirement of "services which are not performed" is not satisfied, and the provision is not applicable. Thus the Supreme Court ruled that the practice of the International Typographical Union in requiring pay for setting so-called "bogus" type which is not used and the practice of the American Federation of Musicians of requiring pay for "standby orchestras" when outside bands play in local theaters were both lawful under this provision.

Loyalty Affidavit

One of the most controversial provisions of the act was directed at Communist officers who have been in power in a few American unions. Section 9(*b*) of the act disqualified a labor organization both as a bargaining agency and as a complainant under the act unless there was on file with the Board an affidavit executed

by each officer of such labor organization and the officers of any national or international labor organization of which it is an affiliate or constituent unit that he is not a member of the Communist Party or affiliated with such party, and that he does not believe in, and is not a member of or supports any organization that believes in or teaches the overthrow of the United States Government by force or by any illegal or unconstitutional methods.

This provision evoked considerable criticism, from both unions and other sources, on the ground that it was unconstitutional to discriminate on the basis of membership in the Communist party when that party was a legal organization entitled to a place on our electoral ballots. However, the Supreme Court settled this issue in 1950 by ruling that Congress had a right to require the oaths to protect the public against the "evils of conduct." Union spokesmen also argued against the one-sided nature of the affidavit provision, which required the loyalty oath from union officers but not from employers.

Noncompliance by many Communist-dominated unions did, however, prove very detrimental to these organizations, and severe membership losses were suffered by many of them. Today, as noted in Chapter 2, only two significant Communist-dominated unions remain—the International Longshoremen's and Warehousemen's Union and the United Electrical, Radio and Machine Workers of America. Although these results derived in part from causes other than the Taft-Hartley Act, there is no question but that the act strengthened the hand of non-Communist elements in unions and paved the way for the decline of Communist influence in the labor movement.

Reports and Financial Accounts

The act also required unions to file with the Secretary of Labor copies of their constitutions, bylaws, reports showing salaries of officers above $5,000, initiation fees, and annual financial statements. The only sanction applied for failure to file reports was denial of use of the machinery of the NLRB. Unfortunately, the unions which did not voluntarily file financial reports were concentrated in the buildings and amusement trades; they were so well entrenched that they had little need to use the NLRB and therefore did not have to comply with such provisions. The reporting provisions of the act were repealed by the Landrum-Griffin Act (see Chapter 22).

Restrictions on Political Contributions

The act made it unlawful for any labor union to make a contribution or expenditure in connection with any election to any federal political office. The prohibition as to contributions corresponded to a similar prohibition applicable to corporations under the Corrupt Practices Act. Addition of the broad term "expenditures," however, in the restriction applicable to unions, raised doubts as to the constitutionality of the provision. The Supreme Court has held that the ban of this section does not apply to expenditure of union funds in publishing the *CIO News*, which advised members to vote for certain candidates in a congressional election.[42]

Contributions to Union Welfare Funds

In recent years, health and welfare funds supported in whole or in part by employer contributions have become increasingly popular as a subject of union-management negotiation. Such funds require the col-

---

[42] *U.S. v. CIO*, 22 LRRM 2194.

lection of very large sums of money. Consequently, Congress felt the need for legislation which would hold union leaders to strict accountability in the administration of such sums. Section 302 of the act attempted to accomplish this purpose by permitting welfare funds maintained by employer contributions only when the payments are held in trust and the fund is administered jointly by employer and employee representatives, with neutral persons available to settle possible disputes. However, funds in existence prior to January, 1946, were exempted. Furthermore, experience demonstrated that employers evidence little interest in the administration of such joint funds, with the result that in some industries, corrupt union officials have been able to utilize to their own personal gain the tremendous sums which build up in such funds over a period of time. Congressional investigation of the handling of certain of these welfare funds led to such shocking disclosures that it became clear that further legislation would be required in order to conserve and protect such funds against possible abuses. The Teller Act of 1958 and the Landrum-Griffin Act were direct results of such investigations.

HOW THE INDIVIDUAL WORKER WAS AFFECTED

A major objective claimed by the framers of the Taft-Hartley Act was to protect individual employees from the arbitrary power wielded by some labor leaders. Consequently, a number of important new privileges were granted to employees, with corresponding limitations on unions, on the theory that the actions of the latter have not always been truly representative of the will of the workers in the collective bargaining unit.

Elections

The Taft-Hartley Act made a number of important changes in election procedure. Under the original Wagner Act procedure, if two or more unions were on the ballot in an election to choose a bargaining representative, the employees voting in a "runoff" election did not have an opportunity to cast a negative vote (i.e., "no union") in the runoff, unless the "no union" choice had received a plurality of votes cast in the first election. In other words, the employees were limited in the runoff election to a choice between two unions, even though one of these unions might have run in third place. Later the NLRB changed this procedure by requiring the two highest choices to be placed on the runoff ballot, so that the "no union" choice could appear on the runoff ballot even if it had not received a plurality of votes in the first election. The Taft-Hartley Act made this procedure a matter of law.

The act also gave employees the right to seek elections to decertify a bargaining representative which no longer represented the majority of workers. In decertification elections held under the act, the bargaining representative has been decertified in about two out of every three elections, indicating that in many cases, unions in the course of time cease to represent the will of the workers.[43] It is interesting to observe that in decertification elections, unions have more success in retaining their bargaining rights in larger employee units than in smaller ones. For example, in decertification elections in 1966, unions won in units averaging 70 employees but lost in units averaging 39 employees.[44]

Representation elections still require a major portion of the Board's time. In the fiscal year ended June 30, 1966, the Board conducted 8,392 elections, a gain of 568 over the previous year. Nearly 76% of the elections involved units of 69 or fewer employees, and 24% were in units of 9 or fewer workers—indicating the difficulty that organized labor now faces in organizing the thousands of small employers. Unions won 61% of the elections in 1966[45] and only 59% in 1967.[46]

The Taft-Hartley Act also made an important change in the rule governing the right of employees on strike to vote in representation elections. Under the Wagner Act the Board had ruled that in a strike caused by employer unfair labor practices, only strikers were eligible to vote, since they were entitled to reinstatement; whereas in a strike over economic issues, both replacements and strikers were eligible to vote. The Taft-Hartley Act, however, contained a specific provision that "employees on strike who are not entitled to reinstatement shall not be eligible to vote." In an economic strike the employer has the legal right to fill jobs of strikers with permanent replacements. Therefore, in an economic strike, strikers who are replaced could lose the right to vote in a representation election. This provision was attacked by union spokesmen, who claimed that it would enable antiunion employers to provoke a strike, recruit nonunion replacements, and then call for an election. The strike breakers could elect "representatives," and this would bar an independent, effective union from calling an election for a year, or they might vote for decertification of the existing union. This provision, which became known as a "union-busting" provision, was amended by the Landrum-Griffin Act, as explained in Chapter 22.

Ban on Compulsory Checkoff

The act prohibited the compulsory checkoff, the method by which union dues are deducted by the employer from the worker's wages and paid directly to the union treasury. The checkoff of membership dues was made lawful only where individual employees execute a written assign-

---

[43] In fiscal 1966, unions won 64 decertification elections and lost 157. *Thirty-First Annual Report, op. cit.,* p. 20.

[44] *Loc. cit.*

[45] *Loc. cit.*

[46] 67 LRR 304.

TABLE 21-1

RESULTS OF NLRB REPRESENTATION ELECTIONS, 1936–67

Fiscal Year	Elections		Employees Involved		
	Total	Percent Won by Unions	Total Eligible	Total Valid Votes Cast	Percent for Union
1936	31	81	9,512	7,572	81
1937	265	94	181,424	164,135	87
1938	1,152	82	394,558	343,687	82
1939	746	77	207,597	177,215	78
1940	1,192	77	595,075	532,955	82
1941	2,568	83	788,111	729,933	81
1942	4,212	86	1,296,567	1,067,037	84
1943	4,153	86	1,400,000	1,126,501	82
1944	4,712	84	1,322,225	1,072,594	77
1945	4,919	83	1,087,177	893,758	79
1946	5,589	80	846,431	698,812	76
1947	6,920	75	934,553	805,474	77
1948	3,222	72	384,565	333,900	77
1949	5,514	70	588,761	516,248	73
1950	5,619	74	890,374	786,382	83
1951	6,432	74	666,556	587,595	75
1952	6,765	73	771,346	667,878	75
1953	6,050	72	737,998	639,739	78
1954	4,663	66	511,430	449,673	70
1955	4,215	68	515,995	453,442	74
1956	4,946	65	462,712	414,568	65
1957	4,729	62	458,904	410,619	64
1958	4,337	61	351,217	315,428	60
1959	5,428	63	430,023	385,794	64
1960	6,380	59	483,964	436,723	64
1961	6,354	56	450,930	403,310	59
1962	7,355	58	536,047	482,558	62
1963	6,871	59	489,365	441,969	60
1964	7,309	58	538,019	486,573	58
1965	7,576	61	531,971	480,280	62
1966	8,103	62	582,212	525,061	58
1967	7,882	60	611,006	542,999	61

SOURCE: National Labor Relations Board statistics.

ment of wages for not longer than one year or for the duration of the applicable union contract, whichever is shorter.

Bargaining Unit Problems

Under the Taft-Hartley Act, as under the Wagner Act, the NLRB continued to be vested with authority to determine the appropriate bargaining unit. This authority, however, was limited in the case of professional employees, craft workers, and guards.

Craft-Industrial Problems. As we have noted in our discussion of the Wagner Act, one of the most difficult problems faced by the NLRB was the contest between AFL and CIO unions as to whether the appropriate bargaining unit should be a craft or an industrial unit. Congress, of course, had been concerned primarily with the question whether employees wanted *any* union to represent them, rather than *which* union. This highly explosive issue was dumped into the lap of the NLRB with little statutory guidance to assist it in its determination. Section 9(*b*) of the Wagner Act simply directed the Board to "decide in each case whether, in order to insure to employees the full benefit of their right to self-organization, and otherwise to effectuate the policies of the Act, the unit appropriate for the purposes of collective bargaining shall be the employer unit, craft unit, plant unit, or subdivision thereof."

In making such determinations, the NLRB found that it had to weigh and balance two often conflicting objectives of labor policy: self-determination and stability in industrial relations. Self-determination, which favored craft severance, could, if carried to an extreme, result in the fragmentation of collective bargaining into a myriad of small, ineffective units. Moreover, it raised the problem of multiplicity of negotiations, more jurisdictional disputes, and possible weakening of industrial unions. On the other hand, the policy of stability, which was frequently synonymous with favored treatment for industrial unions, could mean that individual crafts would be submerged in a large union without regard to their peculiar problems. Moreover, preference for larger industrial unions could lead to dissatisfaction among substantial groups of employees within the union.

The Board wrestled with this problem throughout the Wagner Act period. In the early years, it tended to favor large industrial unions as most conducive to effective collective bargaining. Then, in 1937, this trend was reversed, and the Globe doctrine[47] evolved, which in most instances allowed craftworkers in initial representation elections to determine whether they wanted to be in a plantwide union or have a separate craft. The Board was for a time more reluctant to allow craft severance where craftsmen had already been included in a large industrial union; but in 1942 the Board's policy shifted, and severance was permitted where a "true" craft was involved.

However, the Board's policies on bargaining units did not satisfy either the CIO or the AFL. The Taft-Hartley Act sought to settle this issue by writing into law the restriction that the Board may not decide that a craft unit is inappropriate on the ground that an industrial unit had already been established by a prior Board determination, unless a majority of employees in the proposed craft unit voted against the craft unit. This clause was criticized by CIO officials, who argued that it could be used to permit various splinter craft groups to break off from established industrial unions. These fears proved groundless, however; and in actual prac-

---

[47] The Globe doctrine, which involves the principle of self-determination by a particular group of employees as to their bargaining unit, is so called because it was first enunciated in the case of the *Globe Machine and Stamping Co.*, 3 NLRB 294 (1937).

tice, this provision produced little change in NLRB procedure with regard to representation of skilled crafts. The NLRB wisely interpreted this provision as prohibiting it from using a prior unit determination as the sole ground for decision as to the appropriateness of a craft union, but as still giving it discretion to include skilled workers in a larger industrial union where the work of the skilled group is so integrated with that of the production workers that a separate unit would be inappropriate.

Under its present practice, the Board now considers all relevant factors to determine a severance issue, such as whether the employees sought are skilled journeymen craftsmen or constitute a functionally distinct department; bargaining history at the plant and in the industry; the extent to which the employees have established or maintained their separate identity; the integration of the production process; and the qualifications of the union seeking severance.

Extent of Bargaining Unit. The power of the Board to determine the appropriate bargaining unit can have a material effect upon the ability of unions to organize the unit in question. Generally, the smaller the unit, the easier it is for the union to obtain a majority of the employees, but fragmentation of bargaining units would create a difficult problem for employers, who might find that they have to bargain with many different unions in a multiunit organization. In both the retail industry and the insurance industry, the Board originally believed that wider geographic units were appropriate, but after finding that a large unit inhibited organization, it changed its policy to approve smaller units. Thus, in the retail chain store field, prior to 1961, the Board's policy was to make bargaining units coextensive with the employer's administrative division or the geographic area involved. However, this policy was abandoned in the *Sav-on Drug* case,[48] which involved a group of chain drug stores. Under the Board's present practice in the retail chain store field, the individual store will be found to be an appropriate unit where there is substantial autonomy in each store and no material interchange of employees. Similarly, in the insurance industry, the Board originally concluded that statewide units were appropriate,[49] but after years of experimentation it changed its policy and found the district office to be more appropriate.[50]

The viewpoint of the NLRB is succinctly stated in the following quotation from an article by Board Chairman Frank W. McCulloch, "Looking at the problem of what is an appropriate bargaining unit involves determining what group is appropriate for one purpose—collective bargaining."[51] If the Board establishes policy with respect to a particular size unit and collective bargaining does not result, it believes that in ac-

---

[48] *Sav-on Drugs, Inc.,* 51 LRRM 1152.

[49] *Metropolitan Life Insurance Company,* 56 NLRB 1635.

[50] *Quaker State Life Insurance Company,* 134 NLRB 960.

[51] Frank W. McCulloch, "NLRB Trends," in *NLRB in a Changing Industrial Society,* D. R. Sheriff and V. M. Kuebler (eds.) (Iowa City: Center for Labor and Management, University of Iowa, 1967), p. 16.

cordance with statutory policy it should change the appropriate unit so as to encourage collective bargaining. Critics of the Board claim that the NLRB has gone too far in this direction, as for example, dividing up store units so that there are separate bargaining units for selling and nonselling personnel in department stores. Furthermore, the Board's understanding of the statutory policy appears to be contrary to the provisions of Section 9(c)(5) of the Taft-Hartley Act which tells the Board that in determining whether a unit is appropriate "the extent to which the employees have organized shall not be controlling"—a provision specifically added to the Taft-Hartley Act by Congress to reverse NLRB policy under the Wagner Act.

In appraising the administration by the Board of its duty to determine the appropriate bargaining unit, it is important to realize that the Taft-Hartley Act contains conflicting statements of statutory policy. It was, in a sense, a political instrument which attempted in one law to appease critics of the Wagner Act yet not wholly alienate organized labor. Although the Taft-Hartley Act added many provisions apparently intended to restrict actions of the Board which, under the Wagner Act, had seemed to favor labor unduly or had neglected the rights of individual workers who did not want to be represented by unions, nevertheless Section 1 of the Act, which contains the general statement of statutory policy, retains language clearly affirming it to be the policy of the United States to encourage "the practice and procedure of collective bargaining." Since the determination of the appropriate bargaining unit is a typical kind of administrative decision involving the application of expertise, the Board can exercise wide discretion in its weighing of the relevant issues and can obviously consider the impact of the unit determination on collective bargaining, as long as the extent to which employees have organized is not controlling.

The power of the Board in this area is particularly impressive because it is normally not subject to court review. Although Section 10 of the act provides for court review in the case of any person "aggrieved by a final order of the Board," the Supreme Court has decided that certifications of a bargaining agent are not "final orders" in this sense and therefore cannot be appealed to the courts.[52] Normally, the only way an employer can obtain judicial review of an NLRB order in an election case is to refuse to bargain with the union certified by the Board. When the union brings an unfair labor practice charge, the NLRB's order to bargain can be appealed, and at such time the certification of the bargaining agent and the record of the election are subject to review by the court. However, this process is not open to a union that wishes to challenge an election ruling.

---

[52] If, however, a Board certification violates an express provision of the statute such as improperly grouping together professional and nonprofessional employees in the same bargaining unit, the courts will set aside the action of the Board (*Leedom* v. *Kyne*, 358 U.S. 184, 79 S. Ct. 180 [1958]).

Professional Employees. Under the Wagner Act the NLRB customarily excluded professional employees from all bargaining units of production and maintenance workers. The Board based its policy on the fact that professional employees and production workers had no common history of collective bargaining, and that—from the standpoint of education, experience, economic interest, relation to their employer, and method and amount of compensation—there was little, if any, mutuality of interest between the two groups.

When the bargaining unit problems involved professional employees and subprofessional technicians and/or white-collar workers rather than production workers, the policy was somewhat different. In such instances the Board ruled that its so-called "Globe" doctrine applied. In a key case the Board stated:

Upon the entire record we find that the professional employees might properly be considered either as a separate unit or as part of a larger unit composed of professional and nonprofessional employees. Under such circumstances, we apply the principle that the determining factor is the desires of the professional employees. We shall, therefore, direct separate elections in order that we may ascertain the wishes of the professional employees.[53]

Despite the apparent fairness of this policy, a number of professional associations felt that the NLRB was not giving due consideration to the problems of professional employees. As a result, the Taft-Hartley amendments provided that the NLRB shall not decide that any unit including professional and nonprofessional workers is appropriate for collective bargaining unless a majority of such professional employees vote for inclusion in such unit. In effect, this wrote into law the NLRB's Globe doctrine as far as professional employees are concerned.

Guards. The act also provided that no union could be certified as a bargaining representative if it included both guards or watchmen and other employees or was affiliated with an organization which included both groups. This section accepted *in toto* the arguments of employers that the same union should not be permitted to represent both guards and the rank and file. As a result, unions which included both guards and others had to disaffiliate locals of guards, which, under the Taft-Hartley Act, could be represented only by independent unions, unaffiliated with the AFL or the CIO. This weakened somewhat the union movement among guards.

Discrimination against Minority Groups

The act provided (Section 8[a][3]) that an employer was not justified in discriminating against an employee for nonmembership in a labor organization if he had reasonable ground for believing that such membership was not available to the employee on the same terms and

[53] *Shell Development Company, Inc.,* 38 NLRB 192, 196–97 (1942).

conditions generally applicable to other members. At first glance, this appears to mean that a union-shop contract could not be applied to Negro employees unless Negroes were fully and equally admitted with whites to union membership. However, another section (8[*b*][1]) provided that a union shall have the right to prescribe its own rules with respect to the acquisition or retention of membership. Moreover, the Senate-House Conference Report expressly declared that the act did not disturb arrangements in which Negroes were relegated to an auxiliary local.[54]

For many years the Taft-Hartley Act had little or no effect upon discrimination against Negroes practiced by unions. However, as public opinion focused more and more on this problem, the NLRB gradually evolved the doctrine that a bargaining agent certified by a public authority had a duty to represent all members of the bargaining unit fairly. Thus, in the *Pioneer Bus Company* case (51 LRRM 1546) the Board stated that execution of a contract that discriminates on the basis of race would endanger a union's certification as exclusive bargaining agent and would not bar an election sought by another union. Recently, on the same day that President Lyndon B. Johnson signed into law the Civil Rights Act of 1964, the NLRB in the *Hughes Tool Company* case (56 LRRM 1289) found a union guilty of unfair labor practices and stripped it of its certification as bargaining agent because of its racial discrimination practices. Further emphasizing its new tough line on discrimination, on September 14, 1964, the Board found Local 1367 of the International Longshoremen's Association (148 NLRB No. 44), guilty of unfair labor practices where it had established separate all-white and all-Negro locals and divided work unfairly.

Other Procedural Safeguards

Among other important rights given to individual employees to strengthen their positions relative to the union was the power to sue the union for damages resulting from an illegal strike. Also, the employee was given the right to present grievances directly to his employer and to have such grievances adjusted without the intervention of the union representative. The adjustment could not be inconsistent with the terms of the collective bargaining agreement, and the union was given the right to have its representative present at the adjustment.

HOW THE PUBLIC WAS AFFECTED BY THE LAW

One of the major reasons for enactment of the Taft-Hartley Act was the general recognition on the part of the public and lawmakers that

---

[54] The Conference Report refers specifically to the case of *Larus and Brother Co.*, 62 NLRB 1075 (1945), as an example of an arrangement not disturbed by the act. Any other interpretation would have alienated southern Democrats, who were among the Taft-Hartley Act's most ardent supporters.

some means had to be devised to protect the community from stoppages of the flow of essential commodities and services such as characterized the wave of strikes in 1946. The Wagner Act itself had contained no prohibition against strikes of any kind; instead, it provided a peaceful alternative[55] to the costly strikes which had been fought over the denial of basic rights of union recognition. In 1937, 60% of the workers on strike were involved in organizational disputes. In 1945, only 22% of the strikers were out on organizational strikes.[56] Thus, the Wagner Act was successful in reducing this particular form of work stoppage. At the same time, however, strikes over economic issues—wages, hours, and working conditions—increased in importance. Moreover, industrywide bargaining led to walkouts involving an entire industry instead of merely one plant. Thus, the same number of strikes in 1946 as in 1937 produced four times as many man-days lost in the later year. The Taft-Hartley Act attempted by a number of procedures and prohibitions to narrow and restrict the use by organized labor of the strike weapon.

Prohibited Strikes

Certain types of strikes deemed unduly oppressive to employers and the public were outlawed. These have been considered earlier in this chapter and included secondary strikes and boycotts, jurisdictional disputes, and strikes to upset the certification of a rival union. Any person injured in his business or property as a result of such unlawful strikes could bring suit for damages against the offending union.

Strikes against the federal government were likewise forbidden, and any individual employed by the United States who went on strike was subject to immediate discharge and loss of civil service status. We shall discuss this section in Chapter 23.

Strikes called in violation of no-strike clauses in collective bargaining agreements were not prohibited, but the act provided a procedure whereby the union could be sued by the employer in federal court for damages due to breach of contract. It was hoped that the act, by facilitating the bringing of suits against unions, would make for stricter observance of such clauses and thus lessen the number of work stoppages.

National Emergency Strikes

Finally, the Taft-Hartley Act established procedures to govern so-called "national emergency" strikes. This procedure, which is discussed in Chapter 23, did not, however, forbid such strikes but merely provided for their postponement.

[55] From 1936 to 1945, 10,058,872 employees resorted to the orderly procedures of the act in 32,615 separate representation cases in order to establish their rights to recognition (*Matter of Packard Motor Car Co.*, 61 NLRB 14 [1945]).

[56] National Labor Relations Board, *Eleventh Annual Report* (Washington, D.C.: U.S. Government Printing Office, 1946), p. 2, n. 1.

Cooling-Off Periods

The act also required that at least 60 days' notice had to be given by unions and employers desiring to terminate or modify an existing contract. Within 30 days following such notice, if no agreement had been reached, a second notice was to be given to the Federal Mediation and Conciliation Service and to whatever mediation agency there was within the state.

The difficulties involved in this procedure will be discussed in Chapter 23. Criticism has been directed, in addition, at the sanctions imposed by this section. Employees who walk out in violation of the cooling-off period—the 60 days prior to contract termination—lose their status as employees under the act and therefore are deprived of any protection against unfair practices by an employer. As a practical matter, however, the notice provisions have been of little importance. Notices are perfunctorily given, and the sanctions are so drastic that they are rarely invoked.

APPRAISAL OF THE NLRB UNDER THE TAFT-HARTLEY ACT

Many critics of our present labor policy have aimed their attack not against the Taft-Hartley Act, but rather against the manner in which the NLRB has administered it. It should be recognized that the NLRB is more than an administrative body carrying out the mandate of Congress. It is also a policy-making body, and almost necessarily so; for the Taft-Hartley Act merely sets forth rules in general terms, and it is the function of the Board to amplify this language so that it is applicable to the multitude of diverse cases which present themselves to it for decision.

The present Board has been subject to sharp attack by management spokesmen for alleged bias in favor of labor. The record shows that the present Board has reversed or modified a substantial number of prior Board decisions in representation matters and a substantial number in other fields, which reversals have had the effect of restricting management prerogatives and favoring organized labor. These favorable decisions have fallen into three major categories:

1. Blunting restrictions on union tactical weapons, such as the picket line.
2. Restricting employer counterweapons, such as employer free speech.
3. Defining the bargaining unit to facilitate organizing efforts of unions.

In addition, the Board has expanded the reliance on card checks as opposed to secret ballot elections to determine collective bargaining representatives.

There is no question that the composition of the Board, as changed by Presidential appointments from time to time, has made a difference in its attitude toward labor and management. While employer groups currently blast the Board for being "prolabor," union spokesmen retort that the Board is simply correcting for the promanagement bias of the Eisen-hower Board. If one looks simply at the percentage of elections won by unions in recent years, the composition of the Board does not seem to have made much of a difference (see Table 21–1). Indeed, this is the conclusion reached by one labor economist who studied the results of 63,906 union representation elections held under NLRB auspices from 1955 to 1966.[57] However, union leaders point to the greatly increased number of elections during the Kennedy-Johnson administrations. In their view, unions, under the Eisenhower Board, only filed for election where they had a "sure thing" because they were aware of the power of the employer to exert various forms of pressure on employees, whereas today they are more ready to file for an election even in cases where they know the results will be close.[58]

The lack of regard for *stare decisis* by the Board has made it difficult for management and labor leaders alike to make policy decisions with any assurance that they will comply with what the Board considers lawful practice. Many lawyers argue that if the Board wishes to change a long-standing policy, it should do so by utilizing the process of the Administrative Procedures Act which requires due notice and an oppor-tunity to argue the merits of the new policy. The Board, on the contrary, simply uses a particular case as a vehicle to change its policy, which can be obviously unfair to the participants in that case.

The NLRB in many respects carries out a quasi-judicial function; yet its members are not appointed in a manner like judges, nor do the members purport to act like judges. For this reason, some critics believe that the decision-making power should be taken away from the Board and vested in a labor court, leaving to the NLRB only the purely administra-tive job of holding elections.

Testimony before the Ervin Subcommittee on Separation of Powers, which held hearings in early 1968 to determine whether or not the Board had overstepped its statutory authority, made it clear that the wrath of employer spokesmen was directed not only against the NLRB but also against the courts, including the U.S. Supreme Court. Whether or not one agrees with the policy of the NLRB, it is a fact that many of its most criticized decisions—such as, for example, the subcontracting doctrine enunciated in the *Fibreboard* case—have been sustained by the courts.

APPRAISAL OF THE TAFT-HARTLEY ACT

Whether the Taft-Hartley Act is a "good" or a "bad" law depends in large measure upon the standard by which it is judged. If it is deemed

[57] *Business Week*, December 2, 1967, p. 60.
[58] *Ibid.*

desirable to afford greater freedom and privileges of self-determination to the individual worker, then it would seem that the act constituted a rather hesitant advance in labor legislation. On the other hand, if one believes that progressive social policy requires strengthening labor organizations on the theory that all but a few unions are still at a disadvantage in bargaining with employers, then the various restrictions imposed upon the activities of unions appear less desirable.

Standards, therefore, affect one's view of the act, and such standards frequently reflect the social bias of the individual. However, one standard is at hand which lends itself to a fairly objective appraisal. That is the extent to which the act facilitated the process of effective collective bargaining.

Ways in Which the Act Encouraged Effective Collective Bargaining

Effective collective bargaining may be defined as bargaining which in general represents the will of the majority of workers. The decertification procedure provided by the Taft-Hartley Act enabled employees to rid themselves of a union which because of corrupt leadership or other causes no longer represented the majority of workers. Likewise, the Communist affidavit requirements may have served to lessen industrial disputes which reflected, not the bona fide grievances of workers, but rather the planned intrigues of Communist officials. The prohibition against the closed shop and restrictions on the union shop were intended to eliminate practices such as the selling of jobs through issuance of work permits, which benefited the union bosses rather than the union membership; but these provisions were largely ineffective.

Effective collective bargaining assumes also a balance of power between labor and management. Under the Wagner Act, however, the balance of power in some industries had been so turned in labor's favor that individual employers had no choice but to accept the union's demands. The Taft-Hartley Act sought to remedy this situation by imposing an obligation to bargain upon both the union and the employer. Moreover, on the premise that effective collective bargaining requires responsible parties to the agreement, the act made unions subject to court actions for breach of contract. But this premise ignored the fact that sound industrial relations are not built by running to the courts. Furthermore, as we have already observed in the prior discussion, the plethora of Board and Court decisions on what constitutes good-faith bargaining has probably been detrimental to the establishment of sound voluntary bargaining relations.

Effective collective bargaining assumes that the democratic privilege of self-determination of wages, hours, and working conditions will be reasonably exercised so as not to inconvenience the public by widespread work stoppages. Such union devices as the secondary boycott, jurisdictional strikes, and industrywide strikes in essential industries unnecessarily burden the public. Therefore, the Taft-Hartley Act narrowed the use of the strike weapon within limits deemed consistent with the public interest.

Ways in Which the Act Impeded Effective Collective Bargaining

The act enabled employers to delay peaceful determination of a bargaining representative through the NLRB machinery and therefore encouraged unions to strike to obtain recognition. An employer bent on delaying an election for certification of a bargaining representative could delay proceedings by charging the union with unfair labor practices, and since most organizing campaigns usually involve some "high-pressure" salesmanship by union advocates, a prima facie case of coercion frequently could be made out. On the other hand, recent NLRB rulings have all gone far to eliminate the employers' right of free speech.

The act used as a sanction in a number of provisions the deprivation of rights under the act. Thus, for example, employees who struck in violation of the cooling-off period provisions and unions which failed to sign non-Communist affidavits were forbidden to use the machinery of the Board. Obviously, however, these men and these unions would continue to take part in industrial relations, and their unprotected status only invited attacks by antiunion employers. If the objective of the act was equality between management and unions in collective bargaining, sanctions for enforcement should not have been put in the hands of employers. Such a policy invites industrial unrest rather than compliance with the act.

The act was intended to restore the balance of power in collective bargaining relations. But Congress had in mind the circumstances which exist in highly organized industries, without fully recognizing that in some areas, organization is still in an incipient state and that in such areas the act gave an antiunion employer power to prevent the emergence of effective collective bargaining. Particularly potent in this respect were the provisions which guaranteed the employer "free speech" and enabled him to sue a union in federal court (and thus weaken it financially) and to charge it with unfair labor practices in organizing. Under other provisions of the act an employer could provoke a walkout over economic issues and then be free to replace the strikers with nonunion men. The act stated that the strikers could not vote in an election, but the strikebreakers were given this privilege. Antiunion employers could thus use a strike over wages to change the bargaining representative in their plants. Again recent administration of the Act has re-altered this power balance and particularly left small employers with little recourse to resist large unions.

Effect of Taft-Hartley Act on Growth of Union Organization

There is no question that the rate of growth of unions has slowed down in recent years and that from 1947 to the present, contrary to experience in prior years, unions have grown at a slower rate than the labor force. It is not clear, however, whether the full blame for labor's organizing woes can be put on the Taft-Hartley Act, although labor leaders find this legislation a convenient excuse for lack of progress. As we observed in Chapter 2, it seems likely that more fundamental developments may be responsible for the decline of union membership, among them the shift in employment from manufacturing to service industries; the tremendous growth in white-collar employment; the geographical shift of industry to the South and Midwest, where public opinion has been more hostile to union organization than in the North; the lack of aggressive leadership in unions; and the increasing difficulty of union organization now that most large companies are organized and it is in the smaller companies that unions must seek new members.

The Taft-Hartley Act represented a step in the direction of government dictation of the content of collective bargaining agreements. The act told employers and unions what they could and what they could not include in contracts with respect to welfare plans, union security clauses, and checkoff of dues. While this approach is probably unavoidable if the purpose of the act to protect employees is to be made effective, in the long run this trend may prove detrimental to continuation of voluntary collective bargaining. As we shall see in the next chapter, the Landrum-Griffin Act takes an even bigger step in this direction and subjects the internal affairs of union organizations to governmental regulation.

QUESTIONS FOR DISCUSSION

1. What is meant by the term "unfair labor practice"? How are charges of unfair labor practices handled by the NLRB? How does the Taft-Hartley Act differ from the Wagner Act in its approach toward unfair labor practices?

2. What is meant by "mandatory" and "nonmandatory" subjects of collective bargaining? Give examples of each. Does this distinction make sense in practical collective bargaining? Do you think that the "good-faith" bargaining provisions of the Taft-Hartley Act should be repealed?

3. In what way have recent decisions by the NLRB tended to facilitate union organization? Is this action consistent with the statutory purposes set forth in the Taft-Hartley Act?

4. Discuss the actual and potential effects of the Taft-Hartley Act upon collective bargaining.

SUGGESTIONS FOR FURTHER READING

ABODEELY, PAUL A. *Compulsory Arbitration and the NLRB*. Labor Relations and Public Policy Series Report No. 1, Industrial Research Unit (Philadelphia: University of Pennsylvania Press, 1968).

A concise analysis of how the NLRB is moving to determine the terms and conditions of employment.

BROWNE, HARRY L. "The Labor Board Unsettles the Scales," 42 *Notre Dame Lawyer*, Vol. XLII (1966), p. 133.

An analysis by a Labor Board critic of the effect of recent Board and Court decisions on the principle of free collective bargaining.

GETMAN, JULIUS G. "The Protection of Economic Pressure by Section 7 of the National Labor Relations Act," *University of Pennsylvania Law Review*, Vol. CV (1967), pp. 1195 ff.

A discussion of the extent to which the act protects the rights of employees to engage in concerted activities without interference by employers.

McFARLAND, ALAN. "Union Authorization Cards," *Yale Law Journal*, Vol. LXXV (1966), pp. 805–844.

An excellent résumé of the attitude of the courts and the NLRB toward the use of authorization cards to designate the bargaining representative.

NATIONAL LABOR RELATIONS BOARD. *Annual Report* (Washington, D.C.: U.S. Government Printing Office).

The annual reports of the Board, covering operations for the fiscal year ended June 30, are an excellent source for statistics as well as a summary of action taken by the Board on key issues.

NORTHRUP, HERBERT R., and BLOOM, GORDON F. *Government and Labor*, chaps. v and vi. Homewood, Ill.: Richard D. Irwin, Inc., 1963.

An analysis of some of the major problems which have arisen under the Taft-Hartley Act.

Chapter : THE LANDRUM-GRIFFIN
22 : ACT

In the preceding chapters, we have seen how the role of law and government has evolved in the field of union-management relations. The Norris–La Guardia Act was essentially laissez faire in attitude. The purpose of the statute was to prevent law—in the form of the court injunction—from interfering with union-management relations. Then came the Wagner Act, in which the force of law was used to assist organized labor. Government power was committed to protect the right to organize and to restrict employer interference with such rights. Union tactics were left virtually unregulated. As a result of its favored position, organized labor grew so strong that abuses developed, and the need was recognized for restrictions on the power of unions. The Taft-Hartley Act was enacted, with government now placed in the role of policing certain actions of both labor and management. However, abuses continued to come to light in the internal administration of unions. Since much of the power wielded by unions over individual workers stems from union monopoly over job opportunities provided under both the Wagner and the Taft-Hartley Acts, government has felt a responsibility to safeguard the rights of individual union members. As a result, the conduct of internal union affairs has come to be viewed as a federal problem.

Regulation of internal union procedures is a major purpose of the Labor-Management Reporting and Disclosure Act of 1959, more popularly known as the Landrum-Griffin Act. Passage of this law marked the culmination of the well-publicized hearings of the Senate Select Committee on Improper activities in the Labor or Management Field (McClellan Committee), which revealed that many union officials were guilty of coercion, violence, and denial to union members of basic rights; that small employers were being victimized through use of secondary boycotts, extortion, picketing, and similar techniques; and that employers were guilty of interfering with employee rights through use of "sweetheart" contracts and bribery of union officials by hired consultants.

SCOPE AND COVERAGE OF THE ACT

The Landrum-Griffin Act comprises seven different sections, called "titles," each of which deals with a different phase of the act's coverage. Title I contains a bill of rights for members of labor organizations. Title II requires unions and employers to file various reports[1] with the Secretary of Labor. Title III requires unions to file reports relating to so-called "trusteeships" over other labor organizations. Title IV contains detailed provisions with respect to the term of office of union officials, election procedures, and procedures for removal of union officers. Title V contains provisions relating to the fiduciary responsibility of union officials, requires the bonding of such officials, prohibits loans by unions to employees of such organizations resulting in a total indebtedness in excess of $2,000, and prohibits certain classes of persons with records of crime or Communist affiliation from holding union office. Title VI contains a number of miscellaneous provisions, among them a prohibition against extortionate picketing and a grant of power to the Secretary of Labor to investigate violations of the act.

Title VII contains a number of amendments to the Taft-Hartley Act relating to federal-state jurisdiction, voting rights of economic strikers, and secondary boycotts and recognition picketing. Many congressmen believed that the Landrum-Griffin Act should stand on its own feet and deal only with new areas of regulation, leaving to later enactments the complex task of amending the Taft-Hartley Act. However, so much pressure was brought to bear upon Congress, particularly with respect to the inadequacies of the Taft-Hartley Act prohibitions against secondary boycotts and picketing, that Title VII, embodying such amendments, was finally incorporated in the law as passed.

The act grants to the Secretary of Labor broad powers to investigate possible violations of the law and to institute appropriate civil or criminal action. This authorization does not, however, apply to the bill-of-rights section or to the amendments of the Taft-Hartley Act. In the case of violations of the former section, union members must bring their own civil actions in the U.S. district courts. As to the latter category, enforcement is the responsibility of the National Labor Relations Board. A Bureau of Labor-Management Reports—now called the Office of Labor-Management and Welfare-Pension Reports (LMWP)—was established in

---

[1] None of the above-described reports relate directly to the operation of employee welfare and pension plans. Reporting on the operation of such funds is covered by a different statute—the Welfare and Pension Plans Disclosure Act of 1958, as amended in 1962, more commonly known as the Teller Act. This act requires that a description of every plan covered by the act be filed with the Secretary of Labor; and thereafter, annual reports must be filed, giving details of operation of the funds. Broad powers of investigation and enforcement are granted to the Secretary of Labor; but as noted in previous chapters, major abuses in this area are still extant, and much more money is involved in welfare and pension funds than in union treasuries.

the U.S. Department of Labor to handle the day-to-day administration of the act. This office reported 52,272 active disclosure files as of June 30, 1966.[2]

Like its predecessor, the Taft-Hartley Act, the Landrum-Griffin Act relates to employers and labor organizations in industries "affecting commerce." However, the scope of the latter is broadened by the fact that many of its provisions are applicable to employees and employers covered by the Railway Labor Act, who were expressly excluded from the Taft-Hartley provisions. The definition of "employer" includes anyone considered an employer under any federal law. The definition is thus the most comprehensive to be found in federal law.

HOW THE EMPLOYER WAS AFFECTED

The Landrum-Griffin Act imposes new obligations as well as new benefits upon employers.

Restrictions on Employers

Although the McClellan Committee devoted most of its attention to abuses of labor organizations, it uncovered a number of examples of malpractice by employers in their dealings with employees and unions. Thus, some companies paid union officials in order to obtain so-called "sweetheart" contracts, which permitted continuation of substandard working conditions; or companies conspired with officials of a "friendly" union to permit organizing of the company's workers to the exclusion of other more belligerent unions. The committee also found evidence that some companies were interfering with the rights of employees to organize by using so-called "labor consultants." The committee noted that the Taft-Hartley Act could not deal effectively with such activity because the NLRB had no power to act against independent contractors serving as labor consultants.

Title II of the Landrum-Griffin Act requires employers to file annual reports with the Secretary of Labor disclosing payments and loans to unions, union officers, shop stewards, and employees of unions. The reporting requirement applies to payments and loans, whether direct or indirect, whether in cash or other things of value, but excludes deductions of union dues pursuant to a checkoff and certain other classes of "valid" employer payments. Other subsections require reports by employers of payments to employees, employee committees, or labor consultants which might affect the free choice of employees to exercise their right to organize and bargain collectively. Labor consultants who, pursuant to an arrangement with an employer, undertake to persuade employees in the

---

[2] U.S. Department of Labor, Office of Labor-Management and Welfare-Pension Reports, *Summary of Operations, 1966* (Washington, D.C.: U.S. Government Printing Office, 1966), p. 1.

exercise of their organizing or bargaining rights, or to supply information to the employer concerning employee or union activity in connection with a labor dispute, except information solely for use in legal or arbitration proceedings, must also file detailed reports.

Title V of the law expands Section 302 of the Taft-Hartley Act by broadening the types of payments which are criminal offenses. Payments are now unlawful, for example, if they are made by an employer or his agent to:

1. Any representative of his employees.
2. A union, or its officers or employees, which is seeking to represent or represents or would admit to membership employees of the employer.
3. Employees or committees of employees of the employer in excess of their normal compensation for the purpose of causing them to influence other employees in the exercise of their organizing or bargaining rights.
4. Any officer or employee of a union with intent to influence him with respect to his actions or duties as a union representative or official.

Lawyers have expressed concern that these criminal provisions are very broad—in fact, broader than the corresponding reporting provisions contained in Title II, so that, technically, certain payments which need not be reported may actually be criminal offenses! Furthermore, since certain acts which must be reported are subject to criminal penalties, there is some question as to the constitutionality of these reporting requirements in view of the protection against self-incrimination guaranteed under the fifth amendment. From the date of passage of the act to June 30, 1966, less than 2,000 employer reports had been filed with the LMWP and less than 200 consultant reports.[3] The low incidence in reporting is undoubtedly attributable in large measure to the fact that the clearest examples of reportable activities are often those which constitute a violation of section 8(a) of the Taft-Hartley Act, with the result that persons so involved are understandably reluctant to make a full disclosure.

Benefits of Landrum-Griffin Act to Employers

Although the reporting requirements of the Landrum-Griffin Act are onerous to employers already burdened by reporting requirements of many other federal agencies, nevertheless the benefits to employers conferred by the new law far outweigh its disadvantages. Despite some weakening of the provisions of the act by NLRB and court decisions, the sections of the act further restricting secondary boycotts and organizational picketing by unions are of substantial importance to employers. So also are the sections aimed at eliminating the so-called "no-man's land" in NLRB jurisdiction.

[3] *Ibid.,* p. 13.

Restrictions on Union Secondary Boycotts

We have already observed in the preceding chapter that although the Taft-Hartley Act purported to outlaw secondary boycotts, many loopholes developed in practice. Thus, if a Teamster business agent attempted to persuade X's employees not to handle the goods manufactured by Y, this was unlawful; yet the Taft-Hartley Act did not prohibit the business agent from warning X directly that he had better not handle Y's product! Likewise, the former law permitted boycott action applied through inducement of employees individually, instead of in concert, and inducement of employees of railroads, municipalities, and governmental agencies. The Landrum-Griffin Act closed all of these loopholes.

Under the Taft-Hartley Act, it was common practice for unions to induce employers to sign collective bargaining agreements which contained a so-called "hot cargo" clause. In accepting this provision, the employer agreed that his employees would not handle the goods of anyone with whom the union was having a labor dispute. The act makes it an unfair labor practice for any labor organization and any employer to enter into such agreements. Two exceptions are provided in the statute: agreements in the construction industry relating to contracting or subcontracting of work done at the construction site and agreements relating to jobbers, subcontractors, and the like in the apparel and clothing industry.

Despite the legislative history of the Landrum-Griffin restrictions on "hot cargo" and secondary boycott action by unions, the U.S. Supreme Court in 1967 held that a union did not violate the "hot-cargo" or secondary boycott provisions by maintaining and enforcing contract provisions that (1) gave union members the right to refuse to install prefabricated doors at a construction project and (2) specified that an employer would not subcontract certain construction work. The majority of the Court—with four justices dissenting—said that even if such conduct comes within the broad language of the statutory prohibitions, it was not congressional intent to ban traditional primary activity of unions. In the view of the majority, the action of the union was not "secondary" action but was rather designed to preserve work traditionally done by the union members with the primary employer.[4]

The effect of the statutory restrictions against secondary boycotts has also been weakened by interpretations of the Board and the courts of the so-called "publicity proviso." This proviso appears in the amended Section 8(*b*)(4) of the National Labor Relations Act after enumeration of prohibitions on various forms of strikes and boycotts. The proviso states:

Provided further, that for the purposes of this paragraph (4) only, nothing contained in such paragraph shall be construed to prohibit publicity, other than

---

[4] *National Woodwork Manufacturers Assoc.* v. *NLRB*, 64 LRRM 2801, 386 U.S. 612 (1967).

picketing, for the purpose of truthfully advising the public, including consumers and members of a labor organization, that a product or products are produced by an employer with whom the labor organization has a primary dispute and are distributed by another employer, as long as such publicity does not have the effect of inducing any individual employed by any person other than the primary employer in the course of his employment to refuse to pick up, deliver, or transport any goods, or not to perform any services, at the establishment of the employer engaged in such distribution.

Since the above-mentioned proviso specifically excludes "picketing" from protected union activity, it was generally assumed that picketing in connection with secondary boycott action was unlawful even when directed to the public. However, in a decision handed down by a divided Court, the Supreme Court has indicated that this is not so. In the case before the Court, a Teamsters' union, which had a primary dispute with an organization of fruit packers, set up picket lines in front of retail stores which sold fruit purchased from the packers. The picket signs advised consumers not to buy the fruit because it was nonunion. Pickets were instructed not to patrol delivery entrances or exits, and other precautions were taken not to interfere with the flow of merchandise in and out of the stores. No employees stopped work, and deliveries were not affected. Nevertheless, the NLRB found that the union action was unlawful secondary boycott action intended to force the stores to cease doing business with the packers. However, when the case reached the Supreme Court, the Court reversed the Board and held that so-called "consumer picketing" at neutral stores for the purpose of persuading customers to cease buying *products* of a struck primary employer does not violate the law, even though it may cause economic loss to the stores of the neutral third party.[5] The Court concluded that Congress had not intended to ban all consumer picketing and that it was necessary to distinguish between a union appeal to the public not to trade with the secondary employer (presumably unlawful) and what the Court found existed in the present case—a union appeal to the public not to buy the merchandise of the primary employer.

It is apparent from the foregoing discussion that while the Landrum-Griffin amendments further tightened restrictions on secondary boycott activity, the new language contains its own "loopholes." There will be many years of litigation and possible further congressional legislative revision before the limitations on secondary boycotts are clarified.

Restrictions on Picketing

The same can be said of the Landrum-Griffin restrictions on picketing. The act makes extortionate picketing—picketing intended to "shake down" an employer for the personal profit of a union agent rather than

---

[5] *National Labor Relations Board* v. *Fruit Packers Local 760*, 55 LRRM 2961 (1964).

for the benefit of employees—a federal offense. Furthermore, in perhaps the most controversial section of the law, major restrictions are imposed upon recognition and organizational picketing. The new law makes it an unfair labor practice for a labor organization to picket or threaten to picket an employer where an object thereof is forcing or requiring an employer to recognize or bargain with a labor organization as the representative of his employees, or forcing or requiring the employees of an employer to accept or select such labor organization as their collective bargaining representative, unless such labor organization is currently certified as the representative of such employees, under any of the following circumstances:

(A) Where an employer has lawfully recognized another union and the question of representation may not be legally raised at this time.
(B) Where a Taft-Hartley Act election has been held within the past 12 months.
(C) Where the picketing has been conducted without a petition for a representation election being filed within a reasonable period of time, not to exceed 30 days from commencement of the picketing.

The application of these provisions is made subject to a so-called "consumer picketing" proviso, which has been the source of much controversy. It states, in substance, that nothing in subparagraph (C), quoted above,

. . . shall be construed to prohibit any picketing or other publicity for the purpose of truthfully advising the public (including consumers) that an employer does not employ members of, or have a contract with, a labor organization, unless an effect of such picketing is to induce any individual employed by any other person in the course of his employment, not to pick up, deliver or transport any goods or not to perform any services.

The scope and meaning of these provisions is by no means clear, and a definitive interpretation of the foregoing language must await determination by the Supreme Court. Meanwhile, the National Labor Relations Board, in a series of influential decisions, has laid out these guidelines based upon its construction of the statutory language:

1. *Informational Picketing.* If the sole object of the picketing is to inform the public, and recognition of the union is not an objective of the picketing, the picketing is lawful and is not barred by any of the subsections enumerated above. Furthermore, even if such picketing interferes with deliveries or pickups, it is lawful nonetheless.[6]

2. *Dual-Purpose Picketing.* A picket line frequently has as its purpose both informing the public and securing recognition by an employer. Such picketing is presumably unlawful where the circumstances set out in subsections (A) and (B) above prevail. If (A) or (B) is not applicable,

---

[6] *Crown Cafeteria,* 49 LRRM 1648, reversing 47 LRRM 1321.

such picketing is entitled to the protection of the proviso to subsection (C) unless it interferes with deliveries, etc.[7] The NLRB has further held that mere isolated interferences with deliveries are not enough to make the picketing illegal. Despite the fact that the consumer picketing proviso expressly refers to *"an effect"* and *"any individual"* (italics added), the NLRB has read the language as if Congress were concerned only with a "substantial" effect and has held that there is a violation of the law only if picketing has "disrupted, interfered with or curtailed the employer's business."[8]

3. *Recognition Picketing.* Picketing intended to compel the employer to recognize the union as bargaining representative for his employees is subject to the prohibitions of subsection (C), and the picketing will be enjoined if it continues more than 30 days without a petition for an election being filed.[9] The Board has held, however, that so-called "union standards" picketing is not recognition picketing. Therefore, even if an employer has signed a contract with another certified labor organization, it is not unlawful, according to the NLRB, for another union to picket where the signs carried by the pickets merely state that the employer pays wages lower than the standards set by the picketing union, and there is no attempt by the union to obtain recognition from the employer.[10]

It is apparent from the foregoing brief outline that the NLRB has greatly narrowed the scope of the restrictive provisions contained in the Landrum-Griffin Act as they apply to picketing. Under the present Board, if the evidence shows that a union pickets an employer to protest against wage rates, unfair labor practices, working conditions, or discharge of employees, the NLRB will not interfere with the union action, even if deliveries to the employer are disrupted.

Many of the key decisions have been handed down by a divided Board. The application of the statute is obviously not clear to the members of the Board, and it is even more uncertain for the average union member. Gone are the simple days when the Norris–La Guardia Act granted automatic immunity to such action. By contrast, a union leader who today determines to place a picket line around a plant needs a lawyer at his side to guide him. The legality of the picketing may depend upon the wording of placards which the pickets carry and how people react to them. It may depend upon the relationship between the employer and the union, between the employer and a rival union, or between the employer and other employers with whom the union has a dispute. Most of all, the

---

[7] *Ibid.*

[8] *Barker Bros. Corp. and Golds, Inc.,* 51 LRRM 1053.

[9] The statutory criterion is a "reasonable period of time not to exceed thirty days." The NLRB has held 17 days is a reasonable time in which to file in one case (*International Brotherhood of Teamsters,* 127 NLRB 958, *enf.* 289 F. [2d] 41) and 18 days in another (*Sapulpa Typographical Union,* 45 LRRM 2400).

[10] *Claude Everett Construction Co.,* 49 LRRM 1757.

lawfulness of the picket line may hinge upon what the NLRB interprets the objective and purpose of the picket line to be.[11] To the average laboring man, such examination of motives and objectives seems like a return to the old doctrine of lawful and unlawful objectives, motives, and other mystical criteria which courts found so convenient in the past to justify injunctions against union activity.

Elimination of Jurisdictional No-Man's Land

Another important employer benefit conferred by the Labor Reform Act is the elimination of the so-called "no-man's land" created by the refusal of the National Labor Relations Board to assert jurisdiction over certain labor disputes which did not meet its jurisdictional standards. Under the Taft-Hartley Act the NLRB found it had neither the time nor the money required to handle the great number of labor disputes involving small employers; therefore, it imposed certain jurisdictional limitations on itself, stating in effect that it would not become involved in a dispute if the employer's sales volume was less than a certain prescribed figure. But when the small employer then went to the state court for relief, the U.S. Supreme Court ruled that the state court had no right to hear the case if the NLRB *could* have taken jurisdiction, even if it *did* not! As a consequence, small employers were denied a forum to give them relief from union coercive tactics, even though their larger competitors were protected by the NLRB.

The Landrum-Griffin Act seeks to solve this problem by amending the Taft-Hartley Act so as to permit the states to assert jurisdiction over labor disputes in interstate commerce over which the NLRB declines to take jurisdiction. The law authorizes the NLRB to decline to assert jurisdiction over any labor disputes which it determines would have only a slight impact upon interstate commerce, but it cannot reduce its jurisdiction below the standards prevailing on August 1, 1959. The Board is free, of course, to expand its jurisdiction at any time. The states have always had jurisdiction of labor disputes in intrastate commerce and cases involving violence, mass picketing, or other coercive conduct. This juris-

---

[11] The *Crown Cafeteria* case is a good illustration of how subjective judgments —which reflect the particular bias of the Board member or judge—now determine the lawfulness or unlawfulness of a picket line. In that case a union picketed a new cafeteria which had refused to hire through a union hiring hall or to sign a contract. The picket signs were addressed to "members of organized labor and their friends," stated that the cafeteria was "nonunion," and asked them not to patronize it. No stoppage of deliveries or services took place. In its first hearing of this case, a majority of the NLRB concluded that despite what was said on the signs, the picketing was really conducted for recognition purposes and was therefore not protected by the consumer picketing proviso (47 LRRM 1321). Subsequently, two new members were appointed to the Board, and upon reconsideration of the case the Kennedy Board held that the picketing was lawful because it was conducted merely to advise the public and caused no stoppages (49 LRRM 1648).

diction has now been broadened to include cases in interstate commerce which formerly fell in the "no-man's land" area.

Although the Landrum-Griffin Act appears to have eliminated the question of conflicting jurisdiction over cases of labor disputes, it does not necessarily follow that either management or labor will find that turning these problems back to the states is wholly satisfactory. At this writing, only 15 states and Puerto Rico have comprehensive codes regulating labor relations. In 35 states, parties excluded from protection of the Taft-Hartley Act by reason of the Board's jurisdictional standards do not have recourse to comprehensive labor laws governing labor-management relations. In such cases, these excluded parties will have to rely upon common-law doctrines or their own economic power.[12] The small businessman and the weak union are thus still penalized by lack of size. This problem can be met only by enactment of labor relations laws in all of the states or by a major expansion of the personnel of the NLRB so as to enable that agency to enlarge its jurisdiction. Neither of these possibilities appears to be very likely at this time.

HOW UNIONS WERE AFFECTED

The Landrum-Griffin Act is based upon the premise that unions and officials of unions have in many instances disregarded the rights of individual employees and that individual union members have been powerless to protect themselves against such tactics. The act therefore contains numerous restrictions on unions and union officials while conferring new rights and privileges upon individual union members.

Restrictions on Internal Union Affairs

The Landrum-Griffin Act repeals those provisions of the Taft-Hartley Act that required the filing of information as to the union's constitution, bylaws, and financial reports and also the filing of non-Communist affidavits. It substitutes new provisions requiring more detailed reports concerning the internal operation and financial condition of the union. Most important is the change in approach relative to enforcement. Whereas the Taft-Hartley Act punished failure to file required reports with a denial of the right to use the procedures of the National Labor Relations Board, the Landrum-Griffin Act imposes direct and severe criminal penalties.

Every labor organization is required to adopt a constitution and bylaws and file a copy with the Secretary of Labor. Furthermore, to the extent that the constitution and bylaws do not cover these points, the

---

[12] G. W. Hardbeck, "Federal-State Jurisdictional Issues and Policies under the New Labor Law," *Labor Law Journal*, Vol. XII (February, 1961), p. 106.

union must file a detailed statement as to qualifications for, or restrictions on, membership; procedures with respect to such matters as levying of assessments; audit of the financial transactions of the organization; discipline or removal of officers and agents for breaches of trust; imposition of fines, suspensions, and expulsions of members; and numerous other details as to the internal administration of the union. Unions must also file annually financial reports which, in addition to the usual balance sheet, must disclose loans aggregating more than $250 made to any officer, employee, or member; direct and indirect loans to any business enterprise; payments, including reimbursed expenses, to officers and employees who during the fiscal year received more than $10,000 union compensation; and "other disbursements including the purposes thereof."[13]

Both types of reports which were referred to above must be made available on request to all members of the union. Some union spokesmen have expressed the fear that this provision will enable employers to gain access to such reports and learn the details of their financial condition, which may weaken union bargaining power in negotiations, but there is no evidence that this has as yet occurred.

Restrictions on Union Officials

Under the provisions of many state laws, officers and directors of business corporations are held accountable to strict standards of fiduciary responsibility. The Landrum-Griffin Act applies this principle to officials of unions, stating that officers, agents, stewards, and other representatives of labor unions must conduct themselves in accordance with the rules of law generally applicable to the dealings of a trustee with other people's money. The act establishes a new federal crime—embezzlement or other unlawful conversion of a union's assets by an officer or employee of the union—punishable by a fine up to $10,000, imprisonment up to five years, or both. Drawing on the principle of minority stockholder suits in corporation law, the act provides that if an officer or other representative is accused of violating his fiduciary responsibilities and the union fails to take action against such officer or representative in a reasonable time after being requested to do so by a union member, the latter may, with the court's permission, bring his own suit in state or federal court for an accounting, and attorney's fees may be awarded out of any recovery. In addition, the act establishes detailed bonding requirements for officers, agents, shop stewards, or other representatives of employees of unions who handle funds or other property of the union.

A major objective of the 1959 legislation was to stamp out racketeering, crime, and corruption in labor unions. To this end the act contains provisions designed to bring to light possible conflicts of interest and

---

[13] The latter catchall phrase probably requires reporting on expenditures for political purposes and may therefore provide information on a little-known subject, if enforced. Thus far, however, no enforcement is visible.

similar shadowy transactions through which unscrupulous union officials and employers sacrifice the welfare of employees to personal advantage. Thus, the Landrum-Griffin Act requires officers and employees of labor unions (other than employees performing exclusively clerical or custodial duties) who have engaged in certain transactions enumerated in the act to file annual reports with the Secretary of Labor, covering not only themselves but their wives and minor children, and disclosing payments, stock, or other interests acquired in or from companies which the union represents or seeks to represent. The filing of false reports is made punishable by a fine of up to $10,000, a year in jail, or both. These reports, as well as the reports which employers and labor consultants must file, as discussed previously, are required to be available for public inspection.

Unions are also prohibited from making, "directly or indirectly," any loan or loans to officers or employees which result in a total indebtedness of such individual to the labor organization of more than $2,000. The phrase "directly or indirectly" is included in the act to bar deals such as those used by James R. Hoffa to camouflage his financial manipulations. Hoffa's own Local 299 in Detroit, according to McClellan Committee testimony, once loaned $25,000 to a man who immediately reloaned it to Hoffa!

Persons convicted of serious crimes are barred for a period of five years after conviction from holding any union position other than a clerical or custodial job. This provision was included in the act because the Senate's McClellan Committee had found that a number of unions were under the control of gangsters and hoodlums. Unfortunately, however, the mere fact that the government or individual union members can sue to remove from office an officer with a criminal record does not permit the NLRB to deny certification to such a union when it uses the processes of the Board in a representation procedure. As one NLRB trial examiner put it: "Any thug, gangster, or murderer who is at large can establish himself as a labor organization and, if designated as exclusive bargaining representative by a majority of employees . . . can obtain board certification."[14] Furthermore, the Landrum-Griffin Act lists certain crimes as a bar to holding office, but presumably a union leader convicted of a crime not on the prohibited list would not be barred from continuing to hold office.

The act imposes a similar prohibition against members of the Communist party and ex-Communists for a period of five years after they have quit the party. Violation of these provisions—with respect both to criminals and Communists—is punishable by a fine of not more than $10,000 or imprisonment for not more than one year, or both. Whether these severe penalties will prove more effective than the affadavit requirements formerly included in the Taft-Hartley Act in ridding unions of Communist

[14] *Business Week*, November 7, 1964.

officials remains to be seen. Thus far no effective enforcement has occurred.

The Landrum-Griffin Act prohibits union representatives from requesting or receiving various types of payments from employers or their consultants. The use of force or threats of force against union members to interfere with the exercise of any of their rights under the act is made a federal offense. The act also requires every labor organization "to inform its members concerning the provisions of this Act"—a provision which has led many unions to reproduce the act verbatim in union newspapers.

Trusteeships

The constitutions of many international unions authorize the international officers to suspend the normal processes of government of local unions and other subordinate bodies to supervise their internal activity and to assume control of their property and funds. These so-called "trusteeships" have been widely used by responsible officials to prevent corruption, mismanagement of funds, and infiltration of Communists, and to preserve order and integrity within the union. However, the hearings before the McClellan Committee revealed that trusteeships have been used in some cases as a means of consolidating the power of corrupt union officials, of plundering and dissipating the resources of local unions, and of preventing the growth of competing political elements within the organization. For example, the McClellan Committee found that of the Teamsters' 892 locals, 113 were under "trusteeship"!

Title III of the Landrum-Griffin Act requires national or international unions to file reports with the Secretary of Labor concerning all trusteeships. The act expressly limits trusteeships so that they can be established only in accordance with the constitution and bylaws of the national or international union and can be imposed only for the purpose of "correcting corruption or financial malpractice, assuring the performance of collective bargaining agreements or other duties of a bargaining representative, restoring democratic procedures, or otherwise carrying out the legitimate objects of such labor organizations." In order to limit the duration of trusteeships without imposing a fixed term which would interfere with the legitimate activities of the union, the act merely provides that after a period of 18 months a trusteeship shall be "presumed invalid," and the court is directed to decree its discontinuance unless it is shown by clear and convincing proof that continuation is necessary for an allowable purpose. However, as was pointed out in Chapter 3, despite this provision, the United Mine Workers still maintains trusteeships imposed in the 1920's! The U.S. Department of Labor filed a suit in 1964 to bar these trusteeships, but four years later, it had still not gone to trial.

While trusteeships were abused in some instances prior to adoption of the Landrum-Griffin Act, actually they are relatively uncommon in the total labor movement. On September 14, 1959, the effective date of the act, only 487 subordinate labor organizations, or less than 1% of all reporting organizations, were under some form of trusteeship imposed by a parent body. Since that date, there has been a decline in the number of trusteeships, which now amount to only about half the earlier number.[15]

Restrictions on Union Organizing and Bargaining Tactics

As has already been pointed out, the Landrum-Griffin Act imposes prohibitions and limitations on the use of picketing and boycott tactics by unions. Union spokesmen believe that if the amendments to the Taft-Hartley Act had been brought in as a separate enactment in a different session of Congress, less restrictive provisions would have resulted. However, since the picketing and boycott sections were considered as part of an overall labor reform program aimed primarily at a few corrupt unions, the entire package was adopted into law.

Special Privileges for Unions in Construction Industry

The casual and occasional nature of the employment relationship between employer and employees in the construction industry caused many problems to develop in that industry because of the restrictive provisions of the Taft-Hartley Act. The Landrum-Griffin Act—in one of its few provisions intended to loosen restrictions on unions—recognizes these problems and amends the Taft-Hartley Act so as to make lawful so-called "prehire" agreements in the construction industry. Such agreements may now make union membership compulsory 7 days after employment (rather than 30 days, as is the case in other industries) in states where union shops are permitted. Union contracts also can require an employer to notify the union of job openings and give the union an opportunity to refer qualified applicants for such employment, and can specify minimum training or experience qualifications for employment.

HOW THE INDIVIDUAL WORKER WAS AFFECTED

A major objective of the Landrum-Griffin Act was to rid unions of gangster control and corrupt practices generally. The legislators believed that if they could provide union members with information about what was happening to union funds and other vital aspects of union activities, and if they could protect individual rights through a bill of rights and procedures insuring secret elections, union members would rid themselves of untrustworthy or corrupt officers.

The Bill of Rights

Title I of the law purports to legislate into the internal laws and procedures of unions certain of the essential guarantees contained in the Bill of Rights of the Constitution of the United States. The act provides

---

[15] U.S. Department of Labor, *op. cit.*, p. 15.

that every member of a union shall have equal rights to nominate candidates, to vote in elections or referendums of the union, to attend membership meetings, and to participate in the deliberations and voting upon the business of such meetings, subject to reasonable rules and regulations in the union's constitution and bylaws. Furthermore, every member is guaranteed the right to meet and assemble freely with other members; to express views, arguments, or opinions; and to express at meetings of the labor organization his views upon candidates in a union election or upon any other business before the meeting, subject to the organization's established and reasonable rules pertaining to the conduct of meetings.

Congress wanted to strengthen the hand of the individual member who sought to "buck the machine." Yet, at the same time, it recognized that it could not restrict the legitimate right of unions to carry on business at meetings in an orderly fashion. Therefore, the Landrum-Griffin Act subjected the exercise of individual union members' rights to "reasonable rules" and furthermore provided that nothing in this section of the act should be construed to "impair the right of a labor organization to adopt and enforce reasonable rules as to the responsibility of every member toward the organization as an institution and to his refraining from conduct that would interfere with its performance of its legal or contractual obligations."

The act seeks to limit the extent to which union dues and assessments can be raised without the will of the membership. The act also states that except for nonpayment of dues, no member of any union may be fined, suspended, expelled, or otherwise disciplined by such organization or by any officer thereof unless such member has been served with written specific charges, given a reasonable time to prepare his defense, and afforded a full and fair hearing.[16] Furthermore, unions are prohibited from limiting the right of any union member to sue in court, except that such member may be required to exhaust reasonable hearing procedures (not to exceed a four-month lapse of time) within the union before instituting legal or administrative proceedings against the union or its officers. A Bureau of Labor Statistics study indicates that since enactment of the Landrum-Griffin Act, many unions have amended their constitutional provisions relating to the disciplining of members.[17]

Many persons who favored adoption of other sections of the Landrum-Griffin Act opposed inclusion of the bill of rights in this enactment. They questioned whether or not unions should—or could—operate as model democratic institutions. Unions, they argued, are fighting organizations; in many disputes with employers the very existence of the union

---

[16] These procedural safeguards apply to union members as *members*. They do not relate to suspension or removal from union office. See *Congressional Record*, September 3, 1959, p. 17899.

[17] "Union Disciplinary Powers and Procedures," *Monthly Labor Review*, Vol. LXXXVI (May, 1963), p. 491.

may be in danger. In such cases, organizations typically require strong direction from the top. Furthermore, as unions mature, the role of professionals will become more and more important in determining policy, in much the same way that professional management of corporations has reduced the role of stockholders in decision making.

Whether or not democracy is desirable or feasible in unions, it seems likely that the Landrum-Griffin Act, by encouraging dissent within the local union has promoted some unrest and factionalism within unions which has tended to spill over into contract negotiation and grievance settlement. It is interesting to note that union members are now rejecting about one out of every seven contract agreements between employers and union negotiators. In the first six months of 1967, negotiated settlements

TABLE 22-1

LMRDA Suits Filed by or against the Secretary of Labor,
by Fiscal Year and Type*

Type of Suit	Fiscal Year						Cumulative Sept. 14, 1959—June 30, 1966
	1961	1962	1963	1964	1965	1966	
Election.............	14	9	15	25	12	35	110
Subpoena............	3	4	8	3	8	5	31
Defensive............	6	3	9	4	1	5	28
Reporting...........	2	1	4	6	0	4	17
Trusteeship..........	0	0	1	0	1	1	3
Agreements..........	0	0	0	0	1	0	1
Totals........	25	17	37	38	23	50	190

* No suits were filed prior to fiscal year 1961.
Source: U.S. Department of Labor, Office of Labor-Management and Welfare-Pension Reports, *Summary of Operations, 1966* (Washington, D.C.: U.S. Government Printing Office, 1966), Table 2, p. 6.

were turned down in 14% of the necessary union ratification votes. In 1966, the figure was 11.7%, and it has been rising steadily over the last few years.[18] Furthermore, some employers have expressed concern that union representatives who may now have to contend more strongly to maintain their jobs as union officials will be more inclined to make extreme demands and less likely to strike a bargain which might subject them to criticism by their rivals. More than likely, however, the existence of the act is cited as an excuse by unions and employers who have lost touch with the rank and file.

Certain provisions of the act may hamper union government. For example, suppose the president of a union local believes that one member is an informer for the employer. Technically, he cannot suspend such

[18] *Business Week,* September 9, 1967, p. 61.

member or even keep him from attending meetings, until the full statutory requirements have been complied with—written charges, time for defense, and full hearing. As a practical matter, however, in this and similar circumstances where the bill of rights impedes union action, the officers will probably go ahead and do what they think best, and then "see what happens." The act significantly omits any criminal penalties for violation of the bill-of-rights section, except where there is use of force or threat of violence. Civil remedies, such as an injunction, may not be very effective relief for a member, since there is no way a court can afford a member the right to attend or to speak at a meeting that has already been held. Therefore, although in theory the bill-of-rights section of the new law might be burdensome to unions, in practice this has not occurred nor is it likely to occur.

Fair Elections

Under both the Taft-Hartley Act and the Railway Labor Act, the union which is the bargaining agent has the power, in conjunction with the employer, to fix a man's wages, hours, and working conditions. The individual employee has no right to negotiate directly with the employer if he is dissatisfied with the contract made by his union representatives. The federal government, which conferred these exclusive rights upon unions, has an obligation to insure that the officials of unions who wield this power are responsive to the desires of the membership they represent. The best assurance of this is free and periodic elections—a fact recognized by the AFL–CIO Ethical Practices Committee, which wrote into its code a requirement for frequent elections.

With these principles in mind, the legislators incorporated in the Landrum-Griffin Act detailed provisions relating to union elections. Every national or international union, except a federation of national or international unions, is required to elect its officers not less than once every five years either by secret ballot among the members in good standing or at a convention of delegates chosen by secret ballot. Local unions are required to elect officers not less often than once every three years by secret ballot among the members in good standing. Officers of intermediate bodies between the internationals and the locals must be elected not less often than once every four years by secret ballot among the members in good standing or by labor organization officers representative of such members who have been elected by secret ballot.

The act provides that in any election required to be held by secret ballot, a reasonable opportunity shall be given for the nomination of candidates; and every member in good standing shall be eligible to be a candidate, subject to reasonable qualifications uniformly imposed (except for Communists and persons convicted of certain crimes, who are barred from holding office). Union members are guaranteed the right to vote for, or otherwise to support, the candidate of their own choice without being subject to penalty, discipline, improper interference, or reprisal. All candidates have to be treated equally, and every bona fide candidate is given the right, once within 30 days prior to the union election in which he is a candidate, to inspect the list of names and addresses of "all members of the labor organization who are subject to a collective bargaining agreement requiring membership therein as a condition of employment."[19] Unions are forbidden to spend dues money in support of any candidate, and employers likewise are forbidden to spend money in support of candidates for union office. Detailed requirements are spelled out in the act as to the manner of sending election notices, counting votes, and other safeguards to insure a fair election. The act also establishes a procedure insuring that union officers guilty of serious misconduct may be removed by secret ballot elections.

The Secretary of Labor has ruled that unions may prescribe reasonable rules and regulations with respect to voting eligibility. They may "in appropriate circumstances defer eligibility to vote by requiring a reasonable period of prior membership, such as six months or a year, or by requiring apprentice members to complete their apprenticeship training, as a condition of voting." The Secretary of Labor has expressly stated that such union rules may not be used to create special classes of nonvoting members.

As can be seen from Table 22–1, most of the litigation under the Landrum-Griffin Act involves election procedure. In the fiscal year ended June 30, 1966, the LMWP received 149 complaints about elections, compared with 99 in the previous year. Thirty-five elections were rerun voluntarily during the year after investigation had established that there were violations which might have affected the outcome. Ten others were rerun under the supervision of a court order. At the end of the year, 52 civil suits filed by the Secretary of Labor under the act alleging illegal election procedures were pending.[20] It is noteworthy that approximately 90% of all election complaints investigated to date by LMWP relate to the election of *local* officers. Very few complaints refer to election of intermediate body or national officers.[21] In one significant case, however, an investigation found that James B. Carey, long-time president of the International Union of Electrical, Radio and Machine Workers, whose

---

[19] In 19 states which have so-called "right-to-work" laws, union-shop contracts are unlawful. In these states, it would appear that the lists above referred to would not have to be maintained by the union or made available to candidates. While the language of this particular section raises questions as to both its applicability and its usefulness, another section of the act requires unions to "refrain from discrimination in favor of or against any candidate with respect to the use of lists of members." Therefore, if *any* list of members is available, even in the right-to-work states, it presumably must be made available on equal terms to all candidates.

[20] U.S. Department of Labor, *op. cit.*, p. 1.

[21] U.S. Department of Labor, *Local Union Election Appeals* (Washington, D.C.: U.S. Government Printing Office, 1966), p. 3.

"reelection" had been announced, was in fact defeated by 23,316 votes. Carey promptly "resigned."

As a result of such litigation and the decision of various courts, guidelines are gradually emerging as to the kind of eligibility requirements which unions can impose as a condition of voting in an election. In general, the courts have held that such requirements violate the act if their effect in a particular case is to reduce those eligible to vote to a very small percentage of the membership. For example, in one case involving the Glass Bottle Blowers, the Supreme Court held unreasonable a union rule that only members who have attended 75% of monthly meetings over the last two years could be candidates for office or vote in union elections. It found that such a rule disqualified 490 out of the local union's 500 members! Similarly, the courts have ruled that qualifications in the National Maritime Union and in a local of the Hotel and Restaurant Workers' Union which bar a majority of membership from seeking office violate the Landrum-Griffin Act.[22] Undoubtedly the act has paved the way at least for challenging well-entrenched union officials and for ousting them when they obviously attempt to steal elections.

The perpetuation of what are, in effect, union dictatorships depends upon stifling democratic elections at the local level. The late Senator Robert A. Taft once said that "the employee has a good deal more of an opportunity to select his employer than he has to select his labor-union leader." Certain unions—particularly the Teamsters—have been able to keep the ruling clique in power by various devices which have disqualified opposition candidates or put them at a substantial disadvantage in obtaining votes. The Landrum-Griffin Act strikes at these unfair methods and attempts to insure free and honest elections in unions. The safeguards contained in the law permit rank-and-file union members to express their wishes more freely than was possible in the past, and in some cases they have done so. In most unions, however, there is a general apathy among the membership with respect to union elections. On the other hand, there is among union leaders a strong desire for power and a repugnance to resuming status as an ordinary worker-member. The result is what one writer has called "the iron law of oligarchy."[23] It seems clear that legislation, without active interest on the part of union members, will not suffice to make unions democratic.

As we have noted at the beginning of this section, Congress apparently believed that if it could provide union members with information about the operation of their unions and could protect individual rights through requirement of democratic procedures, union members them-

---

[22] See *Wirtz* v. *Local 153, Glass Bottle Blowers Association*, 389 U.S. 463 (1967); *Wirtz* v. *National Maritime Union*, U.S. Dist. Ct., So. Dist., N.Y. (April 24, 1968), 68 LRRM 2349; and *Wirtz* v. *Hotel, Motel and Club Employees Union*, 88 S. Ct. 1743 (1968).

[23] C. Peter MacGrath, "Democracy in Overalls: The Futile Quest for Union Democracy," *Industrial and Labor Relations Review*, Vol. XII (July, 1959), p. 508.

selves would rid their unions of corruption. Congress thus assumed that a democratic union would be less inclined to corruption. However, experience suggests that this relationship does not always hold. The United Steelworkers, for example, would hardly be classed as a democratic union, yet it handles tremendous trust funds without a hint of corruption. On the other hand, some unions with substantial local autonomy have been infected with corruption. It has been suggested that corruption in a union is more related to economic factors in the industry—such as severe competition and a highly mobile labor force—than to election procedures contained in the union constitution.[24]

Voting by Strikers

Through an amendment of the Taft-Hartley Act, the Landrum-Griffin law eliminates the so-called "union-busting" provision contained in the Taft-Hartley Act. Section 9(c)(3) of that act provided that employees on strike who are not entitled to reinstatement shall not be eligible to vote. This provision had the effect of preventing any "economic striker" (an employee striking for higher wages, better conditions, or any reason other than his employer's unfair labor practices) who had been replaced by a new employee hired during the strike from voting in an NLRB election conducted during the strike. For example, in a case in the rubber industry the United Rubber Workers was certified as bargaining representative in an NLRB election. Following months of fruitless negotiations for a contract, the union struck, and the company replaced the strikers with new employees. Thereafter the employer filed for a new election and succeeded in throwing out the union, because the strikers were not permitted to vote. Under the amendment added by the Landrum-Griffin Act, such economic strikers retain their right to vote in any NLRB election conducted within 12 months of the start of the strike, subject to regulations established by the NLRB. In applying this new statutory provision, the NLRB has ruled that it will presume that economic strikers have retained their interest in struck jobs, and that replacements were employed on a permanent basis, and that both therefore are eligible to vote. This means that the mere fact that a striking worker has taken a job elsewhere does not mean that he cannot vote in an election held in the company at which he and other union men are on strike. The NLRB places the burden of proof on the party challenging his vote to show that he is disqualified from voting.

HOW THE PUBLIC WAS AFFECTED

Because the Landrum-Griffin Act deals primarily with the internal administration of unions, its impact upon the general public is somewhat

[24] David Previant, "Have Titles I–VI of Landrum-Griffin Served the Stated Legislative Purpose? *Labor Law Journal*, Vol. XIV (January, 1963), p. 31.

limited. It was hoped, however, that the procedures it requires, by eliminating corrupt influences in unions, together with the provisions designed
to tighten restrictions on picketing and boycotts, would reduce the area
of industrial strife. There is little evidence one way or the other that this
has occurred.

Beyond this is the strengthening of our democratic processes in the
nation as a whole which comes from the practice of unionism under
conditions where each union member is free to speak his mind and help to
determine the overall policies of union government. Democracy is not
something which can be carried out on rare occasions—like a treasured
antique—and then put back in mothballs. It must be lived daily to survive.
We cannot expect democracy in government to survive when employees
in their daily lives see democratic forces subverted through intimidation
and corruption.

APPRAISAL OF THE ACT

The Landrum-Griffin Act is a law with a very limited purpose. Its
primary object is the reform of labor unions. It does not purport to be a
law covering the broad aspects of collective bargaining, as did the Taft-
Hartley Act. Nor is it intended to effect a broad revision of that act. The
provisions which it includes amending the Taft-Hartley Act were added
as an accident of its legislative history and for the most part bear some
relation to the abuses which were the main object of the legislators'
concern.

Interestingly enough, it is the amendments of the Taft-Hartley Act
—particularly those which deal with restrictions on picketing and secondary boycotts—that have given rise to the most litigation and controversy.
The main body of the Landrum-Griffin law has been incorporated in our
industrial life with a minimum of court action. This does not mean that
this act of Congress has reformed unionism or that many abuses still do
not exist. The fact is, however, that the U.S. Department of Labor has
been called upon to handle fewer complaints of violation of the act than
many labor experts had anticipated.

Analysis of the legislative history of the Landrum-Griffin Act indicates that three basic principles motivated the legislators in drafting it:

1. There should be a minimum of interference by government in the
   internal affairs of any private organization; only essential standards of
   conduct should be established by legislation.
2. Given the maintenance of minimum democratic safeguards and availability of detailed essential information about the union, individual
   members are fully competent to regulate union affairs.
3. Remedies for abuses should be direct. Where the law prescribes
   standards, sanctions for the violation should also be direct.

There can be little argument with the first principle, although there will be considerable dispute as to whether the Landrum-Griffin Act goes too far or far enough in establishing minimum standards. Union spokesmen contend that the act will permit labor spies to obtain confidential information about union finances and to hamstring the internal operation of the union. They contend that the bill-of-rights provisions go so far that they convert the union into a debating society and weaken it as a fighting organization. On the other hand, eight members of the House Labor Committee filed a minority report bitterly attacking the proposed labor reform bill for its omission of a guarantee of civil rights. In their words, "if there is to be a bill of rights in this legislation it must most assuredly include a guarantee of equal rights—the right of every workingman to join a union and not to be segregated within that union because of race, creed, color or national origin." Some union officials oppose the free admission requirement on the ground that a voluntary association such as a union should have a right to choose its members. Others fear that adoption of a bill of rights, as recommended by the minority report, would be equivalent to forced integration and would inhibit unionization of southern members.

With respect to the second principle, some skeptics wonder whether the rank-and-file union member is really concerned about graft and corruption in his union any more than the average citizen really concerns himself about graft and corruption in government. Surveys have indicated, for example, that many Teamster members, despite the disclosure of corruption among their officers, still approve their leadership because they have "produced" for them in terms of high wages and excellent working conditions. Perhaps the conditions affecting the relationship of the average worker and his union are such that we should not expect democratic action to flourish in such an environment. As one writer puts it:

The conditions that currently characterize unions—the complexity of their organization, the increasing tendency to assume functions complementary to those of mangement, the status and salary gap existing between leaders and members, not to mention the psychological compulsion of the leaders to retain power, and the members' expectation that their union is primarily a service institution rather than a way of life—do not provide the soil in which the democratic process can operate.[25]

Nevertheless, maintenance of minimum democratic safeguards seems necessary to protect the rights of individuals and to insure that union action reflects the desire of the membership.

On the subject of the third principle, the Landrum-Griffin law takes a different approach from that of the Taft-Hartley Act. The latter penalized violation by unions of various provisions of the law by denying

[25] MacGrath, *op. cit.,* p. 524.

the union access to the procedures of the NLRB. This has the effect of punishing all the union members for the violations of their officials. The Landrum-Griffin Act, by contrast, imposes direct sanctions in the form of fines, imprisonment, and/or civil remedies through court action to insure compliance with the act. This is certainly a more mature and realistic approach.

The type of legislation embodied in the Landrum-Griffin Act was probably inevitable. Abuses in other aspects of business life—such as the securities market, banking, and drugs—have likewise brought forth detailed federal regulation. Unions thus far have been remarkably free from such internal regulation, despite the fact that they enjoy benefits and privileges under the income tax laws and the antitrust laws which are unique. No association or organization can long expect to enjoy such privileges without assuming major obligations.

Unions in our society are no longer mere private clubs or fraternal organizations whose internal affairs, admission, and fiscal policies are matters of concern to their membership only. On the contrary, they bear more resemblance to public utilities or government entities, subject to legal control of their internal affairs.[26] When a union is certified as a collective bargaining agent, it has conferred upon it a government-sanctioned monopoly and the unusual powers that flow from this privilege. It is incumbent upon government, which granted this power to unions, to insure that it is not abused. Even without special statutory regulation of their internal affairs, there is precedent for holding unions to rules of conduct requiring fair and equal treatment of employees represented by the union. For example, in *Steele v. Louisville & Nashville Railroad*,[27] the U.S. Supreme Court decided that a union certified under the Railway Labor Act could not lawfully make an agreement with an employer which would arbitrarily deprive nonmember Negro employees of their seniority rights. In so holding, the Court stated: "We think that the Railway Labor Act imposes upon the statutory representative of a craft at least as exacting a duty to protect equally the interests of the members of the craft as the Constitution imposes upon a legislature to give equal protection to the interests of those for whom it legislates."[28] Similarly, some state courts have enunciated the view that where a union is acting as a bargaining representative, it is acting as an agency created and functioning under provisions of federal law; therefore, exclusion of persons on the

---

[26] See Joseph R. Grodin, "Legal Regulation of Internal Union Affairs," in Joseph Shister, Benjamin Aaron, and C. W. Summers (eds.), *Public Policy and Collective Bargaining* (Industrial Relations Research Association Publication No. 27 [New York: Harper & Row, Publishers, 1962]), p. 183.

[27] 323 U.S. 192, 65 S. Ct. 226 (1944). See also *Miranda Fuel Company, Inc.*, 51 LRRM 1585.

[28] 323 U.S. 192, 202; 65 S. Ct. 226, 232.

ground of race, for example, deprives such persons of rights guaranteed under the federal Constitution.[29]

Unions have an obligation to maintain democratic processes. They control the conditions under which their members spend most of their productive lives. More and more, they have a captive audience. A truck driver may move from one city to another, but he cannot long escape the far-flung power of the Teamsters' Union. The Landrum-Griffin Act takes a long step in the direction of attempting to insure democratic conditions in unions. Its success in achieving this objective will depend upon the support afforded this legislation by union leaders who profess to be interested in "clean" union government and, most important, upon the rank-and-file union membership who must want democratic government enough to use the tools which Congress has given them.

QUESTIONS FOR DISCUSSION

1. It has been said that a union is an organization that must always be ready for battle. Can such an organization function effectively on democratic basis? Do you consider the operation of most large corporations to be democratic? Why should unions be held to this standard? Discuss.

2. Discuss the so-called "bill of rights" incorporated in the Landrum-Griffin Act. In what way could these provisions handicap union action? Should the bill of rights have been broadened to include other rights, such as the right of free admission to a union? Discuss.

3. Assuming that there were abuses in the internal administration of unions, do you think that the power of the federal government should be invoked to cure such abuses? What other measures might have been taken to accomplish the same objective?

SUGGESTIONS FOR FURTHER READING

Estey, Martin S.; Taft, Philip; and Wagner, Martin (eds.). *Regulating Union Government.* New York: Harper & Row, Publishers, 1964.
  A series of articles analyzing the effect of Landrum-Griffin provisions on union government.

"Picketing and Publicity under Section 8(*b*)(4) of the LMRA," *Yale Law Journal,* Vol. LXXIII (1964), pp. 1265 ff.
  A discussion of the significance of recent Board and Court decisions with respect to the so-called "publicity proviso."

U.S. Department of Labor, Office of Labor-Management Policy Development. *Local Union Election Appeals.* Washington, D.C.: U.S. Government Printing Office, July, 1966.

---

[29] *Betts* v. *Easley,* 161 Kans. 459 (1946); *Thorman* v. *International Alliance of Theatrical & Stage Employees,* 49 Cal. (2d) 629 (1957).

A detailed analysis of challenges to union elections made by union members.

U.S. DEPARTMENT OF LABOR, OFFICE OF LABOR-MANAGEMENT AND WELFARE-PENSION REPORTS. *Summary of Operations*. Washington, D.C.: U.S. Government Printing Office.

This report, issued annually by the agency charged with the responsibility of administering the Landrum-Griffin Act, is an excellent source for statistical data concerning the act's day-to-day operation.

Chapter 23

THE GOVERNMENT IN LABOR DISPUTES—FROM MEDIATOR TO EMPLOYER

The previous chapters have been concerned with key federal legislation. These laws, however, are only part of the total role of the federal government in labor disputes. In this chapter, we shall discuss how the federal government attempts to settle labor disputes or to prevent them from erupting.

In addition to the federal government, 50 states and some municipalities play a significant role in labor disputes by means of "little Taft-Hartley acts," "little Landrum-Griffin laws," and other legislation.

Government enters into labor disputes through one more avenue which needs to be considered—government itself is the largest employer in the country. We shall therefore close our analysis of this subject with a discussion of some of the peculiar problems which arise between government and labor as a result of government being a sovereign employer.

MEDIATION OR CONCILIATION—THE FEDERAL SERVICE

The principal mediation agency in the United States is the Federal Mediation and Conciliation Service.[1] (See Figure 23–1 for definitions.) It dates from the Act of 1913 which created the U.S. Department of Labor. This law contained a paragraph authorizing the Secretary of Labor to mediate labor disputes and to appoint "commissioners of conciliation" for that purpose. This phase of the U.S. Department of Labor's work quickly expanded until a special division was set up in the Department known as the United States Conciliation Service, with headquarters in Washington, D.C., and regional offices in the principal industrial centers of the nation. In 1947, the Conciliation Service, as a division of the Department of Labor, was abolished by the Taft-Hartley Act, and an independent agency, the Federal Mediation and Conciliation Service, whose functions remained basically the same, was substituted for it. This was done largely

---

[1] For a more thorough discussion of mediation, and of the federal, state, and municipal services, see Herbert R. Northrup and Gordon F. Bloom, *Government and Labor* (Homewood, Ill.: Richard D. Irwin, Inc., 1963), chaps. x and xi.

FIGURE 23-1

DEFINITIONS

MEDIATION AND CONCILIATION are used interchangeably to mean an attempt by a third party, typically a government official, to bring disputants together by persuasion and compromise. The mediator or conciliator is not vested with power to force a settlement.

STRIKE NOTICE laws require the union and company to notify each other and certain public officials a specified number of days prior to striking or locking out.

STRIKE VOTE laws require an affirmative vote of either the union members or the employees in the bargaining unit before a strike may be called.

FACT FINDING involves investigation of a dispute by a panel, which issues a report setting forth the causes of a dispute. Usually, but not always, recommendations for settling the dispute are included in the report. Laws requiring fact finding usually provide that the parties maintain the *status quo* and refrain from strikes or lockouts until a stipulated period after the fact finders' report has been made. Once the procedure has been complied with, however, the parties are free to strike and to lock out.

COMPULSORY ARBITRATION requires the submission of an unsettled labor dispute to a third party or board for determination. Strikes or lockouts are completely forbidden, and the arbitrator's decision is binding on the parties for a stated length of time.

SEIZURE involves temporary state control of a business which is or threatens to be shut down by a work stoppage. Strikes or lockouts are forbidden during the period of seizure, which lasts until the threat of work stoppage is abated.

---

at the behest of employer groups who felt that if the Conciliation Service were to remain a division of the Department of Labor, conciliators themselves would inevitably reflect the prolabor bias of the Department.

In establishing a separate Mediation and Conciliation Service, the Taft-Hartley Act gave the Service the statutory base it previously lacked. In addition, Section 201 of the Taft-Hartley Act set forth the policy of the federal government as the peaceful settlement of labor disputes by collective bargaining. Section 203 directed the Service to minimize work stoppages by mediation and encouragement of voluntary arbitration; Section 204 admonished labor and industry to cooperate fully with the efforts of the Service to settle strikes; and Section 205 established a labor-management advisory panel for the Service. Finally, Section 8(d) of the Taft-Hartley Act required labor and management to notify each other of intent to modify a collective agreement at least 60 days prior to the termination date of the agreement, and to notify the Service and any appropriate state agency 30 days later if no agreement had been reached.

The Mediation and Conciliation Service may be called into a dispute by either labor or management, or it may proffer its services. It has, however, no authority to force itself upon a recalcitrant employer or union. Of course, as a federal agency, it carries with it the prestige of the government, so that refusal to participate in a conference called by the Service is not usual.

Mediators often perform a valuable contribution in preventing strikes by bringing the parties together when bargaining has failed. A clever mediator can obtain concessions from the parties by adroit maneuvering, or otherwise find a basis for agreement when it is lacking, as, for example, when the bargaining adversaries are no longer able to communicate directly with one another, or fear to do so.

To accomplish their tasks despite a lack of authority, mediators must time their participation in a dispute correctly. If they enter the dispute too early or too often, the parties may prefer to save concessions for mediation instead of getting down to the business of seeking agreement. If mediators come in too late, the parties' positions may have become too hardened to permit concessions. Mediation is an art, and a valuable one. It cannot be squandered loosely if it is to be effective. The fact that the Mediation Service has been able to attract some excellent men during the last two decades has helped it to increase its ability to accomplish its important task.

State Mediation Agencies

Although almost all states have provisions in their laws for the adjustment of labor disputes, in only a few is it made a full-time job. Nor is this surprising, considering that in many states, there would not be enough work to keep even a single conciliator, let alone a board or commission, occupied. Other states prefer to leave adjustment work to the Federal Mediation and Conciliation Service, with such assistance from the state industrial commissioner, or the state department of labor, as can be rendered by such an agency. The states which, in contrast to the general rule, are most active in the adjustment of labor disputes are California, Connecticut, Massachusetts, Michigan, Minnesota, New Jersey, New York, Pennsylvania, and Wisconsin. In all these states a special agency devotes full time to the job.

The job of the state mediator is no different from that of his federal counterpart. He must be capable of bringing about an agreement by conciliation and persuasion, without authority or power to force compliance with his wishes. The fact that most states have not paid staff mediators anything in excess of a very modest income has made it difficult to find men willing to perform this valuable service. Nevertheless, both authors have encountered some able state mediators over the last several years who have been most helpful in critical disputes.

Municipal Adjustment Agencies

A number of municipalities have at one time or another established machinery for the adjustment of labor disputes. Most have depended upon the volunteer services of public-spirited citizens and have ceased to exist after these citizens retired. Their success has been varied. Experienced mediators have not been available to municipalities, and inexperienced ones have frequently done more harm than good. Strikes which occur on the outskirts of a city or in its suburbs may vitally affect a city, yet be outside the jurisdiction of its adjustment agency. And if state and federal agencies are already in operation, the intrusion of a municipal board may only complicate matters.

Louisville, Kentucky; Toledo, Ohio; and New York City have had the most active municipal mediation agencies. New York City maintains a special labor secretary to the mayor who attempts mediation; and if unsuccessful, he can refer the dispute for further mediation to a panel composed of one labor, one industry, and one public member.

Jurisdictional Hodgepodge in Mediation

Increasing concern has been expressed in recent years by many persons about the competition of mediators to obtain recognition in settling disputes. It is by no means uncommon to find both federal and state mediators, and occasionally, municipal ones also, competing for the job of settling the dispute. The Taft-Hartley Act specifically permits such dual mediation. In recent years, a "code of ethics" requires mediators to cooperate at least on a pro forma basis, but the urge "to get in on the glory" is strong. Moreover, the existence of mediators from different jurisdictions gives labor and management the opportunity to "shop around" in order to try and have the mediation work done by the one judged most sympathetic to the partisan viewpoint of one of the parties.

Mediation is certainly unlikely to be more effective because of the participation by more mediators in a single dispute. The authors have experienced both cooperation and lack of cooperation among state and federal mediators in various disputes. For the most part in our experience, the mediators have cooperated with each other as reasonable people working toward a common goal should. There continues to be, however, sufficient evidence of lack of cooperation to merit consideration both in Washington, D.C., and in the various state capitals of a plan to divide up mediation work so as to achieve optimum efficiency in helping to prevent industrial disputes.[2]

---

[2] For a proposed solution, see Northrup and Bloom, *op. cit.*, pp. 289–91.

ADJUSTMENT IN RAILWAY AND AIR TRANSPORT[3]

Mediation in the railway and air transport industries is conducted by an agency especially set up for this purpose—the National Mediation Board. Moreover, under the procedure set forth in the Railway Labor Act which governs these two industries, mediation is combined with a strike notice and fact-finding procedure. This separate treatment has its historical roots in a series of laws dating back to 1888. Since then, railway labor problems have generally been governed by procedures different from those in other industries. An exception to this rule is the Labor-Management Reporting and Disclosure Act (Landrum-Griffin), which, unlike the basic provisions of the Taft-Hartley Act, applies to both railway and air transport.

The Railway Labor Act makes it the duty of labor and management to exert every reasonable effort to "make and maintain agreements concerning rates of pay and working conditions" and to attempt to adjust all differences by peaceful methods. A three-man, nonpartisan National Mediation Board then attempts mediation if the parties cannot agree among themselves. The Board is further instructed to urge voluntary arbitration if mediation proves unsuccessful. If arbitration is refused and the dispute is such as "substantially to interrupt interstate commerce," the Board is instructed to notify the President, who can create a special emergency board to investigate and publish findings. During the pendency of these various proceedings and until 30 days after the report of the emergency board, neither party may alter "the conditions out of which the dispute arose," except by mutual agreement. The parties, however, are under no legal obligation to accept the recommendations of the emergency board, and strikes or lockouts are permissible after the waiting period has expired.

A unique aspect of the Railway Labor Act is the requirement for compulsory arbitration of grievances and of other disputes arising out of the interpretation of agreements. The agency charged with this task (for the railroads only) is the National Railroad Adjustment Board. This Board is a bipartisan agency composed of 36 members, half of whom are paid and compensated by the carriers and half by the unions "national in scope." (Thus, smaller organizations of workers have no representation on the Adjustment Board.) The work of the Adjustment Board is divided into four divisions, each of which has jurisdiction over certain crafts. If a division deadlocks, referees are appointed by the National Mediation Board or by the division if it can agree on a selection.

The Railway Labor Act also provides elaborate safeguards for the free choice of employee representatives by setting forth a list of unfair

[3] A fuller treatment of this subject is found *ibid.*, chap. xii.

labor practices similar to those contained in the National Labor Relations Act prior to the Taft-Hartley amendments. Enforcement is, however, different from that under the National Labor Relations Act, in that violations are punishable by criminal penalties and prosecution is under the jurisdiction of the U.S. Department of Justice. Because of the difficulties of proving willful intent to commit an unfair labor practice before a jury, there have never been any convictions and only one trial for unfair labor practices. However, railway unions have successfully brought a number of injunctive actions to force employers to cease and desist from alleged unfair labor practices.

Until 1951, the Railway Labor Act prohibited all types of union security and checkoff agreements. This prohibition was placed in the act in 1934 to prevent company unions from obtaining union security and automatic dues support from reluctant workers, and it had the support of the so-called "standard" unions. By 1951, the company unions had been ousted by defeats in representation elections, and the standard unions were able to persuade Congress to legalize union security and checkoff provisions. Unlike the Taft-Hartley Act, the Railway Labor Act provides no machinery for decertifying unions or for voting out union security provisions.

The Railway Labor Act also provides formal machinery for the selection of employee representatives. The National Mediation Board is required to make determinations in this regard and usually does so by representation elections. The bargaining unit under the Railway Labor Act is limited to a "craft or class," but the National Mediation Board has wide discretion in determining the definition of craft or class and in determining voting eligibility in representation elections.

Prior to World War II, the Railway Labor Act was hailed as a "model law," and frequent suggestions were made to enact similar legislation for industry generally. Since 1940, however, a number of strikes or near strikes, which were averted only by Presidential action or special legislation outside the procedures of the Railway Labor Act, have caused many former advocates of the "model law" concept to take a second and deeper look at the Railway Labor Act.

The effect of the elaborate procedure of the Railway Labor Act is to make collective bargaining completely perfunctory prior to the emergency board stage. Neither party tends to concede anything from its original position for fear of prejudicing its case before the emergency board. The procedure of the Railway Labor Act, which is supposed to supplement collective bargaining, has been used instead as a substitute for collective bargaining. Because they know that an important dispute is likely to end up before an emergency board, railway labor and management have just gone through the motions of bargaining until the emergency board hearings took place.

Such a development is probably inevitable. It is the easy way out for the parties to let someone else make the decision for them. In that way, they avoid the responsibility and, under the emergency board procedure, still remain free to act if the board's recommendation is unsatisfactory. In 1963, President John F. Kennedy and Congress refused to permit a strike over the fireman issue, and Congress enacted a special compulsory arbitration law to settle it. Other aspects of the same dispute were settled under the aegis of President Lyndon B. Johnson by mediation in 1964. In 1967, Congress twice passed special legislation to terminate strikes by railway shop employees, and during the previous year the Machinists' union struck five major air carriers for 43 days after rejecting, first, an emergency board report, and then a proposal for settlement by President Johnson. In these cases, the procedure of the Railway Labor Act failed to produce a settlement—as has been the case in almost every major dispute under the act's jurisdiction since 1940.

Experience under the state laws, which also have a fact-finding procedure, is similar to that under the Railway Labor Act.[4] Moreover, nowhere has the appointment of fact-finding or emergency boards been confined to emergencies by any realistic or even generous use of the term "emergency." In the case of the Railway Labor Act, for example, a dispute on the smallest railroad or airline can apparently as easily cause the appointment of an emergency board as a dispute affecting most of the railroads in the nation. Once the appointment of an emergency or fact-finding board becomes commonplace, the public loses interest; and it is then exceedingly difficult, if not impossible, to rally public opinion behind the settlement in the manner which proponents of the fact-finding procedure claim could be effective.

THE TAFT-HARTLEY ACT AND NATIONAL EMERGENCIES

The emergency disputes law which is applicable to industry not covered by the Railway Labor Act is found in provisions of the Taft-Hartley Act. Title I of this law requires that a 60-day notice be given by either union or management to the other party if a change in the collective agreement is contemplated and that such notices also be sent to appropriate federal and state mediation services. This procedure has become perfunctory, since unions generally automatically give notice in order to be free to strike if negotiations do not result in agreement. These notices have, of course, alerted the mediation agencies that a strike could occur, but it is possible that they may also have induced mediation where it was unnecessary.

Title II of the Taft-Hartley Act also requires that the President appoint a Board of Inquiry to investigate and report, without recommen-

---

[4] For an analysis of these state laws, see Herbert R. Northrup, "Factfinding in Labor Disputes: The States' Experience," *Industrial and Labor Relations Review*, Vol. XVII (October, 1963), pp. 114–34.

dations, on the issues of a dispute which "threatens" the national health or safety. The President can then direct the Attorney General to petition a federal district court for an injunction to prevent or terminate the strike or lockout. If the injunction is granted, the conditions of work and pay are frozen for the time being, and the parties are obliged to make every effort to settle their differences with the assistance of the Conciliation Service. If these efforts fail, at the end of 60 days the Board of Inquiry is required to make a public report on the status of the dispute, again without recommendations. The National Labor Relations Board is then required within 15 days to poll employees as to whether they will accept the last offer of the employer and to certify the result to the Attorney General within 5 days. The injunction then must be dissolved. By this time, 80 days will have elapsed since the first application for an injunction. If the majority of workers refuse the employer's last offer, then the President can submit the complete report to Congress, with or without recommendations for action.

As of July 1, 1968, boards of inquiry had been appointed under this section on 28 different occasions. In 15 cases a strike vote on the employer's last offer was taken; and in 7 cases, strikes occurred after the machinery of the act had been completely utilized.

The Taft-Hartley Act thus provides no ultimate sanctions against a national emergency strike after the fact-finding period has elapsed, other than the implied threat of possible congressional action and the force of public opinion. Experience under the Taft-Hartley Act emphasized what experience under the Railway Labor Act had already demonstrated—fact-finding reports have relatively little effect in mobilizing public sentiment so as to compel settlement of labor disputes unless there is really a grave national emergency affecting the entire country, or most of it.[5]

The Last-Offer Vote

Of all the procedures in the act, the one considered the least successful is the last-offer vote. Traditionally, it has been utilized to gain the unions more. They have simply told their memberships to vote no and they will obtain more, *and this has happened in all 15 cases in which a last-offer vote occurred,* more often without a strike than with one. It also happened in eight of the nine cases in which a vote was held under a similar procedure of the now defunct Pennsylvania Utility Arbitration Act (see Table 23–1). The only exception occurred the day before the Korean War wage stabilization program was scheduled to become effective in 1951. The workers voted to accept a settlement for fear of having their wages frozen at pre–last-offer levels. This is to be expected. An

---

[5] For a detailed analysis of cases and effects, see Northrup and Bloom, *op. cit.,* pp. 356–66.

TABLE 23–1

LAST-OFFER VOTES: EXPERIENCE UNDER TAFT-HARTLEY AND
PENNSYLVANIA LAWS TO JANUARY 1, 1963

Law	Number of Votes	Last Offer Accepted	Last Offer Rejected
Taft-Hartley Act.......................15		0*	15
Pennsylvania Utility Arbitration Act....... 9		1†	8

° In one case the employees rejected a subsequent and higher offer after the "last" offer had been rejected. In the West Coast longshore case the union asked employees to boycott the vote; no one voted from this group.
† Vote conducted on January 24, 1951, just prior to 1951 Korean War wage freeze. Employees feared that to reject it would mean freezing existing wages.
SOURCE: National Labor Relations Board and Pennsylvania State Labor Relations Board.

offer, once made, is rarely withdrawn, so why not vote no and probably get more?

Actually, there have been four cases in which the last-offer vote served the purpose of inducing agreement. Professor George W. Taylor has noted that the steel industry settled in 1960 partially because the "last" offer was about to be rejected, according to all forecasts.[6] And in the 1962 Lockheed case the union settled without the union shop because it feared that the employees would not support its insistence on this demand in the last-offer vote. Similarly, in the 1966 strikes of the United Automobile Workers at General Electric's jet engine plant, in Evendale, Ohio, and of the Steelworkers at Union Carbide's defense work facility at Kokomo, Indiana, last minute withdrawal of demands and settlements were probably triggered by the belief of these unions that the employees might accept the companies' last offers.

Despite widespread criticisms of the last offer and other aspects of the Taft-Hartley disputes procedure, there has not been any concerted attempt for change or for repeal. Perhaps this is because the act has not worked as poorly as its critics charge or as well as its proponents claim; and perhaps also because neither the critics nor the proponents believe that substitute legislation which is politically acceptable, would be superior.

Most strike notice and strike vote legislation is not concerned with last offers but rather is designed to prevent "quickie" stoppages. Strike notice legislation usually requires that the employer and a government agency receive notice of an impending stoppage 10 to 60 days before the strike may legally be called. Such notices have been extremely ineffective as strike preventatives because no actual cooling-off period occurs. The

[6] George W. Taylor, "The Adequacy of Taft-Hartley in Public Emergency Disputes," *The Annals,* Vol. CCCXXXIII (January, 1961), p. 79.

general procedure is for the union to give a perfunctory notice as soon as bargaining commences, thus legalizing beforehand any action the union might take, without inhibiting the freedom of such action.

Legislation adopted by the federal government during World War II[7] and by several states not only required notice of a strike but, in addition, an affirmative vote of those involved before a strike is commenced. The purpose of strike vote legislation is to prevent union leaders or a minority of employees from instituting stoppages when a majority of the affected employees are opposed to striking. However, an officially ordered strike vote almost invariably becomes a union weapon. "Vote yes and win a wage increase" is a typical union slogan. A vote to strike does not necessarily mean a strike. It does, however, amount to a vote of confidence in union negotiators and is potent support to the union leader, who can say: "See, the rank and file are really serious. They are ready to strike." During World War II, 82.7% of the employees polled by the federal government voted to strike. In Missouri, which had a typical state law, 88.9% of the employees polled by the state during the law's incumbency in 1948–49 voted in favor of a strike. In each case, only a few strikes actually occurred. The vote was clearly understood as a tactical maneuver.[8]

STATE EMERGENCY DISPUTE LAWS

The states have engaged in a wide variety of experiments designed to cope with strikes which are considered emergencies or which cause serious inconvenience. Twenty-eight states provide for some sort of official investigation and/or fact finding in such instances;[9] 10 have enacted compulsory arbitration;[10] 5 states have provided for seizure of struck facilities;[11] and 1 state—Massachusetts—adopted "choice of procedures," giving the authorities a variety of methods to handle disputes.

These state emergency dispute laws accumulated some very interesting experience, but are now largely inoperative except where they apply to groups not covered by the Taft-Hartley Act, because the courts have ruled that such state laws are in conflict with rights guaranteed under

[7] This was the so-called Smith-Connally, or War Labor Disputes Act of 1943, which expired by its own terms after the war.

[8] Besides Missouri, Florida, Kansas, Michigan, Minnesota, Utah, and Wisconsin had active state strike vote laws. They have been held invalid in interstate commerce because of a conflict with the Taft-Hartley Act and are now largely inactive. See *Automobile Workers* v. *O'Brien*, 339 U.S. 454 (1950). For a discussion of such laws, see Northrup and Bloom, *op. cit.*, pp. 377–88.

[9] See note 4, above.

[10] Kansas enacted a law after World War I; the other laws, which came after World War II, are those of Florida, Indiana, Michigan, Nebraska, New Jersey, Pennsylvania, and Wisconsin. Two laws—those of Minnesota and New York—apply only to hospitals.

[11] Maryland, Massachusetts, Missouri, New Jersey, and Virginia.

federal law.[12] Michigan's fact-finding law, which applies to state and local government and hospital employees; Minnesota's and New York's hospital arbitration acts; and Nebraska's arbitration law, insofar as it covers intra-state and state and local governmental employees—remain in effect because these groups are excluded from the coverage of the Taft-Hartley Act.

Strike control legislation of this character results from a decision that protection of the health and safety of the community requires that strikes and lockouts in essential private as well as public services be either forbidden altogether or permitted only as a last resort after state intervention. Looked at in another manner, there are industries, according to commentators, in which the strike and lockout cannot serve their primary function—to inflict sufficient damage upon the disputants so that they will be willing to compromise and come to an agreement.

In an essential industry, the argument runs, strikes and lockouts do not serve a direct persuasive or coercive purpose because the stoppage tends to injure the public before it injures the parties sufficiently to force a settlement. As a consequence, a strike in an essential industry is likely to create a public emergency or serious inconvenience. This, in turn, is likely to place pressure upon the government to intervene and even to determine the conditions upon which the stoppage is to be ended.

There is no agreement among the states as to which industries should be denied the right to strike. Electric light and power, gas, and water are the most common industries covered by state strike control laws; but Minnesota subjected disputes in charitable hospitals to compulsory arbitration, while it permitted strikes in the three utilities after fact-finding procedure had been complied with. Hawaii placed more drastic controls over disputes in the stevedoring industry than in electric light and power. The fact that supervisors utilizing automated controls can operate utilities during strikes, and have done so, without noticeable effect on output, weakens the "emergency dispute" argument considerably.

Like the wartime emergency legislation discussed below, many of these laws accomplished their purpose of preventing strikes, but at the expense of settlement by collective bargaining. Arbitration and fact-finding laws, in particular, inhibit the bargaining process because concessions made in bargaining may reduce the chances for a favorable arbitration award or fact-finding recommendation. Why concede something which later may be awarded? As the Supreme Court stated in its decision invalidating the Wisconsin law, the so-called "emergency" legislation was

---

[12] The arbitration laws were ruled unlawful in interstate commerce in *Amalgamated Association* v. *Wisconsin Employment Relations Board*, 340 U.S. 383 (1951); the fact-finding laws, in *General Electric Co.* v. *Callahan*, 294 F. (2d) 60 (1962); and the seizure laws, in *Division 1287, Amalgamated Association* v. *Missouri*, 374 U.S. 74 (1963). The Kansas arbitration law was found unconstitutional in 1923 and 1925 cases, and the Michigan arbitration law was invalidated on a procedural defect in 1948.

invoked as soon as a dispute arose, regardless of the extent of the emergency, until the law became "a comprehensive code for the settlement of labor disputes between public utility employers and employees."

Basically, the problem of confining emergency legislation to emergencies remains a difficult one. By various legislative measures the states have gained valuable experience which may aid in pointing the way to a solution of the problem of encouraging free collective bargaining, while at the same time protecting the public against stoppages which create either grave inconvenience or actual emergency.

WARTIME ADJUSTMENT MACHINERY

In peacetime, strikes are costly; but the alternative, once mediation or persuasion has failed, is government direction in place of free collective bargaining. In wartime, however, no industrial strife can be tolerated. During both World War I and World War II, therefore, compulsion substituted for voluntarism in the settlement of labor disputes. To lessen the degree of compulsion, prominent roles in wartime adjustment machinery were given to representatives of labor and industry. Nonetheless, the factor of compulsion remained, and the difficulty of restoring voluntary collective bargaining after compulsory controls are lifted is well illustrated by the great strike waves of both 1919–20 and 1945–46. Moreover, the principles and precedents developed by war labor agencies are likely to have permanent influence on peacetime policy, as the experience of the World War II period illustrates.

The National War Labor Board of World War II

On January 12, 1942, the National War Labor Board of World War II was established by executive order. In June, 1943, it was given statutory backing by the War Labor Disputes Act, passed by Congress over the President's veto. In the previous October, it had been assigned wage control under the Stabilization Act. To aid in administering its functions, the WLB also established 13 regional boards and several industry commissions. Its jurisdiction included virtually all American industry, except rail and air carriers subject to the Railway Labor Act.

Peaceful Settlement. The War Labor Board initially attempted to decide each industrial dispute case on its merits. Gradually, however, it developed official policies on virtually every issue under dispute between the parties. It attempted to maintain peace in settling disputes, as a careful student of War Labor Board policy has noted, by using three basic approaches: (1) appeal to the legal framework governing industrial relations in wartime; (2) appeal to historical precedent, whenever possible; and (3) compromise.

The WLB used the "legal framework" method most frequently in wage cases. The Stabilization Act and the executive orders issued thereunder set forth the law. Hence, when a proposed increase exceeded what the Board had promulgated as allowable under stabilization criteria, the War Labor Board had merely to cite a higher authority as the basis of its decision.

The WLB used historical precedent in refusing to disturb North-South wage differentials, or historical differentials between two plants of the same company located in different parts of the country, or even local differentials between two neighboring plants. Likewise, the WLB refused to alter union- or closed-shop contracts voluntarily agreed to by management.

When the WLB had neither law nor historical precedent to guide it, compromise always remained. The best example is, of course, found in the issue of union security. The principle of maintenance of membership is an obvious compromise between the closed and the open shop. Likewise, compromise guided the War Labor Board when it acceded to unions' demands for such "fringe" issues as paid vacations, paid holidays, and night shift bonuses, but denied demands for paid sick leave and compulsory health and welfare funds.

The Stabilization of Wages. Since changes in wages invariably affect industrial relations, the stabilization duties of the War Labor Board were closely interrelated with its job of maintaining industrial peace.

Unfortunately, wage stabilization was not only related to peaceful labor relations, it often worked at cross-purposes with it. The denial of a voluntary application for wage increases, jointly submitted by an employer and a union, usually caused unrest in a plant, and sometimes a work stoppage. Such stoppages were directed not against employers but against the War Labor Board.

Because of this conflict between wage stabilization and labor peace at a time when the latter was considered paramount, compromise was often permitted to weaken stabilization. For example, when the 17-cent-per-hour general increase demand of the CIO Steelworkers was denied, a variety of fringe issues such as improved vacations, night shift bonuses, and the elimination of interplant inequities was used to mollify the union. In sum, stabilization was made flexible to suit the immediate needs of labor peace. Nevertheless, wages were held in line.

The Heritage of the War Labor Board. The National War Labor Board of World War II rendered decisions for all industry on every conceivable aspect of industrial relations. Its decisions still serve as a guide for rulings in labor disputes. The WLB established the historical precedents and the legal framework for arbitrators to follow, and both labor and management still turn to the WLB's rulings for precedents in solving disputed questions. And this will continue to be true, whether the War Labor Board's decisions have been "sound" or not, primarily because the scope of such decisions includes all industry and all phases of industrial relations.

Likewise, War Labor Board decisions have furthered certain labor goals which have been increasingly accepted in recent years. They include the following: (1) that a "responsible" union deserves union security; (2) that paid vacations, paid holidays, paid sick leave, group health insurance, night shift bonuses, and other benefit issues are proper union objectives; (3) that unions should have a voice in the establishment of benefit plans and that such plans are a proper sphere of collective bargaining; (4) that wage rate structure should be simplified so as to eliminate intraplant differences; and (5) that similar occupations in neighboring areas should be similarly compensated.

The effect of the War Labor Board on postwar labor relations was felt in still another important manner. After four years of seeing the government set the terms and conditions of employment, unions and employers found it difficult to return to collective bargaining. Moreover, many unions and many employers were anxious to "teach the other a lesson." This, combined with the pent-up resentment in wartime, did much to make 1946 the greatest strike year of American history in terms of man-days lost from work.

Both labor and management were surprised at the duration of some of the 1946 strikes. During the war, such strikes as occurred were "quickies." The emphasis was on uninterrupted production, to the exclusion of all else. Union leaders found in the postwar period that management resistance was much greater, particularly when loss of business was compensated for by rebates of wartime excess profits taxes. On the other hand, those employers who felt that unions could not survive postwar strife miscalculated badly. One result of the postwar strike wave was a more realistic appraisal on the part of both labor and management of the effectiveness, costs, and results of strikes.

Another wartime heritage to which the 1946 strikes gave sharp emphasis was the increasing public concern with stoppages of work which interfered with "essential" services or even inconvenienced a portion of the population. Wartime hysteria over strikers was carried over into the postwar period. Moreover, a number of unions exhibited unparalleled irresponsibility and lack of understanding of public sentiment in striking essential services. One result was the election of a Congress with a Republican majority in 1946, which enacted the Taft-Hartley law; and another result was an increasing concern of state legislatures with "emergency" labor settlement machinery, which led to the passage of the laws discussed above.

STATE LABOR RELATIONS ACTS

In 1937, the year in which the Supreme Court sanctioned the Wagner Act, Massachusetts, New York, Pennsylvania, Utah, and Wisconsin adopted legislation patterned on the Wagner Act.

In 1939, however, the Pennsylvania and Wisconsin laws were amended to incorporate restrictions on employers and unions, as well as on employees, thus foreshadowing the Taft-Hartley Act. "Little Taft-Hartley acts" were also adopted by Minnesota and Michigan in 1939, Colorado and Kansas in 1943, Hawaii in 1945, North Dakota in 1961, and Vermont in 1967. In 1947, Utah also converted its law to a Taft-Hartley type, but laws modeled on the Wagner Act were passed by Rhode Island in 1941 and by Connecticut and Puerto Rico in 1945. Oregon passed a labor relations act in 1953, repealed it in 1959, and then in 1961 passed a new labor-management relations act which provides for the selection of bargaining agents and mild restraints against both employers and unions. In 1963, Idaho gave authority to its labor commissioner to hold representative elections, and required unions and employers to bargain in good faith when the commissioner has designated a bargaining agent. The Massachusetts act remains basically a Wagner Act type, although it limits union entrance requirements and union security provisions.

In addition to these comprehensive labor relations laws, a number of states have enacted special- or limited-purpose laws, some of the Landrum-Griffin type.

Jurisdiction

Coverage of the state labor relations acts is limited by (1) the extent of federal preemption and (2) restrictions imposed in the state laws. Between the passage of the Taft-Hartley Act in 1947 and the enactment of the Landrum-Griffin Act of 1959, the jurisdiction of state laws was severely limited to intrastate commerce business not within the purview of the Taft-Hartley law. Amendments contained in the Landrum-Griffin Act specifically gave the states jurisdiction over cases which might fall within the Taft-Hartley Act's jurisdiction, but which the National Labor Relations Board declined to accept under its jurisdictional standards of August 1, 1959. Since only 16 states and Puerto Rico have labor relations laws, this area left to the states is still under common law in most state jurisdictions.

State agencies handle annually only about 10% as many of the 20,000 to 25,000 cases which come before the National Labor Relations Board, and one half of these are New York State labor relations cases. Moreover, the typical state case involves a small shop with few employees.

Unfair Labor Practices

Both the "little Wagner acts" and the "little Taft-Hartley acts" follow the unfair labor practice provisions of the Wagner Act insofar as employer unfair labor practice provisions are concerned. Some include in their proscriptions specific prohibitions against the blacklist, employer espionage, and other matters which were included within the Wagner Act's general restrictions on restraint of employees for union activity.

On the other hand, the state laws of Minnesota and Oregon do not specifically prohibit the employer from restricting or coercing employees in the exercise of their rights. The Wisconsin, Minnesota, and Colorado statutes limit the protection of workers against unions which could conceivably be found to be company dominated under the Taft-Hartley regulations, while the Oregon law provides only the slightest protection in this regard—i.e., the Oregon board may order another election if one has not been conducive to free choice.

The unfair labor practices in the "little Taft-Hartley laws" which are directed against employees and unions may be divided into four categories:

1. Prohibitions of violence and similar activities which were almost universally unlawful before the passage of the labor relations acts—for example, sit-down strikes, sabotage, and mass picketing.
2. Restrictions on peaceful tactics such as picketing and organizing campaigns, especially where coercion is alleged.
3. Limitations on union objectives which make illegal all efforts to achieve a forbidden objective, such as a make-work rule.
4. Regulation of the internal affairs of unions, such as financial matters, election procedure, and eligibility for union office.

Many of these laws thus contain provisions which are similar to those in both the Taft-Hartley and the Landrum-Griffin acts, including the provision in the latter law designed to safeguard the finances and the rights of workers in their relationship with unions. Most provisions controlling union and employee conduct are, however, designed to limit strikes, picketing, or boycotts, or to preclude union interference with the peaceful designation of a bargaining agent.

Representation Disputes

The representation procedure is, in general, similar in most states to that provided under the Taft-Hartley Act, except in Michigan, where elections can be conducted only by agreement of the parties. Decertification procedure is not, however, usually provided for, although Pennsylvania and Wisconsin do have something similar.

Administration

Administration of the state labor relations acts is vested in several different types of administrative establishments. In some, typified by the state labor relations boards of New York and Pennsylvania, a single-purpose agency modeled on the National Labor Relations Board was created to handle only unfair labor practice and representation matters arising under the labor relations acts of the states. A second type of administrative agency, such as that in Colorado, Wisconsin, or North Dakota, is multipurpose. It administers the labor relations act in addition to several other functions—such as mediation of labor disputes, or even functions like workmen's compensation, safety, minimum wages, and other protective legislation. Minnesota and Kansas vest the representative function of their acts in the state mediation agency but leave unfair labor practice enforcement to the courts. Oregon provides for division of the responsibility among a part-time agency, the state attorney general, and the state labor conciliator.

As in the case of the National Labor Relations Board, state labor relations agencies cannot enforce their own orders, but must apply to the courts for enforcement.

Specific Laws Regulating Weapons of Conflict

Besides these comprehensive state laws which have been discussed, many states have enacted legislation outlawing or controlling the weapons of conflict in labor-management relations. Thus, 26 states[13] bar picketing under certain circumstances—for example, by nonemployees or by mass pickets, or picketing the home or where no labor dispute exists. Nine states bar jurisdictional strikes,[14] and 13 restrain secondary boycotts.[15] Sit-down strikes or the seizure of property by strikers are outlawed by 14 states.[16] Montana guarantees sole proprietors and partnerships of two persons in the retail and amusement business the right to work without union "interference" of any kind. Such small businesses are unusually subject to coercive picketing and boycotts.

The constitutionality of many of these provisions remains in doubt, especially in cases in which the Taft-Hartley Act has jurisdiction. As was noted in Chapter 20, governmental regulation of the weapons of conflict involves the difficult question of coercion and free speech, as well as a conflict of state and federal jurisdiction. Hence, it is not surprising that the law is unsettled in these areas of social policy.

On the other side have been the several new laws which prohibit or discourage the recruiting of replacements for strikers. Twelve states now have such laws,[17] as have several cities. The purpose of such laws is, of course, to strengthen union bargaining power by making it more difficult to replace strikers.

Organized labor has now secured the passage of laws in 11 states[18]

[13] Alabama, Arizona, Arkansas, Colorado, Connecticut, Florida, Georgia, Hawaii, Kansas, Louisiana, Maine, Massachusetts, Michigan, Minnesota, Mississippi, Nebraska, New Mexico, North Dakota, Oregon, Pennsylvania, South Carolina, South Dakota, Texas, Utah, Virginia, and Wisconsin.

[14] California, Florida, Iowa, Kansas, Massachusetts, Michigan, Minnesota, Pennsylvania, and Wisconsin.

[15] Arizona, Colorado, Idaho, Iowa, Kansas, Nebraska, North Dakota, Oregon, Pennsylvania, South Dakota, Texas, Utah, and Wisconsin.

[16] Colorado, Florida, Kansas, Maryland, Massachusetts, Michigan, Minnesota, North Dakota, Oregon, Pennsylvania, Utah, Vermont, Washington, and Wisconsin.

[17] Delaware, Hawaii, Iowa, Louisiana, Maine, Maryland, Massachusetts, Michigan, New Jersey, Pennsylvania, Rhode Island, and Washington.

[18] Alaska, California, Connecticut, Delaware, Hawaii, Maryland, Massachusetts, New Jersey, Oregon, Rhode Island and Washington.

making it illegal to require the submission to lie-detector tests as a condition of employment, and in three other states,[19] requiring the licensing of lie-detector machine operators. There is considerable controversy in industry concerning the reliability of such tests and machines.

Finally, in this specific law area, we should note again the existence of 19 state "right-to-work" laws,[20] which were examined in Chapter 6 and which outlaw compulsory unionism.

"Little Norris–La Guardia Acts"

Laws similar to the Norris–La Guardia Act have been enacted by 25 states[21] and Puerto Rico. As on the national scene, these laws have caused the number of injunctions issued in labor disputes to decline sharply. There is, however, tremendous variation in these anti-injunction laws, partially because many have been amended over the years to permit curbs on boycotts, picketing, and other weapons of conflict, and also because some state courts have tended to interpret the laws very narrowly, while others have interpreted them very broadly.

Although there are some exceptions—notably in Massachusetts—the trend seems to be a tendency on the part of state legislatures to reduce the immunities in state anti-injunction acts and a tendency on the part of state courts to interpret laws so as to grant relief when they feel it is warranted. In view of the size and strength of labor unions today as compared with the 1930's and 1940's, when most of these anti-injunction laws were adopted, it is not surprising that both legislatures and courts perceive a greater need to restrain strikes, boycotts, and picketing than was the case 25 years ago.

"Little Landrum-Griffin Laws"—Reporting, Disclosure, and Democracy

We have already noted that the state labor relations acts in a number of jurisdictions provide for safeguards of union finances and members' rights. Reporting and disclosure laws involving union finances are also in effect in other states;[22] but in nearly all cases, enforcement mechanisms are lacking.

---

[19] Arkansas, Florida and Nevada.

[20] Alabama, Arizona, Arkansas, Florida, Georgia, Iowa, Kansas, Mississippi, Nebraska, Nevada, North Carolina, North Dakota, South Carolina, South Dakota, Tennessee, Texas, Utah, Virginia, and Wyoming.

[21] Arizona, Colorado, Connecticut, Hawaii, Idaho, Illinois, Indiana, Kansas, Louisiana, Maine, Maryland, Massachusetts, Minnesota, Montana, New Jersey, New Mexico, New York, North Dakota, Oregon, Pennsylvania, Rhode Island, Utah, Washington, Wisconsin, and Wyoming.

[22] Alabama, Connecticut, Florida, Hawaii, Kansas, Massachusetts, Minnesota, New York, Oregon, South Dakota, Texas, Utah, and Wisconsin. The reporting requirements of the laws of Hawaii, Kansas, Massachusetts, Utah, and Wisconsin are not separate laws, but are included in the "little Taft-Hartley laws" of these states.

In addition, five states—California, Massachusetts, New York, Washington, and Wisconsin—have enacted legislation requiring disclosure about the activities of health and welfare funds set up by labor-management agreements. These laws require full disclosure of the income, disbursements, and operations of the covered funds, but they all lack effective enforcement mechanisms. Connecticut, which once had such a law, repealed it in 1967. As noted in Chapter 3, even the federal law, enacted in 1962, appears inadequate to police effectively the burgeoning welfare funds amassed by unions, and more stringent national legislation is likely to be passed. The states do not appear either to have the will or the means to police union government, so that it has become and will continue to be a federal task except in special cases.

An unusual law is that enacted in 1952 by both New Jersey and New York to regulate waterfront conditions in the port of New York. It established a bistate Authority to control crime on the waterfront by barring those convicted of felonies from serving as waterfront union officials and by regulating waterfront hiring practices. Although considerable success has been achieved by this Authority, particularly in bringing stability and fairness in the hiring of longshoremen, the Authority's own reports emphasize that crime on the waterfront, in New York as in many other ports, still flourishes. Pilfering, loan sharking, and "kickbacks" remain problems difficult to eliminate in a labor market where more men want jobs than there are jobs available and where the opportunity for preying on the job seeker, the customer, and the public is great.

The two most comprehensive state laws aimed at furthering union democracy are the Minnesota Labor Union Democracy Act of 1943 and the New York Labor and Management Improper Practices Act of 1959. The Minnesota law regulates the details of union elections, providing that they must be held at least once every four years by secret ballot. The state can disqualify the union as a bargaining agent in case of violation. The law also gives the state the right to appoint a temporary labor referee to take charge of the union and to conduct a fair election. Although widely heralded when enacted, this law has never been invoked or utilized.

The New York law is very similar to the financial reporting sections of the Landrum-Griffin Act. It requires financial reporting by both employers and unions, imposes a fiduciary obligation on union officers and agents, and forbids conflict-of-interest transactions. The law also applies to employers and to labor relations consultants in a similar manner as the Landrum-Griffin Act by requiring annual reports on expenditures related to interference, restraint, or other attempts to sway employees away from their rights to choose unions as bargaining agents.

The passage of the Landrum-Griffin Act immediately after New York enacted its legislation has tended to overshadow the New York law. Because of the broad coverage of its provisions, few unions are outside the purview of the Landrum-Griffin Act. Congress decided, however, not to bar concurrent state legislation, for it provided in Section 603(*a*) of the Landrum-Griffin Act that "except as explicitly provided to the contrary, nothing in this statute shall reduce or limit the responsibilities of any labor organization . . . or take away any right or bar any remedy to which members of a labor organization are entitled under any other federal law or law of any state." What role a concurrent law like New York's Labor and Management Improper Practices Act can and will play, in view of the far-reaching character of the Landrum-Griffin Act, still remains to be determined. Since Congress decided to exercise the full scope of federal jurisdiction in regulating internal union affairs, the states have not found it desirable to legislate further in this field.

Limits on Union Political Expenditures

A final group of laws aimed at controlling union finances are those which limit a union's right to utilize regular union income from membership dues, fees, etc., for political purposes. Four states—Pennsylvania, Texas, Indiana, and Wisconsin—limit union political contributions. The first two are rather narrow, the latter two rather broad in their restrictions. Like the proscription in the Taft-Hartley Act, however, their aim is to force unions to raise money for political purposes voluntarily and directly, instead of utilizing dues money, which may be contributed by employees who oppose the aims or people for which the contribution is given. In general, these laws have been ineffective.

GOVERNMENT AS EMPLOYER

The biggest American employer is not General Motors Corporation, or the American Telephone and Telegraph Company, but Uncle Sam. As of March, 1964, federal civilian employment was approximately 2.7 million, almost equal to the World War II all-time high of 2.8 million.

But even the number of federal government employees is small compared to the nearly 9 million state and local government employees. Nor is this all. If military personnel are added, the total federal employment rises to 5.8 million, and the number of government employees mounts to 15 million. In addition, another 9 million persons are employed at government expense—in civilian jobs, but receive paychecks which depend directly upon government contracts or grants.

Today, therefore, about 12 million civilians—one out of every seven persons in the civilian labor force—work for government agencies. Almost as many either are in uniform or are supported by government funds —a grand total of more than one fourth of the labor force. Clearly, therefore, the policies of the government *as employer* are of concern not only to government employees but to all American citizens concerned with public policy.

The Sovereign Employer and the Right to Strike

Traditionally, the government, as employer, assumed that since the government represents the sovereign power, it must reserve the sole right to determine the terms and conditions of employment under which its employees labor. In actual fact, however, the second premise does not follow the first. The essence of sovereignty includes the right to delegate authority. Hence, the sovereign power can delegate or share authority to determine the terms and conditions of employment. To a considerable extent, many governmental agencies actually do this, but many do not.

Probably no government body in the United States concedes the right of its employees to strike. A strike of government employees which results from dissatisfaction over wages, hours, and working conditions becomes, in the light of the principle of sovereignty, an insurrection against public authority. Nevertheless, government employees have been involved in many strikes in past years,[23] but it has not been till the mid-1960's that public employee strikes not only became common but affected with some regularity such personnel as teachers, firemen, and policemen whose absence from work either thoroughly disrupt the population or actually endanger it. For example, the U.S. Bureau of Labor Statistics recorded only 35 teachers' strikes in the decade immediately preceding 1966, but 33 in 1966 and 11 in the first quarter of 1967.[24] A total of 142 stoppages of public employees were recorded by the Bureau in 1966, 9 of which concerned state employees, the balance municipal employees, and none federal employees.[25]

Strikes of government employees are manifestations of a changing concept of government-employee relations. Antistrike laws have been enacted by a number of states embodying the same concept set forth in the Taft-Hartley Act, which reads:

It shall be unlawful for any individual employed by the United States or any agency thereof including wholly-owned government corporations to participate in any strike. Any individual employed by the United States or by any such agency, who strikes, shall be discharged immediately from his employment, and shall forfeit his civil service status, if any, and shall not be eligible for reemployment for three years by the United States or any such agency.

More recently, however, legislation has been moving toward union recognition in the public service and machinery to accommodate such

[23] See David Ziskind, *One Thousand Strikes of Government Employees* (New York: Columbia University Press, 1940); and "Strikes of Government Employees, 1942–1961," *Monthly Labor Review*, Vol. LXXXVI (January, 1963), pp. 52–54.

[24] Ronald W. Glass, "Work Stoppages and Teachers: History and Prospect," *Monthly Labor*, Vol. XC (August, 1967), pp. 43–46.

[25] U.S. Department of Labor, Bureau of Labor Statistics, "Work Stoppages Involving Government Employees, 1966," Summary release, n.d.

recognition. The roots of the newer policies go back to the early part of the century.

The Right to Organize and to Bargain Collectively

The right to organize and to bargain collectively has been conceded to its employees by the federal government since the passage of the Lloyd–La Follette Act of 1912. Not until 1961, however, did the federal government have a consistent program of union recognition and collective bargaining for its employees. Some agencies, such as the Tennessee Valley Authority, recognized unions and dealt with them as exclusive bargaining agents, even signing contracts with them. Others, which have less discretion in determining conditions of employment, dealt with unions in much the same manner but did not sign contracts. In such cases, notices were sometimes posted on bulletin boards over the signature of the agency or department manager embodying the substance of what had been agreed to with the government employees' union. Many agencies, however, neither recognized nor dealt with unions.

Outside of the Post Office Department, where union organization in 1961 covered 84% of the employees, government-owned shipyards and arsenals, and special "independent" agencies such as the TVA, the extent of organization in the federal government service was estimated at "only a fraction of the norm in private industry . . . about 10 per cent of . . . employees under the Classification Act are affiliated" with unions.[26] Although this comparison is one of a primarily salaried, white-collar civil service group with industry generally including factory workers, and actually illustrates that a *higher* percentage of salaried employees are unionized in federal employment than in business corporations, the administration of the late President John F. Kennedy determined to make it easier for unions to operate and to receive recognition in the federal government. After a task force report, Executive Order 10988 was issued on January 17, 1962, requiring government agencies to recognize as exclusive bargaining agents unions which, by vote of the employees in an appropriate unit, are shown to represent a majority of the unit. An immediate result has been the recognition of unions as exclusive bargaining agents not only in the Post Office Department, where a form of collective bargaining has long existed, but in such areas as the Military Air Transport Service, the Maritime Administration, and in some more traditional service and white-collar areas; and a substantial growth of union membership in the federal service.

More than one half of the states have now passed laws which provide for union recognition of public employees or some particular group thereof. Some, like Wisconsin or Vermont, provide for coverage

---

[26] Wilson R. Hart, "Government Labor's New Frontier through Presidential Directive," *Virginia Law Review*, Vol. XLVIII (June, 1962), p. 910.

by the basic state labor relations act. Others, such as New York, set up separate public employee relations machinery. Some laws limit the coverage to a particular group, such as nurses, firemen, or teachers, or to municipalities employing more than a minimum number of employees; others are all-inclusive. These laws universally combine provisions for union recognition and procedures for collective bargaining with proscriptions against public employee strikes.

One of the most widely heralded laws is the 1967 so-called "Taylor Law," named after Professor George W. Taylor, of the University of Pennsylvania, its principal author. This law was enacted in New York State after a repressive measure, the Condon-Wadlin Act of 1947 proved unworkable. As amended in 1963, the latter law provided that (1) public employee strikers might be immediately discharged; (2) if such strikers were eventually rehired, they should receive no salary increases for a six-month period; and (3) rehired strikers should be deemed temporary employees for one year and therefore subject to summary discharge. In addition, such rehired strikers could be fined two days' pay for each day on strike up to a total of two months' pay, and they could also be suspended an additional two months without pay after rehiring.

Such laws as Condon-Wadlin have proved unworkable in practice. Not only were flagrant violations of the Condon-Wadlin Act not punished, but on at least two occasions the state legislature enacted special laws exempting strikers from the penalties of the law after strikes had occurred in complete defiance of its provisions. One such case involved New York City transit workers who had tied up the city for over one week with an illegal strike.

The Taylor Law, in contrast to its Condon-Wadlin predecessor, grants all public employees the right to organize and to bargain collectively, reinforces the obligation for public bodies to negotiate, and shifts strike penalties from the individual employees to the union or other employee representative. The law also provides for a disputes and fact-finding procedure similar to that of the Railway Labor Act. It is administered, as already noted, by a special board.

Although widely praised, the Taylor Law has not been without its critics, especially when the state experienced a number of severe strikes after it became effective. The philosophy behind the Taylor Law, as was that behind the Wagner Act, seems to imply that if employees had peaceful means of winning union recognition, strikes would thereby lessen. This is correct, as the experience under the Wagner Act showed, but only for recognition strikes. As a matter of fact, because so many more unions win recognition and so much more bargaining occurs when a government procedure is provided to insure peaceful recognition procedures, more strikes may take place just because there are so many more unions and managements bargaining. The fact of the matter is that strikes have not occurred less often, but more often, among public employees in

New York State since the Taylor Law replaced the Condon-Wadlin Act. This is undoubtedly the result of the tempestuous times as well as of the greater degree of unionism among public employees; but it does illustrate again, as did the Wagner Act and Railway Labor Act in private employment, that providing for union recognition by peaceful means and establishing a fact-finding procedure do not insure labor peace.

Penalties, Strikes, and Collective Bargaining

Penalties do not seem to avoid public employee strikes. The severe ones of the Condon-Wadlin Act were such that politicians literally feared to enforce them. The more mild ones of the Taylor Law (loss of checkoff for unions, and fines for unions, or even jail terms for union leaders) do not seem to act as deterrents either. Some public employee strikes are not too serious in terms of the effects; most however, raise real questions of public safety. Strikes of policemen in Pontiac, Michigan, and Youngstown, Ohio, did not result in disasters, but they could a second time. Garbage and transit strikes completely disrupted New York City and endangered the health of millions. Teacher strikes provoke youngsters to violence and gravely interfere with reasonable learning processes. A democratic order requires that people show restraint as well as exert rights. Certainly, public employees deserve fair treatment and wages; but the public too has its rights, and those include reasonable performance of services for which taxes are expended.

There remains a real question of whether collective bargaining is workable in the public service. In private industry, collective bargaining works because of the obvious costs of failure. If the parties there do not settle on reasonable terms, then the costs of doing business become prohibitive and sales and jobs disappear. In public employment, the economic calculus is missing. An overgenerous settlement forced by a strike or strike threat does not mean economic disaster in public employment. The limits of pressure and the limits of power in the public sphere are not economically defined as yet. Yet the tactics and the pressures involved, the laws and the procedures, and the general aspirations and collective bargaining structure have all been transported from the private sector to the public sector as if the problems and institutional settings were nearly identical.

The difference between public and private collective bargaining is most apparent at the federal level where strikes still remain almost nonexistent. Under present legislative practice, basic wages and conditions of employment at the federal level are set by Congress, not by collective bargaining. Specific salaries, salary grades, basic benefits, and time-off practices are thus established for most federal employees before the employee is hired or a union enters the picture. Most federal employees are, moreover, covered by civil service regulations which govern other conditions of employment. This had led many people to question what useful

purpose a labor organization of federal government employees can perform. Actually, however, in the federal government, as in any other
employment, relations between supervisors and workers result in grievances and other employment problems which are best resolved through
collective bargaining. Much discretion is lodged in the administrators of
government departments and bureaus to promote, penalize, and otherwise
affect the careers of personnel. Often it is only through collective bargaining that the grievances of employees can be satisfactorily adjusted. This is
true for government employees as well as for employees of private concerns.

The general principle followed in collective bargaining in the government service is that administrators may bargain with unions of their
employees on matters over which the administrator has authority or
discretion. Obviously, if Congress provides by statute that the wage for a
certain group of employees shall be a specific amount, the administrator
cannot alter that wage. Obviously, also, if employees are hired pursuant to
civil service regulations, the closed shop or other forms of union security
which make jobs dependent upon union membership are incompatible
with civil service regulations and therefore cannot be entered into. On the
other hand, in such agencies as the Tennessee Valley Authority, to which
Congress has given considerable discretion in handling employee relations,
collective bargaining can be more inclusive. Although some federal departments, such as Labor and Post Office, have signed agreements with
unions, salaries remain to be determined by Congress.

On the state and local level the principles are no different; but in
practice, civil service regulations are often, especially at the local level, not
so widespread. In such cases, collective bargaining can be more flexible
and more nearly include the subjects which are bargained about in private
industry.

In place of reliance on the strike, many unions of government
employees, especially at the federal level, have concentrated their efforts
on the political side. They operate lobbies—often very effective—in Congress, in the state legislative halls, and in municipalities. The Post Office
unions are probably the most effective. With members in every congressional district, they easily command the attention of Congress. Other
union spokesmen pleading the case of their constituents are a common
sight not only before congressional committees but also in the state
capitals, the town meetings, and the school board hearings. And of course,
the more the terms and conditions of employment are fixed by legislative
action, the more must government employee unions concentrate on legislative activity to serve their constituents.

The Future of Union Relations in the Public Service

The fastest growing unions today, and the ones that could be among
the largest in the labor movement, are those in government service.

Already effective lobbyists, they have more recently turned to direct economic action to achieve their goals. Striking teachers, sanitation workers, and even firemen and policemen are no longer a rarity. Such actions have caused deep disquiet among the population. Laws inherently favorable to public employee unions, such as New York's Taylor Law, do not seem to prevent strikes any more than did their more harsh predecessor legislation. Defiance of law by public servants and disruption of public services remain serious matters of public concern for which solutions have not been readily found by our democratic society. It is unlikely, however, that defiance and disruption can be tolerated as a matter of course. The future of collective bargaining in the public service depends, in the last analysis, on public toleration, which in turn would seem to require peaceful and fair dispute settlement as a first condition.

QUESTIONS FOR DISCUSSION

1. Is conciliation a difficult job to do? Explain your answer.
2. Do you think that legislation can be devised which would both protect the country against strikes in emergency situations and maintain normal collective bargaining relationships? What type of legislation would be most advantageous to accomplish these two objectives? Explain your answer.
3. Does state labor legislation now on the books provide a comprehensive body of labor law for intrastate business? Do you think it should? Explain your answer.
4. What type of legislation, if any, would you advocate to govern employee relations in the federal public service and in the public service of your state? Explain your answer by reference to the existing federal executive order and to relevant state legislation.

SUGGESTIONS FOR FURTHER READING

Moskow, Michael H. *Teachers and Unions*. Industrial Research Unit Study No. 42. Philadelphia: University of Pennsylvania Press, 1966.

Shils, Edward B., and Whittier, C. Taylor. *Teachers, Administrators and Collective Bargaining*. New York: Thomas Y. Crowell Co., 1968.
    Two major studies of various aspects of collective bargaining in the public school and general education areas.

Northrup, Herbert R., and Bloom, Gordon F. *Government and Labor*, chaps. ix–xv. Homewood, Ill.: Richard D. Irwin, Inc., 1963.
    A detailed analysis of the subjects treated in this chapter: state labor relations acts, mediation, railway and airline labor legislation, and federal and state emergency disputes procedure.

Vosloo, William B. *Collective Bargaining in the United States Civil Service*. Chicago: Public Personnel Association, 1966.
    A study of the impact of the Kennedy Executive Order on personnel relations and collective bargaining in the federal public service.

WARNER, KENNETH O., and HENNESSY, MARY L. (eds.), *Public Management at the Bargaining Table*. Chicago: Public Personnel Association, 1967.

A series of articles covering nearly all aspects of public employee bargaining, by authors from many points of view.

Chapter 24

CIVIL RIGHTS AND EQUAL
PAY LEGISLATION

During World War II the shortage of labor, successful agitation for fair employment opportunities, and pressure from the government to open up jobs to all those who were being asked to risk their lives in war combined to increase job opportunities for Negroes in areas which had hitherto been closed to them.[1] The booming demand for the products of industry which followed World War II helped to insure further gains for Negroes, as did the industrial expansion which resulted from the Korean War. Then, after some deterioration in their relative position in the late 1950's, Negroes made great gains in the 1960's.

Nevertheless, as the data and analysis in Chapter 14 clearly showed, Negroes continue, even in a period of high employment, to be beset by poverty and unemployment to a far greater degree than do whites. Moreover, if employment should decline and the economy suffer a recession, Negroes, as a group overly concentrated among cylical industries, and also overly concentrated among the last hired, will suffer a disproportionate number of layoffs and have longer periods of unemployment.

Other minorities—Puerto Ricans, Mexican-Americans, Indians, and others—also often suffer discrimination in the labor market. Since the numbers of Negroes are so much greater and their problems usually so much more severe, an analysis of equal opportunity laws in terms of Negro employment problems will provide a sound basis for understanding and evaluating the problems of minorities and the laws designed for their protection. A final section of this chapter analyzes sex and age discrimination, and laws aimed at insuring equal pay for equal work.

BACKGROUND OF CIVIL RIGHTS LEGISLATION—CIVIL RIGHTS AGITATION

The Civil Rights Act of 1964 was the result of developments on both the protest and the legislative front. Besides difficulties in finding

[1] Problems of this period are discussed in Herbert R. Northrup, *Organized Labor and the Negro* (New York: Harper & Bros., 1944); and Robert C. Weaver, *Negro Labor—A National Problem* (New York: Harcourt, Brace & Co., 1946).

jobs, Negroes in the early 1960's were still confronted with segregation in public accommodations in southern and some border states. To the increasing number of educated Negroes, this was particularly unpleasant. In 1961, Negro college students in the South began a series of sit-ins in restaurants and other places of service which denied Negroes equal treatment. Boycotts of businesses, patterned after a most successful one initiated by followers of the late Dr. Martin Luther King, Jr., against a bus company in Montgomery, Alabama, were initiated to fight segregation. The use of these economic weapons resulted in substantial successes in the attack against segregated facilities.

The results achieved by this direct action, combined with the slow results in obtaining school desegregation almost a decade after the United States Supreme Court ruled against such segregation, led to more direct action. In the North the use of the weapons of conflict—the boycott and picketing, especially—was aimed at improving the job opportunities of Negroes. In Philadelphia, for example, the *Bulletin,* one of the three daily papers, the Sun Oil Company, and the A & P supermarket chain all were boycotted into increasing the number of Negro employees. Whereas the fight in the South was initially for equal accommodations, that in the North was for better jobs—a step that the South came to after the goal of equal accommodations has proceeded apace.

As in all protest periods, the direct action of Negroes to assert rights in the early 1960's gave rise to abuses and violence. Alleged school or *de facto* educational segregation stirred emotions resulting in riots and numerous serious clashes of pickets and marchers with counterdemonstrators and police in both the North and South. These outbursts contributed to the intervention of the Kennedy, and later Johnson, administration and to the passage in 1964 of the Civil Rights Act with the first national fair employment or equal employment opportunity legislation incorporated as Title VII of the act.

Legislative Antecedents

The 1964 Equal Opportunity title of the Civil Rights law was based on prior legislative experience in the field. In the early New Deal period, it was found, for example, that Negroes were systematically shut out of employment on public works projects. Accordingly, a program requiring the use of Negro workers consistent with their representation in the area population was inaugurated as early as 1934, and achieved some success. Nondiscriminatory provisions were also incorporated into bills for defense and wartime training.[2]

Presidential Committees

Then, in order to avert a "march on Washington" by Negroes protesting continued job discrimination, President Franklin D. Roosevelt,

[2] Weaver, *op. cit.*, chaps. ii–iv.

by executive order, established a Fair Employment Practice Committee, which operated throughout the war period. Although the Committee held hearings, dramatized the issue of Negro employment, and undoubtedly contributed to the increase in the utilization of Negro manpower, its lack of statutory authority prevented it from securing compliance with its orders when discriminating employers or unions balked. Thus, it failed to make an appreciable change in the employment practices of the railroad or West Coast shipbuilding industries, where employers' discrimination was buttressed by active union support, if not leadership.[3]

The President's Committee on Fair Employment Practice ended its life in 1945, after being denied funds by Congress. It was followed by a succession of committees whose jurisdiction was limited to establishments doing business under contracts with the federal government. These committees were first set up by President Harry S Truman, and then reorganized by each succeeding President. For the most part, they relied on persuasion and publicity. Moreover, they lacked jurisdiction over unions, who are not party to government controls, but who, particularly in the construction industry, are often, as the suppliers of labor under closed-shop contracts,[4] the focal point of discrimination.

The Kennedy Committee was the first to spell out sanctions and to give notice of attempting to enforce them. Such sanctions could lead ultimately to the cancellation of the government contract. At least four contractors were blacklisted, at least temporarily, for noncompliance with fair employment; and threats of similar action were made to obtain results.[5] Such sanctions are often unworkable, because the cancellation of a key contract can endanger the country's defense program or otherwise interfere with the necessary performance of governmental functions.

Plans for Progress and Contract Compliance

One of the most interesting programs in the civil rights field was the "Plans for Progress" program initiated by then Vice President Lyndon B. Johnson early in the Kennedy administration. Today more than 500 major companies are members of this organization which commits them to "affirmative action." In fact, this means that these companies attempt to go out of their way to employ and to train minorities, to give them special consideration to offset past discrimination and otherwise to expand their employment opportunities.

More recently, the government has pursued an affirmative action program by compelling companies which sell to the government—and

---

[3] Northrup, *op. cit.*, chaps. iii and x.

[4] The reader will recall that the ban on the closed shop, as written in the Taft-Hartley Act, and as modified in the Landrum-Griffin Act, has never been effectively enforced in the construction industry.

[5] See Paul H. Norgren and Samuel E. Hill (assisted by F. Ray Marshall), *Toward Fair Employment* (New York: Columbia University Press, 1964), p. 159.

that includes virtually every major and many minor concerns in the country—to institute such programs. This has been carried out aggressively by the Federal Office of Contract Compliance, the latest in the succession of Presidential committees established by Executive Order to deal with equal employment opportunity through the leverage of federal procurement.

State Equal Opportunity Commissions

While the federal government was attempting to improve Negro job opportunities by extralegal executive improvisations, 34 states, the District of Columbia and Puerto Rico enacted enforceable fair employment or equal opportunity laws and several now have official advisory groups promoting equal opportunity. Beginning in 1945 with the enactment of the New York and New Jersey laws, those laws now cover most of the industrial states of the North and West plus the border states of Delaware, Kentucky and Missouri. In addition, several cities, including Baltimore, Cleveland, Minneapolis, Philadelphia, Pittsburgh, St. Paul, and Toledo have enacted laws often before the states in which they are located followed suit. Usually, the state laws then permitted the municipal agencies to handle cases arising within their boundaries.

Most of the state laws provide for a "fair employment," "equal opportunity," or "human rights" commission to administer the laws. These commissions may hear complaints, take testimony, hold hearings, issue orders, and apply to courts for enforcement. They are patterned to a large extent on the administrative model of the National Labor Relations Board or on the state labor relations boards described in Chapters 21 and 23, except that in some states the commissions are specially created divisions of established state government departments instead of independent agencies. Other states—Idaho, Iowa, and Vermont—make discrimination a misdemeanor punishable by fine or imprisonment. In such cases, the aggrieved individual must file his case with the appropriate law enforcement agency, where it is handled like other misdemeanors. The pertinent facts about the state laws are summarized in Table 24–1.

Although state commissions against discrimination have the power to hold public hearings, most have utilized this power very sparingly. Following the lead of its pioneer New York agency, these agencies attempt first to accomplish their aims by conciliation. This is usually successful, because of the threat of bad publicity involved in a public hearing.

State Law Prohibitions and Administration

Most of the state laws are modeled on the pioneer New York law, which prohibits *employers* from discriminating in any way in the employment relationship—hiring, promotion, or discharge conditions, or wages—because of race, color, creed, or national origin; prohibits *unions*

TABLE 24-1

State Fair Employment Practice Laws: Their Coverage and Enforcement

	Type of Illegal Discrimination			Type of Coverage			Type of Enforcement		
	Racial Religious	Sex	Age	Employers	Unions	Employment Agencies	Commission or Department	Criminal Proceedings	Voluntary: No Civil or Penal Enforcement
Alabama									
Alaska	X		X	X(1)	X	X	X		
Arizona	X	X		X(20)	X	X	X		X(f)
Arkansas			X(6)						
California	X		X	X(5)	X	X	X		
Colorado	X		X	X(6)	X	X	X		
Connecticut	X			X(5)	X	X		X	
Delaware	X	X	X	X(a)	X	X	X		
District of Columbia	X			X(a)		X		X	
Florida									
Georgia									
Hawaii	X	X	X	X(1)	X(b)	X(b)	X		
Idaho	X	X	X	X(a)(b)	X(b)	X(b)	X		
Illinois	X			X(50)	X	X	X		
Indiana	X		X	X(6)	X	X	X		
Iowa	X			X(4)	X	X	X		
Kansas	X(e)			X(4)	X	X	X		
Kentucky				X(8)	X	X		X	
Louisiana	X		X	X(25)				X	
Maine	X		X	X(a)	X	X		X	
Maryland	X	X	X	X(c)	X	X	X		
Massachusetts	X	X	X	X(6)	X	X	X		
Michigan	X	X	X	X(8)	X	X	X		
Minnesota	X			X(8)	X	X	X		
Mississippi									

State								
Missouri	X	...	X(25)	X	X	X	...	...
Montana	X	X	X(a)(b)	X(b)	X(b)	...	X	...
Nebraska	X	X(1)	X(c)	X	X	X	...	...
Nevada	X	X	X(15)	X	X	X	...	...
New Hampshire	X	...	X(6)	X	X	X	...	...
New Jersey	X	X(d)	X(a)	X	X	X	...	...
New Mexico	X	...	X(4)	X	X	X	...	...
New York	X	X	X(4)	X	X	X	X	...
North Carolina	...	...	X(a)	...	...	...	...	...
North Dakota	X	X	X(4)	X	X	X	...	X
Ohio	X	X	X(a)	...	...	X	...	...
Oklahoma	X	X	X(6)	X	X	X	...	...
Oregon	X	X	X(6)	X	X	X	...	...
Pennsylvania	X	X	X(a)	X	X	X	...	...
Puerto Rico	X	X	X(4)	X	X	X	...	...
Rhode Island	...	...	...	...	...	X(g)	...	...
South Carolina	...	...	...	...	...	X(g)	...	...
South Dakota	...	...	...	...	...	X(g)	...	...
Tennessee	...	X(d)	...	...	...	X	...	X
Texas	X	X	X(25)	X	X	X	X	...
Utah	X	...	X(a)	X	X	...	X	...
Vermont	...	...	...	...	...	...	...	...
Virginia	X	X(d)	X(8)	X	X	X	...	...
Washington	X	X(d)	X(a)	X	X	X	...	...
West Virginia	X	X	X(a)	X	X	X	...	...
Wisconsin(h)	X	X	X(a)	X	X	X	...	...
Wyoming	X	...	X(2)	X	X	X	...	...

NOTE: *The numbers in parentheses refer to the minimum number of employees required for coverage of an employer.*

(a) No minimum number of employees specified in law.
(b) Coverage stated as "Every person."
(c) Follows pattern of Title VII, being reduced from 100 employees to 25 employees over a three-year period.
(d) Public employees only.
(e) Effective July 1, 1966.
(f) First offense only.
(g) No FEP law, but a Commission on Human Relations to promote equal employment opportunity.
(h) Also prohibits discrimination because of handicap.

SOURCE: Bureau of National Affairs, Inc. Reproduced by permission.

from excluding, expelling, or in any other way discriminating on such a basis; prohibits *employers* or *employment agencies* from advertising or causing to be circulated in any way or placed in an application for employment any such discriminatory limitations or specifications; and prohibits *employers, unions,* and *employment agencies* from discriminating in any way against a person because of that person's opposition to the type of discrimination proscribed under the law.

All the commissions—state and local—were once meagerly staffed except for those of New York State and Philadelphia. New York has always had well-compensated, full-time commission members. Most of the other state or local commissioners are part-time functionaries or governmental personnel who are paid a modest salary or a per diem rate and are free to devote time to other pursuits. Where the commissioners are part-time state employees, there are usually some full-time staff members who do the basic work. After the passage of the 1964 federal Civil Rights Act, state legislatures became more liberal with their civil rights agencies. A trend toward larger staffs and more adequate salaries became apparent, but even today, few approach the New York Commission in terms of budget and staff.

Effectiveness of State Laws against Discrimination

It is difficult to assay directly the effect or effectiveness of state laws against discrimination because other factors have constantly acted and reacted upon employment opportunities of minority groups. It is obvious that many Negroes and members of other minority groups have obtained jobs because of the existence of these laws. For example, soon after the passage of the New York law, banks and department stores in New York City commenced utilizing Negro tellers and clerks to a degree theretofore not done.

It is also obvious that in all of the states which have enforceable fair employment laws, discrimination because of race has not ceased. One still finds companies with sparse minority group employment. A study conducted by one of the authors in the 1938–43 period found substantial discrimination by railroad and building-trades unions;[6] and this applied, with very few exceptions, in the 1960's both in states now having fair employment laws and in those which have not, at least until the passage of the federal Civil Rights Act.

The careful study of state fair employment practice laws by Professors Paul H. Norgren and Samuel E. Hill credited all state agencies with improving minority group employment status, but found that the New York law and agency were by far the most effective.[7] Norgren and Hill point out that the New York Commission has concluded agreements with

---

[6] Northrup, *op. cit.*, chaps. ii and iii.
[7] Norgren and Hill, *loc. cit.*

several thousand firms, where it found discrimination, to alter past practices. The New York Commission follows up these agreements by periodic studies and, as a result, can point to a substantial altering of past practices, including those in areas where Negroes have traditionally not been employed: banking, insurance, other white-collar occupations, supervisory positions in manufacturing, etc. A specific reason for New York's superior progress is, according to this study, the manner in which the New York Commission, on its own initiative, utilizes its superior budgetary and personnel resources to study the racial patterns of an entire industry operating in the state, and then makes recommendations[8] (backed up by possible sanctions) to alter discriminatory practices.

Unions and State Fair Employment Laws

The state fair employment commissions seem to have had less success in dealing with unions, although all unions which barred Negroes by written constitutional provisions had deleted these rules by 1964, and although hundreds of workers are now union members who were excluded before the passage of state fair employment practice laws. Nevertheless, and in spite of the fact that union—and particularly AFL–CIO —support was often a decisive factor in gaining state legislative approval of fair employment laws, some of the most intransigent cases brought before state fair employment commissions, and usually the first cases to go to public hearings or the courts, have involved unions.

Professor F. Ray Marshall's careful appraisal stated that by the fall of 1963, state commissions had "not changed the basic employment patterns in most unionized industries." He found local unions relatively impervious to moral pressures and cited a number of cases where court action—including, in one case, finding of the local by a Connecticut court in a contempt action—was necessary, or where it took mass demonstrations by Negroes to gain union membership. He concluded that "recalcitrant local unions will change their practices when their power sources are threatened by government regulation, retaliation from the Negro community and alienation of public opinion." But to be effective, these sanctions have to be applied directly to the unions and not on the employer when the unions are at fault.[9] In 1964, for example, the New York State antidiscrimination agency was forced to take a large Sheet Metal Workers' local union to court to force it to agree to end confining apprentices to relatives of the all-white membership. Numerous similar

[8] Norgren and Hill buttress their arguments in favor of the Now York State law by citing census data which show much greater improvement for Negroes in New York than in comparable states. But the validity of this is subject to limitations because of various industry mixes, migration, and other factors. Nevertheless, their conclusion that New York has the most effective law seems correct.

[9] See F. Ray Marshall, "Union Racial Policies," in Herbert R. Northrup and Richard L. Rowan (eds.), *The Negro and Employment Opportunity* (Ann Arbor, Mich.: Bureau of Industrial Relations, University of Michigan, 1965), pp. 167–86.

examples can be found and continue to be on the dockets of state commissions.

TITLE VII OF THE CIVIL RIGHTS ACT OF 1964

Despite the relative success of the state commissions, Negro employment progress after 1958 was actually less than that of whites, so that by 1962 the income differential between whites and Negroes had widened. Agitation over employment problems in the North and continued facility segregation in the South resulted in the national consensus which produced the Civil Rights Act of 1964. Title VII of this Act deals with equal employment opportunity and became effective as of July 2, 1965, one year after the passage of the act.

Coverage and Content

The Equal Employment Opportunity title applies to all employers who employed 25 or more persons at least 20 weeks of the preceding year but excludes the federal government (which is nonetheless directed to insure nondiscriminatory employment within its own ranks); state governments or subdivisions thereof; private membership clubs (except unions); religious organizations; and the employment of aliens outside their country. Additional exemptions were granted for one year to employers having less than 100 employees, for two years to those having less than 75 employees, and for three years to those having less than 50 employees. Other than the explicit exemptions, the act applies to employers who are defined as such by the Landrum-Griffin Act, which, as noted in Chapter 22, contains the most comprehensive such definition to be found in federal law.

The Equal Opportunity title also applies to employment agencies, including the United States Employment Service, state and local employment services utilizing federal funds, anyone acting to recruit employees for work, and unions which maintain hiring halls or procure employees for work.

Finally, the law covered unions which have 100 members or more the first year, 75 or more the second year, 50 or more the third year, and 25 or more thereafter. Unions are thus covered in the same manner as employers. Moreover, unions are defined to include locals and national, international, and intermediate bodies.

The basic proscriptions of the law are set forth in Figure 24–1. The coverage of the law extends to joint labor-management committees or other organizations controlling apprenticeship—thus closing a loophole found in many state fair employment laws. It permits religion, sex,[10] or national origin to be utilized where valid occupational classification calls

[10] The question of discrimination by sex is discussed below, pp. 718–19.

FIGURE 24–1

Unlawful Employment Practices under Title VII,
Civil Rights Act of 1964

DISCRIMINATION BECAUSE OF RACE, COLOR, RELIGION, OR NATIONAL ORIGIN

Sec. *703.* (*a*) It shall be an unlawful employment practice for an employer—

(1) to fail or refuse to hire or to discharge any individual, or otherwise to discriminate against any individual with respect to his compensation, terms, conditions, or privileges of employment, because of such individual's race, color, religion, sex, or national origin; or

(2) to limit, segregate, or classify his employees in any way which would deprive or tend to deprive any individual of employment opportunities or otherwise adversely affect his status as an employee, because of such individual's race, color, religion, sex, or national origin.

(*b*) It shall be an unlawful employment practice for an employment agency to fail or refuse to refer for employment, or otherwise to discriminate against, any individual because of his race, color, religion, sex, or national origin, or to classify or refer for employment any individual on the basis of his race, color, religion, sex, or national origin.

(*c*) It shall be an unlawful employment practice for a labor organization—

(1) to exclude or to expel from its membership, or otherwise to discriminate against, any individual because of his race, color, religion, sex, or national origin;

(2) to limit, segregate, or classify its membership, or in any way to classify or fail or refuse to refer for employment any individual, in any way which would deprive or tend to deprive any individual of employment opportunities, or would limit such employment opportunities or otherwise adversely affect his status as an employee or as an applicant for employment, because of such individual's race, color, religion, sex, or national origin; or

(3) to cause or attempt to cause an employer to discriminate against an individual in violation of this section.

(*d*) It shall be an unlawful employment practice for any employer, labor organization, or joint labor-management committee controlling apprenticeship or other training or retraining, including on-the-job training programs to discriminate against any individual because of his race, color, religion, sex, or national origin in admission to, or employment in any program established to provide apprenticeship or other training.

. . . .

OTHER UNLAWFUL EMPLOYMENT PRACTICES

Sec. *704.* (*a*) It shall be an unlawful employment practice for an employer to discriminate against any of his employees or applicants for employment, for an employment agency to discriminate against any individual, or for a labor organization to discriminate against any member thereof or applicant for membership, because he has opposed any practice made an unlawful employment practice by this title, or because he has made a charge, testified, assisted, or participated in any manner in an investigation, proceeding, or hearing under this title.

(*b*) It shall be an unlawful employment practice for an employer, labor organization, or employment agency to print or publish or cause to be printed or published any notice or advertisement relating to employment by such an employer or membership in or any classification or referral for employment by such a labor organization, or relating to any classification or referral for employment by such an employment agency, indicating any preference, limitation, specification, or discrimination, based on race, color, religion, sex, or national origin, except that such a notice or advertisement may indicate a preference, limitation, specification, or discrimination based on religion, sex, or national origin when religion, sex, or national origin is a bona fide occupational qualification for employment.

for such a distinction (e.g., a model, a Kosher butcher, or a teacher in a girls' school or in a religious seminary); it excludes from coverage any protection to members of the Communist party or of any other organization "required to register as a Communist action or Communist front organization by final order of the Subversive Activities Control Board pursuant to the Subversive Activities Control Act of 1950"; and it also excludes from its protection persons who have failed to gain security clearance under any federal security program insofar as access to secret or confidential governmental work is concerned. In order to avert charges of discrimination involving such ordinary employment practices as regional wage differentials, benefits, and seniority, etc., the act permits an employer to apply such different standards to employees in different locations "provided that such differences are not the result of an intention to discriminate because of race, color, religion, sex or national origin." The law also permits employers on Indian reservations to continue to give employment preferences to Indians.

Administration

The act established an Equal Employment Opportunity Commission, a five-man independent agency appointed by the President with the consent of the Senate. Like other federal agencies, this Commission is empowered to establish regional offices and to appoint staff pursuant to civil service regulations, to subpoena records, and to prescribe rules and regulations for carrying out its duties.

Following the provisions of the New York and most other state laws, the Commission is required to attempt first to settle complaints by conciliation. Where there is a state law or municipal ordinance proscribing discrimination or providing for a means of relief, no action may be taken by the Equal Employment Opportunity Commission until it has notified and given the state or local agency 90 days to act or, if the state or local agency is in its first year of existence, 180 days to act. The law specifically permits state laws to exist concurrently, provided such laws do not require or permit the doing of any act which would be an unlawful employment practice. Moreover, the Commission is urged to enter into agreements with state agencies for the utilization of the latter's services to carry out the functions of the federal law. Records are required to be kept by employers, unions, and employment agencies; but if such records must be kept for state agencies or by Presidential Executive Order 10925, pursuant to government contracts, and there is no question of compliance, no additional records need be kept.

Where an alleged violation of the law is not subject to a state or local law, or such state or local agencies have not acted, and where conciliation has not succeeded, the aggrieved person may file a civil action in an appropriate U.S. district court. The court may appoint an attorney free of charge to the complainant, and may permit the U.S. Attorney

General to intervene. The court may enjoin the practice and may order reinstatement, back pay, hiring, union membership for an employee, or other remedies, provided the unlawful practice was found to be *intentional* on the part of the respondent, and provided the discrimination was not for any other reason than what is unlawful under the act. Courts may also appoint masters to determine facts. Continued noncompliance after an order permits the Commission to commence proceedings to compel compliance.

An additional section (707) permits the Attorney General to bring a civil action where he believes that any person or group of persons is engaged in a pattern or practice of resistance to the full enjoyment of any of the rights guaranteed by Title VII, requesting relief, including an injunction, to overcome such resistance. The Attorney General may request the appointment of a three-judge court to hear such a case—in which event, appeal is directly to the Supreme Court, thus bypassing the Court of Appeals.

Before proceeding to court, the Commission may hold a public hearing, examine witnesses, and make findings. Individuals subpoenaed or otherwise objecting to an investigation may appeal to the courts within twenty days after being served.

Analysis

That the federal equal opportunity law has had a profound effect on the policies of employers, there can be no doubt. Where Negroes and other minorities were once excluded, they are now sought. Thousands of minority group individuals have received jobs as a result of the changes effectuated by this law. In addition, patterns of work are being changed. The courts have ruled, for example, that Negroes who have been discriminated against over a period of years can be given a "seniority credit," so that they will have an opportunity to achieve their "rightful place" in the job hierarchy.[11]

Nevertheless, to many Negroes the changes wrought by the law have been painfully slow. They tend to blame continued discrimination and the cumbersome and slow procedures of the law which require a long time period for a case to wind its way through the courts. The real problem, however, is that the publicity about the law seemed to promise more than it could possibly deliver. The Civil Rights Act does not guarantee a man a job. He must have the qualifications for it. Negro educational attainments and skill training remain, on average, far below those of whites. Past neglect and discrimination, continued concentration in the South and in the inner city cores, where education is demonstrably inferior, accentuate the problem for Negroes, who need education or

---

[11] See, for example *Quarles* v. *Philip Morris, Inc.*, U.S. District Court, Eastern District of Virginia, Civil Action No. 4544, January 4, 1968.

training to obtain good jobs. Yet, only through training and development can the qualifications gap be narrowed and the unemployment rate of Negroes—still twice that of whites in spite of gains—be substantially reduced. Perhaps, therefore, the main step forward of the Civil Rights Act is that, besides opening jobs to the qualified, it has demonstrated that there is reason for hope for the unqualified who will obtain and take the necessary training, and it has spurred industry and government to provide that training.

Wagner Act Stage?

There are two other aspects to the Equal Opportunity law which deserve attention. In a real sense, it marks the "Wagner Act" stage of fair employment practice legislation. For the restrictions are entirely on those who might discriminate. But consider what can happen to an employer (or a union or an employment agency) who has a thoroughly fair employment policy by an objective standard. The law would apparently not protect that employer from picketing or boycotts by groups aimed at subverting this policy except that the Equal Employment Opportunity Commission is authorized "upon the request of an employer, whose employees or some of them refuse or threaten to refuse to cooperate in effectuating [the law] . . . to assist in such effectuation by conciliation or such other remedial action as is provided by [the Act] . . . ," which would seem to include a request for a court order.

On the other hand, there is nothing in the law to protect such an employer (or a union or an employment agency) from picketing, boycotts, or other economic action by minority groups who are not satisfied with the policies of such employer *even though the law is satisfied.* Thus, an employer can be severely damaged even though he is in compliance with the law.

This is no remote possibility. There are several national and local organizations vying for support of the Negro community. In Philadelphia the Congress of Racial Equality ordered a boycott of a building project after the unions and contractors had made a settlement on Negro employment agreed to by the National Association for the Advancement of Colored People. In California, CORE has picketed 20 of the Bank of America's 864 branches, even though the bank was the first major employer in California to sign a formal statement of racial equality with the California Fair Employment Practice Commission. CORE justified this action because the Bank declined (1) to waive for Negroes its high school education requirement, which the bank insists upon for all new hires; and (2) to supply CORE with the elaborate statistics on employees which the bank had already supplied to the California Commission. Picketing and boycott pressure led by the followers of the late Martin Luther King, Jr., have forced some retail supermarkets and other retail establishments to employ all Negro staffs, carry products manufactured by Negro-led businesses, and even to hire employees recommended by the organization.

Such occurrences have been sufficiently frequent to remind one of the period when the AFL and the CIO were struggling for power, with the employer caught in the middle. Will the "Wagner Act" type of civil rights law of 1964 be followed by a "Taft-Hartley Act" type some years hence, containing restrictions on minority group activity as well as protecting minority group rights? And later, will there follow a "Landrum-Griffin Act" type, also protecting individuals within minority group organizations?

Relation to Other Laws

As we have noted, the Civil Rights law drafters were very careful to consider the effect of the new law on similar state and local enactments. But there is no mention of Taft-Hartley, Landrum-Griffin, or other federal statutes. For example, a union may be charged with an unlawful employment practice by the Equal Employment Opportunity Commission for discriminating against Negroes at the same time that it is being certified as the bargaining agent for these same discriminated-against employees by the National Labor Relations Board. The Equal Opportunity title also sheds no light on whether picketing or boycotts by racial groups are "labor disputes" within the meaning of the Norris–La Guardia Act, a decision which judges will have to make before deciding whether such demonstrations can be enjoined. Congress also gave no thought as to whether the proscriptions against sex discrimination are compatible with various state laws regulating wages, hours, or conditions of work for women—and therefore technically "discriminate" between the sexes. Thus, our federal labor legislation continues to grow without reference to its impact on existing federal law or the complexities in which labor and management find themselves when caught in the cross fire between two laws or agencies.

Effect on State Employment Services

All states maintain employment offices and related services which are heavily subsidized by the federal government. These offices, like private ones, make little attempt to alter the preferences of their "customers." Federal funds are allocated on the basis of number of placements. Hence, state agencies are anxious to make placements rather than to risk alienating employers.

In the South, these state agencies were either directly segregated or located in neighborhoods and therefore *de facto* segregated. Over 90% of their nonwhite placements were likely to be in service or unskilled work, whereas nearly that percentage of white placements was in higher categories.[12] The Equal Employment Opportunity Commission's policing of

---

[12] Norgren and Hill, *op. cit.*, pp. 35–39.

employment agencies started with those which utilize federal funds, and has already wrought considerable change.

DISCRIMINATION BECAUSE OF SEX

The year 1964 was a banner one for the feminists. In June the "equal pay for equal work" law, enacted in 1963, became effective. And then, just a few weeks later, Congress passed the Equal Opportunity law, which forbade discrimination by sex as well as by race, color, creed, or national origin. This law, as noted, became effective in mid-1965.

Equal Pay for Equal Work

The equal pay law was enacted as an amendment to the Fair Labor Standards Act. Therefore, its coverage is identical with that of the federal minimum wage law (see Table 15–1, p. 447). It is administered and enforced by the Wage and Hour and Public Contracts Division of the U.S. Department of Labor.

The equal pay law, in brief, provides that it is illegal to pay women less than men (or conversely, men less than women) for doing the same work, and it is unlawful for a union or its agents to cause or attempt to cause an employer to discriminate in wages on the basis of sex. Furthermore, elimination of existing differentials by a wage reduction is prohibited. The act contains a general exception for differentials based on any other factor than sex. In addition, three specific exemptions—wage differentials based on merit, seniority, and piece rates or incentives—are specifically permitted.

It may take years of litigation to determine what is or is not equal pay. For example, if the employment of women requires additional material-handling personnel in order to move heavy parts, obviously women are not doing the same work as men who could move the material as well as do the work being done by the women. But there are many gray areas which are not so obvious. The best protection for both employers and unions is to have a well-thought-out, formalized wage structure based on job evaluation, so that rates are as objectively established as possible. The application of such a program can eliminate any vestiges of wage differentials and, perhaps more importantly, preclude charges that they exist.

State Equal Pay Laws

In addition to the federal law, equal pay laws exist in 31 states.[13] The earliest laws were enacted by Michigan and Montana in 1919, the latest by

---

[13] Alaska, Arizona, Arkansas, California, Colorado, Connecticut, Georgia, Hawaii, Illinois, Kentucky, Maine, Maryland, Massachusetts, Michigan, Missouri, Montana, New Hampshire, New Jersey, New York, North Dakota, Ohio, Oklahoma, Oregon, Pennsylvania, Rhode Island, South Dakota, Vermont, Washington, West Virginia, Wisconsin, and Wyoming.

Missouri and Vermont in 1963. These laws vary in coverage and content, and do not seem to have generated either much litigation or any substantial changes in industry's pay practices. Testimony of federal government and union officials maintained that this proved that a federal law was needed. Little evidence was produced before congressional committees that wide wage discrimination against women actually exists, although there is no doubt that women are subject to job discrimination. It is for this reason that the Equal Opportunity law may have a far greater effect on the earnings of women than will the equal pay bill. For the latter is silent on job opportunities—it merely requires equal pay whenever women do equal work.

Equal Opportunity and Sex

The Equal Opportunity law's provision against discrimination because of sex could well have a major impact on industry, unions, and employment agencies. For example, must industry open up its secretarial jobs to men? Can an airline automatically refuse the application of a qualified aviatrix for a pilot's job? Is retirement at age 62 for women and 65 for men discrimination? Will the "help wanted" advertisements no longer be able to be divided into male and female? The Equal Opportunity provisions, unlike those for equal pay, apply to executives, administrators, and professionals, as well as to blue-collar employees. Women may now get their opportunity for top industry jobs! One could go on, adding numerous other questions concerning the manner in which industry has developed a sex-occupational division of employment over the years and the potential for change therein as a result of the Equal Opportunity law.

To be sure, the role of women in the labor market has been fluid, as we have noted several times in the text. But adherence to the patterns of the past will be no guarantee that illegal discrimination will not result.

DISCRIMINATION BECAUSE OF AGE

One more type of discrimination is forbidden by law—age discrimination. In 1967, Congress enacted the Age Discrimination in Employment Act, which became effective six months later. This law is administered under the Secretary of Labor by the Wage and Hour and Public Contracts Division, the same agency which enforces the Fair Labor Standards and Equal Pay Acts. The law applies to about the same jurisdiction as does Title VII of the Civil Rights Act.

In addition to the federal law, about one half of the states have enacted such laws over the years. In general, these laws do not interfere with the operation of a bona fide seniority system, or with compulsory retirement programs. There is, however, a fine line between compulsory early retirement to make way for a younger and more vigorous person, and age discrimination; and between insisting on younger persons for physically strenuous jobs, and age discrimination. It may be many years before legal definitions of where those lines are, can be made. Can, for example, airlines retire stewardesses at age 35 as too old?

QUESTIONS FOR DISCUSSION

1. How will the Equal Opportunity law alter racial patterns in the South? In northern cities? Explain your answer.
2. Assume that you are a construction employer and that you hire through unions. Two of them have never referred a Negro to you. What is your status under the Equal Opportunity law, and what can you do to avoid being charged with an unlawful employment practice without encouraging union antagonism?
3. Which act is more likely to affect employment opportunities for women: the Equal Pay Act or the Equal Opportunity law?

SUGGESTIONS FOR FURTHER READING

MARSHALL, F. RAY. *The Negro and Organized Labor*. New York: John Wiley & Sons, Inc., 1965.
    An analysis of the relations of Negroes and unions prior to the passage of the Civil Rights Act of 1964.

NORTHRUP, HERBERT R.; ROWAN, RICHARD L.; and others. *The Racial Policies of American Industry*, published as ready by the University of Pennsylvania Press, Philadelphia, for the Industrial Research Unit, Wharton School of Finance and Commerce, University of Pennsylvania.
    A series of industry-by-industry studies, sponsored by the Ford Foundation, of Negro employment. Studies on the automobile, aerospace, hotel, petroleum, steel, insurance, retail trade, and several others were completed in 1968, and about 10 others are scheduled for 1969.

SOVERN, MICHAEL I. *Legal Restraints on Racial Discrimination in Employment*. New York: Twentieth Century Fund., Inc., 1966.
    An analysis of equal opportunity laws and their effectiveness.

PART VIII

Concluding Observations

| Chapter | SOME LABOR PROBLEMS |
| 25 | OF THE FUTURE |

Throughout this book, we have stressed the new trends and developments which have modified the context and environment of labor economics during recent years and which promise to affect conditions much more substantially during the balance of this decade. By way of a summary and conclusion, attention is directed to some of these factors once more.

UNEMPLOYMENT—AND INFLATION

From the end of the Korean War in the early 1950's until almost the mid-1960's, the United States was plagued with unemployment which regularly exceeded 5% of the labor force and rose to over 7% in times of recession. Then, under the impetus of government fiscal policy, including a tax decrease, and a business boom, unemployment fell below 4% in 1965 and remained below that figure for several years. But the unemployment and poverty in our large cities and among minority groups continued to remain high, and to complicate the problem, prices moved steadily upward. It is apparent that increasing demand wipes out much of the basic unemployment in society. Yet, the unemployment which remains is hard core and difficult to overcome; and further increases in demand not only do not reach the remaining unemployed but in addition accentuate the inflationary aspects of a high-level economy.

Both the private and the public sectors of our economy have recognized the needs and have attempted to alleviate the structural defects with a variety of aid and training programs. That only the surface has been scratched is obvious; and that much more needs to be learned as to how to make the hard-core unemployed become self-reliant members of our society is equally clear. The fact that Negroes, our largest minority racial group, makes up so disproportionate a number of the disadvantaged unemployed, both complicates the problem and makes its solution more urgent. The race issue is the most serious internal social problem of our age. Finding jobs for Negroes and making the Negro a productive, job-filling member of our society is undoubtedly the key to the solution of this problem.

Perhaps what is needed most is a thorough reexamination of federal and state labor and welfare policies, and an equally hard look on the part of managements and unions at the policies and programs which have developed out of their relationships. It seems obvious that some are in need of revision, that what may have been appropriate in former years may no longer be socially desirable, sound, or even viable.

Minimum Wages and Shorter Hours

Thus, in the area of governmental policy a new look has to be taken at the impact of minimum wage laws. All available data point to a major problem of structural unemployment concentrated among the poorly educated, the least skilled, and the minority group members of the labor force. When we raise minimum wage rates, these workers are the first to lose their jobs. Are these men and women better off when employed at what society concedes to be substandard rates of pay, or either unemployed on temporary grants under our unemployment compensation system or on relief? Or should they be paid a government subsidy and kept at work?

Great strides have been made in training in recent years, but much more needs to be done. The great tragedy revealed by the Civil Rights Act and similar state laws is, now that jobs are open to Negroes, so few are able to make use of opportunities. We need not only greater emphasis on training the unemployed but also on training for upgrading. People with limited education and background who were hired as laborers and expected to be laborers all their lives may be beyond training for better jobs, but we must be sure. Government policies are needed to stimulate such training without the dampening effect of red tape and frustration.

Such problems also pose major challenges for unions. Seniority programs devised in another era need change and flexibility if they are to survive. Moreover, unions have generally not been oriented toward helping the hard-core unemployed; they have been more concerned with obtaining maximum benefits for their members who are already employed. Can union leaders continue to maintain this attitude in view of the nature of the unemployment problem? Can employed union members simply shut their eyes to the fact that union wage policies may restrict employment opportunities? What positive programs for stimulating employment can union leaders logically espouse? Is not the regular advocacy of the shorter workweek as the cure-all an empty hope which, by reason of its costly burden on employers, can only reduce rather than increase job opportunities?

Security and Costs

How much "security" do we crave, and what will it cost? If government-sponsored prepaid medical care is adopted, what will the resultant increased taxes do to the prospects for expansion in our economy and hence to the prospects for a decrease in the rate of unemployment? If, as seems likely, ever-larger fringe benefits induce a preference among employers for overtime rather than new hires, is our security system building more security for the majority and continued insecurity for those unemployed?

Year after year, in prosperity as well as in depression, the welfare costs of our major cities rise, and the number of people on relief increase. Must not our welfare programs be self-defeating? Why cannot welfare recipients be made self-supporting members of society? Are welfare and minimum wage legislation related? How about welfare policies and the impact thereon of union wage policies?

To alleviate poverty, some would make cash handouts in the form of a "negative income tax." This would perhaps simplify record keeping and administration of welfare, but it would not provide either the dignity or the self-reliance of an income-producing job. Moreover, more cash handouts would seem to be inflationary in an economy already concerned about inflation. Would further inflation mean an ever higher negative income tax, and thus would the costs, as in welfare, keep rising?

Collective Bargaining and Unionism

What about collective bargaining in an economy where unemployment, job security, retraining, civil rights, and manpower utilization become the key issues? Can management and unions really deal with these problems as they have dealt with wage issues? If they cannot, what are the alternatives? What has the government to offer as a solution? These very problems are most serious and are certainly not solved in the one industry —railroads—where the government has intervened longest and most consistently.

Can the labor movement contribute to the solution of the basic problems of which unemployment is the central issue? Many observers doubt it. They note that unions have already accomplished their big job: attaining recognition of the dignity of labor. The fact that unions have essentially done the job they set out to do is the very fact that may now bring about their eventual downfall. The late Sumner H. Slichter made this point many times in urging labor to take a broader view of its role in the American economy.

For two decades, unions had a major appeal to workers because union leadership was attuned to the current needs of the labor force. Unions were growing, and their very growth was a dynamic factor of appeal. But after the mid-1950's, unions first lost ground both in terms of total members and proportion of the labor force unionized; then, despite the prosperity which has greatly increased union membership in the mid-1960's, union membership gains failed to keep pace with the growth of the labor force. This leaves the union movement heavily dependent upon the business cycle for growth, membership, and income.

The failure of unions to grow may be blamed on many things. Some AFL–CIO adherents blame it on managerial opposition to unions, although this does not explain why unions grew despite the same opposition in earlier years. Walter Reuther claims that the "stand-pat" leadership of George Meany is at the root of the problem.

Actually, unions may well be suffering from the same inability to please that has harassed many once-popular public figures. Old appeals do not always bring the same results in the entertainment field, the advertising field, the political field, or the union field. Unions have been strangely unable to appeal to many of the new recruits of the labor force. Throughout the 1960's, the labor force will continue to see more additions from the quite young, the older worker, the part-time worker, the previously rural worker, the more highly educated worker, the relatively affluent worker, and the "middle-class-minded" worker. The old appeals that brought workers into unity in unionism in the 1930's are not appropriate to the new workers of the 1960's, even where these workers are occupying jobs of one-time union adherents. Yet, unions have been strangely unable to adapt themselves to the appeals that would be meaningful to the prospective member of the 1960's. When the new workers are in the unions, often as a result of compulsory unionism, the degree of rejection of contracts testifies to the communication gap between leaders and the rank and file.

Beyond the union-centered inability to meet the new prospect on his own terms, there is an added dimension that we pointed out in our description of trends in the labor force. This is the fact that the mix of work has changed as well. Even if there had been no change in the ideas and attitudes of the production worker to whom the union had the greatest appeal in the last generation, a significant shift in ratio toward the predominance of white-collar work has been taking place for at least the last 10 years, and this shift is accelerating daily. This shift is well recognized by union mentors, but not so well seen is what to do about it. At one union convention after another the subject of the organization of white-collar workers is discussed. By now, it is generally conceded that new appeals—and, indeed, new appealers—must be found if the white-collar people are to be organized. Large sums of money have been appropriated for organizing campaigns, and studies have been undertaken to determine the type of appeal which will interest white-collar workers, without evident success.

But if the big unions ever do seriously tackle the organization of white-collar workers, they face a risk far greater than the declining membership rolls that now plague them. The risk is that the unions will have to undergo a change in their own philosophies to become consonant with the contemplated changes in appeals. It is as though a producer were seeking some new advertising technique to reach a new sales market. He sometimes finds—as the unions may, too—that it takes more than just a new appeal: Often, it really requires a new product before the sale is won. If this might be the case in the unions' quest for members in the white-collar ranks, then we could expect the most revolutionary changes in the trends of union thinking.

What would happen, on the other hand, if the union official who is trying desperately to attract white-collar employees to membership should start talking like a conservative in politics after all the years of enunciating a party line in political matters that was so clearly liberal? Would this cause a loss in present membership, or would it bring out a new interest and approval from present members? Nobody knows. The problem is that in many crucial matters of wages and hours and working conditions, there is a broad disparity between what white-collar workers believe and what unions have for many years proclaimed as the belief of their membership. In order to maintain an appeal to both groups, the union would, in effect, have to espouse two philosophies and finally accept a split personality that might be disastrous in its appeal either to blue-collar workers or to white-collar workers.

There is a strange parallel in the present situation to that of the late 1920's. Labor then was on a fading plateau—much smaller, to be sure. Nevertheless, it took depression and the iron will of John L. Lewis to force labor to risk its bureaucracy in order to organize the industrial workers, a risk certainly taken against the will of the craft union leadership, which feared both a new approach and new members.

Mr. Reuther's break with the AFL–CIO has many similarities with that of John L. Lewis' action three decades earlier. Can he revitalize the labor movement and organize the white-collar workers? Perhaps, but one may be doubtful. There is disquiet but no depression. White-collar groups are well compensated, and management is anxious to keep them nonunion and proemployer. Reuther's leadership is scarcely conservative in appeal. His greatest appeal may be rather to workers in local and state government, hospitals, and other areas where unions have already made advances in recent years, but here he would have to confront active unions. In the final analysis, his opportunity to create a new labor movement is much more limited than that which Lewis grasped so effectively in the 1930's.

On the other hand, it is equally difficult for today's union leadership to appeal to the poverty-stricken or for the union rank and file to concern itself with the problems of the poor. With union members having middle-class income, their concerns are less and less those of the slum population and more and more those of the typical suburbanite. A labor movement that has successfully carried its members so fast and so far up the income ladder finds it more and more difficult to represent, or even to communicate with, the downtrodden.

The race issue portends a severe problem for union leadership. They (like most other white people) failed to sense the Negro mood and impending crises which has turned once prounion Negro leaders into sharp critics of unionism. The AFL–CIO has adopted a liberal program. But it has had difficulty selling this program to many of its constituent unions and to the rank and file. Racial antagonism among unionized workers remains strong in many places, and several key unions, particularly in the building trades have obstructed, rather than furthered, employment opportunities for Negroes.

Of all the trends within labor that might have serious portent both as to the future of unions and as to the future of labor-management relations, the most significant seems to be the inability to adjust to changing circumstances. Union leadership appears to be less flexible, less able to reject the old ways and embrace the new ways, than business management. Such, however, may be the fate of a movement as contrasted with an enterprise. The labor movement, perhaps because it is or was a movement—a cause—cannot turn lightly about simply to meet some present and perhaps short-term need. Based as it has been in the conflicts of the old Industrial Revolution, it has difficulty in responding now to the fact that the old Industrial Revolution is over. In the words of A. H. Raskin of *The New York Times*, an astute and sympathetic commentator on the labor scene: "American labor is suffering from an advanced case of hardening of the arteries. It is standing still in membership and organizational vigor at a time when radical changes in technology are revolutionizing industry in ways that may prove as dramatic as the more publicized developments in space travel and nuclear weapons."

Need for New Concepts—and Leaders?

The need for new concepts is not confined to the labor movement but is required on all fronts, in view of the changing direction of the use of the labor force. For example, trends point to an ever-larger percentage of the labor force being occupied in producing "public goods" instead of private products. All one has to do is to look about his city, town, or state to see an increasing share of our productive forces going into such channels as construction of roads, schools, universities, and hospitals. Today, education boasts the biggest payroll in the country; hospitals employ over 2 million persons—more than twice the number of the basic steel industry. The trend of employment in these fields is increasing; that of manufacturing is declining.

What relevance does this have for historical measurements of productivity? Will the concept really be useful for comparable purposes over time when the product of today is ever more one of governmental or quasi-public services? Will this trend accentuate the possibility of inflation because, as otherwise unemployed labor is used in this kind of project, more dollars are put into the income stream as part of payment of wages, but no product emerges that is immediately usable to offset the increased purchasing power?

GOVERNMENTAL INTERVENTION

The same questions may be asked of our governmental labor policies. Are our laws attuned to the economy of the 1960's and 1970's or to that of the 1930's? The labor policy of the United States has developed slowly and haltingly. No one court decision or legislative act can be singled out as representing the beginning of governmental labor policy. Much of our present policy, it is true, stems from the Great Depression and the period of the Roosevelt administration, during which great strides were made toward formulating present labor policies. Nevertheless, each period of history has made some contribution to the present status of labor legislation and governmental action. For example, even the most revolutionary of all labor laws—the National Labor Relations Act—had its roots in state and railway labor legislation of the 1890's.

At various stages of American labor history, different aspects of labor policy have been stressed by legislators and labor leaders. For example, encouragement of collective bargaining by protecting the right of labor to organize was of prime importance in our labor policy in the period from the birth of the National Recovery Administration to enactment of the National Labor Relations Act. Restraints on activities of unions were especially emphasized in the post–World War II era, representing, in part, a reaction to certain alleged excesses of unions during the period of unrestricted union organization. Protection of minority group rights is the dominant theme of the mid-1960's. Labor policy is thus continually evolving. Laws are passed which at the time may represent majority thinking. But majority thinking is not static, and as views alter, labor legislation reflects the changing trend in public opinion.

It is natural to assume, therefore, that labor policy will continue to evolve in the future. While many future developments cannot be predicted, certain trends are already evident. Thus, for example, a developing labor policy will undoubtedly continue to grapple with the amount and coverage of minimum wages and social security, the extent of the workweek and the issue of emerging strikes, and the rights of union members and of minority groups—all issues which have been before the public for several decades.

Actually, the United States has no labor policy but rather a patchwork of policies, comprehensive but not consistent. There is, for example, no uniformity of treatment among the states. State labor relations, workmen's compensation, unemployment insurance, and minimum wage laws differ widely. The accident of location determines the extent of employee protection. Although the Landrum-Griffin Act did define some areas of delegation between federal and state laws, great inconsistencies occur in such areas as picketing, boycotts, mediation, and strike control legislation.

The recent copper strike saw intervention by several governors and at least three senators; a decision by the Johnson administration that the Taft-Hartley Act, which has been utilized in far less significant disputes, did not apply to this case; the appointment of an extralegal fact-finding board; and mediation by three cabinet officers. Not only legislation, but also government action needs to be clear and consistent.

The inconsistency of federal legislation, as noted in previous chapters, is very real. For example, the Norris–La Guardia Act conflicts with the Taft-Hartley Act, and the latter law with the Landrum-Griffin Act. There have been cases in which persons have been sentenced to jail for actions which violated the Landrum-Griffin Act and yet have been recognized as legitimate union officials by the Taft-Hartley Act. This means that management has been required to deal with law violators and racketeers or itself violate a law.

Although the Civil Rights law was made consistent with state legislation of the same type, its relation to the Taft-Hartley Act was not given serious consideration. Other inconsistencies exist in the coverage of various laws. Railway and airline employers and employees who come under the Railway Labor Act have rights and duties different from those of their fellow employees and employers who come under the National Labor Relations Act. Likewise, the railway industry has a separate social security system, while airline pilots have a special (and extraordinary) minimum wage law.

There is also inconsistency of purpose between the two current goals of labor policy: promoting collective bargaining and regulating certain union activities. It remains doubtful that the government at both the federal and state levels can continue to maintain both a spur to union growth and a strong deterrent to certain union activities which can affect union growth.

The fact that there are basic conflicts in the national labor policy should not be surprising. Indeed, all things considered, perhaps it is surprising that there are not more inconsistencies in existing legislation. Labor legislation is enacted in response to pressure of public opinion and influences exerted by various interest groups. In some states, labor's political position is strong; in others, it is weak. State labor laws reflect this fact.

Moreover, neither labor nor industry alone can command sufficient votes to sway Congress. When in disagreement over legislation, both must appeal for support to that huge, vague group known as the "middle class," which holds the balance of power in our society, insofar as such a balance exists. As the electorate shifts first one way and then another, the complexion of Congress and state legislatures changes. Legislation in the highly controversial field of labor relations reflects these changes.

There nevertheless is a real need for a general overhauling of our disjointed system of conflicting and overlapping labor laws. Even if agreement could not be reached as to the basis on which such laws should be improved, it might at least be possible to achieve a greater degree of uniformity than now exists among the various laws. Unfortunately, however, achievement of even such limited agreement is not too likely in view of the basic conflicts of interest, not only between labor and industry but also within both labor and industry groups. The present system of "push and pull" of pressure groups to secure labor legislation favorable to themselves is likely to remain with us for some time to come.

Need for Defining Role of Unions and Management

In Chapter 4, we considered the problem of defining the scope of managerial prerogatives. We need not repeat the considerations there discussed. Suffice it to say that the problem of preserving entrepreneurial freedom to manage business while affording union membership security will be telescoped in importance in coming years by the ever-growing extent of union demands. Although union leaders, by and large, believe in maintenance of the American system of free enterprise, their continuing search for means to afford security to their membership must inevitably produce a narrowing of the area of business initiative. Layoffs, technological change, and production policies are likely to be moved more and more into the orbit of union consultation and control. Union attempts to prove management's ability to pay higher wages and other benefits will lead to increasing interest by unions in company accounting systems and managerial policies.

No one can say where the ever-widening scope of union demands will end. It is safe to hazard a guess, however, that labor and management in the United States will ultimately work out a *modus vivendi* which will differ from that reached in other countries and which will reflect the peculiar character of American democracy and the American industrial environment. Such a compromise must recognize the basic need of the worker to feel secure in his job and to participate fully in the industrial process. At the same time, it is important that management be left free to plan, to invent, and to improve production methods so that not only labor but also the public at large may benefit from the efficiency of the capitalistic system.

The decades ahead will continue to witness a step-up in the tempo of the economic struggle between the United States and the Soviet Union. Soviet spokesmen have clearly stated their objective of surpassing the United States in economic production. They have already startled the world with their progress in space exploration; we cannot dismiss lightly their boast of outproducing us. This very real threat raises the question of whether or not the American economy can any longer afford the make-work rules, the restrictions imposed on new laborsaving devices, the slowdowns and walkouts which have become an accepted part of the labor-management scene in recent years. What is needed is a "new look" for labor, a new *rapprochement* between labor and management, a new recognition by both labor and management that preservation of our way of life requires not only a willingness to fight but also a willingness to produce.

The need for increased efficiency in production is further accentuated by the rapid rise of overseas competition. In the past decade, countries with much lower wage rates than ours have become highly industrialized and now can undercut us on world markets. Japan is a prime example of the new phenomenon of a highly mechanized, low-wage nation; within the next decade, China may also be added to this category. We cannot meet this threat by raising tariffs. The only sound answer is an accelerated rate of increase in output per man-hour in this country through application of the most advanced technology. Can labor leaders rise to this challenge—and if so, can they convince their membership of the necessity for abandoning traditional policies in sharp conflict with the present needs of the nation? Never before in our history has there been such a need for forceful, farseeing labor leadership!

Need for Defining Role of Industry and Government

The problem of demarcating the respective scopes of unions and management has its counterpart in the larger social question of the proper balance between individual initiative and government control. This basic issue is met not only in debates over the merits of government control or ownership of utilities but also in the development of labor policy. It seems clear that in coming years, union organizations will attempt to saddle industry with new and heavy obligations growing out of the worker's need for security. Unions have seized upon the idea that industry should provide for depreciation of the human machine in the same way that it provides for depreciation of capital equipment. This idea has been given concrete form in demands for liberalized pensions, health insurance, life insurance, free dental care, and other benefits. The basic question is whether such benefits, assuming that they are justified, should be provided by industry or government—and in either case, how much of our national income should be devoted to security.

The notion that industry, on its own initiative, should amortize its human costs in the same manner as it has customarily amortized its mechanical costs is an attractive one; yet, it must be recognized that there are definite shortcomings to this view. The primary difficulty in having pensions, supplementary unemployment benefits, or other plans financed and administered by individual firms without any overall supervision or integration by government is that such plans are bound to differ from one company to another. As a consequence, they are likely to be haphazard and incomplete in their coverage, unequal in the amount of their benefits, and unduly favorable to workers who have the good fortune either to be members of strong unions or to work for prosperous concerns. Strong unions, like the United Mine Workers, have already demonstrated their ability to require employers to make enormous contributions to employee welfare funds, but their very success has often brought damaging unemployment and less security to many members of the work force.

A further element of unfairness in leaving the settlement of pensions and other aspects of a welfare program to the processes of collective bargaining is that the costs of such programs must ultimately be borne by all consumers in the form of lower real income, since—to the extent that companies bear the cost of pension plans—costs and prices of their products will tend to rise. This means that the public generally must pay for the disproportionate benefits which may be obtained by strong unions in particular industries. Moreover, as long as welfare plans remain a matter for collective bargaining, there will be constant rivalry among unions in various industries to increase the amount of benefits obtained for their membership, in order to outdo other unions. The consequences of such rivalry upon industrial costs, profits, and employment could be serious.

The alternative to individual company welfare plans is government benefits under an expanded and liberalized social security program. This approach has the advantage of enabling workers to share equally in benefits, regardless of whether they are organized or unorganized, members of strong unions or of weak unions. Moreover, the principle has already been established under the Social Security Act that workers should contribute to support of the cost of the program—a principle which seems to commend itself for its fairness. But an expanded government-administered welfare program for employees also has its drawbacks. It means rising taxes, increasing bureaucracy, and growing intervention by labor in politics so as to make its influence and demands felt in the determination of the extent and disposition of benefits. Pensions are, of course, only the beginning. The politics of union organization require that union leaders, in order to retain the allegiance of their membership, must constantly obtain new benefits for employees. If government, rather than employers, becomes the fount from which new benefits are to be sought, labor may use its political influence to obtain for American workers a "cradle-to-the-grave" welfare program similar to that obtained by British labor from its labor government. Such a development would bring the welfare state to America.

Employee demands for protection against insecurity thus present industry with a challenge and a dilemma. Either industry must accept its responsibilities and take the initiative in developing a broad program designed to protect workers from the risks and hazards of industrial life—with unforeseen consequences upon costs, profits, and employment —or labor may take the other road, which leads to increasing government regulation and taxation of industry, and to increasing dependence by workers upon the government to solve their problems. The decisions made with respect to this aspect of labor policy may thus have profound repercussions upon the pattern of American economic life and may influence the nature of the balance which is ultimately struck between government regulation and individual enterprise in our economy.

Labor Policy in a Democracy

A cornerstone of our democratic form of government has been the use of national policy to control great aggrandizements of power. As a nation, we have long recognized that when particular groups become so powerful that their actions can seriously interfere with market processes and endanger the public interest, government regulation may be required. Thus, the Sherman Antitrust Act recognized the evils inherent in combinations of corporations designed to restrain trade or monopolize an industry. Likewise, our graduated income tax and heavy estate tax were intended, in part, to restrict the concentration of economic and political power which would flow from the amassing of great fortunes passed on from generation to generation without tax.

With this history of the role of governmental regulation in our democratic society, it seems almost inevitable that the extent of regulation of unions will expand as they grow in strength and economic power. To date, the function of government has been primarily to provide the basis for equality of bargaining power between management and labor. The Wagner Act sought to prevent large, strongly entrenched corporations from using their power to throttle unions in their infancy by resort to discriminatory practices. Then, as unions grew in membership and strength, the need for such one-sided intervention in the labor market lessened; and Congress enacted the Taft-Hartley Act in an effort to pare down some of the rights given unions and to equalize bargaining power in the labor market, and the Landrum-Griffin Act to protect members from arbitrary union power. The Civil Rights law, like Landrum-Griffin, is primarily designed to protect individual employees—here members of minority groups.

It might be thought that with the development of strong union organization and the achievement of relative equality in bargaining power between industry and labor, government could now withdraw to the sidelines and let the parties fight it out. Unfortunately, however, the very equality of power between the parties in mass-production industries where strong unions confront large corporations, each with extensive financial resources, increases the possibility of prolonged work stoppages, with their attendant inconvenience to the public.

Although, as has been pointed out in the earlier discussion in this text, few such stoppages actually create national emergencies, nevertheless, the stoppages are serious enough to give rise to a hue and cry that something should be done to prevent such interference with the orderly flow of production.

There are, of course, some persons who believe that the only way to deal with this problem of the battle of the giants is to restore the working of a free market by breaking up unions and large corporations—by "atomizing" competition, as it is called—so that the unions and corporations which are left to deal with each other will be too small seriously to affect the market or the public by reason of their occasional disputes. This possibility, whether or not desirable in theory, is plainly impractical. Our industrial system, as now constituted, is too dependent upon our large, integrated corporations to warrant such a change; and as long as corporate units remain large, union organizations must also be large, in order to bargain effectively for their membership.

The struggle between strong unions and large corporations will lead to a demand by the public for further government regulation of union activities. The pressure for such action is growing as inflation again is with us; for many people have come to believe—either rightly or wrongly—that union demands for wage increases, backed up by the threat of the strike, have been a major cause of the upward trend in prices since World War II. The result may be further restriction of certain rights—such as the right to strike—which unions believe are fundamental to our democracy. But there are few absolute rights in our society. Rights are implicit with obligations. We cherish freedom of speech, but a man cannot yell "fire" without cause in a crowded theater. A democratic society can afford to give rights and privileges to groups only if those rights and privileges will not be abused and the rights of the public will be respected. Twice Congress prevented railway strikes in the middle 1960's—once with the first peacetime compulsory arbitration law, then with a second law which provided almost the same remedy under another name. The more powerful an organization becomes, the greater is the damage it can inflict upon society by abuse of its rights, and therefore the more circumspect must society be to see that such organizations respect their obligations to the community. Today the existence of nonunion and foreign competition is a powerful brake on possible abuses of union bargaining power in many industries, just as the existence of strong competition is a brake on the abuses of corporate power. If unions gradually eliminate such nonunion competition, the chance for abuse of power will be accentuated, and a real test will be presented for enlightened labor leadership. Unless union leaders exercise real self-restraint in the exercise of their powers, they may find that government will prescribe the restraints.

Labor policy in a democracy must also recognize that government regulation is not a panacea. Every walkout which inconveniences the public should not be met with a demand that "there ought to be a law." Free unionism and free collective bargaining are institutions which are worth preserving. By contrast, the growth of government bureaucracy and the intervention of government in the labor market are tendencies which should not lightly be encouraged. In labor policy, as in other national policies, we must follow the middle road. As a general rule, labor and industry should be given every opportunity to work out their problems without government regulation, except in situations where injury to the public is apparent and substantial, and justification from the point of view of legitimate union conduct is lacking.

The obligations of unions in a free society have yet to be clearly defined. The Landrum-Griffin Act is a step in this direction. The Civil Rights law is another. Future delineation of the obligations of unions and of the rights of union members would help to clarify, in part, the role of government and of industry as well. Whatever the ultimate role which government, industry, and unions will play in our society, we may be sure that it will follow a pattern reflecting the needs of our highly integrated industrial economy and the traditional concepts of our democratic society.

QUESTIONS FOR DISCUSSION

1. Write a short statement of what you think the national labor policy should encompass. How does actual policy differ from this?
2. What is the major labor problem today, and why do you think it is so significant?

SUGGESTIONS FOR FURTHER READING

ROWAN, RICHARD L., and NORTHRUP, HERBERT R. *Readings in Labor Economics and Labor Relations* (1968). Part VI, "Public Policy and Labor Relations," pp. 529–72. Homewood, Ill.: Richard D. Irwin, Inc., 1968.

    A series of articles and excerpts from pertinent legislation dealing with the public policy of the United States.

Indexes

INDEX OF AUTHORS CITED

INDEX OF SUBJECTS

This book has been set in 9 and 10 point Janson, leaded 2 points. Part numbers and titles and Chapter numbers and titles are in 18 point Spartan Medium. The size of the type page is 27 x 46½ picas.